WRITING WITH SKILL, LEVEL ONE

The Complete Writer

by

Susan Wise Bauer

INSTRUCTOR TEXT

This book is to be used in conjunction with *Writing With Skill, Level One: Level 5 of the Complete Writer, Student Text*

Level 1 ISBN 978-1-933339-53-5

Available at www.welltrainedmind.com or wherever books are sold

Cover design by Mollie Bauer.

Publisher's Cataloging-In-Publication Data
(Prepared by The Donohue Group, Inc.)

Bauer, S. Wise.
Writing with skill. Level one, Instructor text / Susan Wise Bauer.

p. : ill. ; cm. — (The complete writer ; level 5)

"This book is to be used in conjunction with *Writing With Skill, Level One: Level 5 of the Complete Writer, Student Text.*"—T.p. verso.
Interest grade level: 5-8.
ISBN: 978-1-933339-52-8

1. English language—Composition and exercises—Study and teaching (Elementary) 2. English language—Rhetoric—Study and teaching (Elementary) I. Title. II. Title: Writing with skill. Level one, Instructor Text.

LB1576 .B382 2012
372.62/3

OVERVIEW

TABLE OF CONTENTS

Part III: Sentence Skills 207

Weeks 16–22

Part VII: Final Project 519

Weeks 35–36

INTRODUCTION

Level One of *Writing with Skill* is the first in a four-level writing series designed to prepare students for advanced work in rhetoric and composition. This first level builds basic skills in organization and sentence structure.

The course is designed to "pick up and go." After you read the General Instructions, you may go directly to Week 1 and begin. But I do recommend that you take the time (if not now, soon) to read the Overview of the Year's Sequence that follows (pages xxv-xxvii).

General Instructions

The directions in this course are targeted at the student. As the student moves into the middle grades, she is ready to take on more and more responsibility for her own academic work. Allow her to read the instructions and begin to follow them on her own before you step in with additional help and guidance.

Ultimately, writing is a self-guided activity. This course will develop the student's ability to plan and carry out a piece of writing on her own.

In your text, some instructions will be followed by the notation "(Student Responsibility)." These are to be completed by the student independently, with no assistance from you. When instructions appear without this notation, the student may need you to help with the assignment or to check her work.

When the student sees the symbol ✦, she should stop and answer the question asked before going on. Encourage her to answer these questions out loud; this will force her to come up with a specific answer rather than a vague idea.

NOTE TO INSTRUCTOR: Train the student to read the instructions thoroughly! Students who are transitioning into independent work will be inclined to skim instructions and then tell you that they don't understand. Your first step, when the student is confused, should *always* be to say "Read the instructions out loud to me." Often, you'll find that the student skipped or misunderstood the directions.

The student will need to keep a Composition Notebook. She should use a three-ring notebook divided into six sections. The sections should be labelled "Narrations," "Outlines," "Topoi," "Copia," "Literary Criticism," and "Reference." However, the student will be instructed to label only the first three sections and the last section. The "Copia" and "Literary Criticism" sections will not be used until later in the course (and we're anxious not to scare young writers by making them think that they're going to be writing research papers about novels).

The student should plan on studying writing four days per week. It is appropriate for students at this level to begin to type their assignments. Before the student begins to use any word processing program, **make sure that all grammar and spell check options are turned off.** These crutches make it easy for the young student to write carelessly, depending on the program to pick up any errors. Our goal is to teach students to write carefully, paying close attention to both mechanics and organization.

Beginning in Week 3, the student will need a thesaurus. Although any comprehensive thesaurus will work, the most recent version of the classic *Roget's International Thesaurus* is recommended. Avoid condensed or pocket-sized thesaurii, since these are less complete.

Many young writers may need to continue with regular handwriting (penmanship) practice at a different time during the day.

Evaluation

Rubrics (guides for evaluation) are provided for your use. In my opinion, giving a "grade" is not useful at this level. Use the rubric to decide whether the student has done an adequate job by following the instructions for the assignment. If the student has not followed the instructions, show him specifically where his composition falls short, and ask him to revise the assignment.

Samples of acceptable answers are also given when appropriate. These acceptable answers have the minimum level of complexity and information you should require from the student; if the student wishes to answer with more detail and subtlety, encourage him to do so.

Customizing the Course

You should feel free to adapt the assignments and pace to fit your student.

The first three weeks of the course progress slowly in order to build confidence and accustom the student to working independently. If the student has no difficulty writing narratives, you may skip Week 1. Weeks 2 and 3 should be completed, but the student may do more than one lesson per day.

During the rest of the course, the student may progress faster or slower than the recommended pace. You should also adjust required word lengths and complexity to suit your own needs.

OVERVIEW OF THE YEAR'S SEQUENCE

This course has five elements that are introduced gradually over the first 24 weeks of study.

Narrations. First, the student will review how to write narrations; the ability to summarize a story in three or four sentences is a basic skill which should be in place before middle-grade writing begins. In the first three weeks of the course, the student will review this basic skill. In the next 12-week unit, 11 of the weeks begin with a more difficult one-day narration exercise (the exception is the second week, when an unfamiliar skill introduced in Week 4 is carried over into Week 5 so that the student has additional time to understand it). When these exercises are completed, the student should place them in the first section of the notebook.

It is normal for a student at this level to find one or two of the narrations unusually challenging; sometimes a story just doesn't make sense to a particular reader. But if the student struggles with more than two or three of the narrations, you may need to spend a few weeks working on this skill before continuing with *Writing with Skill.* Additional narration practice is provided in the preceding level of this series, *Writing with Ease, Level Four.* (A placement test for *Writing with Ease* is available on the Writing with Ease page at welltrainedmind.com.)

Outlines. Instead of immediately starting to write compositions, the student will begin by working on skills that need to be in place *before* she begins to write.

Writing involves two difficult tasks. First, the student has to decide what she's writing about—the general topic, the information to include, and where to find that information. Second, the student must put that information into correct order before setting it down on paper.

Instead of asking the student to do both difficult tasks at the same time, this curriculum will give her the chance to learn them separately. She will begin by practicing the second task: setting information down in order.

The student will complete 26 outlining exercises over the course of the year. Outlining helps the student put information in the correct order; once she has ordered her facts, she can begin to write about them. When the student practices outlining, she is developing her ability to carry out the second task in writing.

In this level of the course, the student will concentrate on finding the main idea in each paragraph or section of a composition. This is the most important step in learning to outline. Later levels of this course progress on to more complex outlining skills; the final weeks of this course will prepare the student for the next level by introducing very basic two-level outlining.

These outlines should be placed in the second section of the notebook.

Topoi. *Topoi* is the plural form of the Greek word *topos*, from which we get the English word "topic." The study of topoi develops the student's ability to carry out the first step in the writing process: figuring out what to say.

In classical rhetoric—the study of writing in ancient and medieval times—topoi helped writers and speakers to come up with arguments. An Athenian who wanted to convince his listeners that the leaders of Athens were better than the rulers of Rome might have begun his speech by telling the story of what happened to Rome when it had insane or evil emperors. Then, he might have gone on to explain that the reason why Athens was flourishing was because it had sane, virtuous leaders.

Both parts of the argument are topoi. The first (telling the story of what happened to Rome) is a topos called "chronological narrative"—a story told from beginning to end in the same order that it happened in time. The second is a topos called "cause and effect sequence"—connecting something that happened (Athens flourished!) with whatever caused it (sane, virtuous leaders).

Topos literally means "place," and topoi are places that the young writer goes in order to find material for composition. If the student's assignment in history is "Read this chapter about the Great Pyramid and then write a brief composition," having a list of topoi in mind helps the student come up with the subject of the composition. She might think "Can I tell a story about the Great Pyramid from beginning to end? Yes, I could write about its construction." (That would be a chronological narrative on a historical topic.) Or she might think "Can I explain cause and effect about the Great Pyramid? Yes, I could write about Egyptian views on the afterlife, and how those views caused the Great Pyramid to be built." (That would be a cause and effect sequence for a historical event.)

Over the course of the year, the student will learn how to construct four basic (and valuable) topoi in history and science: chronological narrative, description, descriptive sequence, and cause and effect sequence. These are simplifications of topoi that Aristotle first proposed as tools for debators, adapted for the use of middle-grade writers. Chronological narratives make use of the skills developed in the narration exercises; the other forms make use of the skills developed in outlining.

Copia. Beginning in Week 16, copia exercises will replace the narration assignments. These exercises are intended to improve the student's prose style.

Copia ("abundance") is the widely accepted nickname for the famous writing text *Brevis de copia praeceptio* ("A Short Rule for Copiousness"), written by the Renaissance scholar and theologian Desiderius Erasmus and printed in 1512. In *Copia,* Erasmus offered students a detailed analysis of prose style, encouraging them to develop many different prose patterns ("abundant" ways of expression). He then took a single sentence, "Your letter pleased me greatly," and rephrased it 195 different ways, including:

> Your epistle exhilarated me intensely.
> At your words a delight of no ordinary kind came over me.
> How exceedingly agreeable did we find your epistle!

Your brief note made me burst with joy.
Your by no means displeasing letter has arrived.[1]

The copia exercises in *Writing with Skill* ask students to rephrase, recast, and reword assigned sentences. The practice of copia forces students to use variety and encourages them to be alert to the patterns of sentences. Copia exercises were a staple of grammar-school education in Erasmus's day; they trained students to be "resourceful in language" and "served as a basis for all future literary education."[2]

The copia exercises assume a basic knowledge of grammar. *Writing With Skill* should be used in conjunction with a thorough grammar course.

Literary Criticism. Beginning in Week 23, the student will begin to learn how to write about literature: fiction and poetry.

Basic literary criticism is a type of writing that most students will be asked to perform at some point in their academic career; even engineering students are usually required to take a literature course in the first year of college, and will be assigned "reaction" or "literary analysis" papers. In the first year of this curriculum, students will begin to gently build the skills needed for writing about imaginative literature. They will spend four weeks learning to write the answers to basic questions about fiction, and three weeks doing the same for poetry. These written answers will form the foundation of more advanced skills, taught in later years of this course.

Documentation. In the first 26 weeks of the course, the student's focus will be on learning the basic forms, or topoi, that can be used to construct a longer composition. Once these basic forms are learned, an additional skill will be added: properly documenting the sources of information. Starting in Week 27, the student will continue to practice the topoi but will also begin to add footnotes and in-text citations to his compositions. Through this, she'll also learn to avoid plagiarism.

Final Project. In the last two weeks of the course, the student will put all of the skills she's learned together to produce an original composition. Although source material for assignments is provided in the first 34 weeks of the course, the student will need to find her own source material for the final project. Suggestions for possible topics and sources are provided in this instructor text only.

---

1. Desiderius Erasmus, *Copia: Foundations of the Abundant Style: De duplici copia verborum ac rerum Commentarii duo*, trans. and ed. Betty I. Knott, in *Collected Works of Erasmus: Literary and Educational Writings 2*, ed. Craig R. Thompson, vol. 28 (Toronto: University of Toronto Press, 1978), ch. 33.
2. Desiderius Erasmus, *Colloquies*, trans. Craig R. Thompson (Toronto: University of Toronto Press, 1997), p. 164.

Part I

BASIC SKILLS
WEEKS 1–3

Overview of Weeks 1–3

The first three weeks of this course will review and practice three basic skills: finding the main idea in a story, finding the main idea in a paragraph, and using a thesaurus to find synonyms.

The student has been instructed to label the first section of the Composition Notebook "Narrations" and the second "Outlines."

Narrations. First, the student will review how to write narrations.

Summarizing forces the student to identify the central story, or plot, of a narrative. This story-line is the *skeleton* of a narrative fiction; it lies underneath all of the details, dialogue, and actions, and organizes them into a particular order. Finding the story-line in narrative fiction will make it easier for the student, later on, to write her own compositions. This review will also equip the student for the lessons in beginning literary criticism (Weeks 23–26).

Finished narrations should be placed in the first section of the student's Composition Notebook.

Outlines. Before the student begins to write her own compositions, she will study how other writers organize *their* work—what order they put their information in. She will learn how to *outline* their work by noting down the main idea in each section of their compositions. This will teach her the basic skills of outlining, which she can then use to organize her own compositions.

Finished outlines should be placed in the second section of the student's Composition Notebook.

In the third week, the student will practice using the thesaurus as she writes both a narration and an outline. She will need her own thesaurus. Although any comprehensive thesaurus will work, the most recent version of the classic *Roget's International Thesaurus* is recommended. Avoid condensed or pocket-sized thesaurii, since these are less complete. Free online thesaurii, as well as the "thesaurus" tool in most word processors, are also very incomplete. (With reference books, you get what you pay for.) Use a print thesaurus instead.

Week 1: Narrative Summaries

Day One: Original Narration Exercise

Focus: Summarizing a narrative by choosing the main events and listing them chronologically

The steps that say "Student Responsibility" should be completed by the student with no assistance or feedback from you. Other steps may require you to help the student and/or check the student's work.

The student instructions are reproduced below for your convenience.

STEP ONE: **Read (Student Responsibility)**

Student instructions for Step One:

Read the following excerpt from the beginning of the first chapter of *The Pepins and Their Problems* by Polly Horvath.

At the end of the excerpt, you will see a small number that sits up above the last word. This small number is called a *superscript* number. *Super* means "above, over," so a superscript number sits up above the regular script, or print.

When you see the superscript number, look down at the bottom of the page. You will see a line of smaller type beginning with the same number. This is called a *footnote,* because it is a note at the foot, or bottom, of the page. The footnote tells you the title of the book that the excerpt comes from, the author, the publisher, the year of publication, and the page numbers in the book where the excerpt is found.

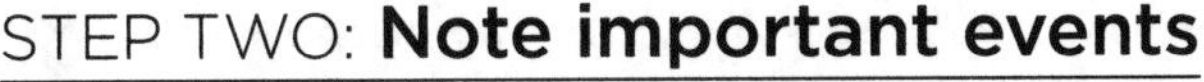

STEP TWO: **Note important events**

Student instructions for Step Two:

This is a short and simple passage—a warm-up for you!

When you summarize a narrative, it's often best to start by jotting down a few phrases or short sentences that remind you of things that happened in the story. Although you may not need to do this with such a short passage, practice this now. On scratch paper, write down four or five phrases or short sentences that will remind you of the things that happened in the passage. *Do not use more than five phrases or short sentences!*

Be sure to write the events down in the same order that they happen in the story.

If you have trouble with this assigment, ask your instructor for help.

HOW TO HELP THE STUDENT WITH STEP TWO

The student should have written down on scratch paper four or five short phrases or sentences that summarize the main events. The phrases/sentences should resemble a few of the following (these are given only as a guide):

The Pepins always have problems.
The Pepins and their bizarre problems
Toads in their shoes
Couldn't put on their shoes
No one knew what to do.
They went next door to ask their neighbor for help.
Their neighbor had toads in his shoes too.
No one knew how to get the toads out.

This should be an easy assignment, but if the student is having difficulty getting started, ask him:

Who are the main characters in this story? *(The Pepins)*
What problem do they have? *(There are toads in their shoes.)*
How do they try to solve the problem? *(They go ask their neighbor.)*
Does the solution work? *(No, it does not.)*

STEP THREE: **Write summary sentences**

Student instructions for Step Three:

After you've written down your four or five phrases or sentences, try to combine them into two or three sentences. You can do this by putting two phrases in the same sentence (for example, "Toads in their shoes" and "They couldn't put on their shoes" could be combined into "They couldn't put on their shoes because there were toads in the shoes"). Or you may find that one or more of your jotted notes turns out to be unnecessary. (If you leave out the detail that Mr. Bradshaw was eating corn cereal, the summary will still make sense!)

Say your two or three sentences out loud several times before writing them down. After you've written the sentences down, ask your instructor to check them. Remember to proofread the sentences first. Reading them out loud *after* you've written them is an excellent way to check your own work.

If you have trouble, ask your instructor for help.

HOW TO HELP THE STUDENT WITH STEP THREE

In this step, the student practices turning the jotted phrases and sentences into two or three smooth, coherent sentences. She should say her sentences out loud several times before she writes; listen to make sure that you hear her talking out loud, and if necessary remind her that she should be speaking before she writes.

An acceptable narration might sound like one of the following:

The Pepins were always having strange problems. One morning, they woke up to find toads in their shoes. None of them knew what to do.

OR

The Pepins woke up one morning to find out that their shoes were full of toads. So were their neighbor's, Mr. Bradshaw. None of them knew how to get the toads out of the shoes.

OR

The Pepins found toads in their shoes and couldn't get them out. They went next door to see Mr. Bradshaw, but he didn't know how to get the toads out either.

When the summary is finished, check it using the following rubric (guide to evaluation). This rubric focuses only on the skills emphasized in this lesson. Future rubrics will build on this, as the student learns more about both organization and mechanics.

Week 1 Narration Rubric

Organization

1 Events should be in chronological order.

2 If two or more events are listed in a single sentence, they should have a cause and effect relationship.

For example:

The Pepins didn't know what to do, so they went next door to ask Mr. Bradshaw

is acceptable; they went next door *because* they didn't know what to do.

The Pepins had toads in their shoes, and they went next door

is not acceptable. There is no clear causal relationship between the two sentences.

Mechanics

1 Each sentence should make sense on its own when read aloud.

2 Each proper name should be capitalized.

Day Two: Original Narration Exercise

Focus: Summarizing a narrative by choosing the main events and listing them chronologically

STEP ONE: **Read (Student Responsibility)**

Student instructions for Step One:

Read the following excerpt from *The Wolves of Willoughby Chase* by Joan Aiken. In this passage, young Sylvia is travelling to stay with her wealthy cousin Bonnie at the country house known as Willoughby Chase. She has not had enough to eat, and her clothes are old and thin, so she is both hungry and cold—but she knows that she should be suspicious of the strange man who is sharing the railway carriage with her. When he offers her a box of chocolates, she refuses, even though her mouth waters.

STEP TWO: **Note important events**

Student instructions for Step Two:

On scratch paper, write down five or six phrases or short sentences that will remind you of the things that happened in the passage. *Do not use more than six phrases or short sentences!* There are many vivid details in this passage (like the "jam tarts, maids of honor, lemon cheese cakes, Chelsea buns, and numerous little iced confections"). Remember that details should not be included in a summary—try to stay focused on the main events.

Be sure to write the events down in the same order that they happen in the story.

If you have trouble with this assigment, ask your instructor for help.

HOW TO HELP THE STUDENT WITH STEP TWO

Today's exercise is designed to remind the student that details should not go into a summary. The details in this passage—the description of the cakes, the wolves, Sylvia's dream—are so vivid that the student will be tempted to include them. If you see him writing many more than five or six short phrases or sentences, check to make sure that he is not listing details instead of main events.

The student's phrases/sentences should resemble some of the following (these are given only as a guide):

The man offered Sylvia cakes to eat.
Sylvia was uncomfortable with the man.
Sylvia ignored man.
Stranger offered her cakes but she refused.
Sylvia fell asleep in the train.
Train stopped because of wolves.

Wolves got on the line.
Train stopped.
Wolves tried to get into the train.
A wolf broke the window.
A wolf broke into the train compartment.
The stranger stabbed the wolf.

If the student is having difficulty condensing the story, ask him:

How does Sylvia react to the man in the train? *(She tries to ignore him/feels uncomfortable.)*
What happens to stop the train? *(Wolves are on the line.)*
What happens after the train stops? *(A wolf breaks in through the window.)*
How does the man react? *(He stabs the wolf with a piece of glass.)*

STEP THREE: **Write summary sentences**

Student instructions for Step Three:

> After you've written down your five or six phrases or sentences, try to combine them into three or four sentences. Remember: you can do this by putting two phrases or sentences together (for example, "Sylvia was uncomfortable" and "The man offered her cakes but she refused" could be combined into "Sylvia was uncomfortable with the man, so when he offered her cakes she refused"). Or you may find that one or more of your jotted notes turns out to be unnecessary. (If you completely leave out the information that the man offered her cakes, the summary will still make sense!)
>
> Say your three or four sentences out loud several times before writing them down. After you've written the sentences down, ask your instructor to check them. Remember to proofread the sentences first by reading them out loud.
>
> If you have trouble, ask your instructor for help.

HOW TO HELP THE STUDENT WITH STEP THREE

In this step, the student practices turning the jotted phrases and sentences into three or four smooth, coherent sentences. She should say her sentences out loud several times before she writes; listen to make sure that you hear her talking out loud, and if necessary remind her that she should be speaking before she writes.

An acceptable narration might sound like one of the following:

Sylvia found herself on the train with a stranger. He offered her cakes, but she tried to ignore him. After they had been travelling for a while, wolves on the line stopped the train. One wolf broke into the train car, but the stranger stabbed it to death.

OR

Sylvia was very uncomfortable with the stranger who was in her compartment, so she tried to ignore him and went to sleep. She woke up when the train stopped. Wolves were on the line, and one of them broke into the compartment. The man threw his cloak over the wolf and stabbed it with a piece of glass.

OR

When Sylvia took the train to see her cousin, she had to share her compartment with a stranger. Then wolves on the line stopped the train. One wolf broke into the compartment, but the man killed it.

When the summary is finished, check it using the Week 1 Narration Rubric from Day One.

Day Three: Original Narration Exercise

Focus: Summarizing nonfiction by choosing the main events and listing them chronologically

In Days One and Two, the student wrote narrations summarizing two excerpts from novels—long works of creative fiction. However, narrations can also be used to summarize nonfiction (history, science, biography, etc.).

STEP ONE: **Read (Student Responsibility)**

Student instructions for Step One:

> The following passage about the Russian czar Peter the Great, who ruled 1682–1725, comes from *The Story of the World, Volume 3: Early Modern Times* by Susan Wise Bauer.

STEP TWO: **Note important events**

Student instructions for Step Two:

> On scratch paper, write down six or seven phrases or short sentences that will remind you of the things that happened in the passage. Do not use more than seven phrases or short sentences! Make sure that you focus on the main events in the passage (like the Russian army's conquest of Azov) rather than the smaller details (the weather started to grow colder).
>
> Be sure to write the events down in the same order that they happen in the story.
>
> If you have trouble with this assignment, ask your instructor for help.

HOW TO HELP THE STUDENT WITH STEP TWO

The student should have written down on scratch paper six or seven short phrases or sentences that summarize the main events. The phrases/sentences should resemble some of the following:

Peter the Great wanted to sail to Europe.
Peter fascinated by the West
Peter the Great wanted his merchant ships to visit the West.

He needed a port.
His only port city was frozen for half the year.
The Russians needed a warmer port.
Peter wanted to capture the Port of Azov.
The Port of Azov was on the Sea of Azov which led to the Black Sea and Mediterranean.
The Turks controlled the Port of Azov.
Peter thought he could defeat the Turks.
Peter took his army to Azov and laid siege to it.
The Russian siege didn't work.
Turkish ships kept sailing in and out.
The Russians built warships and barges.
The Russians spent the winter building a fleet.
The new Russian navy drove off the Turkish galleys.
The Russians got into the fortress on a pile of rubble.
The Russian army defeated the Turks.
Peter and his army captured Azov.

If the student is having difficulty condensing the passage, ask her:

What does Peter the Great want at the beginning of the passage? *(To visit the West)*
Why can't the Russian ships visit the West? *(They don't have a port to sail in and out of.)*
What does Peter decide to do? *(Take Azov away from the Turks)*
Why doesn't the siege work at first? *(Turkish ships can sail into Azov with food and weapons.)*
How do the Russians stop the Turkish ships? *(They build a navy and block the Turkish galleys.)*
What is the end result? *(They conquer Azov.)*

STEP THREE: **Write summary sentences**

Student instructions for Step Three:

> After you've written down your six or seven phrases or sentences, try to combine them into four sentences. Remember: you can do this by putting two phrases or sentences together, or you may find that one or more of your jotted notes turns out to be unnecessary.
>
> Say your sentences out loud several times before writing them down. After you've written the sentences down, ask your instructor to check them. Remember to proofread the sentences first by reading them out loud.
>
> If you have trouble, ask your instructor for help.

HOW TO HELP THE STUDENT WITH STEP THREE

In this step, the student practices turning the jotted phrases and sentences into four smooth, coherent sentences. She should say her sentences out loud several times before she writes; listen to make sure that you hear her talking out loud, and if necessary remind her that she should be speaking before she writes.

An acceptable narration might sound like one of the following:

Peter the Great was fascinated by the West. He wanted his ships to sail to Europe, but the only Russian port was frozen for half the year. So he laid siege to the Port of Azov, which was held by the Turks. After the Russians built a navy to drive off the Turkish ships, Azov was conquered.

OR

Peter the Great wanted his ships to sail to the West. His only port was frozen for much of the year, so he laid siege to the Port of Azov. At first, the Russians could not conquer it because the Turkish ships resupplied it from the water. So over the winter the Russians built a new navy and used it to conquer Azov.

OR

Peter the Great wanted to sail to the West, but first he had to conquer the Port of Azov. The port was held by the Turks, and without ships, the Russians were not able to besiege it successfully. After they built a navy, though, they were able to drive off the Turkish warships. Then they conquered Azov by building a mound of rubbish and using it to climb over the walls.

When the summary is finished, check it using the Week 1 Narration Rubric from Day One.

Day Four: Challenge Exercise

Focus: Summarizing a complete narrative by choosing the main events and listing them chronologically

In the final review exercise of this week, the student will practice summing up an entire story, from beginning to end. While the story is not difficult, there are many details, and it may take the student some time to sort out the main events.

STEP ONE: **Read (Student Responsibility)**

Student instructions for Step One:

> This traditional folktale is German in origin—but it is so old that no one knows for sure where it came from (or what it means). The Brothers Grimm included it in their 1812 collection of fairy tales, but this version is from Andrew Lang's classic collection *The Red Fairy Book*.

STEP TWO: **Note important events and write summary sentences**

Student instructions for Step Two:

You can summarize a long story like this in one of two ways.

If you're able to, just list the six or eight most important events in the story, in the same order that they happen in the story. But because there are so many details in the story, you might have to write down *each* event first—even though this will make a much longer list. However, once you've written down the longer list, you should be able to group events together and condense them so that you end up with only six or eight *main* events.

Here's an example. You might be able to look at the first five paragraphs of the story and sum them up in a single sentence:

Dullhead had two older brothers who refused to share their food with a stranger.

But you might have to list each event instead, like this:

Dullhead was the youngest of three sons.
All three brothers met a little man in the forest.
He asked them to share their food and drink.
The two oldest would not share their food with him.
The two oldest brothers hurt themselves after they refused to share.

Then you would need to work at condensing those five sentences into one or two sentences. You could start by crossing out the repetition:

Dullhead was the youngest of three sons.
~~All three brothers~~ met a little man in the forest.
He asked them to share their food and drink.
The two oldest ~~would not share their food with him.~~
~~The two oldest brothers~~ hurt themselves after they refused to share.

Then, cross out the details that aren't necessary for the understanding of the story.

Dullhead was the youngest of three sons.
met a little man ~~in the forest~~
He asked them to share their food ~~and drink~~.
The two oldest
~~hurt themselves after they refused~~ to share

Now, the first part of your summary might sound like this:

Dullhead was the youngest of three sons who met a little man in the forest. He asked to share their food, but the two oldest refused.

Your finished summary should not be more than eight sentences in length.

You should expect this exercise to take you some time, so don't get frustrated! When you have finished your summary, read it aloud. If it is still too long, read through it a second time, looking for unnecessary information or repeated phrases. Cross these out and try to combine sentences.

If you have trouble with this assignment, ask your instructor for help. And when you are finished with your summary, check your work with your instructor.

HOW TO HELP THE STUDENT WITH STEP TWO

The student has been given the choice of either summarizing directly or writing down on scratch paper a list of main events and *then* summarizing. If the student chooses to list the main events, his phrases/sentences should resemble some of the following:

Dullhead was the youngest of three sons.
Dullhead had two brothers and was the youngest.
All three brothers met a little man in the the forest.
He asked them to share their food and drink.
The two oldest would not share their food with him.
The two oldest brothers hurt themselves after they refused to share.
Dullhead shared his food.
He was given a golden goose.
He stayed at an inn.
The inn-keeper's daughters tried to pluck the feathers.
They stuck to the goose when they touched it.
Dullhead took the goose with the three girls attached to it.
Four more people touched them and stuck to each other.
They came to a town ruled by a king with a serious daughter.
The king had promised that whoever could make his daughter laugh would marry her.
The princess laughed when she saw Dullhead and the people stuck to him.
The king did not want Dullhead to marry his daughter.
He told Dullhead to find a man who could drink a whole cellar of wine.
Dullhead found a man who could drink it.
He told Dullhead to find a man who could eat a mountain of bread.
Dullhead found a man who could eat all the bread.
He told Dullhead to find a ship that could sail on land or water.
Dullhead found the little man.
The little man gave him the ship.
The king gave Dullhead his daughter.
Dullhead and the princess ruled the kingdom for many years.

An acceptable finished summary might resemble one of the following:

Dullhead was the youngest of three sons who met a little man in the forest. He asked to share their food, but the two oldest refused. Dullhead shared his food, and was given a golden goose as a reward. Seven people tried to touch the goose and stuck to it instead. When Dullhead took the goose and the seven people into a nearby town, the princess of the town laughed at him. The king had promised that she could marry anyone who made her laugh, but he did not want Dullhead to be his son-in-law. So he gave Dullhead three impossible tasks. The little man helped Dullhead finish the tasks, and he was able to marry the princess.

Dullhead met a little man in the forest and was kind to him. The little man gave him a golden goose as his reward. Then Dullhead discovered that anyone who tried to steal a feather from the goose stuck to it. Soon he had seven people stuck to the goose. He took the goose and the seven people into a nearby town, which was ruled by a king with a serious daughter. The king had promised that whoever made the princess laugh could marry her. Dullhead and his goose made the princess laugh, but instead of giving him the princess, the king asked him to do three tasks. Dullhead finished the tasks with the help of the little man and married the princess.

Dullhead received a magical golden goose as a reward because he was kind to a little man in the forest. Everyone who tried to steal a feather from the goose stuck to it. So Dullhead took the goose and all of the people who were stuck to it into a nearby town. The town was ruled by a king who had promised his daughter to anyone who could make her laugh. She laughed when she saw Dullhead, but the king did not want him to to marry the princess. So he told Dullhead to find a man who could drink a cellarfull of wine, a man who could eat a mountain of bread, and a ship that could sail on land or water. With the magical help of the little man, Dullhead found all three and married the princess.

If the student is unable to trim his summary down to eight sentences, ask him to answer the following questions in one sentence each.

What good thing did Dullhead do?
What did he get as a reward?
What was strange about it?
Where did he go?
What promise had been made?
Was it kept? If not, what happened instead?
How did Dullhead react?
What was the end result?

Check the student's summary using the following rubric.

Week 1 Challenge Narration Rubric

Organization

1 Events should be in chronological order.
2 If two or more events are listed in a single sentence, they should have a cause and effect relationship.
3 The summary must not be more than eight sentences in length.
4 It should mention the little man, the goose, Dullhead, the king, and the princess; the other characters do not need to be named as long as the series of events is clear.
5 It should end with Dullhead's marriage to the princess.

Mechanics

1 Each sentence should make sense on its own when read aloud.
2 Each proper name should be capitalized.
3 The student may choose to capitalize *King* and *Princess* (since the story does) or to leave them lowercase, but should be consistent throughout the story.

Week 2: One-Level Outlines

Day One: Introduction to Outlining

Focus: Understanding the basic principles of outlining

For the last week, the student has reviewed writing narrations—three or four sentences summarizing the central story, or plot, of a narrative. Now the student will begin to work on a new form of summary writing: outlining.

Before the student begins outlining, he will become familiar with two terms: *paragraph* and *topic sentence.*

The student will work independently today; his instructions are reproduced below for your convenience.

STEP ONE: **Understand paragraphs**

A paragraph is a group of sentences that are all related to a single subject. You can recognize a paragraph because the first sentence is *indented* (begins half an inch farther to the right than all the other sentences).

Look at the following paragraph from the book *Inside of a Dog: What Dogs See, Smell, and Know*:

All of the sentences in this paragraphs are related to one subject: the fight between the wolfhound and the Chihuahua. (Notice that the first sentence is indented.)

Now read the following three paragraphs, found in *Understanding Light: The Science of Visible and Invisible Rays:*

The sentences in these three paragraph are also all related to a single subject. What object does the paragraph describe?

All of the paragraphs tell us something about *the human eye.* But you can't just use "The human eye" as the subject for each paragraph, because *all* of the paragraphs talk about the human eye.

Instead, each paragraph tells us about a different part or function of the human eye. In the first paragraph, all of the sentences are related to the subject "What the human eye can do." In the second paragraph, all of the sentences are related to the subject "What people understand about how the human eye works." What is the subject of the third paragraph? Remember: it will have something to do with the human eye.

✦

The subject of the third paragraph is "The structure of the human eye" or "What the human eye looks like."

When you start to outline, you will try to summarize the subject of each paragraph in one or two phrases or in one sentence. Your summary sentence or phrases should be specific enough to show how the paragraph is different from other paragraphs that might have the same *general* subject.

STEP TWO: **Understand topic sentences**

Sometimes, paragraphs have *topic sentences.* A topic sentence does your work for you, because it states the subject of the paragraph outright. Topic sentences are usually found near the beginning or end of a paragraph.

Read the following four paragraphs. In each paragraph, the topic sentence is in bold print.

The first paragraph is about the discovery of the Pacific Ocean by Balboa—which is exactly what the topic sentence tells you. The second paragraph is about the clusters of galaxies in the universe. The third paragraph tells the story of the camera. And the fourth paragraph is all about distraction.

In each of these paragraphs, the topic sentence sums up the subject of the paragraph. But many paragraphs do not have a single topic sentence. Look again at the three paragraphs from *Understanding Light* that you looked at in Step One. Beside each paragraph, you will see the summary phrases or sentence that explain the paragraph's main subject.

These are perfectly good paragraphs—but none of them have a single topic sentence that sums up the main subject. Not every good paragraph has a topic sentence, but in every good paragraph, all of the sentences relate to a single main subject.

You will not be required to identify or write topic sentences in this year of study. However, you will often see the term *topic sentence* used, so you should know what it means.

STEP THREE: **Understand basic outlining**

In the final step of today's lesson, you'll study the basic principles of outlining.

When you outline a passage of writing, you begin by finding the main idea in each paragraph and assigning it a Roman numeral. Your goal is not to write a single sentence that incorporates *all* (or even most) of the information in the paragraph. Instead, you should try to write a sentence (or several phrases) that sums up the paragraph's central theme, or subject.

You can often find the central subject of the paragraph by asking two questions for each paragraph:

1. What is the main thing or person that the paragraph is about?
2. Why is that thing important?

Read the following paragraph from *The Story of Canada* by Janet Lunn and Christopher Moore.

Now answer the following questions before looking at the answers.

What is the main thing that the paragraph is about?

Buffalo. The paragraph does talk about the Blackfoot people as well—but notice that the paragraph begins with the *buffalo,* and that all of the references to the Blackfoot people are made to explain how the *buffalo* were used.

Why is the buffalo important?

Because the Blackfoot people used it for food, clothing, and other purposes.

If you were to put together these two answers in one sentence, it would look something like this:

I. The Blackfoot people used buffalo for food, clothing, and many other purposes.

(Notice that I is the Roman numeral for "1" or "first paragraph.")

You might be tempted to write a whole list of things that the Blackfoot people used buffalo for ("The Blackfoot used the buffalo for meat, tipis and clothing, thread, clubs, spoons, needles, and fuel"), but when you are constructing an outline, you should *not* include *all* of the information in the paragraph. Instead, you should summarize. If you

The next paragraph in *The Story of Canada* reads:

Ask the question: What is the main thing that the paragraph is about?

Horses.
Why are horses important?

The Blackfoot tribe learned how to ride them in the 1700s.
So your sentence would sound like this:

II. The Blackfoot tribe learned to use horses in the 1700s.
(Note that II is the Roman numeral for "2" or "second paragraph.")

Remember: you are not trying to summarize every detail in the entire paragraph. You are finding the central idea in it.

In the next day's work, you'll try to find the central idea in each paragraph for yourself.

Day Two: Outlining Exercise

Focus: Finding the main idea in each paragraph of a passage about history

In today's exercise, the student will construct his first one-level outline.

As you help the student with the rest of this year's outlining exercises, keep this principle in mind: There may be several different, but valid, ways to outline any given paragraph. If the student can give good reasons why he's chosen his points, don't worry about whether he's constructed the best possible outline.

STEP ONE: **Read (Student Responsibility)**

Student instructions for Step One:

This excerpt is from a biography called *Hatshepsut: Egypt's First Female Pharaoh,* by Pamela Dell.

You'll find the passage easier to understand if you have a little background information. Hatshepsut's father, Thutmose I, died around 1492 BC and left two heirs: his daughter Hatshepsut and his son Thutmose II. Hatshepsut had the best claim to the throne, because she was the daughter of Thutmose I's most important wife. But Thutmose I wanted his son, Thutmose II, to be the next ruler of Egypt instead. Unfortunately, Thutmose II was the son of a much less important wife.

To make Thutmose II more acceptable to the people as the next pharoah, Thutmose I arranged for him to marry Hatshepsut—his half-sister. The Egyptian royal pharaohs often did this. They believed that their blood was divine, so they were reluctant to marry anyone from outside the royal family—that would be like mixing divine and human blood.

STEP TWO: **Begin to construct a one-level outline**

Student instructions for Step Two:

> The passage selected for today's outlining exercise has short, easy paragraphs. Remember, you should begin by asking one simple question:
>
> 1. What is the main thing or person that this section is about?
>
> In this passage, every single paragraph is about Hatshepsut, Thutmose II—or both of them.
>
> Begin your outline by deciding whether each paragraph is about Hatshepsut, Thutmose II, or both. Write your answers on the outline below, remembering that each Roman numeral stands for a paragraph of the reading. The first point is done for you.
>
> I. Hatshepsut and Thutmose II
> II.
> III.
> IV.
> V.
> VI.
> VII.
>
> When you are finished, check your work with your instructor.

HOW TO HELP THE STUDENT WITH STEP TWO

The student's answers should be:

I. Hatshepsut and Thutmose II
II. Hatshepsut
III. Hatshepsut
IV. Thutmose II
V. Thutmose II
VI. Hatshepsut
VII. Hatshepsut

Paragraphs II-V should be very straightforward, since only one of the two characters is mentioned. In the sixth and seventh paragraphs, Thutmose is mentioned, but the focus is very clearly on Hatshepsut's roles as wife and mother.

STEP THREE: **Finish constructing a one-level outline**

Student instructions for Step Three:

> Now finish your outline by asking the second question: In each paragraph, what did these people *do?* Or to put it another way: What event or part of their lives or accomplishment does the entire paragraph talk about?
>
> Remember, you should not be listing individual details from the paragraphs. Instead, try to think of the single word or phrase that sums up what all the details have in common.
>
> Consider the first paragraph:
>
> No one knows for sure whether Hatshepsut and Thutmose II were married when their

father died. But at the time of their marriage, neither of them was an adult. Hatshepsut was probably between 12 and 15, and Thutmose was probably a few years older or younger.

You wouldn't finish out the first main point on your outline by writing:

I. Hatshepsut and Thutmose II may have married before their father died, were both very young

Both the timing of their marriage, and the *age* at which they were married, are details. But both of those details tell you more about their *marriage*. So your first point should be:

I. Hatshepsut and Thutmose II and their marriage

or

I. Hatshepsut and Thutmose II's marriage

Try now to finish your outline by finding the main subject of each paragraph. You can use the answer above for I.

If you have trouble, ask your instructor for help. When you are finished, check your work with your instructor.

HOW TO HELP THE STUDENT WITH STEP THREE

The student's answers should resemble the following:

I. Hatshepsut and Thutmose II get married OR Hatshepsut and Thutmose II's marriage
II. Hatshepsut and her vows OR Hatshepsut's vows
III. Hatshepsut and her titles OR Hatshepsut's titles
IV. Thutmose II and his battles OR Thutmose II's battles
V. Thutmose II and his buildings OR Thutmose II's buildings
VI. Hatshepsut and her duties OR Hatshepsut and her duties as King's Wife
VII. Hatshepsut and her role as mother OR Hatshepsut and her children

If the student struggles with this assignment, use the following dialogues:

Paragraph 2

Instructor: Hatshepsut promised to do five things. What were they?

Student: Be feminine, exude fragrance, speak in musical tones, make herself loved, tend her lord

Instructor: What word do the writers use for these promises? They say that Hatshepsut took traditional. . .

Student: Vows

Instructor: So this paragraph is all about Hatshepsut's five. . .

Student: Vows

Paragraph 3

Instructor: There are four proper names for Hatshepsut listed in this paragraph. What does the paragraph call these names? Hint: they are King's Daughter, King's Great Royal Wife, God's Wife of Amun, King's Sister.

Student: They are titles.

Instructor: So this paragraph is all about Hatshepsut's four. . .

Student: Titles

Paragraph 4

Instructor: This paragraph tells you all about one kind of success that Thutmose II may—or may not—have had. What kind of success was that?

Student: Success in battle OR *Military success*

Instructor: So the paragraph is all about Thutmose II's battles. That is your main point.

Paragraph 5

Instructor: What three things did Thutmose II build, according to this paragraph?

Student: Monuments, other works, the temple complex at Karnak

Instructor: So this paragraph is about Thutmose II's success at. . .

Student: Building

Instructor: That is your main point.

Paragraph 6

Instructor: The main point of this paragraph is found in the very first sentence. What did Hatshepsut perform?

Student: Her royal wifely duties

Instructor: "Hatshepsut's duties" are the main subject of the paragraph.

Paragraph 7

Instructor: This paragraph is all about another kind of job that Hatshepsut had. What was that job or role?

Student: To be a mother

Instructor: So you could say that this paragraph is all about Hatshepsut's role as a. . .

Student: Mother

Day Three: Outlining Exercise

Focus: Finding the main idea in each paragraph of a passage about science

The student will continue to practice basic outlining skills for the rest of this week.

STEP ONE: **Read (Student Responsibility)**

Student instructions for Step One:

This excerpt, from the basic geology text *The Round World* by Michael Dempsey, discusses the metals found in the crust of the Earth (the outermost layer of the Earth).

STEP TWO: **Understand how to outline science writing (Student Responsibility)**

Student instructions for Step Two:

When you outline science writing, you may need to ask slightly different versions of the questions suggested at the beginning of this week. Remember, those questions are:

1. What is the main thing or person that the paragraph is about?
2. Why is that thing important?

For a science text, you might sometimes find it more useful to ask:

1. What is being described or defined in this paragraph?
2. Is there one central thing which is most important about it?

Look at the first paragraph again and ask yourself: What is being described or defined in this paragraph?

This isn't an easy question to answer, because the paragraph starts out with a *negative* definition. What is *not* (or rarely) found in the Earth's crust?

Pure metals.

This paragraph is centered around describing what is found in the Earth's crust *instead of* pure metals. Pure metals aren't found in the Earth's crust—what is found instead?

Metals combined with other elements.

That answers both questions—metals are being described in this paragraph, and the most important thing about those metals is that they're combined with other elements.

So the first point in your outline would look like this:

I. Metals combined with other elements

There may be more than one good way to phrase a main point. If, for example, you wrote

I. The makeup of metals in the crust

that could also sum up the main idea of the paragraph—which then goes on to define exactly *what* the makeup of metals in the crust is.

STEP THREE: **Construct a one-level outline**

Student instructions for Step Three:

Now finish your outline by finding the main point for each of the remaining three paragraphs.

If you have difficulty, use the hints below. When you are finished, check your work with your instructor.

I. The makeup of metals in the crust (this point was already covered for you!)
II. This point has to do with amounts.
III. This paragraph has a definition in it. What is being defined? (You don't have to give the *content* of the definition.)
IV. How many kinds of what?

HOW TO HELP THE STUDENT WITH STEP THREE

The student's answers should resemble the following:

I. Metals combined with other elements OR The makeup of metals in the crust
II. The quantity of metals in the crusts
III. The definition of ore
IV. The three kinds of rock

Note that the student should *not* put the following level of detail into the outline:

III. Ore is a rock with enough metal to make extraction worthwhile.
IV. The three kinds of rock are igneous, sedimentary, and metamorphic.

Those details belong in a two-level outline:

III. The definition of ore
A. Geological processes concentrated the metal.
B. Rocks with concentrated metal are called ore.
IV. The three kinds of rock
A. Igneous
B. Sedimentary
C. Metamorphic

If the student has difficulty with the outline, use the following dialogue:

Paragraph 2
Instructor: In this paragraph, there are two words repeated twice (each). What are they?

Student: Quantity and metal

Instructor: The main point of this paragraph is "The quantity of metal in the earth's crust."

Paragraph 3
Instructor: What do we call a rock with enough metal in it to make extraction worthwhile?

Student: Ore

Instructor: The main point is "The definition of ore."

Paragraph 4
Instructor: How many kinds of rock are there?

Student: Three

Instructor: The main point is "Three kinds of rock."

Day Four: Outlining Exercise

Focus: Finding the main topic in each paragraph of a passage about science

STEP ONE: **Understand topical outlines (Student Responsibility)**

Student instructions for Step One:

In the last passage you outlined, each paragraph talked about the same basic topic: metals in the Earth's crust. But even though *every* paragraph talked about metals in the Earth's crust, you couldn't outline it by writing:

I. Metals
II. Metals
III. Metals
IV. Metals

Instead, you had to identify what was being *said* about metals in each paragraph. The first paragraph talked about metals combined with each other, the second about how *much* metal was in the crust, the third about metal in rock (ore), and the fourth about the kinds of rock that have metal in them.

But sometimes a writer will use each paragraph of an essay to talk about a different topic. Look at the following paragraphs, adapted from a popular book about birds published at the beginning of the last century:

Each one of these paragraphs describes a different bird. The simplest way to outline the passage is:

I. The road runner
II. Petrels
III. Crows
IV. The dusky grouse

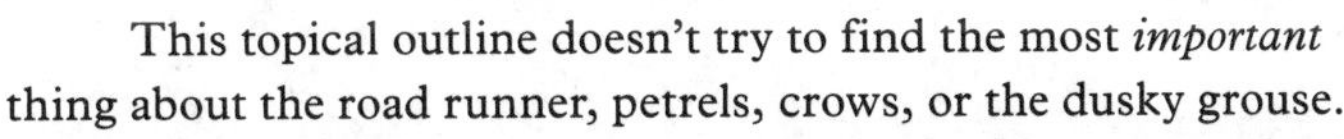

This topical outline doesn't try to find the most *important* thing about the road runner, petrels, crows, or the dusky grouse. Since the paragraphs go on to give a whole list of facts about each bird, it would be almost impossible to figure out which fact is the most "central." What's central in each paragraph is the bird itself.

So the topical outline simply lists the topics: one kind of bird for each paragraph.

STEP TWO: **Read (Student Responsibility)**

Student instructions for Step Two:

This excerpt is taken from the science book *Real Things in Nature* by Edward S. Holden. After you've read the passage, you will construct a basic topical outline of its paragraphs.

STEP THREE: **Construct a one-level topical outline**

Student instructions for Step Three:

Now write a one-level outline for the passage, listing only the main topic discussed in each paragraph. If you have difficulty, ask your instructor for help.

When you are finished, check your work with your instructor.

HOW TO HELP THE STUDENT WITH STEP THREE

The student's outline should resemble the following:

I. The sun
II. The corona
III. Meteors
IV. Shooting stars
V. Comets

The topics of the paragraphs are fairly simple to find, but if the student has difficulty, ask the following questions:

I. What is a huge, intensely hot globe made of gases and vapors and 5,000 times more brilliant than white-hot boiling iron?
II. What is the envelope, or crown, of the sun?
III. What are the clouds of stone that travel in orbits and are usually invisible?
IV. What do we call a meteor that moves into the atmosphere and burns up?
V. What are crowds of stones that move in a swarm around the sun and then never come back?

Week 3: Using the Thesaurus

Day One: Original Narration Exercise

Focus: Summarizing first-person nonfiction

This week, the student will review the skills of narration and outlining and will be introduced to the use of a thesaurus. In today's narration exercise, the student will write a summary that she will make use of in the next lesson.

STEP ONE: **Read (Student Responsibility)**

Student instructions for Step One:

> Read the following excerpt from *The Story of My Life*, the autobiography (a biography written by the person herself) of Helen Keller. Helen Keller was born in 1880. She lost both her hearing and sight after a serious illness when she was 19 months old. Because she could neither see nor hear, she couldn't communicate with others. When she was six years old, her parents asked the Perkins Institute for the Blind in Boston to help them by sending Helen a teacher. The teacher who came was Anne Sullivan, aged 20. Sullivan took on the job of trying to communicate with Helen. In this part of the autobiography, Helen describes the moment when her teacher suddenly found a way to make contact with her.

STEP TWO: **Understand the use of first and third person (Student Responsibility)**

Student instructions for Step Two:

> You will notice that the passage is written in the *first person*—from the point of view of Helen Keller herself. Look at the following quote from the story and circle each bolded pronoun. These are first person pronouns.
>
>> **We** walked down the path to the well-house, attracted by the fragrance of the honeysuckle with which it was covered. Some one was drawing water and **my** teacher placed **my** hand under the spout. As the cool stream gushed over one hand she spelled into the other the word *water*, first slowly, then rapidly. **I** stood still, **my** whole attention fixed upon the motions of her fingers.

Now read another version of the quote, in which the first person pronouns have been changed to third person pronouns and names.

> **Helen and Miss Sullivan** walked down the path to the well-house, attracted by the fragrance of the honeysuckle with which it was covered. Some one was drawing water and **Helen's** teacher placed **her** hand under the spout. As the cool stream gushed over one hand she spelled into the other the word *water*, first slowly, then rapidly. **Helen** stood still, **her** whole attention fixed upon the motions of her fingers.

When you write your summary, you may either use the first person (as though *you* were Helen, summarizing her own story) or the third person point of view. Whichever you choose, be sure to use the same point of view all the way through the summary.

STEP THREE: **Note important events**

Student instructions for Step Three:

Now jot down six or seven phrases or short sentences that remind you of the main events in the passage. Remember, you can use either the first or third person. You can write

Miss Sullivan gave Helen a doll

or

Miss Sullivan gave me a doll

as long as you keep the same point of view in every phrase or sentence.

Do not use more than seven phrases or short sentences! Be sure to write the events down in the same order that they happen in the passage.

If you have trouble with this assignment, ask your instructor for help.

HOW TO HELP THE STUDENT WITH STEP THREE

The student's list of events should resemble six or seven of the following. (The examples below are in the third person; it's fine for the student to use the first person instead.)

Miss Sullivan gave Helen a doll.
She spelled "doll" into Helen's hand.
Helen spelled "doll" too.
Helen showed her mother how to spell "doll."
She didn't understand what she was doing.
She learned to spell many words but didn't know what they meant.
Miss Sullivan tried to teach her what "doll" meant.
Helen could not understand that words stood for things.
Helen broke her doll.
She wasn't sorry.
Her teacher took her outside.
They walked to the well house.
Miss Sullivan put Helen's hand under the water.
She pumped water over Helen's hand and spelled "water" into it.
Helen understood that the word "water" meant water.

Helen understood what a name was for the first time.
She could think with words for the first time.
She felt sorrow for the first time.

If the student has difficulty locating the central events, ask her to answer the following questions in one complete sentence each:

What did Miss Sullivan bring Helen?
In the first paragraph, what did Miss Sullivan teach Helen to do?
Did Helen understand this?
Where did Miss Sullivan take her, and what did they do there?
What two things did Miss Sullivan do at the same time?
What was the result?

STEP FOUR: **Write summary sentences**

Student instructions for Step Four:

> After you've written down your six or seven phrases or sentences, try to combine them into four sentences. Remember: you can do this by putting two phrases or sentences together, or you may find that one or more of your jotted notes turns out to be unnecessary.
>
> Say your sentences out loud several times before writing them down. After you've written the sentences down, ask your instructor to check them. Remember to proofread the sentences first by reading them out loud.
>
> If you have trouble, ask your instructor for help.

HOW TO HELP THE STUDENT WITH STEP FOUR

In this step, the student practices turning the jotted phrases and sentences into four smooth, coherent sentences. She should say her sentences out loud several times before she writes; listen to make sure that you hear her talking out loud, and if necessary remind her that she should be speaking before she writes.

An acceptable narration might sound like one of the following:

When Miss Sullivan came to teach Helen Keller, she gave Helen a doll and tried to teach her what the word "doll" meant. Helen learned the word, but she didn't understand what it meant. So Miss Sullivan took her outside, pumped water over her hand, and spelled "water" at the same time. Finally, Helen understood what a name was.

I learned how to spell words, but I didn't understand what they meant. One day, my teacher pumped water over one of my hands and spelled "water" into the other. Suddenly I understood that the word stood for the cool thing flowing over my hand. I had words for the first time.

When the summary is finished, check it using the following rubric.

Week 3 Narration Rubric

Organization

1 Events should be in chronological order.
2 If two or more events are listed in a single sentence, they should have a cause and effect relationship.
3 The summary should end with a statement about Helen's new understanding of words/names.

Mechanics

1 Each sentence should make sense on its own when read aloud.
2 Each proper name should be capitalized.
3 Either first or third person should be used consistently throughout.
OPTIONAL
4 Quotation marks should be used to set off words that are spelled out to Helen

Note: The student is probably not familiar with the grammar rule governing #4. The rule is: When words are referred to as words, they are set off with either quotation marks or italics. "Word as word" means that the focus is on the word *itself,* not on the meaning, so:

I felt water on my hand.

She spelled "water" on my hand.

You may explain this rule to the student if you choose, but if you think the student will be confused, feel free to ignore it.

Day Two: Thesaurus Use

Focus: Understanding and using the thesaurus

Today's lesson introduces the student to the thesaurus. If you are not familiar with thesaurus use, be sure to read the student instructions carefully.

The student will not begin the copia exercises (rewriting sentences with the help of the thesaurus) until Part III of this course. However, she may sometimes find it helpful to consult a thesaurus in Part II, so the skill is introduced here.

Choosing the correct synonym is a skill that takes time, maturity, and plenty of exposure to good writing. Beginning writers will often choose a synonym that has the wrong shade of meaning. For example, the thesaurus gives the following synonyms for "sad":

oppressed, unhappy, sorry, dejected, woebegone, inconsolable

If I write "I was angry and sad," the following synonyms would be appropriate:
I was angry and oppressed.
I was angry and unhappy.
I was angry and dejected.
I was angry and inconsolable,

But "sorry" and "woebegone" are not good choices, because those emotions—while they *do* involve sadness—aren't likely to coexist with anger.

The exercises that follow give the student some guidance in choosing good synonyms. However, at this level, it's important not to overcorrect or overexplain. The more the student reads, explores, and experiments, the better her sense for the correct word will become.

As a completely optional exercise, you can help the student develop word sense using Google Books (books.google.com).[3] Type a single word or expression into the search box. When the search results load, choose the "Preview Available" option. The results will reload, including only books that you can click on to read an entire page (as opposed to "snippet view," which only gives you the view of a single line).

Skimming down the results will help the student gain a sense of the ways in which particular words are used. For example, the exercise that follows asks the student to distinguish between "zealous" and "willing," but this may be difficult if the student hasn't seen the word "zealous" used in different contexts. A quick search for "zealous" on Google Books starts with a number of books that have "zealous" in the title. You want to see how the word is used in sentences, though, so you would scroll down past these books and look for "zealous" in the actual text that appears as a brief excerpt next to the book cover. These include:

> Johnson was truly zealous for the success of "The Adventurer."
> —James Boswell, *The Life of Samuel Johnson*

> Every year some zealous Frenchman exposes the iniquities of the Tudors. . .
> —John Acton, *Letters of Lord Acton to Mary Gladstone*

> . . . his zealous and unwearied exertions. . .
> —United States War Department, *Report of the Secretary of War*

> Attorneys also owe an obligation to be zealous advocates for their clients.
> —O. Russel Murray, *The Mediation Handbook*

3. The following instructions use the Google Books search as it worked in the spring of 2011. Websites change constantly, so you may need to adapt the instructions.

Simply reading these sentences will begin to give the student a sense of the word's exact meaning.

If you come up with too many archaic uses, you can also limit the search to books published within the twenty-first (or another) century.

STEP ONE: **Understand thesaurus use (Student Responsibility)**

Student instructions for Step One:

A thesaurus is a reference book that groups together words with similar but different shades of meaning. (A dictionary, on the other hand, contains definitions of single, particular words.) When you write, you can use the thesaurus to find the exact word you need. (Note: The numbers in the following description are based on the fourth edition of *Roget's International Thesaurus*. You will probably use a different edition, but the organization of your thesaurus will be the same even if the numbers are a little different.)

A thesaurus contains two types of lists.

The first half of the thesaurus contains words grouped by meaning and part of speech. These word groups all have numbers. For example, the list headed

475. Knowledge

might contain:

1. **nouns** that name different kinds of knowledge (information, facts, experience, perception, insight, understanding, wisdom, literacy), as well as names for fields of knowledge (literature, science, art, techonology) and names of people who know things (scientist, scholar, authority, expert, intellectual),

2. **verbs** for the act of knowing (know, perceive, recognize, discern, be learned in, be expert in), and

3. **adjectives** that describe both people who are knowledgeable (informed, instructed, trained, familiar with, learned, educated, bookish) and things which are known (well-known, recognized, familiar, grasped, common, public).

The second half of the thesaurus contains an alphabetical listing of thousands of vocabulary words. This is the part of the thesaurus that you'll go to first as you write.

In the last lesson, you learned that Helen Keller "left the well-house eager to learn." Suppose that, while writing your summary, it seemed most natural to write "After Helen Keller learned that words stood for things, she was eager to learn." That's true, but when writing a summary you should try not to copy the exact wording in the passage. So instead, you could turn to the second half of your thesaurus and look up *eager* in the *e* section.

Beneath the word *eager,* you would find a series of other adjectives with different shades of meaning, each followed by a number: for example,

consenting *775.4*
desirous *634.21*
willing *622.5*
zealous *635.9*

Which of these comes closest to the meaning of *eager,* as Helen Keller used it? Probably not "consenting," because that just implies that she wouldn't *refuse* to learn if offered the opportunity—but in the passage, Keller is anxious to learn. "Willing" also fails to show how eager Keller was. But "desirous" and "zealous" both imply a real desire and need to learn.

If you decide that "zealous" is the closest to "eager," you would then turn back to the group of words numbered 635 in the first half of the thesaurus. That group of words is headed "Eagerness," so all of the nouns, adjectives, and verbs in it will have something to do with being eager. Glancing down the group, you would see that Section 635 has 15 different subgroups. The first six subgroups contain nouns; the next two contain verbs; the five after that, adjectives;

and the final two, adverbs.

Since the word "zealous" was followed by the number 635.9, you would then look down to subgroup 9 of Section 635. There, you would find a series of adjectives closely related to the adjective *zealous:*

eager, anxious, avid, keen, prompt, ready, lively, vital, champing at the bit, and many more.

You could choose one of these adjectives to substitute for *eager* and write one of the following:

She was anxious to learn.

She was keen to learn.

She was champing at the bit to learn.

Sometimes you'll find that the word you chose to follow leads you to a section where none of the words seem to fit. That's normal; using a thesaurus is sometimes a process of trial and error. But reading through the lists will help expand your vocabulary and fill your memory with words.

STEP TWO: **Practice thesaurus use**

Student instructions for Step Two:

Begin to practice your thesaurus skills now, using two sentences from Helen Keller's memoir.

For each underlined noun, adjective, and verb, find four synonyms in your thesaurus. List those synonyms on the lines provided. Remember that you must provide noun synonyms for nouns, adjective synonyms for adjectives, and verb synonyms for verbs.

When you look up a verb, remember that you'll need to look it up in the present tense. "Felt" is in a past tense. The present tense of "felt" is "feel." "Feel" is the word you'd look up in the second half of the thesaurus.

After you've found the synonyms, rewrite each sentence one time on your own paper, choosing from among the listed synonyms. Do not repeat any of the synonyms. When you've finished, read your sentences out loud and listen to how the sound and rhythm change. Remember to put your verbs back in the past tense!

If you're not sure which subsections of the thesaurus you should go to, ask your instructor for help.

When you're finished, show your work to your instructor.

HOW TO HELP THE STUDENT WITH STEP TWO

The student's answers should resemble the following, although other synonyms are certainly acceptable. "Sorrow" and "regret" are often used as synonyms; if necessary, explain to the student that since Keller uses both, she means that she felt two different emotions. Synonyms for "sorrow" should highlight sadness; synonyms for "regret" should highlight pangs of conscience.

Suddenly I felt a misty consciousness as of something forgotten—a thrill of returning thought; and somehow the mystery of language was revealed to me.

felt *sense, feel, experience, perceive, apprehend, be aware of*

misty *faint, pale, weak, dim, shadowy, obscure, hazy, blurry, uncertain mystery* *enigma, puzzle, problem, riddle, miraculousness, sealed book, unknown quantity*

Neither sorrow nor regret followed my passionate outburst.

sorrow *grief, care, woe, sadness, unhappiness, dejection, melancholy, gloom*
regret *shame, contrition, scruples, self-reproach, penitence*
outburst *outbreak, flare-up, blaze, explosion, eruption, fit, upheaval*

The student's sentences might resemble the following:

Suddenly I sensed *a* shadowy *consciousness as of something forgotten—a thrill of returning thought; and somehow the* enigma *of language was revealed to me. Neither* grief *nor* shame *followed my passionate* explosion.

You may need to remind the student that verbs should be put in the past tense.

Day Three: Outlining Exercise

Focus: Finding the main idea in each paragraph of a passage about science

STEP ONE: **Read (Student Responsibility)**

Student instructions for Step One:

The following passage has two parts. The first four paragraphs all deal with the same topic (earthworms); each paragraph explores a different part or feature of the earthworm. The last three paragraphs describe different relatives of the earthworm, so each one has a different topic.

STEP TWO: **Construct a one-level outline**

Student instructions for Step Two:

Now write a one-level outline for the passage on the worksheet below.

Because the passage shifts from a detailed discussion of earthworms to a more topical description of other worms, you should also shift your outlining style when you get to the last three paragraphs. For the first four paragraphs, use the questions

1. What is being described or defined in this paragraph?
2. Is there one central thing which is most important about it?

to find the main point. For the last three paragraphs, simply list the topic covered.

Two of the points are done for you.

If you have difficulty, ask your instructor for help. And when you're finished, check your work with your instructor.

HOW TO HELP THE STUDENT WITH STEP TWO

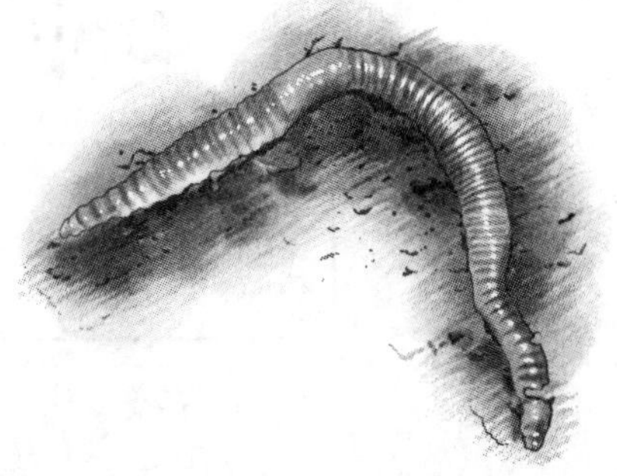

The student's outline should combine the two kinds of outlining the student has already practiced; the first four points should give the main idea of each paragraph, while the last three should list the topic of each paragraph. The finished outline should resemble the following:

I. The difference between earthworms and insect larvae
II. How earthworms benefit the soil OR The earthworm and the soil
III. What happens when the worm is cut in two OR Cutting the worm in half
IV. The structure of the earthworm
V. Hairworms
VI. The lugworm
VII. The leech

If the student has difficulty, use the following dialogues

Paragraph 2
Instructor: This paragraph is all about the ways in which an earthworm benefits one particular thing. What is it?

> *Student: The soil*

Instructor "How earthworms benefit the soil" is the main idea.

Paragraph 3
Instructor: What happens to the worm in this paragraph?

> *Student: It gets cut in half.*

Instructor: Everything else in the paragraph is related to that main idea.

Paragraph 4
Instructor: The main idea of this paragraph is stated in the very first sentence. Read the first part of that sentence out loud.

> *Student: The structure of the animal is very simple.*

Instructor: Breathing organs, blood, the blood system, eyes, and hearing all have to do with the structure of the earthworm.

Paragraphs 6 and 7
Instructor: What kind of worm is described?

> *Student: The lugworm* and *the leech.*

Instructor: Those are the topics of those two paragraphs.

Day Four: Thesaurus Use

Focus: Using the thesaurus

STEP ONE: **Practice thesaurus use**

Student instructions for Step One:

> For each underlined noun, adjective, and verb, find four synonyms in your thesaurus. (You only need to use two for "loosened.") List those synonyms on the lines provided. Remember that you must provide noun synonyms for nouns, adjective synonyms for adjectives, and verb synonyms for verbs.
>
> When you look up a verb, remember that you'll need to look up the active form and the present tense. "Is loosened" is the present tense and passive form of "loosen." "Is aired" is the present tense and passive form of "air." (Make sure you look at the *verb* "air," not the *noun* "air"!) What is the active, present form of "is enriched"?
>
> After you've found the synonyms, rewrite each sentence one time on your own paper, choosing from among the listed synonyms. Do not repeat any of the synonyms. When you've finished, read your sentences out loud and listen to how the sound and rhythm change. Remember to put your verbs back in the past tense!
>
> When you are finding synonyms for science writing, you should be particularly careful to pick words close in meaning. Leeches are found in pools, not oceans—even though "pool" and "ocean" may both be found in the same section of your thesaurus. In this exercise, work hard to find the *right* synonyms.
>
> When you're finished, show your work to your instructor.

HOW TO HELP THE STUDENT WITH STEP ONE

This exercise is challenging, not because the words are difficult, but because the student must find very close equivalents; "soil" is the same as "dirt," but in this context it is not the same as "dust" or "soot." You may need to encourage the student to look at more than one thesaurus entry; for example, the thesaurus entry for "soil" includes "dirt" but no other useful synonyms, so the student will then need to look up "dirt." The entry for "dirt" includes "land," and the entry for "land" includes "ground" and "earth."

Thus the <u>soil</u> is <u>loosened,</u> <u>aired</u> and <u>enriched</u> by the same process.

soil	*dirt, land, earth, ground*
loosened	*break up, separate, work loose*
aired	*aerate, aerify, give air, freshen, oxygenate, ventilate*
enriched	*cultivate, enhance, upgrade, augment, build up, fertilize*

The leech is a wormlike <u>animal</u> often <u>found</u> in pools.

animal	*being, creature, living thing, wild thing, entity, thing, invertebrate*
found	*discover, encounter, identify, locate, observe, spot, see*

Part II

BUILDING BLOCKS FOR COMPOSITION WEEKS 4–15

Overview of Weeks 4–15

In the next 12 weeks of this course, the student will spend one day working on a review of narration skills. On the second day of each week, he will complete an outlining exercise; on the third and fourth days, he will learn about topoi by analyzing and copying a model. The first 12 topoi lessons cover the most basic composition elements: chronological narration and description.

The only exception to the pattern is in Weeks 4–5, when the first assignment to copy a model is extended over two days so that the student is not overwhelmed.

Weekly pattern:

Review of Year 4 Skills, One-Level Outlines, Foundational Topoi

Day 1: Narrative summary
Day 2: Outlining exercise
Day 3: Analyze topos model
Day 4: Practice topos model

Topoi, Weeks 4–15

Chronological narration in history (Weeks 4, 6, 11)
Chronological narration in science (Weeks 5, 7, 15)
Description of a place (Weeks 8–11)
Scientific description (Weeks 12-15)

Week 4: Chronological Narrative of a Past Event

Day One: Original Narration Exercise

Focus: Summarizing a narrative by choosing the main events and listing them chronologically

STEP ONE: **Read (Student Responsibility)**

Student instructions for Step One:

Read the following excerpt from Edith Nesbit's short story "The Deliverers of Their Country," found in *The Book of Dragons.*

STEP TWO: **Note important events**

Student instructions for Step Two:

You will now summarize the passage in three or four sentences and write those sentences down on your own paper.

Before you can write a brief summary of a lengthy passage, you'll need to identify the most important events in the passage. On your scratch paper, write down five or six phrases or short sentences that will remind you of the things that happened in the story. *Do not use more than six phrases or short sentences!* Remember, you're not supposed to write down *everything* that happens in the story—just the most important events. The most important events are the ones that help the story make sense; if you took them out of the original passage, you wouldn't understand the rest of the story. (For example, if you left out the fact that the dragons were everywhere, would the reactions of the people make sense to you?)

Be sure to write the events down in the same order that they happen in the story.

Here's a head start: begin with the sentence "Effie got a dragon in her eye."

If you have trouble with this assigment, ask your instructor for help.

HOW TO HELP THE STUDENT WITH STEP TWO

The student should have written down on scratch paper five or six short phrases or sentences that summarize the main events. The phrases/sentences should resemble five or six of the following (these are given only as a guide):

Effie got a dragon in her eye.
Her brother found a dragon in his tea.
Doctor and father amazed by dragons
Soon there were dragons all over the place.
Dragons—looked the same, all different sizes
At first the newspapers called them lizards.
The large dragons went to bed early.
The small dragons got everywhere.
Got into everything, larger ones bit and got into beds
No point in offering a reward, everybody wanted to kill them
Everyone killed the dragons.
The police caught the dragons on sticky wood and canvas towers.
The stores were full of dragon poison and other remedies.
But there were more dragons than ever.

(Remember, the student should not provide more than five or six phrases/sentences.)

Beginning writers often have difficulty telling the difference between main events and supporting details. Watch the student as he writes down his phrases. If he's writing too many phrases, or the sentences are long and complex, stop his before he goes on. Ask him the following questions to help him distinguish between main events and supporting details:

Is the story about Effie and her family, or about the dragons? *(Dragons)*

How did the characters in the story react to the dragons when they first appeared? *(They were interested/curious, they kept them as specimens, they were pleased with them.)*

What changed their reaction to the dragons? *(There were dragons everywhere.)*

How did people try to get rid of the dragons? Just list two things. *(They killed them; the police set up sticky towers to catch them; they poisoned them.)*

What was the result? *(There were more dragons than ever.)*

If the student is still having trouble deciding what events to leave out, ask him: If you left this event out, would the rest of the story still make sense? If it would, it's a minor detail and can be eliminated.

STEP THREE: **Write summary sentences**

Student instructions for Step Three:

> After you've written down your five or six phrases or sentences, try to combine them into three or four sentences. You can do this by putting two phrases in the same sentence (for example, "Effie got a dragon in her eye" and "Her brother got a dragon in his tea" could be combined into "Effie and her brother both found small dragons"). Or you may find that one or more of your jotted notes turns out to be unnecessary. (If you wrote down "Everyone killed the dragons" as well as "Police caught dragons and burned them," you don't really need the second sentence. If everyone was killing the dragons, that includes the police.)

Try to avoid listing minor details; instead, stick to main events. If you took a main event out of the original story, the rest of the story wouldn't make sense. It doesn't really matter what the newspapers first called the dragons—without that detail, the story still makes sense. But if we didn't know that the dragons were everywhere, we wouldn't understand why they were such a big problem.

Say your three or four sentences out loud several times before writing them down. After you've written the sentences down, ask your instructor to check them.

If you have trouble, ask your instructor for help.

HOW TO HELP THE STUDENT WITH STEP THREE

In this step, the student practices turning the jotted phrases and sentences into three or four coherent, smooth sentences. He should say his three or four sentences out loud several times before he writes; listen to make sure that you hear him talking out loud, and if necessary remind him that he should be speaking before he writes.

You may need to help him combine two phrases into one sentence. (For example, *Soon there were dragons all over the place* and *Dragons—looked the same, all different sizes* could be combined into "Soon there were dragons of all different sizes all over the place.") Encourage him to eliminate those phrases which seem unnecessary; in the list above, *At first the newspapers called them lizards* should be cut because the subject of naming the dragons never comes up again.

When the summary is finished, check it using the following rubric.

Week 4 Narration Rubric

Organization

1 Events should be in chronological order.

2 If two or more events are listed in a single sentence, they should have a cause and effect relationship.

For example:

The dragons were everywhere, and everyone killed them

is acceptable; because the dragons were everywhere, everyone killed them.

The newspapers called the dragons lizards at first, and everyone killed them

is not acceptable. There is no causal relationship between the two sentences.

3 Each event of major importance should be in the summary (if it were missing from the original passage, the narrative would no longer make sense).

Mechanics

1 Each sentence should make sense on its own when read aloud.

2 Each proper name should be capitalized.

Day Two: Outlining Exercise

Focus: Finding the main idea in each paragraph of a historical narrative

STEP ONE: **Read (Student Responsibility)**

Student instructions for Step One:

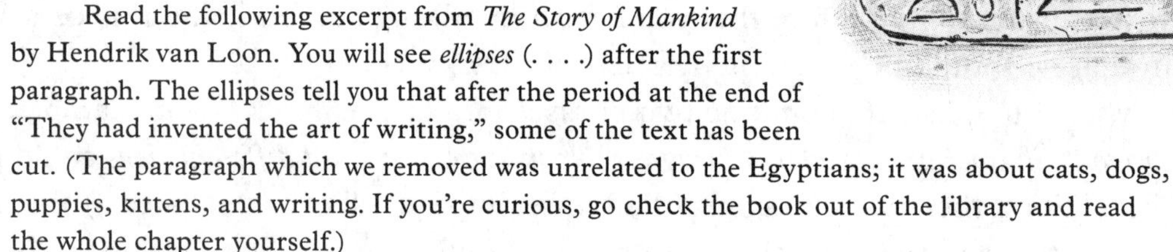

Read the following excerpt from *The Story of Mankind* by Hendrik van Loon. You will see *ellipses* (. . . .) after the first paragraph. The ellipses tell you that after the period at the end of "They had invented the art of writing," some of the text has been cut. (The paragraph which we removed was unrelated to the Egyptians; it was about cats, dogs, puppies, kittens, and writing. If you're curious, go check the book out of the library and read the whole chapter yourself.)

STEP TWO: **Construct a one-level outline**

Student instructions for Step Two:

Instead of simply summarizing this passage, you will outline it.

Let's review the outlining process. You'll begin by looking for the main idea in each section of text. The passage above is divided into four sections (there's an extra space between each section). For each section, try to come up with a single sentence that states the main idea. In previous lessons, you did this for single paragraphs; often, though, a single main idea will be explored in more than one paragraph.

Don't try to include as much information as possible in this single sentence. Ask yourself two sets of questions:

1. What is the main thing or person that this section is about? *Or* Is the section about an idea?
2. Why is that thing or person important? *Or* What did that thing or person do/what was done to it? *Or* What is the idea?

Try that for the first section. What is the main thing or person that this section is about? If you're not sure, ask yourself: Who was responsible for all the inventions and discoveries in that first paragraph?

The Egyptians.

Now look at everything else in the passage, which tells you why the Egyptians were important: they were important because of all the things they did.

You can't list each individual invention or discovery, because you're not trying to include *all* the information in a single sentence. If you knew someone who played basketball, football, soccer, volleyball, and field hockey, you wouldn't summarize by saying "She plays basketball, football, soccer, volleyball, and field hockey." You'd say "She plays many sports."

Try finishing your sentence now. What did you come up with?

Your sentence should sound like one of these:

I. The Egyptians invented and discovered many things. OR
I. The Egyptians made many inventions and discoveries.

(Be sure not to simply copy the first sentence in the paragraph. Remember, this is supposed to be a summary in *your own words*.)

Now work on coming up with a summary sentence for each one of the remaining four sections. (You can use the sentence we gave you for the first section.) When you write an outline, you should use Roman numerals for the summary sentences, like this:

I. The Egyptians made many inventions and discoveries.
II. Second sentence
III. Third sentence
IV. Fourth sentence

For this assignment, try to use complete sentences (although this isn't always necessary in an outline).

When you are finished, check your assignment with your instructor.

HOW TO HELP THE STUDENT WITH STEP TWO

For each section of text, the student should pick out a major point by asking himself two sets of questions:

1. What is the main thing or person that this section is about? *Or* Is the section about an idea?
2. Why is that thing or person important? *Or* What did that thing or person do/what was done to it? *Or* What is the idea?

Suggested answers (the student's sentences should resemble the following but don't need to be identical):

I. The Egyptians invented and discovered many things.
II. Egyptian writing could not be read.
III. A French officer discovered a stone with writing on it.
IV. Champollion discovered the main principles of Egyptian writing.

If the student struggles with this assignment, use the following dialogues:

Section 2
Instructor: What is the main thing this section is about? Hint: it is mentioned in every single sentence.

Student: Egyptian writing or hieroglyphs [the student may use this name even though it is not in the passage]

Note to Instructor: If the student answers "strange pictures" or "queer figures," point out that these are synonyms for the same thing and ask: What is that thing?
Instructor: What is important about this writing? Hint: the answer is suggested in the first and third sentences and stated clearly in the last sentence.

Student: No one could read or *decipher* or *understand it.*

Instructor: Make sure that your main point has "Egyptian writing" as the subject of the sentence.

Section 3
Instructor: It may be a little harder for you to find the main idea of this section. Is Bonaparte's visit to Africa the most important thing that happens? Hint: do we hear any more about it after this one section?

Student: No.

Instructor: What is the other important event in this section?

Student: A French officer discovers a stone with writing on it or *A French officer found the Rosetta Stone* or *A French officer found a slab of basalt with three inscriptions on it.*

Instructor: That is the main idea of the passage, because if you don't know about the discovery of the stone, you won't understand the next section.

Note to Instructor: Encourage the student to put his sentence in the past tense, since the passage itself is in the past tense.

Section 4
Instructor: This last section tells you about Champollion [this should be pronounced *sham-poe-LYAHN,* with the "ly" slurred together to make a single sound]. What did he discover?

Student: He discovered the meaning of Egyptian writing or *He discovered the main principles of hieroglyphs.*

Day Three: Analyzing the Topos

Focus: Understanding the form of a chronological narrative of a past event

The passage the student outlined in the last writing session is an example of this week's topos: a **chronological narrative of a past event** (the deciphering of Egyptian writing). Remember, a topos is a form of writing: a "place" that the student can go to find topics in history and science.

A chronological narrative of a past event explains *what happened in the past*, and *in what sequence*. A chronological narrative can stand on its own as a history composition or can be a smaller part of a larger paper.

In today's assignment, the student will examine how a chronological narrative is put together. The work should be done independently; the student's directions are reproduced below for your reference.

STEP ONE: **Examine model passages**

When you set out to write a chronological narrative in history, you aim to answer two simple questions:

Who did what to whom? (Or *What was done to what?*)

In what sequence?

Look again at the outline you made of the passage from *The Story of Mankind*. The exact words you used will be different, but the outline probably looks something like this:

I. The Egyptians invented and discovered many things.
II. Egyptian writing could not be read.
III. A French officer discovered a stone with writing on it.
IV. Champollion discovered the main principles of Egyptian writing.

Notice that each one of these main points answers the first question: *Who did what to whom?* (Or *What was done to what?*)

I. *Who?* The Egyptians *Did what?* invented and discovered *To what?* many things.
II. *What?* Egyptian writing *What was done to it?* could not be read.
III. *Who?* A French officer *Did what?* discovered *what?* a stone with writing on it.
IV. *Who?* Champollion *Did what?* discovered *To what?* the main principles of Egyptian writing.

The points are also put into chronological order (in other words, the oldest event comes first, the next oldest second, and so on). First, Egyptians invented writing. After that, the ability to read the writing faded away. Long after that, a French officer discovered the stone. And after the discovery of the stone, Champollion cracked the code of Egyptian writing.

Here is a second example of a **chronological narrative of a past event,** from *Albert Einstein and the Theory of Relativity* by Robert Cwiklik. It describes a village festival that Albert Einstein went to when he was four years old.

This chronological narrative about a past event introduces a discussion about Albert Einstein's early interest in electricity. Because chronological narratives sound like stories, they seize the reader's attention.

Glance back over the four sections and notice the order of events.

In the first section, nothing has happened yet; the crowd is just waiting for an event. With your pencil, underline "the crowd" (the *who*) once. Underline the phrase "they were waiting" twice (this answers the question *did what?*).

The second section happens right after the first section. You know this because of the word "suddenly." Draw a box around "suddenly." Underline "gas lamps" once and "dimmed" twice. These words answer the question *What did what?*

In the third section, underline "The band" and "The people" (the *who*) once. Underline the phrase "grew so quiet" twice (this answers the question *did what?*).

In the final section, draw a box around "then." This time word tells you that the last section comes *after* the events listed earlier. Underline "electric lights" once and "exploded in a blaze" twice. These words answer the question *What did what?*

Now look at the summary below:

> At first, the crowd was waiting.
> Suddenly the gas lamps dimmed.
> The band and the people grew quiet.
> Then electric lights exploded in a blaze.

The original narrative has a lot more details in it—but this summary shows you exactly how the writer tells each main event in chronological order.

STEP TWO: **Write down the pattern of the topos**

Now copy the following chart onto a blank sheet of paper in the "Reference" section of your Composition Notebook. You will be adding to this page as you learn more about chronological narratives, so leave plenty of room at the bottom of the page; also leave blank space under the "Remember" column.

Chronological Narrative of a Past Event

Definition: A narrative telling what happened in the past and in what sequence

Procedure	Remember
1. Ask *Who did what to whom?* (Or *What was done to what?*)	
2. Create main points by placing the answers in chronological order.	

Day Four: Practicing the Topos

Focus: Learning how to write a chronological narrative of a past event

A chronological narrative of a past event can be used in many different kinds of writing. If the student is asked to write about history, he can decide to tell, in order, what happened during a battle, or when a king died and his heir fought for the throne, or when an explorer set off to find a new land. But he can also use a short chronological narrative as the introduction to a scientific composition, or as a way to grab the reader's interest in a composition on any other subject. Here's the beginning of Susan Casey's book *The Wave: In Pursuit of the Rogues, Freaks, and Giants of the Ocean:*

> *57.5° N, 12.7° W, 175 miles off the coast of Scotland*
> *February 8, 2000*
> The clock read midnight when the hundred-foot wave hit the ship, rising from the North Atlantic out of the darkness. Among the ocean's terrors a wave this size was the most feared and the least understood, more myth than reality—or so people had thought. This giant was certainly real. As the RRS *Discovery* plunged down into the wave's deep trough, it heeled twenty-eight degrees to port, rolled thirty degrees back to starboard, then recovered to face the incoming seas. . . . Captain Keith Avery steered his vessel directly into the onslaught, just as he had been doing for the past five days. . . . He stood barefoot at the helm, the only way he could maintain traction after a refrigerator toppled over, splashing out a slick of milk, juice, and broken glass (no time to clean it up—the waves just kept coming). . . . [The] waves suddenly grew even bigger and meaner and steeper. Avery heard a loud bang coming from *Discovery's* foredeck. He squinted in the dark to see that the fifty-man lifeboat had partially ripped from its two-inch-thick steel cleats and was pounding against the hull.[4]

That's a much more interesting beginning than "The significant wave height, an average of the largest 33 percent of the waves, was sixty-one feet, with frequent spikes far beyond that," which the writer gets to after the story is over.

Today, the student will practice putting together a chronological narrative of his own.

Note to Instructor: The "Practicing the Topos" exercises provide you with detailed answers and a script to help guide the student. However, if you feel comfortable guiding the student on your own, you may always allow the student to practice the topos by drawing material from his current history or science reading and using the same principles outlined below.

In later weeks, the "Practicing the Topos" exercise will be completed in a single session.

4. Susan Casey, *The Wave: In Pursuit of the Rogues, Freaks, and Giants of the Ocean* (New York: Doubleday, 2010) pp. 3–4.

Since this is the first time the student has attempted to use this skill, this first exercise will be divided between today and the first day of next week's lesson.

STEP ONE: **Plan the narrative**

Student instructions for Step One:

Your first step is to plan out the narrative by choosing a theme (this will also serve as your title) and selecting the events you'll write about.

On the next page, you'll see a list of events, written out chronologically for you, from the life of Alexander the Great. The bolded entries are main events; the indented entries are further details about those main events. (These details are taken from Plutarch's "Life of Alexander," written in AD 75.)

Your assignment is to write a chronological narrative based on these events. This chronological narrative can be one paragraph or several paragraphs, but it must be at least 150 words long and no longer than 300 words.

You may choose where your narrative begins and ends, but the narrative must progress chronologically forward at all times. Do not try to include all of the events! Instead, you will need to select which events to use and which ones to leave out. This will force you to pick a "theme" for your chronological narrative.

For example: if you decide that your chronological narrative will be about "Alexander's Invasions," you might want to start your chronological narrative at 334 BC, the invasion of Persia, and only include the following events:

Invaded Persia in 334 BC
Invaded Egypt in 332 BC
Defeated Darius for a second time
Declared himself king of Persia
Invaded India in 326 BC

because all of those events have something to do with Alexander's invasions.

If, on the other hand, you wanted to write a chronological narrative about "Alexander's Early Life," you might choose the following events:

Born in 356 BC
Son of Philip II, king of Macedon
Tamed the horse Bucephalus at age 10
Taught by Aristotle from ages 13 to 16
Fought at his father's side beginning in 338 BC

and ignore the Persians completely.

Because this is the first time you've written a chronological narrative, you may use either of the lists above. Here are other possible themes:

"Alexander's Reign"
"The End of Alexander's Life"
"Alexander and Persia"

Choose a theme and select four or five main (bolded) events to use in your chronological narrative. (You can also come up with a theme of your own.)

If you have difficulty, ask your instructor for help.

EVENTS IN ALEXANDER THE GREAT'S LIFE

Born in 356 BC
  Mother, Olympia
Son of Philip II, king of Macedon
  Philip conquered most of Greece

Greek cities added to Macedonian kingdom

Tamed the horse Bucephalus at age 10

Philip intended to buy horse
Horse: wild, unmanageable
Alexander asked to ride the horse
Promised his father: If I can't ride it, I'll pay for it
Horse was afraid of shadow
Turned horse towards sun, rode horse

Taught by Aristotle from ages 13 to 16

Most famous philosopher in the world at this time
Gave Alexander lifelong thirst for knowledge
Interested in medicine, philosophy, history

Fought at his father's side beginning in 338 BC

Led his father's army to victory, Battle of Chaeronea

Father assassinated in 336 BC

Assassin was bodyguard, Pausanias
Pausanias then killed by rest of bodyguard

Succeeded his father to the throne

Twenty years old
Had all of his rivals to the throne murdered
Greek cities rebelled, had to reconquer them

Invaded Persia in 334 BC

Went to the city of Gordium
Untied the Gordian knot (impossible to untie) by cutting it
Defeated the Persian king Darius at the Battle of Issus
Darius fled, left his wife, mother, and daughters behind
Alexander treated the women with respect

Invaded Egypt in 332 BC

Proclaimed pharaoh
Founded Alexandria

Defeated Darius for a second time

Darius and army defeated at the Battle of Gaugamela
Darius once again forced to flee
Alexander captured Babylon and Susa
Darius was assassinated by his own kinsman, Bessus

Declared himself king of Persia

Invaded India in 326 BC

Crossed the Indus River
Fought against Indian king Porus and troop of elephants
Troops mutinied and refused to go any farther
Alexander, furious, shut himself into his tent
Finally Alexander agreed to go home

Returned to Babylon

Marched back through the Gedrosian Desert
Famine, thirst, disease killed 3/4 of men before he got home

Died in 323 BC

Came down with a fever in early June
Fever lasted for weeks
In the last few days, unable to speak or name a successor
Died on June 28th

Kingdom divided among his generals

HOW TO HELP THE STUDENT WITH STEP ONE

In this step, the student will simply choose how many events to include in his chronological narrative. You may need to help him select the correct events. Encourage him to include four or five main (bolded) events, but no more. Remind him that he can leave out main events that do not go with his theme.

Two themes are already described in the assignment. The following events belong with the three remaining suggested themes:

"The Beginning of Alexander's Reign"

(These are simply the first five events of Alexander's independent rule, but if necessary, you can explain to the student that the final conquest of the Persians marked the end of Alexander's first great royal campaign.)

Succeeded his father to the throne

Twenty years old

Had all of his rivals to the throne murdered

Greek cities rebelled, had to reconquer them

Invaded Persia in 334 BC

Went to the city of Gordium

Untied the Gordian knot (impossible to untie) by cutting it

Defeated the Persian king Darius at the Battle of Issus

Darius fled, left his wife, mother, and daughters behind

Alexander treated the women with respect

Invaded Egypt in 332 BC

Proclaimed pharaoh

Founded Alexandria

Defeated Darius for a second time

Darius and army defeated at the Battle of Gaugamela

Darius once again forced to flee

Alexander captured Babylon and Susa

Darius was assassinated by his own kinsman, Bessus

Declared himself king of Persia

"The End of Alexander's Life"

(These four events follow Alexander's assumption of the Persian crown, which was the high point of his power; the refusal of his troops to go farther into India was the first check to his power, and each of the following events decreased his authority a little more.)

Invaded India in 326 BC

Crossed the Indus River

Fought against Indian king Porus and troop of elephants

Troops mutinied and refused to go any farther

Alexander, furious, shut himself into his tent

Finally Alexander agreed to go home

Returned to Babylon
Marched back through the Gedrosian Desert
Famine, thirst, disease killed 3/4 of men before he got home
Died in 323 BC
Came down with a fever in early June
Fever lasted for weeks
In the last few days, unable to speak or name a successor
Died on June 28th
Kingdom divided among his generals
"Alexander and Persia"
(The three following events are the only ones having to do directly with Persia. If the student chooses this theme, point out that he should eliminate the invasion of Egypt because, even though it happened between the first invasion of Persia and the second defeat of Darius, it doesn't directly relate to the theme; this would be a good time to explain that a chronological narrative doesn't have to include *every* event, as long as the events that *are* present are covered in chronological order. You can also tell the student that a narrative containing only three events is acceptable because there are so many details following the first and second events.)
Invaded Persia in 334 BC
Went to the city of Gordium
Untied the Gordian knot (impossible to untie) by cutting it
Defeated the Persian king Darius at the Battle of Issus
Darius fled, left his wife, mother, and daughters behind
Alexander treated the women with respect
Defeated Darius for a second time
Darius and army defeated at the Battle of Gaugamela
Darius once again forced to flee
Alexander captured Babylon and Susa
Darius was assassinated by his own kinsman, Bessus
Declared himself king of Persia

STEP TWO: **Become familiar with time and sequence words (Student Responsibility)**

Student instructions for Step Two: The student will work independently for Step Two, but the instructions are reproduced below for your reference.

> Remember, when you write a chronological narrative of a past event, you ask: Who did what to whom? (Or What was done to what?) In this exercise, most of this information is supplied so that you can concentrate on making the narrative flow smoothly forward in chronological order. (In later assignments, after you've had a little more practice, you'll take more responsibility for finding the information as well.)
>
> In this first chronological narrative assignment, concentrating on using **time** and

sequence words to turn the listed events into clear, straightforward prose. For example, if you were writing a narrative that included this main event:

Invaded Persia in 334 BC

Went to the city of Gordium
Learned myth about Gordian knot (who untied it would rule the world)
Cut the knot
Defeated the Persian king Darius at the Battle of Issus
Darius fled, left his wife, mother, and daughters behind
Alexander treated the women with respect

one part of your narrative might end up sounding like this:

Alexander invaded Persia in 334. **Eventually,** he travelled to the city of Gordium. In the city was a knot known as the Gordian knot; according to myth, whoever could untie the knot would rule the world. **As soon as** he heard the myth, Alexander drew his sword and cut the knot instead.

After some time, Alexander met the Persian king, Darius, and the Persian army at the Battle of Issus. He defeated Darius in battle. **Immediately afterwards,** Darius fled. He fled so quickly that he left his wife, mother, and daughters behind him. But **when** Alexander realized this, he treated the women with respect.[5]

Look back at the words in bold print. All of them are **time** and **sequence** words—words that you use in a chronological narrative to show the order in which events happen.

Plan on using the following list of time words as you construct your chronological narrative. Try to use at least three of them, without repeating any. Finish today's work by reading the time words out loud.

***SEE APPENDIX I, TIME AND SEQUENCE WORDS** in student workbook.*

You've finished a long assignment today. At the beginning of next week, you'll return to your list of events and use it to write brief chronological narrative.

5. Note: If you know other details about Alexander (more about the Gordian knot, or the Battle of Issus, or the Persian king Darius), you may certainly use them to make the narrative more interesting. But remember: this isn't required, and you can't go over 300 words for the entire composition.

Week 5: Chronological Narrative of a Scientific Discovery

Day One: Finishing the Chronological Narrative of a Past Event

Focus: Learning how to write a chronological narrative of a past event

At the end of last week, the student began to work on writing a chronological narrative of a past event. She selected events from a list, and also read through time and sequence words.

Today, she will finish this narrative.

STEP ONE: Review the topos (Student Responsibility)

Student instructions for Step One:

Turn to the Chronological Narrative of a Past Event chart in your Composition Notebook. Add the bolded events below under the "Remember" column.

Chronological Narrative of a Past Event

Definition: A narrative telling what happened in the past and in what sequence

Procedure	Remember
1. Ask *Who did what to whom?* (Or *What was done to what?*)	**1. Select your main events to go with your theme.**
2. Create main points by placing the answers in chronological order.	**2. Make use of time words.**

You will find a copy of the Time and Sequence Words reference sheet in Appendix I. Take it out and place it in the Reference section of your Composition Notebook, just after the Chronological Narrative of a Past Event page.

STEP TWO: **Write the narrative**

Student instructions for Step Two:

Now use the events list you worked on at the end of last week and write your own chronological narrative, based on it.

Here's a summary of your assignment:

1. This chronological narrative can be one paragraph or several paragraphs, but it must be at least 150 words long and no longer than 300 words.
2. You may choose where your narrative begins and ends, but the narrative must progress chronologically forward at all times.
3. Do not try to include all of the events! Instead, you will need to select which events to use and which ones to leave out. This will force you to pick a "theme" for your chronological narrative.
4. Use three or more time words in your narrative.

Try not to use the identical words of the events list. For example, if you are using the following events:

Son of Philip II, king of Macedon

Philip conquered most of Greece

Greek cities added to Macedonian kingdom

try not to write:

Alexander was the ***son*** *of Philip II,* ***king*** *of Macedon. Philip conquered most of Greece. He added the* ***Greek cities*** *to the* ***Macedonian kingdom.***

Changing the common nouns and their adjectives (the words in bold print) is a simple and straightforward way to make your narrative sound different:

Alexander was the ***heir*** *of Philip II,* ***ruler*** *of Macedon. Philip conquered most of Greece. He added the* ***city-states of Greece*** *to* ***his realm.***

If you have difficulty, ask your instructor for help. And when you're finished, show your composition to your instructor.

HOW TO HELP THE STUDENT WITH STEP TWO

There are three possible areas of difficulty with this assignment.

1. The student may need encouragement to leave out some of the details related to her main events. For example, if she is using this main event:

Invaded India in 326 BC

Crossed the Indus River

Fought against Indian king Porus and troop of elephants

Troops mutinied and refused to go any farther

Alexander, furious, shut himself into his tent

Finally Alexander agreed to go home

and her composition is running too long, you could point out that any of the following combinations of details makes sense:

Invaded India in 326 BC
Troops mutinied and refused to go any farther
Alexander, furious, shut himself into his tent
Finally Alexander agreed to go home
Invaded India in 326 BC
Crossed the Indus River
Troops mutinied and refused to go any farther
Finally Alexander agreed to go home
Invaded India in 326 BC
Crossed the Indus River
Fought against Indian king Porus and troop of elephants
Troops mutinied and refused to go any farther
Finally Alexander agreed to go home

Use your judgment in suggesting details that can be left out; the point of this exercise is not to pick the "right" details, but to practice moving the narrative forward.

2. The student may need help choosing the correct time words. If necessary, go over the Time and Sequence Words reference list with her and suggest six or seven appropriate words for her to choose from. If the student has difficulty moving from one topic to the next, encourage her to use his Time and Sequence Words for transitions.

3. The student may have trouble using her own phrasing. If necessary, help her find synonyms for the nouns and adjectives in the event list. Don't be afraid to give her two or three alternatives to choose from.

Right now, the student has only been asked to look at nouns and adjectives. This is intentional. Remember: the focus of this lesson is the form of the chronological narrative, and trying to learn two new skills at the same time can discourage a young writer. There are many ways to rephrase sentences, and these will be covered in detail in the copia exercises that begin in Week 16.

When the narrative is finished, check it using the following rubric.

Week 4/5 Rubric
Chronological Narrative of Past Events

Organization

1 Events should be in chronological order.
2 Three or more time words should be used.
3 The composition should use more than 150 but fewer than 300 words.

Mechanics

1 Each sentence should make sense on its own when read aloud.
2 Each proper name should be capitalized.
3 The exact words of the source material should not be used in every sentence.

Day Two: Outlining Exercise

Focus: Finding the main idea in each paragraph of a scientific narrative

STEP ONE: **Read (Student Responsibility)**

Student instructions for Step One:

Read the following excerpt from *100 Greatest Science Discoveries of All Time* by Kendall Haven.

STEP TWO: **Construct a one-level outline**

Student instructions for Step Two:

Begin to outline this passage by looking for the main idea in each section of text. You'll see that the passage above is divided into five sections (there's an extra space between each section). For each section, try to come up with a single sentence that states the main idea.

Remember, you shouldn't try to include as much information as possible in this single sentence. Ask yourself two sets of questions:

1. What is the main thing or person that this section is about? *Or* Is the section about an idea?

2. Why is that thing or person important? *Or* What did that thing or person do/what was done to it? *Or* What is the idea?

Try that for the first section. What is the main thing or person that this section is about? (That should be easy—whose name is mentioned three times?)

Vesalius (of course).

Now look at everything else in the passage, which tells you a number of different facts about Andreas Vesalius's early life—where he was born, what he read, what he did, what field of study he decided to pursue. All of these facts don't belong in your sentence. But the last three (he read medical books, he dissected animals, he went to medical school) all tell you about a single quality that Vesalius had—a quality that makes him important. He was important because he was. . .

Try finishing that sentence now.

What did you come up with? It should sound like one of these:

I. Vesalius was curious about living things.
I. Vesalius was interested in living things.
I. Vesalius was curious about how living things functioned.

Now work on coming up with a summary sentence for each one of the remaining four sections. (You can use the sentence we gave you for the first section.) Continue to use Roman numerals for the summary sentences, like this:

I. Vesalius was curious about living things.
II. Second sentence
III. Third sentence
IV. Fourth sentence
V. Fifth sentence

For this assignment, try to use complete sentences (although this isn't always necessary in an outline).

If you have difficulty, ask your instructor for help. And when you are finished, check your assignment with your instructor.

HOW TO HELP THE STUDENT WITH STEP TWO

For each section of text, the student should pick out a major point by asking herself two sets of questions:

1. What is the main thing or person that this section is about? OR Is the section about an idea?
2. Why is that thing or person important? OR What did that thing or person do/what was done to it? OR What is the idea?

Suggested answers (the student's sentences should resemble the following but don't need to be identical):

I. Vesalius was curious about living things OR Vesalius was curious about how living things functioned.
II. Dissection was not done in medical school OR Anatomy was not taught through dissection.

III. Vesalius was known for dissection OR Vesalius learned through dissection.
IV. Vesalius then gave lectures based on dissection OR Vesalius then gave lectures about the human body.
V. Vesalius showed that Galen was wrong.

If the student struggles with this assignment, use the following dialogues:

Section 2
Instructor: What is the main thing this section is about?

Student: Dissection.

Instructor: What do we learn about dissection? Hint: it has to do with a negative (something *not* done).

Student: Dissection was not done.

Instructor: Dissection was not done where?

Student: Dissection was not done in medical school.

Note to Instructor: The student might answer "Anatomy" to the first question. This is acceptable, since dissection and anatomy are so closely related. If the answer is "anatomy," ask "How was anatomy *not* taught?" ("It was not taught through dissection.") "Anatomy was taught through books" is not acceptable because it does not include dissection, which is the main theme not only of this section, but of the whole excerpt.

Section 3
Instructor: Who is this section about? (Again?)

Student: Vesalius

Instructor: What did Vesalius do? Hint: it's something others did *not* do.

Student: Vesalius dissected bodies OR *Vesalius learned through dissection.*

Note to Instructor: If the student starts to give individual details, such as "Vesalius took over dissecting at his second lecture" or "Vesalius raided graveyards for bodies," say "What does that tell us about the single most important thing Vesalius did that others did not?"

Section 4
Instructor: What did Vesalius do after he graduated?

Student: Vesalius gave lectures.

Instructor: What were those lectures about?

Student: The lectures were about dissection OR *The lectures were about the human body.*

Note to Instructor: If the student starts to list the specific topics of the lectures (muscles, arteries, nerves, etc.), say "What do muscles, arteries, and nerves all belong to?" ("The human body.")

Section 5
Instructor: There are two important people in this section. Who are they?

Student: Vesalius and Galen

Instructor: What did Vesalius do to Galen?

Student: He showed that Galen was wrong.

Day Three: Analyzing the Topos

Focus: Understanding the form of a chronological narrative about a scientific discovery

The passage the student outlined in the last writing session is an example of this week's topos: a **chronological narrative of a scientific discovery** (Vesalius's disproving Galen's theories about anatomy).

A chronological narrative about a scientific discovery (or event) explains *what happened* and *in what sequence*—just like a chronological narrative of a past event (last week's topos). There are two major kinds of scientific events that can be narrated chronologically:

1. a scientific discovery or advance, and
2. a scientific process that happened in the past.

Vesalius's disproving of Galen's theories is an example of the first kind of scientific event. The birth of a star, the retreat of glaciers, and the fossilization of a fallen *T. rex* are examples of the second kind.

Later in the year, the student will work on chronological narratives about scientific processes. This week, the focus will be on chronological narratives about scientific *discoveries.*

The student will do today's work independently; her directions are reproduced below for your reference.

STEP ONE: **Examine model passages**

When you set out to write a chronological narrative about a scientific discovery, you aim to answer two questions:

What steps or events led to the discovery?
In what sequence did these steps or events happen?

Look again at the outline you made of the passage from *100 Greatest Science Discoveries of*

All Time. The exact words you used will be different, but the outline probably looks something like this:

I. Vesalius was curious about living things.
II. Dissection was not done in medical school.
III. Vesalius learned through dissection.
IV. Vesalius then gave lectures based on dissection.
V. Vesalius showed that Galen was wrong.

Notice that each one of these main points, except for the second, lists a step or event that led to Vesalius's contradiction of Galen. The points are also put into chronological order. First, young Vesalius was curious; because he was curious, he dissected and learned; after he learned, he lectured; finally, the lectures showed that Galen was wrong.

So what is the second point doing in the narrative?

Because a chronological narrative about a scientific discovery tells us how a scientist moves from one understanding of the world to another (in this case, from Galen's old understanding of anatomy to Vesalius's new understanding), you will often need to provide a paragraph or section that explains what the old understanding of the world was *before* the discovery. The second point in the narrative tells us about the old approach to anatomy; we need to know this so that we can appreciate just how different Vesalius's new ideas were.

So a chronological narrative about a scientific discovery usually includes a "background point" somewhere near the beginning—a paragraph that gives necessary background information.

Here is a second example of a **chronological narrative about a scientific discovery,** from *Seven African-American Scientists* by Robert C. Hayden and Richard Loehle. You may not be familiar with the term "Far East," which generally refers to China, Japan, Korea, and other eastern Asian countries.

In this chronological narrative about a scientific discovery, the very first paragraph is the "background point"—the one that gives you the information you need to understand *why* George Washington Carver set out to discover new uses for the peanut. With your pencil, underline "George Washington Carver" once and "faced a real dilemma" twice. Carver had talked farmers into growing peanuts instead of cotton—and now, they had too many peanuts.

Each of the following sections describes, in order, the steps Carver took to discover more about peanuts.

In the second section, draw a box around the word "began." This is the beginning—the first step Carver took. Now ask yourself: What did Carver begin to do? Did he discover anything? Use your pencil to underline the following verbs twice: "to shell," "ground," "heated," "put." These verbs show you that Carver's first step was simply to *process* the peanuts—to turn them into powder, mash, and oil.

In the third section, draw a box around the word "then." This time word shows you that the third section happened, chronologically, after the second. Circle the word "oil" in the first sentence, and then circle "soap, cooking oil, and rubbing oil" in the second sentence. After Carver processed the peanuts, he was able to turn the oil into three other products.

In the fourth section, draw a box around the word "remained." Then circle "dried peanut cake" in the first sentence and "cheese" in the second sentence. Carver's next step, after he used the oil, was to make use of what was left *after* the oil was drained away; he made cheese out of the remaining peanut material.

In the fifth section, draw a box around the word "Next." This time word shows you that Carver's final actions took place *after* he made cheese from the peanut cake. Circle "peanut cake left in the press" in the first sentence and "protein" in the last sentence. The last thing Carver did with the leftover peanut cake was analyze it for protein.

Now look at the summary below:

> There were too many peanuts.
> Carver began by processing the peanuts.
> Then Carver drained off the oil and used it.
> Afterwards, Carver made cheese from the peanut cake.
> Next, Carver analyzed the leftover peanut cake for protein.

The original narrative has a lot more details in it—but this summary shows you exactly how the writer tells each step in Carver's discoveries in chronological order.

STEP TWO: **Write down the pattern of the topos**

Now copy the following onto a blank sheet of paper in the Reference section of your Composition Notebook. You will be adding to this page as you learn more about chronological narratives of scientific events, so leave plenty of room at the bottom of the page.

Chronological Narrative of a Scientific Discovery

Definition: A narrative telling what steps or events led to a discovery, and in what sequence

Procedure	Remember
1. Ask, *What steps or events led to the discovery?*	1. May need a background paragraph explaining the circumstances that existed before the discovery.
2. Ask, *In what sequence did these steps or events happen?*	
3. Create main points by placing the answers in chronological order.	

Day Four: Practicing the Topos

Focus: Learning how to write a chronological narrative about a scientific discovery

Like a chronological narrative about a past event, a chronological narrative about a scientific discovery can be used as a science composition on its own, or as an introduction to a paper which then goes on to examine scientific concepts. The astronomy textbook *In Quest of the Universe* begins like this:

> On the night of March 23, 1993, amateur astronomer David Levy photographed part of the sky near the planet Jupiter. His friends, fellow astronomers Carolyn Shoemaker and her husband Eugene Shoemaker, spotted something unusual in the picture: a comet that had broken up into about 20 pieces. The comet became known officially as Comet Shoemaker-Levy 9 (the ninth comet discovered by these three sky-watchers) and unofficially as the "string of pearls" comet.

When astronomers announced the news of the comet on June 1, 1993, they had traced its path closely enough to tell that it had come under the influence of Jupiter's powerful gravitational field. They had deduced that the comet was pulled apart by Jupiter's gravity in July of 1992. They predicted that the comet would crash into Jupiter on or about July 25, 1994. . . .

By the time of the predicted impacts, the entire world was watching, linked together by the Internet and the television. The Hubble Space Telescope was trained on Jupiter, as was the Galileo space probe then approaching the Jupiter system, as well as most major observatories around the world and untold numbers of amateur telescopes. It has been said that more telescopes were aimed at the same spot—Jupiter—than ever before or since, and the viewers were not disappointed.[6]

This is definitely a more gripping beginning than "Comets are thought to be material that coalesced in the outer solar system, the remnants of small eddies. These objects would feel the gravitational forces of Jupiter and Saturn, and many would fall onto those planets."[7]

Today, the student will practice putting together a chronological narrative of her own.

STEP ONE: **Plan the narrative**

Student instructions for Step One:

Your first step is to plan out the narrative.

You'll need to approach the chronological narrative about a scientific discovery a little differently than the narrative about a past event. Because a scientific discovery is reached by a related series of steps, you can't pick and choose among the main events as easily as you did when you wrote about Alexander the Great. (You could leave out Alexander's invasion of India and still have a good historical narrative—but if you left out Vesalius's determination to find corpses and dissect them, his new discoveries about human anatomy wouldn't make sense.)

Instead, when you write the narrative of a scientific discovery, you make three choices:

1. Where to begin and end.
2. How much detail to use.
3. Where to put the "background paragraph," and how much information to include in it.

Below you'll see a list of events, written out chronologically for you, covering Edward Jenner's discovery of the smallpox vaccine. The information for this list was taken from *Doctors and Discoveries: Lives That Created Today's Medicine* (Houghton Mifflin, 2002) by John G. Simmons and *Diseases: Finding the Cure* by Robert Mulcahy (The Oliver Press, 1996).

Your assignment is to write a chronological narrative based on these events. This chronological narrative can be one paragraph or several paragraphs, but it must be at least 150 words long and no longer than 300 words.

1. Begin planning out your narrative by circling the events that belong in the "background information" paragraph of your composition.
2. Next, mark a beginning and ending place for your composition.

---

6. Theo Koupelis, *In Quest of the Universe,* sixth ed. (Jones and Bartlett, 2010), pp. 1–2.
7. Koupelis, p. 198.

3. Each main event in bold print is followed by details about that main event. Draw a light line through the details you don't intend to include.

EVENTS LEADING TO JENNER'S DISCOVERY
OF THE SMALLPOX VACCINE

Smallpox was a great danger in the eighteenth century

Killed 40 million people in the eighteenth century
Half of the people who caught smallpox died
Smallpox victims kept in "smallpox houses"

No reliable way to avoid smallpox

Many doctors gave people mild cases of smallpox to protect them
The "mild cases" sometimes killed the patients

Edward Jenner born in 1749

Inoculated against smallpox as a child
Inoculation made him sick
Kept in a smallpox house while he was sick

Jenner began to train as a doctor in 1762

Apprentice to a surgeon for eight years
Entered St. George's Hospital in 1770
Studied surgery and anatomy

Jenner began to practice medicine in his home town in 1773

Jenner noticed that milkmaids were not getting smallpox

Knew milkmaids often had cowpox
Cowpox gave cows blisters on their udders
Milkmaids sometimes got blisters on hands and arms
Cowpox gave patients a fever that lasted 4 days
Many local people believed that cowpox gave them immunity to smallpox

Jenner investigated relationship between smallpox and cowpox

Kept records of cowpox outbreaks
Discovered two forms of cowpox
Decided only one form of cowpox gave immunity to smallpox

Jenner inoculated James Phipps on May 14, 1796

James Phipps was eight years old
Jenner used pus from a cowpox blister
Jenner scraped Phipps's arm and put pus into it
Phipps had a small fever
Jenner tried to give Phipps a mild case of smallpox
Phipps was immune

Jenner tested his vaccine on 23 other people

Did not know why vaccination worked
Believed his observations were correct

Jenner published his results

At first, other doctors skeptical
Royal Society of Medicine refused to accept his findings
Some people afraid cowpox would make them act like cows

Vaccine slowly accepted

Parliament gave Jenner money in 1802 to continue his research
12,000 people vaccinated in 1804
British government began to give the vaccines in 1808
Deaths decreased to 600 per year

HOW TO HELP THE STUDENT WITH STEP ONE

The student should have circled the first two main events to use in her "background information" paragraph.

If she needs assistance choosing beginning and ending points, you may suggest one of the following:

Begin with ***Edward Jenner born in 1749*** and end with ***Jenner inoculated James Phipps on May 14, 1796.*** (This allows the student to tell the story of Jenner's own experience with smallpox and then to end with Jenner's first "victory" over the disease.)

Begin with ***Jenner noticed that milkmaids were not getting smallpox*** and end with ***Vaccine slowly accepted.*** (This focuses in more narrowly on the discovery of the vaccine itself.)

STEP TWO: **Use time and sequence words (Student Responsibility)**

Student instructions for Step Two:

You'll use time and sequence words in this composition, just as you did in last week's assignment.

Turn to the Chronological Narrative of a Scientific Discovery chart in your Composition Notebook. Add the bolded events below under the "Remember" column.

Chronological Narrative of a Scientific Discovery

Definition: A narrative telling what steps or events led to a discovery, and in what sequence

Procedure	Remember
1. Ask, *What steps or events led to the discovery?*	1. May need a background paragraph explaining the circumstances that existed before the discovery.
2. Ask, *In what sequence did these steps or events happen?*	**2. Make use of time words.**
3. Create main points by placing the answers in chronological order.	

Now pull out your Time and Sequence Words list and keep it in view as you write. Refer to your list of time words as you construct your chronological narrative. Try to use at least three of them, without repeating any.

STEP THREE: **Write the narrative**

Student instructions for Step Three:

Here's a summary of your assignment:

1. This chronological narrative can be one paragraph or several paragraphs, but it must be at least 150 words long and no longer than 300 words.

2. You may choose where your narrative begins and ends, but the narrative must progress chronologically forward at all times.

3. The only exception is your "background paragraph," where you describe what the world was like before the smallpox vaccine. This paragraph should come early in the composition (first or second).

4. Do not include all of the details.

5. Use three or more time words in your narrative.

6. Try not to use the identical words of the events list. As you did last week, change the common nouns and adjectives if necessary so that your narrative is not a direct copy of the events list.

If you have difficulty, ask your instructor for help. And when you're finished, show your composition to your instructor.

HOW TO HELP THE STUDENT WITH STEP THREE

There are three possible areas of difficulty with this assignment.

1. If the student needs assistance deciding what details to leave out, refer to the following; the marked-out details add color and interest but do not advance the narrative.

EVENTS LEADING TO JENNER'S DISCOVERY
OF THE SMALLPOX VACCINE

Smallpox was a great danger in the eighteenth century
Killed 40 million people in the eighteenth century (Either use this detail
Half of the people who caught smallpox died or this one; not both)
~~Smallpox victims kept in "smallpox houses"~~
No reliable way to avoid smallpox
Many doctors gave people mild cases of smallpox to protect them
The "mild cases" sometimes killed the patients
Edward Jenner born in 1749
~~Inoculated against smallpox as a child~~
~~Inoculation made him sick~~
~~Kept in a smallpox house while he was sick~~
~~**Jenner began to train as a doctor in 1762**~~
~~Apprentice to a surgeon for eight years~~
~~Entered St. George's Hospital in 1770~~
~~Studied surgery and anatomy~~
Jenner began to practice medicine in his home town in 1773
Jenner noticed that milkmaids were not getting smallpox
Knew milkmaids often had cowpox
~~Cowpox gave cows blisters on their udders~~
~~Milkmaids sometimes got blisters on hands and arms~~
~~Cowpox gave patients a fever that lasted 4 days~~
Many local people believed that cowpox gave them immunity to smallpox
Jenner investigated relationship between smallpox and cowpox
~~Kept records of cowpox outbreaks~~
~~Discovered two forms of cowpox~~

~~Decided only one form of cowpox gave immunity to smallpox~~

Jenner inoculated James Phipps on May 14, 1796

~~James Phipps was eight years old~~

Jenner used pus from a cowpox blister

Jenner scraped Phipps's arm and put pus into it

Phipps had a small fever

Jenner tried to give Phipps a mild case of smallpox

Phipps was immune

Jenner tested his vaccine on 23 other people

~~Did not know why vaccination worked~~

~~Believed his observations were correct~~

Jenner published his results

~~At first, other doctors skeptical~~

~~Royal Society of Medicine refused to accept his findings~~

~~Some people afraid cowpox would make them act like cows~~

Vaccine slowly accepted.

~~Parliament gave Jenner money in 1802 to continue his research~~

~~12,000 people vaccinated in 1804~~

~~British government began to give the vaccines in 1808~~

Deaths decreased to 600 per year

As before, use your judgment in suggesting details that can be left out; the point of this exercise is not to pick the "right" details, but to practice moving the narrative forward.

2. The student may need help choosing the correct time words. If necessary, go over the Time and Sequence Words reference list with her and suggest six or seven appropriate words for her to choose from.

3. The student may have trouble using her own phrasing. If necessary, help her find synonyms for the nouns and adjectives in the event list. Don't be afraid to give her two or three alternatives to choose from.

When the narrative is finished, check it using the following rubric.

Week 5 Rubric
Chronological Narrative of Scientific Discovery

Organization

1 Events should be in chronological order.
2 The paragraph giving "background information" should be the first or second paragraph in the composition.
3 Three or more time words should be used.
4 The composition should use more than 150 but fewer than 300 words.

Mechanics

1 Each sentence should make sense on its own when read aloud.
2 Each proper name should be capitalized.
3 Possessive forms should be written properly. (Note that the possessive of "Phipps" is "Phipps's.")
4 The exact words of the source material should not be used in every sentence.

Week 6: Chronological Narrative of a Past Event

Day One: Original Narration Exercise

Focus: Summarizing a narrative by choosing the main events and listing them chronologically

STEP ONE: **Read (Student Responsibility)**

Student instructions for Step One:

Read the following excerpt from *The Once and Future King* by T. H. White. The "Once and Future King" is King Arthur; the first half of the novel describes Arthur's boyhood. White imagines that young Arthur (known as "the Wart" by his adoptive family) was tutored by the magician Merlin, who taught him about the natural world by turning him into different animals. Archimedes is Merlin's pet owl.

STEP TWO: **Note important events**

Student instructions for Step Two:

On your scratch paper, write down four or five phrases or short sentences that will remind you of the things that happened in the story. *Do not use more than five phrases or short sentences!* Remember, you're not supposed to write down *everything* that happens in the story—just the most important events. The most important events are the ones that help the story make sense; if you took them out of the original passage, you wouldn't understand the rest of the story. (For example, if you left out the fact that the Wart turned into an owl, would the flying scenes make sense to you?)

Be sure to write the events down in the same order that they happen in the story.

If you have trouble with this assigment, ask your instructor for help.

HOW TO HELP THE STUDENT WITH STEP TWO

The student should have written down on scratch paper four or five short phrases or sentences that summarize the main events. The phrases/sentences should resemble four or five of the following (these are given only as a guide):

Wart turned into a bird.
Ate a magic mouse
Magic mouse turned Wart into an owl.
Archimedes the owl came to get Wart.
Wart practiced flying.
Archimedes told Wart how to fly.
World looked strange to Wart.
Saw like an owl
Saw everything as the same color
Archimedes told Wart how to land.
Wart managed to land on a branch.
Landing—going upward and then sitting down

(Remember, the student should not provide more than four or five phrases/sentences.)

Watch the student as he writes down his phrases. If he's writing too many phrases, or the sentences are long and complex, stop him before he goes on.

In this excerpt, the student may be tempted to write down too many details about exactly how birds fly and land. Remind him that it isn't necessary to include all of the details in the speeches made by Archimedes and the Wart; the summary should focus on what *happens* in the story, not on what is said.

You may ask the following questions to help distinguish between main events and supporting details:

What happened to the Wart? *(He turned into a bird.)*
After he turned into a bird, what did he and Archimedes do together? *(They practiced flying.)*
What did the Wart notice about the world? *(He could see in the dark OR The world all looked like shades of the same color.)*
What did the Wart do successfully at the end of the story? *(He was able to sit on the branch.)*

STEP THREE: **Write summary sentences**

Student instructions for Step Three:

> After you've written down your four or five phrases or sentences, try to combine them into three or four sentences. You can do this by putting two phrases in the same sentence (for example, "Wart ate a magic mouse" and "Wart turned into an owl" could be combined into "Wart ate a magic mouse that turned him into an owl"). Or you may find that one or more of your jotted notes turns out to be unnecessary. (If you wrote down "Wart saw like an owl" and

"Wart could see in the dark," you don't really need one of those sentences; both describe the same change.

Try to avoid listing minor details; instead, stick to main events. Minor details don't change the sense of the story. (It doesn't really matter that the Wart learned to flick his wings and stall—without that detail, we can still understand the story.)

Say your three or four sentences out loud several times before writing them down. After you've written the sentences down, ask your instructor to check them.

If you have trouble, ask your instructor for help.

HOW TO HELP THE STUDENT WITH STEP THREE

In this step, the student practices turning the jotted phrases and sentences into three or four coherent, smooth sentences. He should say his three or four sentences out loud several times before he writes; listen to make sure that you hear him talking out loud, and if necessary remind him that he should be speaking before he writes.

You may need to help him combine two phrases into one sentence. (For example, "Wart practiced flying" and "Archimedes told Wart how to fly" could be combined into "Archimides helped Wart practice his flying.")

When the summary is finished, check it using the following rubric.

Week 6 Narration Rubric

Organization

1 Events should be in chronological order.

2 If two or more events are listed in a single sentence, they should have a cause and effect relationship.

For example:

Wart ate a magic mouse and turned into an owl

is acceptable, because the mouse turned Wart into the owl.

Archimedes taught the Wart to fly and the Wart could see like an owl

is not acceptable. There is no causal relationship between the two sentences.

3 Each event of major importance should be in the summary (if it were missing from the original passage, the narrative would no longer make sense).

Mechanics

1 Each sentence should make sense on its own when read aloud.

2 Each proper name should be capitalized. (Note that "Wart" is a proper name in this context. It may be written either as "Wart" or "the Wart," since White uses both.)

3 Personal pronouns should have clear antecedents and be of the proper gender (Archimedes and the Wart are "he," while the mouse is "it").

Day Two: Outlining Exercise

Focus: Finding the main idea in each paragraph of a historical narrative

STEP ONE: **Read (Student Responsibility)**

Student instructions for Step One:

Read the following excerpt from *Historical Catastrophes: Hurricanes and Tornadoes* by Billye Walker Brown and Walter R. Brown. This passage is about Colonel Joseph Duckworth, the first man to fly a plane into a hurricane.

STEP TWO: **Construct a one-level outline**

Student instructions for Step Two:

Begin to outline this passage by looking for the main idea in each section of text. You'll see that the passage above is divided into five sections (there's an extra space between each section). For each section, try to come up with a single sentence that states the main idea.

Remember: don't try to include as much information as possible in this single sentence. Ask yourself two sets of questions:

1. What is the main thing or person that this section is about? *Or* Is the section about an idea?
2. Why is that thing or person important? *Or* What did that thing or person do/what was done to it? *Or* What is the idea?

You'll notice that this passage, unlike the others you've outlined, has dialogue in it; some parts of the passage are written more like a story. This dialogue makes the passage more interesting to read, but it shouldn't affect the answers to these questions.

Try asking the first question about the first section now. What is the main thing or person that this section is about?

The answer should be obvious:

Joseph Duckworth.

Now look at everything else in the passage. There are many details about Joseph Duckworth's life—but you're not trying to include all of the information about Joseph Duckworth in a single sentence. Remember, you're trying to find the *main idea only.*

You may remember that you had a similar challenge in the first passage you outlined from *The Story of Mankind;* the passage contained a whole list of inventions and discoveries made by the Egyptians, and you summarized by saying something like "The Egyptians invented many things." In this passage, you need to take a similar approach. What important, single idea can you draw from all of these details about Joseph Duckworth?

If you're still puzzled, try finishing this sentence: "Joseph Duckworth was a very. . . ."

What did you come up with? Your sentence should sound like one of these:

I. Joseph Duckworth was a very experienced pilot. OR

I. Colonel Joseph Duckworth knew how to fly in many different situations.

Now work on coming up with a summary sentence or phrase for each one of the remaining sections. Don't worry about sticking to either sentences or phrases exclusively—use whichever form seems most natural. Remember to use Roman numerals.

If you have difficulty, ask your instructor for help. And when you are finished, check your assignment with your instructor.

HOW TO HELP THE STUDENT WITH STEP TWO

For each section of text, the student should pick out a major point by asking himself two sets of questions:

1. What is the main thing or person that this section is about? Or Is the section about an idea?
2. Why is that thing or person important? Or What did that thing or person do/what was done to it? Or What is the idea?

Suggested answers (the student's sentences should resemble the following but don't need to be identical):

I. Joseph Duckworth was a very experienced pilot OR Colonel Joseph Duckworth knew how to fly in many different situations.

II. The morning of the flight OR A hurricane moves inland OR Duckworth decides to fly into a hurricane.

III. The flight into the hurricane OR Duckworth and O'Hair fly into the hurricane.

IV. The second flight with a meteorologist on board OR They make a second flight with a meteorologist.

V. Flights into other hurricanes OR More hurricane air reconnaissance

Note to Instructor: Although many guides to outlining will insist that outlines be in the form of either phrases or sentences, this requirement often pushes students into forming unnatural and awkward sentences or phrases. The student is learning to outline as a *tool*: the outline should help him organize his thoughts so that he can become a better writer. Since the outline is a tool, not an end in itself, you should let the student mix phrases and sentences and use whichever form seems most natural.

If the student struggles with this assignment, use the following dialogues:

Section 2

Instructor: What's the single most important thing that happens in the second section? Hint: it's a decision that Duckworth makes.

Student: Duckworth decides to fly into the hurricane.

Note to Instructor: Since the entire section describes the scene of Duckworth's decision, rather than just telling about the decision itself, "The morning of the flight" is acceptable. The student could also argue that the most important thing in the second section is the arrival of the hurricane, since the flight wouldn't have taken place unless the hurricane had moved inland. "A hurricane moves inland" is also acceptable.

Outlining is not an exact science; as noted before, it is a tool that helps the student organize thoughts. Don't get stalled on trying to find an exact or "correct" answer for any one section, as long as the student can make a reasonable argument for the main point he has selected.

Section 3
Instructor: There are a lot of details in this third section, but there's one thing that happens that ties the whole section together. Without this one act, the details in the section wouldn't make any sense.

Note to Instructor: If the student is still puzzled, say "What did Duckworth and O'Hair do?"

Student: The two men flew into the hurricane.

Section 4
Instructor: What happens for the second time in this section?

Student: They fly into the hurricane.

Instructor: How is this flight different? What makes it worth mentioning?

Student: A meteorologist was aboard.

Note to Instructor: "A meteorologist measured the hurricane" should not be listed as the main point; this is a detail about what happens on the flight. The existence and importance of the flight must be established before we can find out details about what happened on it.

Section 5
Instructor: What was the result of Duckworth's flights into the hurricane? Hint: it was something that happened three more times in 1943.

Students: There were more flights into hurricanes.

Note to Instructor: The student could argue that the result was "hurricane air reconnaisance"; this is acceptable.

Day Three: Analyzing the Topos

Focus: Understanding the form of a chronological narrative about a past event

The passage outlined in the last writing session was a **chronological narrative of a past event.** The student studied and practiced this form in the first week of this program; in this week, he will review and practice some more.

STEP ONE: **Review time and sequence words**

Student instructions for Step One:

> Remember, a chronological narrative of a past event explains *what happened in the past* and *in what sequence.* Each one of the main points in your outline describes something that happened, and the passage itself presents these happenings in chronological order.
>
> Your points probably sound something like the points below (although your exact words will be different):
>
> I. ________ Joseph Duckworth was a very experienced pilot.
> II. ________ A hurricane moves inland.
> III. ________ Duckworth and O'Hair fly into the hurricane.
> IV. ________ They make a second flight with a meteorologist.
> V. ________ Flights are made into other hurricanes.
>
> Pull out your Time and Sequence Words sheet. Using your pencil, write an appropriate time word on the blank in front of each point. When you are finished, check your work with your instructor.

HOW TO HELP THE STUDENT WITH STEP ONE

The student may need assistance choosing the correct time and sequence words from his list. If necessary, you may give the following hints:

I. Choose a word from the "events that happen before any others" category on the list.
II. Choose a word from the "event that happens after a previous event—but you're not exactly sure whether a long or short period of time elapsed first" category.
III. and IV. Choose a word from the "event that happens very soon after a previous event" category.
V. Choose a word from the "event that happened after another event—AND was caused by the previous event" category.

Encourage the student to read the time and sequence word and then the entire sentence out loud to see whether the word fits the sentence.

The following answers are the most natural:

I. *At first, in the beginning*
II. *Next, after some time, subsequently*
III. *and IV. Shortly afterwards, before long, not long after, immediately*
V. *As a result, as a consequence*

STEP TWO: **Add dialogue and actions (Student Responsibility)**

Student instructions for Step Two:

In this passage, the authors *dramatize*—use dialogue (the words characters actually speak) and actions to move the narrative forward. First, they tell you about Duckworth's past. Then, when the narrative reaches the morning of the flight, the authors change techniques. Rather than simply listing events, they begin to tell a story.

Dialogue can make chronological narratives more interesting. Look at the following example from Harold Lamb's history of the Mongol invasions, *Genghis Khan and the Mongol Horde*. In this section, Genghis Khan's warriors are pursuing the defeated king Muhammad Shah, who has been driven from his country by the Mongol armies.

You will notice ellipses (. . .) in the passage below. Remember, ellipses show that words in the original have been left out of the excerpt.

The author could have written "Muhammad Shah wondered if he would be safe anywhere." But instead, he gave Muhammad Shah dialogue—an actual speech that moves the narrative forward by showing why Muhammad Shah took sail to an island in the Caspian Sea (where he would die—although you should read the book if you want to find out how).

STEP THREE: **Add to the pattern of the topos (Student Responsibility)**

Student instructions for Step Three:

Turn to the Chronological Narrative of a Past Event chart in your Composition Notebook. Add the bolded point below under the "Remember" column.

Chronological Narrative of a Past Event

Definition: A narrative telling what happened in the past and in what sequence

Procedure	Remember
1. Ask *Who did what to whom?* (Or *What was done to what?*)	1. Select your main events to go with your theme.
2. Create main points by placing the answers in chronological order.	2. Make use of time words.
	3. Consider using dialogue to hold the reader's interest.

Day Four: Practicing the Topos

Focus: Learning how to write a chronological narrative about a past event

Today, the student will practice putting together another chronological narrative about a past event.

STEP ONE: **Plan the narrative**

Student instructions for Step One:

Below you'll see a list of events, written out chronologically for you, about the sinking of the *Titanic.* The bolded entries are main events; the indented entries are further details about those main events. (Those details are taken from Logan Marshall's 1912 account, *The Sinking of the Titanic,* and Jack Winocour's *The Story of the Titanic: As Told by Its Survivors.*)

Your assignment is to write a chronological narrative based on these events. This chronological narrative can be one paragraph or several paragraphs, but it must be at least 150 words long and no longer than 300 words.

Remember that you should not try to include every event. For example, you could construct a narrative with only the following events:

Collision with the iceberg
Captain realized ship was sinking
Lifeboats launched
Ship sank between 2:05 and 2:20 AM

Leaving out the ice sightings, the initial flooding of the ship, and the sending of distress signals doesn't confuse the narrative at all; it is still clear that the ship collided with the iceberg, began to sink, and then sank after lifeboats were launched.

Look over the following events now, and mark three or four main (bolded) events to include in your narrative. If you have difficulty, ask your instructor for help.

EVENTS IN THE SINKING OF THE TITANIC

Ice sightings on April 14, 1912
- Captain Edward Smith received six ice warnings earlier
- Icebergs reported in *Titanic*'s path at 9:30 PM
- Report never reached captain
- *Titanic* continued at top speed
- Night was moonless and dark
- Lookouts had no binoculars
- Ice warning sent to *Titanic* from nearby ship *Californian*
- *Titanic* radio operator Jack Phillips ignored warning
    - "Shut up! Shut up! I am busy!" (Reported by *Californian*)

Collision with the iceberg
- Iceberg sighted straight ahead at 11:40 PM
- Lookouts telephoned first officer on the bridge
- First officer (William Murdoch) ordered ship turned to port (left)
- Ship collided with iceberg 37 seconds after sighting

Sharp edge of berg cut starboard (right) side of ship open
Passengers on deck played with ice chunks from berg

Ship began to flood

Officers told passengers there was no danger

"Oh, no, nothing at all, nothing at all. Just a mere nothing. We just hit an iceberg." (Reported by survivor Edith Louise Rosenbaum Russell)

Five separate compartments filled with water
Sixth compartment began to flood
Pumps in sixth compartment began to work
Pumps could remove 2,000 tons of water per hour
24,000 tons of water flooding into ship per hour

Captain realized ship was sinking

Shipbuilder Thomas Andrews told captain ship would sink in 1 1/2 hours

Captain Smith: "Give the command for all passengers to be on deck with life-belts on." (Reported by Logan Marshall)

Lifeboats readied just after midnight, in early hours of April 15
Lifeboats could only carry half the passengers on *Titanic*
Second officer Charles Lightoller asked captain for permission to fill boats

"Hadn't we better get the women and children into the boats, sir?" (Reported by Lightoller himself)

Lifeboats filled with women and children beginning 12:25 AM

Distress signals sent

White distress rocket launched 12:50 AM
Wireless operators sent out old distress signal CQD

"We have struck an iceberg. Badly damaged. Rush aid." (Reported by Logan Marshall)

Later also began to send new SOS signal as well

"Sinking by the head." (Reported by Jack Winocour)

Other ships received signal but were far away
Closest ship, *Carpathia,* responded but was four hours away
Signal transmitted to New York (*Titanic* destination)

Shipline official announced, "We are confident that there will be no loss of life." (Reported by Logan Marshall)

Lifeboats launched

First lifeboats launched beginning 1:10 AM
Passengers reluctant to leave ship

Many said, "This ship cannot sink; it is only a question of waiting until another ship comes up and takes us off." (Reported by Jack Winocour)

First lifeboats only 1/4 full
Deck began to tilt, more passengers left ship
Later lifeboats overloaded
Last lifeboat launched 2:05 AM
Captain Smith went down with ship but told officers to save themselves.

"You have done your duty, boys. Now every man for himself." (Reported by survivor W. J. Mellers)

Ship sank between 2:05 and 2:20 AM

Propellers rose above water 2:05 AM
First funnel of ship fell into water
Water broke windows and flooded into bridge
Stern (rear) of ship rose above water
Electricity failed 2:18 AM
Second funnel fell

Ship split in half
Bow (front) section sank
Stern rose back up in water
Stern sank 2:20 AM
Only one lifeboat returned for people in water

Rescue arrived 4:10 AM

711 of 2,222 people in lifeboats
Carpathia arrived 4:10 AM
Carpathia picked up passengers until 8:50 AM
Five passengers died on board *Carpathia*
Carpathia set out for New York 8:50 AM

Survivors reached New York April 18

HOW TO HELP THE STUDENT WITH STEP ONE

You may need to help the student select which events to include. Encourage him to include three or four main (bolded) events but no more.

If necessary, point out to the student that as long as two main events make sense when put together, events between them can be eliminated. For example, the following sequences make sense:

Ice sightings on April 14, 1912
Collision with the iceberg
Lifeboats launched
Ship sank between 2:05 and 2:20 AM

and

Collision with the iceberg
Ship sank between 2:05 and 2:20 AM
Rescue arrived 4:10 AM
Survivors reached New York April 18

However, going from

Ice sightings on April 14, 1912 to
Ship began to flood

doesn't make sense, because the collision has to happen in order for the ship to flood; in the same way, the student cannot go from

Lifeboats launched to
Rescue arrived 4:10 AM

because unless the ship sinks, rescue isn't needed.

STEP TWO: **Choose details and dialogue (Student Responsibility)**

Student instructions for Step Two:

> When you write your chronological narrative, you won't include every detail listed under the main events; this would make your narrative too long and complicated. Instead, choose the details you want to highlight, and leave others out. Be sure that you include at least one line of dialogue.

For example, if you chose the following events:

Captain realized ship was sinking

Shipbuilder Thomas Andrews told captain ship would sink in 1 1/2 hours

Captain Smith: "Give the command for all passengers to be on deck with life-belts on." (Reported by Logan Marshall)

Lifeboats readied just after midnight, in early hours of April 15

Lifeboats could only carry half the passengers on *Titanic*

Second officer Charles Lightoller asked captain for permission to fill boats

"Hadn't we better get the women and children into the boats, sir?" (Reported by Lightoller himself)

Lifeboats filled with women and children beginning 12:25 AM

Lifeboats launched

First lifeboats launched beginning 1:10 AM

Passengers reluctant to leave ship

Many said, "This ship cannot sink; it is only a question of waiting until another ship comes up and takes us off." (Reported by Jack Winocour)

First lifeboats only 1/4 full

Deck began to tilt, more passengers left ship

Later lifeboats overloaded

Last lifeboat launched 2:05 AM

Captain Smith went down with ship but told officers to save themselves.

"You have done your duty, boys. Now every man for himself." (Reported by survivor W. J. Mellers)

you might write:

Captain Smith realized that the ship was sinking. The first lifeboats were launched at 1:10 AM, but many passengers refused to leave the ship. They said, "This ship cannot sink; it is only a question of waiting until another ship comes up and takes us off."

Or you might write:

The captain realized the Titanic *was doomed when the shipbuilder told him that the ship would sink in an hour and half. "Give the command for all passengers to be on deck with life-belts on," he ordered. The lifeboats were filled with women and children, and then were launched.*

Notice that only two or three details were included for one main event—and that another main event was simply stated with no details at all.

Read through your selected main events and mark which details and dialogue you intend to include. (You may find that you need to adjust your choices when you begin to write.)

STEP THREE: **Write the narrative**

Student instructions for Step Three:

As you begin to write, don't forget to include time and sequence words (as you learned in Week 4's lesson).

Here's a summary of your assignment:

1. This chronological narrative can be one paragraph or several paragraphs, but it must be at least 150 words long and no longer than 300 words.
2. The narrative must progress chronologically forward at all times.
3. Include at least one line of dialogue, but do not try to include all of the details!
4. Use two or more time words in your narrative.
5. If necessary, review the following rules about how to write dialogue:

Use quotation marks to surround a speaker's exact words.

If a dialogue tag ("he said," "Captain Smith said") comes before a speech, use a comma after the dialogue tag. The punctuation at the end of the speech itself goes *inside* the closing quotation mark.

Captain Smith said, "Put on your life jackets."

If the dialogue tag comes after the speech, place a comma, question mark, or exclamation point (but *not* a period) before the closing quotation mark.

"Put on your life jackets," Captain Smith said.

"Put on your life jackets!" Captain Smith said.

"Should we put on our life jackets?" Captain Smith said.

Do *not* write

"Put on your life jackets." Captain Smith said.

Dialogue should never just sit in the middle of a paragraph as an independent sentence, with no dialogue tag. Don't write,

The ship began to sink. Captain Smith was concerned. "Put on your life jackets." The passengers began to obey.

Instead, write

The ship began to sink. Captain Smith was concerned. "Put on your life jackets," he told the passengers.

If you have difficulty, ask your instructor for help. And when you're finished, show your composition to your instructor.

HOW TO HELP THE STUDENT WITH STEP THREE

There are three possible areas of difficulty with this assignment.

1. The student may need help choosing which details to leave out. Remind him if necessary that if he's writing a narrative with three or four main events, he can leave out most of the details for all of the events except for one. A sample composition based on these main events:

Collision with the iceberg
Ship began to flood
Ship sank between 2:05 and 2:20 AM
Rescue arrived 4:10 AM

might sound like this:

The Titanic *collided with an iceberg at 11:40 PM.* ***Immediately****, the ship started to flood, but officers told the passengers that there was no danger. One survivor reported that officers said, "Just a mere nothing. We just hit an iceberg." But five compartments were already filling with water. A sixth compartment began to flood as well. The pumps in that compartment started to work, but they could not remove the water in time. They could only remove 2,000 tons of water every hour, and 12 times that much water was pouring into the ship.*

Before long, *the ship began to sink. Between 2:50 and 2:20 AM, the* Titanic *split in half. The bow sank* ***first****, and* ***then*** *the stern.*

The rescue ship Carpathia *did not arrive until 4:10 PM. Only 711 of the 2,222 people on board made it into the lifeboats. The* Carpathia *picked them up until 8:50 AM and* ***then*** *set out for New York.*

This is an acceptable length, but more details could be included to bring the composition closer to the 300 word maximum.

2. The student may need help choosing the correct time words (examples are bolded in

the sample composition above). If necessary, go over the Time and Sequence Words reference list with him and suggest five or six appropriate words for him to choose from.

3. If the student has not studied the proper punctuation for direct dialogue, he may need your help understanding the dialogue rules given in his instructions.

Note to Instructor: This assignment introduces a new skill (using dialogue). To avoid overwhelming the student with instructions, the directions do not specifically tell the student to avoid using the direct words of the events list. If the student seems to be completing the assignment with ease, however, you may choose to add this to the requirements. In that case, help him find synonyms for the nouns and adjectives in the events list, as in previous assignments.

Week 6 Rubric
Chronological Narrative of Past Events

Organization

1 Events should be in chronological order.
2 Two or more time words should be used.
3 The composition should use more than 150 but fewer than 300 words.

Mechanics

1 Each sentence should make sense on its own when read aloud.
2 Each proper name should be capitalized.
3 At least one line of dialogue should be included; dialogue and dialogue tags should be properly punctuated.

Week 7: Chronological Narrative of a Scientific Discovery

Day One: Original Narration Exercise

Focus: Summarizing a narrative by choosing the main events and listing them chronologically

STEP ONE: **Read (Student Responsibility)**

Student instructions for Step One:

Read the following excerpt from *Tik-Tok of Oz* by L. Frank Baum. Baum wrote a whole series of books set in the magical land of Oz. In this chapter, Betsy Bobbin and her friend the Shaggy Man have joined up with the sky fairy Polychrome, daughter of the Rainbow (in Oz, the Rainbow is a person!), and the Princess Rose, who has been driven from her throne in the Rose Kingdom and is now in exile. Travelling together, the four find an old well. The Shaggy Man tries to draw water out of it using a windlass (a mechanism for cranking a bucket up out of a well), but the hook on the end of the windlass doesn't hold a bucket. Instead, the hook creaks up out of the well with a pile of copper junk on the end of it.

STEP TWO: **Note important events**

Student instructions for Step Two:

On your scratch paper, write down five or six phrases or short sentences that will remind you of the things that happened in the story. *Do not use more than six phrases or short sentences!* Remember, you're not supposed to write down *everything* that happens in the story—just the most important events. The most important events are the ones that help the story make sense; if you took them out of the original passage, you wouldn't understand the rest of the story.

Be sure to write the events down in the same order that they happen in the story.

If you have trouble with this assigment, ask your instructor for help.

HOW TO HELP THE STUDENT WITH STEP TWO

The student should have written down on scratch paper five or six short phrases or sentences that summarize the main events. The phrases/sentences should resemble five or six of the following (these are given only as a guide):

Shaggy Man pulled up a bundle of copper.
Shaggy pulled a copper man from the well.
Shaggy, Betsy, Polychrome, Rose Princess
Copper bundle was a man.
Sign on the back of the copper man
Mechanical man pulled up out of well
Copper man had clockwork mechanism.
Engraved plate with directions
Directions for winding clockwork man
Guaranteed for thousand years
Had to be propped up
Shaggy's old friend Tik-Tok
Copper man was Tik-Tok.
Wound him up with key
Wound up thoughts first
Flashes of light showed when he started to think.
Wound up phonograph
Copper man talked.
Still fell over until action wound
Wound up action clockwork
Man could think, talk, walk.

Remember, the student should not provide more than five or six phrases/sentences.

Watch the student as she writes down her phrases. If she's writing too many phrases, or the sentences are long and complex, stop her before she goes on.

In this excerpt, the student may be tempted to write down too many details about the labels on the clockwork man. Remind her that it isn't necessary to include all of the details; instead, she can focus on what *happens* in the story (once Tik-Tok is wound up, he can think, talk, and walk) or simply summarize the *type* of information on the labels ("The labels described Tik-Tok and told how to wind him").

STEP THREE: **Write summary sentences**

Student instructions for Step Three:

> After you've written down your five or six phrases or sentences, try to combine them into three or four sentences. You can do this by putting two phrases in the same sentence, or you may find that one or more of your jotted notes turns out to be unnecessary.
>
> Try to avoid listing minor details; instead, stick to main events. Minor details don't

change the sense of the story. (It doesn't really matter that when Tik-Tok first walked, he went in a circle; without that detail, we can still understand the story.)

Say your three or four sentences out loud several times before writing them down. After you've written the sentences down, ask your instructor to check them.

If you have trouble, ask your instructor for help.

HOW TO HELP THE STUDENT WITH STEP THREE

In this step, the student practices turning the jotted phrases and sentences into three or four coherent, smooth sentences. She should say her three or four sentences out loud several times before she writes; listen to make sure that you hear her talking out loud, and if necessary remind her that she should be speaking before she writes.

You may need to help her combine two phrases into one sentence.

When the summary is finished, check it using the following rubric.

Week 7 Narration Rubric

Organization

1 Events should be in chronological order.

2 If two or more events are listed in a single sentence, they should have a cause and effect relationship.

For example:

After he was wound up, Tik-Tok could think, talk, and walk

is acceptable.

The Shaggy Man recognized Tik-Tok, and Betsy wound him up

is not acceptable. There is no causal relationship between the two sentences.

3 Each event of major importance should be in the summary (if it were missing from the original passage, the narrative would no longer make sense).

Mechanics

1 Each sentence should make sense on its own when read aloud.

2 Each proper name should be capitalized.

3 Personal pronouns should have clear antecedents and be of the proper gender (Tik-Tok is "he," while Polychrome and the Rose Princess are both "she").

Day Two: Outlining Exercise

Focus: Finding the main idea in each paragraph of a scientific narrative

STEP ONE: **Read (Student Responsibility)**

Student instructions for Step One:

Read the following excerpt from *Discoverer of the Unseen World: A Biography of Antoni van Leeuwenhoek* by Alma Payne Ralston. In this passage, Ralston explains how Leeuwenhoek became the first scientist to see single-celled organisms. The "new contrivance" Leeuwenhoek wanted to test was a tiny, clear tube of glass that would allow him to examine a drop of water underneath the lens of his microscope.

"Leeuwenhoek" is pronounced "leh-ven-hook."

STEP TWO: **Construct a one-level outline**

Student instructions for Step Two:

Begin to outline this passage by looking for the main idea in each section of text. You'll see that the passage above is divided into four sections (there's an extra space between each section). For each section, try to come up with a single sentence that states the main idea.

Remember, you shouldn't try to include as much information as possible in this single sentence. Ask yourself two sets of questions:

1. What is the main thing or person that this section is about? *Or* Is the section about an idea?
2. Why is that thing or person important? *Or* What did that thing or person do/what was done to it? *Or* What is the idea?

Try that for the first section. What is the main thing or person that this section is about?

If your answer was "Leeuwenhoek," look again. The details in the section don't tell you about Leeuwenhoek. What do they tell you about?

Once you've answered that question, answer the second: Why is it important?

Use the same strategies to come up with summary sentences for each of the remaining three sections. Remember to use Roman numerals for the summary sentences.

For this assignment, try to use complete sentences (although this isn't always necessary in an outline).

If you have difficulty, ask your instructor for help. And when you are finished, check your assignment with your instructor.

HOW TO HELP THE STUDENT WITH STEP TWO

For each section of text, the student should pick out a major point by asking herself two sets of questions:

1. What is the main thing or person that this section is about? OR Is the section about an idea?
2. Why is that thing or person important? OR What did that thing or person do/what was done to it? OR What is the idea?

Suggested answers (the student's sentences should resemble the following but don't need to be identical):

I. Berkelse Mere was a lake that changed color in the summer OR The inland lake Berkelse Mere became white and green in the summer.

II. Leeuwenhoek decided to test the lake OR Leeuwenhoek wanted to know why.

III. He scooped up water to test it OR He collected a water sample to observe.

IV. He saw animalcules OR He saw figures the size of a strand of hair OR He saw microscopic life forms OR Microscopic creatures were in the water.

If the student struggles with this assignment, use the following dialogues:

Section 1

Instructor: What did Leeuwenhoek think of, in this section?

Student: He thought of the inland lake.

Instructor: What was the lake like in winter?

Student: It was clear.

Instructor: What was the lake like in summer?

Student: It became cloudy OR *It became whitish with green clouds.*

Instructor: So what is the most important thing in this passage?

Student: The lake.

Instructor: What was strange about the lake?

Student: It changed during the summer.

Section 2

Instructor: What did Leeuwenhoek decide to do about the lake?

Student: He decided to test it OR *He was curious about it.*

Section 3

Instructor: What did Leeuwenhoek do, once he got to the lake?

Student: He scooped up water to test OR *He collected a water sample to observe.*

Instructor: The rest of the section contains details about *how* Leeuwenhoek observed the water sample. That information would go into subpoints supporting this main point.

Note to Instructor: If the student simply says "He scooped up water" or "He collected a water sample," ask "Why did he collect the water sample?"

Section 4

Instructor: What did Leeuwenhoek see?

Student: He saw microscopic creatures OR *Microscopic creatures were in the water.*

Instructor: The rest of the section contains details about the creatures Leeuwenhoek saw. That information would go into subpoints supporting this main point.

Note to Instructor: The answer to the question "What is the most important thing in this section?" is "Microscopic creatures." The answer to "Why are they important?" can either be, "Because Leeuwenhoek saw them" or "Because they were there."

Day Three: Analyzing the Topos

Focus: Understanding the form of a chronological narrative about a scientific discovery

The passage the student outlined in the last writing session is an example of this week's topos: a **chronological narrative of a scientific discovery**. The student has already studied several examples of this (Vesalius's discoveries in anatomy, George Washington Carver's work with the peanut, the sighting of Comet Shoemaker-Levy 9). Today, she'll expand her knowledge of this form.

The student will do all of today's work independently; her directions are reproduced below for your reference.

STEP ONE: **Review the pattern of the topos (Student Responsibility)**

Student instructions for Step One:

> Turn to the Chronological Narrative of a Scientific Discovery page in your Composition Notebook. Read through the pattern of the narrative again.

STEP TWO: **Examine the model (Student Responsibility)**

Student instructions for Step Two:

Your chart should have reminded you that a chronological narrative about a scientific discovery answers two questions:

What steps or events led to the discovery?

In what sequence did these steps or events happen?

and puts those answers in chronological order.

Look again at the outline you made of the passage from *Discoverer of the Unseen World.* The exact words you used will be different, but the outline probably looks something like this:

I. Berkelse Mere was a lake that changed color in the summer.
II. Leeuwenhoek decided to test the lake.
III. He collected a water sample to observe.
IV. He saw microscopic life forms.

Points II, III, and IV list, in chronological order, steps that led to the discovery of microscopic life forms.

Your chart should also have reminded you that you may need a paragraph giving background information. Point I gives you necessary background information; it describes an existing phenomenon (the cloudy lake) that no one in Leeuwenhoek's day understood.

Finally, your chart reminded you to make use of time and sequence words.

Below, you will see an expanded version of the passage about Leeuwenhoek's discovery. Read through the passage one more time and follow these simple instructions:

1. Look for the time and sequence words, which have been bolded.
2. When you read the additional paragraphs, ask yourself "What new element do these paragraphs bring into the narrative?"

You will notice that most of the time and sequence words occur in the middle of the passage, where Leeuwenhoek is actually going through the steps of the discovery.

What do you think the additional paragraphs add to the narrative?

They do add to the description of the microscopic world Leeuwenhoek discovered. But you should have noticed a new element in the final paragraph. It is bolded below:

The writer of this narrative has decided to use Leeuwenhoek's exact words, found in a letter Leeuwenhoek wrote to the scientists of the Royal Society.

Last week, you learned that dialogue—the words characters actually speak—can add interest to a chronological narrative about a past event. A chronological narrative about a scientific discovery can also become more vivid and real when dialogue is used.

Many scientists wrote letters, essays, and even books about their discoveries, so often you can find the exact words that scientists have used about their own work. Introducing a sentence or two from the scientist herself *about* her discovery adds color and interest to a chronological narrative about a scientific discovery.

Now add the bolded point below under the "Remember" column on your Chronolgoical Narrative of a Scientific Discovery chart:

Chronological Narrative of a Scientific Discovery

Definition: A narrative telling what steps or events led to a discovery, and in what sequence

Procedure	Remember
1. Ask, *What steps or events led to the discovery?*	1. May need a background paragraph explaining the circumstances that existed before the discovery.
2. Ask, *In what sequence did these steps or events happen?*	2. Make use of time words.
3. Create main points by placing the answers in chronological order.	3. **If possible, quote directly from the scientist's own words.**

Note to Instructor: In the next lesson, the student will practice quoting directly from a scientist as she constructs her chronological narrative. The quotes are provided. The student has not yet been taught how to find primary sources, and it is important not to overwhelm her with too many new skills simultaneously.

The following directions are provided for you, in case you wish to assign another topic for the composition—or feel that your student is ready to find primary sources on her own.

FINDING PRIMARY SOURCES IN SCIENCE FOR MIDDLE-GRADE WRITERS

1. Anthologies

The following anthologies contain multiple excerpts from the writings of scientists in different disciplines. Although they are designed for older readers, they may be useful references to have on hand.

Bynum, W. F., and Roy Porter. *Oxford Dictionary of Scientific Quotations.* New York: Oxford University Press, 2006.

Carey, John. *Eyewitness to Science: Scientists and Writers Illuminate Natural Phenomena from Fossils to Fractals.* Cambridge, Mass.: Harvard University Press, 1997.

Mackay, Alan L. *A Dictionary of Scientific Quotations,* second expanded ed. Bristol: Institute of Physics, 1992.

Oster, Malcolm. *Science in Europe, 1500–1800: A Primary Sources Reader.* New York: Palgrave Macmillan, 2002.

2. Internet resources

a. Websites

Dictionary of Science Quotations at
http://www.todayinsci.com/Quotations/QuotationsIndex.htm

This website, sponsored by Today in Science, can be searched for direct quotes by topic or by scientist name.

A Short Dictionary of Scientific Quotations at

http://naturalscience.com/dsqhome.html

Briefer than the website listed above, but useful.

b. Google Books

Search print books for letters, essays, and translations.

1. Go to http://books.google.com.
2. Click on the "Advanced Book Search" link.
3. On the Advanced Book Search screen, enter the name of the scientist and the scientific topic in the "with all the words" field.

   For example, entering Antoni van Leeuwenhoek and microscopic brought up, among other titles, The Select Works of Antony van Leeuwenhoek, *containing his letters about his discoveries. Although you can also enter the scientist's name in the "Return books written by" blank, this will limit your search and only bring up books authored by the scientist; often, the most accessible quotes are found in books authored or edited by someone else.*
4. Click on the Google Search button.
5. When the search results appear, look down the left-hand side of the page and click on "Preview and full view." (The default, "Any view," lists books that can't be accessed online.)

Day Four: Practicing the Topos

Focus: Learning how to write a chronological narrative about a scientific discovery

In the last lesson, the student saw an example of a chronological narrative about a scientific discovery that made use of the scientist's own words. Here is another, from *Doctors and Discoveries: Lives That Created Today's Medicine* by John G. Simmons. This narrative tells how the sixteenth-century French surgeon Ambroise Pare learned to use antiseptic on wounds to keep them from getting infected. (The first paragraph gives background information.)

> The years of Pare's youth were marked by the ascendancy of Francis I, who, four years after becoming king in 1515, lost his bid to become emperor of the Holy Roman Empire. This led him into a series of wars with Charles of Hapsburg that were fought largely on the Italian peninsula. There, at the siege of Turin in 1537, Pare made his first and most famous innovation.
>
> As was customary, Pare and his fellow surgeons treated gunshot wounds by cauterizing[8] them with boiling oil of elder, which was thought to prevent death from "gunpowder poisoning." This method caused terrible agony and more damage to

8. Cauterization is the burning of tissue in order to seal off a wound and prevent infection.

the flesh than the projectile had. At Turin, the oil ran out. As a stopgap, Pare covered the wounds with a salve composed of egg yolk, turpentine, and oil of roses. One night he wrote, "I could not sleep . . . for I was troubled in minde, and the dressing of the precedent day, (which I judged unfit) troubled my thoughts; and I feared that the next day I should finde them dead, or at the point of death by the poyson of the wound, whom I had not dressed with the scalding oyle." In fact, these patients were still alive and in better condition than the men who had been treated with cauterization. Pare continued to treat casualties in this way, he added, and "When I had many times tryed this in divers others I thought this much, that neither I nor any other should ever cauterize any wounded with Gun-shot."[9]

Today, the student will practice putting together a chronological narrative of her own, making use of direct quotes.

If necessary, review last week's rules for writing dialogue with the student.

STEP ONE: **Plan the narrative**

Student instructions for Step One:

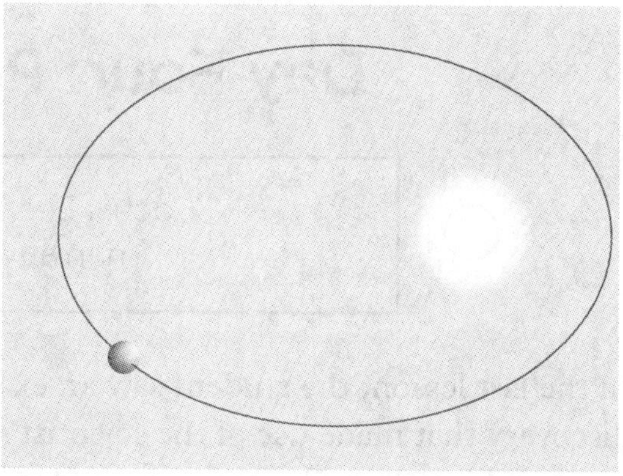

Your first step is to plan out the narrative. On the next page, you'll see a list of events, written out chronologically for you, covering Johannes Kepler's discovery that planets move in elliptical orbits. This information was taken from *Star Maps: History, Artistry, and Cartography* by Nick Kanas (Praxis, 2007); *Johannes Kepler and the New Astronomy* by James R. Voelkel; and *Tycho & Kepler: The Unlikely Partnership that Forever Changed Our Understanding of the Heavens* by Kitty Ferguson (Bloomsbury, 2002).

You'll need to make three choices:

1. Which main events and details to use in your narrative.
2. Where to put the "background paragraph," and how much information to include in it.
3. Which time and sequence words to use.

Your chronological narrative can be one paragraph or several paragraphs, but it must be at least 150 words long and no longer than 300 words.

Begin to plan out your narrative now by following these three instructions:

1. Circle the events that belong in the "background information" paragraph of your composition.
2. Draw a light line through the main events and details you do not intend to include. (Remember, you can eliminate an entire main event plus all its details. If you want to include a main event, you can also include only one of its details—or all of them.)

---

9. John G. Simmons, *Doctors and Discoveries: Lives That Created Today's Medicine* (Houghton Mifflin, 2002), p. 120.

3. Consult your chart of Time and Sequence Words. Make an initial selection of four or five words that you might be able to use in your narrative (you'll only need to use two or three in your actual draft).

EVENTS LEADING TO KEPLER'S DISCOVERY
OF ELLIPTICAL PLANETARY ORBITS

Johannes Kepler studied at university in the 1590s
He studied heliocentrism
One of his teachers was a follower of Copernicus
Heliocentric world view of Copernicus vs. geocentric world view
Heliocentrism=sun at center of solar system
Copernicus said sun at *exact* center of solar system
Copernicus said all orbits completely circular
Geocentrism=Earth at center of solar system
Geocentric world view still popular
Copernicus's theory still rejected by many
Most astronomers believed Earth at center of solar system
Geocentrism=Earth had no orbit because it remained still
Worked as assistant to astronomer Tycho Brahe 1600–1601
Helped Brahe observe orbits for planets
Assumed all orbits were circles
Observed Mars at different times
Mars seemed to speed up and slow down
Could not explain why the planet Mars moved as it did
Tycho Brahe died in 1601
Told Kepler to keep on trying to understand orbit
Kepler tried to find mathematical explanation for movement of Mars
Failed 40 times to find formula that explained Mars orbit
Struggled with Mars orbit for five years
In 1605, Kepler realized orbit must be an ellipse
Formulated "Kepler's first law of planetary motion"
Law: Planets move in elliptical orbits, sun is one focal point of orbit
Published findings in *Astronomia Nova* in 1609
Contained theory that all planets move in elliptical orbits
Planets move faster when close to sun, slower when farther away
Argued that sun pulls on planets
Intended to prove heliocentrism once and for all
Argued that Earth behaved like other planets

HOW TO HELP THE STUDENT WITH STEP ONE

The student should have circled the first two main events to use in her "background information" paragraph.

The student may need assistance identifying unnecessary events and details. In the list below, everything that can be left out of the composition is marked through for your reference.

~~Johannes Kepler studied at university in the 1590s~~
~~He studied heliocentrism~~
~~One of his teachers was a follower of Copernicus~~
Heliocentric world view of Copernicus vs. geocentric world view

Heliocentrism=sun at center of solar system
~~Copernicus said sun at *exact* center of solar system~~
Copernicus said all orbits completely circular
Geocentrism=Earth at center of solar system
~~Geocentric world view still popular~~
~~Copernicus's theory still rejected by many~~
Most astronomers believed Earth at center of solar system
~~Geocentrism=Earth had no orbit because it remained still~~
Worked as assistant to astronomer Tycho Brahe 1600–1601
Helped Brahe observe orbits for planets
~~Assumed all orbits were circles~~
~~Observed Mars at different times~~
~~Mars seemed to speed up and slow down~~
Could not explain why the planet Mars moved as it did
~~**Tycho Brahe died in 1601**~~
~~Told Kepler to keep on trying to understand orbit~~
Kepler tried to find mathematical explanation for movement of Mars
~~Failed 40 times to find formula that explained Mars orbit~~
~~Struggled with Mars orbit for five years~~
In 1605, Kepler realized orbit must be an ellipse
Formulated "Kepler's first law of planetary motion"
Law: Planets move in elliptical orbits, sun is one focal point of orbit
~~**Published findings in *Astronomia Nova* in 1609**~~
~~Contained theory that all planets move in elliptical orbits~~
~~Planets move faster when close to sun, slower when farther away~~
~~Argued that sun pulls on planets~~
~~Intended to prove heliocentrism once and for all~~
~~Argued that Earth behaved like other planets~~

STEP TWO: Write a draft of the narrative

Student instructions for Step Two:

Your next step is to write a first draft of your narrative. Here's a summary of your assignment:

1. This chronological narrative can be one paragraph or several paragraphs, but it must be at least 150 words long and no longer than 300 words.
2. The narrative must progress chronologically forward at all times. The only exception is your "background paragraph," where you describe what most people believed about the Earth and sun during Kepler's day. This paragraph should come early in the composition (first or second).
3. Do not include all of the main events and details.
4. Use two or more time words in your narrative.
5. Try not to use the identical words of the events list. In previous lessons, you were told to look at nouns and adjectives and to change them if possible. This events list contains

a number of verbs; when you write this narrative, concentrate on changing the verbs.

For example, if you are writing a paragraph based on the following events:

Worked as assistant to astronomer Tycho Brahe 1600–1601

Helped Brahe observe orbits for planets

Assumed all orbits were circles

try not to write:

Kepler ***worked*** *as an assistant to the astronomer Tycho Brahe from 1600–1601. He* ***helped*** *Brahe* ***observe*** *orbits for planets. Both men* ***assumed*** *all orbits* ***were*** *circles.*

Instead try to use original verbs in place of the verbs (bolded) in the events list.

Kepler **became** *the assistant of the astronomer Tycho Brahe in 1600 and worked with Brahe for a year. His job was to* **track** *the orbits of the planets. Both men* **believed** *that all planets* **orbited** *the sun in a perfect circle.*

If you have difficulty, ask your instructor for help.

HOW TO HELP THE STUDENT WITH STEP TWO:

There are two possible areas of difficulty with this step:

1. The student may need help choosing the correct time words. If necessary, go over the Time and Sequence Words reference list with her and suggest four or five appropriate words.

2. The student may have trouble using her own phrasing. If necessary, help her find synonyms for the verbs in the event list. Don't be afraid to give her two or three alternatives to choose from.

STEP THREE: Add direct quotes

Student instructions for Step Three:

Now that you've completed a rough draft of your narrative, consider how you might use Johannes Kepler's actual words to make some part of it more vivid.

Read through these five direct quotes from Kepler himself.

DIRECT QUOTES FROM KEPLER

"First, therefore, let my readers grasp that today it is absolutely certain . . . that all the planets revolve around the sun, with the exception of the moon, which alone has the Earth as its centre."[10]

"The planetary orbit is elliptical and the sun, the source of movement, is at one of the foci of this ellipse."[11]

"I was almost driven to madness considering and calculating this matter. I could not find out why the planet would rather go on an elliptical orbit."[12]

"I am moved by an exceedingly powerful desire for knowledge of the heavens."[13]

"If God is concerned with astronomy, which piety desires to believe, then I hope that I shall achieve something in this domain."[14]

---

10. Johannes Kepler and Charles G. Wallis, *The Harmonies of the World* (BiblioBazaar, 2008), p. 22.
11. Kepler and Wallis, p. 25.
12. Quoted in Owen Gingerich, *The Eye of Heaven: Ptolemy, Copernicus, Kepler* (American Institute of Physics, 1993), p. 344.
13. Quoted in Max Caspar and Clarisse Doris Hellman, *Kepler* (Dover, 1993) pp. 120–121.
14. Caspar and Hellman, p. 123.

Now look over your list of main events, and try to decide which main events each of these quotes belong to. (Some of the quotes might be usable in more than one part of the composition.)

For example, consider this quote: "I am moved by an exceedingly powerful desire for knowledge of the heavens." The quote tells you why Kepler spent his life studying the sky. So it might fit into a paragraph based on the following events:

Johannes Kepler studied at university in the 1590s
Worked as assistant to astronomer Tycho Brahe 1600–1601
Kepler tried to find mathematical explanation for movement of Mars

If the draft of your paragraph based on the first event read like this:

Johannes Kepler became a university student in the 1590s. He was taught heliocentrism, because one of his teachers believed Copernicus's theories of the universe.

you could add the quote as follows:

Johannes Kepler became a university student in the 1590s and studied astronomy. He said of his own studies, "I am moved by an exceedingly powerful desire for knowledge of the heavens." He was taught heliocentrism, because one of his teachers believed Copernicus's theories of the universe.

Now decide which quote you want to use and add it in to the appropriate paragraph. If you have difficulty, ask your instructor for help.

When you are finished, check your work with your instructor.

HOW TO HELP THE STUDENT WITH STEP THREE

The student should begin by deciding which main events each quote illustrates. For your reference, the answers are:

QUOTE	EVENTS	REASONS
"First, therefore, let my readers grasp. . ."	**Johannes Kepler studied at university in the 1590s**	He learned this at university.
	Heliocentric world view of Copernicus vs. geocentric world view	Describes the heliocentric world view
	Worked as assistant to astronomer Tycho Brahe 1600–1601	His work was based on this assumption.
"The planetary orbit is elliptical. . ."	**In 1605, Kepler realized orbit must be an ellipse**	This theory explained the orbit.
	Formulated "Kepler's first law of planetary motion"	This realization led him to formulate the law.
	Published findings in *Astronomia Nova* in 1609	This was the finding he published.

QUOTE	EVENTS	REASONS
"I was almost driven to madness. . ."	**Worked as assistant to astronomer Tycho Brahe 1600–1601**	This was his reaction to the observations he made of Mars while working for Brahe.
	Tycho Brahe died in 1601	This continued to be his experience as he worked on the orbits after Brahe's death.
	Kepler tried to find mathematical explanation for movement of Mars	This was his experience as he looked for the explanation.
"I am moved by an exceedingly powerful desire. . ."	**Johannes Kepler studied at university in the 1590s**	This motivated his studies.
	Worked as assistant to astronomer Tycho Brahe 1600–1601	This motivated his work.
	Tycho Brahe died in 1601	This motivated his continued work after Brahe's death.
	Kepler tried to find mathematical explanation for movement of Mars	This continued to motivate him.
	Published findings in *Astronomia Nova* in 1609	This lay behind his desire to share his findings.

QUOTE	EVENTS	REASONS
"If God is concerned with astronomy. . ."	**Johannes Kepler studied at university in the 1590s**	He believed this about his studies.
	Worked as assistant to astronomer Tycho Brahe 1600-1601	He believed this about his work.
	Tycho Brahe died in 1601	He continued to believe this about his work.
	Kepler tried to find mathematical explanation for movement of Mars	He continued to believe this about his work.
	Published findings in *Astronomia Nova* in 1609	This lay behind his desire to share his findings.

You may need to remind the student to add a dialogue tag (see the rules for writing dialogue in Week 6, pages 80-81). All of these quotes are drawn from Kepler's writings, so it is appropriate to use "He thought," "he said," "he believed," or "he wrote."

When the narrative is finished, check it using the following rubric.

Week 7 Rubric
Chronological Narrative of Scientific Discovery

Organization

1 Events should be in chronological order.
2 The paragraph giving "background information" (heliocentric vs. geocentric world view) should be the first or second paragraph in the composition.
3 Two or more time words should be used.
4 The composition should use more than 150 but fewer than 300 words.

Mechanics

1 Each sentence should make sense on its own when read aloud.
2 Each proper name should be capitalized.
3 Possessive forms should be written properly.
4 The exact words of the source material should not be used in every sentence.
5 At least one direct quote should be included; quote and accompanying dialogue tags should be properly punctuated.

Week 8: Description of a Place

Day One: Original Narration Exercise

Focus: Summarizing a narrative by choosing the central details

STEP ONE: **Read (Student Responsibility)**

Student instructions for Step One:

Read the following excerpt from George MacDonald's modern fairy tale *The Princess and the Goblin.*

STEP TWO: **Note central details**

Student instructions for Step Two:

You may notice that this passage is a little different than the narratives you've been summarizing. Instead of listing a series of chronological events, George MacDonald sets the stage for his story by describing the world Princess Irene lives in. The passage should have given you a clear picture in your mind.

On your scratch paper, write down five or six phrases or short sentences that identify the most important things about this world. If a detail doesn't add significantly to the mental picture of the princess's world, you should leave it out. (For example, it doesn't really matter that the people in the world mistook animals for the goblins. But if you don't mention that the goblins were "misshapen in body," your picture of the world will be incomplete.)

If you have trouble with this assignment, ask your instructor for help.

HOW TO HELP THE STUDENT WITH STEP TWO

The student should have written down on scratch paper five or six short phrases or sentences that sum up the central details about the Princess Irene's world. The student can choose to include or leave out the descriptions of the princess herself; either is acceptable.

The phrases/sentences should resemble five or six of the following (these are given only as a guide):

Many mountains and valleys
Princess had eyes as blue as night sky.
Princess eight years old
Princess lived in a half-castle, half-farmhouse.
Mountains filled with caverns and mines
Miners found caverns and hollows under the mountains.
Goblins lived in caverns.
Goblins misshapen in body but cunning and mischievous
Goblins dwarfed and misshapen
Goblins grew in knowledge and cleverness.
Could do things people couldn't do
Had a king and government of their own

(Remember, the student should not provide more than five or six phrases/sentences.)

Watch the student as he writes down his phrases. If he's writing too many phrases, or the sentences are long and complex, stop him before he goes on. You may need to point out that the legend about where the goblins came from and why they lived under the mountain doesn't add anything to the picture of the world itself; the student should stay focused on the details about what the world looks like at the time of the story itself.

If necessary, you may ask the student the following question:

What is the most important geographical feature of the princess's world? *(Mountains)*
What were in those mountains? *(Caverns, mines)*
What lived in the mines? *(Goblins)*
What did the goblins look like? *(Misshapen, dwarfed, ugly, strong)*
What were the non-physical characteristics of the goblins?
(What were they *like*?) *(Mischievous, clever, annoying to people who lived on the surface, had their own government)*

STEP THREE: **Write summary sentences**

Student instructions for Step Three:

> After you've written down your five or six phrases or sentences, try to combine them into three or four sentences. You can do this by putting two phrases in the same sentences (for example, "Many mountains and valleys in kingdom" and "Mountains filled with caverns and mines" could be combined into "There were many mountains filled with caverns and mines in the kingdom"). Or you may find that one or more of your jotted notes turns out to be unnecessary (if you wrote down "Mountains filled with caverns and mines" and "Miners found caverns," you can eliminate one of those sentences).
>
> Say your three or four sentences several times before writing them down. After you've written the sentences down, ask your instructor to check them.
>
> If you have trouble, ask your instructor for help.

HOW TO HELP THE STUDENT WITH STEP THREE

In this step, the student practices turning the jotted phrases and sentences into three or four coherent, smooth sentences. He should say his three or four sentences out loud several times before he writes; listen to make sure that you hear him talking out loud, and if necessary remind him that he should be speaking before he writes.

You may need to help him combine two phrases into one sentence and eliminate those phrases which seem unnecessary. If helpful, remind him that describing the princess herself is optional. An acceptable summary would be:

> *The Princess Irene lived in a country filled with mountains, valleys, and caverns. Goblins lived in the caverns. They were ugly and misshapen, but clever and filled with mischief.*
>
> or
>
> *The kingdom was mountainous. Beneath the mountains, miners discovered caverns where goblins lived. The goblins were misshapen and hideous, but very strong. They had a kingdom and king of their own and caused trouble for the people above.*

The student's answer may vary; these are simply examples. When the summary is finished, check it using the following rubric.

Week 8 Narration Rubric

Organization

1 Sentences should describe the world at the time the story takes place.
2 If two or more details are listed in a single sentence, they should be related.
For example:
The kingdom was filled with mountains, and caverns were below the mountains
is acceptable;
Caverns were under the mountains, and the goblins caused mischief
is not acceptable. There is no stated relationship between the caverns and the goblins.

Mechanics

1 Each sentence should make sense on its own when read aloud.
2 Each proper name should be capitalized.
3 Possessive forms should be written properly.
4 Personal pronouns should have clear antecedents and be of the proper gender.

5 Consistent verb tense should be used throughout.
For example, the student should not write
The kingdom was full of mountains, and caverns are in the mountains
because the first verb is in the simple past and the second is in the simple present.
The kingdom is full of mountains, and caverns are in the mountains and
The kingdom was in the mountains, and caverns were in the mountains
are both acceptable.

Day Two: Outlining Exercise

Focus: Finding the central topic in each paragraph of a description

STEP ONE: **Read (Student Responsibility)**

Student instructions for Step One:

Read the following excerpt from *The Mississippi Bubble* by Thomas B. Costain.

You may find the following background information useful: In the seventeenth century, France, Spain, and England were competing for control of the new land on the North American continent. The French wanted to build a great city on the Mississippi River so that they could control which ships went up and down the river. But the English and Spanish navies might appear at any moment to attack a French settlement. So might the Native Americans, known to the French as Indians, who already lived along the Mississippi. So any settlement would need a strong fort to defend it.

The leader the text refers to, Sieur d'Iberville, was a famous French general sent by King Louis XIV to establish this French colony.

STEP TWO: **Construct a one-level outline**

Student instructions for Step Two:

You've already practiced outlining passages that tell events in chronological order. For these outlines, you have been asking yourself two questions:

1. What is the main thing or person that this section is about?
2. Why is that thing or person important?

This passage is a little different; it describes a *place*. Although you can certainly use the same two questions when you outline a passage of description, you can also take a simpler approach. Instead of asking these two questions and writing a sentence that answers each one, you can ask yourself: What part of the place does this paragraph focus on?

Try that for the first section now.

Were you able to come up with an answer?

This first paragraph tells about Iberville's descision to build the fort and city at Biloxi. So the first section tells you about the *location* of the fort and city. Your first outline point would be:

I. The location

Look at the second section. This paragraph focuses on one specific part of the location. (Hint: it involves water.)

Did you come up with an answer?

This second paragraph tells you about the bay itself. Your second outline point can be either

II. Biloxi Bay itself

or

II. The bay and harbor

If you were doing a two-level outline of this paragraph (something you won't practice until later on), the subpoints—points that tell you more about the *main* point—would all describe the bay and the harbor formed by the bay.

Now try to complete this exercise by providing points III and IV. You can continue to use phrases rather than complete sentences. If you have difficulty, ask ask your instructor for help. And when you are finished, check your assignment with your instructor.

HOW TO HELP THE STUDENT WITH STEP TWO

For this passage, the student will be coming up with phrases that describe the main focus of each passage. The first two points have been provided, since the student hasn't outlined passages of description before.

Suggested answers (the student's answers should resemble the following but don't need to be identical):

I. The location
II. Biloxi Bay itself or *The bay and harbor*
III. The site for the fort or *The high bank where the fort would be built*
IV. The fort itself

If the student struggles with this assignment, use the following dialogues:

Paragraph 3
Instructor: The first two paragraphs described the overall location where the city and the fort would be built. But this paragraph focuses on only one of those things. What is it?

Student: The fort

Instructor: Does the paragraph describe the fort itself?

Student: No

Instructor: What does Iberville choose, in this paragraph, to prepare for the building of the fort?

Student: The site for the fort

Instructor: That is the focus of the paragraph. The bank, the ravines, and the forest are all details about the site where the fort would be built.

Paragraph 4
Instructor: What do the wooden buildings, barricade, bastions, and ditches combine to make up?

Student: The fort

Instructor: All of these details about about the fort itself. That is the focus of this paragraph.

Day Three: Analyzing and Practicing the Topos, Part One

Focus: Understanding the form of a description of a place

The passage the student outlined in the last writing session is an example of this week's topos: a **description of a place.** In today's assignment, the student will begin to understand the elements that go into a good place description.

The first two steps of the assignment should be done independently; the student's directions are reproduced below for your reference. The student may need your assistance on the third step.

STEP ONE: **Understand the purpose of descriptions (Student Responsibility)**

Student instructions for Step One:

> Like chronological narratives, descriptions of places can sometimes stand on their own; a detailed description of a medieval castle, an ancient city, or a modern submarine could be a short history composition in its own right. More often, though, a description of a place fits into a larger piece of writing. Thomas Costain's description of the fort in *The Mississippi Bubble* is part of a chapter about the bitter wars between European countries over the New World. The

description of the fort's many walls, towers, ditches, and defenses helps give you an idea of just how hard the French were prepared to fight for control of the Mississippi River.

Here is another description of a place, this one from a book by Jonathan Kozol called *Savage Inequalities.* Kozol's book is about the dreadful condition of schools in poor, inner-city neighborhoods. In this passage, he is being driven through East St. Louis on his way to visit a neighborhood where the schoolchildren live.

After you read the description of this bleak wasteland, you're not at all surprised when Kozol arrives at the school itself and finds disintegrating classrooms, no heat, no equipment, damaged textbooks, and bathrooms that don't work.

As you can see from the two examples you've looked at, a description of a place is more than just a listing of details. When you write a description, you decide what details to include. But you also decide what *emotion* the description should help the reader feel, or what *idea* the reader should begin to understand.

Read the following description of the field where the Battle of Hastings was fought in 1066.

The writer goes on to contrast the peace of the field *now* with the struggle of the battle itself, *long ago.* He wants us to feel, sharply, the difference between the present and the past, so he uses quiet, slow, peaceful words in his description: *little, low, sluggishly, small, gently, forlorn.*

This is the first element in a well-written description: the writer has in mind a *specific purpose* that he wants the description to fulfill. Thomas Costain wanted the reader to understand just how strong and well-defended the French fort on the Mississippi would be; Jonathan Kozol wanted the reader to focus on the poverty of East St. Louis; James Hosmer, who wrote the description of the field above, wanted the reader to appreciate the peace and quiet of the present-day spot.

STEP TWO: **Write down the pattern of the topos (Student Responsibility)**

Student instructions for Step Two:

Now copy the following onto a blank sheet of paper in the Reference section of your Composition Notebook. You will be adding to this page as you learn more about chronological narratives, so leave plenty of room at the bottom of the page; also leave blank space under the "Remember" column.

The definition of this topos may seem very obvious. Copy it down anyway—you'll be learning, in later lessons, about descriptions that *aren't* simply physical and visual.

Description of a Place

Definition: A visual description of a physical place

Procedure	Remember
1. Ask, *What specific purpose should this description fulfill?*	

STEP THREE: **Practice the topos**

Student instructions for Step Three:

> You'll end today's lesson by writing two brief descriptions, each with a different purpose.
>
> Look closely at the second sentence in James Hosmer's description of the battlefield of Hastings:
>
> *Through it, in low ground, sluggishly flows a small brook, and from the brook ridges slope up gently on either hand.*
>
> Now imagine that Hosmer had wanted us to feel the urgency and danger of the Battle of Hastings himself. He might have written:
>
> *The sunken field was gashed by a thin stream of water, and from the stream's edges, ridges rose up on either hand.*
>
> What if Hosmer had written a description of the field without any particular purpose in mind? The sentence might sound like this:
>
> *A brook ran through the field. There were hills on both sides of the water.*
>
> which would have been incredibly boring (and not very descriptive). Descriptions that have purpose are always more vivid and engaging.
>
> Your assignment is to take the following description and rewrite it twice. The first time, imagine that you're using this description of a room in the first chapter of a ghost story: make it creepy, frightening, or suspenseful. The second time, imagine that the description is coming at the conclusion of a romance in which the hero and heroine have finally fallen in love and decided to marry.
>
> > *The room was large and the ceiling was high and vaulted. The windows were long and high, with arches at the tops. The floor was made of oak boards. The sun was setting outside, and the light that came through the windows was red and gold, but it did not reach all the way into the corners of the room. Curtains hung at the windows, and there was a lot of furniture in the room.*
>
> As you write, remember that you can make use of vivid adjectives (the "shining windows" or the "gloomy windows"), synonyms ("The room was large" could become either "The room was echoing" or "The room was spacious and welcoming"), and vivid verbs (did the light "flood" or "struggle" through the windows?).
>
> If you need assistance, ask your instructor for help. And when you are finished, show your two descriptions to your instructor.

HOW TO HELP THE STUDENT WITH STEP THREE

The student may need assistance finding appropriate adjectives and verbs for the passage.

For a student who is a reluctant writer, use the thesaurus to suggest appropriate adjectives and verbs. Give the student three or four choices and encourage him to pick one. Don't feel that you are making the assignment "too easy" for a struggling student; you are instead modelling for the student the process of considering different words and choosing the best one. *Give the student as much help as necessary.* A student who is having a difficult time with this new skill should not be asked to exercise another relatively new skill at the same time.

Students who are not struggling can use the thesaurus themselves.

Don't expect the student to change every verb and add adjectives to every noun; this would clutter up the passage. Instead, focus on whether the verbs or adjectives chosen are appropriate to the purpose of the passage. The student may also leave out words and phrases, and combine or divide sentences.

An acceptable sample rewrite might be:

Ghost Story Rewrite

> *The room was vast and dim; the ceiling was almost out of sight. The windows were narrow and out of reach, the floor made of dark dusty wood. Night had almost come, and the last light of the sun was lurid crimson; it struggled through the glass, but the corners of the room remained dark. Tattered dirty curtains blocked all other light. Dark sofas, battered chairs, and unfriendly clusters of tables and rugs cluttered the room.*

Romance Rewrite

> *The room was spacious and lofty, with huge arched windows; the floor was made of golden oak. The glowing light of the setting sun spilled through the windows and lit the middle of the room, leaving the corners cozy and dim. White curtains billowed at the windows. A squashy comfortable sofa sat in the middle of the room, with a loveseat on one side.*

When the student has finished this assignment, tell him that the description provided is a paraphrase of a passage from Edgar Allan Poe's ghost story "The Fall of the House of Usher." Ask him to read aloud the passage below.

> The room in which I found myself was very large and lofty. The windows were long, narrow, and pointed, and at so vast a distance from the black oaken floor as to be altogether inaccessible from within. Feeble gleams of encrimsoned light made their way through the trellised panes, and served to render sufficiently distinct the more prominent objects around; the eye, however, struggled in vain to reach the remoter angles of the chamber, or the recesses of the vaulted and fretted ceiling. Dark draperies hung upon the walls. The general furniture was profuse, comfortless, antique, and tattered. Many books and musical instruments lay scattered about, but failed to give any vitality to the scene. I felt that I breathed an atmosphere of sorrow. An air of stern, deep, and irredeemable gloom hung over and pervaded all.[15]

15. Edgar Allan Poe, "The Fall of the House of Usher," in *Prose Tales of Mystery and Imagination* by Edgar Allan Poe (Henry Frowde, 1903), p. 204.

Day Four: Analyzing and Practicing the Topos, Part Two

Focus: Understanding the form of a description of a place

Today, the student will add an additional element to the model of the "Description of a Place."

STEP ONE: **Understand space and distance words and phrases (Student Responsibility)**

Student instructions for Step One:

Read these three excerpts from the passages you've already examined this week. Notice which words are bolded.

Biloxi Bay was a safe harbor, well screened by Deer Island. The bay extended **back** into the mainland for several miles and Deer Island lay **across** the mouth of the bay, blocking it off except a channel at either end.

A seemingly endless railroad train rolls **past** us **to the right**. **On the left:** a blackened lot **where** garbage has been burning. **Next to** the burning garbage is a row of twelve white cabins, charred by fire.

The windows were long, narrow, and pointed, and at so vast **a distance from** the black oaken floor as to be altogether inaccessible from **within.** Feeble gleams of encrimsoned light made their way **through** the trellised panes . . . Dark draperies hung **upon** the walls.

When you studied chronological narratives, you learned that time and sequence words can help you put events into chronological order. When you write a description, **space and distance words and phrases** can help you create a clear picture of a place.

Pull out the list of Space and Distance Words/Phrases found in Appendix I. This is not an exhaustive (complete) list, and many of the words on it can work in more than one way (if, for example, you wanted to explain that a tree stood three feet to the right of a house, you could say, "The tree was next to the house" or "The tree was to the right of the house" or even "The tree was a short distance from the house"). But the categories on the list will give you a starting place as you write your descriptions.

Before you go on with the next step, look up from your paper and choose one object or piece of furniture in the room. Now look down your list of Space and Distance Words/Phrases and count how many of them could accurately describe your relationship to that object.

STEP TWO: **Add to the pattern of the topos**

Student instructions for Step Two:

These space and distance words and phrases can help you write a more precise, and so more interesting, description.

Read the following description and underline each of the space and distance words and phrases.

When you are finished, ask your instructor to check your work.

Now turn to the Description of a Place chart in your Composition Notebook. Add the bolded point below under the "Remember" column.

Description of a Place

Definition: A visual description of a physical place

Procedure	Remember
1. Ask, *What specific purpose should this description fulfill?*	**1. Make use of space and distance words.**

HOW TO HELP THE STUDENT WITH STEP TWO

Check the student's work using the following key:

In a hole **in** the ground **there** lived a hobbit. Not a nasty, dirty, wet hole, **filled with** the ends of worms and an oozy smell, nor yet a dry, bare, sandy hole **with** nothing **in** it to sit **down on** or to eat; it was a hobbit-hole, and that means comfort.

It had a perfectly round door like a porthole, painted green, **with** a shiny yellow brass knob **in** the exact middle. The door opened **on to** a tube-shaped hall like a tunnel: a very comfortable tunnel **without** smoke, **with** panelled walls, and floors tiled and carpeted, provided **with** polished chairs, and lots and lots of pegs for hats and coats—the hobbit was fond of visitors. The tunnel wound **on and on,** going fairly but not quite straight **into** the side of the hill—The Hill, as all the people for many miles **round** called it—and many little round doors opened **out of** it, first on **one side**, and then **on another.** No going **up**stairs for the hobbit: bedrooms, bathrooms, cellars, pantries (lots of these), wardrobes (he had whole rooms devoted to clothes), kitchens, dining-rooms, all were **on** the same floor, and indeed **on** the same passage. The best rooms were all **on** the left-hand side (going in), for these were the only ones to have windows, deep-set round windows looking **over** his garden, and meadows **beyond,** sloping **down to** the river.[16]

---

16. J. R. R. Tolkien, *The Hobbit* (Random House, 1982), p. 1.

STEP THREE: **Practice the topos**

Student instructions for Step Three:

> Look carefully at the picture of Neuschwanstein Castle in Germany. King Ludwig of Bavaria had it built between 1869 and 1884 on the ruins of a medieval castle. The palace was designed to have more than 200 rooms, but fewer than 20 were finished before the king's death. If the castle looks familiar to you, it may be because Disney used it as the model for the castle in *Sleeping Beauty*.
>
> Write a description of at least four but not more than seven sentences describing this place. Use at least four different space and distance words and phrases in your description. Be sure to describe the castle itself *and* also to include some detail about the surrounding landscape.
>
> The purpose of your description should be to convey how spectacular the castle is. If you need help with this purpose, ask your instructor.
>
> When you are finished, ask your instructor to check your work.

HOW TO HELP THE STUDENT WITH STEP THREE

The student may need assistance with the purpose of this description. If necessary, suggest that he make use of some of the following words:

ADJECTIVES	*VERBS*
monstrous	*tower*
enormous	*soar*
gigantic	*rise*
lofty	*overlook*
elevated	*surmount*
eminent	*command*
steep	*dominate*
prominent	*crown*
towering	*cap*
soaring	*crest*
ascending	*peak*
high-pitched	*plunge*
skyscraping	*drop*
gigantic	*ascend*
colossal	*tower*
plunging	
precipitous	
immense	
vast	
stupendous	
mammoth	
roomy	
sheer	

When the description is finished, check it using the following rubric:

Week 8 Description Rubric

Organization

1 The description should use appropriate adjectives and verbs to convey a sense of vastness.

EXAMPLE: *The castle sits on top of a* ***gigantic*** *rock whose sides* ***plunge steeply*** *down.*

2 The description should mention both the castle itself and the landscape.

3 At least four space and distance words and phrases should be used.

EXAMPLE: Far **below** the castle, **to the right**, a white road stretches **into** the distance.

4 The composition should use at least three and not more than seven sentences.

Mechanics

1 Each sentence should make sense on its own when read aloud.

2 Verbs should have consistent tense (all past or all present).

Rows of windows line the white walls, and spires reach sharply upwards is acceptable.

Rows of windows lined the white walls, and spires reach sharply upwards is not.

Week 9: Description of a Place

Day One: Original Narration Exercise

Focus: Summarizing a narrative by choosing the central details and actions

STEP ONE: **Read (Student Responsibility)**

Student instructions for Step One:

Read the following excerpt from *Mary Poppins in the Park* by P. L. Travers. Travers wrote a series of books about Mary Poppins, the magical British nanny, and her charges: Michael and Jane, the two older children in the Banks family; the twins John and Barbara; and baby Annabel. In this chapter, Michael and Jane are playing in the park, with Mary Poppins nearby—which always means that something mysterious is about to happen.

"Plasticine" is a kind of modelling clay. In the story, Michael thinks that a statue looks like "Neleus." Neleus was a minor Greek god, one of the sons of the sea god Poseidon.

STEP TWO: **Note central details**

Student instructions for Step Two:

Like last week's story, this week's narrative contains a description. At the end of the description, something happens that moves the story forward.

On your scratch paper, write down six or seven phrases or short sentences that describe Jane's Park for Poor People. You don't need to summarize the conversation between Jane and Michael (so, for example, you don't need to note "Michael asked Jane who the little plasticine woman was"), but you can use details within the conversation (so you might want to write "The little woman was named Mrs. Hickory").

After you've written down your phrases, add a final sentence describing the most important thing that happens at the end of the story.

If you have trouble with this assignment, ask your instructor for help.

HOW TO HELP THE STUDENT WITH STEP TWO

The student should have written down on scratch paper six or seven short phrases or sentences that sum up the central details about Jane's Park for Poor People. The phrases/sentences should resemble six or seven of the following (these are given only as a guide):

Square of green with pebbled paths
Paths made of pebbles as wide as fingernail
Flowerbeds of petals
Little house of twigs
Flowers were trees.
Benches and houses made of twigs
Little man made of clay with round face, body, arms, legs
Little round man made of plasticine
Little woman named Mrs. Hickory
Lake made out of pebbles and milk
Statue of plasticine at lake
Swing of sticks and wool
Cardboard table and stools
Table and stools made of cake box
Feast of plasticine on table
Cake, fruits, meats made of plasticine
Buttercup tree over table
Plasticine doves

After the student finishes her descriptive phrases, she should have written a final sentence telling the important event that happens at the story's end. This sentence should resemble one of the following:

The little plasticine figure began to talk.
The park came to life.
Mr. Mo came to life and the food in the park became real.
The little man began to talk to Jane and Michael.

Watch the student as she writes down her phrases. If she's writing too many small details, stop her before she goes on. She shouldn't list each one of the foods made out of plasticine; you may need to remind her to summarize by either saying "Jane made foods" or else listing the major categories of the feast. You may also need to remind her not to give a blow-by-blow recounting of the conversation between Jane and Michael.

If necessary, you may ask the student the following questions:

What did Jane make in the park? *(A Park for Poor People)*
What kinds of things did Jane make out of plasticine? *(Two little people, a feast, a statue)*
What did Jane make out of sticks and flowers? *(Houses, benches, and trees)*
What was under the buttercup? *(A cardboard table and a plasticine feast)*
What did Mr. Mo suddenly do at the end of the story? *(He started to talk or He came alive.)*

STEP THREE: **Write summary sentences**

Student instructions for Step Three:

> After you've written down your phrases, try to combine them into three or four sentences. (Your last sentence doesn't count.) Because there are so many details about the park, experiment with putting three phrases into one sentence; for example, "Little house of twigs," "Flowers were trees," and "benches made of twigs" could all be combined into "Twig benches and a twig house were surrounded by trees made of flowers."
>
> Say your three or four sentences several times before writing them down. When you've finished, add your last sentence to the end of your summary. You will probably need to use a time word to connect the last sentence to the summary, since the park itself and all of its details were already in existence *before* the event at the end of the story happened.
>
> After you've written the sentences down, ask your instructor to check them. If you have trouble, ask your instructor for help.

HOW TO HELP THE STUDENT WITH STEP THREE

In this step, the student practices turning the jotted phrases and sentences into three or four coherent, smooth sentences. She should say her three or four sentences out loud several times before she writes; listen to make sure that you hear her talking out loud, and if necessary remind her that she should be speaking before she writes.

You may need to help her combine two or more phrases into a single sentence. An acceptable summary would be:

> *Jane made a Park for Poor People on a square of green, with paths made of pebbles. She made benches and a house of twigs and stuck flowers in the ground for trees. There was a lake made of pebbles and milk, with a plasticine statue. A feast of cake, fruit, and meat lay on a cardboard table. Then the little man she had made from plasticine came to life.*

or

> *Jane's Park for Poor People had pebble paths, flower trees, and twig benches. A little man made out of plasticine lived in a twig house. She also made a huge feast of plasticine food and set it on a cardboard table with cardboard chairs. At the end of the story, the little man began to talk to her.*

The student's answer may vary; these are simply examples. When the summary is finished, check it using the following rubric.

Week 9 Narration Rubric

Organization

1 The summary should describe the park, with a single sentence at the end describing the final event.
2 A time word should link the final sentence to the rest of the summary.
3 Details of conversations should not be listed.
4 If two or more details are listed in a single sentence, they should be related.

For example,

Flowers were trees, and flowerbeds were made of petals

is acceptable;

Flowers were trees, and a little round man sat on a bench

is not.

Mechanics

1 Each sentence should make sense on its own when read aloud.
2 Each proper name should be capitalized.
3 Possessive forms should be written properly.
4 Personal pronouns should have clear antecedents and be of the proper gender.
5 Consistent verb tense should be used throughout.

Day Two: Outlining Exercise

Focus: Finding the central topic in each paragraph of a description

STEP ONE: **Read (Student Responsibility)**

Student instructions for Step One:

Read the following excerpt from *Life in a Medieval Castle* by Gary Blackwood. You have probably studied before about the "feudal system." Under this system, a lord granted land to farmers, who then became his *vassals* and owed him crops and military service.

The words in brackets [ ] have been inserted to make the excerpt clearer.

STEP TWO: **Construct a one-level outline**

Student instructions for Step Two:

As in last week's outlining assignment, this week's passage describes a place. Last week, you learned that although you can ask two questions about each section:

1. What is the main thing that this section is about?
2. Why is that thing or person important?

you can also ask a simpler question when outlining a passage of description:

What part of the place does this paragraph focus on?

As you work on finding the major points for your outline, you may want to use a combination of the two methods.

The reason is simple. When a passage of description is narrowly focused on one area, the single question "What part of the place does this paragraph focus on?" can give you a straightforward answer. But often, a passage of description will contain sections that have a slightly different focus.

Look at the first section in the description and ask yourself "What part of the place does this paragraph focus on?"

What answer did you come up with?

You probably came up with a single word:

Castles

That's not a very good major point; it's too broad, too vague, and too general. Imagine that you were using an outline to write, and your first outline point merely said "Castles." How would you know what to write—or even where to start? This question doesn't work because although the passage goes on to describe each major part of a medieval castle, the first *section* of the passage is an introduction that talks about castles *generally.*

Try asking the two other questions now. What main thing is the section about?

Castles.

Why are the castles important?

Castles were common or *Castles served many purposes* (these two points are similar—they were common because they served many purposes). That's a good first main point for the passage.

Follow this rule as you look for a major point for the remaining sections: First, ask "What part of the place does the section focus on?" If the answer is a single common word, go back to the two-question procedure instead.

Now try to complete this exercise by providing points II through VII. You can mix phrases and sentences if necessary. If you have difficulty, ask your instructor for help. And when you are finished, check your assignment with your instructor.

HOW TO HELP THE STUDENT WITH STEP TWO

In this assignment, the student has been encouraged to try two different methods of finding the main idea in each section. It is acceptable for her to mix phrases and sentences in her outline.

Suggested answers (the student's answers should resemble the following but don't need to be identical):

I. *Castles were common* or *Castles served many purposes.*
II. *Fortifications before the Norman invasion OR Early fortifications OR Early fortifications were crude.*
III. *The appearance of castles with towers OR Castles in the early tenth century*
IV. *How a castle was built OR Building a castle*
V. *The mound or motte*
VI. *The bailey*
VII. *Inside the tower or donjon OR Cramped life inside the tower*

If the student struggles with this assignment, use the following dialogues.

Section 2
Instructor: This section isn't exactly about castles. What is it about?

Student: Fortifications

Instructor: When did these fortifications exist?

Student: Before the Norman invasion or *In the ninth century*

Instructor: This section describes the fortifications before the Norman invasion. Remember, when you're writing an outline, you shouldn't include details in the major points of the outline. The ring of mounded earth, the ditch, and the fence are all details.

Section 3
Instructor: In this section, something new appeared. What was it?

Student: Castles with towers or *Structures with towers*

Note to Instructor: If the student answers "Castles," say "What was new about the castles?"
Instructor: Put that into a sentence. What appeared?

Student: Castles with towers appeared.

Section 4
Instructor: This section has quite a few details about what the finished castle looks like, but it isn't really describing a castle. All of the details together describe a *process.* What is the process?

Student: Building a castle

Section 5
Instructor: What part of the castle does this section describe?

Student: The motte OR *mound*

Section 6
Instructor: What part of the castle does this section describe?

Student: The bailey OR *The area inside the palisade*

Section 7
Instructor: What part of the castle does this section describe?

Student: The tower or *What was inside the tower*

Day Three: Analyzing and Practicing the Topos, Part One

Focus: Understanding the form of a description of a place

The passage the student outlined in the last writing session is another example of this week's topos: a **description of a place.** The student studied and practiced this form in the last week of this program; this week, she'll study and practice some more.

STEP ONE: Review the use of space and distance words and phrases

Student instructions for Step One:

> Read the following descriptions and underline the space and distance words and phrases. The first description was written by the Greek historian Herodotus; the second, by the modern historian Stephen Blake; the third, by the secretary to the sixteenth-century Spanish conquistador Hernan Cortes.
>
> When you are finished, check your work with your instructor. In the first two lines of the assignment, the space and distance words and phrases have been bolded as an example.

HOW TO HELP THE STUDENT WITH STEP ONE

The answer key for Step One is below:

> The sanctuary is situated **in the center of** the city, and one can walk **around** it and look **down into** it from all sides, because the city has risen . . . with the accumulation of soil over time but the sanctuary has remained undisturbed since it was first built, and therefore it is possible to look **down into** it. **Surrounding** it is a dry wall carved **with** reliefs, and **within** that wall is a grove of very tall trees growing **around** a large temple which contains the cult statue. The sanctuary is square and measures 583 feet **on** each side. Extending **from** the entrance is

a stone road about 1,750 feet long and 400 feet wide, leading **through** the marketplace **to the east**. Trees so tall that they seem to touch the sky grow **on either side of** the road, which continues **until** it reaches the sanctuary of Hermes. That is what the sanctuary of Boubastis looks like.[17]

In its plan and build, Peking, like the other sovereign cities, reflected the dominance of the imperial household. **At** its very heart, a fortress **within** a fortress **within** a fortress, lay the Forbidden City, a 385-acre enclosure that contained audience halls, private apartments, religious shrines, and about 15,000 persons—the imperial family, personal servants, privileged retainers, and eunuchs. **At the center of** the Forbidden City stood the Hall of Supreme Harmony. **In the middle of** this hall **on** a great throne the Ming emperor exercised absolute power.[18]

Mexico-Tenochtitlan is completely **surrounded by** water, standing as it does **in** the lake. It can be approached by only three causeways: one, about half a league long, entering **from the west**; another **from the north**, about a league long. There is no causeway **from the east**, and one must approach by boat. **To the south** is the third causeway. . . . The lake **upon** which Mexico is situated, although it seems to be one, is really two, very different from each other, for one is saline, bitter, and stinking, and has no fish in it, while the other is of sweet water and does have fish, although they are small. The salt lake rises and falls, and has currents caused by the winds. The fresh-water lake is **higher**, so that the good water flows **into** the bad, and not the other way around, as some have thought . . . **On** its shores are more than fifty towns, many of them of five thousand houses, some of ten thousand, and one, Texcoco, as large as Mexico.[19]

If the student has difficulty finding space and distance words and phrases, tell him which line the missing words are located in, and how many words he's overlooked. This exercise is simply intended to increase the student's awareness of how these words are used; it isn't meant to be a test.

STEP TWO: **Understand point of view**

Student instructions for Step Two:

If you were Herodotus, where would you be standing while describing the sanctuary of Boubastis?

Herodotus gives you a hint in the first sentence of the description, when he says "One can walk around and look down into it from all sides." As he describes the sanctuary, he is doing so from the point of view of someone who is above the place, looking down over it and seeing all of its different parts.

The second passage has a different point of view. Imagine that the narrator of this passage is walking through the walls of Peking, towards the center. He arrives at the Forbidden City, at the "heart" of the city, and walks through the walls of the Forbidden City, still heading towards the center. He arrives at the Hall of Supreme Harmony, at the center of the Forbidden Center, and walks through its door. Right at the middle of the Hall is the throne of the Ming emperor.

This point of view is of someone moving forward, getting closer and closer to the center. The first narrator can see the whole place he's describing all at once. The second narrator can't

17. Herodotus, *The Landmark Herodotus: The Histories,* trans. Robert B. Strassler (Random House, 2009), p. 180.

18. Stephen P. Blake, *Shahjahanabad: The Sovereign City in Mughal India 1639–1739* (Cambridge University Press, 2002), p. 206.

19. Francisco Lopez de Gomara, *Cortes: The Life of the Conqueror by His Secretary,* trans. Lesley Byrd Simpson (University of California Press, 1964), p. 159.

see the Hall, or the throne, until he arrives at it.

There are four basic points of view for a description:

1. From above, as though you were hovering over the place. This is sometimes called the "impersonal" point of view, because you're not directly involved in the place itself; you're looking over it as a detached observer.
2. From inside it, as though you were part of the place, standing still in the middle of it at a particular point and looking around.
3. From one side, as though you were standing beside the place looking at it from one particular angle.
4. Moving, as though you were walking through the place, or around it.

You can choose to use any one of these points of view when you write a description, but once you've settled on one, keep asking yourself: Am I still describing this place from the *same* point of view? You shouldn't (for example) be describing a mountain from above, and then suddenly leap into an inside cave without telling the reader how you got there.

Now look back at the third description. Try to figure out which point of view this passage is written from. When you've decided, check your answer with your instructor.

HOW TO HELP THE STUDENT WITH STEP TWO

The third description is written from a moving point of view, but rather than moving into the city, as the narrator in the second description does, this narrator is circling around the city. You may point out to the student that this is the point of view Cortes himself would have had when approaching the city of Tenochtitlan by boat.

If the student has difficulty, suggest that he draw a square on paper, to represent Tenochtitlan, and then a circle around it, to represent the lake. Label the diagram with N, S, E, and W to represent the points of the compass. Tell the student to put his pencil on the W, since the narrator mentions the causeway from the west first. Then the narrator mentions the north causeway, so now he must be standing at the north. Tell the student to move his pencil from the west to the north. Continue on to the next direction mentioned (the east) and then the final direction (south). The student should have traced three quarters of a circle, showing that the narrator is circling the city.

STEP THREE: **Add to the pattern of the topos (Student Responsibility)**

Student instructions for Step Three:

Pull Appendix II, Points of View, from the back of your workbook. Place it in your Composition Notebook. (You will learn about the other points of view in Appendix II later.)

Now turn to the Description of a Place chart in your Composition Notebook. Add the bolded point below under the "Procedure" column.

Description of a Place

Definition: A visual description of a physical place

Procedure	Remember
1. Ask, *What specific purpose should this description fulfill?*	1. Make use of space and distance words and phrases.
2. Choose a point of view.	

Day Four: Analyzing and Practicing the Topos, Part Two

Focus: Understanding the form of a description of a place

Today the student will review the material from the last lesson and will write her own description from two different points of view.

STEP ONE: **Review point of view**

Student instructions for Step One:

> In the last assignment, you learned about the four basic points of view that descriptions can be written from. Glance at your Points of View appendix and review those now.
>
> When you've finished, read the following three descriptions. The first comes from the French writer Rene Auguste Constantin de Renneville, who was imprisoned in the French prison known as the Bastille from 1702 to 1713. The second was written by the nineteenth-century English novelist Charles Dickens. The third is from American Jon Krakauer's account of climbing Mount Everest in 1996.
>
> In the margin beside each description, write which point of view is being used. When you are finished, check your work with your instructor.

HOW TO HELP THE STUDENT WITH STEP ONE

The first description is written from *inside* a Bastille prison cell. If necessary, ask the student whether anything in the description can be seen from outside the Bastille.

The second description is written from the *above/impersonal* point of view. If necessary, ask the student to underline the words "Scrooge," "court outside," "pouring in," and "dense without." Then, ask where you would need to be standing in order to see all of these things simultaneously.

The third description is written *from one side or angle*—it describes only what Krakauer can see while standing on the peak and facing the Tibetan plateau. If the student selects "Moving through or around," ask her if the description changes as the narrator moves. (It doesn't; the first sentence mentions movement, but is there only to show how the narrator arrives at his particular vantage point.) If the student selects "Above/impersonal," ask two questions:

1. Is the narrator present in the place? (Yes. In an above/impersonal narration, the narrator is not part of the scene.)
2. Can the narrator see what's behind him? (No. He is only looking down one side of the mountain, which means that he is narrating from a particular angle rather than seeing the entire scene.)

STEP TWO: **Practice the topos**

Student instructions for Step Two:

Now you'll experiment with writing a description of the same place from three of the four points of view.

Choose the most interesting room in your house (or if you can go outside, the most interesting section of yard, park, field, or forest). Your goal will be to describe this place in no more than three or four sentences for each point of view, giving a sense of peace, calm, tranquility, belonging, and contentment.

The first time you describe the place, do so from an *abstract/impersonal* point of view. You should not be present in the description at all (in other words, you would write "Photographs hang along the living room wall," as opposed to "I can see pictures of my family on the wall"). Imagine that you're hovering above the place and can see everything in it simultaneously.

The second time you describe the place, do so from *one side or angle.* Choose a place to stand, and describe only what you can see from that particular spot. You should put yourself in the description (so you would write "A beech tree stands on my left, with a holly half-hidden behind it," as opposed to "There is a beech tree with a holly behind it").

Finally, describe the place one last time. This time, describe what you can see as you walk through it *or* as you walk around it. Be sure to list details in the same order that you see them as you move. You can choose to either put yourself in the description ("As I walk past the kitchen table, the refrigerator comes into view on my right") or leave yourself out ("The refrigerator stands on the right, just past the kitchen table").

When you are finished, check your work with your instructor.

HOW TO HELP THE STUDENT WITH STEP TWO

The student will complete today's work by writing three descriptions of the same place. The first should be written from the above/impersonal point of view, the second from one side or angle, and the third from a moving point of view, either through or around.

Begin by helping the student choose an appropriate place to describe. An ideal place would be a room or portion of the outdoors that the student can see from an elevated place—a yard which can be seen from a second-story window or the top of a slide, or a room which can be seen from a staircase or from the top of a piece of furniture. While the "above/impersonal" point of view doesn't require the narrator to physically *be* above the place being described (generally, writers use their imaginations and background knowledge instead), it can be very helpful for beginning writers to experience the difference between what a place looks like from above and what it looks like as you walk through it.

Whether or not you're able to find an "above" angle on the chosen place, make sure that it is large enough for the student to walk through and describe (a small room will look pretty much the same from the doorway and from the far side, which takes some of the distinctives of the "walking through" point of view away). It's also best if some of the details of the place are invisible or blocked from certain points of view.

The student has been assigned the task of conveying a sense of peace, tranquillity, calm, and contentment. Don't worry too much about how clearly this comes through. The focus of this assignment should stay firmly on point of view.

The descriptions should be brief (after all, the student has to write three of them). Acceptable descriptions might resemble the following:

From above/impersonal (note that the student herself should not be present in this description):

> *The garden basks under a warm sun. Flowers twine over the gate, and beds of lettuce and carrots lie on either side of the path. Sunflowers nod along the front fence, and fruit trees lean over the back wall; in the distance, chickens cluck and a rooster crows.*

From one side or angle (the student *should* be present in this description):

> *I sit with my back against the garden fence. Carrots grow to my left, and beyond them I can see the garden path and the corner of a bed of lettuce. Above my head, a sunflower nods. I can hear invisible chickens clucking somewhere behind me.*

Walking through:

> *(The student is present) I open the gate and step into the garden. Carrots grow in a carefully tilled bed on my right; on my left, lettuce is green against the rich dirt. As I walk down the path, I see asparagus growing in a bed just off the path. Beyond the asparagus, a row of sunflowers leans over the right-hand fence.*

> *(The student is absent.) The garden gate leads under an arbor covered with hibiscus vine. On the other side of the gate, the path winds through beds of carrots and lettuce. Asparagus grows in the middle of the garden; along the back, apples and peaches lean over the fence, dropping their fruit on the ground.*

When the description is finished, check it using the following rubric:

Week 9 Description Rubric
Summary of Description of a Place

Organization

1 The descriptions should use appropriate adjectives and verbs to convey peacefulness (or at least the absence of violence!).
2 At least two space and distance words and phrases should be used in each description.
3 Point of view should remain consistent throughout each description.
4 The details described should differ in each description, depending on the point of view.

Mechanics

1 Each sentence should make sense on its own when read aloud.
2 Verbs should have consistent tense (all past or all present).
3 Subjects and verbs should be in agreement.

Week 10: Description of a Place

Day One: Original Narration Exercise

Focus: Summarizing a narrative by choosing the central events and details

STEP ONE: Read (Student Responsibility)

Student instructions for Step One:

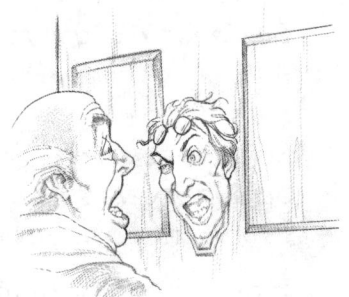

Read the following excerpt from *A Christmas Carol,* by Charles Dickens. You've already seen a description from *A Christmas Carol* in last week's lesson. Dickens was a master of vivid, detailed descriptions, and *A Christmas Carol* is probably his best-known work.

In this passage, the miser Scrooge is coming home in the dark after a long day's work—on Christmas Eve. He has just walked up the steps of his own house and is getting ready to open his own front door.

Jacob Marley was Scrooge's former partner, but when the story begins, he's been dead for seven years. "Livid" means ashen colored, pale, deathly white; you should also know that some bacteria found in decaying seafood can give off a very faint luminescent glow.

STEP TWO: Note central events and details

Student instructions for Step Two:

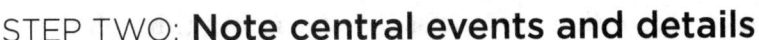

This week's story contains a series of events, *and* at least one description which should be included in your narrative summary.

Begin by writing down on scratch paper five or six phrases or short sentences that will remind you, in order, of the things that happened in the story. After you've put these sentences down in order, ask yourself: If you hadn't read the story, would you need a few more *visual* details about any of these phrases or sentences? Underline one or two phrases or sentences that would be clearer if you provided a few more descriptive details. Draw a line from the phrase(s) or sentence(s) to the other side of your paper. At the end of this line, write down three or four central details about the place where the event happened.

If you have trouble with this assignment, ask your instructor for help.

HOW TO HELP THE STUDENT WITH STEP TWO

The passage combines a series of events with at least one vital description; the narrative summary will be incomplete without a brief description of the door knocker/Marley's face. The student may also choose to provide a brief description of Scrooge's room, if this seems necessary to make the ringing of the bell clear. The description of Scrooge's empty house is *not* central to the narrative. The entire narrative should be no more than four sentences.

The student should begin by noting down five or six phrases or short sentences that sum up the main events. The phrases/sentences should resemble five or six of the following (these are given only as a guide):

Scrooge opened door with key.
Saw Marley's face in the knocker
The knocker changed to Marley's face and back again.
Scrooge went upstairs in the dark.
Went through all the rooms to see if anyone was there
Double locked himself in his room
Sat close to fire
Bell in room began to ring.
Bells all over house began to ring.
Bells stopped.
Scrooge heard chain dragging below.
Scrooge heard sound like dragging chain.
Sound came towards his door.

If the student has trouble locating the main events in the narrative, ask the following questions:

What happened on Scrooge's front doorstep? *(The knocker turned into Marley's face.)*
What did Scrooge do when he got into the house? *(He looked through all the rooms.)*
What did Scrooge do when he got to his room? *(He double locked himself in.)*
What did he hear? *(He heard a chain dragging down below.)*

Note that this entire narrative is organized according to *place:* as Scrooge moves through the house, a major event happens in each place.

After jotting down the major events, the student should identify the points at which more visual description is necessary. The appearance of Marley's face on the front door is absolutely central to this passage; without it, there's no reason for Scrooge to be nervous, or to suspect that the chain-dragging sound is caused by a ghost. The details about Marley's face might include:

Face had a dismal light.
Face glowed.
Not angry or ferocious
Spectacles on forehead
Hair blowing slightly

Open, motionless eyes
Livid in color
Turned back to knocker

It is also possible that the student may decide to expand on Scrooge's locking himself in his room by explaining that the room had a low fire and also a bell hanging against one wall. However, the summary will make perfect sense without these details.

STEP THREE: **Write summary sentences**

Student instructions for Step Three:

> Now try to combine your phrases or sentences about the main events into three sentences (your narrative shouldn't be more than four sentences, and you'll need to keep one sentence for the additional descriptive details). Say your three sentences out loud several times. Then decide which details to include in your additional sentence. Write down all four sentences, putting the sentence with the additional details directly after the sentence that mentions the main event connected to those details. (If you can incorporate the details into one of other sentences, that's fine.)
>
> After you've written the sentences down, ask your instructor for help. And if you have trouble, ask your instructor for help.

HOW TO HELP THE STUDENT WITH STEP THREE

In this step, the student practices turning the jotted phrases and sentences into three or four (probably four) coherent, smooth sentences. He should say his sentences out loud several times before he writes; listen to make sure that you hear him talking out loud, and if necessary remind him that he should be speaking before he writes.

The summary should include a sentence describing Marley's face and should not be more than four sentences. It should mention Scrooge's seeing the face, entering the house, locking himself in, and hearing the "bells and clanking sound." An acceptable summary would be:

Scrooge was unlocking his door when the knocker turned into Marley's face. The face was deathly pale, staring at him with wide eyes, and was glowing slightly. The face turned back into a knocker, but Scrooge was so frightened that he searched the whole house. He locked himself into his room, but then heard chains dragging from down below.

OR

Scrooge came home in the dark on Christmas Eve. His door knocker turned into the glowing, ghostly face of his dead partner Jacob Marley. Scrooge went upstairs and locked himself into his room. Then the bells all over the house began to ring, and he heard a ghostly chain dragging towards his door.

When the summary is finished, check it using the following rubric.

Week 10 Narration Rubric

Organization

1 Events should be in chronological order.
2 If two or more events are listed in a single sentence, they should have a cause and effect relationship.
3 Each event of major importance should be in the summary (if it were missing from the original passage, the narrative would no longer make sense).
4 Vital details should be listed immediately after (or in the same sentence as) the connected event.
5 The summary should not be more than four sentences long.

Mechanics

1 Each sentence should make sense on its own when read aloud.
2 Each proper name should be capitalized.
3 Personal pronouns should have clear antecedents and be of the proper gender.
4 Consistent verb tense should be used throughout.

Day Two: Outlining Exercise

Focus: Finding the central topic in each paragraph of a description

STEP ONE: **Read (Student Responsibility)**

Student instructions for Step One:

Read the following excerpt from *The Travels of Marco Polo,* describing the palace of the Mongol khan Kublai Khan, who established the Yuan Dynasty in China. Marco Polo was a Venetian merchant who travelled to China between 1271 and 1295; when he returned, he wrote a book about his adventures.

STEP TWO: **Construct a one-level outline**

Student instructions for Step Two:

> This week's passage is one last example of a place description—Kublai Khan's palace in China. As in the first description you outlined, some sections in this passage can be outlined fairly easily if you simply ask "What part of the place does this paragraph focus on?" If this question doesn't give you a simple answer, you can instead ask:
>
> 1. What is the main thing this section is about?
> 2. Why is that thing or person important?
>
> Use the following hints as you work through the sections.
>
> *Section 1.* All of the sentences in this section refer to the same *thing*. This is an introductory section, giving the reader an overview of . . . what?
>
> *Section 2.* The sentences in this section all refer to the same *quality* or *characteristic* shared by the parts mentioned.
>
> *Sections 3–5.* These sections refer to specific parts of the place.
>
> As in the last lesson, you can mix phrases and sentences if necessary. If you have difficulty, ask your instructor for help. When you are finished, check your assignment with your instructor.

HOW TO HELP THE STUDENT WITH STEP TWO

Clear, vivid writing is never cookie-cutter in its organization—something the student is being taught from the very beginning of the outlining process. Rather than merely describing individual parts of Kublai Khan's palace, this description begins with two sections that have slightly different purposes. The first section gives a general overview of the entire palace; the second focuses on the decorations that occur throughout the palace, rather than describing a particular spot within it. Sections 3 through 5 return to the familiar pattern; the third section describes the buildings to the rear of the the palace, the fourth the artificial north mount of the palace, and the fifth the water feature nearby.

It is acceptable for the student to mix phrases and sentences in this outline.

Suggested answers (the student's answers should resemble the following but don't need to be identical):

I. The palace OR The size of the palace OR The overall plan of the palace
II. The ornaments and decorations in the palace OR What makes the palace beautiful
III. The buildings to the rear OR The apartments behind the palace
IV. The artificial mount OR The Green Mount
V. Streams and ponds nearby OR The water features OR The fishponds and streams

If the student struggles with this assignment, use the following dialogues.

Section 1
Instructor: What is situated on the southern side of the city?

Student: The palace

Instructor: What has no upper floor, but a lofty roof?

Student: The palace

Instructor: What stands on a paved foundation or platform?

Student: The palace

Instructor: What does the wall surround?

Student: The palace

Instructor: It should be pretty clear to you what the main focus of this section is . . . the palace! This section gives an overall view of the palace, before the writer begins to focus on particular *parts* of the palace—like seeing something from up high before zooming in.

Section 2

Instructor: What *kinds* of decorations are on the sides of the halls and apartments?

Student: Carved work and gilt, figures, representations

Note to Instructor: The student shouldn't answer by describing dragons, warriors, birds, beasts, and battles—these are the subjects of the decorations, not the *kinds.*

Instructor: What is on the exterior of the roof?

Student: Colors

Instructor: What do the windows look like?

Student: Crystal

Instructor: Carved work, colors, crystal—all of these tell you about what makes the palace beautiful. Instead of describing a particular place within the palace, this section tells you about the ornaments and decorations that turn the entire palace into something magnificent.

Section 3

Instructor: What is to the rear of the palace?

Student: Large buildings containing apartments

Instructor: What does the monarch keep there?

Student: His treasure

Instructor: Who lives there?

Student: His wives and concubines

Instructor: This section describes the buildings behind the palace by telling you what happens there.

Section 4
Instructor: What is on the northern side of the palace?

Student: A mount of earth

Instructor: Everything in this section describes this Green Mount.

Section 5
Instructor: Rather than describing a single place, this section describes two related places. What are they? Hint: both of them are described as large and deep.

Student: Excavations [or ponds]

Instructor: What are they connected by?

Student: A stream [or aqueduct]

Instructor: What do ponds and streams have in common?

Student: Water

Instructor: Your main point could be phrased either as "Water features at the palace" or simply as "Streams and ponds."

Day Three: Analyzing and Practicing the Topos, Part One

Understanding the use of figurative language in a description of a place

The student has already learned three things about the description of a place: it should serve a particular purpose, it should use space and distance words, and it should be written from a particular point of view. This week, he'll add one more element to his descriptions.

STEP ONE: **Understand metaphor and simile (Student Responsibility)**

Student instructions for Step One:

Look again at these excerpts from the descriptions you studied last week.

Trees **so tall that they seem to touch the sky** grow on either side of the road, which continues until it reaches the sanctuary of Hermes. That is what the sanctuary of Boubastis looks like. (Herodotus)

In addition, the room was filled with rotten and unhealthy fumes, and every quarter of an hour, the sentry tolled a bell that was so close to my room that **it seemed it was hanging from my ears.** (de Renneville)

The city clocks had only just gone three, but it was quite dark already—it had not been light all day—and candles were flaring in the windows of the neighbouring offices, **like ruddy smears upon the palpable brown air.** The fog came pouring in at every chink and keyhole, and was so dense without, that although the court was of the narrowest, **the houses opposite were mere phantoms.** (Dickens)

All three of these descriptions use *figurative language.* Herodotus's trees don't really touch the sky; the bell wasn't really hanging from de Renneville's ears; and if you were in Dickens's London during a fog, you wouldn't see smears on palpable (touchable) brown air or phantom houses. Figurative language exaggerates some part of the description in order to make it even more vivid in the reader's mind.

There are two major categories of figurative language (or "figures of speech"). A simile compares two things *explicitly* by using the words "like" or "as," or otherwise spelling out for you that figurative language is being used:

like ruddy smears upon the palpable brown air

In the first simile, the word "like" says clearly, "Hey, this is figurative language!" The candle light isn't a smear; it's *like a smear.* In the second simile, the trees don't touch the sky. They just *seem* to touch the sky.

A metaphor doesn't announce itself by using the words "like" or "as" or by saying that one thing "seems like" or "resembles" another. Instead, the writer simply speaks about one thing in terms of another. When Dickens writes "palpable brown air," he is talking about the air as though it were a thing to be touched and held. This is his way of telling you that the air is smoggy and impossible to see through. If he were to spell the metaphor out, he might write,

like ruddy smears upon the air, which was like a thing that could be touched.

It's much simpler and more elegant for him to use an adjective which means "able to be touched" (palpable) and just apply it to the air. In the same way, he doesn't write

the houses opposite were almost invisible but not quite, like transparent ghosts.

Instead, he writes

the houses opposite were mere phantoms.

STEP TWO: Identify figurative language in descriptions

Student instructions for Step Two:

Read the following descriptions. Underline each metaphor and simile. In the margin, write "m" for metaphor and "s" for simile.

Remember this rule: A simile announces itself ("Look here! Figurative language being used!"). A metaphor simply speaks about one thing in terms of another.

If you have difficulty, ask your instructor for help. And when you are finished, check your work with your instructor.

HOW TO HELP THE STUDENT WITH STEP TWO

There are two levels of figurative language in today's passages. There are actual metaphors and similes, but there are also individual nouns, verbs, and adjectives which imply a word picture—for example, referring to the Matterhorn as a "dark finger." The metaphors and similes the student should be able to identify are underlined in the passages below. The student may also identify the italicized words, but this isn't required.

Explanations and teaching suggestions are found beneath each passage below; if necessary, go over the explanations with the student.

> The summer heat has withered everything except the mesquite, the palo verde, the grease wood, and the various cacti. Under foot there is a little dry grass, but more often patches of bare gravel and sand roll in shallow beds that *course* toward the large valleys. In the draws and flat places the fine sand lies thicker, is tossed in *wave forms* by the wind, and banked high against clumps of cholla or prickly pear. In the wash-outs and over the cut banks of the arroyos it is sometimes heaped in mounds and crests like driven snow.[20]

Course: The beds of gravel and sand are compared to streams that flow downwards to rivers.

Wave forms: A second use of water imagery.

Like driven snow: Simile. If the student cannot find the simile, suggest that he look for the word "like." The sand is heaped like snow, but whiteness is also implied.

> In the center . . . is the river Nile. On both sides of the river is the black rich soil of the land of Egypt. We can see the wide fields that have been planted by . . . men of the village. Those fields will soon be covered with a bright carpet of green and, later in the season, will be brilliant with waving grain. Farther to the westward are the sandstone mountains, which glitter in the bright sunshine.[21]

Bright carpet: Metaphor. The fields will be completely concealed, as a rug conceals floorboards. If the student cannot find the metaphor, ask him to find the one thing in the passage that belongs inside a house and not outdoors.

"Brilliant" is not a metaphor, simply a descriptive word; if the student identifies it as a metaphor, ask him what the grain is being compared to. (Identifying metaphors isn't an exact science, so if he can make a convincing argument, accept it.)

> When approaching the Alps from the air, on a clear day, we look down on their highest point within the massive snows of Mont Blanc. We also identify the *dark finger* of the Matterhorn and the great north wall of the Bernese Alps. Beyond these familiar landmarks, virtually endless rows of snow peaks recede to a misty horizon. They resemble white-capped waves on a windblown sea.[22]

Dark finger: The Matterhorn juts upward like a raised finger.

White-capped waves on a windblown sea: A straightforward simile, highlighting the

20. John Charles Van Dyke, *The Desert: Further Studies in Natural Appearances* (Charles Scribner's Sons, 1913), p. 3.
21. Walter Scott Perry, *With Azir Girges in Egypt* (Atkinson, Mentzer & Co., 1913), p. 37.
22. Nicholas Shoumatoff and Nina Shoumatoff, *The Alps: Europe's Mountain Heart* (University of Michigan Press, 2001), p. 3.

contrast between the mountains and their white peaks. If the student is unable to find it, ask him to find the one thing in the passage that doesn't belong in the Alps.

> The land had meantime been thickly enveloped in its pure white mantle, and wreaths of snowdrifts lay over the rocks scattered over its surface. The light became fainter. Sometimes the precipitous faces of the glaciers seemed to glow in subdued rose through the leaden grey of the atmosphere. When new "ice holes" appeared, a frosty vapour rose and spread over the surface of the ice; the ship and surrounding objects were covered as if with down; even the dogs were *frosted* white.[23]

Pure white mantle: A metaphor, comparing snow with an all-covering cloak.

Wreaths: A metaphor, implying that the snowdrifts decorate the rocks.

If the student has difficulty, tell him that there are two metaphorical words in the first sentence, neither of which have to do directly with snow; you may also say that one is a clothing metaphor, the other a decoration metaphor.

> Mount Shasta rises in solitary grandeur from the edge of a comparatively low and lightly sculptured lava plain near the northern extremity of the Sierra. . . . Go where you may, within a radius of from fifty to a hundred miles or more, there stands before you the colossal cone of Shasta, *clad* in ice and snow, the one grand unmistakable landmark—the pole star of the landscape.[24]

Clad: A clothing metaphor.

Pole star: Metaphor, implying that the mountain is the central, most important part of the landscape, the one that all travellers use to orient themselves. If necessary, ask the student to identify the thing in the passage that belongs in the sky, not on earth.

STEP THREE: **Add to the pattern of the topos (Student Responsibility)**

Student instructions for Step Three:

> Turn to the Description of a Place chart in your Composition Notebook. Add the bolded point below under the "Remember" column.
>
> Description of a Place
>
> Definition: A visual description of a physical place

Procedure	Remember
1. Ask, *What specific purpose should this description fulfill?*	1. Make use of space and distance words and phrases.
2. Choose a point of view	**2. Consider using vivid metaphors and similes.**

23. Julius Payer, *New Lands Within the Arctic Circle* (Macmillan & Co., 1876), p. 294.

24. John Muir, *Nature Writings* (Library of America, 1997), p. 634.

Day Four: Analyzing and Practicing the Topos, Part Two

Focus: Understanding the use of figurative language in a description of a place

STEP ONE: **Review the form of the description**

Student instructions for Step One:

Read the following description of London, written by the nineteenth-century journalist Blanchard Jerrold. Jerrold teamed up with the French artist Gustave Dore to write a book about London that would combine written descriptions with engraved pictures of the city.

At every corner there is a striking note for the sketch-book. A queer gateway, low and dark, with a streak of silver water seen through the stacks of goods beyond, and bales suspended like spiders from their web; a crooked narrow street with cranes over every window, and the sky netted with ropes as from the deck of a brig. . . . An apple stall surrounded by jubilant shoe-blacks and errand-boys. A closed, grass-grown church-yard, with ancient tomb stones lying at all angles like a witch's fangs.[25]

Now answer the following questions:

1. What is the point of view of the narrator?
2. How many space and distance words does the description use? Underline them.
3. What metaphors and similes does the description use? Underline them.
4. What quality of the city of London do you think the narrator is trying to bring out? (In other words, can you guess at the purpose of the description?)

Ask your instructor for help if you have difficulty with any of the questions. When you are finished, check your answers with your instructor.

HOW TO HELP THE STUDENT WITH STEP ONE

Suggested answers and student guidance for each question:

1. Moving through or around OR *From above (impersonal)*

If this short description were set into context, it would be clearer that the narrator is personally involved in the scene and walking through the city. Missing context, the student may classify the description as from above (impersonal).

This is reasonable, but you may want to point out that the first sentence suggests that (1) the narrator is personally involved, since he's thinking about carrying his sketchbook with him, and (2) the mention of "every corner" suggests that the narrator is walking from corner to

25. Blanchard Jerrold and Gustave Dore, *London: A Pilgrimage* (Anthem Press, 2005), pp. 22–24.

corner; in addition, the perspective on the details given (seeing through the low gateway; looking up at a sky netted with ropes) implies that the narrator is at ground level. Only go into this level of detail, though, if the student is not struggling with the assignment.

2. There are ten space and distance words/phrases used, bolded below:

> **At** every corner there is a striking note for the sketch-book. A queer gateway, low and dark, with a streak of silver water seen **through** the stacks of goods **beyond**, and bales suspended like spiders **from** their web; a crooked narrow street with cranes **over** every window, and the sky netted **with** ropes as **from** the deck of a brig. . . . An apple stall **surrounded by** jubilant shoe-blacks and errand-boys. A closed, grass-grown church-yard, **with** ancient tomb stones lying **at** all angles like a witch's fangs.

If necessary, tell the student how many space and distance words are on each line, and have him use the Space and Distance Words/Phrases list to find them.

3. There are three metaphors/similes:
like spiders from their web
netted with ropes as from the deck of a brig
like a witch's fangs

STEP TWO: **Practice avoiding cliches**

Student instructions for Step Two:

> Although metaphors and similes can make descriptions more vivid, using figurative language that's cliched (used too often) can have the opposite effect. When Herodotus wrote that a tree seemed to touch the sky, he wasn't using a cliche. But after Herodotus, thousands (maybe tens of thousands) of writers also wrote that trees seemed to touch the sky. After thousands of writers use the same simile or metaphor, it becomes a cliche.
>
> When you write a description, you may be tempted to describe a peak as "sharp as a needle," a stream as "chattering merrily," or the sides of a limestone pyramid as "white as snow." But because these images are so often used, they don't cause the reader to stop and picture in his mind exactly what you're describing; his eye just skims over it and he moves on.
>
> In the description above, did the sentence about the tomb stones lying at angles like witch's fangs make you stop for a moment to picture exactly what that would look like?
>
> You can avoid using cliches by rejecting the first image that pops into your head; it's usually the most familiar one. Imagine that you want to express just how white something is. Your first thought will probably be "White as snow." Instead of using that metaphor, stop and think for a moment. Exactly what *sort* of whiteness are you trying to describe? Is it the hard, shiny whiteness of marble? Think about what else is not just white, but also hard and shiny. Pearls? Dried toothpaste? The paint on a Chevrolet?
>
> Or maybe it is the soft, dull whiteness of cotton. What else is not just white, but also soft and dull? A marshmallow? Chicken feathers?
>
> When you use figurative language, you have to think about the *exact* qualities you are trying to convey. Practice doing that now. In the sentences below, cross out each cliche. Then spend some time thinking about the exact quality described in brackets. Come up with a metaphor that's new and vivid, and write it in over the crossed-out cliche.

When you are finished, check your work with your instructor. And if you have difficulty, ask your instructor for help.

HOW TO HELP THE STUDENT WITH STEP TWO

The first part of the assignment—locating the cliches—should be simple for the student; all of the comparisons except for the first ("white as snow") use the word "like." Expect the second part of the assignment to take some time. The student's new similes don't have to be brilliant, but they should be *different*. You may need to remind the student to keep the *exact* quality in brackets in mind.

If the student needs inspiration, you may want to direct him to the nineteenth-century reference work *A Dictionary of Similes* by Frank Jenners Wilstach. Full texts are available online from books.google.com and elsewhere.

When the student has finished the assignment, you may show him the original versions of these sentences below.

The beaches are as hot and white as molten glass but the ocean is blue and numbingly cold.
—Mark Helprin, *The Pacific and Other Stories* (Penguin Press, 2004), p. 168

White beaches glistened in the tropic sunlight as if their sands were polished grains of silver.
—Charles H. Johnston, *Famous Discoverers and Explorers of America* (L. C. Page & Co., 1941), p. 67

The gallant ship, surrounded by enemies, lay like a great fortress on the sea, scattering death on every side from her hundred and four portholes.
—Thomas Babington Macaulay, *The History of England* (Penguin, 1979), p. 472

Lower away in the south . . . there lay a black squall-cloud with a rounded outline, like a big windbag, resembling nothing so much as a fat boy's face with its cheeks blown out, when he tries to fill a football with the pressure from his lungs.
—Frederick Philip Grove, *Over Prairie Trails* (Random House, 2010), p. 106

The castle, which stood on the highest platform of the clustered hills, was built of rough-hewn limestone, full of lights and shadows made by the dark dust of lichens and the washings of the rain. Masses of beech and fir sheltered it on the north, and spread down here and there along the green slopes like flocks seeking the water which gleamed below.
—George Eliot, *Daniel Deronda* (William Blackwood and Sons, 1878), pp. 144–145

Glare ice, black ice they call it, polished the road and reflected first my headlights and then the rising sun. . . . The land stretched flat and frozen on either side, slicked with hoarfrost and gleaming like washed china.
—Michael Doris, *A Yellow Raft in Blue Water* (Macmillan 2003), p. 201

In front of the line . . . the forest was cut down, and the trees left lying where they fell among the stumps, with tops turned outwards . . . like a forest laid flat by a hurricane. But the most formidable obstruction was immediately along the front of the breastwork, where the ground was covered with heavy boughs, overlapped and interlaced, with sharpened points bristling into the face of the assailant like the quills of a porcupine.

—Francis Parkman, *Rivals for America* (Little, Brown, and Co., 1916), p. 143

Week 11: Combining Chronological Narrative of a Past Event and Description of a Place

Day One: Original Narration Exercise

Focus: Summarizing a narrative by choosing the main events and listing them chronologically

STEP ONE: **Read (Student Responsibility)**

Student instructions for Step One:

Read the following excerpt from Mark Twain's *Tom Sawyer.*

STEP TWO: **Note important events**

Student instructions for Step Two:

You will now summarize the passage in three or four sentences and write those sentences down on your own paper.

On your scratch paper, write down five or six phrases or short sentences that will remind you of the things that happened in the story. *Do not use more than six phrases or short sentences!* Remember, you're not supposed to write down *everything* that happens in the story—just the most important events.

Be sure to write the events down in the same order that they happen in the story.

If you have trouble with this assigment, ask your instructor for help.

HOW TO HELP THE STUDENT WITH STEP TWO

The student should have written down on scratch paper five or six short phrases or sentences that summarize the main events. The phrases/sentences should resemble the following (these are given only as a guide):

Tom Sawyer didn't want to go to school.
Tom hated Monday mornings.
Tom tried to think of a way to stay home from school.
Wanted to be sick
Front tooth was loose.
Tom had a sore toe.
Decided to pretend his sore toe hurt
Tom woke up Sid by groaning about his sore toe.
Sid went downstairs to get Aunt Polly.
Aunt Polly came to see Tom's toe.
The toe wasn't actually sore.
Tom told Aunt Polly he had a loose tooth.
Tom didn't want his tooth pulled out.
Aunt Polly pulled the tooth.
Pulled tooth with a loop of silk tied to the bedpost
Tom could spit through his front teeth.
Popular at school because of missing tooth

(Remember, the student should not provide more than five or six phrases/sentences.)

Watch the student as he writes down his phrases. If he's writing too many phrases, or the sentences are long and complex, stop him before he goes on. Ask him the following questions to help him distinguish between main events and supporting details:

What was Tom's problem at the beginning of the story? *(He didn't want to go to school.)*
What did he decide to do? *(He decided to pretend to be sick* OR *He pretended his sore toe hurt.)*
Who was sharing the room with Tom? How did that person react? *(Sid went down to get Aunt Polly OR Sid thought Tom was dying and ran for Aunt Polly.)*
What did Aunt Polly tell Tom about his toe? *(Aunt Polly told him that his toe was fine OR Aunt Polly told him he wasn't going to die.)*
What did Aunt Polly do then? *(She pulled out Tom's tooth OR She pulled the loose tooth out with a loop of silk.)*
What was the result of Tom's losing his tooth? *(He could spit through his teeth* OR *He became very popular at school.)*

If the student is still having trouble deciding what events to leave out, ask him: If you left this event out, would the rest of the story still make sense? If it would, it's a minor detail and can be eliminated.

STEP THREE: **Write summary sentences**

Student instructions for Step Three:

After you've written down your five or six phrases or sentences, try to combine them into three or four sentences. You can do this by putting two phrases in the same sentence (for example, "Tom Sawyer didn't want to go to school" and "Decided to pretend his sore toe hurt" could be combined into "Tom Sawyer didn't want to go to school, so he pretended that his toe hurt"). Or you may find that one or more of your jotted notes turn out to be unnecessary.

Say your three or four sentences out loud several times before writing them down. After you've written the sentences down, ask your instructor to check them.

If you have trouble, ask your instructor for help.

HOW TO HELP THE STUDENT WITH STEP THREE

Now the student will practice turning the jotted phrases and sentences into three or four coherent, smooth sentences. Her instructions tell her to practice saying three or four sentences out loud several times before she writes; if necessary, remind her that she should be speaking before she writes.

You may need to help her combine two phrases into one sentence.

When the summary is finished, check it using the following rubric.

Week 11 Narration Rubric

Organization

1 Events should be in chronological order.

2 If two or more events are listed in a single sentence, they should have a cause and effect relationship.

For example:

Tom woke up Sid, and Sid ran downstairs for Aunt Polly

is acceptable; Sid ran downstairs because Tom woke him up.

Tom woke up Sid and Aunt Polly came upstairs

is not acceptable. There is no obvious causal relationship between the two events.

3 Each event of major importance should be in the summary (if it were missing from the original passage, the narrative would no longer make sense).

It is acceptable for the student to describe the exact method by which the tooth was pulled; although it would make sense to just say "Aunt Polly pulled the tooth," this is one of the most memorable parts of the passage.

Mechanics

1 Each sentence should make sense on its own when read aloud.

2 Each proper name should be capitalized.

3 Personal pronouns should have clear antecedents and be of the proper gender.

4 Verb tense should be consistent throughout.

Day Two: Outlining Exercise

Focus: Finding the central topic in each paragraph of a chronological narrative that includes description

STEP ONE: **Read (Student Responsibility)**

Student instructions for Step One:

Read the following excerpt from *The History of Puerto Rico: From the Spanish Discovery to the American Occupation* by R. A. Van Middeldyk. "The Admiral" is Christopher Columbus, who made his first visit to Puerto Rico in November 1493. This was Columbus's second voyage to the Americas; he had returned from his first journey not long before and had convinced the Spanish government to pay for a second trip of exploration.

STEP TWO: **Construct a one-level outline**

Student instructions for Step Two:

This week's passage combines two of the topics you've been studying: the chronological narrative and the description of a place.

As in previous weeks, you'll need to find a major point for each section. Because the sections alternate between chronological narrative and description, you'll have to use both of the methods you've studied. If the section seems to be chronological narrative, ask:

1. What is the main thing or person that this section is about? *Or* What is the major event in this section?
2. Why is that thing, person, or event important?

If the section seems to be primarily descriptive, ask:

What part of the place does this paragraph focus on?

If you're not sure which method will work best, try both.

You may mix phrases and sentences if necessary. If you have difficulty, ask your instructor for help. And when you're finished, check your assignment with your instructor.

HOW TO HELP THE STUDENT WITH STEP TWO

In this assignment, the student has been encouraged to ty try two different methods of finding the main idea in each section. It is acceptable for her to mix phrases and sentences in her outline.

Suggested answers:

I. The islands Columbus found OR The islands discovered on the voyage

II. Chanca's account of their arrival OR Chanca's description of their journey
III. The first islands they discover OR Landing on the islands OR The Admiral claims the islands
IV. The island vegetation OR Fruits and trees on the island
V. Journey to Basse Terre OR Another island with inhabitants OR Travelling to another island with people

This passage mixes description of a place with chronological narrative of a historical event, so expect the student to need help with some sections. Encourage the student to identify each section as either narrative or description. If a section is narrative, she should follow the two-question method ("What is the main thing/event? Why is it important?"). If description, she can try asking the simple question "What part of the place does this describe?"

Section 1 (description)
Instructor: What group of things does this section describe? (Hint: they are named four different times.)

Student: The islands

Instructor: Which islands? The answer is in the first sentence.

Student: The islands discovered on the voyage

Instructor: The rest of this passage gives you more details about those islands. "The islands discovered on the voyage" is your main point.

Section 2 (narrative)
Instructor: Who is the most important person in this section?

Student: Chanca

Instructor: What important thing did he do?

Student: He wrote a description of their journey OR He wrote about their arriving at the islands.

Section 3 (narrative)
Instructor: What is the most important event in this section?

Student: They landed on the islands OR *Columbus landed on an island.*

Section 4 (description)
Instructor: What *kind* of thing is described in this passage? Remember, in a main point you should try not to list individual details about particular things.

Student: Vegetation OR Plants OR *Trees and fruit*

Instructor: You would not make your main point something like "Poisonous fruits" because that's a detail from only one part of the section. Everything in the passage refers to trees, plants and fruit. Where were these trees, plants, and fruit?

Student: On the islands OR *On Marie-Galante*

Section 5 (narrative)
Instructor: Something new and different happens in this section. What is it?

Student: They travel to another island.

Instructor: What new and different thing is on that island?

Student: People

Instructor: Put those two things together for your main point.

Student: They travel to another island with people.

Day Three: Analyzing the Topos

Focus: Understanding the form of a chronological narrative that includes description

The passage outlined in the last writing session was a **chronological narrative of a past event** that made use of a **description of a place**—a combination of two forms already learned. Today, the student will review the elements that make up both forms, and look at the ways in which writers combine them. Tomorrow, she will write his own chronological narrative, making use of a place description.

The student will complete Steps One and Two independently before asking for assistance with Step Three.

STEP ONE: Review the elements of a chronological narrative (Student Responsibility)

Student instructions for Step One:

> In studying the form of a chronological narrative of past events, you've learned:
>
> 1. A chronological narrative answers the questions: Who did what to whom? (Or what was done to what)? And in what sequence?
> 2. Time and sequence words make the narrative flow smoothly forward.
> 3. Dialogue and actions help hold the reader's interest.
>
> Look back at your outline of the passage from *The History of Puerto Rico.* It probably looks something like this:
>
> I. The islands discovered on the voyage
> **II. Chanca's description of their journey**
> **III. Landing on the islands**

IV. Fruits and trees on the island
V. Travelling to another island with people

The first and fourth sections contain descriptions, but points II, III, and V tell you who did what and in what order:

First, Chanca and the others made a journey.
Second, they landed on the islands.
Third, they travelled to other islands nearby.

The passage makes use of time and sequence words to help move the narrative forward—not just the time and sequence words on your chart, but also verbs and phrases that show the passage of time. Look at the sections below, and circle the bolded words, saying each word aloud as you circle it.

Finally, notice how the writer makes use of dialogue. Rather than putting in speeches made by Columbus and the other travellers, the writer chooses to use the exact words of someone who was on the voyage. When Chanca, the fleet physician, writes "It was marvelous to see and hear the people's manifestations of joy," we are brought much closer to the actual event than if the writer had simply put "The people were glad to see land."

STEP TWO: **Review the elements of a description of a place (Student Responsibility)**

Student instructions for Step Two:

The writer of *The History of Puerto Rico* inserts passages of description into his narrative whenever he wants the reader to picture the places that the exploreres are discovering. The first and fourth sections:

I. The islands discovered on the voyage
IV. Fruits and trees on the island

are place descriptions, but the final section also contains an important single-sentence description of a place.

Each description has a particular purpose. The first section acts as an introduction to the entire journey; it's a little like being given a map to look at as the story goes on. The fourth section makes clear to the reader just how strange and foreign the unfamiliar landscape looked to the explorers. And the sentence in the final section gives the reader a sense of the awe felt by the explorers when they saw the beauty of the new land.

Go through the descriptions below and circle the bolded space and distance words and phrases, saying each one out loud. As you read, think about the point of view of the narrator in each section. Is the narrator above the scene and uninvolved in it, inside it, looking at it from one side, or moving through it? (Each section has a different point of view.) Jot a note identifying the point of view beside each section before going on to read the explanations below the descriptions.

Did you identify the point of view of each section? If so, read on.

The "introduction/map" section is very definitely written from above the scene. The narrator of this section is the writer of the history, Rudolph Adams Van Middeldyk. He's describing the scene as though looking down on a map, and he's certainly not personally involved with it.

The "unfamiliar land" section is written by Chanca, the fleet physician, and he seems to be inside the scene. You could also argue that he's moving through it, but we're not given any space or distance words that imply he's walking through the island as he describes it; he sounds more as if he's standing next to the tree with the laurel leaves, looking around.

In the "natural beauty" section, the narrators are the sailors who've just dropped anchor on the southern coast, and they are looking at the island as a whole from the side angle.

Finally, the "unfamiliar land" and "natural beauty" sections both contain figurative language. Chanca says that the sailors "behaved like madmen"; although this has more to do with the people than with the place itself, the simile certainly makes the scene vivid. In the final section, Van Middeldyk uses one of those cliches; you can do better when you write tomorrow.

STEP THREE: **Analyze a model passage**

Student instructions for Step Three:

Your final assignment for today is to go through the following chronological narrative and description and do the same analysis that was done for you above. You don't have to construct another outline, but you do have to:

1. Identify each paragraph as either *primarily* narrative or *primarily* description and write the label in the right-hand margin.
2. Circle each time and sequence word in the narrative paragraphs.
3. Underline each space and distance word in the description paragraphs.
4. In the left-hand margin, write the purpose and point of view of any descriptive paragraph.
5. Draw a box around any figurative language (this may occur either in the descriptive or narrative passages).
6. Underline any lines of dialogue twice.
7. Check your answers with your instructor.

This passage is from *Nelson's Trafalgar: The Battle That Changed the World*, by Roy Adkins. The Battle of Trafalgar was fought on October 21, 1805, just off the coast of Spain. The British fleet was one one side; the French and Spanish (the "Combined Fleet") were allied on the other. Rear-Admiral Dumanoir [doom-ah-nwhar] commanded part of the French fleet. The *Victory* was the flagship of the British fleet and was commanded by Admiral Lord Nelson, who was killed during the battle. Captain Lucas, who commanded the *Redoubtable* (also spelled *Redoutable* in some histories), was a French officer.

HOW TO HELP THE STUDENT WITH STEP THREE

Check the student's answers, and if necessary prompt her with the information below.

1. Paragraph 1: Description
   (paints a picture of the place on the sea where the battle is taking place)
   Paragraph 2: Narrative
   (tells of battle events)
   Paragraph 3: Narrative
   (tells how the French and Spanish sailed away)

Paragraph 4: Narrative
(tells about the fight between the Victory *and the* Redoubtable*)*

2. Paragraph 2 time and sequence words, in order of occurrence: *now, while, as, no longer*
   Paragraph 3 time and sequence words, in order of occurrence: *in the meantime, still, longer, afterwards, till*
   Paragraph 4 time and sequence words, in order of occurrence: *by now, frequently*
3. Paragraph 1 space and distance words, in order of occurrence: *at, where, from, into, out, through, down, by, from, by*
4. Purpose of Paragraph 1: as an introduction, to set the scene, to give a sense of the horror and carnage of the battle
   Point of view: from above and uninvolved (this is the only perspective from which one could see the movement of the ships, the sea, and the sides of the ships simultaneously)
5. Figurative language:
   Paragraph 1: *heart* of the fighting, *cut* the French and Spanish line
   (These may be difficult for the student to locate; if he misses them, ask "What body part is used to refer to something else?" and "Are the British columns actually holding knives?")
   Paragraph 2: *kaleidoscope*
6. Lines of dialogue: "Oh! you belong to one of the ships that did not come up till the battle was nearly over."

Day Four: Practicing the Topos

Focus: Learning how to write a chronological narrative of a past event that includes a description of a place

Today, the student will put together a chronological narrative of a past event; one of the paragraphs will also describe a place that's central to the event.

STEP ONE: **Plan the narrative**

Student instructions for Step One:

> On the next page, you'll see a list of events, written out chronologically for you, about the sixteenth-century Russian tsar Ivan IV ("Ivan the Terrible"). Bolded entries are main events; the indented entries are futher details about those main events. These details are taken from *The Cambridge History of Russia* (Cambridge University Press, 2006) edited by Maureen Perrie and from *Russia: The Once and Future Empire from Pre-History to Putin* by Philip Longworth (Macmillan, 2006).
>
> Your chronological narrative will be based on these events. This chronological narrative must be at least 150 words long and no longer than 300 words.

As in previous assignments, you will not include every event. Look over the following events now, and mark three or four main (bolded) events to include in your narrative. **You must include the construction of St. Basil's Cathedral as one of your main events.**

After you have chosen your main events, mark which details and dialogue you intend to include. You won't include all of the details under any main event (pick and choose), but you must include at least one line of dialogue in your final composition.

EVENTS IN THE LIFE OF TSAR IVAN IV

Ivan's childhood

Born August 25, 1530

His father was Grand Prince of Moscow

Father died 1533

Ivan became Grand Prince at age 3

His mother ruled for him

Mother poisoned in 1538

Russian noblemen struggled over the throne

Ivan's family fought to keep the throne for Ivan

They drove out opposition by 1547

Crowned Emperor (Tsar) of Russia in 1547

First Russian ruler to use the title "tsar"

"Tsar" was Russian form of "Caesar," old Roman title

Believed he was God's anointed and should have complete power

The medieval history called the *Nikon Chronicle* says: "From that time on, the princes began to regard him with fear."

Enlarged his kingdom through conquest

Fought against the Mongols

Fought against his western neighbors

Fought north into Siberia

Conquered the Tatar city of Kazan in 1552 (Tatars=Turkish people group)

Russia now spread across vast territories

Russia now had many different races inside it

Ordered the building of a new church to celebrate his military victories

Commanded the church built in 1552

Construction began in 1555

Construction went on until 1679

The church was called Cathedral of the Intercession of the Virgin

Later its name was changed to honor Basil the Blessed

Church now known as St. Basil's Cathedral

Became known as "Ivan the Terrible"

"Terrible" really means "dreaded" or "awe-inspiring"

Given the title because of his punishment of wrongdoers

Began a "reign of terror" in 1564

Began to suffer from mental breakdown

Formed secret police to hunt out his enemies

Ivan wrote, "If a tsar's subjects do not obey him they will forever be at war with one another."

An Italian ambassador wrote home, "Since he tries to find out everything his subjects do, very few of them dare to say anything." He also wrote that the Russian "people fear their lord, and are more obedient to their ruler than any other people in the world."

Secret police known as *oprichnina* wore black cloaks and carried brooms (brooms represented "sweeping clean")

Had political opponents murdered

Attacked his own city of Novgorod and massacred the population

Ivan IV said, "We are free to show favor to our servants and are free to put them to death."

Killed his own son in 1581

His son Ivan was 27

Argued with his son about the clothes his son's wife wore

Son contradicted him

Ivan the Terrible struck his son with an iron-tipped staff

Son was in coma for several days before dying

Died in 1584

Had been ill—could no longer walk and was carried in a litter

Was getting ready to play chess

Died suddenly

Left his country poorer and in chaos

HOW TO HELP THE STUDENT WITH STEP ONE

You may need to help the student select which events to include. Encourage her to include three or four main (bolded) events but no more.

The main events in this particular list are more or less interchangeable. The student could choose:

Ivan's childhood
Crowned Emperor (Tsar) of Russia in 1547
Enlarged his kingdom through conquest
Ordered the building of a new church to celebrate his military victories

or

Enlarged his kingdom through conquest
Ordered the building of a new church to celebrate his military victories
Began a "reign of terror" in 1564

or a number of other combinations. However, since she has to include the main point about the church, she should include either "Crowned Emperor" or "Enlarged his kingdom through conquest" in her events list. Otherwise, it won't make sense that the church celebrated Ivan's military victories; both of these points show how powerful he was.

You may also need to remind the student that she can leave out as many details as necessary. For example, she could write:

Ivan was crowned emperor of all Russia in 1547. He enlarged his kingdom through conquest and ordered the building of a new church to celebrate his military victories.

and follow this with her description of the cathedral. This paragraph would only include information from the main (bolded) points.

Then as her final point, she could write a paragraph on the reign of terror that includes almost all of the events under the main event "Began a 'reign of terror' in 1564." Alternately, the student could include only one or two details under each main event and end up with a composition of equal length.

STEP TWO: **Plan the description**

Student instructions for Step Two:

As part of your composition, include a description of St. Basil's Cathedral. On the next page, you will see some pictures of the cathedral. Use these images and write a brief description of the cathedral. (If possible, go online and do a search at images.google.com for "St. Basil's Cathedral." The domes and towers are painted bright colors; a description without this detail is acceptable, but the colors make the cathedral much more interesting.)

You will include this description in your narrative, either as part of the paragraph where you tell us that Ivan IV ordered the cathedral built, or as a separate paragraph following this main event.

Note that the pictures show the cathedral in its present form; it has been added onto, restored, and repainted since Ivan's day. When you write your description, you may want to mention that you are describing the cathedral as it now looks.

Write down a few phrases now that give details about the cathedral's size, shape, and appearance. Your final description should follow these guidelines:

1. It should be written from above, with an impersonal perspective.
2. It should include at least two space and distance words.
3. The cathedral's design was unusual and unique; the description should give a sense of the cathedral's being out of place, looking like nothing else in the city, shocking onlookers with its strangeness.
4. The description should contain at least one clear use of figurative language.

HOW TO HELP THE STUDENT WITH STEP TWO

There are two likely areas of difficulty with this assignment:

First, the student may have difficulty with the purpose of the description. If necessary, suggest that she make use of some of the following adjectives and nouns:

ADJECTIVES	*NOUNS*
odd	*oddity*
peculiar	*curiosity*
rare	*anomaly*
unique	*marvel*
out of the ordinary	*spectacle*
offbeat	
unexpected	
singular	
curious	
fantastical	
striking	
astonishing	
spectacular	
unprecedented	
foreign	
outlandish	

Second, the student may have trouble finding the appropriate metaphor or simile.

Suggest that she focus on the following:

1. The shape of the domes; they are swirled, fat, twisted, sharp.

Possible similes: like candy (gumdrops, kisses, meringues), Christmas ornaments, onions (these are known as "onion domes")

2. The number of the domes: they cluster.

Possible similes: fruit, flowers

3. The colors: bright, multicolored

Possible similes: flowers, stained glass, sunset

The following descriptions are from two travelogues; *Through Russia in War-time* by Charles Fillingham Coxwell, published in 1917, and *Through Russia: From St. Petersburg to Astrakhan and the Crimea,* by Katharine Blanche Guthrie, published in 1894. Allow the student to read both when her own description is finished. If she is completely blocked, you may also choose to let her read them for inspiration—but don't allow her to look at them as she writes.

> *Returning to the Red Square through the Redeemer's Gate, I marvelled at the boldness and originality of St. Basil's Cathedral. The designer, determining upon a startling combination of qualities, summoned strangeness and variety of shape, design, and colouring to create a temple which should tell Heaven of man's gratitude for Nature's bounty. Eleven cupolas and spires crown as many small and dark chapels crowded together, but distributed in two stories, the whole, despite crudeness of tints, producing a result highly effective. The employment of pillars and arches and lines inclined at a sharp angle is here altogether subsidiary to that of towering, bulb-like masses, fantastically imitative. Conical scales and graceful curves and spiral markings suggest fruits and vegetables; among others, the pineapple and onion.*
>
> *—Charles Fillingham Coxwell*

> *It is certainly the most eccentric pile in Europe, and utterly unlike anything we had ever seen. It has a coloured spire, so twisted that it is impossible to tell whether it is in immediate danger of falling, or whether its crooked appearance is the result of an optical illusion. Then it has eleven bulb-shaped domes, each surmounted by the crescent and the cross, and secured by the usual streaming chains. One dome was larger than the others, which were of different sizes, and not placed symmetrically. They cropped up anywhere, and were either deeply indented or patterned in bold relief. These were picked out in the most gorgeous colours; there was nothing delicate in the tracery, which was, on the contrary, coarse and solid, and so all the more effective. One had a twisted design, red, on a green ground (red and green predominated) ; another, all prickly angles, yellow and black; a third was ornamented with scales of blue and crimson; a fourth was in quarters like a melon. There were outside flights of stairs, which appeared to lead to nothing; doors which were unattainable, and would have been all the better for the steps; and slits of windows, which the crows alone could have found useful.*
>
> *—Katharine Blanche Guthrie*

STEP THREE: **Write**

Student instructions for Step Three:

> As you begin to write, don't forget to include time and sequence words and dialogue. Don't forget to incorporate your description of the cathedral into your composition. When you are finished, show your composition to your instructor.

HOW TO HELP THE STUDENT WITH STEP THREE

The student may need assistance in:

Reviewing the rules for dialogue (see p. 80–81);

Choosing time and sequence words (you may need to remind her to use at least two); and

Choosing space and distance words.

When the student is finished, check her work using the following rubric.

Week 11 Rubric
Chronological Narrative of a Past Event Incorporating Description of a Place

Organization

1 Events should be in chronological order.
2 Two or more time words should be used.
3 There should be a clear connection between an event that shows Ivan IV's power and the construction of the cathedral.
4 The description of the cathedral should immediately follow the main event "Ordered the building of a new church to celebrate his military victories."
5 At least one metaphor or simile should be used in the description of the cathedral.
6 At least two space and distance words should be used.
7 The description should be written from the point of view of an outside, impersonal observer.
8 The composition should be at least 150 and not more than 350 words.

Mechanics

1 Each sentence should make sense on its own when read aloud.
2 Each proper name should be capitalized.
3 Possessive forms should be written properly.
4 Verbs should be in consistent tense.
5 Subjects and verbs should be in agreement.
6 The exact words of the source material should not be used in every sentence.
7 At least one direct quote should be included; the quote and accompanying dialogue tags should be properly punctuated.

Week 12: Scientific Description

Day One: Original Narration Exercise

Focus: Summarizing a narrative that combines two narrative voices

STEP ONE: **Read (Student Responsibility)**

Student instructions for Step One:

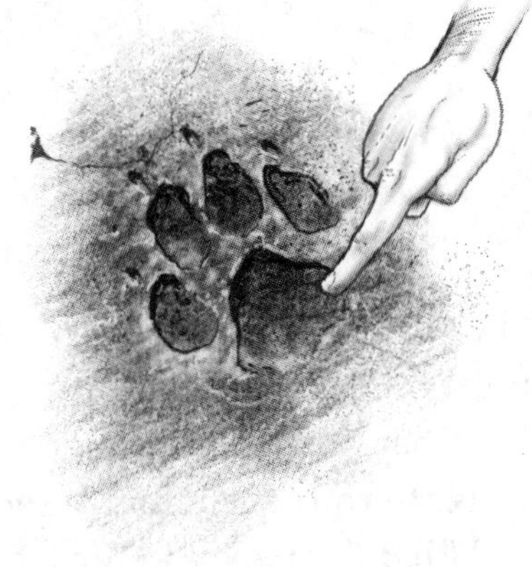

Read the following excerpt from *The Hound of the Baskervilles* by Arthur Conan Doyle. In this passage, a country doctor named James Mortimer has come to London to see the great detective Sherlock Holmes and his friend, Dr. Watson at 221B Baker Street. James Mortimer has just finished explaining to Sherlock Holmes that he needs helping solving a mystery; his friend Sir Charles Baskerville died suddenly and tragically, three months before. His body was found lying on the moor (the high, open area of land) near his house, late at night. James Mortimer thinks that the death is connected, somehow, to the legend that the entire Baskerville family is cursed to be haunted and pursued by a giant, ghostly hound.

As this excerpt begins, James Mortimer has already told Holmes and Watson all about the legend. Now he is describing the circumstances of Charles Baskerville's death.

"Chimerical" means "unreal, imaginary, fantastic" (it comes from the name of a mythological Greek beast, the chimera, which had the head of a lion, the body of a goat, and the tail of a snake).

STEP TWO: **Note important events in the two different stories**

Student instructions for Step Two:

You will now summarize the passage in three or four sentences, and write those sentences down on your own paper.

This may be a challenge because there are actually two different stories in the excerpt. The first is the story that James Mortimer is telling about Charles Baskerville; the second is the story that the author, Arthur Conan Doyle, is telling about James Mortimer and Sherlock Holmes.

Begin by jotting down, on the left-hand side of your paper, five or six phrases or sentences that will remind you of the things that happened in James Mortimer's story. Draw a vertical line down the middle of the paper. On the right-hand side, jot down two or three phrases or sentences that will remind you of the things that happen in Arthur Conan Doyle's story.

If you have trouble with this assignment, ask your instructor for help.

HOW TO HELP THE STUDENT WITH STEP TWO

The student should have written down two sets of phrases or sentences. On the left-hand side of his paper, the phrases/sentences summarizing James Mortimer's story about Charles Baskerville should resemble the following (these are given only as a guide):

Sir Charles was afraid to go out on the moor.
Sir Charles thought that a curse was on his family.
Three weeks before he died, he saw something.
He saw a giant black creature.
Dr. Mortimer told Sir Charles to go to London.
Intended to go to London to see a doctor
Dr. Mortimer found Sir Charles's body.
Sir Charles died on the moor.
No injury on the body
There were footprints all around the body.
Footprints of a giant hound were all around.

If the student has difficulty, ask him the following questions to help him isolate the most important events in the story.

What was Sir Charles's great fear? *(He was afraid of the giant hound.)*
Note to Instructor: If the student says, "He was afraid to go out on the moor," say "Why?"
What happened to Sir Charles? *(He died.)*
What was unusual about his body? *(There was no injury to his body.)*
What was all around the body? *(The footprints of a giant hound)*

On the right-hand side of his paper, the phrases/sentences summarizing Arthur Conan Doyle's story should resemble the following:

Holmes asked Dr. Mortimer many different questions.
Dr. Mortimer described the scene.
Mortimer described yew hedge, walk, and gate.
Mortimer told Holmes where the prints were.
Mortimer told them what he had seen.

Watch the student as he writes his phrases and sentences. If you see that he is carefully summarizing each line of the dialogue (*It was not a sheep dog; damp cold night; gate leading to the moor was four feet,* etc.) stop him. Remind him that he is supposed to be summarizing what *happens* in the story. Use the following questions:

What is actually happening in the story itself—that is, in Sherlock Holmes's house at 221B Baker Street? *(Holmes and Mortimer are talking.)*
What are they talking about? *(The night Sir Charles died)*
What is Holmes doing? *(Asking questions about the scene)*
What is Mortimer doing? *(Answering the questions)*

STEP THREE: **Write summary sentences**

Student instructions for Step Three:

> After you've written down your phrases and sentences, try to combine them into three or four sentences. The first part of your summary should begin with, "According to Dr. Mortimer" (or a similar phrase). The second part of your summary should begin with, "After Dr. Mortimer finished his story" (or a similar phrase).
>
> Say your three or four sentences out loud several times before writing them down. After you've written the sentences down, ask your instructor to check them.
>
> If you have trouble, ask your instructor for help.

HOW TO HELP THE STUDENT WITH STEP THREE

Now the student will practice turning the phrases and sentences into three or four coherent, smooth sentences. His instructions tell him to practice saying three or four sentences out loud several times before he writes; if necessary, remind him that he should be speaking before he writes.

The summary should move from Dr. Mortimer's story to the narrative about what's actually happening at Baker Street; a sample acceptable narration might be

According to Dr. Mortimer, Sir Charles Baskerville was afraid of the giant hound that haunted his family. He refused to go out the moor, but one night he was found dead there. The footprints of a giant hound were all around his body. After Dr. Mortimer had finished his story, Sherlock Holmes asked him several more questions about the scene of the death.

OR

Dr. Mortimer told Holmes and Watson that his friend Charles Baskerville was afraid of a giant ghostly hound. Mortimer wanted Baskerville to go to London. Before Baskerville could leave, his body was found on the moor with giant hound footprints around it. After Dr. Mortimer had told his story, Holmes asked him to describe the path, the gate, and the moor more closely.

When the summary is finished, check it using the following rubric.

Week 12 Summary of Narrative Fiction Rubric

Organization

1 Events should be in chronological order.
2 If two or more events are listed in a single sentence, they should have a cause and effect relationship.
3 Dr. Mortimer's story should be distinct from the events actually taking place at Baker Street.
4 The second part of the summary should describe Mortimer and Holmes having a conversation, not the details of the scene recounted by Mortimer.

Mechanics

1 Each sentence should make sense on its own when read aloud.
2 Each proper name should be capitalized.
3 Personal pronouns should have clear antecedents and be of the proper gender: for example, in the sentences "Mortimer wanted Baskerville to go to London. Before he could leave. . . ," the antecedent of "he" is unclear.
4 Verb tense should be consistent throughout.
5 The perfect past (pluperfect) should be correctly used: "When Dr. Mortimer had finished" or "After Dr. Mortimer had told his story" indicates that Dr. Mortimer's story happened *before* the scene at Baker Street.

Day Two: Outlining Exercise

Focus: Finding the central topic in each paragraph of a scientific description

STEP ONE: **Read (Student Responsibility)**

Student instructions for Step One:

Read the following excerpt from *The Illustrated Encyclopedia of Astronomy and Space*, edited by Ian Ridpath. An astronomical unit is 92,955,807.27 miles (149,597,870.7 kilometers), approximately the same as the average distance between the Earth and the sun.

STEP TWO: **Construct a one-level outline**

Student instructions for Step Two:

This week's passage is a slightly different kind of description: a scientific description of an object or phenomenon.

When you first outlined a descriptive passage in Week 8, you learned that you can sometimes ask a simpler question of a descriptive paragraph than of a narrative paragraph. When you're reading a narrative, you're following a series of events, so you need to know not only what a paragraph is *about,* but what is happening in it. You have been finding this information by asking: What is the main thing or person that this section is about? Why is that thing or person important?

In a descriptive passage, though, a writer often describes a place or object one part or *aspect* at a time. "Aspect" refers to some specific characteristic or quality of the object that's not actually physical; so, for example, if a description of a fort began by discussing the fort's walls, that would be a *part* of the fort; if the description began by describing the *need* for the fort, or the importance of the fort, that would be an *aspect.*

Often you can find the central topic in a section of scientific description by asking: What aspect or part of the whole does this section describe?

Let's try this for the first paragraph of your description. First, experiment with the original method: What is the most important thing in this paragraph?

The answer's obvious: *a comet.*

Why is that thing important?

This doesn't turn out to be a very useful question, because there are a number of important things listed (orbits, heads and tails, names) and they all seem to have equal importance in the passage. Instead, ask yourself: What aspect or part of the whole does this section describe?

Think about this for a moment before looking at the next line.

The whole thing.

This paragraph tells you what a comet *is* by giving an overall description of the parts of a comet, where a comet comes from, and how a comet gets its name. If you were going to give this paragraph a title, it might be "Introduction to comets" or "All about comets." Often, a scientific description will start with an introductory paragraph that gives a basic definition and overview of the object (or phenomenon) under study.

So your first point might look like this:

I. *Definition of comets*

or

I. *What a comet is*

Now look at the second paragraph. Once again, asking "What's the most important thing in this passage?" would probably give you the answer "Comets." But which of the discoveries about comets listed in this paragraph would qualify as the *most important one?* Instead, ask yourself: What part or aspect of the comet does this paragraph describe? No specific parts are mentioned—but how about *aspect?* What is happening in this paragraph, all centered around the comet?

Or, to put this another way, what did Tycho Brahe, Isaac Newton, Edmond Halley, and Wilhelm Olbers all do?

✦

They all studied comets. So your second point might look like this:

II. *The study of comets*

or

II. *How the study of comets developed*

Now go through the rest of the paragraphs, asking yourself: What part or aspect of the comet does this section describe?

If you have difficulty, ask your instructor for help. When you're finished, check your work with your instructor.

HOW TO HELP THE STUDENT WITH STEP TWO

In this assignment, the student has been encouraged to consider what *part* (physical element) or *aspect* (nonphysical quality) is the main topic of each section.

Suggested answers (the student's answers should resemble the following but don't need to be identical):

I. Definition of a comet or What comets are
II. The study of comets or How the study of comets developed
III. The three parts of a comet or The structure of a comet
IV. Nucleus
V. Head, or coma
VI. Tail
VII. Number of comets or How many comets there are

If the student struggles with this assignment, use the following dialogues:

Paragraph 3
Instructor: Like the first paragraph, this one gives a kind of overview. What is the overview *of?*

Student: A comet

Instructor: But what about the comet? Its size? Where it is in the solar system? Its structure? The chemicals that make it up?

Student: Its structure

Paragraphs 4, 5, and 6
Instructor: Which of the three parts of the comet does this paragraph focus on?

Paragraph 7
Instructor: What aspect of the comet is explored in this section? Hint: what do 10 million, 20,000 to 60,000, and 100 billion all have in common?

Student: They are numbers.

Instructor: That is the aspect—the number of the comets, or how many there are.

Day Three: Analyzing the Topos

Focus: Understanding the form of a scientific description of an object or phenomenon

The passage the student outlined in the last writing session is an example of this week's topos: **a scientific description of an object or phenomenon** (a thing that can be seen). Today's assignment is to understand the elements that go into a good scientific description.

In today's assignment, the student will work independently; the student's directions are reproduced below for your reference.

STEP ONE: **Examine model passages**

Look back at your outline. Although your exact wording won't be the same, your outline probably resembles this one:

I. What comets are
II. How the study of comets developed
III. The structure of a comet
IV. Nucleus
V. Head, or *coma*
VI. Tail
VII. Number of comets

Now look at the pattern this writer has followed:

I. What comets are	Brief definition
II. How the study of comets developed	History of discovery
III. The structure of a comet	Description of physical parts
IV. Nucleus	
V. Head, or coma	
VI. Tail	
VII. Number of comets	Amplitude (this is a general word for measures of size, height, width, quantity)

Sections III–VI make up the scientific description of the comet. Like a description of a place, a scientific description is often part of a longer composition; in this piece, the scientific description is part of a longer encyclopedia entry.

Here's another scientific description, this one from Bill Bryson's *A Short History of Nearly Everything.*

You should see a similarity between this passage and the description of comets in the first section. Both descriptions are *structural:* They describe the different parts that make up the whole.

The description of the comet tells us about the nucleus, the head (or *coma*), and the tail; all three of those things together make up a comet. Look at the two paragraphs about the cell.

In the first paragraph, Bryson describes three parts that make up a cell. What are those parts? Go back and underline them.

In the second paragraph, Bryson mentions one more element that goes into the structure of a cell (and helps support it). What is it? Underline it now.

What did you underline?

In the first paragraph, you should have underlined outer casing or membrane, nucleus, and cytoplasm. In the second paragraph, you should have underlined cytoskeleton. These are the different parts that make up a cell.

When you write a scientific description, you can begin by describing each of the separate parts that make up the whole. Now look again at these sentences from this week's descriptions:

A comet's nucleus is made of dust particles loosely compacted with water ice, together with frozen carbon monoxide and methane.

If a comet becomes very active, the solar wind carries away dust and gas to form its tail.

The membrane is not, as most of us imagine it, a durable, rubbery casing, something that you would need a sharp pin to prick. Rather, it is made up of a type of fatty material known as a lipid . . .

Each one of these sentences describes the nucleus, the tail, and the membrane by telling you *what it is made of.*

STEP TWO: Understand the use of figurative language

When you write a scientific description, you can describe the parts of an object and tell what each part is made of—and still not give the reader a clear picture of it. Read the following sentences:

Galaxies are made up of collections of stars, dust, nebulae, and other cosmic materials. Each one has a nucleus. The nucleus is a bulge consisting of very tightly packed groups of stars. Some galaxies have spiral arms; others are elliptical or irregular in shape.

The sentences tell you about the different parts of a galaxy, but they don't create a clear picture in your head. Compare those sentences with this paragraph, which begins by describing spiral galaxies like our Milky Way:

At the center of the nucleus of our galaxy . . . is an enormous black hole—perhaps one million times the size of the sun. Moving outward, we come to the "spiral arms". . . . Stars form in the spiral arms from clouds of dust and interstellar gas, and the entire galaxy rotates in space like a giant pinwheel. . . . Not all galaxies are like the Milky Way, however. Some are elliptical in shape, like giant footballs floating in space. Others are small, irregular things, like the dough left on a cookie tray after all the cookies have been cut.[26]

There are three useful similies in that paragraph. (Remember, a simile is figurative language that uses "like" or "as" to draw a comparison between two things.) Underline them now.

Did you underline the following?

like a giant pinwheel

26. James Trefil, ed., *Encyclopedia of Science and Technology* (Routledge, 2001), p. 211.

<u>like giant footballs floating in space</u>
<u>like the dough left on a cookie sheet</u>

All of these similes allow you to picture the appearance of the galaxies described.

Bill Bryson also uses figurative language in his description of a cell. He could just write "Proteins, chemicals, and other agents move around through the cell." Instead, he imagines what the cell would look like if you could stand in it:

Blown up to a scale at which atoms were about the size of peas, a cell itself would be a sphere roughly half a mile across, and supported by a complex framework of girders called the cytoskeleton. Within it, millions upon millions of objects—some the size of basketballs, others the size of cars—would whiz about like bullets.

When you are writing a scientific description, you are often trying to give a picture of something that's outside of regular everyday experience. It's not easy to fully understand the structure of a galaxy, or a comet, or a cell if you've never actually *seen* one. Figurative language keeps scientific descriptions from being abstract and technical by giving the reader a vivid, simple picture.

STEP THREE: **Write down the pattern of the topos**

Copy the following onto a blank sheet of paper in the Reference section of your Composition Notebook. You will be adding to this page as you learn more about scientific descriptions, so leave plenty of room.

Scientific Description

Definition: A visual and structural description of an object or phenomenon

Procedure	Remember
1. Describe each part of the object or phenomenon and tell what it is made from.	1. Consider using figurative language to make the description more visual.

Day Four: Practicing the Topos

Focus: Learning how to write a scientific description of an object or phenomenon

Today, the student's assignment is to write a scientific description following the pattern of this week's topos.

STEP ONE: **Plan the description**

Student instructions for Step One:

Look carefully at the labelled diagram of the parts of the volcano. Then read the excerpts that follow. Your assignment is to write a description of a volcano that describes each important part of the volcano's structure by explaining what it is made of and what it looks like. This description should be at least 200 words but not more than 400.

You should not try to include details about every part of the volcano. As you read through the excerpts, decide which parts of the volcano your description will include, and which you will leave out. Cross lightly through the parts that you will not use in your description.

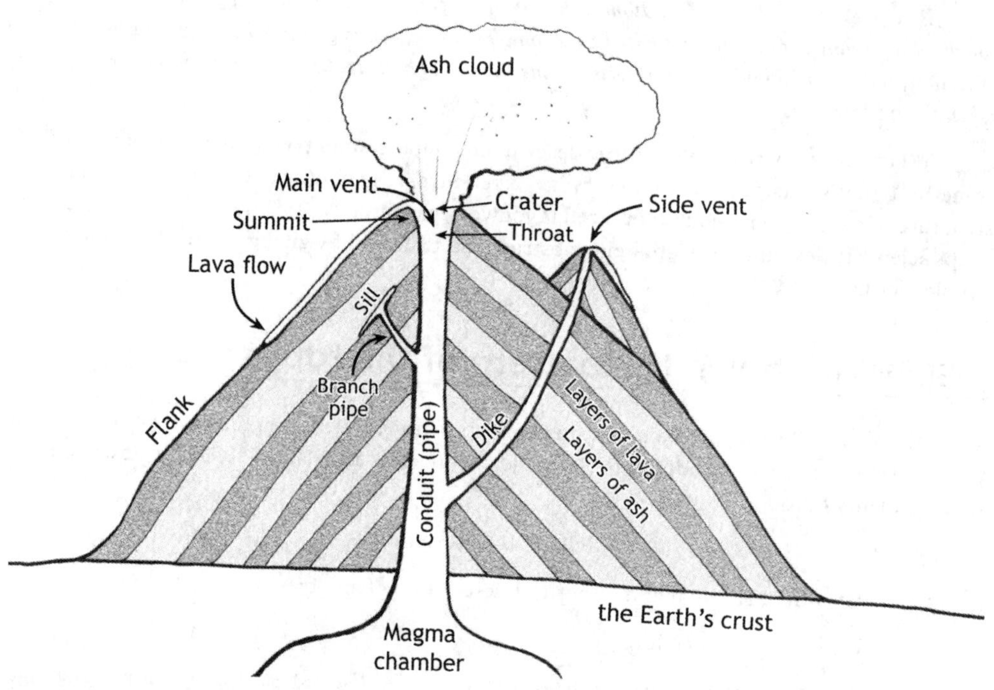

HOW TO HELP THE STUDENT WITH STEP ONE

The student should be able to complete this step without assistance. If he feels that he doesn't have enough detail to write his description, or if he wants to add to the information given, he may do additional reading in his science texts or online.

STEP TWO: **Choose a metaphor or simile**

Student instructions for Step Two:

> As you write your description, you should include at least one metaphor or simile.
> Jot down at least one metaphor or simile that could help describe each of the following:
> The ash cloud
> The layers inside the volcano
> The magma chamber and main conduit
> If you have difficulty, ask your instructor for help.

HOW TO HELP THE STUDENT WITH STEP TWO

If the student has difficulty coming up with figurative language, suggest he focus on the following:

1. The shape of the ash cloud: it is round, puffy, billowing
   Possible similes: like balloons or something else inflated, featherbeds
   The thickness of the ash cloud: it is dark, opaque, threatening
   Possible similes: like weather (night, thunderhead, rain cloud)
2. The appearance of layers inside the volcano
   Possible similes: baked goods (layer cake, baklava)
3. The shape of magma chamber and main conduit
   Possible simile: bulb (flower, light) and stem
   water balloon and straw, well and water pipes

STEP THREE: **Write the description**

Student instructions for Step Three:

> Here's a summary of your assignment:
> 1. This description can be one paragraph or several paragraphs, but it must be at least 200 and not more than 400 words.
> 2. You may choose which parts of the volcano to include in your description.
> 3. As part of your description, explain what the selected parts are made from.
> 4. Use at least one metaphor or simile in your description.
> If you have difficulty, ask your instructor for help. And when you're finished, show your composition to your instructor.

HOW TO HELP THE STUDENT WITH STEP THREE

This should be a fairly straightforward writing assignment. If the student is completely blocked, you may allow him to read the classic definition below, but do not allow him to look at it as he writes.

> A volcano is usually in the form of a cone, at the summit of which is a circular basin or depression called a crater. From the mouth of this crater there is a perpendicular shaft leading to the interior of the earth, and from this passage issue the products of the volcano; steam, gases, ashes, fragments of heated rock, and sometimes streams of melted rock called lava.
>
> These materials form themselves into a series of layers around the mouth of the crater, and it is to these layers that the conical form of the volcano is due. The more liquid the ejected materials, the broader and flatter are the cones.
>
> Ashes from volcanoes, when examined, show no resemblance to real ashes, but are found to be simply pulverized lava. These ashes sometimes form a powder and

are carried by the winds for hundreds of miles. At times, huge fragments of rock are thrown out with great violence. It is said that during an eruption of Cotopaxi, in Ecuador, a mass of several tons weight was hurled a distance of seven miles.

A stream of white hot lava flowing from a crater bears a great resemblance to molten iron escaping from a furnace. The surface of the lava soon forms into a crust, but the interior remains in the melted state and continues to flow. It is said if the stream is thick, the molten lava will remain warm for ten or even twenty years.

—J. L. Wellington, *Popular Science News,* Vol. 36
(Science News Co., 1902), p. 133

When the student is finished, check his work using the following rubric:

Week 12 Rubric
Scientific Description

Organization

1 The description should include at least three or four major parts of the volcano.
2 The description should explain what each part of the volcano is made from.
3 At least one metaphor or simile should be used.
4 The description should be at least 200 words long but no longer than 400 words.

Mechanics

1 Each sentence should make sense on its own when read aloud.
2 Verbs should have consistent tense (all past or all present).
3 Possessive forms should be written properly.
4 Subjects and verbs should be in agreement.

Week 13: Scientific Description

Day One: Original Narration Exercise

Focus: Summarizing a narrative with several parts

STEP ONE: **Read (Student Responsibility)**

Student instructions for Step One:

Read the following complete folktale, "Why the Sea Is Salt." This tale is a pourquoi story—a genre (type) of story that tells why something in nature is as it is. "Pourquoi" is pronounced *puh-quaa*, with the accent on the second syllable, and means "why" in French. You may be familiar with the *Just So Stories* by Rudyard Kipling; these are also pourquoi stories.

STEP TWO: **Find the different stories in the narrative**

Student instructions for Step Two:

You will now summarize the passage in five or six sentences, and write those sentences down on your own paper.

Last week, your narrative had two different stories told by two different people—one told by a character within the story (Dr. Mortimer), and the other told by the writer himself, Arthur Conan Doyle, *about* Dr. Mortimer, Sherlock Holmes, and Dr. Watson. This week, your narrative only has one point of view and one narrator—but there is still more than one story in it. Each story has many different details, so whittling the summary down to the most central events will be a challenge.

There are actually three different narrative strands, or stories, in this tale. Try to locate them now. Jot down the major characters in each narrative strand. Use these two hints:

Hint #1: The same major character occurs in the first two stories, but not in the third.

Hint #2: The second story in the narrative occurs in the *middle* of the first story (or, to put it another way, the first story begins, the second story begins and finishes, and then the first story ends).

Don't hestitate to ask your instructor for help. Show your instructor your answers before continuing on.

HOW TO HELP THE STUDENT WITH STEP TWO

Although this story seems simple, almost elementary, summarizing it can be difficult because of the number of events that take place within it. The student will need to identify the three separate narrative strands in the story in order to find the most central events *only*—otherwise she will probably come up with a laundry list of 20–25 events. This exercise also continues to familiarize the student with the presence of multiple stories/points of view within a single piece of writing.

The student should come up with the follow major characters for each narrative strand:

#1: The poor man and his brother/wife/friends
Story: Poor man gets the mill and amazes everyone with his new wealth
#2. The poor man, the woodchopper, and the dwarves
Story: Poor man goes to land of dwarves and gets mill
#3: The merchant
Story: Merchant steals mill and sinks it to the bottom of the sea

If she has difficulty, ask the following questions:
You meet the first two characters in the first story in the very first paragraph.
Who are they? *(The rich brother and the poor brother)*
What is the problem between them? *(The poor brother needs food. The rich brother doesn't want to give it to him.)*
Once the poor brother returns home with the mill, how is the problem solved? *(The mill gives him food and other things that he needs.)*

The second story comes between the problem in the first story and its resolution. In the second story, who does the poor brother meet? *(The woodchopper)*
What group of characters does he then encounter? *(The dwarves)*
In the third story, there's really only one major character—and he isn't the brother. Who is he? *(The merchant)*

STEP THREE: **Note the main events in each story**

Student instructions for Step Three:

> Now that you've found the three stories in the narrative, write down *only the two central events* in each story. If you cannot find them, ask your instructor for help.

HOW TO HELP THE STUDENT WITH STEP THREE

The student's main events should resemble the following:

Story #1: Poor brother needed food from rich brother.
Poor brother returned home with mill that made him rich.
Story #2: Poor man met a woodchopper who sent him to the land of dwarves.

Poor man bargained for magic mill in land of dwarves.
Story #3: Merchant stole the mill and didn't know how to turn it off.
Mill sank to the bottom of the sea and kept grinding salt.

The student may have difficulty eliminating other, less central, details and events. If necessary, ask her the following questions. Tell her she must answer each question with only one sentence.

Story #1
What happened between the poor brother and rich brother at the beginning of the story?
What did the mill do that changed the relationship between the two brothers?
Story #2
How did the poor man know to go to the land of the dwarves?
What did he get there?
Story #3
In the third story, what two things happened to the mill?

STEP FOUR: **Write summary sentences**

Student instructions for Step Four:

> Use your notes to write a summary with no more than six sentences. You may put each main event into its own sentence, but you may also combine two events into a single longer sentence.
>
> Remember that you will need to place the two events in the second story *between* the first and second events in the first story!
>
> When you are finished, show your work to your instructor.

HOW TO HELP THE STUDENT WITH STEP FOUR

The student's final summary should resemble the following (these are only examples):

A poor man had so little food that he went to beg food from his older brother. When he was returning home, he met a woodchopper who sent him to the land of the dwarves. He got a magic mill from the dwarves, and the mill gave him food, clothing, and wealth. Finally a merchant stole the mill to grind salt. The mill sank to the bottom of the sea and is still grinding out salt.

OR

There were once two brothers, one poor and one rich. The poor brother was returning home from his brother's house when he met a magic woodchopper. The woodchopper sent him to the land of the dwarves, where he got a magic mill. The magic mill made him wealthy. Later, a merchant stole the magic mill and took it to sea to grind salt. The mill ground so much salt that it sank the merchant's ship.

You may need to point out to the student that the "pourquoi" part of the story ("That is why the sea is salt") isn't an actual *event* and doesn't belong in the summary of events.

Use the following rubric to check the student's work.

Week 13 Rubric
Summary of Narrative Fiction

Organization

1 Events should be in chronological order; the two events in the first story should occur before and after the events in the second story.
2 The summary must mention the poor brother, the rich brother, the dwarves, and the merchant; other characters may or may not be present.
3 If two or more events are listed in a single sentence, they should have a cause and effect relationship.
4 The summary should not be longer than six sentences.

Mechanics

1 Each sentence should make sense on its own when read aloud.
2 Each proper name should be capitalized.
3 Personal pronouns should have clear antecedents and be of the proper gender.
4 Verb tense should be consistent throughout.
5 Subjects and verbs must be in agreement.

Day Two: Outlining Exercise

Focus: Finding the central topic in each paragraph of a scientific description combined with a chronological narrative

STEP ONE: **Read (Student responsibility)**

Student instructions for Step One:

> Read the following excerpt from *The Greely Arctic Expedition: As Fully Narrated by Lieut. Greely, U.S.A., and Other Survivors.* This passage comes from Greely's account of his disastrous 1881 expedition to the Arctic, which ended with 19 of his 25-man crew dead. The account was first published in 1884.

When the writer uses the word "fantasia" in the fourth paragraph, he means that the crashing of the ice sounds unreal, fantastic, strange.

In the fifth paragraph, Point Barrow is a headland (a piece of land surrounded by water on three sides) on the northern coast of what is now Alaska. It is the northernmost point in the United States. Many Arctic expeditions used Point Barrow as a starting point for their journeys toward the North Pole. Point Barrow is blocked by ice for as much as nine months of the year.

There is also some technical language in the fifth paragraph. To "steam up a long lead" means to follow a particular path through the water under steam power. "Grounded ice" is an ice wall, found in shallow water, which rests on the ground beneath the surface. An "ice cape" or ice cap is a blanket of ice that covers less than 50,000 square kilometers (31,000 square miles) of land (if a blanket of ice covers more than that, it is called an "ice sheet"). A "fathom" is a nautical measurement six feet long (so 15 fathoms is the same as 90 feet).

In the sixth paragraph, "the pack" refers to pack ice or drift ice; this is floating ice which has been blown by the wind into a large single cluster.

STEP TWO: **Construct a one-level outline**

Student instructions for Step Two:

This week's passage, like last week's, is a scientific description of an object or phenomenon. The thing being described is *the Arctic Ocean*, which is both an object and a phenomenon; it is an object filled with ice, but it is also incredibly cold (that is the phenomenon).

You can find the central topic in the first four paragraphs by asking yourself, as you did last week, "What aspect or part of the whole does this paragraph describe?" Remember; a part is a physical element of the whole; an aspect is a characteristic or quality.

In the fifth and sixth paragraphs, the writer illustrates one particular aspect of the Arctic Ocean (its danger) by changing techniques. Instead of continuing with his scientific description, he inserts a brief chronological narrative. When you outline a chronological narrative, you should ask:

1. What is the main thing or person that this section is about? *Or* Is the section about an idea?
2. Why is that thing or person important? *Or* What did that thing or person do/what was done to it? *Or* What is the idea?

Try this for the last two paragraphs in the excerpt.

If you have difficulty, ask your instructor for help. When you're finished, check your work with your instructor.

HOW TO HELP THE STUDENT WITH STEP TWO

The first four paragraphs of this passage are scientific description, while the last two are chronological narrative.

Suggested answers (the student's answers should resemble the following but don't need to be identical):

I. The ice-filled water OR The cold ocean ("The icebergs" is also acceptable)
II. The cold OR What happens in the cold
III. Extreme cold OR What happens in extreme cold

IV. The sound of the sea OR What ice-filled water sounds like
V. The steam whaler North Star *arrives OR The* North Star *arrives at Point Barrrow OR The* North Star *anchors on the ice.*
VI. The ice destroys the North Star *OR The* North Star *is crushed by the ice.*

If the student struggles with this assignment, use the following dialogue:

Paragraph 1
Instructor: Name for me all of the objects which are named in this paragraph. By "objects," I mean actual different *things* that you would see if you were standing there, looking at the scene.

Student: Icebergs, ice-fields, sea-gulls, whale, rocks

Instructor: Where do all of those things live (or exist)?

Student: In the ocean

Instructor: That is the aspect or part of the Arctic Ocean which is being described—the ocean itself. Like the paragraph section in last week's passage about comets, this paragraph gives an overall description—of the ocean.

Paragraph 2
Instructor: In this paragraph, one particular aspect of the Arctic Ocean is being described. What is it?

Student: The cold

Note to Instructor: If the student says "Ice-smoke," point out that the first four sentences all describe the cold, and explain that "ice-smoke" is simply an illustration of just how cold the air is.

Paragraph 3
Instructor: The third paragraph also describes the cold. What is the difference between the cold in this paragraph, and the cold in the paragraph above?

Student: It is colder.

Instructor: How cold? Use an adverb to describe the adjective *cold:* It is *how cold?*

Student: It is extremely *cold* OR *It is* incredibly *cold.*

Instructor: "The extreme cold" (or The incredible cold) is the main topic of this paragraph.
Note to Instructor: If the student says "very cold," explain that "very" is an overused word that doesn't convey any real meaning. Ask the student to come up with another word in its place.

Paragraph 4
Instructor: In this paragraph, what aspect of the cold ocean is being described? Hint: it's not something you can *see*. It is an aspect that's understood with another one of the senses.

Student: How it sounds OR *The sounds*

Paragraph 5

Instructor: In this paragraph, the writer begins to tell you a chronological narrative in order to give you a better picture of just how dangerous the ice-filled sea is. What is the most important thing in this paragraph?

Student: The steam whaler North Star

Instructor: After the *North Star* arrives at Point Barrow, what does she do?

Student: She anchors OR She goes into an inlet.

Paragraph 6

Instructor: What happens to the *North Star* in this paragraph?

Student: The North Star *is destroyed by the ice.*

Instructor: All of the details in this paragraph are about the *North Star*'s destruction; that is definitely the main event.

Day Three: Analyzing the Topos

Focus: Understanding the form of a scientific description of an object or phenomenon

The passage the student outlined in the last writing sesson was a scientific description of an object or phenomenon, combined with a brief chronological narrative. But the student is not quite ready to practice combining the two; first, she'll study another way of putting together a scientific description.

Last week, the student learned that when she writes a scientific description, she can describe each separate part of the object or phenomenon and tell what it is made from; she can also use figurative language to make the description more visual. Today, the student will add another element to that pattern.

STEP ONE: **Understand point of view in scientific description (Student Responsibility)**

Student instructions for Step One:

Look again at this excerpt from *The Greely Arctic Expedition:*

These sentences describe an aspect of the Arctic Ocean—the cold—in a very specific way; they tell the reader how the cold looks, sounds, and feels to an observer.

When you write a scientific description, you can always explain what an object (or phenomenon) is made from. But you should also consider describing exactly how an observer would *see, hear,* or *sense* the object or phenomenon.

Read the following description of an atom, written by physicist Hans Christian Von Baeyer after he has travelled to the National Institute of Standards and Technology in Colorado to see the "atom trap" used by scientist David Wineland to catch and view atoms.

Later in the book, Von Baeyer describes the parts of an atom. But in this passage, he describes how *he,* the observer, *experiences* the atom. He tells us where he was while he was looking at the atom, exactly how it appeared to him, and what his thoughts were as he watched it.

Like place descriptions, scientific descriptions have a point of view. When you studied place descriptions, you learned that a place can be described from four different points of view:

1. From above (impersonal)
2. From inside
3. From one side or angle
4. Moving through or around

A scientific description is a little bit different. When you describe each part of an object or phenomenon and tell what it is made of, you are using a removed point of view. Look again at this paragraph from last week's description of a comet:

Try to picture where the author of this passage might be standing while he describes a comet. Where do you think he is?

If you can't quite figure it out, you're on the right track. The writer isn't standing *anywhere* while he looks at the comet. He's describing it from a removed position—as though he's home, in his study, looking at diagrams, scientific studies, charts, and tables.

This can be a very effective way to describe a scientific object or phenomenon. When you're writing about science, you'll often find yourself describing something you haven't actually seen—like a cell, or an atom. Even if you've seen a comet through a telescope, it was probably indistinct and fuzzy. And although you may have seen a volcanic eruption on television, you probably haven't *been* at one, so you haven't smelled, heard, or felt the effects of an eruption.

But sometimes you'll find it more effective to describe an object or phenomenon as though you are actually present: seeing, hearing, smelling, and feeling what you're describing. Maybe you'll be lucky enough to see the thing you're describing with your own eyes, like Hans Christian Von Baeyer did. If not, you'll have to use the information and photographs you find in books, plus your imagination. The authors of the popular health guide *100 Questions & Answers about Influenza* probably never saw a flu virus with their own eyes, but here's what they wrote:

Even if the writers haven't actually looked at a flu virus through an electron microscope, in this description they are imagining what they would see through the lens. This description is written from the point of view of someone who is present, in the same place as the flu virus, looking at it.

STEP TWO: **Identify point of view in scientific description**

Student instructions for Step Two:

Read the following descriptions, which are taken from the nature books *Trees That Every*

Child Should Know by Julia Ellen Rogers and *The Yosemite* by John Muir. In the margin next to each description, write "Removed" or "Present." Remember, in a "present" point of view, the narrator is describing what he sees as he stands and looks at a particular object. In a "removed" point of view, the narrator tells you what an object is like and what it is made of—but he is writing as if he were home in his study, looking at reference books and charts.

You may have some difficulty with this assignment—it is supposed to be challenging! Don't worry too much about how many you get "right" or "wrong"; you're just trying to develop a deeper understanding of what makes an effective description.

When you're finished, show your work to your instructor. Your instructor will discuss your answers with you.

HOW TO HELP THE STUDENT WITH STEP TWO

The student should identify each paragraph of description as coming from either a "present" or "removed" point of view.

Discuss any incorrect answers with the student, using the information below. Note that there is some room for interpretation in this assignment; if the student can offer a reasonable defense of her choice, you may accept different answers.

"Of all the world's eighty or ninety species of pine tree . . ."
Point of view: Present
Everything described is something that the observer could see if standing next to the tree, looking up at it; in addition, the first-person pronoun in the last line suggests that the narrator is comparing his present view of the tree to other trees he has personally seen.

"First, willows have slender, flexible twigs . . ."
Point of view: Removed
Although there are some visual details in this paragraph, the narrator makes general statements about *all* willows ("nearly always," "always") that she couldn't possibly know by looking at a single tree that is present in her view. In addition, she makes observations about the nature of the wood and what a hypothetical old tree, not in her field of view, might be like.

"The manzanita [shrub] never fails to attract particular attention. . . ."
Point of view: Present
The narrator describes only what he can see by looking at a shrub; in addition, the last sentences ("they look as if they had been peeled") suggests that this is exactly what the narrator is doing—looking.

"The scrawny, grey, digger pines, with cones as big as a man's head. . ."
Point of view: Present
The narrator is travelling along the road, describing each band of trees as she comes to it.

"The white ash is a tall, handsome, stately tree. . ."

Point of view: Removed

There are visual details in this paragraph, but the narrator is describing an abstract tree, not a particular one; if she were looking at one specific tree, who would say that the tree's bark is "often" pale grey—that particular tree would either be pale grey or not. In addition, she describes the tree at different times during the year—spring (when the seeds come out) and late summer.

STEP THREE: **Add to the pattern of the topos (Student Responsibility)**

Student instructions for Step Three:

Turn to the Scientific Description chart in your Composition Notebook. Add the bolded point below under the "Remember" column.

Scientific Description

Definition: A visual and structural description of an object or phenomenon

Procedure	Remember
1. Describe each part of the object or phenomenon and tell what it is made from.	1. Consider using figurative language to make the description more visual.
2. Choose a point of view.	

Day Four: Practicing the Topos

Focus: Learning how to write a scientific description of an object or phenomenon

STEP ONE: **Review point of view (Student Responsibility)**

Student instructions for Step One:

Last week, you read this description of a pyroclastic flow from the reference book *Volcanoes* by Robert Wayne Decker and Barbara Decker:

Compare this to the following description of a pyroclastic flow, written by the Roman lawyer Pliny the Younger after he lived through the eruption of Mount Vesuvius in the year 79.

The first description is written from the removed point of view, the second from the present point of view. The removed point of view tells you about the makeup, behavior, and qualities of a pyroclastic flow. The present point of view tells you what a pyroclastic flow looks and feels like.

(You may notice that the second description is organized almost like a chronological narrative. The forms of a description and a chronological narrative can overlap, but we will study this a little later. For now, just pay attention to the difference betwen a removed and a present point of view.)

STEP TWO: **Understand the aspects of a present point of view**

Student instructions for Step Two:

A description written from the present point of view tells the reader what the narrator is seeing, hearing, feeling, smelling, and even tasting. When you write a description from the present point of view, you should think of each one of these senses: sight, sound, touch, smell, and taste. A description written from the present point of view won't include all of them—but it will include at least two or three.

Read the following sentences from present point-of-view descriptions of a forest fire. Write in the margin which of the five senses (sight, smell, taste, feeling, hearing) is being used. More than one sense may be used in the same sentence.

After you've written the answers, check them with your instructor.

HOW TO HELP THE STUDENT WITH STEP TWO

The student should identify each descriptive sentence as using one of the five senses. Discuss any incorrect answers with the student, using the information below.

"When the back fire . . ."
Sense: Hearing
"Roar" tells you that the fire and flame made a sound. Sight is also used in this sentence, since the narrator can see just how high up the eruption of smoke and flame goes.

"As we scrambled after the crown fire . . ."
Sense: Taste
"Tang" is a taste sensation; also, only tastes are sensed "between" the teeth.

"The fire was rushing through the trees . . ."
Sense: Sight
Everything in this sentence is seen only.

"The acrid stink of burning logs lingered . . ."
Sense: Smell
"Stink" is a scent word. Sight is also used in this sentence, since the narrator can see that the ground is black.

"The ground still radiated heat . . ."

Sense: Touch

Only touch can register the presence of heat. Sight is also used in this sentence, since the narrator can see that the fire has disappeared.

STEP THREE: **Write the description**

Student instructions for Step Three:

> Your last assignment for this week is to rewrite last week's description so that it comes from a present, rather than a removed, point of view.
>
> Pull out last week's description now. Look at each part of the volcano described. For each one, ask yourself: If I were standing right there, looking at the volcano itself, what would this part look, sound, smell, feel, and taste like? Then rewrite your description as though you were standing next to the volcano, using all five senses.
>
> This description can be one paragraph or several paragraphs, but it must be at least 150 and not more than 300 words. You do not need to use all of the senses in your description, but you must use at least three of the five.
>
> For your reference, the senses are:
>
> sight
> smell
> taste
> touch
> sound
>
> If you have difficulty, ask your instructor for help. And when you're finished, show your composition to your instructor.

HOW TO HELP THE STUDENT WITH STEP THREE

The final form of the student's present point-of-view description will depend on the form of last week's description. However, you can help the student if she appears to be stalled by making the following suggestions.

Sight. Both the lava and the ash are spectacular—literally, amazing to look at. The student should think in terms of light and dark. Lava can be described as bright, gleaming, glowing, burning, flaring, kindling, crimson, white-hot, red-hot, radiant, incandescent; ash can be described as dark, sooty, leaden, livid, gloomy, murky, black, pitch-dark, starless, dusky.

Smell. Observers of volcanoes have used the following adjectives to describe the smell of ash and lava: acrid, bitter, biting, burning, harsh, sulfuric, metallic, caustic, stinging, thick, sharp, irritating.

Taste: Suggest that the student take in a deep breath through her mouth, and then think about what she might taste in the air. Taste and smell are closely related; the adjectives used for smells above can also describe taste.

Touch: The student should concentrate on heat: the ground and air may be blistering, boiling, burning, fiery, flaming, roasting, scalding, scorching, searing, sizzling, smoking, sweltering, baking, too hot to touch, painfully hot.

Sound: Both the eruption of lava and the pyroclastic flow are *loud:* roaring, blasting, booming, crashing, rumbling, thundering, booming, detonating, shattering; a din, roar, smash, explosion, crash, eruption, outbreak, rumble.

If the student is stalled, you may allow her to read the following descriptions. (Allow her to read them after her work is finished, even if she doesn't need the inspiration as she writes.)

Instead of exploding straight up through the summit, the pent-up pressure blasted through the north side of the mountain, sending a blizzard of rock, ash, and chunks of glacial ice northward with a velocity that approached the speed of sound. A black cloud poured out of the mountain, hugging the ground as it rolled over ridges and churned down valleys. the lateral blast pulverized, incinerated, or blew away virtually everything in a fan-shaped swath of destruction that extended as far as 17 miles from the crater. The noise of the explosion was heard as far away as Saskatchewan, and shock waves were clearly felt throughout the Puget Sound area, where many people described the impacts as "whumps." Windows rattled 100 miles away. Dishes fell from shelves; cracks opened in masonry walls. A vertical plume rose 16 miles into the atmosphere and continued unabated for nine hours.[27]

I felt a thunder, the trees trembled, and I turned to speak to Paula; and it was then I saw how, in the hole, the ground swelled and raised itself two or 2.5 meters high, and a kind of smoke or fine dust—gray, like ashes—began to rise up in a portion of the crack that I had not previously seen near the [hole]. Immediately more smoke began to rise, with a hiss or whistle, loud and continuous; and there was a smell of sulfur.[28]

. . . . [T]he sides of the volcano opened out with a terrible explosion. A wall of fire swept over the town and the bay. . . . Hearing the awful report of the explosion and seeing the great wall of flames approaching the steamer, those on deck sought shelter wherever it was possible. . . . I was in the chart room, but the burning embers were borne by so swift a movement of the air that they were swept in through the door and port holes, suffocating and scorching me badly. I was terribly burned by these embers about the face and hands, but managed to reach the deck . . . the atmosphere being charged with ashes, it was totally dark. The sun was completely obscured, and the air was only illuminated by the flames from the volcano and those of the burning town and shipping.[29]

---

27. Rob Carson, *Mount St. Helens: The Eruption and Recovery of a Volcano* (Seattle: Wash.: Sasquatch Books, 1990), p. 39.

28. John P. Lockwood and Richard W. Hazlett, *Volcanoes: Global Perspectives* (New York: John Wiley and Sons, 2010), pp. 295–296.

29. Alexander E. Gates and David Ritchie, *Encyclopedia of Earthquakes and Volcanoes* (New York: Checkmark Books, 2001), p. 309.

When the student is finished, check her work using the following rubric

Week 13 Rubric
Scientific Description

Organization

1 The description should explain what the eruption looks like from the perspective of at least three of the five senses: sight, sound, smell, taste, touch.
2 The description should be at least 150 words and no longer than 300 words.

Mechanics

1 Each sentence should make sense on its own when read aloud.
2 Each proper name should be capitalized.
3 Personal pronouns should have clear antecedents and be of the proper gender.
4 Verb tense should be consistent throughout.
5 Subjects and verbs must be in agreement.
6 Adjectives and adverbs should refer to heat, sound, light, and dark.

Week 14: Scientific Description

Day One: Original Narration Exercise

Focus: Summarizing a narrative by choosing the central events and details

STEP ONE: **Read (Student Responsibility)**

Student instructions for Step One:

Read the following excerpt from the first chapter of *The Adventures of Baron Munchausen*. *The Adventures of Baron Munchausen* is a collection of tall tales about a real man, Karl Friedrich Hieronymous, Baron Munchausen. He was born in Germany in 1720 and, after joining the Russian army in 1739, rose to the rank of captain. Munchausen died in 1797.

Baron Munchausen was well known for telling exciting stories about his adventures. Between 1781 and 1783, a series of stories about Baron Munchausen's exploits appeared, anonymously, in the German magazine *Vademecum für lustige Leute*. However, although some of the adventures described were based on Munchausen's own stories, others were actually drawn from folktales told about other German heroes long before Munchausen was even born.

Although no one knows for sure, the anonymous writer may have been the German writer and scientist Rudolf Erich Raspe, who was a friend of Munchausen's but had moved from Germany to England in 1775. In 1785, Raspe published an English version of the *Adventures of Baron Munchausen* in which he expanded and added to many of the tales—over Munchausen's strong objections. A year later, Raspe's friend Gottfried August Burger borrowed Raspe's book, with his approval, and translated the stories back into German—adding yet more fantastic detail as he did so.

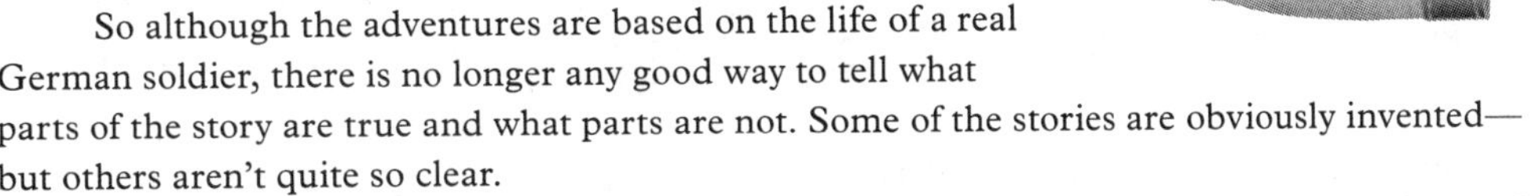

So although the adventures are based on the life of a real German soldier, there is no longer any good way to tell what parts of the story are true and what parts are not. Some of the stories are obviously invented—but others aren't quite so clear.

Your excerpt is taken from the 1902 English translation of Burger's adaptation of Raspe's translation of the anonymous 1781 stories! It includes the following preface. No one knows *who* wrote this preface.

STEP TWO: **Find the different stories in the narrative**

Student instructions for Step Two:

> You will now summarize the story in three or four sentences, and write those sentences down on your own paper.
>
> Like last week's narrative, this passage has more than one story in it. Try to locate them now. Use the following hint: what are the unlikeliest events in the passage? Each one marks the center of a different story.
>
> Once you've found the different stories, draw lines through the passage above to separate the stories. When you've finished, show your work to your instructor.
>
> If you have difficulty, ask your instructor for help.

HOW TO HELP THE STUDENT WITH STEP TWO

This passage has two stories in it: the story of Munchausen's journey to Ceylon, and the story of his encounter with the tiger and crocodile. All other details are contained within one of these two frames.

To separate the two stories, the student should have drawn a line in the following place:

> After we had repaired the damages we sustained in this remarkable storm, and taken leave of the new governor and his lady, we sailed with a fair wind for the object of our voyage.

> In about six weeks we arrived at Ceylon, where we were received with great marks of friendship and true politeness. The following singular adventures may not prove unentertaining.
>
> After we had resided at Ceylon about a fortnight I accompanied one of the governor's brothers upon a shooting party. He was a strong, athletic man, and being used to that climate (for he had resided there some years), he bore the violent heat of the sun much better than I could. In our excursion he had made a considerable progress through a thick wood when I was only at the entrance.

The student has not been told how many stories are in the passage. If he has difficulty finding the correct place to divide the passage, ask him the following questions:

What unlikely event happens first in the story? *(A storm roots up enormous trees and they float through the sky.)*

What is Baron Munchausen doing when this happens? *(He is sailing on a ship OR He is on a voyage.)*

What is the second unlikely event in the story? *(The crocodile and lion eat each other.)*

What is Baron Munchausen doing when this happens? *(He is hunting.)*

Then say to the student, "Mark the place where the story of the voyage ends and the story of Baron Munchausen *on* the island begins."

STEP THREE: **Note the main events in each story**

Student instructions for Step Three:

> Now write down only three events from each story. You may *not* write down more than three! If you have difficulty, ask your instructor for help.

HOW TO HELP THE STUDENT WITH STEP THREE

The student's main events should resemble three (for each story) following:

Story #1 (The voyage)
The Baron went on a journey to the island of Ceylon.
A storm tore up enormous trees that floated like feathers.
Enormous trees were ripped up by the wind and then fell back into place.
One of the trees killed the chief of the island.
The storm killed the oppressive chief, and the people chose cucumber-gatherers in his place.
The storm damaged the ship, and the ship had to be repaired.

Story #2 (The hunting trip)
They arrived at Ceylon.
The Baron went on a hunting party in Ceylon.
He saw a lion on one side and a crocodile on the other.
A lion tried to kill him, but jumped into the mouth of a crocodile on the other side.
The Baron cut off the lion's head and killed the crocodile.

The student may have difficulty eliminating other, less central, details and events. If necessary, ask him the following questions. Tell him that he must answer each question with only one sentence.

Story #1 (The voyage)
Where was the Baron going?
What strange thing happened while they were at anchor?
What was the result of this storm?
Story #2 (The hunting trip)
Where did the Baron and the others arrive?
What did the Baron see on his hunting trip?
What happened to them?

STEP FOUR: **Write summary sentences**

Student instructions for Step Four:

> Use your notes to write a summary with no more than six sentences. You may put each main event into its own sentence, but you may also combine two events into a single longer sentence.
>
> When you are finished, show your work to your instructor.

HOW TO HELP THE STUDENT WITH STEP FOUR

The student's final summary should resemble the following (these are only examples):

Baron Munchausen set out on a journey to Ceylon. On the way, he saw a storm so huge that it ripped enormous trees up like feathers and then set them right back down again. The storm damaged the ship, but once it was repaired, the Baron continued on to Ceylon. When he arrived, he went hunting. A lion and crocodile trapped him, but the lion jumped into the crocodile's mouth by accident and the Baron killed them both.

OR

When he was young, Baron Munchausen sailed to Ceylon. On the way, his ship anchored at an island. A terrible storm hurled trees into the air like feathers, and one of them fell on the island's oppressive chief. The voyage continued until the Baron reached Ceylon. He went hunting, but he was trapped when a lion attacked him from one side and a crocodile on the other. He fell on the ground, and the lion jumped into the crocodile's mouth instead.

You may need to point out to the student that the very beginning (the Baron's desire to go travelling) and the very end (the speeches made by the museum curator in Amsterdam) of the story contain no actual *events* and do not belong in the summary.

Use the following rubric to check the student's work.

Week 14 Rubric
Summary of Narrative Fiction

Organization

1 Events should be in chronological order.
2 The summary must mention the two extraordinary events in the passage.
3 The summary should not also cover the first and last paragraphs.
4 If two or more events are listed in a single sentence, they should have a cause and effect relationship.
5 The summary should not be longer than six sentences.

Mechanics

1 Each sentence should make sense on its own when read aloud.
2 Each proper name should be capitalized.
3 Personal pronouns should have clear antecedents and be of the proper gender.
4 Verb tense should be consistent throughout.
5 Subjects and verbs must be in agreement.
6 Any predicate nominatives or adjectives must agree with their subjects in person, number, and gender.

Day Two: Outlining Exercise

Focus: Finding the central topic in each paragraph of a scientific description

STEP ONE: Read (Student Responsibility)

Student instructions for Step One:

Read the following excerpt from Anna Botsford Comstock's classic guide to observing and understanding nature, *Handbook of Nature Study.*

STEP TWO: Construct a one-level outline

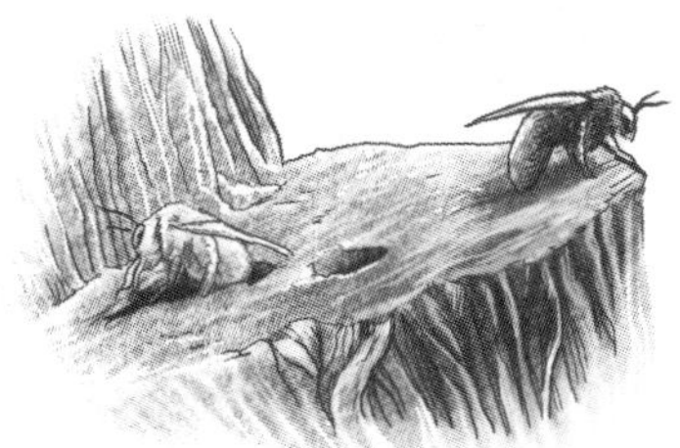

Student instructions for Step Two:

This week's passage is yet another example of scientific description. For each section, decide whether it would be more productive to ask yourself "What aspect or part of the whole does this section describe?" or "What is the main thing that this section is about? Why is that thing important?"

If you have difficulty, ask your instructor for help. When you're finished, check your work with your instructor.

HOW TO HELP THE STUDENT WITH STEP TWO

Although these sections are filled with detail, each has a fairly simple main theme. The student has been given the task of deciding whether it would be more productive to ask the simple question "What aspect or part of the whole does this section describe?" or whether it would be better to ask the two-part "What is the main thing that this section is about? Why is that thing important?"

If necessary, you may help the student by pointing out that while the first section is completely descriptive, the second, third, and fourth sections contain *actions.* Whenever an action is involved, the two-part question should be asked.

Suggested answers (the student's answers should resemble the following but don't need to be identical):

I. Insect apartment house OR Inside an insect apartment house
II. The carpenter bee builds an insect apartment house OR The carpenter bee makes her home.
III. The grubs hatch OR The grubs struggle to get out.
IV. The bees emerge.

If the student struggles with this assignment, use the following dialogue:

Section 1
Instructor: What is inside the dead twigs?

Student: An insect apartment house

Note to Instructor: If the student says "A tunnel," say "What is the tunnel?"
Instructor: The rest of the section tells us how to find out something more about the insect apartment house. What question about the insect apartment house does the rest of the section try to answer?

Student: Who made it?

Instructor: The information about who made it gives futher detail about the insect apartment house. The main topic of the paragraph still remains: the insect apartment house itself.

Section 2
Instructor: There is a very clear main character in this section. Who is it?

Student: The carpenter bee

Instructor: Tell me in one sentence what the carpenter bee is doing. All of the little details in the section give more information about this one central activity.

Student: Building her house

Section 3
Instructor: Who are the main characters in this section? Hint: they are all the same kind of thing.

Student: The grubs

Instructor: What are they doing, one at a time?

Student: Hatching or *Trying to get out*

Section 4
Instructor: What do all the bees do in the final section?

Student: They escape.

Day Three: Analyzing the Topos

Focus: Understanding the form of a scientific description of an object or phenomenon

The scientific description that the student outlined last week mixed together the removed and present point of view. Today, the student will study mixing points of view.

STEP ONE: **Understand combined points of view in scientific description (Student Responsibility)**

Student instructions for Step One:

Look again at the first paragraph of the description from *The Handbook of Nature Study.* It begins with the personal point of view, as though you and the narrator were both standing together, looking at the twig containing the "apartment house":

Take a dozen dead twigs from almost any sumac or elder, split them lengthwise, and you will find in at least one or two of them a little tunnel down the center where there was once pith.

However, as it continues, the writer shifts to a removed point of view, telling us about the parts of the "apartment house" and what each part is made of:

[I]f it is made of tiny chips, like fine sawdust glued together, a bee made it and there are little bees in the cells; if it is made of bits of sand or mud glued together, a wasp was the architect and young wasps are the inhabitants.

If you're writing a description of a place, it is usually a good idea to keep a consistent point of view; the reader can easily understand what it might be like to look down on a pyramid from above, or at an Incan city from the side, and it can be very disorienting if the viewpoint suddenly shifts. (Not always; as you become a more skilled writer, you may find that you need to suddenly change your point of view as you describe a place. But for now, "don't change point of view" is a good rule to follow.)

When you're writing a scientific description, though, you're often attempting to give a clear picture of something that that the reader has never seen—and in many cases, will *never* see. (How many of us will get to see an atom? A magma chamber? The inside of a cell?) Describing the parts of an atom, or a cell, will give the reader an idea of what the object is like, but not necessarily a clear and *vivid* idea.

Compare these two descriptions of a cell. The first is an impersonal, removed description, from the popular science book *How We Live and Why We Die: The Secret Lives of Cells* by Lewis Wolpert; the second is Bill Bryson's description of a cell, which you read back in Week 12.

Even though Bill Bryson isn't actually looking at a cell, he uses his imagination. After he uses the removed point of view to describe the parts of the cell and what they're made of, he thinks about what a cell might look like if it were large enough for someone to stand inside. Then he finishes his description from the personal point of view.

Lewis Wolpert's description of a cell is clear and useful. But Bryson's is more vivid, more gripping, and more likely to keep the reader's attention.

STEP TWO: Identify combined points of view

Student instructions for Step Two:

In the following descriptions, underline the sentences which come from a personal point of view.

HOW TO HELP THE STUDENT WITH STEP TWO

The underlined sentences in the descriptions below come from the personal point of view. Explanations follow each description; if necessary, use these explanations to help the student.

There are mountains and volcanoes on Venus, and evidence of plate tectonics that have shifted vast sections of the crust. There must be Venus-quakes, as well. <u>Imagine trying to walk on the surface of Venus! The very ground is red-hot. The atmosphere is so thick that it warps light like a fisheye lens. The sky is perpetually clouded. Yet there is no real darkness: even during the long Venusian night there is an eerie, sullen glow from the red-hot ground.</u>[30]

The first two sentences describe aspects of Venus that could not be seen by an observer; the description then changes to describe only what someone walking on the surface of Venus could see.

The red cells [carry oxygen] for about one hundred eighty days, then they die. The white blood cells roam around looking for intruders, like bacteria and viruses, to

---

30. Ben Bova, *Venus* (Tor, 2000), p. 11.

> attack and kill. There are also platelets . . . sticky plugs that often take on amorphous shapes and are reformed every seven days. Imagine that you've just been created in bone marrow. But instead of being limited to being a red cell, white cell, or platelet, you belong to an elite cadre of cells, unique and gifted, because you have the power to become any cell you desire. . . . You're called a "pluripotential-stem" cell. Most of your life is spent bathed in blood in the marrow. But every once in a while you may slip away into freely circulating blood and travel through the body.[31]

The first three sentences explain the functions of the cell. Beginning with the fourth sentence, the reader is asked to imagine herself *inside* the bone marrow with the other cells.

> . . . . Jupiter is a liquid world that has no surface. The gaseous atmosphere blends gradually with the liquid hydrogen interior. Below the clouds of Jupiter lies the largest ocean of the solar system—and it has no surface and no waves. When you look at Jupiter, all you see are clouds. These cloud layers lie deep inside a nearly transparent atmosphere of hydrogen and helium. You can detect this hydrogen atmosphere by noticing that Jupiter has limb darkening. . . . When you look near the limb of Jupiter (the edge of its disk) the clouds are much dimmer . . . because it is nearly sunset or sunrise along the limb. If you were on Jupiter at that location, you would see the sun just above the horizon, and it would be dimmed by the atmosphere. In addition, light reflected from clouds must travel out at a steep angle through the atmosphere to reach Earth, dimming the light further. Jupiter is brighter near the center of the disk because the sunlight shines nearly straight down on the clouds.[32]

This description goes back and forth between the removed and personal points of view. The first three sentences describe the different parts of Jupiter's atmosphere and surface. The fourth sentence encourages the reader to imagine herself looking at Jupiter from the outside—but the fifth sentence goes on to describe something that an observer couldn't possibly see. The sixth, seventh, and eighth sentences return to explaining what you would see from two different perspectives—looking at Jupiter from the outside in the sixth and seventh sentences, then moving to stand *on* Jupiter in the eighth. The final two sentences return to explaining how light affects Jupiter, rather than explaining what the light would *look like* on Jupiter.

> Hot springs are defined as springs of water that issue onto the earth's surface at temperatures "appreciably" above the average temperature of the air at their exit point. This means that if you sat in one in Hawaii you might be boiled like a lobster, whereas in Minnesota you could be turned into a giant ice cube.[33]

The first sentence tells what a hot spring is; the second encourages the reader to imagine herself *in* a hot spring.

---

31. Mehmet Oz, *Healing from the Heart* (Dutton, 1998), p. 17.
32. Michael A. Seeds, *The Solar System,* 6th ed. (Thomson Brooks/Cole, 2008), pp. 515–516.
33. Ron L. Morton, *Music of the Earth: Volcanoes, Earthquakes, and Other Geological Wonders* (Plenum Press, 1996), p. 125.

> The process that caused Antarctica—and all the other continents—to drift over time is known as plate tectonics. Understanding plate tectonics starts with knowing Earth's basic structure. <u>If you could slice through our planet, you'd find it is made up of three major layers. The innermost layer is a very hot core of iron and nickel. The inside of this core is solid, and the outside is liquid. The middle layer, the mantle, is composed of rock that flows very, very slowly, like toothpaste. The outermost layer is the crust. Oceanic crust forms the ocean floor, while continental crust forms the continents.</u> The crust and the upper part of the mantle, which is cooler and more rigid than the mantle's deeper parts, together make up what geologists call the lithosphere. The lithosphere is broken up into more than a dozen huge rocky slabs called tectonic plates. These plates are slowly moving.[34]

After the introductory two sentences, the reader is placed in the position of standing over an imaginary Earth with a knife in hand. The underlined sentences tell what the reader would see by looking at the static, sliced-open earth. The final sentences, however, describe aspects of the layers that can't be seen—the coolness of the mantle, the definition of the combined layers as "lithosphere," and moving of plates. (The student may make the argument that the plates can be seen moving from the reader's imaginary position; this is a judgment call, so you may accept this argument if it is presented convincingly.)

STEP THREE: **Add to the pattern of the topos (Student Responsibility)**

Student instructions for Step Three:

> Turn to the Scientific Description chart in your Composition Notebook. Add the bolded point below under the "Remember" column.
>
> Scientific Description
>
> Definition: A visual and structural description of an object or phenomenon

Procedure	Remember
1. Describe each part of the object or phenomenon and tell what it is made from.	1. Consider using figurative language to make the description more visual.
2. Choose a point of view.	**2. Consider combining points of view.**

34. Rebecca L. Johnson, *Plate Tectonics* (Lerner Publications, 2006), p. 6.

Day Four: Practicing the Topos

Focus: Learning how to write a scientific description of an object or phenomenon

Today, the student will write a scientific description of the planet Mars that mixes points of view. This description should have three elements:

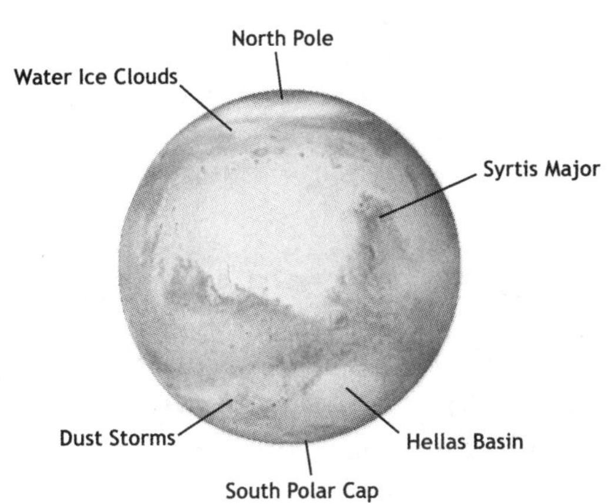

1. A section that describes, from a removed point of view, each part of an object or phenomenon and tells what it's made from.
2. A section that also describes at least one part of the object or phenomonon from a present, personal point of view, using at least three of the five senses (smell, taste, touch, hearing, sight).
3. A metaphor, simile, or some other use of figurative language that makes some part of the object or phenomenon more vivid and real to the reader.

STEP ONE: **Write a draft of the description of Mars**

Student instructions for Step One:

> Look carefully at the labelled diagrams of the planet Mars on the next page. Then, read the facts and excerpts that follow. Finally, write a rough draft of a description of Mars. This should describe each important part of the planet by explaining what it is made of and what it looks like. You should not try to include details about every part of Mars; you can focus on the exterior, the interior, or a few selected major features of both. This description should be at least 200 words but not more than 400.
>
> You will insert the present point of view into this rough draft in the second step of your lesson.

HOW TO HELP THE STUDENT WITH STEP ONE

You may need to help the student decide which parts to leave out of the description. If necessary, encourage him to leave out the more abstract facts about the planet (temperature, diameter, atmosphere, makeup of the mantle and core) since these will be more difficult to use as the basis of the present point-of-view section (the next step).

STEP TWO: **Write a draft of the present point-of-view section of the description**

Student instructions for Step Two:

> Look back at the draft you wrote in Step One. Choose one part of the description and ask yourself: If I were standing in space or in the atmosphere, looking *at* Mars, what would this part of the planet look, sound, smell, feel, or taste like? Or ask yourself: If I were standing *on* Mars and looking around, or looking up, what would this part of Mars look, sound, smell, feel, or taste like?
>
> Write two or three sentences describing your chosen part of Mars, using the present point of view.
>
> If you have difficulty, ask your instructor for help.

HOW TO HELP THE STUDENT WITH STEP TWO

The student's present point-of-view description will vary, depending on the part of Mars he chooses to describe. However, you can help the student if he appears to be stalled by making the following suggestions.

If he is looking at Mars from the outside: Suggest that he think of the planet's color (red-orange with blue-gray streaks, dark areas, and white polar caps); of the differences in the landscape (volcanoes in the northern hemisphere are vast, high, broad, spreading, colossal, gigantic, immense, mammoth, massive, monstrous, spread out, titanic, impressive; craters in the southern hemisphere are huge, broad, deep, yawning, vast, etc., and also could be described as pockmarks, hollows, pits, pockets, dents, depressions); or of the different conditions of the surface (dusty, dust-masked, swirling, stormy, gritty, masked by dust, veiled by dust, obscured by dust).

If he is standing on Mars looking around: He may also think of color, landscape, and the surface, as well as the temperature around him (hot and cold, or various synonyms), the Martian winds (gusting, torrential, raw, squally, tempestuous, wild), the textures he can feel (gritty, sandy, metallic, stony), and the metallic (iron, tangy) tastes of the wind and air.

STEP THREE: **Settle on a metaphor or simile**

Student instructions for Step Three:

> Jot down at least one metaphor or simile that could help describe one of the following:
>
> The dryness of the planet (no free water)
>
> The bleak, bare surface of the planet (no vegetation, all rock and desert)
>
> The contrast between the orange-red dusty surface of the planet and the white polar caps
>
> The size of the moons
>
> If you have difficulty, ask your instructor for help.

HOW TO HELP THE STUDENT WITH STEP THREE

If the student has difficulty coming up with figurative language, you may suggest the following metaphors:

Dryness: clay, ashes, crumbs, granite, death, parched mouth, bone
Bleak and bare: shore, winter, snow-covered field, wasteland
Orange and red/white: clown's paint, markings of a bird or animal, paint
Size/shape of the moons: marbles, eggs, pebbles, nuts, Play-Doh balls

STEP FOUR: **Complete the final draft**

Student instructions for Step Four:

> Now you will combine the three elements of the description. Insert the present point-of-view sentences into your removed point-of-view description at the appropriate place; then insert your metaphor, simile, or figurative language.
>
> If necessary, read back over the examples in the last three weeks to see the different ways in which writers make use of figurative language and mixed point of view.
>
> Your finished draft should be more than 200 words but not more than 500 words in length.
>
> If you have difficulty, ask your instructor for help. And when you are finished, show your composition to your instructor.

HOW TO HELP THE STUDENT WITH STEP FOUR

You may need to help the student integrate the three elements together. For example, if the student has written:

The surface of Mars is dry because there is no free water on the planet. All the water is frozen into the ice caps at the poles

as a removed point-of-view description, as well as

Standing on the surface, you can see the dry red dust stretching away towards the distant white gleam of the poles

as a present point-of-view description, you might suggest that the present point-of-view description be placed *inside* the removed point-of-view description, like this:

The surface of Mars is dry because there is no free water on the planet. Standing on the surface, you can see the dry red dust stretching away towards the distant white gleam of the poles, where all the planet's water is frozen.

If the student also wrote that the surface was "as dry as the ashes of a dead fire," the final sentences might read:

The surface of Mars is as dry as the ashes of a dead fire, because there is no free water on the planet. Standing on the surface, you can see the dry red dust stretching away towards the distant white gleam of the poles, where all the planet's water is frozen.

It may be helpful to require the student to read the sentences out loud, experimenting with different ways of fitting the elements together.

When the student is finished, check his work using the following rubric.

Week 14 Rubric
Scientific Description

Organization

1. The description should describe what at least three separate parts of Mars are made from, what they look like, and what function they have.
2. The description should include at least one present point-of-view description of at least one part of Mars from the perspective of at least three of the five senses: sight, sound, smell, taste, touch.
3. At least one metaphor or simile should be used.
4. The final description should be at least 200 words and no longer than 500 words.

Mechanics

1. Each sentence should make sense on its own when read aloud.
2. Each proper name should be capitalized.
3. Personal pronouns should have clear antecedents and be of the proper gender.
4. Verb tense should be consistent throughout.
5. Subjects and verbs must be in agreement.

Week 15: Combining Chronological Narrative of a Scientific Discovery and Scientific Description

Day One: Original Narration Exercise

Focus: Summarizing a narrative by choosing the main events and listing them chronologically

STEP ONE: **Read (Student Responsibility)**

Student instructions for Step One:

Read the following excerpt from the adventure novel *Big Red* by Jim Kjelgaard. Danny, the novel's main character, works for a rich man named Mr. Haggin who owns a kennel of champion Irish Setters. Danny's favorite dog in the kennel is the show dog Big Red. Mr. Haggin won't allow Big Red out to hunt, because he's afraid the dog will be injured and no longer be able to win ribbons in dog shows.

In this excerpt, Big Red has escaped from the kennel and is on the trail of the legendary killer bear Old Majesty. Danny needs to catch Big Red and get him back home before Mr. Haggin notices that his prize dog is out in the wilderness.

STEP TWO: **Write summary sentences**

Student instructions for Step Two:

You will now summarize the passage in three or four sentences and write those sentences down on your own paper.

This is the last narration summary exercise in this year's workbook. In the last 11 weeks, you've practiced summarizing by noting down important events and then combining those events into three or four sentences. In this last exercise, try to streamline the process by combining the two steps. Write three or four sentences summarizing the main events in the story, and then show them to your instructor.

You may find it helpful to underline the most important events in the excerpt above, and then look only at those events as you write. You may also need to write five or more sentences and then edit them by cutting out unnecessary details and combining sentences.

If you have difficulty with this assignment, ask your instructor for help. When you're finished, show your work to your instructor.

HOW TO HELP THE STUDENT WITH STEP TWO

The student has been encouraged to cut out the middle step of jotting down phrases and sentences about the main events before writing her summary. She'll still have to make a mental note of the most important events before she writes, however.

Although the passage is fairly straightforward, much of it describes Danny's pursuit of the dog and the bear, and the student may get bogged down in the details of the chase. Watch her as she writes, and if she seems to be writing more than five or six sentences, stop her. Ask her the following questions:

What problem does Danny have? *(Big Red has escaped and is chasing the bear.)*
What is he afraid will happen to Big Red? *(Big Red will be injured or killed.)*
What does Danny spend most of the passage doing? *(Tracking the bear)*
When he finds Big Red, what is the dog doing? *(The dog is stalking the bear.)*
What happens to Big Red at the end? *(Danny gets him back.)*
What happens to the bear? *(The bear gets away.)*

An acceptable summary of this passage might sound like this:

Big Red, the prize Irish Setter, escaped and chased the bear Old Majesty through the mountains. Danny was afraid Big Red would be injured. He spent all day and night tracking Big Red and the bear. When he found them, he was able to catch Big Red, but the bear got away.

OR

Big Red disappeared into the forest, chasing the bear. Danny followed his tracks, but he couldn't catch up to either Big Red or the bear. Finally, he found Big Red getting ready to attack the bear. He caught Big Red by the collar, and the bear escaped without hurting the dog.

When the summary is finished, check it using the following rubric.

Week 15 Rubric
Summary of Narrative Fiction

Organization

1 Events should be in chronological order.
2 If two or more events are listed in a single sentence, they should have a cause and effect relationship.
3 The summary should not go into detail about Danny's actions in tracking Big Red and the bear.
4 The summary should not be longer than four sentences.

Mechanics

1 Each sentence should make sense on its own when read aloud.
2 Each proper name should be capitalized.
3 Personal pronouns should have clear antecedents and be of the proper gender.
4 Verb tense should be consistent throughout.
5 Subjects and verbs must be in agreement.
6 Any predicate nominatives or adjectives must agree with their subjects in person, number, and gender.

Day Two: Outlining Exercise

Focus: Finding the central topic in each paragraph of a chronological narrative that includes a scientific description of an object or phenomenon

STEP ONE: **Read (Student Responsibility)**

Student instructions for Step One:

Read the following excerpt from *Changes in the Wind: Earth's Shifting Climate* by Margery and Howard Facklam. The first paragraphs take place during World War II, a time when the United States and Japan were at war.

An "incendiary bomb" is a bomb intended to start a fire by exploding and spreading some sort of fast, hot-burning fuel all over the target area. In World War II, most incendiary bombs had the chemical phosphorus in them.

The "troposphere" is the lowest part of the Earth's atmosphere; that is, the section closest to the ground. It has a depth of anywhere between 7 and 20 kilometers (about 4.5 to 12.5 miles). Most of the phenomena we associate with day-to-day weather occur in the troposphere. The next layer up is called the "stratosphere." It runs up to 50–60 kilometers (about 31–38 miles) above the Earth's surface.

STEP TWO: **Construct a one-level outline**

Student instructions for Step Two:

This week's passage combines two of the topics you've been studying: a chronological narrative, and a scientific description of a phenomenon (the jet stream).

As in previous weeks, you'll need to find a major point for each section. Because the sections alternate between chronological narrative and description, you'll have to use both of the methods you've studied. If the section seems to be chronological narrative, ask:

1. What is the main thing or person that this section is about? *Or* What is the major event in this section?
2. Why is that thing, person, or event important?

If the section seems to be primarily descriptive, ask:

What part or aspect of the jet stream does this section describe?

If you're not sure which method will work best, try both.

You may mix phrases and sentences if necessary. If you have difficulty, ask your instructor for help. And when you're finished, check your assignment with your instructor.

HOW TO HELP THE STUDENT WITH STEP TWO

In this assignment, the student has been encouraged to try two different methods of finding the main idea in each section. It is acceptable for her to mix phrases and sentences in her outline as she answers.

Suggested answers:

I. Bombers pushed off course by high winds OR The bombing mission fails OR 1944 bombing mission

II. Discovery of Japanese balloons OR Japanese balloons discovered in trees OR Balloons that rode the jet stream to America

III. The jet stream

IV. The loops of the jet stream

If the student has difficulty, encourage her to identify each section as either narrative or description before attempting to find the main idea. The first two sections are narrative; the last two, descriptive. The chronological narrative in the passage is very brief; it tells a three-paragraph story about what the jet stream made happen, as a lead-in to the description of the jet stream itself.

If necessary, use the following dialogue to help the student.

Section 1 (narrative)
Instructor: What is the most important group of things in this passage?

Student: The bombers

Note to Instructor: If the student says that the jet stream is the most important thing, point out that "jet stream" isn't actually mentioned in the section.
Instructor: What happened to the bombers?

Student: They were pushed off course by high winds.

Section 2 (narrative)
Instructor: What is the most important group of things in *this* passage?

Student: The balloons

Note to Instructor: The jet stream is mentioned in this passage, but it still isn't the most important *thing:* the balloons are mentioned seven times, the jet stream only twice.
Instructor: What country did the balloons belong to?

Student: Japan

Instructor: What is the most important thing about the balloons?

Student: The balloons were stuck in the trees OR *The balloons were carried by the jet stream.*

Note to Instructor: Both answers are acceptable; the second explains what carried the balloons to the trees, while the first explains where the balloons ended up after riding the jet stream.

Section 3 (description)
Instructor: Does the first sentence tell you about a specific aspect of the jet stream? What aspect?

Student: The loops OR *The shape* OR *The place where the jet stream is*

Instructor: Does the second sentence tell you about a specific aspect of the jet stream? What aspect?

Student: The speed

Instructor: What aspect do you find out about in the third sentence?

Student: The size

Instructor: The fourth?

Student: Speed again

Instructor: When a section tells you about many different aspects of an object or phenomenon, it is giving you an overview. Remember, a scientific description often starts with an introductory paragraph that gives a basic definition and overview of the phenomenon. So what phenomenon is being surveyed here?

Student: The jet stream

Instructor: That is the main point of the section.

Section 4 (description)
Instructor: This section focuses on one particular aspect of the jet stream. Hint: that aspect is mentioned four times.

Student: The loops

Instructor: That is the main point of the section.

Day Three: Analyzing the Topos

Focus: Understanding the form of a chronological narrative that includes a scientific description of an object or phenomenon

The passage the student outlined in the last writing session was a brief chronological narrative that made use of a scientific description of a phenomenon—a combination of two forms the student has already learned. Today, the student will examine two different ways of combining chronological narrative with scientific description.

The first two steps should be done by the student independently; the student's instructions are provided below for your reference.

STEP ONE: **Chronological narrative of a past event as an introduction to scientific description (Student Responsibility)**

Student instructions for Step One:

> In Week 4 of this course, you learned that a chronological narrative can serve as an introduction to a longer piece of writing. In the passage about the jet stream, the first two sections are a brief chronological narrative about a historical event; this serves as an introduction to a longer description and explanation of the jet stream. (You only have three paragraphs of this description, but the book itself has much more.)
>
> A chronological narrative from history can be an excellent introduction to a scientific description. The story of the failed bombing mission and the strange discovery of Japanese balloons in Montana tells you what the jet stream can *do*; once you know this, the description of the jet stream itself makes much more sense.
>
> Look again at this excerpt from Susan Casey's book *The Wave: In Pursuit of the Rogues, Freaks, and Giants of the Ocean*, which you saw for the first time in Week 4 of this course.

> After this chronological narrative of past events, Casey goes on to a scientific description of an object or phenomonon—the waves themselves ("The significant wave height, an average of the largest 33 percent of the waves, was sixty-one feet, with frequent spikes far beyond that . . .").

In both of these passages, a chronological narrative about past events is used as an attention-getting introduction to a scientific description of objects or phenomona.

STEP TWO: **Chronological narrative of scientific discovery combined with a scientific description (Student Responsibility)**

Student instructions for Step Two:

In Weeks 4–7 of this course, you studied two kinds of chronological narratives: chronological narratives about a past event, and chronological narratives about scientific discoveries.

A chronological narrative about a past event can serve as an interesting introduction to a scientific description—but the introduction isn't completely *necessary.* You could understand both the description of the jet stream and the description of the wave perfectly well without the chronological narration that introduces each.

But a chronological narrative about a scientific discovery often *needs* a scientific description to round it out. Read again this chronological narrative about the scientific discoveries of Antoni van Leeuwenhoek, from Alma Payne Ralston's book *Discoverer of the Unseen World:*

Notice that the chronological narrative of scientific discovery leads seamlessly into the description of what Leeuwenhoek saw through his microscope: a scientific description of an object or phenomenon (the microscopic creatures in the water).

STEP THREE: **Examine the models**

Student instructions for Step Three:

Read the following three passages. In each one, a chronological narrative is combined with a scientific description of an object or phenomenon. In each passage, draw a line between the chronological narrative and the scientific description. Then, write in the margin beside the chronological narrative whether it is about "past events" or "scientific discovery."

HOW TO HELP THE STUDENT WITH STEP THREE

The student should have identified the following chronological narratives and descriptions. Explanations for each answer follow.

In November 1609, he invented a telescope that was 15 times more powerful than the human eye. Within the next five months, he created a telescope twice as powerful as that one.

The telescope that Galileo created is known today as a refracting telescope. It was about five or six feet in length. It was about five or six feet in length. In a refracting telescope, light

TYPE OF NARRATIVE: Chronological narrative of scientific discovery

EXPLANATION: The chronological narrative describes the steps that Galileo took towards a greater understanding of the telescope: first, finding out about the "optical device built in Holland"; next, building a telescope with 3x–4x magnification; next, building a telescope with 8x–9x magnification; then a telescope with 15x magnification; and then, finally, the refracting telescope with twice that power. These steps show a continuing progress towards the "discovery" (creation) of a powerful telescope.

> . . . legs. Peg spent the next year of her life struggling to regain mobility. After months of intense physical therapy, she succeeded. Not every poliomyelitis victim was as fortunate. . . .

> Today we know that polio is caused by a virus. A virus is a submicroscopic agent made up of a protective shell of proteins surrounding the virus's genetic material. Viruses are parasitic,

TYPE OF NARRATIVE: Chronological narrative of past events

EXPLANATION: The narrative doesn't reveal the steps that were taken towards a greater knowledge of the polio vaccine; instead, it tells the vivid story of one individual polio sufferer, a story which has nothing to do with the discovery or invention of anything having to do with polio or a polio vaccine or treatment.

> . . . right into them. In a series of four papers published in 1952, Hodgkin and Huxley showed that the mechanism of the nerve impulse worked with positively-charged atoms ("ions") of

---

> When an axon is resting, it maintains a considerable excess of sodium ions outside it, and a similar excess of potassium ions inside. As an action potential sweeps along an axon, its outer

TYPE OF NARRATIVE: Chronological narrative of scientific discovery

EXPLANATION: The narrative explains, era by era (1930s, 1940s, 1952), how Hodgkin and Huxley progressed towards a greater understanding of the ways in which nerves work. It is followed by a scientific description of just *how* those nerves work.

Day Four: Practicing the Topos

Focus: Learning how to write a chronological narrative that includes a scientific description of an object or phenomenon

Today, the student will put together a composition that includes both a chronological narrative about a scientific discovery and a scientific description of an object or phenomenon. The student has already practiced both of these forms in previous lessons; encourage her to work as independently as possible in Steps One through Three.

STEP ONE: **Write a rough draft of the description**

Student instructions for Step One:

> You'll begin today's assignment by writing a brief description of a deep-ocean vent.
> First, turn to the Scientific Description chart in your Composition Notebook and read the "Procedure" and "Remember" points out loud.
> Next, read the facts that follow, and study the pictures.
> Finally, write a rough draft of your description. This description should contain at **least two** of the following three elements:
>
> 1. A section that describes, from a removed point of view, each part of an object or phenomenon and tells what it's made from.
> 2. A section that also describes at least one part of the object or phenomenon from a present, personal point of view, using at least three of the five senses (smell, taste, touch, hearing, sight).
> 3. A metaphor, simile, or some other use of figurative language that makes some part of the object or phenomenon more vivid and real to the reader.
>
> Your description should be at least 150 and not more than 250 words.

HOW TO HELP THE STUDENT WITH STEP ONE

Listen to the student; if you do not hear her reading the Scientific Description chart, remind her to read the chart out loud.

If the student has difficulty with the description, allow her to read the following passages. The first begins with the removed point of view and then moves to the present point of view; the second is written entirely from the present point of view.

> Cold, heavy seawater penetrates kilometers downward through cracks in the volcanic rocks that underlie the seafloor; is heated up by the upswelling molten rocks; expands; becomes lighter and buoyantly rises. . . . Black smokers . . . resembling factory smokestacks belching black smoke . . . occur at widely spaced sites, each typically up to the size of a football field. The surrounding deep seafloor is like a desert covered with freshly frozen lava flows, their glassy surfaces glaring like ice in the submersible's floodlights. Here one finds an oasis of life—clusters of tube worms with red plumes containing blood similar to ours protruding from white stalks the height of a person; crabs clinging to the stalks and grazing on the plumes, which retract in response. Rows of giant white clams, each up to .3 meter long, filter microbes from warm water pouring from cracks in the dark lava seafloor. Clusters of yellow-shelled mussels hang from the rocks like large grapes on a vine. Mats of microbes resemble splashes of whitish paint on the dark rocks. The

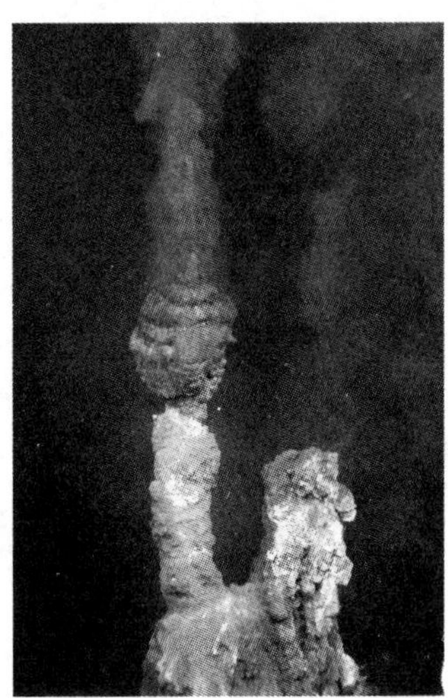

Black smoker called "The Brothers." Public domain photo from the Oceanic and Atmospheric Administration

chimney is coated with the excrement of worms, each several centimeters long, with their heads darting in and out of tubes that tap hot water through the chimney wall.[35]

A long fissure in the seabed seems devoid of life where it begins as a small crack in the muddy bottom. As one moves along the widening crevice to the place where thick plumes of what look like coal plant smoke bellow from the center of the earth itself. Here, suddenly, unexpectedly, without logic, springs to life a colorful, odd, diverse assemblage of life forms. Giant mussels, sea feathers and tube worms crowd around the vent opening. We might as well be on the surface of the moon.[36]

STEP TWO: **Write a rough draft of the chronological narrative**

Hydrothermal vents on the deep ocean floor. Public domain photo from the National Oceanic and Atmospheric Administration

Student instructions for Step Two:

> Now that you know what a deep-ocean hydrothermal vent is, you'll go back and write the first part of your composition—the chronological narrative about the discovery of the vents.
>
> Before you begin, turn to the Chronological Narrative of a Scientific Discovery chart in your Composition Notebook. Read the points under the "Procedure" and "Remember" columns out loud.
>
> Next, look through the list of events covering the 1977 discovery of deep-ocean hydrothermal vents. Decide which main events and details you will include. (This is a brief list, so you may decide to include most of them.)
>
> Finally, write your brief narrative. This should be at least 100 and no more than 300 words. Remember, you don't need to to include *every* element on the chart; you can choose, for example, to leave out the paragraph of background information.

HOW TO HELP THE STUDENT WITH STEP TWO

If the student gets bogged down in details, remind her that she does not need to include every event on the list. She should include the 1977 expedition, but she only needs to include one of the three main events listed before that ("Scientists predicted 'hot spots' on the ocean floor," "The 1975 expedition," and "1976 experiments") in order to write a chronological narrative.

You may need to remind her to make appropriate use of time words. You may also need to remind her of the proper punctuation for direct quotes.

---

35. Sylvia A. Earle and Linda K. Glover, *Ocean: An Illustrated Atlas* (National Geographic Society, 2009), p. 159.
36. Tundi Agardy, *Marine Protected Areas and Ocean Conservation* (Elsevier, 1997), p. 5.

STEP THREE: **Finalize the composition**

Student instructions for Step Three:

> Now read your entire composition out loud. Listen to each sentence. If any of your phrases or sentences sound rough or awkward, try phrasing them in different ways until you find a combination of words that sounds smoother or easier to understand.
>
> When you are satisfied with your composition, show it to your instructor.

HOW TO HELP THE STUDENT WITH STEP THREE

Remind the student to read her composition out loud before handing it in to you.

Check the final composition using the following rubric.

Week 15 Rubric
Chronological Narrative of a Scientific Discovery Incorporating Description of a Place

Organization

1 Events in the narrative should be in chronological order.
2 Two or more time words should be used.
3 The events of the 1977 expedition should be included, as well as at least one other main event on the list.
4 The description should make use of one or both points of view: removed, present.
5 Present point-of-view descriptions should incorporate at least three of the five senses: sight, sound, smell, taste, touch.
6 Removed point-of-view descriptions should describe each part of the object or phenomenon and tell what it is made of.
7 At least one metaphor or simile may be used.
8 The entire composition should be at least 250 and no longer than 550 words.

Mechanics

1 Each sentence should make sense on its own when read aloud.
2 Each proper name should be capitalized.
3 Possessive forms should be written properly.
4 Personal pronouns should have clear antecedents and be of the proper gender.
5 Verb tense should be consistent throughout.
6 Subjects and verbs must be in agreement.
7 The exact words of the source material should not be used in every sentence.
8 At least one direct quote should be included; quote and accompanying dialogue tags should be properly punctuated.

Part III

SENTENCE SKILLS WEEKS 16–22

Overview of Weeks 16–22

Beginning in Week 16, the student will continue to practice one-level outlines; she will also continue to learn and practice new topoi. However, she will no longer be completing narration exercises. Summarizing stories is a basic writing skill, practiced throughout the elementary years, that prepares the student for the more advanced skill of outlining.

However, students who are still struggling with narration exercises should continue to practice this skill once a week. *Writing with Ease, Level 4* provides 36 weeks of additional narration exercises.

The copia exercises described in the introduction will now replace narrations as the fourth day of writing practice. The student has been instructed to label the fourth section of her notebook "Copia," and to file all copia exercises in this section.

Weekly pattern:

One-Level Outlines, Further Topoi, Copia Exercises

Day 1: Outlining exercise
Day 2: Analyze topos model
Day 3: Practice topos model
Day 4: Copia exercise

Topoi, Weeks 16–22

New topoi:

Description of a person
Descriptive sequence in history
Descriptive sequence in science

Review:

- Chronological narration in history
- Chronological narration in science
- Spatial description of a place
- Scientific description of an object or phenomenon

Week 16: Description of a Person

Day One: Outlining Exercise

Focus: Finding the central topic in each paragraph of a character study

STEP ONE: **Read (Student Responsibility)**

Student instructions for Step One:

Read the following description of Queen Elizabeth I (1533–1603), from a biography written at the beginning of the twentieth century. Most of the passage is self-explanatory, but you may want to know that Zucchero is an alternate spelling of Zuccari; Federico Zuccari (1543–1609) was an Italian painter. William Camden (1551–1623) was the first historian to chronicle the reign of Queen Elizabeth. A "contemporary historian" is a historian who lived at the same time as the person or event the historian is writing about.

STEP TWO: **Construct a one-level outline**

Student instructions for Step Two:

You will notice that this passage is not divided into sections. Treat each paragraph as a separate section and find the main idea in each one.

Like the passages you've seen in the last few weeks, this passage is a description. When finding the main idea, you will probably want to ask "What part or aspect of Queen Elizabeth does this paragraph describe?" However, there are two paragraphs that will need a slightly different approach: the second and the sixth.

See if you can figure out how to word the main idea in each of those paragraphs on your own. If you need help, though, you may ask your instructor.

When you're finished, check your assignment with your instructor.

HOW TO HELP THE STUDENT WITH STEP TWO

Most of the paragraphs in this description talk about a different aspect of Queen Elizabeth. However, the second and sixth paragraphs are slightly different in format; each gives the opinion of a contemporary of Queen Elizabeth. The main idea in these paragraphs is "What a contemporary of Elizabeth's thought of her," rather than "An aspect of Elizabeth's character."

Suggested answers:

I. Queen Elizabeth's overall appearance OR Queen Elizabeth's appearance
II. Sir Francis Bacon's description
III. Elizabeth's appearance in portraits OR Portraits of Queen Elizabeth
IV. Queen Elizabeth's clothes OR How Queen Elizabeth dressed
V. Elizabeth's mental endowments OR Elizabeth's intelligence
VI. Camden's description
VII. Elizabeth's writings

If necessary, use the following dialogues to help the student.

Paragraph 1
Instructor: In this paragraph, the writer describes Elizabeth's form, height, hair, eyes, complexion, nose, and mouth. What aspect of Elizabeth do all of these cover? Hint: it isn't her personality or her mind.

Student: The way she looks

Paragraph 2
Instructor: This paragraph also describes the way Elizabeth works. What is the difference between the first and second paragraphs? Hint: who wrote each description?

Student: The author wrote the first description, and Sir Francis Bacon wrote the second description.

Instructor: Since the second paragraph repeats much of the description given in the first paragraph, the main idea isn't, once again, "Elizabeth's appearance." Instead, the main idea is "Here is what Francis Bacon wrote about Elizabeth."

Paragraph 3
Instructor: Although this paragraph once again gives physical details about Elizabeth, the focus of the paragraph is on how Elizabeth appears in a certain setting. What is that setting?

Student: Paintings OR *Portraits*

Instructor: That is the main idea in this paragraph.
Note to Instructor: If the student says "A painting by Zucchero," point out that this is not the only painting mentioned in the paragraph; the specific painting by Zucchero is simply an illustration of the main idea, which is "Portraits of Elizabeth."

Paragraph 4
Instructor: What part of Elizabeth's behavior (something she liked to do) is described in this paragraph?

Student: Her love of clothes

Paragraph 5
Instructor: What aspect of Elizabeth's personality (something about her character) is described in this paragraph?

Student: Her intelligence

Paragraph 6
Instructor: Compare this paragraph to the second paragraph. The main idea is very similar. Not "What Francis Bacon wrote about Elizabeth," but . . .

Student: What Camden wrote

Paragraph 7
Instructor: This paragraph mentions poetry, translations, and commentaries. What do all of those things have in common?

Student: Elizabeth wrote them.

Note to Instructor: If the student says that the main idea is "Elizabeth's poetry" or "Elizabeth's translations," point out that there are three specific kinds of writing mentioned in the passage. Each is an illustration of the overall topic, "Things Elizabeth wrote."

Day Two: Analyzing the Topos

Focus: Understanding the form of a description of a person

In the last few weeks, the student has learned the forms of two types of description: description of a place, and scientific description of an object or phenomenon. The passage outlined in the last writing session introduces the student to a third type: description of a person.

STEP ONE: Examine model passages (Student Responsibility)

Student instructions for Step One:

When you think "description of a person," you probably think of appearance: hair and eye color, age, height and weight, nose, chin, etc. But a description of a person can include *many* details that aren't just about physical appearance.

Look back at your outline. Although you will have phrased many of the points differently, your outline probably sounds something like this:

I. Queen Elizabeth's appearance
II. Sir Francis Bacon's description
III. Portraits of Queen Elizabeth
IV. Queen Elizabeth's clothes
V. Elizabeth's intelligence
VI. Camden's description
VII. Elizabeth's writings

Each paragraph of the description deals with a different aspect of Queen Elizabeth. They could be categorized as this:

Topic of paragraph	**Aspect**
I. Queen Elizabeth's appearance	*Physical appearance*
II. Sir Francis Bacon's description, VI. Camden's description	*What others thought of her*
III. Portraits of Queen Elizabeth	*How she was portrayed*
IV. Queen Elizabeth's clothes	*How she behaved*
V. Elizabeth's intelligence, VII. Elizabeth's writings	*Her mind*

Here's another description of a person—this one a fictional person. You're probably familiar with him already.

Like the passage about Queen Elizabeth, this description tells us something about what Scrooge looks like—and much more

Look at the first paragraph. This tells you that Scrooge is old, with a pointed nose, wrinkled skin, a stiff walk, red eyes, blue lips, and a thin wiry beard. Dickens also tells you how Scrooge *sounds:* he has a grating voice. But while Dickens is giving you these details about Scrooge's personal appearance, he is also describing Scrooge's strongest character quality. He is tight-fisted, squeezing, wrenching, grasping, scraping, clutching, covetous: all adjectives that tell you of his *miserliness.*

The next paragraph tells you about another character quality of Scrooge: he isn't affected by anything outside him. And the final paragraph, like the quotes from Francis Bacon and the historian Camden, tells you what *others* thought of Scrooge.

STEP TWO: **Write down the pattern of the topos (Student Responsibility)**

Student instructions for Step Two:

Copy the following onto a blank sheet of paper in the Reference section of your Composition Notebook. You will be adding to this page, so leave plenty of room.

Description of a Person

Definition: A description of selected physical and non-physical aspects of a person

Procedure	Remember
1. Decide on which aspects will be included.	

They may include:

- Physical appearance
- Sound of voice
- What others think
- Portrayals and portraits
- Character qualities
- Challenges and difficulties
- Accomplishments
- Habits
- Behaviors
- Expressions of face and body
- Mind/intellectual capabilities
- Talents and abilities
- Self-disciplines
- Religious beliefs
- Clothing, dress
- Economic status (wealth)
- Fame, notoriety, prestige
- Family traditions, tendencies

STEP THREE: **Identify aspects in descriptions of persons**

Student instructions for Step Three:

Read through the following descriptions. There are spaces in the margins next to each aspect covered in the description. Write in the margins the aspect that those particular sentences of the description are covering; use the list above.

When you are finished, show your work to your instructor.

HOW TO HELP THE STUDENT WITH STEP THREE

Check the student's work using the following key (brief explanations are also provided):

Unable to walk, unwilling to stand, Roosevelt made a virtue of immobility. Because he sat, the great figures of the world sat with him. No more did they pose strolling through formal gardens or striding down great halls. Instead, they posed with the President for formal portraits or, unbending, for informal chatty poses.

EXPRESSIONS OF FACE AND BODY
(This has to do with Roosevelt's usual physical posture—expression of body)

Roosevelt's face changed expression with the quickness, the sureness, of a finished actor's. It was amused, solemn, sarcastic, interested, indignant. It was always strong and confident and it was never dull.[37]

EXPRESSIONS OF FACE AND BODY
(Facial rather than bodily expression)

Cleopatra may be one of the most recognizable figures in history but we have little idea of what she actually looked like. Only her coin portraits—issued in her lifetime, and which she likely approved—can be accepted as authentic. . . .

TALENTS AND ABILITIES
(These are all things that Cleopatra was able to *do*)

37. "America Loved the Roosevelts," in *Life* Magazine, Nov. 25, 1946 (Vol. 21, No. 22), p. 110.

A capable, clear-eyed sovereign, she knew how to build a fleet, suppress an insurrection, control a currency, alleviate a famine. An eminent Roman general vouched for her grasp of military affairs. Even at a time when women rulers were no rarity she stood out, the sole female of the ancient world to rule alone and to play a role in Western affairs. She was incomparably richer than anyone else in the Mediterranean.	ECONOMIC STATUS (WEALTH)
And she enjoyed greater prestige than any other woman of her age as an excitable rival king was reminded when he called, during her stay at court, for her assassination. (In light of her stature, it could not be done.)	FAME, NOTORIETY, PRESTIGE
Cleopatra descended from a long line of murderers and faithfully upheld the family tradition but was, for her time and place, remarkably well behaved.[38]	FAMILY TRADITIONS, TENDENCIES
The next day, Monday, is Gandhi's "day of silence." He does not speak, but he listens. As he said once laughingly, it is the best opportunity to impose upon him all things one wants him to hear. He must hear without replying (though he does not forbid himself certain brief written answers).	SELF-DISCIPLINES (requirements Gandhi made for himself)
Precisely at 10 AM he arrives. His irregular chuckle announces him as he ascends the stairs; and I seat him in a big folding arm chair next to my table upon which I rest my elbows and from my swivel chair I lean towards him.	SOUND OF VOICE (chuckle/laughter is a voice sound)
Immediately he pulls his naked feet from his sandals, and, enveloped in his cloak, he folds his legs under him.	CLOTHING, DRESS
He wears big bifocal glasses which allow him to see far and near. . . . The ears stand out. The forehead is wide and well built; it is deeply wrinkled when he speaks. . . . This first impression of frailty is deceiving; the man is solid. His big, thin hands which clutch his cloak over his arms are all bones, veins and . . . muscles.[39]	PHYSICAL APPEARANCE

Day Three: Practicing the Topos

Focus: Learning how to write a description of a person

In the last writing session, the student learned that a description of a person can include many aspects besides physical appearance. Today, he will practice writing a description, following this pattern.

38. Stacy Schiff, *Cleopatra: A Life* (Little, Brown and Company, 2010), pp. 1–2.
39. *Rolland's Journal*, quoted in *The Gandhi Reader: A Source Book of His Life and Writings,* by Gandhi and Homer Alexander Jack (Indiana University Press, 1956), pp. 385–386.

STEP ONE: **Review the pattern of the topos**

Student instructions for Step One:

Read the description of Beethoven below, from the classic reference *Grove's Dictionary of Music and Musicians.* Using the Description of a Person chart in your Composition Notebook, write the aspects covered by the description on the lines in the margin.

When you are finished, show your work to your instructor.

HOW TO HELP THE STUDENT WITH STEP ONE

Use the key below to check the student's work. Give any necessary help; some of the parts of the description can be understood in more than one way.

Those who saw him for the first time were often charmed by the eager cordiality of his address, and by the absence of the bearishness and gloom which were attributed to him by others.	BEHAVIOR ("What others think" is also acceptable)
His face may have been ugly, but all admit that it was remarkably expressive. "Every change of feeling," says the painter Klober, who painted him in 1818, "in his mind, showed itself at once unmistakably in his features."	EXPRESSIONS OF FACE AND BODY ("What others think" also acceptable)
When lost in thought and abstracted his look would naturally be gloomy, and at such times it was useless to expect attention from him; but on recognising a friend his smile was peculiarly genial and winning. . . .	EXPRESSIONS OF FACE AND BODY
His head was large, the forehead both high and broad, and the hair abundant. It was originally black, but in this last years of his life, though as thick as ever, became quite white, and formed a strong contrast to the red colour of his complexion. . . . His teeth were very white and regular, and good up to his death; in laughing he showed them much.	PHYSICAL APPEARANCE
When in pleasant frame of mind his voice was soft, but on occasion he could raise it, and in singing we read of him roaring. . . .	SOUND OF VOICE
His hands were much covered with hair, the fingers strong and short (he could barely span a tenth), and the tips broad, as if pressed out with long practising from early youth.	PHYSICAL APPEARANCE
He was very particular as to the mode of holding the hands and placing the fingers. . . . His attitude at the piano was perfectly quiet and dignified, with no approach to grimace, except to bend down a little towards the keys as his deafness increased. . . .	BEHAVIOR ("Expressions of face and body" also acceptable)
Though so easily made angry, his pains as a teacher must have been great. "Unnaturally patient," says one pupil, "he would have a passage repeated a dozen times till it was to his mind"; "infinitely strict in the smallest detail," says another, "until the right rendering was obtained."[40]	WHAT OTHERS THINK ("Behavior" also acceptable)

40. Sir George Grove, *Grove's Dictionary of Music and Musicians,* Vol. 1 (Macmillan & Co., 1904), pp. 224–225.

STEP TWO: **Plan the description**

Student instructions for Step Two:

> Like a description of a place or a chronological narrative, a description of a person can act as a building block in a larger composition. If you were writing a paper about the attack of the Spanish Armada, you might use portraits and the accounts of contemporary historians to describe Philip II of Spain, or the English admiral Sir Francis Drake; the descriptions would make your paper more interesting. If you were writing about the solar system, you might decide to describe Galileo or Copernicus; if you were writing about art or music, you might use a description of Handel or Picasso as a way to make your composition more vivid.
>
> In future lessons, you'll practice using portraits and accounts to write descriptions of people from the past. Today, you'll begin to develop this skill by writing a description of a real person—someone you know in person. This description can be of you, one of your family members, or an acquaintance. The purpose of this exercise is to help you become more aware of the different aspects that can be included in a vivid, well-written description.
>
> Start to plan out your description by brainstorming. On a piece of scratch paper, jot down as many words, phrases, and short sentences as you can think of for each of the aspects listed in the Description of a Person chart.
>
> You'll probably think of several words or phrases for some of the aspects, and none at all for others. Your brainstorming will let you know which aspects to concentrate on, and which to avoid. No description should try to cover *all* aspects of a person. (Notice that in the description of Beethoven, family tradition, religious beliefs, self-disciplines, and several other aspects aren't addressed at all.) However, your description *should* include physical appearance.
>
> If you're unable to think of more than five or six words/phrases/sentences overall, you might want to consider describing a different person.

HOW TO HELP THE STUDENT WITH STEP TWO

This basic exercise isn't intended to produce a great piece of literature; it's designed to help the student widen his perspective past the physical appearance of a person as the most important element of a description.

In this step of the exercise, the student is simply brainstorming. However, you should glance at his scratch paper occasionally to see whether the brainstorming is effective. If the student seems to be stalled, suggest that he choose another person to describe. A description is easiest to write when it includes both positive and negative (or unflattering) aspects of the person; if the student chooses to describe you, or someone else very close to him, he may have trouble coming up with vivid and realistic adjectives.

You may also need to help the student think through some of the more abstract aspects listed in the Description of a Person chart. If necessary, use the following questions:

FOR	**ASK**
What others think	If you were a stranger who met this person in a store or public place, what would your impression be? Think of a friend who also knows this person. How would they describe the person?

Character qualities	Do any of the following words apply to the person? *Brave, cautious, diligent, contented, compassionate, impatient, generous, enthusiastic, respectful, creative, worried, careful, loving, forgiving, friendly, organized, happy, loyal, truthful, ambitious, patient, responsible, hardworking, thrifty*
Behavior	What particular actions, speeches, habits, or events show that the character qualities listed above apply to the person?
Expressions of face and body	When you picture the person in your mind, what expression is on his/her face? What position is he/she in? Standing, sitting, walking, running? Is he or she making a particular hand or arm gesture?
Self-disciplines	When you think about the person, do you think about promises he or she has made to others? Resolutions that he or she is determined to keep? Virtues or responsibilities that he or she is committed to?

STEP THREE: **Write the description**

Student instructions for Step Three:

> Now use your notes and write your description, following these directions:
>
> 1. Include at least five but no more than eight of the aspects listed on the Description of a Person chart.
> 2. The physical appearance of the character should be one of the aspects included.
> 3. The description should be at least 200 but not more than 600 words in length.
> 4. The description should be based in fact—but you have the freedom to exaggerate or invent *two* (no more!) aspects of the description.
> 5. You may not use any of the following words: *nice, good, bad, beautiful, lovely, attractive, handsome, pretty, ugly, sparkling, twinkling, soft, loud, famous, poor, rich, smart,* and *dumb*. These words are so common that they convey no specific image to the reader's mind.
>
> If necessary, ask your instructor for help. When you are finished, check your work with your instructor.

HOW TO HELP THE STUDENT WITH STEP THREE

When the student has finished his description, check it using the following rubric.

Week 16 Rubric
Description of a Person

Organization

1 At least five but no more than eight of the aspects listed on the Description of a Person chart should be used.
2 Physical appearance of the character should be included.
3 The entire composition should be at least 200 and no longer than 600 words.

Mechanics

1 Each sentence should make sense on its own when read aloud.
2 Each proper name should be capitalized.
3 Possessive forms should be written properly.
4 Personal pronouns should have clear antecedents and be of the proper gender.
5 Verb tense should be consistent throughout.
6 Subjects and verbs must be in agreement.
7 The following words may not be used: *nice, good, bad, beautiful, lovely, attractive, handsome, pretty, ugly, sparkling, twinkling, soft, loud, famous, poor, rich, smart,* and *dumb.*

Day Four: Copia Exercise

Focus: Using the thesaurus to improve writing

This week, the student will begin copia exercises by reviewing and practicing thesaurus use.

STEP ONE: **Review thesaurus use (Student Responsibility)**

Student instructions for Step One:

> Back in Week Three, you were introduced to thesaurus use. Remember, a thesaurus is a reference book that groups together words with similar but different shades of meaning.
>
> If you are comfortable with using the thesaurus, you can go on to Step Two. Otherwise, review the following:
>
> A thesaurus contains two types of lists.
>
> The first half of the thesaurus contains words grouped by meaning and part of speech.

These word groups all have numbers. For example, the list headed

630. Imagination

might contain

1. **nouns** that name different sorts of imagination (fantasy, creative thought, inventiveness, illusion, wishful thinking, daydreaming) as well as names for people who imagine (poet, visionary, prophet, dreamer) and names for things that are imagined (pipe dream, castle in the sky, imagistic poetry);

2. **verbs** for the act of imagining (imagine, fancy, dream up, envision, idealize); and

3. **adjectives** that convey a quality of imagination (imaginary, fanciful, make-believe, ideal, otherworldly, enchanted, spellbound).

The second half of the thesaurus contains an alphabetical listing of thousands of vocabulary words. This is the part of the thesaurus that you'll go to first as you write.

When you worked on the description in your last writing session, you were told not to use the common (and almost meaningless) word *nice.* Suppose that *nice* was the first word that came to your mind when you were writing. To find a better word, you would turn to the second half of the thesaurus and look up *nice* in the *n* section.

Beneath the word *nice,* you would find a series of other adjectives with different shades of meaning, each followed by a number: for example,

attentive	*530.15*
conscientious	*974.15*
kind	*938.13*
pleasant	*863.6*
tasty	*428.9*

Which of these comes closest to the meaning of *nice* that came to your mind as you wrote? Once you've decided (the person you're thinking of probably isn't "tasty," but "attentive" is much closer!), you would turn back to the group of words that matches the number.

If you chose "attentive," you would find that Section 530 contains words having to do with *attention.* There are 23 different subgroups under Section 530. The first four subgroups contain nouns; the next ten contain verbs; the six after that, adjectives; and the final three, adverbs and interjections. If you looked down to subgroup 15 of Section 530, you would find a series of adjectives closely related to the adjective *attentive:*

heedful, mindful, diligent, interested, concerned, fascinated

and many more.

STEP TWO: **Explore synonyms for basic noun, verb, and adjective forms**

Student instructions for Step Two:

Begin to practice your thesaurus skills now, using the following two sentences from the descriptions studied this week. The first describes Elizabeth; the second, Cleopatra.

For each underlined noun, adjective, and verb, find four synonyms in your thesaurus. List those synonyms on the lines provided. Remember that you must provide noun synonyms for nouns, adjective synonyms for adjectives, and verb synonyms for verbs.

After you've found the synonyms, rewrite each sentence twice on your own paper, choosing from among the listed synonyms. Do not repeat any of the synonyms. When you've finished, read your sentences out loud and listen to how the sound and rhythm change with each new set of adjectives, nouns, and verbs.

When you're finished, show your work to your instructor.

Her face was <u>striking</u> and <u>commanding</u> rather than delicately <u>beautiful,</u> the countenance of one born to <u>rule.</u>

A capable, clear-eyed sovereign, she knew how to build a fleet, suppress an insurrection, control a currency, alleviate a famine.

HOW TO HELP THE STUDENT WITH STEP TWO

The student may need to be reminded to select the proper part of speech for each underlined word. Acceptable answers that might be found in the thesaurus include:

striking (adj): astonishing, compelling, distinguished, fascinating, unusual, memorable
commanding (adj): arresting, assertive, autocratic, decisive, imperious, imposing
beautiful (adj): alluring, charming, dazzling, gorgeous, radiant, ravishing
rule (verb): administer, be in authority, dictate, lead, prevail, dominate

suppress (verb): check, contain, crush, extinguish, put down, repress, stop
insurrection (noun): coup, disorder, mutiny, revolt, rising, uprising
alleviate (verb): mitigate, mollify, make better, relieve, ease, allay, lighten

You may need to discuss word choices and shades of meaning with the student. For example, the word choices for "beautiful" include *fascinating, magnetic,* and *striking;* however, it's clear from the sentence that "beautiful" is here used to describe conventional loveliness, as opposed to attractive qualities such as "compelling" and "imposing" which aren't necessarily related to physical prettiness. "Alleviate" in the sentence about Cleopatra means "make better," not "pacify" or "encourage."

It's acceptable for the student to construct final sentences that have different shades of meaning than the original. Ideally, though, the student should be aware of the differences. If necessary, help the student look up definitions in a dictionary if he's unsure of the particular meaning of a word.

Don't overwhelm the student with additional dictionary work if the thesaurus exercise takes significant time, and don't expect perfect comprehension of all shades of meaning from the student. This year's thesaurus work is introductory. An acceptable sentence about Elizabeth that preserves the meaning of the original might sound like this:

Her face was fascinating and imposing rather than delicately charming, the countenance of one born to lead.

An acceptable sentence about Cleopatra might sound like this:

A capable, clear-eyed sovereign, she knew how to build a fleet, crush a revolt, control a currency, ease a famine.

Week 17: Description of a Person

Day One: Outlining Exercise

Focus: Finding the central topic in each paragraph of a character study

STEP ONE: **Read (Student Responsibility)**

Student instructions for Step One:

> Read the following description of Abraham Lincoln, written by one of his contemporaries: Isaac Newton Arnold (1815–1884), a congressman who was a strong supporter of Lincoln. Arnold introduced the 1862 bill that abolished slavery in the United States territories; he also drafted the original document that eventually became the Thirteenth Amendment to the Constitution.

STEP TWO: **Construct a one-level outline**

Student instructions for Step Two:

> Like last week's reading, this passage isn't divided into sections. Treat each paragraph as a separate section; each one addresses a different aspect of Abraham Lincoln.
>
> When you're finished, check your work with your instructor.

HOW TO HELP THE STUDENT WITH STEP TWO

This description is very similar to last week's. The student may find it helpful to refer to the aspects on the Description of a Person chart as she looks for the main idea in each paragraph.

Suggested answers:

I. Abraham Lincoln's physical appearance
II. Portraits of Lincoln
III. Lincoln's mental powers OR Lincoln's reasoning ability

IV. His memory
V. His reading
VI. His public speaking ability
VII. How he investigated subjects OR His decision making OR How he made up his mind

If necessary, use the following dialogues to help the student.

Paragraph 1
Instructor: This paragraph mixes together physical descriptions of Lincoln and comments about his manner and behavior. You need to decide which one is more central. Look at the first two sentences in the paragraph. The first tells you about Lincoln's height—his physical appearance. What does the second tell you about?

Student: How he walked

Instructor: The second sentence is about manner and behavior. But why did Lincoln stoop and lean forward as he walked? (Hint: would a short person feel the need to stoop?)

Student: Because he was tall

Instructor: So the sentence about his manner and behavior was really an illustration of his physical appearance. Look at the next three sentences. Is the sentence beginning "He was very athletic" about physical appearance or manner?

Student: Physical appearance

Instructor: In this paragraph, physical descriptions are often connected with Lincoln's character. But the *main* aspect being described is Lincoln's physical appearance.

Paragraph 2
Instructor: Caricatures, sculptures, and paintings of Lincoln all fall under a single category that's on your list of aspects. Which one is it?

Student: Portraits

Note to Instructor: "What others thought" often overlaps with "Portraits." In this paragraph, though, we don't find out anything about the *opinions* of others—just about the existence of various portraits of Lincoln. This makes "Portraits" the best option.

Paragraph 3
Instructor: Your clue to the main idea in this paragraph is found in the first line. There are two forms of the same word in this line. What are they?

Student: Mentally, mental

Instructor: Everything else in this paragraph describes Lincoln's mental powers. His reasoning powers were located in his mind. What were his reasoning powers like?

Student: They were keen and logical.

Instructor: What kind of conclusions did his reasoning powers lead him to?

Student: Correct conclusions

Instructor: All of the details given in this paragraph tell you more about Lincoln's mental powers and Lincoln's reasoning ability. Either one of those phrases could be used to express the main idea.

Paragraph 4

Instructor: This paragraph focuses on one particular mental power. It starts by describing this mental power, and then gives a brief story showing how strong that mental power was. What mental power does the paragraph focus on?

Student: Lincoln's memory

Instructor: That is the main idea of the paragraph.

Paragraph 5

Instructor: What did Lincoln do with both the Bible and Shakespeare?

Student: He read them.

Instructor: All of the details in this paragraph are about Lincoln's reading—what he read, and when he read it. So "Lincoln's reading" is the main idea of the paragraph.

Paragraph 6

Instructor: In this paragraph, the aspect being described is stated in the very first sentence. What ability of Lincoln's does the first sentence describe?

Student: His public speaking

Instructor: Every sentence that follows tells you more about Lincoln's public speaking: how it affected people, what he said, and how those saying were remembered. So the main focus of the paragraph is "Lincoln's public speaking."

Paragraph 7

Instructor: In this final paragraph, the writer is describing a *process* that Lincoln went through. It is a process that required time. What is that process?

Student: Investigating subjects

Instructor: The other details in the passage tell you *how* Lincoln investigated subjects. His investigation was the way in which he made up his mind about decisions, so you could phrase this main point in two different ways: either "How he investigated subjects" or "How he made up his mind."

Day Two: Analyzing the Topos

Focus: Understanding the form of a description of a person

In last week's lessons, the student learned that a description of a person includes more than simply physical appearance; descriptions can also include personality, habits, behaviors, place in society, the perceptions of others, and more. Today, the student will see how a description can be written to give either a positive or negative impression.

STEP ONE: **Examine model passages (Student Responsibility)**

Student instructions for Step One:

Before you go on, answer a quick question about the description of Lincoln from the last lesson. Just off the top of your head, do you think that the author admired Lincoln or despised him?

The author, Isaac Newton Arnold, admired Lincoln tremendously.

How do you know this? Arnold makes several direct statements about Lincoln that are highly complimentary; for example, that he was "an earnest, sincere man," that his "taste and judgment" in poetry and eloquence "was exquisite," that he had "sound judgment," and more. But Arnold shows his admiration for Lincoln indirectly, too.

Read again Arnold's lines describing Abraham Lincoln's height and his habit of hunching over:

Now read a description of Lincoln from a book published, after the Civil War, by a southern writer who blamed Lincoln for the devastation caused by the war:

Portraits of Lincoln tell us that both of these descriptions are more or less accurate—but they give very different impressions of Lincoln! Each one is *slanted,* or biased, in a different direction. The first description makes the reader inclined to like Lincoln; the second, to despise him.

Both writers choose their words very carefully. With your pencil, underline the word "athletic" in the first description (third sentence) and "thin in the chest" in the second description (second sentence). Both descriptions tell you that Lincoln was "sinewy," meaning that he didn't have much fat on him, so that his tendons showed. But the first writer is careful to tell you that he was strong and sinewy, while the second implies that he was frail.

Now look at the descriptions of Lincoln's forehead. In the first description, underline "high." In the second, underline "high and narrow." A high forehead can imply intelligence—but a high and narrow forehead means that Lincoln had a pointy head, implying less space for his brain.

The positive description tells us that Lincoln's hair was dark, black, stiff, and coarse.

Underline those words. The negative description also adds the unflattering word "unkempt"; underline it now.

Underline "cheek bones high and projecting" in the first description and "cheeks were flabby, the loose skin in folds" in the second description. Both of those things are true. But which is the more flattering detail—and which one makes Lincoln sound hideous?

The flattering description talks about Lincoln's eyes but ignores his complexion. Underline "expressive and varied" in the first description. The unflattering description doesn't contradict this—instead, the writer doesn't mention Lincoln's eyes at all. Instead, the writer describes Lincoln's complexion as "yellow, shriveled and leathery." Underline those words.

Finally, underline the words in both descriptions that tell about Lincoln's physical behavior: "leaning forward as he walked" in the first description and "extremely ungainly and awkward" in the second. The first description is neutral, but along with all the good things in the first description, it adds to the positive impression of Lincoln. The second description uses two unflattering words, "ungainly" and "awkward," to describe this leaning forward.

Glance back at all the underlined words. Can you see how each writer carefully chooses his words to steer the reader towards an opinion of Abraham Lincoln?

STEP TWO: **Identify word choice in descriptions**

Student instructions for Step Two:

> In the following descriptions, circle the words that seem "slanted" in one direction or another. In the margin of each description, write P for positive (the writer wants us to *like* the person being described) or N for negative (the writer wants to encourage *dislike*).
>
> The books from which these quotes are taken are listed at the end of the lesson, so that you will not know the identity of the people described until the exercise is finished.

HOW TO HELP THE STUDENT WITH STEP TWO

In the passages below, the words which are clearly slanted to convey positive or negative impressions are underlined. Ask the student to try to verbalize the reasons for her choices; points for discussion are below.

It is acceptable for the student to choose additional words as long as she can offer an explanation.

After the student has explained her choices, tell her the identity of the person described in each passage.

N

> This man is darkness. All you have to do is look at him. Lank hair flapping sideways on the forehead; cold malicious eyes full of hate; the strained pouting lips . . . a bitter closed tightness of expression and narrowness—above all narrowness.[41]

Darkness, cold, malicious, bitter, closed, narrowness are clearly negative. *Lank* implies limpness and lifelessness. (*Flapping* could also be construed as negative; it is an undignified and

---

41. William E. Leuchtenburg, *The White House Looks South: Franklin D. Roosevelt, Harry S. Truman, Lyndon B. Johnson* (Louisiana State University Press, 2005), p. 125.

uncontrolled action.) The description is of Gene Talmadge, a notoriously racist politician from Georgia who opposed civil rights and encouraged whites to openly intimidate black voters in order to scare them away from the polls. Talmadge died in 1946.

P Large lustrous dark brown eyes, kindly eyes—honest, earnest eyes—which you saw at once were the windows of a great soul. Eyes that gleamed with a high unfaltering purpose, and a dauntless courage, and could serenely look impending disaster and death in the face.[42]

Large, lustrous, kindly, honest, earnest, high unfaltering purpose, dauntless courage, serenely are clearly positive. For the eyes to be "windows" to the soul implies an honest, open personality with no deception in it. *Gleamed* is a light metaphor; illumination (as opposed to darkness) is a good thing. The description is of of the Confederate general Robert E. Lee, written by a southerner who hero-worshipped Lee.

P [He] was by nature a bold and free thinker . . . all his sympathies were warmly enlisted with the party of resistance.[43]

N He was a confirmed infidel, a howling atheist, and a lover of French revolutionary excess.[44]

Both of these descriptions are of Thomas Jefferson, and focus on his religious beliefs. Jefferson was not an orthodox Christian, but these authors take a very different approach. The first comes from a biography of Jefferson written by a Freethinker who wants to claim Jefferson's beliefs as *bold, free,* and *warm.* The "party of resistance" refers to the French revolution, but is probably meant to remind the reader of the American revolution (which, for American readers, was a positive). The second is a line used by Jefferson's contemporary opponents, who were horrified by his rejection of Christian doctrine. *Confirmed* implies that Jefferson was damned, *infidel* was a term of abuse also applied in the eighteenth century to Muslims, *howling atheist* implies that atheists had no more intelligence than beasts, and the French revolution is referred to in terms of its *excess* (the bloodshed). (For many contemporaries of Jefferson, *French* was also a negative as well.)

P Her hair is of a rich chestnut tint. Her complexion is that of a delicate brunette, and this accords with the darkness of her eyes, hair, and majestic eyebrows.[45]

Rich, delicate, and *majestic* all imply that the person is royalty; this nineteenth-century description is of Mary Queen of Scots. *Chestnut* hair is generally a sign of beauty in this century (brown hair that isn't beautiful is often described as *dull* or *mousy*).

---

42. Franklin Lafayette Riley, *General Robert E. Lee after Appomattox* (New York: The Macmillan Company, 1922), p. 197.
43. John Torrey Morse, *Thomas Jefferson* (Houghton Mifflin, 1885), p. 15.
44. Contemporary critics of Jefferson, quoted by Francis G. Couvares in *Interpretations of American History: Through Reconstruction* (Simon & Schuster, 2000), p. 6.
45. Agnes Strickland, *Life of Mary, Queen of Scots*, vol. 1 (George Bell and Sons, 1873), p. 34.

N Almost skeletal in appearance, dark eyes hooded in a sallow complexion, untrimmed moustache, sitting in a corner buried in a newspaper, occasionally taking a sip of tea, seldom joining in the banter of the group.[46]

Skeletal, hooded, and *sallow* all imply ugliness. *Untrimmed* implies untidyness or lack of personal awareness; *buried* suggests withdrawal and unsociableness, as does *seldom joining.* The description is of the young Adolf Hitler.

STEP THREE: Add to the pattern of the topos (Student Responsibility)

Student instructions for Step Three:

Turn to the Description of a Person chart in your Composition Notebook. Add the bolded part below under the "Remember" column.

Description of a Person

Definition: A description of selected physical and non-physical aspects of a person

Procedure	Remember
1. Decide on which aspects will be included. They may include: Physical appearance Sound of voice What others think Portrayals and portraits Character qualities Challenges and difficulties Accomplishments Habits Behaviors Expressions of face and body Mind/intellectual capabilities Talents and abilities Self-disciplines Religious beliefs Clothing, dress Economic status (wealth) Fame, notoriety, prestige Family traditions, tendencies	**1. Descriptions can be "slanted" using appropriate adjectives.**

46. Ian Kershaw, *Hitler: A Biography* (W. W. Norton, 2008), p. 55.

Day Three: Practicing the Topos

Focus: Summarizing nonfiction by choosing the main events and listing them chronologically

Today, the student will practice rewriting two descriptions, changing the slant of each one.

STEP ONE: **Read the description (Student Responsibility)**

Student instructions for Step One:

Begin by reading carefully through the following description of the great scientist Isaac Newton, drawn partly from the writings of his admirer John Conduitt. John Conduitt married Isaac Newton's niece Catherine; Newton lived with the couple towards the end of his life.

Read with pencil in hand, and mark each word or phrase that seems to be slanted. The first one is done for you.

STEP TWO: **List the qualities described**

Student instructions for Step Two:

When you studied descriptions of places, you learned that a description of a place can serve a purpose. You can describe a castle in a way that shows the reader how spectacularly beautiful the building is—or you can describe its walls and moats and towers so that the reader will see how strong the castle is. The castle is the same—but the reader comes away with a different impression.

The same is true of descriptions of people.

Imagine that you're babysitting your favorite two-year-old cousin. This cousin is very persistent if she wants something. She's cute and smart, but if she wants a cookie, she'll ask for it over and over again (very sweetly) until you give up and hand her a cookie. If you were describing this aspect of your cousin, you might tell the story of the cookie and then say "She is so determined!" But someone who doesn't like children would tell the story and then say "She is so demanding!"

Being determined and being demanding are actually two sides of the same aspect of your cousin. She's persistent. Depending on the circumstances (and on who's around), persistence can be a good thing—or an annoying thing.

Many aspects of people can be viewed from two different angles. Someone who is hard-working can be diligent—or she can be driven. Someone who is easygoing can be peaceful—or he can be lazy.

To rewrite a description from the opposite point of view, you have to examine each aspect described by the writer and figure out what the flip side of each one is. Look at the chart below. Down the left-hand side are listed the different aspects (described in a positive way) of Isaac Newton. In the center column, you will need to write the positive way to look at that aspect. In the right-hand column, you will try to figure out what the negative side of that aspect is.

Look at the first entry in the chart. The description tells you that Isaac Newton lived in a "handsome generous" way, which is an old way of saying "very generous." Newton's hospitality, willingness to pay for "splendid entertainments," and his charitability are all examples of one aspect: his generosity.

What's the flip side of generosity? If you give away too much, spend too much on entertainment, and feed too many people who want to stay for the night, you'll go broke. If you were looking at Isaac Newton critically, you might say "He's wasting money and overspending."

Work on finishing the chart now. A few of the other spaces in the columns are filled out to help you. If you have trouble thinking of the flip side of any of these qualities, try looking them up in the thesaurus.

This is a challenging assignment, so use your imagination. And ask your instructor for help if necessary.

HOW TO HELP THE STUDENT WITH STEP TWO

Some students will find it easy to see the opposite side of each of these qualities, but others will struggle. This assignment is merely intended to make the student familiar with the idea of a slanted personal description. Give as many hints as necessary; you may want to give the student one of the words listed in the answers and have her consult her thesaurus to find synonyms.

ISAAC NEWTON

DESCRIPTION	GOOD THING	BAD THING
handsomely generous, hospitable, gave entertainments, charitable	generosity	overspending wasting money
meek and sweet easily moved to tears	sensitive softhearted, warmhearted	melancholy, moody, overemotional teary, sentimental
happy and vigorous constitution strong, vigorous, lively	energetic, healthy active	fidgety, restless, overbusy
comely and gracious aspect	handsome	too interested in looks
thick hair, white as silver	striking, attention-grabbing	theatrical, showy
bloom and colour	rosy, glowing	red-faced, flushed
retained his senses	alert, intelligent, clear-witted	artful, knowing, crafty, sly
wrote and studied every day	diligent, hardworking, studious	drudging away, grinding away, toiling, slaving

STEP THREE: **Write the description**

Student instructions for Step Three:

Now use your chart to rewrite the description, making all of Isaac Newton's good qualities sound like bad qualities. For example, instead of

He always lived in a very handsome generous manner . . . always hospitable, and upon proper occasions gave splendid entertainments. He was generous and charitable without bounds,

you might begin by writing,

He always lived in a wasteful, spendthrift fashion, allowing anyone who asked to come and stay, eat his food, and drink his wine. He lavished huge amounts of money on elaborate parties, and gave away money to any gambler or beggar who asked.

Feel free to use your imagination.

You'll probably feel like you're being very unkind to Isaac Newton. Don't worry; you're not actually writing a description of the real Isaac Newton. You're reacting to John Conduitt's exaggerated description of a perfect old man. (You might be interested to know that at least one of Newton's friends described the scientist as rarely smiling, grave, and withdrawn).

Check your work with your instructor when you're finished.

HOW TO HELP THE STUDENT WITH STEP THREE

The student should go through the chart from top to bottom, writing one or two sentences about each of the qualities on it. If she gets stuck, encourage her to go back to the original and paraphrase each part of it, replacing verbs, adjectives, and nouns with new verbs, adjectives, and nouns with the help of the thesaurus.

For example, if the student reaches

DESCRIPTION	GOOD THING	BAD THING
thick hair, white as silver	*striking, attention-grabbing*	*theatrical, showy*

and can't think of what to write, she could take the following part of the sentence:

He had a . . . fine head of hair, as white as silver, without any baldness

and consult the thesaurus for each verb, adjective, and noun, and write:

He possessed a spectacular mane, snow white, with no bare patches.

Do not worry about originality at this point: each sentence that the student writes in careful consultation with the thesaurus is building the student's ability to express an idea in words.

An acceptable description might sound like this:

He always lived wastefully, allowing anyone who asked to come and stay. He spent huge amounts of money on elaborate parties, and gave away money to any gambler or beggar who asked. He was so moody and sentimental that a sad story would make him cry. He was restless and overbusy, even as he got old. He worried about his looks and was proud of his theatrical snow-white mop of hair. He was burdened by work, toiling away for hours every day until he died.

Check the student's work using the following rubric.

Week 17 Rubric
Description of a Person

Organization

1 The description should include the eight qualities/aspects listed on the chart from Step Two.
2 Qualities listed in the same sentence should be related. For example,
He spent money on elaborate parties and gave away money
is acceptable, because both of those actions show wastefulness.
He spent money and worried about his looks
is not, because wastefulness and vanity are different qualities.
3 The description should be negative.
4 The entire composition should be at least 100 and no longer than 250 words.

Mechanics

1 Each sentence should make sense on its own when read aloud.
2 Each proper name should be capitalized.
3 Possessive forms should be written properly.
4 Personal pronouns should have clear antecedents and be of the proper gender.
5 Verb tense should be consistent throughout.
6 Subjects and verbs must be in agreement.

Day Four: Copia Exercise

Focus: Transforming nouns and adjectives

In the last few weeks, the student has practiced using the thesaurus to find synonyms for nouns, adjectives (and adverbs), and verbs. Replacing a word with a synonym is the simplest way to change a sentence. When Erasmus rephrased his sentence "Your letter pleased me greatly," the first thing he did was replace "letter," "pleased," and "greatly" with synonyms, like this:

noun verb adverb
Your <u>letter</u> <u>pleased</u> me <u>greatly</u>.

noun verb adverb
Your epistle exhilarated me intensely.

The student will continue to practice this kind of substitution, but now will also begin to vary sentences by altering their grammatical structure.

The following weeks assume that the student can identify the parts of speech and understand how they function in a sentence. The copia lessons should be paired with a thorough grammar program that will supply the necessary background knowledge.

STEP ONE: **Understand how to transform nouns to adjectives and adjectives to nouns (Student Responsibility)**

Student instructions for Step One:

Look carefully at these descriptive phrases, drawn from this week's descriptions.

adj adj noun
a bold and free thinker

____

(prep phrase)
noun prep noun
seldom joining in the banter of the group

____

(prep phrase)
adj adj noun prep noun
a bitter closed tightness of expression

____

In the first phrase, the adjectives "bold" and "free" both modify the noun "thinker." But both of those adjectives could be turned into nouns:

bold—boldness free—freedom

and made into a prepositional phrase following the noun "thinker." Write

a thinker of boldness and freedom

on the line to the right of the original phrase.

Here's your first rule for transforming sentences: Most descriptive adjectives can be turned into nouns and placed into a prepositional phrase that modifies the original noun.

This works in reverse as well. When a prepositional phrase modifies a noun, you can usually turn the noun of the phrase into a descriptive adjective. In the second phrase, the prepositional phrase "of the group" modifies the noun "banter." Write

the group banter

on the line to the right of the original phrase. In this case, you don't even have to change the form of the word, because "group" can be either an adjective or a noun.

Be sure that you say the sentence variations out loud when you do this; sometimes your variation will sound so awkward that you'll need to make other changes. Look at the third phrase. The prepositional phrase "of expression" modifies the noun "tightness," but if you were to change this to:

adj adj adj noun
a bitter closed expressive tightness

the phrase becomes very confusing! Instead, you could leave "expression" as a noun and change the noun "tightness" to an adjective:

adj adj adj noun
a bitter closed tight expression

You could then change the adjective "bitter" to a noun and put it in a prepositional phrase that modifies "expression." Write

a closed tight expression of bitterness

on the line to the right of the phrase.

STEP TWO: **Begin the Sentence Variety chart (Student Responsibility)**

Student instructions for Step Two:

Write "Sentence Variety" on the top of a blank sheet of paper. Write the following principle and illustration on the first line:

descriptive adjectives ⟷ nouns   an eloquent man
a man of eloquence

You will be adding to this chart in future lessons. Place it in the Reference section of your Composition Notebook.

STEP THREE: **Practice sentence variety**

Student instructions for Step Three:

Complete the following exercise on the lines provided. Avoid awkward phrases! When you are finished, check your work with your instructor.

In the following phrases, identify the descriptive adjectives. Where possible, turn the descriptive adjectives into nouns and rewrite the phrases, using prepositional phrases where necessary.

his reasoning powers were keen and logical
an earnest and sincere man

In the following phrases, identify the nouns which can be turned into descriptive adjectives. Rewrite the phrases, turning the nouns into adjectives; you may need to eliminate prepositions and other words.

in reply to the expression of their delight
the party of resistance
such a meekness and sweetness of temper
this man is darkness

The following phrase can be altered in two ways. Write them on the lines provided. If necessary, ask your instructor for help.

her hair is of a rich chestnut tint

HOW TO HELP THE STUDENT WITH STEP THREE

Check the student's work using the answers below. You may need to explain the answers to the student.

his reasoning powers were keen and logical	*his powers of reasoning were keen and logical* *OR his powers of keen, logical reasoning*

"Keen" and "logical" are also descriptive adjectives, but "of keenness and logicality" is too awkward.

an earnest and sincere man	*a man of earnestness and sincerity*

Most descriptive adjectives can be turned into nouns with the suffix -ness, but some (like "sincere") use the suffix -ity instead.

in reply to the expression of their delight	*in reply to their delighted expression*
the party of resistance	*the resistance party*
such a meekness and sweetness of temper	*such a meek, sweet temper*

Abstract nouns ending in -ness are turned back into adjectives by removing the suffix.

this man is darkness	*this dark man*

The noun "darkness" is a predicate nominative, so there is no prepositional phrase to eliminate.

her hair is of a rich chestnut tint	*her rich chestnut hair* *her hair is tinted rich chestnut*

This sentence is a trick; the descriptive adjectives "rich" and "chestnut" cannot be easily transformed into nouns ("tint of richness" is awkward). However, the noun "tint" can either be eliminated or changed into the predicate adjective "tinted."

STEP FOUR: **Vary one of your own sentences**

Student instructions for Step Four:

> From your own written work this week, choose a sentence that contains either descriptive adjectives that can be transformed into nouns, or a prepositional phrase that can be turned into a descriptive adjective. Write the transformed sentence on the lines below.

HOW TO HELP THE STUDENT WITH STEP FOUR

This exercise is primarily the student's responsibility. If she has difficulty finding a sentence to transform, encourage her to go back through her work, underlining descriptive adjectives and circling prepositional phrases. She can then try transforming these adjectives and phrases out loud until she finds a sentence which doesn't sound awkward when changed.

Week 18: Using a Metaphor to Organize a Character Description

Day One: Outlining Exercise

Focus: Finding the central topic in each paragraph of a biographical sketch

STEP ONE: **Read (Student Responsibility)**

Student instructions for Step One:

> Read the following biographical sketch of the Flemish painter Jan Brueghel (pronounced BROY-gull), known for his detailed, exact landscapes and still life paintings. A biographical sketch is a combination of character description and chronological narrative; it gives chronological details of the subject's life, but also includes paragraphs that are organized around aspects of the subject's character, personality, appearance, and accomplishments.
>
> "Subject" is also a grammatical term, but in this context, "subject" refers to the person the biographical sketch is about.

STEP TWO: **Construct a one-level outline**

Student instructions for Step Two:

> Find the main idea in each paragraph of the biographical sketch. You will probably find it most useful to ask "What aspect of Jan Brueghel's life or character does this paragraph focus on?"
>
> Try to word the main idea of each paragraph on your own; if you need help, though, you may ask your instructor. When you're finished, check your work with your instructor.

HOW TO HELP THE STUDENT WITH STEP TWO

Although this biographical sketch combines the techniques of character description with chronological narrative, the student will find it easiest to ask "What aspect of Brueghel is being described?" for each paragraph. The chronological narratives are mostly *within* the paragraphs—so, for example, the aspect of Jan Brueghel described in the second paragraph is "His training as a painter," and the training is then described in the form of a chronological narrative.

This technique will be examined in more detail in the next week's lessons.

Suggested answers:

I. Jan Brueghel's family OR The Brueghel family of painters
II. His training as a painter OR How he learned to paint
III. The subjects of his paintings OR What Brueghel painted
IV. His techniques OR How he painted OR The way he painted
V. His collaboration with other painters OR His work for other painters
VI. A few of his paintings OR His paintings

If necessary, use the following dialogues to help the student.

Paragraph 1

Instructor: Besides being painters, what did Pieter Brueghel the Elder, Pieter Brueghel the Younger, Jan Brueghel, and Jan Brueghel the Younger all have in common?

Student: They were related.

Instructor: All of the details in this paragraph tell you about Jan Brueghel and his family; Brueghel's family is the main idea that the paragraph is organized around.

Paragraph 2

Instructor: What does the writer point out about Jan at the time that his father died?

Student: He was too young to learn from him.

Instructor: What did his grandmother do for him?

Student: She taught him the first principles of art.

Instructor: What did he do in Italy?

Student: Studied and painted

Instructor: What did Peter Goetkint [pronounced HOOT-kintd] do for him?

Student: Taught him to paint in oils

Instructor: All of the details in this passage tell you more about how Jan Brueghel learned what?

Student: How to paint

Instructor: That is the main idea of the passage.

Paragraph 3
Instructor: What do fruit, flowers, landscapes, sea-ports, markets, figures, biblical scenes, mythical scenes, and historical scenes all have in common?

Student: Brueghel painted them all.

Instructor: The main idea in this paragraph is "What Brueghel painted."

Paragraph 4
Instructor: *Delicate, correct, realistic, detailed,* and *exact* are all descriptive adjectives. What do they tell you more about?

Student: The way Brueghel painted

Instructor: That is the main idea of the paragraph.
Note to Instructor: If the student says "Brueghel's paintings," say "Yes, but what *aspect* of the paintings? Not the subjects of the paintings—that was covered in the previous paragraph."

Paragraph 5
Instructor: Brueghel did the same thing for Rubens and four other painters. What was it?

Student: He painted their landscapes OR *He helped them with their paintings.*

Instructor: His work with other painters is the topic of this paragraph.

Paragraph 6
Instructor: There are six separate things described in this paragraph. What are they?

Student: Brueghel's paintings

Instructor: That is the topic of this paragraph.
Note to Instructor: If the student begins to describe the fig tree, the figures, or other parts of the paintings, say "That is a small part of what?" The six paintings described are: *Vertumnus and Pomona,* an unnamed desert landscape, an unnamed portrait of Mary, an unnamed picture of Noah's Ark, *The Blind Leading the Blind,* and *A Vase of Flowers.*

Day Two: Analyzing the Topos

Focus: Using a metaphor to organize a description

This week, the student will investigate one more way of organizing a description: using a *governing metaphor.*

Remember: Similes are comparisons that announce themselves by using "like" or "as," or by otherwise spelling out that figurative language is being used. The Iraqi writer Juman Kubba uses a simile when she describes her mother:

> . . . *[S]he was like a tent and a shield that we all hid under and took shelter beneath.*[47]

Metaphors speak about one thing in terms of another, without using "like," "as," or other signals. Here is how Victor Hugo describes a group of aristocratic young ladies in *The Hunchback of Notre-Dame*:

> . . . *these fair damsels, with their keen and envenomed tongues, twisted, glided, and writhed around . . .*[48]

He never says "They are like snakes!" Instead, he simply describes them in the same terms he would use for a snake.

STEP ONE: **Examine a model passage**

Student instructions for Step One:

> Look at the first paragraph of Charles Dickens's description of Scrooge in *A Christmas Carol*:

Dickens begins with two similes: Scrooge is "as hard and sharp as flint" and "secret, and self-contained, and solitary as an oyster."

But the rest of the description is a metaphor. When Dickens says that Scrooge is "cold within," he's describing Scrooge's character. "Cold" is an adjective which we often use for someone who has no love or compassion ("warmth") for others. When we say someone is "cold," we don't mean *physically* cold. A person with a cold personality still has a body temperature of 98.7 degrees.

So does Scrooge—but when Dickens writes this description, he uses *physical cold* as the governing metaphor. He doesn't say "Scrooge was as cold as an iceberg." Instead, he describes Scrooge's physical appearance and his actions *in terms of* physical cold.

Look carefully at how Dickens describes Scrooge's nose, cheeks, walk, eyes, and lips:

The cold within him froze his old features	*nipped his pointed nose*
	shrivelled his cheek
	stiffened his gait
	made his eyes red
	his thin lips blue

All of these phrases are *metaphorical.* Scrooge's nose, cheeks, eyes, and lips are a perfectly normal temperature, but Dickens speaks of them as though they were physically cold.

Take a few minutes now to investigate Dickens's method. Look up "cold" in your thesaurus. In the following chart, write synonyms for "cold" that mean *physically cold* in the first column. Write synonyms for cold that mean *uncaring, unresponsive* in the second column. (Some synonyms may appear in both columns.)

---

47. Juman Kubba, *The First Evidence: A Memoir of Life in Iraq under Saddam Hussein* (McFarland & Co., 2003), p. 172.
48. Victor Hugo, *The Hunchback of Notre-Dame* (Carey, Lea and Blanchard, 1834), p. 194.

COLD (physically cold) | COLD (uncaring, unresponsive)

_______________ | _______________

When you are finished, show your chart to your instructor.

Now look back at the description of Scrooge. Dickens wants to describe Scrooge's character as *cold (uncaring, unresponsive),* so he has imagined what *physical cold* would do to Scrooge's appearance. Then, he has described Scrooge's nose, cheeks, eyes, lips, and walk as though *physical cold* made them what they were.

In the same way, he has described Scrooge's white beard, eyebrows, and hair as though *physical cold* changed their color:

A frosty rime was on his head, and on his eyebrows, and his wiry chin.

He also writes of Scrooge's actions as if Scrooge carried actual freezing temperatures around with him.

He iced his office in the dog-days; and didn't thaw it one degree at Christmas.

By using a single metaphor (physical cold) to describe every aspect of Scrooge's appearance, character, and action, Dickens is able to organize his description and make it effective. Imagine if Dickens had written the description of Scrooge like this:

His nose was pointed, his cheeks were shrivelled, and he walked stiffly. His eyes were bloodshot, his lips were blue, and his voice was low and rough. His hair, eyebrows, and beard were white.

You still might be able to picture Scrooge in your mind, but this physical description wouldn't tell you anything about what Scrooge is like.

Of course, Dickens could have just added:

Scrooge was cold and distant

to his description of Scrooge's physical appearance. But good writers always try to do more than one thing at the same time. Instead of writing a physical description, and then writing a separate character description, Dickens makes his writing more effective, more powerful, and more memorable by using a metaphor to do both at the same time.

A metaphor doesn't have to take up a whole paragraph. In *Les Misérables,* the novelist Victor Hugo describes the bandit Gueulemer as if he were a gigantic stone and metal statue—just as huge, hard, and impossible to destroy—in just two lines:

> Gueulemer was a Hercules without a pedestal. . . . He was six feet high and had a marble chest, brazen biceps, cavernous lungs, a colossus's body, and a bird's skull.[49]

49. Victor Hugo, *Les Misérables* (Carleton, 1862), p. 94.

HOW TO HELP THE STUDENT WITH STEP ONE

Acceptable answers to the exercise in Step One might include the synonyms listed below:

COLD (physically cold)

arctic
freezing
chill
cutting
frosty
frozen
icy
raw
wintry
numb
bleak

COLD (uncaring, unresponsive)

apathetic
cool
distant
emotionless
frosty
glacial
impersonal
joyless
lukewarm
reserved
stony
unconcerned
unfeeling
indifferent
heartless
coldhearted

STEP TWO: Add to the pattern of the topos (Student Responsibility)

Student instructions for Step Two:

Turn to the Description of a Person chart in your Composition Notebook. Add the bolded point below under the "Remember" column.

Description of a Person

Definition: A description of selected physical and non-physical aspects of a person

Procedure	Remember
1. Decide on which aspects will be included. They may include: Physical appearance Sound of voice What others think Portrayals Character qualities Challenges and difficulties Accomplishments Habits Behaviors Expressions of face and body Mind/intellectual capabilities Talents and abilities	1. Descriptions can be "slanted" using appropriate adjectives. **2. An overall metaphor can be used to organize the description and give clues about character.**

Self-disciplines
Religious beliefs
Clothing, dress
Economic status (wealth)
Fame, notoriety, prestige
Family traditions, tendencies

Day Three: Practicing the Topos

Focus: Using a governing metaphor in a character description

Today, the student will work on using a governing metaphor in a character description. A metaphor has been provided, but if the student shows an interest in finding and using a different metaphor, allow him to do so (while still following the steps laid out in this lesson).

STEP ONE: **Review the connection between character and description (Student Responsibility)**

Student instructions for Step One:

Read the following description of the eighteenth-century Frenchman Joseph Fouché, who served the dictator Napoleon Bonaparte as Minister of Police. This description was written by historian Alan Schom in his biography of Napoleon.

In this description, Alan Schom is describing both the character and the appearance of the Minister of Police. The minister is completely ruthless (without pity, without feeling, without mercy) and hard-hearted. He doesn't feel, he doesn't react; he doesn't even *move.*

In the second line of the description, circle *pale, colorless, expressionless.*

In the third line, circle *dead, bloodless.*

In the fourth line, circle *cold.*

Now think for a minute. What is pale, colorless, expressionless, bloodless, and cold?

A dead man.

A man who is as ruthless and merciless as the Minister of Police isn't *actually* dead, but he is dead to the sufferings of others; so Alan Schom uses the metaphor of a dead man to describe Joseph Fouché.

STEP TWO: **Prepare to write the description (Student Responsibility)**

Student instructions for Step Two:

Today, you'll write a description of the English king Henry VIII, as he was in his later years. The description should follow the same pattern as the descriptions of Scrooge and Joseph Fouche; it should tell the reader about Henry's physical appearance and character, and should also include a sentence or two about an action that Henry habitually performed (like Scrooge's "icing" his office, and Fouche standing motionless at official receptions).

Prepare to write the description by reading the following excerpts about Henry VIII and studying the portrait of him. Mark lightly with a pencil those aspects of Henry that you might want to include in your description. Be sure to glance at the aspects listed on your Description of a Person chart; you should include at least three of them in your description.

Pick and choose from the details in the excerpts; you shouldn't try to include all of them.

STEP THREE: **Plan the governing metaphor**

Student instructions for Step Three:

You'll write your description of Henry VIII using the governing metaphor of a *wounded lion.* Nowhere in your description will you use the word "lion" (just as Victor Hugo never came out and said "These damsels are snakes"). Instead, as you write about Henry VIII, you'll use some of the same verbs, nouns, and adjectives that you would use to write about a lion.

Take some time now to brainstorm these words. On a piece of scratch paper, jot down the following:

VERBS	NOUNS	ADJECTIVES
prowl	mane	dangerous

Under these headings, write down as many lion-related words as you can think of. You've been given a starter word in each category. For verbs, think about what lions do; for nouns, think not only about the parts of a lion, but about other names for lions ("predator," for example). For adjectives, think of any words that would describe a lion.

Reading the entry about "lion" in an encyclopedia or online source will give you plenty of ideas. You may also find it helpful to look up the word "lion" in your thesaurus. In what word groups does the word "lion" appear? Turn to those word groups and read through them for ideas.

Once you've thought of a few words in each category, use your thesaurus to look up additional words. If you look up "dangerous," for example, you might find two subgroups listed, "perilous" and "unreliable." "Perilous" is a much better word for a lion than "unreliable," so you would turn to that subgroup. Along with "perilous," you would find "menacing" and "threatening," both of which you could use in your description.

Try to find eight to ten words to list in each category. If you have difficulty, ask your instructor for help.

HOW TO HELP THE STUDENT WITH STEP THREE

Possible verbs, nouns, and adjectives are listed below. (This isn't an exhaustive list; the student may come up with others.) If the student needs help, suggest one or two words in each category and encourage him to look each word up in the thesaurus.

VERBS	NOUNS	ADJECTIVES
prowl	mane	dangerous
roar	fur	perilous
stalk	teeth, jaws, mouth	menacing
tear	wild cat	threatening
attack	den	majestic
devour	predator	commanding
lurk	king	bold
pounce	claws	fierce
rule	pride	greedy
kill	prey	ravening
maul		roaring
break		devouring
crush		strong
roam		tawny
eat		courageous
gorge		terrible
		heavy
		imposing

STEP FOUR: Use the governing metaphor to write the description

Student instructions for Step Four:

> Now write your description, following these directions:
>
> 1. It should be at least 50 words long and no more than 150.
> 2. Aim to use at least four or five of the words from your list.
> 3. Cover at least three of the aspects in your Description of a Person chart.
> 4. Use at least one adverb.
>
> You can use your imagination in describing Henry and his actions. Remember that not every single part of the description needs to fit into the metaphor. Schom tells us that Fouche has reddish-blond hair, which doesn't fit his "dead man" metaphor; Dickens says that Scrooge is hard, tight-fisted, and secretive, none of which have anything to do with cold. The metaphor should guide you in writing *much,* but not all, of your description; you can write about Henry VIII as if he were a lion and still add that he liked music, without trying to make it sound as if lions like music.
>
> Here is a starting line for you, in case you're stuck: "In his later years, King Henry VIII was still majestic and commanding, with an auburn mane and kingly manner."
>
> If you need help, ask your instructor. When you're finished, show your description to your instructor.

HOW TO HELP THE STUDENT WITH STEP FOUR

You're not expecting the student to produce great literature, and his final description may sound strained and unnatural. That is acceptable; this exercise is only meant to introduce the student to the skill of writing metaphorically.

If the student has trouble getting past the first sentence, make one of the following suggestions:

Describe Henry eating.

Imagine that Henry is walking through the halls of his palace and a servant displeases him. What happens?

Describe Henry losing his temper.

You may also read the student individual sentences from the sample descriptions below.

Acceptable descriptions might resemble the following:

In his later years, King Henry VIII was still majestic and commanding, with a broad face surrounded by an auburn mane. He was dangerously short-tempered, roaring at anyone who made him angry. A wound on his leg had not healed, and it oozed and stank. He could no longer roam through his castle. Instead he lurked in his den, gorging himself and growing fat. But he could still entertain himself with music, which he had always loved.

As he grew older, King Henry VIII grew fat. He devoured his meals greedily. He was often sick, and the ulcer on his leg made him short-tempered. He pounced on his servants for the smallest mistake and roared at them fiercely. His gold mane began to turn gray. He became fiercer and more terrible, attacking anyone who made him angry.

Check the student's work using the following rubric.

Week 18 Rubric
Description of a Person

Organization

1 The description should include at least three of the qualities/aspects listed on the Description of a Person chart.

2 Qualities listed in the same sentence should be related. For example,

He was often sick, and the ulcer on his leg made him short-tempered

is acceptable, because the ulcer is a kind of sickness.

He was short-tempered, and his gold mane began to turn gray

is not, because his temper and his hair are unrelated.

3 The description should use at least four of the words from the student's list of verbs, adjectives, and nouns.
4 The entire composition should be at least 50 and no longer than 150 words.
5 The composition may include imaginary scenes and actions not described in the source excerpts.

Mechanics

1 Each sentence should make sense on its own when read aloud.
2 Each proper name should be capitalized.
3 Possessive forms should be written properly.
4 Personal pronouns should have clear antecedents and be of the proper gender.
5 Verb tense should be consistent throughout.
6 Subjects and verbs must be in agreement.
7 At least one adverb should be used (in the above samples, "**dangerously** short-tempered" and "he devoured his meals **greedily**").

Day Four: Copia Exercise

Focus: Transforming active and passive verbs

STEP ONE: **Review**

Student instructions for Step One:

In the following sentence, identify the descriptive adjectives. Turn the descriptive adjectives into nouns and rewrite the phrases. Hint: you will need to change the verb "be" to "have."

Kings were expected to be masterful, proud, self-confident, and courageous.

In the following phrase, identify the nouns which can be turned into descriptive adjectives. Rewrite the phrase, turning the nouns into adjectives and eliminating the prepositional phrase.

errands of peace or war ____________________

Check your work with your instructor.

HOW TO HELP THE STUDENT WITH STEP ONE

The student should have answered:

Kings were expected to have mastery, pride, self-confidence, and courage.

peaceful or warlike errands

If the student has trouble finding the noun form of "masterful," tell him to look the adjective up in the thesaurus, and then to look in the noun subgroup of the entry. He should do the same for "peace" and "war."

STEP TWO: **Understand how to transform passive verbs into active verbs (Student Responsibility)**

Student instructions for Step Two:

Look carefully at these sentences, drawn from this week's descriptions.

The figures themselves were painted by Rubens.

His suspicion was aroused on the slightest pretext.

Underline the subject of each sentence once and the complete verb (main verb plus helping verbs) twice.

You should have underlined:

figures were painted
suspicion was aroused

Both of these verbs are in the passive voice, which means that the subject *receives* the action of the verb. The figures didn't paint anyone; someone else painted the figures. Write "p" over the verb "were painted" in the first sentence. The suspicion doesn't arouse anything; other things arouse the subject. Write "p" over the verb "was aroused" in the second sentence.

In a sentence with a verb in the active voice, the subject *does* the action of the verb. Most sentences can be rewritten so that the voice changes from passive to active. Read the next two sentences out loud:

subject passive verb prepositional phrase
The figures were painted by Rubens.

subject active verb direct object
Rubens painted the figures.

The first sentence is the original, with the verb in the passive voice. A verb in the passive voice often needs a prepositional phrase following it. Since the subject isn't doing the action, the prepositional phrase can tell you more about who is actually *causing* the action of the verb.

When you rewrite a passive verb to make it active, the object of the prepositional phrase can become the subject. The subject, which is receiving the action of the verb anyway, then becomes the direct object.

prep. phrase

subject passive verb (preposition object of preposition)

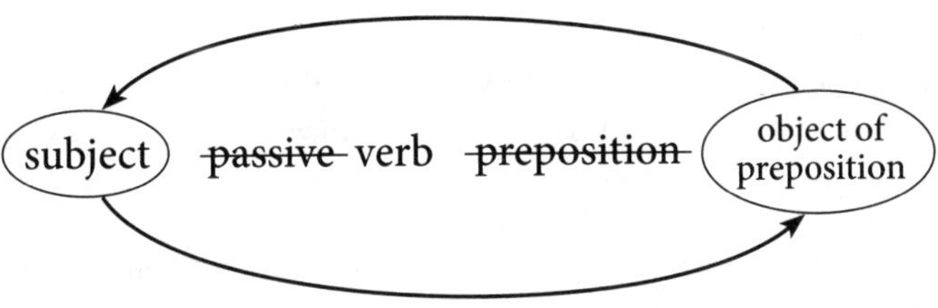

subject (old o.p.) active verb direct object (old subject)

Now read the next three sentences out loud.

subject / passive verb / prepositional phrase
His suspicion was aroused on the slightest pretext.

subject / active verb / direct object
The slightest pretext aroused his suspicion.

subject / active verb / direct object / prepositional phrase
The courtiers aroused his suspicion with the slightest action.

In the second and third sentences, the passive voice has been changed to active voice. But in the second sentence, it isn't completely clear *who* is arousing suspicion. "Pretexts" can't really arouse anything—a pretext is an excuse, a reason for doing something that isn't the *true* reason. So if you rewrite this sentence, you have to invent a new subject for it.

Writers often use the passive voice when they want to avoid giving the responsibility for causing the verb to any one subject. Sometimes this is a good idea; the third sentence puts all the blame on the courtiers, but the truth about Henry VIII was that *everyone* and *everything* made him suspicious. In this sentence, the passive voice allows the writer to be more accurate.

STEP THREE: **Add to the Sentence Variety chart (Student Responsibility)**

Student instructions for Step Three:

Add the following principle and illustration to the Sentence Variety chart you started in Week 17:

passive verb ⟷ active verb	The kingdom was ruled by its king. The king ruled his kingdom.

STEP FOUR: **Practice sentence variety**

Student instructions for Step Four:

> In the following sentences, underline the subject once and the complete passive verb (main verb plus any helping verbs) twice. Circle any prepositional phrases that tell you more about who or what caused the action of the verb.
>
> On your own paper, rewrite each sentence, making the passive verbs active, making the subjects into direct objects, and providing a subject—either from the prepositional phrases in the sentences, or from your imagination.
>
> When you're finished, read both the original sentences and your sentences out loud. Sometimes, the revised sentence will sound better—and sometimes the original will be much clearer than the rewritten sentence! Place a checkmark by any of your sentences that sound like improvements on the original.
>
> Show your work to your instructor.

HOW TO HELP THE STUDENT WITH STEP FOUR

The student should have identified the subjects, verbs, and prepositional phrases marked below. Suggestions for rewritten versions, along with explanations, follow each sentence.

Whether or not the sentence is "improved" is a judgement call; there are no wrong answers for that part of the assignment.

She was almost petrified with fear.
Fear almost petrified her.

This sentence is straightforward and follows the pattern in the lesson.

Hodgkin's research was interrupted by the Second World War.
The Second World War interrupted Hodgkin's research.

This sentence also follows the pattern in the lesson. You may need to remind the student that "Hodgkin's" is not the subject; it is a proper adjective modifying the subject, "research."

He had even found an old, rotten English sailboat in a shed, and was fascinated by it.
He had even found an old, rotten English sailboat in a shed, and it fascinated him.
OR He had even found an old, rotten English sailboat in a shed. The sailboat fascinated him.

The only tricky aspect to this sentence is that it has two verbs. The first verb is active, and the student has been asked to underline only *passive* verbs. The subject pronoun "He" has to remain in the sentence, since it is also the subject of the first verb, so the student will need to add a second personal pronoun as the direct object of the active verb "fascinated."

The youngest of them was called Dullhead, and was sneered and jeered at and snubbed on every possible opportunity.
They called the youngest of them Dullhead, and sneered and jeered at him and snubbed him on every possible opportunity.

There are several pitfalls in this sentence. First: the subject is "youngest," not "Dullhead." Second, there are four passive verbs in this sentence, but the last three all share the same helping verb. Third, the verbs "sneered" and "jeered" should both be followed by "at," "snubbed" should not be (so the student cannot just write "sneered and jeered and snubbed"). Fourth, the student will need to invent a subject for the sentence. Alternate words for the first clause could be:

> *The brothers called the youngest of them Dullhead OR They called the youngest Dullhead.*

> An alternate phrasing for the second clause could be:

> *and sneered at him, jeered at him, and snubbed him on every possible opportunity.*

> *The ill-fated* Star *was caught and ground to pieces as if she were no stronger than a child's cardboard toy.*
> *The ice caught the ill-fated* Star *and ground her to pieces as if she were no stronger than a child's carboard toy.*

The student will need to supply the subject; if necessary, you can refer him back to page 166 (Week 13, Day Two) for context. If the student writes

> *The ice caught and ground the ill-fated* Star *to pieces,*

this is not incorrect, but it is slightly more awkward than the first option.

> *If the food in the cells is pollen paste, it was placed there by a bee.*
> *If the food in the cells is pollen paste, a bee placed it there.*

This sentence is straightforward, but the first clause should remain unchanged.

Week 19: Biographical Sketch

Day One: Outlining Exercise

Focus: Finding the central topic in each paragraph of a biographical sketch

STEP ONE: **Read (Student Responsibility)**

Student instructions for Step One:

> Read the following biographical sketch of the nineteenth-century writer Edgar Allan Poe. Remember: a biographical sketch is a combination of character description and chronological narrative.

STEP TWO: **Construct a one-level outline**

Student instructions for Step Two:

> Even though this biographical sketch moves forward chronologically, it is still a descriptive piece. If you ask the chronological narration question, "What is the main thing or person that this paragraph is about?" the answer is always going to be "Poe." Instead, ask the description question, "What aspect of Poe's life does this paragraph describe?"
>
> When you're finished, check your assignment with your instructor.

HOW TO HELP THE STUDENT WITH STEP TWO

Suggested answers:

I. Poe's life of struggle OR Poe's unfortunate life
II. Poe's childhood OR Poe's early years
III. Poe at school
IV. Poe at college OR Poe fails to stay in college
V. Poe turns to literature OR Poe as editor and writer
VI. His wife's accident

VII. Poe in New York OR Poe fails in New York
VIII. Poe and his wife die

If necessary, use the following dialogues to help the student. Remember that the student can use phrases, sentences, or a mix of both in his outline.

Paragraph 1
Instructor: This is an introductory paragraph. Most of the descriptions you've outlined begin with an introductory paragraph that gives an overview or summary of the subject. This subject is Edgar Allan Poe. What is the central theme of Poe's life, summed up in this paragraph?

Student: His unhappiness OR His struggle

Instructor: "Poe's unfortunate life" is the central point in this paragraph.
Note to Instructor: If the student says "His genius," say "Does the rest of the passage talk more about Poe's genius, or more about his misfortunes?"

Paragraph 2
Instructor: What period in Poe's life does this paragraph tell you about?

Student: His childhood

Note to Instructor: If the student answers with "Poe's parents" or "Poe's adoption," point out that this paragraph covers both sets of Poe's parents (biological and adoptive). The broader answer "His childhood" encompasses the entire paragraph, not just part of it.

Paragraph 3
Instructor: In this paragraph, you find out about Poe's experiences in two different institutions—one in Amerca and one in England. What are those institutions?

Student: Schools

Instructor: You could call this "His school experience" or "Poe at school."

Paragraph 4
Instructor: This paragraph also tells you about Poe's experiences at two different institutions. What kind of institutions are these?

Student: Colleges

Instructor: You could call this main point "Poe at college." Or you could phrase your main point so that it tells you what happened to Poe at both colleges. Did he succeed or fail?

Student: He failed.

Instructor: So you could also call this main point "Poe fails to stay in college."

Paragraph 5
Instructor: The organizing idea of this paragraph is in the very first sentence. What is it?

Student: Poe turns to literature.

Instructor: Writing a short story, editing the *Southern Literary Messenger*, writing for papers, writing for *Graham's Magazine*, and doing other editing and writing jobs—all of those are details about Poe's decision to turn to literature.

Paragraph 6
Instructor: What tragic event causes everything else that happens in this paragraph?

Student: Poe's wife has an accident.

Instructor: That is the main idea in the paragraph.

Paragraph 7
Instructor: This paragraph also tells you about a period in Poe's life—a period where he lived in one particular place. Where is that place?

Student: New York

Instructor: You could phrase this main point as "Poe in New York." Or you could follow the same strategy as in the paragraph about Poe at college, and say what happened to Poe in New York. What happened to him?

Student: His paper failed.

Instructor: You could also make the main point "Poe fails in New York."

Paragraph 8
Instructor: Something bad happens to both Poe and his wife in this final paragraph; what is it?

Student: They die.

Instructor: "Poe and his wife die" is the main point in the paragraph.

Day Two: Analyzing the Topos

Focus: Understanding the form of a biographical sketch

Both this week and last week, the student's outlining assignment was based on a biographical sketch. Today, the student will study the form of a biographical sketch.

A biographical sketch combines elements of both character description and chronological narrative. It gives chronological details of the subject's life, but also includes paragraphs that are organized around aspects of the subject's character, personality, appearance, and accomplishments.

The student will need two colored pencils for this lesson. (The instructions say "green" and "red," but any two colors will work.)

Today's assignment should be completed independently. The student's directions are reproduced below for your convenience.

STEP ONE: **Examine model passages**

Read the following brief biographical sketch of the poet John Milton. ("Pamphleteering" means that Milton helped support the cause of Oliver Cromwell, who helped drive Charles I off the throne of England, by writing short essays which were printed on flyers and distributed to the public.)

This biographical sketch only has two parts! In the first paragraph, the writer lists chronologically some of the important events in John Milton's life. In the second paragraph, he describes John Milton's most famous writings.

In the left-hand margin beside the first paragraph, write "Chronological life events" with your green pencil. In the margin beside the second paragraph, write "Greatest accomplishments" with your red pencil.

This is a very simple form of a biographical sketch: a summary of life events, followed by a survey of the subject's accomplishments. You can see how the sketch combines elements from two forms you've already studied. The list of life events is a condensed chronological narrative; the paragraph about greatest accomplishments describes an aspect of John Milton's character and personality. The green pencil represents the techniques taken from your Chronological Narrative of Past Events chart; the red pencil represents aspects taken from the Description of a Person chart.

Here is another version of a simple biographical sketch, written about a very different subject.

Like the sketch of John Milton, this combines elements of description and chronological narrative. The first paragraph tells you what others said about Sargon, and about his fame and notoriety. With your red pencil (Description of a Person), write "What others think/Fame, notoriety" in the margin beside the first paragraph.

The second paragraph lists Sargon's conquests (which is about all we know about him) in chronological order. With your green pencil (Chronological Narrative of Past Events), write "Chronological conquests" in the margin beside the second paragraph.

Look at a slightly more complicated biographical sketch, this one of the Canadian medical pioneer Maude Elizabeth Abbott (1869–1940).

This biographical sketch, like the others, contains chronological events in the subject's life, but it also uses more elements from the Description of a Person format than the previous two.

With your green pencil, write "Chronological events" next to the second paragraph, the fourth paragraph, and the sixth paragraph. Together these three paragraphs tell, in chronological order, the most important events in Abbott's life as a physician.

With your red pencil, write "Introduction" next to the first sentence in the first paragraph. Like many descriptions, this paragraph begins with an introductory statement that sums up the subject.

This paragraph also covers two other aspects of description—Abbott's family and her mind/intellectual capabilities (her intense yearning for education). With your red pencil, write "Family" and "Mind" next to the first paragraph.

The third paragraph talks about the difficulties Abbott faced in her education—another aspect of description. With your red pencil, write "Challenges and Difficulties" next to the third paragraph.

In the fifth paragraph, you learn about Abbott's talents and abilities; write "Talents and abilities" in red next to the fifth paragraph. And in the final paragraph, the sketch sums up Abbott's accomplishments. Write "Accomplishments" in red next to the final paragraph.

Notice that whatever else is included (or left out), a biographical sketch *always* includes a chronological summary of important life events.

STEP TWO: **Write down the pattern of the topos**

Copy the following onto a blank sheet of paper in the Reference section of your Composition Notebook.

Biographical Sketch

Definition: A chronological summary of the important events in a person's life combined with description of aspects of the person

Procedure	Remember
1. Decide on the life events to list in the chronological summary.	
2. Choose aspects from the Description of a Person chart to include.	

Day Three: Practicing the Topos

Focus: Learning how to write a biographical sketch

Today, the student will write a brief biographical sketch. This can be as short as 125 words (about the length of the Milton biography) or as long as 400 words (the Abbott biography). It should contain a chronological list of important life events as well as at least one paragraph describing an aspect found on the Description of a Person chart.

STEP ONE: **Choose important life events**

Student instructions for Step One:

Read down this list of important events in the life of the frontiersman Daniel Boone. With your pencil, lightly mark the events that you might want to include in your chronological narrative of life events. You should include at least four but not more than eight events.

Remember, as in your other chronological narrative assignments, that you can pick and choose as long as your final narrative makes sense. However, you should include Boone's birth and death.

You may find it helpful, as you're selecting events, to focus on one of four themes:

Boone as a soldier
Boone as a hunter/explorer
Boone as a family man
Boone and the Native American tribes

HOW TO HELP THE STUDENT WITH STEP ONE

The student may need help choosing which events to include. Sample acceptable events for each theme are listed below; the italicized events can be left out if the student is planning a shorter composition.

Boone as a soldier

1734	Born in Berks County, Pennsylvania; at this time Pennsylvania was still a British colony
1755–1756	Fought on the side of the British during the French and Indian War (1754–1763) (French and Indian War was fought between Great Britain and France, in North America, over possession of North American territory; the Native Americans were allied with the French)
1759	*Fought against the Cherokee during the "Cherokee Uprising" (Cherokee Uprising was a struggle between the British colonists in North America and the Cherokee tribes)*
1774	*Fought with other colonists against the Shawnee and forced them to give up their claim to Kentucky. A new settlement in Kentucky was now planned.*
1775–1782	Fought in the American Revolutionary War
1780	*Boone became a lieutenant colonel in the local militia.*
1782	*Fought the Battle of Blue Licks, one of the last of the American Revolution; his son Israel was killed during the battle.*
1820	Died in Missouri at the age of 85

Boone as a hunter/explorer

1734	Born in Berks County, Pennsylvania; at this time Pennsylvania was still a British colony
1746	*Given his first rifle*
1762	*Started to explore farther westward because of the number of people settling nearby.*
1767	First went out of colonial territory into what is now Kentucky, during a hunting trip
1774	*Fought with other colonists against the Shawnee and forced them to give up their claim to Kentucky. A new settlement in Kentucky was now planned.*
1775	To prepare for a new settlement, Daniel Boone set out to blaze a new trail into

Kentucky; with 30 others, he began to mark out the Wilderness Road, through the Cumberland Gap in the Appalachian Mountains, into what is now Kentucky. He founded Boonesborough, Kentucky, on the Kentucky River

1799 *Moved out of the current United States into the frontier country; settled in what is now Missouri*

1820 Died in Missouri at the age of 85

Boone as a family man

1734 Born in Berks County, Pennsylvania; at this time Pennsylvania was still a British colony

1756 Married his neighbor Rebecca Bryan and settled in North Carolina, on the Yadkin river

1759 *Fought against the Cherokee during the "Cherokee Uprising" (Cherokee Uprising was a struggle between the British colonists in North America and the Cherokee tribes). Forced to leave North Carolina by the Cherokee; moved with his family to Virginia*

1773 *Daniel Boone took his family and 50 settlers to establish a colony in Kentucky; his son James and another young man were killed by the Shawnee and their allies, and the colony was abandoned.*

1775 To prepare for a new settlement, Daniel Boone set out to blaze a new trail into Kentucky; with 30 others, he began to mark out the Wilderness Road, through the Cumberland Gap in the Appalachian Mountains, into what is now Kentucky. He founded Boonesborough, Kentucky, on the Kentucky River. In September, he brought his family to Boonesborough.

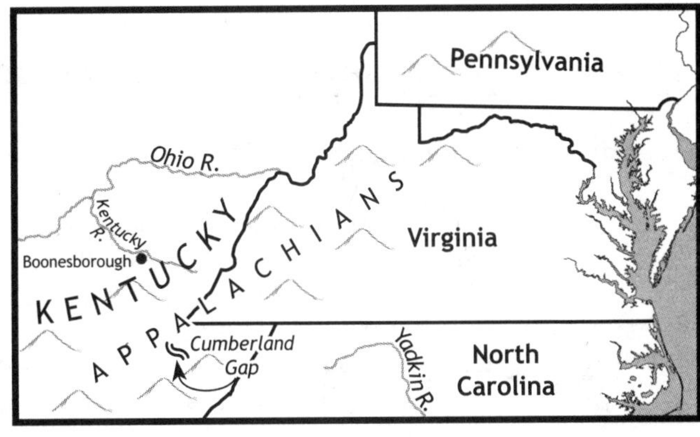

1776 *Boone's daughter Jemima and two other girls were captured by a Native American war party; Boone and others followed and captured the girls back.*

1782 *Fought the Battle of Blue Licks, one of the last of the American Revolution; his son Israel was killed during the battle.*

1820 Died in Missouri at the age of 85

Boone and the Native American tribes

1734 Born in Berks County, Pennsylvania; at this time Pennsylvania was still a British colony

1759 *Fought against the Cherokee during the "Cherokee Uprising" (Cherokee Uprising was a struggle between the British colonists in North America and the Cherokee*

	tribes). Forced to leave North Carolina by the Cherokee; moved with his family to Virginia
1773	*Daniel Boone took his family and 50 settlers to establish a colony in Kentucky; his son James and another young man were killed by the Shawnee and their allies, and the colony was abandoned.*
1774	*Fought with other colonists against the Shawnee and forced them to give up their claim to Kentucky. A new settlement in Kentucky was now planned.*
1775	To prepare for a new settlement, Daniel Boone set out to blaze a new trail into Kentucky; with 30 others, he began to mark out the Wilderness Road, through the Cumberland Gap in the Appalachian Mountains, into what is now Kentucky. He founded Boonesborough, Kentucky, on the Kentucky River. In September, he brought his family to Boonesborough.
1776	*Boone's daughter Jemima and two other girls were captured by a Native American war party; Boone and others followed and captured the girls back.*
1778	On an expedition to get salt for Boonesborough in February, Boone was captured by Shawnee warriors who were allies of the British. They took him back to their town of Chillicothe and adopted him to replace a warrior who had been killed. He escaped on June 16 and returned to Boonesborough.
1820	Died in Missouri at the age of 85

STEP TWO: **Choose aspects to include (Student Responsibility)**

Student instructions for Step Two:

The quotes below are taken from several different biographies of Daniel Boone. They give you more information about three different aspects that might appear in a description of Boone. You will need to include at least one of these aspects in your biographical sketch, using your own words. (You may include more than one, as long as your composition is 400 words or shorter.)

Read through these and make a tentative decision about which aspect you'll include in your composition.

You can choose where to place the descriptive paragraph or paragraphs in the composition, but there should be some connection between the events and the description. If you decide to describe habits and behavior, the paragraph should come just after an event in which Boone has been hunting, trapping, or exploring.

If you describe Boone's education, the paragraph should come early in the sketch, before the events in Boone's adult life.

A description of Boone's appearance doesn't really connect to any particular event; it shouldn't interrupt the narrative, though, so you should place it at the beginning or end.

STEP THREE: **Write the sketch**

Student instructions for Step Three:

Now write your sketch, using the information from the last two steps and following these directions:

1. The sketch should begin with an introductory sentence that gives an overview of who Daniel Boone was and why he was important. Here are three introductory sentences from biographical sketches you've studied; you can model your introduction after these if necessary.

    Maude Elizabeth Abbott spent her life both making and preserving medical history.

    Sargon of Akkad (reigned c. 2340–2284) was king and founder of the Akkadian Dynasty.

    Few men of genius have ever lived a sadder or more unfortunate life than Edgar Allan Poe.
2. The chronological narrative should include at least four but not more than eight events from the chronological list.
3. You must also describe at least one aspect of Daniel Boone.
4. The paragraph(s) of description should be placed near a related event.
5. The sketch should be at least 125 but not more than 400 words in length.
6. Do not use the exact words of the source material—use your thesaurus! Remember that you can also rephrase by transforming descriptive adjectives to nouns (and vice versa), and by turning passive verbs into active verbs.

If necessary, ask your instructor for help. When you are finished, check your work with your instructor.

HOW TO HELP THE STUDENT WITH STEP THREE

This sketch should be brief and not too detailed. An acceptable short biographical sketch with four main events and one paragraph of description might sound like this:

> *Daniel Boone was a frontiersman and explorer who led the way into Kentucky. He was born in 1734 in Pennsylvania. He married a neighbor, Rebecca Bryan, and settled in North Carolina in 1756. Nineteen years later, after he blazed his way through the Cumberland Gap into Kentucky, he took his family to live in the new town of Boonesborough. Boone died in 1820, at the age of 85.*
>
> *People who met Daniel Boone described him as tall, strong, and broad-chested. According to his son Nathan, he had dark hair and blue eyes, although when he grew older his hair turned pure white. He was known to be quiet, kind, and friendly. Although he is often pictured with a coonskin cap, he never wore one; he preferred a beaver hat.*

This is the minimum amount of detail required, but the student can include more events and description as long as the composition is 400 words or shorter.

Incidentally, don't worry if the student begins all her sketches with "My subject was born in. . . ." This is only the first stage of her skill development. In future lessons, she'll learn more about how to vary sentences. Mastering the structure of compositions is a foundational step; it comes before style.

In the next few weeks, the student will use source materials in most lessons. Don't worry about plagiarism; the student will be taught proper documentation in the second half of this course. Right now, she is learning to glean information from published sources, so she'll only be required to practice one new skill at a time.

Week 19 Rubric
Biographical Sketch

Organization

1 The sketch should begin with an introductory statement about Daniel Boone.
2 The chronological narrative should have at least four but not more than eight events from the chronological list, including Boone's birth and death. These events should be listed in chronological order.
3 One aspect of Boone should be described.
4 The paragraph(s) of description should be placed near a related event. Appearance can be described either at the beginning or end of the composition.
5 The sketch should be at least 125 but not more than 400 words in length.
6 The composition should not use the exact words of the source material.

Mechanics

1 Each sentence should make sense on its own when read aloud.
2 Each proper name should be capitalized.
3 Possessive forms should be written properly.
4 Personal pronouns should have clear antecedents and be of the proper gender.
5 Verb tense should be consistent throughout.
6 Subjects and verbs must be in agreement.

Day Four: Copia Exercise

Focus: Transforming active and passive verbs

STEP ONE: **Review**

Student instructions for Step One:

> In the following sentence, turn the appropriate descriptive adjectives into nouns and rewrite the sentence.
>
> He was a brilliant and successful editor.
>
> In the following sentence, turn the appropriate noun into a descriptive adjective and

rewrite the sentence.

Poe published a little volume of poems.

In the following sentences, transform the passive verbs into active verbs. Remember: you will need to provide a subject (you may find one in a prepositional phrase following the verb), and the current subject will become an object.

He was taken to England by his new parents.

He was made the editor of the *Southern Literary Messenger.*

HOW TO HELP THE STUDENT WITH STEP ONE

The correct transformations are:

He was an editor of brilliance and success.
Poe published a little poetry volume.
His new parents took him to England.
The Southern Literary Messenger *made him the editor.*

The student may come up with a different subject, such as "The owners of the *Southern Literary Messenger* made him the editor." This is acceptable. The student may decide to change the verb itself: "He became editor of the *Southern Literary Messenger.*" This is not incorrect, since the passive verb has been replaced with an active verb, but ask the student to rephrase the exact verb in the sentence out loud as well.

STEP TWO: **Understand how to transform active verbs into passive verbs (Student Responsibility)**

Student instructions for Step Two:

Last week, you practiced turning passive verbs into active verbs. You can also transform sentences by turning active verbs into passive verbs.

Look carefully at these sentences:

Sargon subdued Elam to the east.
Some of these accounts also credit him with a mysterious birth.

Underline the subject of each sentence once and the complete verb (main verb plus helping verbs) twice. Write DO over each direct object.
You should have marked the following words:

DO
Sargon subdued Elam
DO
Some credit him

If you underlined "accounts" as the subject of the second sentence, remember that the subject of a sentence cannot be in a prepositional phrase. "Accounts" is the object of the preposition "of."

In both of these sentences, the verbs are in the active voice, which means that the subject *does* the action of the verb. The action of the verb is then received by the direct object.

Sentences with active verbs and direct objects can usually be rewritten so that the verb becomes passive and the direct object becomes the subject. Read the next two sentences out loud:

subject active verb DO
Sargon subdued Elam to the east.

subject passive verb prepositional phrase
Elam, to the east, was subdued by Sargon.

The first sentence is the original, with the verb in the active voice. In the second sentence, I have done the reverse of what you learned to do last week.

The direct object "Elam," which was receiving the action of the active verb "subdued," becomes the subject. It is still receiving the action of the verb, because the helping verb "was" makes the verb into a passive verb. The subject moves to the end of the sentence and becomes the object of the preposition (which I added) in a prepositional phrase that shows who causes the action to happen.

subject active verb direct object

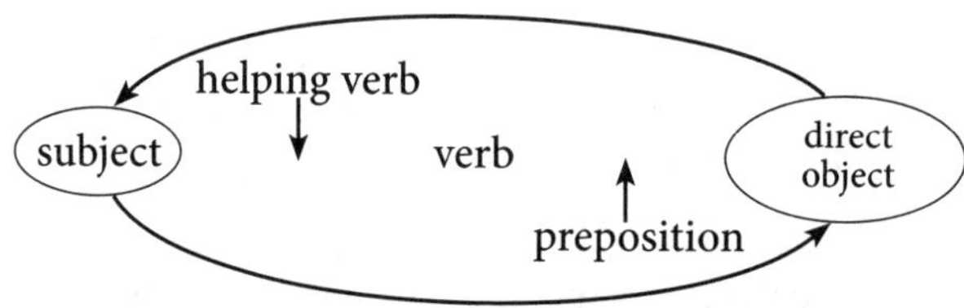

prep. phrase
subject passive verb (preposition object of preposition)
(old d.o.)

Why would you decide to do this? The original sentence comes from a paragraph about Sargon. But if you were writing a paragraph about Elam, it would seem more natural for Elam to be the subject of the sentence. Read the next two sets of sentences out loud and listen for the difference.

Elam was constantly under attack. Its soldiers fought off many assaults, but then Elam was subdued by Sargon.

Elam was constantly under attack. Its soldiers fought off many assaults, but then Sargon subdued Elam.

The passive verb in the first set of sentences keeps the focus on Elam instead of switching it to Sargon.

Now read the next two sentences out loud.

subject active verb DO
Some of these accounts also credit him with a mysterious birth.

subject passive verb prepositional phrases
He is credited with a mysterious birth by some of these accounts.

You would make this change if you wanted to keep the focus on Sargon rather than shifting it over to the accounts that talk about him. (Notice that the object pronoun "him" has to become the subject pronoun "he" when it moves from being the object of the preposition to the subject of the sentence.)

Passive verbs can be the sign of a sloppy writer. If you're working on a science essay, it's much easier to write "Oxygen was first recognized as an element over 200 years ago" than to go to the trouble to find out *who* discovered it (and when) so that you can write "Carl Scheele first identified oxygen in 1771." But using a passive verb often helps you keep an essay focused. So whenever you use a passive verb, you should be sure that you know exactly why you've decided to go with the passive instead of the active voice.

STEP THREE: **Practice sentence variety**

Student instructions for Step Three:

In the following sentences, underline the subject once and the complete active verb (main verb plus any helping verbs) twice. Write DO above each direct object.

On your own paper, rewrite each sentence, making the active verbs passive, transforming direct objects into subjects, and moving the subjects into prepositional phrases. Make any other necessary changes (such as using an object pronoun instead of a subject pronoun).

When you're finished, read both the original sentences and your sentences out loud. Sometimes, the revised sentence will sound better—and sometimes the original will be much clearer than the rewritten sentence. Place a checkmark by any of your sentences that sound like improvements on the original.

Show your completed work to your instructor.

HOW TO HELP THE STUDENT WITH STEP THREE

The student should have identified the subjects, verbs, and direct objects marked below. Suggestions for rewritten versions, along with explanations, follow each sentence.

Whether or not the sentence is "improved" is a judgement call; there are no wrong answers for that part of the assignment (except for the last sentence, which is much better in its original form).

DO

The king wore a coat of raised gold.

A coat of raised gold was worn by the king.

This sentence is straightforward and follows the pattern in the lesson.

DO

His Italian paintings also include scenes from the Bible.

Scenes from the Bible are also included in his Italian paintings.

This sentence also follows the pattern in the lesson, slightly complicated by the prepositional phrase "from the Bible" and the adverb "also." "In his Italian paintings" could also be phrased as "on his Italian paintings."

DO
Cleopatra enjoyed greater prestige than any other woman of her age.

Greater prestige was enjoyed by Cleopatra than by any other woman her age.

You may need to point out to the student that an additional preposition has to be added in order to make "by Cleopatra" and "by any other woman" parallel. The preposition "than" compares Cleopatra and other women; whenever two things are compared, they should have the same form:

by Cleopatra
Greater prestige was enjoyed *than*
by any other woman her age.

DO
Pare covered the wounds with a salve composed of egg yolk, turpentine, and oil of roses.

The wounds were covered by Pare with a salve composed of egg yolk, turpentine, and oil of roses.

The first part of this sentence follows the pattern in the lesson; the second half of the sentence should remain unchanged.

DO DO DO
The cold within him froze his old features, nipped his pointed nose, shrivelled his cheek,
DO
stiffened his gait.

His old features were frozen, his pointed nose was nipped, his cheek was shrivelled, his gait was stiffened by the cold within him.

This sentence has four verbs and four direct objects; each direct object must become a subject, and the current subject "cold" should go at the end to show that the cold was causing each one of these verbs to happen.

STEP FOUR: **Vary one of your own sentences**

Student instructions for Step Four:

> From your own written work this week, choose a sentence that contains an active verb and a direct object. Transform this sentence by making the active verb passive. Write the transformed sentence on the lines below.

HOW TO HELP THE STUDENT WITH STEP FOUR

This exercise is primarily the student's responsibility. If she has difficulty finding a sentence to transform, encourage her to go back through her work, underlining action verbs and circling direct objects. Only sentences with action verbs *and* direct objects can be transformed.

Week 20: Biographical Sketch

Day One: Outlining Exercise

Focus: Finding the central topic in each paragraph of a biographical sketch

STEP ONE: **Read (Student Responsibility):**

Student instructions for Step One:

Read the following short account of the life and work of the ancient mathematician Archimedes (pronounced *ark-eh-MEED-ease)*. If you haven't read before about the Punic Wars, you should know that the three Punic Wars were fought between Rome and the North African city of Carthage between 264 and 146 BC. Both the Romans and the Carthaginians wanted to control the city of Syracuse, on the island of Sicily (which fell right between the two powers). A *quinquereme* (third paragraph) was a heavy warship.

There are only five paragraphs in this passage, but there is a lot of detail in each paragraph. In Step Two, you'll be given some help outlining it.

STEP TWO: **Construct a one-level outline**

Student instruction for Step Two:

This passage is a biographical sketch of Archimedes. Like the other biographical sketches you've studied, it mixes aspects of description with a narrative of important events in Archimedes's life.

Use the following hints to construct your outline.

Paragraph 1. The main idea here is an aspect of description. You last saw this aspect in the biographical sketch of Sargon.

Paragraph 2. This paragraph does *not* cover an aspect.

Paragraph 3. Archimedes created a lot of them.

Paragraph 4. The focus in this paragraph shifts away from Archimedes to something else.

Paragraph 5. You're on your own.
When you're finished, check your work with your instructor.

HOW TO HELP THE STUDENT WITH STEP TWO

Because there is a lot of detail (and many long sentences) in this passage, the student has been given outlining hints. The final outline should resemble this:

Suggested answers:

I. What others know about Archimedes OR Famous stories of Archimedes
II. Main events in Archimedes's life
III. Archimedes's war inventions OR The war machines Archimedes invented
IV. The Roman reaction OR The inventions frightened the Romans
V. The death of Archimedes

If the student needs further help with the outline, use the following dialogues:

Paragraph 1
Instructor: This paragraph contains three different stories about Archimedes. What adjective does the writer use for the stories? (Hint: it's hyphenated.)

Student: Well-known

Instructor: The main point of the paragraph is that people *know* these stories. Look at the aspects listed in your Description of a Person chart. Which aspect has to do with what people *know* about the subject of a description?

Student: What others think ["fame" is also an acceptable answer]

Instructor: The main point can be phrased as "What people know about Archimedes" or "Famous stories about Archimedes."

Paragraph 2
Instructor: This paragraph contains a birth and death date. That should clue you in to the function of the paragraph: it contains the important events of Archimedes's life. This is the chronological narrative paragraph.

Paragraph 3
Instructor: This paragraph has to do with one kind of invention. Catapults, war machines, cranes, missile launchers—what are all of these for?

Student: Fighting

Instructor: The main topic of the paragraph is "Archimedes's war inventions."

Paragraph 4
Instructor: How did the Romans react?

Student: They were scared.

Instructor: That is the main point of the paragraph.

Paragraph 5
Instructor: This whole paragraph gives four different versions of what event?

Student: The death of Archimedes

Instructor: That is the main point of the paragraph.

Day Two: Analyzing the Topos

Focus: Understanding the form of a biographical sketch

This week, the student will learn one last way to construct a biographical sketch: focusing on what the subject is best known for (his work, profession, and achievements).

The student will need green and red colored pencils again for this lesson, as well as a regular pencil.

Today's assignment should be completed independently. The student's directions are reproduced below for your convenience.

STEP ONE: **Examine model passages**

Read the following paragraphs about the Persian scholar Omar Khayyám. Khayyám wrote a very famous book of poems, now known as *The Rubáiyat of Omar Khayyám.* But he was also an accomplished mathemetician, although this work is not as well known.

This passage has mathematical terms in it that will probably be unfamiliar to you. But you don't need to know what a third-degree equation or binomial coefficient is in order to read about Khayyám's accomplishments.

This sketch has two elements: an introductory paragraph with basic information about Khayyám's life (where and when he was born, what his life was like), and then three more paragraphs describing all of the things Khayyám discovered in mathematics and science.

There are very few life events in this sketch—because we don't *know* very much about Khayyám's life. A biographical sketch focusing almost completely on the subject's work is a good choice if you're writing about an ancient or little-known subject. Often, you'll find that you just don't have enough information to construct a full chronological narrative, or to cover more than one or two aspects of a description. We don't know what Khayyám did every day; we don't know anything about his family, his appearance, his habits, or his behavior.

But we do have the work he left behind—and that's what we can use to write a sketch about him.

Even if you *do* know quite a lot about someone's life, you can still write a biographical sketch that focuses on the subject's work. Read the following sketch of Noah Webster. As you read, use your regular pencil to lightly underline every sentence that discusses Webster's *writings*.

A *philologist* is someone who studies the historical development of languages and how they have changed over time.

We know plenty of facts about Noah Webster's life. Any encyclopedia can tell you that Webster's family was descended from William Bradford, leader of Plymouth Plantation; that he was sixteen when he went to Yale; that he married a wealthy woman; that he was involved in politics, opposed slavery, helped found Amherst College, and had eight children. But none of those life events appear in this sketch, because the sketch is about Webster's writings, and particularly those writings that had to do with language.

If you underlined the sentences dealing with Webster's writing career, you should have ended up underlining every single sentence in the second, third, and fourth paragraphs. All the other aspects of Webster's life mentioned, as well as the chronological narrative, are in the first and last paragraphs only.

Using your green pencil to represent the chronological narrative of Webster's life, underline all three sentences in the first paragraph, and the very last sentence of the last paragraph. These four sentences cover the important life events in the biographical sketch.

Using your red pencil, underline the first two sentences of the last paragraph. These descriptive sentences tell you about two aspects of Webster: his character and his religious beliefs.

Now go back to your red pencil. In the three central paragraphs, circle each date. You should find six dates. Notice that Webster's work, the focus of this whole part of the sketch, is covered in chronological order. This is an excellent way to organize paragraphs that talk about the subject's work: write about each major achievement in chronological order.

Finally, look back one last time at the sketch about Omar Khayyám. Since we don't know what order Khayyám made his discoveries in, the writer organizes this part of the sketch another way. Using your regular pencil, write "Algebra" next to the second paragraph. Write "Geometry and Calendar" next to the third paragraph. Write "Other" next to the fourth paragraph. These paragraphs are organized around the different types of work Khayyám did.

STEP TWO: Add to the pattern of the topos

Turn to the Biographical Sketch chart in your Composition Notebook. Add the bolded points below under the "Remember" column.

Biographical Sketch

Definition: A chronological summary of the important events in a person's life combined with description of aspects of the person

Procedure	Remember
1. Decide on the life events to list in the chronological summary. 2. Choose aspects from the Description of a Person chart to include.	**1. The main focus can be on the subject's work/accomplishments** **a. Listed chronologically** **b. Listed by subject/topic**

Day Three: Practicing the Topos

Focus: Learning how to write a biographical sketch

Today, the student will write a biographical sketch of Shakespeare, organizing most of the composition around his accomplishments.

STEP ONE: **Draft the chronological narrative**

Student instructions for Step One:

This biographical sketch should begin with a paragraph giving a basic chronological narrative of Shakespeare's life. This should be followed by at least three paragraphs discussing Shakespeare's works.

You can either put all of the chronological narrative in the first paragraph or divide it into two parts (like the Webster sketch does). If you divide it, the first paragraph would cover Shakespeare's life through 1599, when his company began acting at the Globe and his plays really moved to the center of his life. Then you would stop, write your paragraphs about his work, and then write a final paragraph about the last years of Shakespeare's life, when he went back to Stratford and then finally died.

Pattern
Chronological narrative, birth to death
Paragraphs about work

Pattern 2
Chronological narrative, birth to 1599
Paragraphs about work
Chronological narrative, 1613–1616

Using the following list of events, write a rough draft of your chronological narrative now. Try to use your own wording. The chronological narrative can be as short as 50 words or as long as 150.

If you have trouble, ask your instructor for help. If not, you can continue on to Step Two without showing your work.

HOW TO HELP THE STUDENT WITH STEP ONE

The student should be comfortable with writing chronological narratives by now. If he has trouble turning the brief facts into sentences, make two suggestions.

First, it provides variety to give the subject's age instead of the date for some events. Instead of writing

Shakespeare was born in 1564. In 1571, he started school in Stratford.

the student could write

Shakespeare was born in 1564. When he was seven years old, he started school.

Second, ask the student to think about the unwritten things that *must* have happened between these major events. He had to meet Anne Hathaway before he married her, for example; so instead of just writing,

He married Anne Hathaway in 1582,

he could write

In 1582, he met Anne Hathaway and fell in love with her. They were married, and the following year their daughter Susanna was born.

Instead of writing,

He started school in 1571 and became apprentice to a butcher in 1577,

he could write

He started school in 1571, but he was only able to attend for six years. When he was thirteen years old, his father took him out of school and apprenticed him to a butcher.

The student does not need to check his draft with you before going on. For your reference, though, an acceptable chronological narrative of life events would be:

William Shakespeare was born in Stratford-upon-Avon in 1564. He began school in Stratford when he was seven, but when he was thirteen he left school and was apprenticed to a butcher. Five years later, he met and married Anne Hathaway. They had three children, a daughter and then twins. In 1585, Shakespeare was caught poaching deer in Stratford, so he left his town and went to London instead. There, he worked in a theater and helped to found a theater company. After 1599, his company acted at the Globe Theatre. When it burned down in 1613, Shakespeare retired and went back to Stratford. He died there on April 23, 1616.

A shorter version is also acceptable:

William Shakespeare was born in Stratford-upon-Avon in 1564. In 1585, he went to London and began to work in the theater. He founded a theater company which began to perform at the Globe Theatre. When the Globe burned down in 1613, Shakespeare retired and went back to Stratford. He died there on April 23, 1616.

STEP TWO: **Draft the paragraphs about work**

Student instructions for Step Two:

Now, you'll work on writing the paragraphs about Shakespeare's work.

Below, you'll see three separate pieces of information. The first is a chronological list of Shakespeare's major works. The second is a list of Shakespeare's plays, divided by type (comedy, tragedy, history). The third is part of an essay telling more about each play. (It would be a boring sketch if you just listed the plays; you should be able to give a little more detail, but I'm assuming that you haven't yet *read* all 36 plays.)

As you read through this information, keep two things in mind.

First, there are two ways to organize these paragraphs. You can write one paragraph about the tragedies, one about the comedies, and one about the histories—the method followed in the biographical sketch of Omar Khayyám. Definitions of each type of play are provided; you would want to use some of this information.

Or you can put the plays in chronological order and and write about each one—the method followed in the Noah Webster sketch. If you follow this second method, you may want to know that Shakespeare's plays are traditionally divided into three periods: 1590–1594 (early or first), 1595–1600 (middle or second), and 1601–1609 (late or third). The essay below tells a little more about these periods.

You don't need to put in the dates for every single play, but try to use at least three dates. You may use either commas or parentheses to set off the dates.

Pattern 1	*Pattern 2*
The histories	First period works (1590–1594)
The comedies	Second period works (1595–1600)
The tragedies	Third period works (1601–1609)

Second, don't try to list all of the plays! An essay with a long list of titles is boring and hard to read. Pick at least six but not more than eight or ten plays to mention, and make sure that you say something specific about each one. If you are already familiar with some of Shakespeare's work, use your background knowledge as well as the information in the essay.

If you have trouble, ask your instructor for help. If not, you can continue on to Step Three without showing your work.

HOW TO HELP THE STUDENT WITH STEP TWO

Encourage the student to draw on any knowledge he may have of Shakespeare; he can summarize plots and discuss characters of familiar plays. Where he uses the essay to fill in information, remind him not to use the exact words of the source material.

The student does not need to check his draft with you before going on. For your reference, though, an acceptable draft organized by chronology would be:

During the first period of Shakespeare's work (1590-1594), Shakespeare was improving his skills. His play Love's Labour's Lost *tells the story of a king and three lords who give up the company of women so that they can study.* The Comedy of Errors *is about mistakes in identity. The three parts of the history play* Henry VI *tell what happened during the Wars of the Roses.*

In the second period (1595-1600) Shakespeare wrote more comedies. A Midsummer Night's Dream *and* The Merchant of Venice *both have three plots woven together.*

In the last period, Shakespeare wrote some of his greatest plays. He wrote Hamlet, *which has amazing poetry.* Macbeth *is about a man who causes his own downfall.* King Lear *is about old age.*

An acceptable description divided by type of play would be:

Shakespeare wrote many comedies that end with a wedding. In The Taming of the Shrew *(1596), a young woman with a bad temper marries a man with an even worse temper.* As You Like It *has both serious and funny elements.* Twelfth Night *weaves together high comedy and low comedy.*

Shakespeare's tragedies tell about suffering and death. In Romeo and Juliet, *the hero and heroine fall in love and then die.* Hamlet *is about revenge, a ghost, and madness. In* King Lear, *the old king is deceived by his daughters.*

Shakespeare also wrote plays based on history. Henry V *(1598) is about the ideal king of England.* Henry IV *has two parts and stars Hotspur and Falstaff.* Richard III *(1593) tells the story of the duke of Gloucester, who murdered his nephews so he could become king.*

STEP THREE: **Finish the sketch**

Student instructions for Step Three:

> Now put your composition together. Read through it out loud, listening for any awkward sentences. Then read it again, looking for mistakes in spelling, punctuation, and capitalization. If you used any passive verbs, ask yourself whether an active verb would be better.
>
> When you are content with your work, show it to your instructor.

HOW TO HELP THE STUDENT WITH STEP THREE

This assignment blends together skills that the student has been developing over the past 19 weeks: the ability to read a piece of writing and summarize it in his own words; construction of chronological narratives; description; and organization.

Remember that the student is still a beginner, though, and don't expect poetic literary summaries. ("This play is about" is a perfectly adequate paragraph opener.) Transitions and other more advanced techniques will be addressed in later lessons.

Full versions of acceptable sample compositions are below, followed by the rubric.

William Shakespeare was born in Stratford-upon-Avon in 1564. He began school in Stratford when he was seven, but when he was thirteen he left school and was apprenticed to a butcher. Five years later, he met and married Anne Hathaway. They had three children, a daughter and then twins. In 1585, Shakespeare was caught poaching deer in Stratford, so he left his town and went to London instead. There, he worked in a theater and helped to found a theater company. After 1599, his company acted at the Globe Theatre.

During the first period of Shakespeare's work (1590–1594), Shakespeare was improving his skills. His play Love's Labour's Lost *tells the story of a king and three lords who give up the company of women so that they can study.* The Comedy of Errors *is about mistakes in identity. The three parts of the history play* Henry VI *tell what happened during the Wars of the Roses.*

In the second period (1595–1600) Shakespeare wrote more comedies. A Midsummer Night's Dream *and* The Merchant of Venice *both have three plots woven together.*

In the last period, Shakespeare wrote some of his greatest plays. He wrote Hamlet, *which has amazing poetry.* Macbeth *is about a man who causes his own downfall.* King Lear *is about old age.*

When the Globe burned down in 1613, Shakespeare retired and went back to Stratford. He died there on April 23, 1616.

William Shakespeare was born in Stratford-upon-Avon in 1564. In 1585, he went to London and began to work in the theater. He founded a theater company which began to perform at the Globe Theatre. When the Globe burned down in 1613, Shakespeare retired and went back to Stratford. He died there on April 23, 1616.

Shakespeare wrote many comedies that end with a wedding. In The Taming of the Shrew *(1596), a young woman with a bad temper marries a man with an even worse temper.* As You Like It *has both serious and funny elements.* Twelfth Night *weaves together high comedy and low comedy.*

Shakespeare's tragedies tell about suffering and death. In Romeo and Juliet, *the hero and heroine fall in love and then die.* Hamlet *is about revenge, a ghost, and madness. In* King Lear, *the old king is deceived by his daughters.*

Shakespeare also wrote plays based on history. Henry V *(1598) is about the ideal king of England.* Henry IV *has two parts and stars Hotspur and Falstaff.* Richard III *(1593) tells the story of the duke of Gloucester, who murdered his nephews so he could become king.*

Week 20 Rubric
Biographical Sketch

Organization

1 The sketch should begin with a brief chronological narrative. This should be at least 50 and not more than 150 words. The chronological narrative can either cover all of Shakespeare's life in one paragraph, or can cover birth to 1599 in the first paragraph and 1613–1616 in a paragraph at the end of the composition.
2 The events in the narrative should be listed in chronological order.
3 The sketch should contain three paragraphs describing Shakespeare's works. The three paragraphs should either describe the works in the order they were composed, or should describe them by type (history, comedy, tragedy).
4 At least six but not more than ten plays should be named.
5 The sketch should give specific details about each play listed.
6 The sketch should not use the exact words of the source material.

Mechanics

1 Each sentence should make sense on its own when read aloud.
2 Each proper name should be capitalized.
3 Possessive forms should be written properly.
4 Personal pronouns should have clear antecedents and be of the proper gender.
5 Verb tense should be consistent throughout.

When the student is talking about Shakespeare's life, past tense should be used. When he is describing the action of a play, he may use either past or present tense—but he should always use the *same* tense when describing a play.

Shakespeare wrote many comedies that end with a wedding. In The Taming of the Shrew *(1596), a young woman with a bad temper marries a man with an even worse temper.* As You Like It *has both serious and funny elements.* Twelfth Night *weaves together high comedy and low comedy.*

is correct. The first verb is past because it describes something Shakespeare did in the past. The other verbs, describing the actions in the plays, are all present tense.

Shakespeare wrote many comedies that end with a wedding. In The Taming of the Shrew *(1596), a young woman with a bad temper married a man with an even worse temper.* As You Like It *had both serious and funny elements.* Twelfth Night *weaves together high comedy and low comedy.*

is not correct because the first two play descriptions use past tense while the third uses present.

6 Subjects and verbs must be in agreement.

Day Four: Copia Exercise

Focus: Indirect objects and prepositional phrases

STEP ONE: **Review**

Student instructions for Step One:

In the following sentence, turn the appropriate descriptive adjective into a noun and rewrite the sentence.

Webster published a number of political pamphlets.

In the following sentence, turn the appropriate noun into a descriptive adjective and rewrite the sentence.

He did not accept the patronage of a king.

In the following sentence, transform the passive verb into an active verb and rewrite the sentence.

His studies were interrupted by the outbreak of the War of Independence.

In the following sentence, transform the active verb into a passive verb and rewrite the sentence.

Archimedes contrived all sorts of engines against the Romans.

HOW TO HELP THE STUDENT WITH STEP ONE

The correct transformations are:

Webster published a number of pamphlets about politics.
He did not accept kingly patronage. OR He did not accept a king's patronage.
The outbreak of the War of Independence interrupted his studies.
All sorts of engines against the Romans were contrived by Archimedes.

STEP TWO: **Understand how to transform indirect objects into prepositional phrases (Student Responsibility)**

Student instructions for Step Two:

When you learned how to make a passive verb into an active verb, you also learned how to take the subject of a sentence and transform it into the object of a preposition. So, when the sentence

Regan deceives King Lear

becomes

King Lear is deceived by **Regan**

the subject, Regan, becomes the object of the preposition "by."

There is another part of speech that can be transformed into the object of a preposition: the indirect object. This is a simple transformation, but you can use it to bring some variety to your sentences.

An indirect object is a word that is indirectly affected by an action verb. In the sentence

S V IO DO

Annie Sullivan gave Helen a doll.

"doll" is the direct object; it receives the action of the verb "gave" (meaning that the doll itself was the thing given). "Helen" is the indirect object. Helen didn't get given. No one picked her up and handed her over. But the action of giving the doll *did* affect Helen; she ended up with a new doll.

Indirect objects can be taken out of their place (between the verb and the direct object), and paired up with a preposition to express the same meaning:

S V DO OP

Annie Sullivan gave a doll to Helen.

In this transformed sentence, the indirect object has become the object of the preposition "to."

STEP THREE: **Add to the Sentence Variety chart (Student Responsibility)**

Student instructions for Step Three:

Write the following principle and illustration on the next line of your Sentence Variety chart:

indirect object ⟶ object of the preposition	The mother gave the baby a bottle. The mother gave a bottle to the baby.

STEP FOUR: **Practice sentence variety**

Student instructions for Step Four:

In the following sentences, transform each indirect object into an object of a preposition and rewrite the sentence on the line below.

HOW TO HELP THE STUDENT WITH STEP FOUR

These transformations are not complicated. The second sentence may slow the student up; it is an imperative sentence with an understood subject. However, the subject isn't affected by the transformation.

His mother gave him a fine rich cake.

His mother gave a fine rich cake to him.

Mary, get me a silk thread and a chunk of fire.

Mary, get a silk thread and a chunk of fire for me.

They offered him gold and silver.

They offered gold and silver to him.

Jane showed Michael a little pebbly hollow.

Jane showed a little pebbly hollow to Michael.

Week 21: Sequence: Natural Process

Day One: Outlining Exercise

Focus: Finding the central topic in each paragraph of a sequence of events

STEP ONE: Read (Student Responsibility)

Student instructions for Step One:

Read the following passage.

STEP TWO: Construct a one-level outline

Student instructions for Step Two:

This passage walks you through the spawning cycle of salmon. Each paragraph explains a different part of the cycle. The exception is the first paragraph; like an introduction to a description, the first paragraph gives an overview of the entire process.

Construct your one-level outline now. If you have difficulty, ask your instructor for help. When you are finished, show your outline to your instructor.

HOW TO HELP THE STUDENT WITH STEP TWO

Each paragraph is centered around a different part of the spawning process.

Suggested answers:

I. Salmon spawning OR Salmon reproduction
II. How they find their way OR Theories about how they find their way
III. Getting ready for the journey OR Changes before the journey
IV. The journey itself OR The journey home
V. Getting ready to mate OR Preparing the mating bed

VI. The mating process OR The spawning itself
VII. The salmon die OR After the spawning
VIII. The salmon hatch OR The salmon grow
IX. The process begins again OR The young salmon begin to spawn.

If necessary, use the following dialogues to help the student.

Paragraph 1
Instructor: This paragraph sums up the whole process that the passage is about, from beginning to end. What process is this whole passage about?

Student: Salmon spawning

Paragraph 2
Instructor: What are the theories in the second paragraph about?

Student: How salmon find their way home

Instructor: That is the topic of the paragraph.

Paragraph 3
Instructor: When do all of the changes described in this paragraph happen? Hint: right before something important starts.

Student: Before the salmon journey back

Instructor: This paragraph focuses on the changes that happen before the journey.

Paragraph 4
Instructor: What aspect of the journey is discussed in this paragraph? Hint: the answer is in the first sentence of the paragraph.

Student: The journey is long and tiring.

Instructor: The topic of the paragraph is "The journey itself" or "The long, tiring journey."

Paragraph 5
Instructor: What action is described in the fifth paragraph?

Student: Making the mating bed

Instructor: That is the topic of the paragraph.

Paragraph 6
Instructor: What action is described in the sixth paragrah?

Student: The mating OR Fertilizing the eggs

Instructor: That is the topic of the paragraph.

Paragraph 7
Instructor: What happens after the spawning?

Student: Most salmon die.

Instructor: You could phrase the main point either as "The salmon die" or "After the spawning."

Paragraph 8
Instructor: What is the process described in this paragraph?

Student: The salmon grow up.

Instructor: That is the main topic of the paragraph.

Paragraph 9
Instructor: What process is described in this final paragraph? Hint: it's the same one described in the first paragraph.

Student: The salmon spawn.

Instructor: You could phrase the main topic either as "The process starts over" or "The young salmon spawn."

Day Two: Analyzing the Topos

Focus: Understanding the form of a sequence describing a natural process

Today, the student will examine the elements of a sequence. The assignment should be completed independently. The student's directions are reproduced below for your convenience.

> The passage you read for the last exercise is an example of a *sequence,* a form you haven't seen before.
>
> A sequence has something in common with a chronological narrative of past events; both list a series of events in the order that they happened. A chronological narrative tells you about events that happened *once.* The Rosetta Stone was only found once; Leeuwenhoek only discovered microscopic creatures for the first time once; Genghis Khan's men only pursued Muhammad Shah to his final hiding place one time.
>
> But a sequence lists events that happen over and over and over again. In science, a sequence can describe the steps in a natural process—like the birth of a star, the transformation of peat into coal, or the germination of a seed. In history, a sequence can describe the way that a past process worked—the way a seventeenth-century mill ground grain into flour, or how a navigator on a sailing ship read the sky and set his course. Or a sequence can tell *how* to do something in the future: do a magic trick, train a dog, roast a chicken.

STEP ONE: **Examine model passages**

Your outline of the sequence about salmon probably looked something like this:

I. Salmon spawning
II. How salmon find their way
III. Changes before the journey
IV. The journey itself
V. Getting ready to mate
VI. The spawning itself
VII. After the spawning
VIII. The salmon grow.
IX. The process begins again.

Like the first sentence in a description, the first paragraph sums up the whole process of salmon spawning. With your pencil, write on the first line to the right "Introduction/summary."

The second paragraph tells you what scientists known and don't know about the process. On the second line, write "Scientific background."

The next six paragraphs each describe one step in the process, moving chronologically from the beginning to the end. Turn your paper sideways, and write "Step-by-step process" on the lines.

The final paragraph tells you when the process will happen again. Remember, a sequence describes a series of steps that repeats itself over and over. On the final line, write "The cycle repeats."

Read the following description carefully, looking for the same elements.

You should have recognized three of the same elements in this sequence.

The first paragraph is an introduction and summary: what honey is, where it comes from, and where bees live. Write "Introduction/Summary" in the margin next to the first paragraph.

The next four paragraphs progress, step by step, through the honey-making process. Write "Step-by-step process" in the margin next to those paragraphs.

The last paragraph tells you that the process repeats itself "whenever there are flowers in bloom." Write "The cycle repeats" in the margin next to the final paragraph.

This sequence doesn't tell you what scientists think about bees, but it contains the other three elements.

Like descriptions and chronological narratives, sequences can stand on their own or form a small part of a longer composition. If a sequence stands on its own, it should have at least three of the elements listed above. But a sequence that's part of a larger essay can have just one element: the step-by-step process. The following simple sequence appears in a much longer chapter about growth and decay in nature:

The step-by-step process of cell division is the only element in that sequence. Write "Step-by-step process" in the margin next to the paragraph.

A short sequence can also have just two elements, like the following:

Next to the first paragraph, write "Introduction/summary." Next to the second, write "Step-by-step process."

STEP TWO: **Write down the pattern of the topos**

Copy the following onto a blank sheet of paper in the Reference section of your Composition Notebook.

Sequence: Natural Process

Definition: A step-by-step description of a cycle that occurs in nature

Procedure	Remember
1. Describe the natural process chronologically, step by step. 2. Decide which other elements to include: a. Introduction/summary b. Scientific background c. Repetition of the process	

Day Three: Practicing the Topos

Focus: Learning how to write a sequence describing a natural process

Today, the student will work on constructing the core element of a sequence: the step-by-step process.

STEP ONE: **Plan the step-by-step process**

Student instructions for Step One:

Using the following paragraphs of information, list all of the events, in the order in which they occur, that happen to a star as it begins to age and then dies. Not all of the steps are listed in each paragraph, and some of the paragraphs overlap. You'll have to figure out the order in which the steps occur.

Try to use phrases and very brief sentences rather than complete detailed sentences on your list. If you copy down complete sentences from the paragraphs, you'll make it much harder to use your own words rather than the words of the source material when you actually write your paragraphs.

When you are finished with your list, check it with your instructor before continuing on.

HOW TO HELP THE STUDENT WITH STEP ONE

The student's list should resemble the following. The italicized events are optional; some students will include them, but leaving them out is acceptable.

1. Stars burn hydrogen.
2. Heavier core forms.
3. Star shrinks, gets hotter.
4. *Star gets hungry.*
5. *Helium sitting at core*
6. Star begins collapse.
7. Core shrinks.
8. Outer layers expand, cool.
9. *Star gets brighter and cooler.*
10. Now is red giant
11. *Goes on shrinking and expanding*
12. Helium core ignites OR Helium flash
13. Helium fuel all burns OR Fire at core goes out.
14. Outer core keeps burning.
15. *Outer envelope moves outward.*
16. Planetary nebula forms.
17. *Has small core with shell OR Has carbon core and glowing outer ring*
17. Star becomes white dwarf.
18. All fuel is burned up.
19. Star becomes black dwarf.

Note: either 6 or 7 should be present, but both are not necessary (although acceptable)

It may take the student several tries to list all of the events. Feel free to prompt as much as necessary. Ways to prompt might include:

Read a missing event to the student and say "Where do you think this goes on your list?"

Say "What happens *immediately before* [OR *just after*] this event?" (while pointing to event on student's list).

Tell the student "You should have at least 12 or 13 separate events."

If the student just lists a stage without explanation ("Planetary nebula, white dwarf, black dwarf"), point out that these are names and not events and that the *events* creating these stages must be listed.

STEP TWO: **Divide the list into paragraphs**

Student instructions for Step Two:

> In Step Three, you'll write a step-by-step sequence that tells how a hydrogen-burning star dies. This sequence should be organized into paragraphs: one paragraph for each stage in the star's death. Looking at your list, draw lines between the events to separate them into stages. Jot down the name of the stage beside each set of events.
>
> Hint: the first stage is *not* "red giant." You'll have to make up your own name for the first stage. When you are finished, check your work with your instructor.

HOW TO HELP THE STUDENT WITH STEP TWO

The student should have separated the list into the approximate divisions below. Notice that the first part of the list can be divided into either one or two stages, depending on whether not the student wants to describe the star before the aging process starts.

These divisions are not hard and fast. Some events go equally well at the end of one stage or at the beginning of the next.

Give the student any help needed (including telling her the answers, if you have to). The student is essentially constructing an informal two-level outline to write from; this may be challenging for some students.

1. Stars burn hydrogen.	*Star before it ages*
2. Heavier core forms.	OR *Main sequence*
3. Star shrinks, gets hotter.	*star* (optional)
4. Star gets hungry.	
5. Helium sitting at core	
6. Star begins collapse.	*Aging star* OR
7. Core shrinks.	*Death sequence*
8. Outer layers expand, cool.	*starts*
9. Star gets brighter and cooler.	
10. Now is red giant	*Red giant*
11. Goes on shrinking and expanding	
12. Helium core ignites OR Helium flash	
13. Helium fuel all burns OR Fire at core goes out.	
14. Outer core keeps burning.	*Planetary nebula*
15. Outer envelope moves outward.	
16. Planetary nebula forms.	
17. Has small core with shell OR Has carbon core and glowing outer ring	
17. Star becomes white dwarf.	*White dwarf*
18. All fuel is burned up.	
19. Star becomes black dwarf.	*Black dwarf*

STEP THREE: **Write the sequence**

Student instructions for Step Three:

> Using your list and referring back to the source material for details, write five (or six) paragraphs about the death of a star. Each stage should be described in a separate paragraph.
>
> Don't use the exact words of the source material; use your thesaurus to find synonyms, and rephrase where possible.
>
> Give at least one descriptive detail about the star in each stage (color, temperature, size, mass, etc.)
>
> When you are finished, check your work with your instructor.

HOW TO HELP THE STUDENT WITH STEP THREE

An acceptable sample paragraph from this sequence might resemble this (the "aging star" section of the sequence):

> *As the star begins to get older, the core gets heavier and hotter. The core collects helium, but the star isn't hot enough to burn it. As the core shrinks, the outer layers of the star expand and grow cooler.*

This is the mimimal amount of detail the student should aim to include. More detailed and longer paragraphs are also acceptable.

Check the student's work using the following rubric:

Week 21 Rubric
Sequence: Natural Process

Organization

1 There is no specific word count for this exercise, but it should be either five or six paragraphs in length.
2 The paragraphs should be, in order: hydrogen stars (optional), the beginning of the death process, red giant, planetary nebula, white dwarf, black dwarf.
3 Within each paragraph, the events should be listed in chronological order.
4 Each paragraph should contain some descriptive detail about the star at that stage (color, temperature, size, mass, etc.).
5 The sequence should not use the exact words of the source material.

Mechanics

1 Each sentence should make sense on its own when read aloud.
2 Possessive forms should be written properly.
3 Each paragraph should have at least two sentences.
4 Verb tense should be consistent throughout.
5 Subjects and verbs must be in agreement.

Day Four: Copia Exercise

Focus: Transforming infinitives into participles

STEP ONE: **Review**

Student instructions for Step One:

Rewrite the following sentences according to the instructions. Check your work with your instructor.

Turn the appropriate descriptive adjective into a noun.

Water droplets in the atmosphere act like prisms.

Turn the appropriate two nouns into descriptive adjectives.

Rainbows form when beams of sunlight break through a shower of rain.

Transform the passive verb into an active verb.

The common honey bee from the earliest period has been kept by people.

Transform the active verb into a passive verb.

From these flowers, the bees collect the nectar and honey.

Transform the indirect object into the object of a preposition.

Twenty thousand bees can bring the hive a pound of nectar.

The correct transformations are:

Droplets of water in the atmosphere act like prisms.
Rainbows form when sunlight beams break through a rain shower.
People have kept the common honey bee from the earliest period OR From the earliest period, people have kept the common honey bee.
The nectar and honey are collected from these flowers by the bees OR The nectar and honey are collected by the bees from these flowers.
Twenty thousand bees can bring a pound of nectar to the hive.

STEP TWO: **Understand how to transform infinitives into participles (Student Responsibility)**

Student instructions for Step Two:

Read the following two sentences out loud.

The star begins **to grow** hungry for a new energy source.
The star begins **growing** hungry for a new energy source.

In the first sentence, the main verb *begins* is followed by an *infinitive*. An infinitive is a verb form that starts with *to*. Write *inf.* over the bolded "to grow" in the first sentence.

In the second sentence, the main verb is followed by a *participle*. A participle is a verb form that ends with *ing*. Write *part.* over the bolded "growing" in the second sentence.

When a main verb is followed by an infinitive, you can often change that infinitive to a participle. In the next two sentences, underline the main verb twice. Write *inf.* over the infinitive and *part.* over the participle.

The outermost part of the star continues to expand.
The outermost part of the star continues expanding.

In both sentences, you should have underlined the main verb "continues." "To expand" is the infinitive; "expanding" is the participle.

When you change an infinitive to a participle, you might have to make other changes to the sentence. The changes might be minor, like inserting punctuation:

The male salmon patrols the area to keep away intruders.
The male salmon patrols the area**,** keeping away intruders.

Or you might need to rearrange the words in the sentence so that it's easier to understand. Read the next three sentences out loud:

The darker color makes it easier to blend into the water.
(The darker color makes it easier blending into the water.)
The darker color makes blending into the water easier.

Not every infinitive can be changed into a participle. Read the next two sentences out loud.

Only a few salmon live to mate again.
Only a few salmon live mating again.

Always read your transformed sentences out loud to make sure that they still make sense!

STEP THREE: **Add to the Sentence Variety chart (Student Responsibility)**

Student instructions for Step Three:

Write the following principle and illustration on the next line of your Sentence Variety chart:

infinitives ←→ participles	The truth needs saying. The truth needs to be said.

STEP FOUR: **Practice sentence variety**

Student instructions for Step Four:

> In the following sentences, transform each infinitive into a participle and rewrite the sentence on the line below. The last sentence will require you to make another change as well; be careful!
>
> Check your finished work with your instructor.
>
> When a red giant starts to expand, its core temperature is still low.
> The core contracts until the helium begins to ignite.
> The hydrogen shell continues to burn as the core contracts.

HOW TO HELP THE STUDENT WITH STEP FOUR

These transformations are straightforward:

When a red giant starts expanding, its core temperature is still low.
The core contracts until the helium begins igniting.
The hydrogen shell continues burning as the core contracts.

Week 22: Sequence: Natural Process

Day One: Outlining Exercise and Topos Review

Focus: Finding the central topic in each paragraph of a sequence of events; reviewing the form of a sequence

Today's assignment will combine outlining with a brief review of the form of a sequence. This will give the student two days to work on a sequence that includes all four of the elements studied so far.

STEP ONE: Read (Student Responsibility)

Student instructions for Step One:

Read the following passage about severe weather. Some of the terms and abbreviations may be unfamiliar, so review them before you read:

Condensation point: the temperature at which water in the air will turn liquid.

Latent heat: heat released or absorbed during a change of state (such as condensation, melting, or boiling).

Tropopause: the boundary between the troposphere (the lowest layer of the Earth's atmosphere) and the stratosphere (the second layer of the atmosphere).

Supercooled: when a liquid is chilled past its usual freezing point but remains liquid (usually because it has been chilled so quickly).

-40° C (-40°F): Celsius and Farenheit are two different temperature scales, but this isn't a mistake; -40° is the point at which the two scales meet.

m/s: meters per second.

ft/s: feet per second.

STEP TWO: **Review the pattern of the topos**

Student instructions for Step Two:

> Before you try to outline this passage, look back over the elements that are often present in a sequence:
>
> Introduction/summary
> Scientific background
> Step-by-step process
> Repetition of the process
>
> A sequence often has so much detail in each paragraph that it's hard to locate the most important point. Knowing what each paragraph is doing can help you with your outline.
>
> Decide which element of the sequence each paragraph belongs to, and jot the answer down in the margins of the passage. Before you go on to the next step, check your work with your instructor.

HOW TO HELP THE STUDENT WITH STEP TWO

The student has been asked to identify the element of the sequence that each paragraph belongs to. There is no scientific background in this passage. Be alert to how much time the student is spending on this assignment; if he seems to be struggling, tell him that one of the elements isn't used in this sequence.

The student should have written the following answers in the margins next to each paragraph:

Paragraph 1 Introduction/summary
Paragraph 2 Step-by-step process
Paragraph 3 Step-by-step process
Paragraph 4 Step-by-step process
Paragraph 5 Repetition of the process

STEP THREE: **Construct a one-level outline**

Student instructions for Step Three:

> Now that you know what each paragraph is doing, outlining the passage should be easier.
>
> Start with the first paragraph. You can't just outline this by writing:
>
> I. Introduction/summary
>
> because that doesn't say anything about the *content* of the passage. Ask yourself "What is this paragraph introducing me to?" The answer could become your first major point.
>
> As you outline the next three paragraphs, ask yourself "Which stage of the process does this paragraph describe?"
>
> Then ask yourself "In that stage of the process, what is the first, or most important, or biggest thing that happens?"
>
> See if you can figure out how to approach the last paragraph.
>
> If you're still confused, you can ask your instructor for help. When you are finished, show your work to your instructor.

HOW TO HELP THE STUDENT WITH STEP THREE

The student's outline should resemble the following:

Suggested answers:

I. Introduction to thunderstorms OR When and where thunderstorms happen
II. Warm air begins to rise OR The storm begins to form OR Conditions that cause storms
III. Air forms a cumulonimbus cloud OR Cumulonimbus cloud forms.
IV. Rain or snow begins to fall OR The storm reaches maturity.
V. The end of the storm OR The storm in decline OR More thunderstorms form

If necessary, use the following dialogues to help the student.

Paragraph 1
Instructor: Where can thunderstorms happen?

Student: Anywhere

Instructor: The passage tells you something else about thunderstorms. What is it?

Student: When they happen OR How long they last

Instructor: So you could sum this paragraph up by saying "Where and when thunderstorms happen."

Paragraph 2
Instructor: This paragraph describes the first stage of the storm. During the first stage of the storm, what starts to happen? Hint: the answer is in the second sentence.

Student: The air starts to rise.

Instructor: Everything else that happens during the first stage of the storm comes from that rising air. So you could make your main point "Warm air begins to rise." Since that is the beginning of the storm, you could also use "The beginning of the storm." Both answers refer to the same thing.

Paragraph 3
Instructor: This paragraph describes the second stage of the storm. Both sentences in the paragraph describe the same thing. Hint: it forms, and the droplets and ice crystals and snowflakes are inside it.

Student: The cumulonimbus cloud

Instructor: The formation of the cloud is the most important thing that happens during the second stage. So that should become your main point: "The cumulonimbus cloud forms."

Paragraph 4
Instructor: What's the big thing that happens during the third phrase of the storm? Everything else in the passage explains or describes it.

Student: Rain or snow falls.

Instructor: That is the main point.

Paragraph 5
Instructor: What repeats, in this last paragraph?

Student: Thunderstorms

Instructor: That is the main point of this last paragraph: "The process repeats."

Day Two: Practicing the Topos, Part One

Focus: Learning how to write a sequence describing a natural process

Over the next two days the student will write about the life of the octopus, putting together a full sequence with all four elements. Today the student will work on on the step-by-step process. Tomorrow, he will add the other three elements plus a brief physical description.

The plural of *octopus* can be either *octopi* or *octopuses*. Both are used.

STEP ONE: **Plan the step-by-step process**

Student instructions for Step One:

> Follow the same instructions as last week: use the following paragraphs of information and list all of the events, in the order in which they occur, that happen in an octopus's life. As before, try to use phrases and very brief sentences rather than complete detailed sentences.
>
> When you are finished with your list, check it with your instructor before continuing on.

HOW TO HELP THE STUDENT WITH STEP ONE

The student's list should resemble the following. The italicized points are optional.

1. Eggs have cushion, yolk, shell
2. *Eggs are size of rice*
3. Eggs hatch
4. *Baby is size of flea*
5. Drifts around in the water
6. Many are eaten
7. *Enjoys light*

Note: "Mother guards eggs" does not go here. This early section is about the baby octopus; mother's behavior goes later on, in section on adult octopus.

8. Settles to floor
9. Lives in crevices and caves
10. Stays in same nest
11. Comes out to hunt
12. Finds a mate
13. Male stops eating, organs deteriorate
14. Male leaves den and is often eaten
15. Male dies after mating
16. Female finds den
17. Female lays eggs
18. Female closes up den
19. Female guards eggs
20. Does not eat
21. Washes eggs with water
22. Babies hatch 1–3 months
23. Mother dies

This detail can also go above, in the first part.

It may take the student several tries to list all of the events. Feel free to prompt as much as necessary. Ways to prompt might include:

Read a missing event to the student and say "Where do you think this goes on your list?"

Say "What happens *immediately before* [OR *just after*] this event?" (while pointing to event on student's list).

Tell the student "You should have at least 14 or 15 separate events."

The information in the paragraphs is out of chronological order; many of the details about the baby octopi are found in the paragraphs about the mother's aging and death, and the male's aging is described after the hatching of the eggs, although the male dies soon after it mates (before the eggs are hatched). Remind the student that details about young octopi go in the first part of the list. If necessary, point out the order in which the male and female octopi die.

STEP TWO: **Divide the list into paragraphs**

Student instructions for Step Two:

> Before you write your sequence, you'll need to organize your information into paragraphs: one paragraph for each major stage of an octopus's life.
>
> The stages are:
>
> embryo/egg
> hatchling/young
> mature
> reproducing
> old age
>
> Looking at your list, draw lines between the events to separate them into stages. Jot down the name of the stage beside each set of events.
>
> When you are finished, check your work with your instructor.

HOW TO HELP THE STUDENT WITH STEP TWO

The student should have separated the list into the approximate divisions below. These divisions are not hard and fast; some events go equally well at the end of one stage or at the beginning of the next.

Give the student any help needed (including telling him the answers, if you have to).

1. Eggs have cushion, yolk, shell	
2. Eggs are size of rice	*Embryo/egg*
3. Eggs hatch	
4. Baby is size of flea	
5. Drifts around in the water	*Hatchling/young*
6. Many are eaten	
7. Enjoys light	
8. Settles to floor	
9. Lives in crevices and caves	*Mature*
10. Stays in same nest	
11. Comes out to hunt	
12. Finds a mate	
13. Male stops eating, organs deteriorate	*Old age (male)*
14. Male leaves den and is often eaten	
15. Male dies after mating	
16. Female finds den	
17. Female lays eggs	
18. Female closes up den	*Reproducing*
19. Female guards eggs	
20. Does not eat	
21. Washes eggs with water	
22. Babies hatch 1–3 months	*Old age (female)*
23. Mother dies	

The student may wonder what to do with “finds a mate,” which seems to go with “reproducing” but comes out of order. Instead of having a one-sentence paragraph about finding a mate so that reproduction comes before both old age stages (male and female), suggest that “finding a mate” be treated as part of the mature octopus’s behavior.

A Note From Susan

This problem comes up because the paragraphs don't provide any information about the mating process itself. "Reproducing" should actually be two stages—mating and egg-laying. I decided to leave the mating process out because most of the descriptions are detailed and graphic, and middle-grade students are so easily embarrassed by anything having to do with sex, even octopus sex. Writing is hard enough; I didn't want the student cringing over the paragraphs as well. (And lest you think I'm exaggerating, all of the descriptions say things like "The octopus spermatophor contains about seven billion sperm, equal to thirty human ejaculations" and "The octopus uses several penetration techniques.")

If you have a mature student, you can always send him to the encyclopedia or another reference book (about octopi, that is) to find the missing information.

STEP THREE: **Write the step-by-step process**

Student instructions for Step Three:

> Using your list and referring back to the source material for details, write six paragraphs about the life cycle of an octopus. Each stage should be described in a separate paragraph. Don't use the exact words of the source material: use your thesaurus to find synonyms, and rephrase where possible.
>
> Give at least one descriptive detail about the octopus in each stage (behavior, habits, appearance).

HOW TO HELP THE STUDENT WITH STEP THREE

An acceptable sample paragraph from this sequence might resemble this (the "female dies" section of the sequence):

> *After the eggs hatch, the female octopus dies. She doesn't care for the baby octopi. Instead, the end of her life cycle comes when she has finished guarding the eggs.*

This is probably the most difficult paragraph to write because there's only one event in it. If necessary, prompt the student to go back and find additional information in the source material.

Other paragraphs will be longer and contain more detail.

Check the student's work using the following rubric.

Week 22 Rubric Sequence: Natural Process

Organization

1 There is no specific word count for this exercise, but it should be six paragraphs in length.
2 The paragraphs should be, in order: embryo/egg, hatchling/young, mature, reproduction, old age.
3 Within each paragraph, the events should be listed in chronological order.
4 Each paragraph should contain some descriptive detail about the octopus at that stage (behavior, habits, appearance).
5 The sequence should not use the exact words of the source material.

Mechanics

1 Each sentence should make sense on its own when read aloud.
2 Possessive forms should be written properly.
3 Each paragraph should have at least two sentences.
4 Verb tense should be consistent throughout.
5 Subjects and verbs must be in agreement.

Day Three: Practicing the Topos, Part Two

Focus: Learning how to write a sequence describing a natural process

Today, the student will finish the composition by adding the other three elements of the sequence, plus a brief description of what the mature octopus looks like.

STEP ONE: **Write the introduction**

Student instructions for Step One:

> Go back now and read the first paragraphs of the salmon essay (p. 279), the honey essay (p. 282), and the passage on thunderstorms (p. 291). All three of these sequences have an

introductory paragraph that tells you what the subject of the sequence is. Each paragraph also draws you into the composition by telling you something interesting about that subject.

Using the information below, write a similar introductory paragraph that has two to five sentences. This paragraph could use one of two themes:

The octopus is a very intelligent creature OR

People have always been fascinated by the octopus.

If you have trouble getting started, you can use one of the sentences above as your first sentence.

HOW TO HELP THE STUDENT WITH STEP ONE

To write this paragraph, the student can simply summarize the information in the first two paragraphs (octopus intelligence) or the last three (what has fascinated people about the octopus). If she has trouble, tell her to think about the assignment as if she were writing one of the narrative summaries from earlier in the course.

The paragraph should be two to five sentences long. Acceptable paragraphs might be:

The octopus is a very intelligent creature. It can escape from almost any aquarium, and knows how to make an escape plan. One octopus even got out of its aquarium and was found in the library, turning the pages of books!

The octopus is known for its intelligence. It knows how to make plans for escape. The French scientist Jacques Cousteau once watched an octopus climb out of a tank, find a way down a table leg, get to the edge of a boat, and jump into the water! Another octopus escaped, slid into the library, and paged through the books there.

The octopus has always fascinated and frightened us. People have told stories about boats being attacked by a giant octopus. Octopi have been accused of drowning swimmers and grabbing sailors. They have been called terrible, ferocious monsters.

If the student has difficulty, say "How do we know that the octopus is intelligent? Give me two examples OR What stories have people told about the octopus? What have they called it?"

STEP TWO: **Write the paragraph about scientific knowledge**

Student instructions for Step Two:

Go back now and read the second paragraph of the salmon essay (page 279). This paragraph tells you something about the current state of scientific knowledge. You'll write a similar paragraph now about the octopus, after reading the passages below.

Your paragraph should be two to five sentences in length. It should say two things:

People have known about the octopus for a long, long time.

Not enough actual scientific study has been done.

If you have trouble getting started, you can use the two sentences above. After each sentence, give an example or detail.

When you're finished, show your paragraph to your instructor.

HOW TO HELP THE STUDENT WITH STEP TWO

An acceptable short paragraph would be:

People have known about the octopus since the time of the Egyptians. Aristotle described it, and so did other Greek and Roman writers. But not enough scientific study has been done on the octopus. Other fish have been studied more, because they are worth more money.

A longer and more detailed paragraph is also acceptable, as long as it is no more than five sentences.

If the student has difficulty, say "Who knew about the octopus in the past? Give me two examples. Why haven't more scientific studies been done in the present?"

STEP THREE: **Write about the repetition**

Student instructions for Step Three:

> You already have enough source material to write your final paragraph, about the repetition of the whole process.
>
> Three of the sequences you've read have finished with this sort of paragraph. Those paragraphs have told you:
>
> *When the thunderstorm is over, more thunderstorms continue to form.*
>
> *Bees keep on collecting nectar all summer.*
>
> *Young salmon start the process all over again.*
>
> Your paragraph should tell the reader, in two or three sentences, that once the octopus eggs have hatched, the whole cycle will begin again.
>
> If you have trouble getting started, ask your instructor for a prompt. When you're finished, show your composition to your instructor.

HOW TO HELP THE STUDENT WITH STEP THREE

An acceptable one-sentence paragraph would be:

Now that the babies have hatched, they will drift through the water until they are old enough to settle on the bottom and begin the whole process again.

An acceptable three-sentence paragraph would be:

As soon as the babies grow to be adults, they will go through the whole process again. The female will lay eggs, guard them, and then die. The octopus does not live long!

If the student needs a prompt, say "Tell me in one sentence what the babies will do now that they've hatched."

STEP FOUR: **Add a brief physical description**

Student instructions for Step Four:

Now you'll write a brief description—three to six sentences—of the adult octopus. You'll put this description into your sequence in one of two places:

1. Right after the paragraph about the mature octopus.
2. Between the scientific knowledge paragraph and the beginning of the step-by-step process.

You can decide where the paragraph sounds most natural.

To describe an octopus, use the model for a scientific description of an object or phenomenon. You can take a minute to review that chart in the Reference section of your Composition Notebook.

When you write this description, use the removed impersonal point of view.

Use any details from the source material you've already seen, plus the paragraphs and photos below.

HOW TO HELP THE STUDENT WITH STEP FOUR

This should be a fairly straightforward description. It should be three to six sentences in length. An acceptable description might be:

The grown octopus has a short round body and a huge head which contains most of its organs. It uses its eight tentacles to move and to hold its prey. It has a sharp vicious beak and two large eyes on top of its body.

STEP FIVE: **Put the composition together**

Student instructions for Step Five:

Now put your composition together in the following order:

Introduction
Scientific knowledge
(Description)
Step-by-step process
(Or description here)
Repetition

Read it out loud, checking for grammatical errors and awkward sentences.
When you are finished, show your composition to your instructor.

HOW TO HELP THE STUDENT WITH STEP FIVE

When the student is finished, check his work using the following rubric.

Week 22 Rubric
Sequence of a Natural Event with Brief Description

Organization

1 There is no specific word count for this exercise, but it should contain the following elements, in order: introduction, scientific knowledge, description (this may also go after the step-by-step process), step-by-step process, repetition.
2 Within each paragraph of the step-by-step process, the events should be listed in chronological order.
3 The description should contain at least three details about the octopus's appearance.
4 The exact words of the source material should not be used.

Mechanics

1 Each sentence should make sense on its own when read aloud.
2 Possessive forms should be written properly.
3 Each paragraph should have at least two sentences.
4 Verb tense should be consistent throughout.
5 Subjects and verbs must be in agreement.

Day Four: Copia Exercise

Focus: Review transforming sentences

Today, the student will review transforming sentences and the Sentence Variety chart.

STEP ONE: **Read**

Student instructions for Step One:

> Read the following excerpt, adapted from the accounts of a nineteenth-century naturalist. As you read, underline any phrases that can be easily transformed, using the principles you've already learned. ("Easily" means that the transformation doesn't sound incredibly awkward and stilted.)

HOW TO HELP THE STUDENT WITH STEP ONE

The following phrases should have been underlined:

> Professor Beale, a distinguished naturalist, was searching for shells on a North Pacific island when he found a small octopus, creeping with its eight tentacles over some rocks towards the sea. Curious to find out how strong the animal was, the professor tried to stop its progress by pulling on one of its tentacles. Finally, with a huge effort and a jerk, he separated the octopus from the rock. The moment the arms came free, the octopus flew directly at the naturalist and fixed with the same strength on his bare arm. When the creature was finally pried away, its powerful suckers had drawn blood wherever they attached.[50]

adjective can become noun
adjective can become noun
infinitive can become participle
active verb can become passive
passive verb can become active

If the student cannot find the phrases, tell him which sentences the phrases are in. If he still needs help, tell him which construction is in that sentence.

STEP TWO: **Transform sentences**

Student instructions for Step Two:

> Rewrite the excerpt on your own paper, transforming each marked sentence. When you are finished, show your work to your instructor.

HOW TO HELP THE STUDENT WITH STEP TWO

Use the following key to check the student's work:

Professor Beale, a naturalist of distinction, was searching for shells on an island in the North Pacific when he found a small octopus, creeping with its eight tentacles over some rocks toward the sea. Curious to find out how strong the animal was, the professor tried stopping its progress by pulling on one of its tentacles. Finally, with a huge effort and a jerk, the octopus was separated by the professor from the rock. The moment the arms came free, the octopus flew directly at the naturalist and fixed with the same strength on his bare arm. When he finally pried the creature away, its powerful suckers had drawn blood wherever they attached.

50. Freely adapted from *Appleton's Journal*, Vol. 11 (D. Appleton & Co., 1874), p. 146.

Part IV

BEGINNING LITERARY CRITICISM: PROSE WRITING ABOUT STORIES WEEKS 23–26

Overview of Weeks 23–26

Over the next four weeks, the student will begin to learn how to write about literature. This unit will focus on fiction.

Basic literary criticism is a type of writing that most students will be asked to perform at some point in their academic career; even engineering students are usually required to take a literature course in the first year of college, and will be assigned "reaction" or "literary analysis" papers. In the first year of this curriculum, students will begin to gently build the skills needed for writing about imaginative literature by writing the answers to basic questions about fiction. These written answers will form the foundation of more advanced skills, taught in later years.

An essay of literary criticism, even a beginning essay written by a middle-school student, is not quite the same as the traditional "book report." Book reports, as they're usually taught, have very little purpose; they consist of a lengthy summary of the plot along with a couple of sentences of "evaluation" ("Here's what I thought about the book"). There's an essential element missing: *analysis*. Book reports tend to encourage students to leap straight past information-gathering (reading—the first step) to an opinion (evaluation—the last step) while skipping the all-important middle step: thinking logically about how and why the story works. In a book report, the plot summary is 90% of the composition; in literary criticism, a brief overview of the story is given in two or three sentences (narration exercises have prepared the student to do this) and the bulk of the composition is taken up with critical analysis.

These four lessons are not a "literature course." Instead, this unit is simply intended to give the student a model for writing about books. The student should be able to take the approach laid out here and apply it to other literature.

The student should label the last section left in the Composition Notebook "Literary Criticism."

Week 23: Hero/Villain, Protagonist/Antagonist

Day One: Read

Focus: Reading

The first step in doing literary criticism is to read the story. *All* the student should do today is go to a comfortable place and read the story.

When you're doing basic literary criticism with a young student, it is very easy to over-analyze literature—to spend too long on any one work, ask too many questions, and criticize too many elements. This can have two unfortunate effects. It can inadvertently train the student to approach literature first as a puzzle to be solved, rather than an imaginative experience to be enjoyed. And it can make the student *dread* literary criticism.

Right from the beginning, encourage the student to enjoy literature first, and analyze it second. The first day of every week should be spent reading the story for enjoyment—and not criticizing or talking about it at all.

STEP ONE: **Understand the background (Student Responsibility)**

Student directions for Step One:

> The first story you'll read for this unit is " Rikki-Tikki-Tavi" by Rudyard Kipling. The story is found in Appendix III.
>
> Rudyard Kipling was born in 1865. His parents were English, but Kipling was born in Bombay, India. At that time, much of India was controlled by the British Empire. The British government sent colonists from England to live in India, and the Indian government was controlled by British officials and the British army. Many writers at Kipling's time wrote about English families who lived in India. (You may have read *A Little Princess,* by Frances Hodgson Burnett. Sara Crewe's father is an Englishman living in India who sends his daughter back to England to school.)
>
> Kipling died in 1936, at the age of 70. He wrote *The Jungle Book, Kim, Captains Courageous,* many other short stories, and poems.

STEP TWO: **Read (Student Responsibility)**

Student instructions for Step Two:

> Read and enjoy.
> Eat a cookie while you're reading.

Day Two: Think

Focus: Hero and villain, protagonist and antagonist, conflict

Today, the student will examine how this story works; tomorrow; she will write about the story.

It's always easier to write about a piece of literature after *talking* about it; putting ideas into spoken words is a little easier than putting them down directly on paper. In Steps Two–Four below, you will need to direct the lesson by carrying on the suggested dialogue with the student. At the end of each dialogue, the student will write a brief observation; these will be used in tomorrow's brief essay assignment.

There is much more that could be said about this story, but this discussion is for beginners, and is intended to be simple and straightforward. The focus is on learning the correct terms for elements of the story, and identifying the villain.

In your discussions, you may need the following pronunciations:

Nag: In Hindi, this is pronounced more like "narg" than the English "nag," but since you're reading in English, you can choose which pronunciation to use.
Nagaina: Nah GYE nah
Karait: Ker ITE
Chuchundra: Chew CHUN drer
Chua: CHEW er

STEP ONE: **Identify the characters**

Student instructions for Step One:

> On a piece of scratch paper, list all of the characters in the story—even the minor ones—in two columns.
>
> There is a very basic division in this story: it has two different kinds of characters. What are they? Identify them, and write this at the top of each column.
>
> When you're finished, you should have a short column and a long column. Check your work with your instructor.

HOW TO HELP THE STUDENT WITH STEP ONE

The student's columns should look like this:

ANIMAL	*HUMAN*	
Rikki-tikki-tavi	*Big man*	
Darzee	*Teddy*	
Chuchundra	*Teddy's mother*	
Darzee's wife		
Nag		
Nagaina		
Karait		
The Coppersmith		
(Chua)		This character is only mentioned, and does not appear; inclusion optional

The student is supposed to identify and name the two different kinds of characters. This is a very basic question unless she overthinks and tries to divide them by "weak and strong" or some other conceptual method. If necessary, say "Which characters wear clothes?"

STEP TWO: **Identify the protagonist**

Carry on the following dialogue with the student. If the student answers as suggested, continue on with the main dialogue and skip the optional dialogue; if the student is confused, use the optional dialogue.

MAIN DIALOGUE / **OPTIONAL DIALOGUE**

Instructor: The first question to ask about a story is: *Who* is the story about? Who is the central character?

Student: Rikki-tikki-tavi

(Answers with another character)

Instructor: Who is the most active character in the whole story—the one who actually solves the problem of the snakes?

Instructor: In any story, the central character is the one who has a problem that needs solving. What is Rikki-tikki-tavi's problem?

Student: The snakes OR Nag and Nagaina

(If the student answers with a specific scene, such as, "Nagaina tried to bite Teddy")

Instructor: What about Nagaina and Karait? Aren't they problems too? What is the overall name for Nagaina, Karait, and Nag?

Instructor: Of course, the people in the story have a problem with the snakes as well. But there's a good reason why Teddy or his parents are *not* the central characters of the story. What do you think that reason is?

Student: They don't solve the problem.

(If student can't answer the question easily)

Instructor: What do Teddy and his parents do to solve the problem of the snakes?

Student: Nothing

Instructor: They are *passive*—which means that they don't do anything to solve the problem.

Instructor: What does the big man do to Karait, the little dust snake?

Student: Beats him with a stick

Instructor: Why doesn't this solve the problem?

Student: He's already dead.

Instructor: What does the big man do to Nag the cobra?

Student: Shoots him

Instructor: That does help solve the problem—but if Rikki-tikki-tavi hadn't already attacked the cobra, the man would have come into the bathroom in the morning without his gun or stick, and Nag would have killed him. What does the man do to Nagaina?

Student: Nothing

Instructor: Rikki-tikki-tavi kills Nagaina and Karait, and he makes it possible for the man to kill Nag. So he's the central character, because he solves the problem of the snakes. There are two different names for the central character of a story. Sometimes, you'll see the central character called a "hero" or a "heroine." A hero or heroine is a central character who's admirable—brave, loving, unselfish, self-sacrificing, and so on. Does Rikki-tikki-tavi have admirable qualities?

Student: Yes

Instructor: What are they?

Student: He is brave [courageous, loyal, etc.].

(If student cannot answer question easily)

Instructor: He follows Nagaina into her hole even though he's frightened. Doing something even though you're scared is . . .

Student: Brave

Instructor: Not all stories have heroes or heroines. A story can also be about someone who is weak, or cowardly, or vain. So there's another term for the central character of a story—a term that lets the central character be less than a heroine. The term is *protagonist.* Read the definition of *protagonist* in your workbook.

Student: The character who wants to get, become, or accomplish something.

Instructor: Draw a line between *pro* and *agonist.* This word is from the Greek. An "agonist" is someone who's active, doing something, fighting, striving, struggling. "Pro" means "first." So the protagonist is the first actor, the most important fighter, the one with the biggest goal to accomplish. What does Rikki-tikki-tavi want to accomplish?

Student: He wants to get rid of the snakes.

Instructor: Look at page 501 of the story. Read me the conversation that begins with "My cousin Chua, the rat" and ends with "Can't you hear, Rikki-tikki?"

Student: *"My cousin Chua, the rat, told me—" said Chuchundra, and then he stopped.*

"Told you what?"

"H'sh! Nag is everywhere, Rikki-tikki. You should have talked to Chua in the garden."

"I didn't—so you must tell me. Quick, Chuchundra, or I'll bite you!"

Chuchundra sat down and cried till the tears rolled off his whiskers. "I am a very poor man," he sobbed. "I never had spirit enough to run out into the middle of the room. H'sh! I mustn't tell you anything. Can't you hear, Rikki-tikki?"

Instructor: Chuchundra knows that the snakes are a problem, but he just tries to stay out of the way. Rikki-tikki-tavi makes a plan to get rid of them. That's the difference between a protagonist and a minor character. Now, on the lines in your workbook, write down what Rikki-tikki-tavi wants to accomplish. Also list three or four adjectives that describe Rikki-tikki-tavi. They should be mostly positive adjectives—but you might also include a word that is less than complimentary about Rikki-tikki-tavi.

Suggested adjectives: brave, loyal, courageous, reckless, cocky or arrogant, proud

STEP THREE: **Identify the antagonist**

Carry on the following dialogue with the student.

Instructor: If Rikki-tikki-tavi had just been adopted by a nice family with no snakes in their garden, there wouldn't really be a problem for the mongoose to solve—and you'd have a very short and boring story. Read me the definition of "antagonist" in your workbook.

Student: The character, force, or circumstance that opposes the protagonist

Instructor: Draw a line between "ant" and "agonist." "Anti" means against, opposing. So the antagonist is the active opponent of the protagonist. An antagonist doesn't have to be another character. In the book *Into Thin Air,* the protagonist wants to climb Mount Everest. The mountain is the antagonist, because the mountain itself is keeping the protagonist from reaching his goal. However, in this story, the antagonist *is* another character. Who is it?

Student: Nag [or Nagaina, or both]

Instructor: Nag and Nagaina together are the antagonists. They oppose Rikki-tikki-tavi. Now read me the definition of "villain" in your workbook.

Student: An antagonist with evil motives

Instructor: Are Nag and Nagaina villains?

Student: Yes.

Instructor: Except in cartoons, villains aren't evil just for the sake of being evil. They too have something that they want to get, or something that they need to accomplish, or something that they want to be. What do Nag and Nagaina want?

Student: They want to have the garden for themselves OR *They want room and quiet*

(If the student answers "To kill the people")
Instructor: What will they get once the people are dead?
Student: The garden for their babies

Instructor: On the lines in your workbook, write down what Nag and Nagaina want, and what they intend to do in order to get it.

STEP FOUR: **Identify the conflict**

Carry on the following dialogue with the student.

Instructor: Now that you know who the protagonist and antagonist are, the last important question about the story will be easy to answer. Read me the definition of "conflict" in your workbook.

Student: The clash between protagonist and antagonist

Instructor: Conflict is what happens when the protagonist wants something and the antagonist wants something—and only one of them can succeed. The conflict *is* the story. If Rikki-tikki-tavi wanted to go swimming and Nag and Nagaina wanted the house to be empty, they might still be enemies, but there wouldn't be much of a story. But Rikki-tikki-tavi wants to kill snakes. If he succeeds, do Nag and Nagaina succeed?

Student: No

Instructor: Nag and Nagaina want the house to be empty—so they intend to kill the people who live there. What do they think Rikki-tikki-tavi will do if the house becomes empty? Look back at the story if you can't remember; the answer is in one of Nag's speeches. [Page 502]

Student: Rikki will go.

Instructor: The snakes and the mongoose can't *both* get what they want. The struggle between them is what creates the story. On the lines in your workbook, write down a brief description of two points in the story at which the cobras and the mongoose clash.

(If the student has difficulty)

Instructor: Why does Nag go into the bathroom?

Student: To kill the man

Instructor: Why does Rikki go into the bathroom?

Student: To kill Nag.

Instructor: You would write "When Nag goes into the bathroom to kill the man, Rikki follows and attacks him."

AND

Instructor: Why does Nagaina go to the house?

Student: To kill the people

Instructor: Why does Rikki follow?

Student: To kill Nagaina

Optional

If the student is still interested, you may add the following:

Instructor: At the very end of the story, Kipling makes the conflict even more intense. Nagaina and Rikki-tikki-tavi are struggling with each other, but Rikki-tikki-tavi also has a conflict with himself. When Nagaina goes to the house, what does she intend to do?

Student: Kill the people

Instructor: She has a new reason to kill the people now; what is it?

Student: They killed her husband.

Instructor: Rikki-tikki-tavi still wants to kill the cobra. But he also has another want: to protect the people. If he leaps forward and bites Nagaina, what will she do?

Student: She will bite Teddy.

Instructor: Rikki might be able to kill her, but only by risking Teddy's life. So there is a conflict between what he wants and what Nagaina wants—but there is also a conflict between Rikki's desire to kill the snake and his desire to protect Teddy. He can't just kill the snake; he has to figure out another solution. What does he do?

Student: He tells Nagaina that he will destroy the last egg.

STEP FIVE: **Begin the Literary Terms chart (Student Responsibility)**

Student instructions for Step Five:

> On the top of a blank piece of paper, write "Literary Terms." Underneath, write the terms learned in this lesson, along with the definitions provided. Place the chart in the Reference section of your notebook.

Day Three: Write

Focus: Writing about the story

Today, the student will write a brief essay of literary criticism. This essay will have two parts: a brief summary of the story and two or three paragraphs discussing the protagonist, antagonist, and conflict.

STEP ONE: **Write the summary**

Student instructions for Step One:

> Begin by writing a narrative summary of the story, just as if you were writing one of the narrations you practiced earlier in the year. This summary should be at least three but not more than eight sentences long.
>
> If you have trouble, ask your instructor for help. When you are finished, check your summary with your instructor.

HOW TO HELP THE STUDENT WITH STEP ONE

The student may use either present or past tense for the summary, but should keep the same tense all the way through.

The student does not need to use the title of the story, but if she does, you may need to remind her that story titles are surrounded by quotation marks, while book titles are italicized (in handwriting, underlined):

The story "Rikki-Tikki-Tavi" is part of The Jungle Book *by Rudyard Kipling.*

The narration should resemble one of the following:

In the story "Rikki-Tikki-Tavi" by Rudyard Kipling, the mongoose Rikki-tikki-tavi is rescued by a boy and his parents and goes to live with them. He discovers that there are cobras in the garden, Nag and Nagaina. The cobras want to kill the people so that they can have the garden for their young. Rikki-tikki-tavi kills Nag and destroys the nest of eggs, but Nag's wife Nagaina goes into the house to kill the family. Rikki gets her to leave the house by showing her the last egg. When she takes the egg and tries to escape, he follows her into her hole and kills her.

Rikki-tikki-tavi was adopted by a family who lived in a bungalow in India. He wanted to protect the family from the cobras who lived in the garden. The male cobra, Nag, tried to kill the father of the family, but Rikki killed Nag instead. Nag's wife Nagaina then tried to kill Teddy, the son. Rikki destroyed Nagaina's eggs, chased Nagaina into her hole, and killed her there.

Rikki-tikki-tavi was a mongoose who lived with a family in an Indian bungalow. Two cobras, Nag and Nagaina, lived in the garden. They wanted to kill the family so that they could have the garden for themselves. Rikki killed Nag when Nag came into the bathroom. Nagaina was so angry about her husband's death that she went to the house to kill the boy, Teddy. Meanwhile, Rikki was destroying Nagaina's eggs. When he heard that Nagaina was in the house, he went after her and lured her away with the last remaining egg. Nagaina took the egg and fled, but Rikki followed her into her hole and killed her beneath the ground.

Because of the length of the story, the student may struggle with a brief summary. Remind him that only Rikki, Nag and Nagaina, and the family need to be in the summary; the other minor characters do not. If he needs additional help, ask him the following questions:

How did Rikki come to live in the bungalow?
Who lived in the garden?
What did Rikki do to Nag?
What did Rikki do to Nagaina?

STEP TWO: **Write the analysis**

Student instructions for Step Two:

Now answer the following questions in two short paragraphs:

First paragraph:

1. Who is the protagonist? What does he want? Why?
   Hint: try not to use the word "protagonist" in your paragraph.
2. Who is the antagonist? What does he/they want? Why?
   Hint: don't use the word "antagonist"!

Second paragraph:

3. How do these wants result in conflict? In what scenes does this conflict most clearly appear?
   When you are finished, show your work to your instructor.

HOW TO HELP THE STUDENT WITH STEP TWO

The paragraphs should resemble the following:

Rikki-tikki-tavi wanted to kill snakes—any snakes. All mongooses want to kill snakes. Two snakes, Nag and Nagaina, lived in the garden of Rikki's bungalow. They wanted to kill the people who lived in the bungalow, so that the garden would be empty. If the people were dead, Rikki would go away, and the garden would be safe for their children.

Nag hid in the bathroom to try to kill the man of the family, but Rikki found him there and attacked him. He was holding onto Nag's hood when the man ran into the bathroom and shot the cobra. Then Rikki found Nagaina's eggs. He was destroying them one at a time when Nagaina went into the house to kill the family because Nag was dead. Rikki

> *went after her. He saved the boy in the family by showing Nagaina the one egg that was left. She left the boy, grabbed the egg, and ran away. But Rikki chased her into her hole underground and killed her there.*

Although the student's paragraphs may be phrased differently, the following information *must* be included:

1. That Rikki wants to kill snakes (all snakes, not just the cobras).
2. That the cobras want the bungalow empty so that their children can grow up safely.
3. That Nag went into the bathroom in order to kill the man.
4. That Rikki killed Nag.
5. That Nagaina went into the house to kill the family *because* Nag was dead.
6. That Rikki tempted her away with the last egg.
7. That Rikki followed her and killed her.

The emphasis is on the *reasons* for the character's actions. If the student leaves one of these out, ask a *why* ("Why did Nagaina go into the house?") or *how* ("How did Rikki kill Nagaina?") question to point this out.

While the student will probably use past tense, it is not incorrect to use present tense: "Rikki wants to kill snakes. Two snakes live in the garden . . ."

Notice that it is correct to say "Rikki wanted [past tense] to kill snakes. All mongooses want [present tense] to kill snakes." The first sentence is in the past because it summarizes the past action of the story. The second is in the present because it is a statement that still holds true for mongooses in the present. The third sentence should return to using past tense.

STEP THREE: **Assemble the essay**

Student instructions for Step Three:

> Compare the analysis with the narrative summary. They are similar—but while a narrative summary tells you what happened, an analysis tells you *why*. Your narrative summary *might* have mentioned what the cobras wanted, or what Rikki-tikki-tavi wanted, but it could still be a perfectly good narrative summary if you didn't mention either.
>
> Look carefully at the beginning of the narrative summary. There is information in this first sentence (or maybe the first two sentences) that does not appear in your analysis. What is this information? Take that sentence(s) and make it the first line of your first paragraph. This sentence "sets the scene" for your analysis by telling the reader who the characters are.
>
> When you are finished, show your finished essay to your instructor.

HOW TO HELP THE STUDENT WITH STEP THREE

The purpose of asking the student to write both a summary and an analysis is to point out the difference between summarizing actions and analyzing motives. However, the first sentence of the essay does need to introduce the reader to the world of the story by telling who Rikki is and how he came to live in the bungalow. The final version of the essay should begin:

In the story "Rikki-Tikki-Tavi" by Rudyard Kipling, the mongoose Rikki-tikki-tavi is rescued by a boy and his parents and goes to live with them. Rikki-tikki-tavi wants to kill snakes—any snakes. All mongooses want to kill snakes . . .

Rikki-tikki-tavi was adopted by a family who lived in a bungalow in India. Rikki-tikki-tavi wanted to kill snakes—any snakes. All mongooses want to kill snakes. . . .

Rikki-tikki-tavi was a mongoose who lived with a family in an Indian bungalow. He wanted to kill snakes—any snakes. All mongooses want to kill snakes. . . .

Notice that both the introduction and the analysis should use the same tense. The student may also substitute pronouns for proper names to avoid unnecessary repetition.

Check the final version of the essay using the following rubric.

Week 23 Rubric
Brief Literary Essay

Organization

1 The essay should begin with an introduction to the world of the story.
2 Next should come the explanation of what Rikki wants and why.
3 Next should come the explanation of what the cobras want and why.
4 Next should come a chronological description of the scene where Rikki kills Nag, including the reason why Nag went into the bathroom.
5 The essay should end with a chronological description of the scene where Rikki kills Nagaina, including the reason why Nagaina went into the house.

Mechanics

1 Each sentence should make sense on its own when read aloud.
2 Possessive forms should be written properly.
3 Verb tense should be consistent throughout.
4 Subjects and verbs must be in agreement.
5 Rikki-tikki-tavi may be abbreviated as Rikki.
6 Antecedents of pronouns should be clear.
7 The titles of short stories should be in quotation marks; the titles of books, italicized (in handwriting, underlined).

Day Four: Literary Language

Focus: Synecdoche

In previous lessons, the student has studied two major kinds of figurative language: metaphors and similes. Remember, a simile compares two things *explicitly* by using "like" or "as," or otherwise spelling out that figurative language is being used:

like ruddy smears upon the palpable brown air

A metaphor doesn't announce itself by using the words "like" or "as," or by saying that one thing "seems like" or "resembles" another. Instead, the writer simply speaks about one thing in terms of another:

the houses opposite were mere phantoms

Today the student will learn about a particular kind of metaphor called *synecdoche* (pronounced sih-NEK-du-kee). The first two steps should be done independently, but the directions are reproduced below for your convenience.

STEP ONE: Understand synecdoche (Student Responsibility)

Student instructions for Step One:

Read the following passage from "Rikki-Tikki-Tavi" out loud:

When Rikki becomes angry with the bird Darzee, what does he call him? Underline the phrase "stupid tuft of feathers."

Synecdoche is a particular kind of metaphor in which a writer uses *part* of a thing to represent the *whole.* The bird Darzee *has* tufts of feathers, but when Rikki uses one part of Darzee as a name for the whole bird, he is using synecdoche.

You have probably heard synecdoche many times without knowing it. When a sea captain in a book or movie calls "All hands on deck!" he is using synecdoche. What he really means is "All sailors on deck!" But the sailors have hands, and their hands are the most important part of them—so he calls for their *hands* (the part) when he really wants *the whole sailor.* If a hero in a story shouts "Beware my blade!" what he really means is "Watch out for my sword!" or "Watch out for my skill with the sword!" "Blade" is just one *part* of the *whole* sword.

Wise sayings and proverbs often use synecdoche. In the Old Testament proverb "A lying tongue hates its victims," "lying tongue" is one body part of a person who tells lies. Using "lying tongue" in place of the whole person highlights one particular characteristic of that person. In the Danish proverb "A hearth of your own is worth gold," "hearth" stands for "your own home"—a hearth (fireplace) is just one part of that home.

STEP TWO: **Add to the Literary Terms chart (Student Responsibility)**

Student instructions for Step Two:

> On your Literary Terms chart, write the following three definitions:
>
> simile: a comparison that uses "like," "as," or similar words
> metaphor: a comparison that speaks of one things in terms of another
> synecdoche: a kind of metaphor that uses a part to represent the whole

STEP THREE: **Identify synecdoche**

Student instructions for Step Three:

> In the following sentences, underline the words or phrases that use synecdoche. On the line next to each sentence, write the name of the whole that the word or phrase refers to. The first is done for you.

HOW TO HELP THE STUDENT WITH STEP THREE

Use the following key to check the student's work.

In came Mrs. Fezziwig, <u>one vast substantial smile</u>. In came the three Misses Fezziwig, beaming and lovable.
—Charles Dickens, *A Christmas Carol* — *Mrs. Fezziwig herself*

The uncle sat down with his niece and went over the individual qualities of the many suitors who sought her <u>hand</u>.
—Miguel de Cervantes, *Don Quixote* — *the niece herself*

Some men never enter a <u>church door</u> til they die.
—English proverb — *whole church*

The <u>White House</u> claimed that President Nixon was "under great strain."
—W. Dale Nelson, *Who Speaks for the President?* — *the United States government*

The third fleet, equipped by the Goths in the ports of Bosphorus, consisted of five hundred <u>sails</u>.
—Edward Gibbon, *The Decline and Fall of the Roman Empire* — *ships*

There were eager ears, understanding ears, stubborn ears, and ignorant ears which failed to make sense of what he was saying.
—Ronald Blythe, *Talking to the Neighbours*

people who were listening

New faces greet me at the door.
—*Scribners Monthly,* Vol. 22

people

All around him, he saw small farmers suffering: too many mouths to feed and never enough bread.
—David Laskin, *The Long Way Home*

children or family

food

Week 24: Hero/Villain Protagonist/Antagonist

Day One: Read

Focus: Reading

Today's work should be done independently. The student's instructions are reproduced below for your convenience. You should review the pronunciations in preparation for tomorrow's dialogue.

STEP ONE: **Understand the background (Student Responsibility)**

Student instructions for Step One:

> This week, you'll read the short story "The Necklace" by Guy de Maupassant (pronounced *ghee duh moh pah SAWHN).*
>
> Guy de Maupassant and Rudyard Kipling lived at the same time; de Maupassant was born in 1850, so he was 15 years older than Kipling. He died in 1893, at the early age of 42.
>
> Maupassant (his full name was Henri René Albert Guy de Maupassant) was a French writer, famous for his short stories. "The Necklace," one of his best-known stories, is set in Paris.
>
> The French names in the story might not be familiar to you. The pronunciations are below. Try saying them out loud a few times before you read.

Georges Ramponneau	*Zhorzh RAM pon no*
M. and Mme. Loisel	*MUH syuh* and *MAH dahm Lwazel*
Mathilde	*ma TEEL duh*
Mme. Forestier	*MAH dahm for ES tee ay*
Seine	*Sen*
coupés	*COOP ay*
Rue des Martyrs	*roo deh MAH tear*
Palais Royal	*pah lay roy AHL*
francs	*fhraw*
Champs Élysées	*SHAHN zay lee zay*
Jeanne	*Zhahn*

STEP TWO: **Read (Student Responsibility)**

Student instructions for Step Two:

> Read and enjoy.

Day Two: Think

Focus: Hero and villain, protagonist and antagonist, conflict

Today, the student will examine how this story works; tomorrow, he'll write about the story.

STEP ONE: **Identify the characters**

Student instructions for Step One:

> There are only three characters in this story who have names and speeches. List them on a piece of scratch paper.
>
> In Steps Two–Four your instructor will carry on a dialogue with you. At the end of each dialogue, you'll write a brief observation on the lines. These observations will help you construct your brief essay tomorrow.

HOW TO HELP THE STUDENT WITH STEP ONE

The student should have listed three names on his paper: M. Loisel, his wife Mme. (Mathilde) Loisel, and Mme. (Jeanne) Forestier.

STEP TWO: **Identify the protagonist**

Carry on the following dialogue with the student. If the student answers as suggested, continue on with the main dialogue and skip the optional dialogue; if the student is confused, use the optional dialogue.

MAIN DIALOGUE

Instructor: Turn to your Literary Terms chart and read me the definition of "protagonist."

Student: The character who wants to get, become, or accomplish something

Instructor: Who is the protagonist?

Student: Madame [or Mathilde] Loisel

OPTIONAL DIALOGUE

(Answers with another character)

Instructor: What are the first two words of the first sentence in the story?

Student: She was

Instructor: What are the first two words of the second sentence?

Student: She had

Instructor: What are the first two words of the third sentence?

Student: She dressed

Instructor: Right from the beginning, this story focuses on one character—the protagonist. Who is she?

Instructor: Madame Loisel wants something—very badly. The second paragraph describes what she wants. The third paragraph sums it up. Can you put into your own words what she wants? Use at least two phrases to to describe her wants. [Note: the student should include both the desire to be rich, to *have* possessions, and the desire to be looked up to, envied, and respected—the good opinion of others towards those who *are* rich.]

Student: She wants to be rich and sought after OR *envied* OR *important* OR *aristocratic* OR *a member of high society . . . [etc.].*

(If student cannot find the right phrases)

Instructor: If she suffers from poverty, what does she want to be?

If she were to have dresses, jewels, and salons filled with important people, how would she appear to others?

She was born into one kind of life, but there is another kind of life that she longs for. What is it?

Instructor: On the lines in your workbook, jot down one sentence explaining what Madame Loisel wants to *get*, and a second sentence explaining what she wants to *become.*

SAMPLE ACCEPTABLE ANSWERS

Madame Loisel wants possessions—a beautiful house, jewels and dresses, delicious food and drink and servants. She wants to become rich, admired, and pampered.

OR

Madame Loisel wants to be rich and have beautiful rooms and furniture, fancy meals, furs and jewels. She also wants to be charming and sought after and envied.

STEP THREE: **Identify the antagonist**

Carry on the following dialogue with the student.

Instructor: Read me the definition of "antagonist" from your Literary Terms chart.

Student: The character, force, or circumstance that opposes the protagonist

Instructor: Last week's story had two very obvious protagonists—two villains. This story is a little more difficult, because there's not exactly a "bad guy" in it. So to figure out who the antagonist is, answer this series of questions for me. First: what happens to the necklace?

Student: Madame Loisel loses it.

Instructor: What do she and her husband do in order to cover up the loss?

Student: They buy a new necklace.

Instructor: Because the new necklace is so expensive, they have to borrow—which means that they end up paying much more than the cost of the necklace, because they have to pay interest on the loan. Look back at the story and tell me three things they do so that they can scrape together enough money to pay back the loan.

Student: They dismiss their servant and rent a garret; Madame Loisel does her own housework; she does the shopping and looks for bargains; her husband copies accounts and manuscripts.

Instructor: Madame Loisel wants to be rich and admired; instead, she becomes poor and old before her time. Some character, force, or circumstance keeps her from achieving her goal. Does Madame Forestier keep her from achieving her goal?

Student: No

(If the student answers yes)

Instructor: Does Madame Forestier tell them to replace the necklace?

Student: No

Instructor: Does she even know that it's lost?

Student: No

Instructor: So she doesn't cause the catastrophe.

Instructor: Does losing the necklace keep Madame Loisel from achieving her goal?

Student: No

(If the student answers yes)

Instructor: She could have reacted to the loss of the necklace in a different way. What if she had been honest with Madame Forestier and said, "I lost your necklace." What would her friend have told her?

Student: That the necklace was a fake

Instructor: Losing the necklace didn't ruin her life. Keeping the loss a *secret* ruined her life.

Instructor: Paying back the loan is what keeps Madame Loisel from becoming rich and admired. But she only agrees to take out the loan because she refuses to admit that she lost the necklace. Why doesn't she just tell her friend that the necklace was lost?

Student: She is too proud OR *She is ashamed* OR *She is afraid.*

Instructor: We don't know exactly why she won't tell—but we can guess that she is just too embarrassed to tell her friend how careless she was. She conceals the loss because she is proud, and because she is afraid. Concealing the loss means that she never has the chance to find out how little the necklace is worth. So the force or circumstance or character that keeps her poor and obscure is . . . [give the student a chance to answer]

Student: Herself. *(If the student is still confused, finish the sentence for him.)*

Instructor: Madame Loisel is the protagonist—but she is also the antagonist. The story describes how a character is, literally, her own worst enemy. So this story is *very* different from last week's. In "Rikki-Tikki-Tavi," the antagonist is an outside character, and there is a real physical struggle. But in this story, the struggle all happens within one character's personality. Now write on the lines in your workbook two sentences about Madame Loisel as protagonist. In those sentences, tell us about the character qualities that keep her from being honest about the loss of the necklace. You may speculate if necessary!

SAMPLE ACCEPTABLE ANSWERS:

She is afraid to tell her friend that she has lost the necklace because she doesn't know what will happen. She is also embarrassed that she took such poor care of the diamonds.

OR

She is too embarrassed to tell her rich friend that she has lost the jewels. She is also too proud to admit that she can't pay for the necklace.

STEP FOUR: **Identify the conflict**

Carry on the following dialogue with the student.

Instructor: Read me the definition of "conflict" from your workbook.

Student: The clash between protagonist and antagonist

Instructor: In this story, the protagonist and antagonist are the same person. Madame Loisel wants to be rich and admired. Because she wants to be rich and admired *at the ball*, what does she do?

Student: She borrows the necklace.

Instructor: But borrowing the necklace leads to losing the necklace. And because she is proud and afraid, she won't admit that she lost the necklace. This produces the conflict in the story—between the protagonist side of Madame Loisel, which wants to be rich and admired and taken care of and surrounded with luxury, and the antagonist side, which is proud and fearful. In "Rikki-Tikki-Tavi," who wins the conflict—the protagonist or the antagonist?

Student: The protagonist

Instructor: In "The Necklace," who wins the conflict—the protagonist side of Madame Loisel or the antagonist side?

Student: The antagonist side

Instructor: In this story, the protagonist doesn't win the conflict! It's as if the cobras killed Rikki and took over the bungalow. At the end of the story, what has happened to the protagonist side of Madame Loisel—the side that wants to be rich and taken care of?

Student: It has disappeared. (If student is confused, tell him the answer.)

Instructor: The writer shows you that the protagonist has been completed defeated. In the last scene, what happens when Madame Loisel speaks to Madame Forestier?

Student: Madame Forestier doesn't recognize her. *(If the student is confused)* Instructor: Does Madame Forestier even recognize her?

Instructor: That shows you how thoroughly the protagonist side of Madame Loisel—the side that wants to be rich and pampered—has been defeated. That part of her has completely disappeared. So the result of the conflict is that the antagonist wins. Here's a final question for you. Is this a good outcome? Is the protagonist in this story better than the antagonist? Is there a hero, or a villain?

[Note: There is no right or wrong answer to this question. The story is ambiguous.]

Instructor: In this story, the conflict happens over the ten years that it takes to pay back the loan. There's not a single struggle, like Rikki's battle with Nag in the bathroom or Nagaina underground. All we know is that, during those ten years, the part of Madame Loisel that wanted to be rich and admired is defeated. In your workbook, write two or three brief sentences about the results of the conflict between the two sides of Madame Loisel.

Optional

If the student is still interested, you may add the following.

Instructor: Madame Loisel gave up on wanting to be rich. But did she give up on wanting to be admired?

[Note: Give the student a chance to think about this before continuing on.]

Instructor: Why did she tell Madame Forestier about the necklace?

Student: She was proud of paying the money back.

Instructor: She was proud—and she wanted Madame Forestier to admire her. The two sides of Madame Loisel have been struggling, and her pride and fear won out. But by the end of the story, she still wants to be admired. That side of her is not completely defeated!

SAMPLE ACCEPTABLE ANSWERS (additional descriptive details are acceptable; these are minimum sentences):

She gave up her desire to be rich and admired and instead spent ten years, with her husband, paying back the loan. She grew old and plain and weary. By the time the loan was paid, she no longer looked anything like the old Madame Loisel.

OR

Madame Loisel and her husband gave up their house, their servants, and their whole way of living to pay back the loan. Ten years of struggle changed Madame Loisel completely.

Day Three: Write

Focus: Writing about the story

Like last week's essay, the student's assignment will have two parts: a brief summary of the story and two or three paragraphs discussing the protagonist, antagonist, and conflict.

STEP ONE: **Write the summary**

Student instructions for Step One:

> Begin by writing a brief narrative summary of the story on your scratch paper. This summary should be four to eight sentences long. You don't need to talk about the characters' wants and plans, because you'll cover this in the second part of the essay; focus on what actually *happens* in the story (this will help you keep the story short).
>
> If you have trouble, ask your instructor for help. When you are finished, check your summary with your instructor.

HOW TO HELP THE STUDENT WITH STEP ONE

The student may use either present or past tense for the summary, but should keep the same tense all the way through. As in last week's exercise, the student does not need to use the title of the story, but should set it off by quotation marks if it does appear.

The narration should resemble one of the following:

In "The Necklace" by Guy de Maupassant, Madame Loisel is asked to a ball, but she cannot go unless she has a beautiful dress and necklace. She borrows a diamond necklace from a friend. The ball is a success, but on the way home, she loses the necklace. She and her husband borrow a huge amount of money to buy a replacement necklace. It takes them ten years to pay back the loan. After the money is paid back, she sees her friend in the park. Madame Loisel is old and worn, but her friend is still beautiful. She tells her friend that they replaced the necklace, and her friend tells her that the original necklace was a fake.

Madame Loisel borrows a beautiful diamond necklace to go to a ball. During the evening, she loses the necklace. She and her husband go into debt to replace it and work ten years to pay off the debt. Afterwards, she finds out that the necklace was made of paste.

Madame Loisel was invited to a ball, but she was embarrassed to go without jewelry. Her rich friend lent her a diamond necklace. On the way home from the ball, she lost it. She sold everything and went to work to replace the necklace. Her entire life changed. After she replaced the necklace, she found out that the original necklace wasn't even real.

If the student has difficulty writing a *short* summary, ask the following questions:
What invitation did Madame Loisel receive?
What did she do to make herself fine enough for the ball?
What happened to the necklace?
How did she react to the theft?
What did she find out afterwards?
Tell the student to answer each question in one sentence.

STEP TWO: **Write the analysis**

Student instructions for Step Two:

Now write about the following topics in three short paragraphs. You may draw on the notes you made in the last writing session.

First Paragraph

Describe what Madame Loisel, the protagonist, wants. At the end of the paragraph, tell briefly how the necklace fits into these wants.

Second Paragraph

Describe what Madame Loisel, the antagonist, wants. Begin your paragraph by mentioning the loss of the necklace. End the paragraph by describing the actions that Madame Loisel, the antagonist, takes.

Third Paragraph

Describe the outcome of the conflict between Madame Loisel's two sides. This paragraph can be as short as one sentence, but you can also choose to make it longer.

When are you are finished, show your analysis to your instructor.

HOW TO HELP THE STUDENT WITH STEP TWO

The paragraphs should resemble the following:

Madame Loisel wanted to be rich and admired by all. When she was invited to the ball, she had a chance to look both beautiful and rich.

After she lost the necklace, she was too embarrassed and too proud to tell her friend what had happened. So she gave up everything she wanted and became poor and hard-working. The ten years of labor made her coarse and old before her time.

Because her pride was stronger than her desire to be rich, Madame Loisel's life was changed forever.

OR

Madame Loisel lives an ordinary, everyday life, but she wants to be rich, admired, and pampered. She wants to be charming, sought after, and envied. She borrows the necklace for the ball so that she can pretend to be wealthy for one evening.

When she loses the necklace, she is too embarrassed to tell her friend, and ashamed to admit how careless she was. Instead she works for ten years to pay back the loan she takes out to replace the necklace.

The ten years wear her out and make her rough and plain. Her shame and her embarrassment are stronger than her wish to be charming, so she gives up everything she has.

Although the student's paragraphs may be phrased differently, the following information *must* be included:

1. That Madame Loisel wished to be rich, envied, admired, beautiful.
2. That she had a chance to appear this way at the ball.
3. That she lost the necklace.
4. That her pride, embarrassment, or shame kept her from admitting the truth.
5. That she worked for ten years/gave up everything to replace the necklace.
6. That her shame was stronger than her desire to be admired/rich/beautiful.

Either past or present tense may be used, but the three paragraphs should all use the same tense consistently.

STEP THREE: **Assemble the essay**

Student instructions for Step Three:

> Compare the analysis with the narrative summary. Notice that the two pieces of writing do *not* overlap nearly as much as the narrative summary and analysis from last week. This is because a narrative summary describes actions (external, outside the character), and an analysis describes wants and desires (internal, inside the character's head). The real conflict in this story is internal, inside Madame Loisel herself, so the narrative summary does not tell you everything you need to know about the conflict.
>
> Make your narrative summary the first paragraph of your essay. You should now have a four-paragraph essay. Read the essay out loud. Eliminate any unnecessary repetition by cutting phrases or substituting synonyms and pronouns. If any sentences sound awkward, correct them.
>
> Show your final essay to your instructor.

HOW TO HELP THE STUDENT WITH STEP THREE

In this essay, the narrative summary will not need to be shortened as much as in the last essay assignment; the narrative summary gives information about the actual events in the story, while the analysis focuses on the internal motivations. The student will need to cut any repetition and will also need to substitute synonyms and pronouns where necessary, as in the example below:

> *Madame Loisel was invited to a ball, but she was ~~embarrassed~~* ashamed *to go without jewelry. Her rich friend lent her a diamond necklace. On the way home from the ball, she lost it. She sold everything and went to work to replace the necklace. Her entire life changed. After she replaced the necklace, she found out that the original necklace wasn't even real.*
>
> *~~Madame Loisel~~* She *wanted to be rich and admired by all. When she was invited to the ball, she had a chance to look both beautiful and rich.*
>
> *After she lost the necklace, she was too embarrassed and too proud to tell her friend what had happened. So she ~~gave up everything she wanted and~~ became poor and hardworking. The ten years of labor made her coarse and old before her time. Because her pride was stronger than her desire to be rich, Madame Loisel's life was changed forever.*

Notice that both the narrative summary and the analysis should use the same tense.

Week 24 Rubric
Brief Literary Essay

Organization

1 The essay should begin with a short summary of the story's plot.
2 Next should come the explanation of Madame Loisel's wish to be rich and admired.
3 Next should come the explanation of Madame Loisel's pride and embarrassment.
4 The essay should end by explaining that her life changed forever because the second set of wants was stronger than the first.

Mechanics

1 Each sentence should make sense on its own when read aloud.
2 Possessive forms should be written properly.
3 Verb tense should be consistent throughout.
4 Subjects and verbs must be in agreement.
5 Antecedents of pronouns should be clear.
6 Unnecessary repetition of the same nouns, adjectives, and proper names should be avoided.
7 The title of the story should be in quotation marks if used.
8 The title "Madame" may be written out or abbreviated as "Mme."

Day Four: Literary Language

Focus: Inversion/surprise

The student will work independently today. The directions are reproduced below for your convenience.

STEP ONE: **Understand inversion**

The first time you read "The Necklace," you were probably surprised by the last two sentences. Like Madame Loisel, you believe through most of the story that the diamond necklace is real. Like Madame Loisel, you don't find out the truth until the very end.

This is called *inversion*, and a story that uses inversion is often called a *surprise story*.

When you read a story, you often have information that the main characters don't. For example, in "Rikki-Tikki-Tavi" you discovered something about Nag that Rikki doesn't know:

> . . . though Rikki-tikki had never met a live cobra before, his mother had fed him on dead ones, and he knew that all a grown mongoose's business in life was to fight and eat snakes. Nag knew that too and, at the bottom of his cold heart, he was afraid.

Because you know that Nag is afraid, it isn't really a surprise to you when Rikki is able to kill him.

But in "The Necklace," neither you *nor* Madame Loisel know that the necklace is fake. You spend the whole story believing that she is doing something necessary and noble in replacing the necklace with real diamonds. In the last two sentences, both you and Madame Loisel find out how pointless her ten years of struggle have been. Your whole opinion of her actions changes—or *inverts*.

When a writer uses inversion, he or she withholds information until the end. When you receive this information, your point of view suddenly changes. To invert something is to turn it inside out or upside down; inversion causes you to turn your initial opinion of the story completely around because you have received new information.

In "The Necklace," the inversion is very sudden and unexpected. But sometimes inversion can be more gradual, as you and the character slowly discover together that your original point of view was wrong.

The American short story writer O. Henry[51] was a master of inversion. Some of his stories have sudden inversions, but others are more gradual. "The Ransom of Red Chief" is a surprise story in which the inversion takes place over the whole course of the story.

Take some time now to read "The Ransom of Red Chief" in Appendix III. After you have finished, read Step Two below.

You'll notice that the narrator uses a number of

51. "O. Henry" is a pen name (the invented name a writer uses for his work). His real name was William Sydney Porter.

unusual words that you may not be familiar with. This is part of his character (and he doesn't always use them correctly either). You don't need to know the meaning of all of the words to enjoy the story. Mark words that you don't know lightly with a pencil and keep reading. When you've finished, you can look up any words that have made the story unclear to you.

STEP TWO: **Understand the surprise story**

The inversion in this surprise story takes place in several steps. The first comes almost as soon as Sam and Bill kidnap their victim. Instead of being frightened, the boy starts having "the time of his life."

The second inversion comes when Bill, instead of frightening the boy, becomes so frightened that "from that moment" his "spirit was broken."

The third inversion comes when the boy's father asks for the ransom—instead of paying it.

And the fourth and final inversion comes when Bill and Sam decide to pay the ransom just to get rid of Red Chief.

By the time Bill and Sam hand over the money and run, the kidnapping story has been completely inverted. They are the captives—not the captors! But you're not suddenly surprised, because O. Henry has been leading you up to this moment all along.

STEP THREE: **Add to the Literary Terms chart**

On your Literary Terms chart, write the following two definitions:

inversion (plot): an unexpected revelation that reverses the meaning or action of the story
surprise story: a story that uses inversion to change the reader's point of view

("Plot" is inserted in parentheses because "inversion" can also be used as a grammatical term.)

Week 25: Supporting Characters

Day One: Read

Focus: Reading

In the last two weeks, the student has practiced answering basic literary analysis questions about complete short stories—stories that have a beginning, a middle, and an end.

But you can also use these same questions to help the student write about *part* of a book. Often, you'll need to encourage the student to write about a book she is still reading: writing about each section or chapter as she finishes it. This can help the student remember what she's read, as well as provide her with source material for a longer essay. The student's point of view about a particular character may also change between the beginning and end of the book.

Today's work should be done independently. The student's instructions are reproduced below for your convenience.

STEP ONE: **Understand the background.**

This week, you'll read a single chapter—Chapter III—from *Anne of Green Gables* by Lucy Maud Montgomery. The chapter is in Appendix III.

Lucy Maud Montgomery (1874–1942) was Canadian and wrote many of her stories and novels about Prince Edward Island, the smallest province in Canada. *Anne of Green Gables* was the first novel about the orphan Anne Shirley. Set in the late 1800s, it told how Anne Shirley came from the orphanage (called the "orphan asylum") to live with the childless Marilla Cuthbert and her brother Matthew. Montgomery later wrote seven more novels about Anne and her family.

In Chapter I of *Anne of Green Gables,* Marilla and Matthew ask their friend Mrs. Spencer to go to the orphan asylum in Nova Scotia, about two hundred miles away, and pick out a boy who can come and help them on the farm. At this time, it was common for couples to give a home to orphans in exchange for work; the orphans weren't formally adopted, but in better homes, they became part of the family. (In worse situations, they were treated like unpaid servants.)

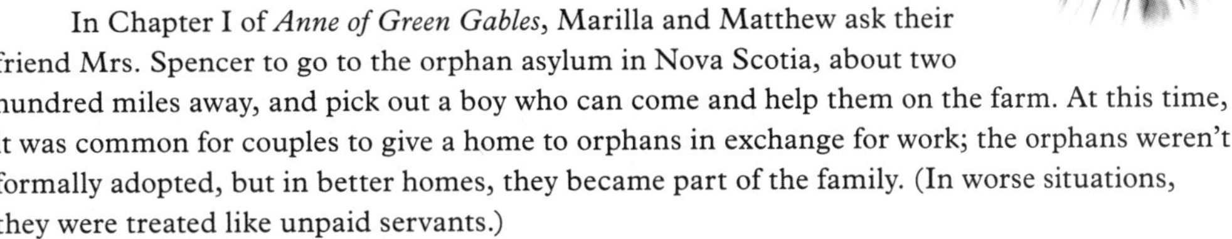

The boy is supposed to arrive on the train from Nova Scotia. But when Matthew arrives at the station, he finds that Mrs. Spencer has misunderstood their request. Instead of a boy, the orphan asylum has sent a little girl. Chapter II describes her as a "child of about eleven, garbed in a very short, very tight, very ugly dress of yellowish-gray wincey. She wore a faded brown sailor hat and beneath the hat, extending down her back, were two braids of very thick, decidedly red hair. Her face was small, white and thin, also much freckled; her mouth was large and so were her eyes, which looked green in some lights and moods and gray in others."

Matthew knows that Marilla won't be happy about this, but he can't leave the little girl alone in the train station, so he brings her home for the night. On the way, her imagination and cheerful conversation win him over.

In Chapter III, the two arrive back at Green Gables, where Marilla Cuthbert is waiting for Matthew to bring home a boy.

STEP TWO: **Read**

Read and enjoy.

Day Two: Think

Focus: Shifting protagonists and antagonists; supporting character

Today the student will examine a single chapter of a book; tomorrow she'll write about that chapter.

STEP ONE: **Identify the first protagonist-antagonist pair**

Carry on the following dialogue with the student. If the student answers as suggested, continue on with the main dialogue and skip the optional dialogue; if the student is confused, use the optional dialogue.

MAIN DIALOGUE

Instructor: See if you can remember the definition of "protagonist" without looking at your Literary Terms chart. If you can't, turn to the chart and read the definition out loud.

Student: The character who wants to get, become, or accomplish something

Instructor: It wasn't too hard to identify the protagonists in "Rikki-Tikk-Tavi" and "The Necklace." But finding the protagonist in this chapter isn't quite as easy. You know that the book is called *Anne of Green Gables,* so it's safe to assume that Anne Shirley is the central character in the book. But is she the *protagonist in this chapter?* You can start to figure this out by asking "What does Anne Shirley want to get, or become, or accomplish *in this chapter?*"

Student: She wants a home OR She wants to become part of Marilla and Matthew's family OR She wants to stay with Matthew and Marilla.

OPTIONAL DIALOGUE

(If the student gives an unrelated answer)

Instructor: Why does Anne burst into tears as soon as she comes into the Cuthbert home?

Student: She finds out that she isn't wanted.

Instructor: She *wants* to belong. That is her biggest desire—to be part of the family.

Instructor: Now see if you can remember the definition of "antagonist" without looking at your Literary Terms chart. If you can't, read the definition out loud.

Student: The character, force, or circumstance that opposes the protagonist

Instructor: Something or someone is trying to keep Anne Shirley from staying with Matthew and Marilla. Is Matthew keeping Anne from staying at Green Gables?

Student: No.

Instructor: Is Marilla?

Student: Yes.

Instructor: Why?

Student: Because Anne isn't a boy

Instructor: Marilla is the antagonist because she opposes Anne's desire to stay at Green Gables. She opposes Anne's desire to stay—because Anne isn't a boy. So this chapter has both a character and a circumstance as the antagonist. The character is Marilla; the circumstance is Anne's being a girl instead of a boy. In Step One of your workbook, write down one sentence explaining what Anne wants and one sentence explaining why Marilla opposes her.

SAMPLE ACCEPTABLE ANSWERS:

Anne wants to stay at Green Gables and be part of the Cuthbert family. But Marilla doesn't want her to stay, because she wants a boy to help on the farm.

OR

Anne hoped that Marilla and Matthew would want her to come and stay at Green Gables. But Marilla wanted a boy to work with Matthew—not a girl.

STEP TWO: **Identify the second protagonist-antagonist pair**

Instructor: You can think of Anne as the protagonist and Marilla as the antagonist—but the situation's more complicated than that. Marilla wants something too. What does she want?

Student: A boy to help on the farm

Instructor: But that's not the whole answer. She wants a boy to help Matthew on the farm—but even after Matthew offers to hire some help, Marilla wants Anne to go back to the orphan asylum. Look at the last page of the story and read Marilla's speech to Matthew that begins with "Oh, she can talk fast enough."

Student: "Oh, she can talk fast enough. I saw that at once. It's nothing in her favour, either. I don't like children who have so much to say. I don't want an orphan girl and if I did she isn't the style I'd pick out. There's something I don't understand about her. No, she's got to be despatched straight-way back to where she came from."

Instructor: There are two things about Anne that Marilla doesn't like. What are they?

Student: She talks too much, and Marilla doesn't understand her.

Instructor: When Matthew says "She'd be company for you," what does Marilla say?

Student: "I'm not suffering for company."

Instructor: Marilla likes quiet; she likes to be alone; and she likes to understand people easily. Marilla wants each day to be simple and uncomplicated. In that way, she is also a protagonist in the story. She wants to achieve something: a quiet, orderly life. Now, there's an antagonist opposing her. Who is opposing her?

Student: Anne

Instructor: Anne isn't quiet; she would keep Marilla from being alone; and she is certainly unpredictable. If she stays, Marilla can't have the life she wants. One reason *Anne of Green Gables* is such a satisfying book is because the author doesn't just tell a story about one protagonist and one antagonist. Instead, she tells a story about two protagonists who both want something important—and who end up blocking each other! If you want to see how the author resolves this, you'll have to read the whole book. Now, in Step Two of your workbook, write down one sentence explaining what Marilla wants and one sentence explaining how Anne opposes her.

SAMPLE ACCEPTABLE ANSWERS:

Marilla wants to be alone and have a quiet peaceful life. If Anne stays at Green Gables, Marilla will have noisy company.

OR

Marilla wants a quiet, orderly life that is simple and uncomplicated. If Anne stays, she will make Marilla's life complicated and unpredictable.

STEP THREE: **Identify the supporting character**

Instructor: There's a third character in the chapter. Who is it?

Student: Matthew

Instructor: Matthew wants something too. What does he want?

Student: He wants to keep Anne.

(Gives an unrelated answer)

Instructor: Does he want to send Anne back?

Instructor: Matthew's not the protagonist because he's not *actively trying* to get what he wants. He wants to keep Anne, but listen to what he says: "It's kind of a pity to send her back when she's so set on staying here." That's not a very strong statement! And what does he say when Marilla questions him? Read me what Matthew says on page 526, beginning with "Well, now, no, I suppose not."

Student: "Well, now, no, I suppose not—not exactly. . . . I suppose—we could hardly be expected to keep her."

Instructor: Listen to what Marilla says: "I don't want an orphan girl. She's got to be despatched." And listen to how strongly Anne tells us what she wants: "You don't know how delighted I was. I couldn't sleep all last night for joy!" Finally, listen to what Matthew says: "Well, now, it's just as you say, of course, Marilla." Matthew doesn't have strong desires and he doesn't try hard to get what he wants, so he's not a protagonist. Is he opposing anyone?

Student: No.

Instructor: So he's not an antagonist. Matthew is a *supporting character.* Read me the definition of "supporting character" in your workbook.

Student: a character who helps, supports, or hinders the protagonist or antagonist

Instructor: How does Matthew support Anne?

Student: He says that she should stay OR *He says that they might be good for her.*

Instructor: You may not see it very clearly, but he also hinders Marilla. He makes her doubt her decision to send Anne back. The author tells you, in the last paragraph, that Marilla goes to bed "frowning most resolutely." That's because she's started to wonder if she *should* keep her resolution to send Anne away. Now, in Step Three of your workbook, write down two sentences explaining how Matthew helps, supports, or hinders Anne and how he helps, supports, or hinders Marilla.

SAMPLE ACCEPTABLE ANSWERS:

Matthew wants Anne to stay, so he tells Marilla that he can hire a boy to help him. He won't contradict Marilla, but he does make Marilla wonder if she should keep Anne.

OR

Matthew says that it would be a pity to send Anne away. This supports Anne, but it also makes Marilla question her decision to send Anne back to the orphan asylum.

STEP FOUR: **Add to the Literary Terms chart (Student Responsibility)**

Student instructions for Step Four:

Write the definition of "supporting character" on your Literary Terms chart, using the same format as your other definitions.

Day Three: Write

Focus: Writing about the chapter

By now, the student should be familiar with the structure of the essay she'll be writing: first, a brief summary of the chapter; then, several paragraphs discussing the protagonist, antagonist, and conflict. Today, the student will also add a paragraph about the supporting character.

STEP ONE: **Write the summary**

Student instructions for Step One:

> Begin by writing a brief narrative summary of the chapter on your scratch paper. This summary should be three to six sentences long. You don't need to talk about the characters' wants because you'll cover this in the second part of the essay; focus on what actually *happens* in the chapter. You will need to include some of the information given about Chapters I and II of the book.
>
> Remember that chapter titles go in quotation marks but that book titles are italicized (or underlined).
>
> If you have trouble, ask your instructor for help. When you are finished, check your summary with your instructor.

HOW TO HELP THE STUDENT WITH STEP ONE

The student may use either present or past tense for the summary, but should keep the same tense all the way through. The student does not need to use the title of either the chapter or the book, but if she does, they should be punctuated properly:

In Chapter III of *Anne of Green Gables*, "Marilla Cuthbert Is Surprised," Anne arrives at Green Gables.

The narration should resemble one of the following:

Matthew and Marilla Cuthbert expected to get a boy from the orphan asylum. When Matthew arrived at the train station, though, he found a little girl. He took her home, but Marilla insisted that they still needed a boy. The little girl, Anne Shirley, burst into tears and told Marilla that it was the most tragic day of her life. Matthew suggested that Anne stay and be company for Marilla, but Marilla refused to keep her.

Marilla and Matthew meant to give a home to an orphan boy in exchange for help in the fields, but the orphan asylum sent Anne Shirley instead. When Anne realized that Marilla didn't want to keep her, she burst into tears and couldn't eat her dinner. Marilla put Anne to bed that night in the guest room, but she intended to send Anne back the next day. Meanwhile, Matthew had begun to think that they should keep Anne. He told Marilla that he could hire a boy to work on the farm, and that Anne could be company for her. But Marilla refused, because Anne talked too much and was hard to understand.

Anne Shirley comes to Green Gables by mistake. When she arrives, she finds out that Marilla Cuthbert wants a boy instead. Anne is crushed, but Marilla insists that she only wants a boy—even though Matthew changes his mind and suggests that Anne stay.

STEP TWO: **Write the analysis**

Student instructions for Step Two:

Now write about the following topics in three short paragraphs. Each paragraph must be at least two sentences long but can be as long as five or six sentences. You may draw on the notes you made in the last writing session.

First Paragraph

Discuss what Anne, as the protagonist, wants; then describe what opposes her.

Second Paragraph

Discuss what Marilla, as the protagonist, wants; then describe what opposes her.

Third Paragraph

Discuss how Matthew, as a supporting character, supports or hinders at least one of the other characters.

When you are finished, show your analysis to your instructor.

HOW TO HELP THE STUDENT WITH STEP TWO

The student's paragraphs should resemble the following:

Anne desperately wants to stay at Green Gables, but Marilla insists that they need to have a boy instead. She tells Anne that there is no place for a girl at Green Gables.

Marilla doesn't want to keep Anne because Anne talks too much and is hard to understand. Marilla likes her life to be peaceful and orderly; Anne would make her life noisy and chaotic.

Matthew is on Anne's side. He wants her to stay, and he thinks that he and Marilla could be good for Anne.

OR

Anne wanted to have a home, and she thought that Green Gables would be her new home. She begged Marilla for the chance to stay. Marilla wanted a boy to help on the farm, though, so she refused to listen.

Marilla wanted a boy to help, but she also wanted her life to stay quiet and predictable. She knew that Anne would talk too much, and it bothered her that she didn't understand Anne.

Matthew told Marilla that they should keep Anne. He offered to hire a boy to help on the farm instead. He wasn't willing to argue with Marilla, but Marilla began to doubt herself.

Although the student's paragraphs may be phrased differently, the following information *must* be included:

1. That Anne wanted to stay at Green Gables.
2. That she was opposed by Marilla's wanting a boy.
3. That Marilla wanted a peaceful, quiet life.
4. That Anne's noise and unpredictability would oppose this want.
5. That Matthew wanted Anne to stay (this can be phrased either as support for Anne or hindrance to Marilla).

Either past or present tense may be used, but the three paragraphs should all use the same tense consistently.

STEP THREE: **Assemble the essay and provide transitions**

Student instructions for Step Three:

Make your narrative summary the first paragraph of your essay. You should now have a four-paragraph essay. Eliminate any unnecessary repetition.

The paragraphs all make sense individually, but they probably don't seem to flow into each other. The narrative summary isn't related to the three paragraphs, and although the three paragraphs all make sense, the reader might wonder: Why is the writer telling me this?

In order to make a literary essay readable, you may need to provide transitions. For example, imagine that the first two paragraphs in your essay are:

NOTE: DO NOT READ THE FOLLOWING UNLESS YOU HAVE FINISHED YOUR OWN SUMMARY AND ANALYSIS!

Anne Shirley comes to Green Gables by mistake. When she arrives, she finds out that Marilla Cuthbert wants a boy instead. Anne is crushed, but Marilla insists that she only wants a boy—even though Matthew changes his mind and suggests that Anne stay.

Anne desperately wants to stay at Green Gables, but Marilla insists that they need to have a boy instead. She tells Anne that there is no place for a girl at Green Gables.

Individually, those paragraphs are fine. But you need to explain to the reader why you're going back, in the second paragraph, to talk some more about Anne. After all, the reader probably figured out from the first paragraph that Anne wants to stay at Green Gables.

To do this, you need to provide a *transition.* Your transition should explain to the reader that you're getting ready to examine the author's use of literary techniques.

At the beginning of your second paragraph, insert a sentence that expresses one the following:

In *Anne of Green Gables,* Lucy Maud Montgomery tells more than one story.

"Marilla Cuthbert Is Surprised" tells us about two protagonists and a supporting character.

You may use one of these sentences, but try to rephrase and use synonyms so that you do not repeat the *exact* words. You may also write a sentence of your own.

Now read your essay out loud. If any sentences sound awkward, correct them.

When you are finished, show your essay to your instructor.

HOW TO HELP THE STUDENT WITH STEP THREE

Since this is the student's first introduction to writing transitions, the student may use a version of one of the sentences provided. Acceptable rephrasings can be as simple as:

Lucy Maud Montgomery tells about more than one character in Anne of Green Gables.

This chapter tells us about three characters—two protagonists and a supporting character.

The student may also write a more original sentence resembling one of the following:

In Anne of Green Gables, *Lucy Maud Montgomery tells a complex story about more than one set of wants.*

In "Marilla Cuthbert Is Surprised," both Anne and Marilla are protagonists and *antagonists.*

The third chapter introduces us to the main characters as well as an important supporting character.

Day Four: Using Direct Quotes

Focus: Using direct quotes to support conclusions

Today, the student will examine the use of direct quotes in a literary essay and will then go back to add quotes to yesterday's composition.

Steps One and Two should be completed independently. The directions are reproduced below for your convenience.

STEP ONE: Understand the use of direct quotes in a literary essay (Student Responsibility)

Student instructions for Step One:

Read the following excerpts from essays about *Tom Sawyer, The Once and Future King,* and *Ozma of Oz* by L. Frank Baum.

Tom's struggle with the adult world is brought out in his relationship with Aunt Polly, who has to play the dual role of a loving mother and a strict father, and she expresses her dilemma: "Every time I let him off, my conscience does hurt me so, and every time I hit him my old heart most breaks."[52]

Merlin teaches Wart the important lessons of life he will need when he is king: how to use his imagination and how to use his intellect to outwit the strong who "will try to conquer you." Other lessons are "Always look before you leap," "Love is a powerful thing," and "Get an education" by learning to read.[53]

The book starts with Dorothy Gale of Kansas on a boat, then being washed overboard and clinging to a chicken-coop, whose only other occupant is a hen named, by Dorothy, Billina. Unexpectedly, the hen can talk, and when Dorothy says, "I thought hens could only cluck and cackle," the hen replies, "I've clucked and cackled all my life, and never spoken a word before this morning, that I can remember. But when you asked a question, a minute ago, it seemed the most natural thing in the world to answer you. So I spoke, and I seem to keep on speaking, just as you and other human beings do. Strange, isn't it?" Thus, at the beginning of the book, the question of the defining quality of language—humans have language, and hens generally don't—is put before us.[54]

In each one of these paragraphs, the writer makes a statement about the book:

> "Aunt Polly has to be both loving mother and strict father."
> "Merlin teaches Wart the lessons he will need to be king."
> "The difference between animals and humans is the ability to talk."

But instead of just making the statement, the writer gives you *proof* for it—by quoting directly from the book itself.

From now on, whenever you write a literary essay, you should include at least one direct quote from the book. Direct quotes tell the reader that you're not just making up the points in your essay; they're actually based on something *in* the literature itself.

For example, the third paragraph of your literary analysis of *Anne of Green Gables* might have sounded something like this:

Matthew is on Anne's side. He wants her to stay, and he thinks that he and Marilla could be good for Anne.

Compare that paragraph with *this* one:

Matthew is on Anne's side. He wants her to stay; he tells Marilla, "It's kind of a pity to send her back when she's so set on staying here." He also thinks that he and Marilla could be good for Anne. When Marilla says, "What good would she be to us?" Matthew answers, "We might be some good to her."

The second paragraph is not only more interesting, but sounds more authoritative (as though the writer really knows what he's talking about).

52. K. Balachandran, *Critical Essays on American Literature* (Sarup & Sons, 2005), p. 172.
53. Kevin J. Harty, *Cinema Arthuriana* (McFarland & Co., 2002), p. 119.
54. Ronald Chrisley and Sander Begeer, *Artificial Intelligence: Critical Concepts*, Vol. 1 (Routledge, 2000), p. 148.

STEP TWO: **Review the rules for using direct quotes (Student Responsibility)**

Student instructions for Step Two:

A direct quote can be either a quote from the story itself ("And to bed, when she had put her dishes away, went Marilla, frowning most resolutely") or a speech made by one of the characters ("Oh, she can talk fast enough. I saw that at once").

The rules for using direct quotes are similar to the rules for using dialogue—but not exactly the same. Read through the following rules now. Don't worry about memorizing these rules. Just refer back to them as you use direct quotes in your own work, and the correct form will soon become familiar to you.

1. Use quotation marks to surround an exact quote.
   "To bed went Matthew."
2. If the exact quote contains dialogue, use double quotation marks around the exact quote and single quotation marks around the dialogue.
   "'There wasn't any boy,' said Matthew wretchedly. 'There was only her.'"
3. A direct quote should never just sit in the middle of a paragraph as an independent sentence, with no tag. (In quotations, the "dialogue tag" is called an "attribution tag.") Don't write
   Matthew wanted Anne to stay. "Well now, she's a real interesting little thing," persisted Matthew.

   Instead, write
   Matthew wanted Anne to stay. When Marilla said that Anne should go back to the asylum, Matthew said, "Well now, she's a real interesting little thing."
4. If an attribution tag ("the author writes" or "Anne said") comes before a direct quote, use a comma after the tag:
   The author tells us, "Anne looked around her wistfully."

   UNLESS the direct quote is preceded by "that":
   The author tells us that "Anne looked around her wistfully."
5. If there is no attribution tag, just put direct quotes around the quote but do not use a comma; the quote can simply become part of your sentence.
   When Anne was alone in the room she "looked around her wistfully."
6. The punctuation at the end of the speech itself goes *inside* the closing quotation mark. Exceptions: exclamation points and question marks go inside the closing quotes if they are part of the original quote, but outside of the closing quotation mark if not.
   When Anne looked around, she saw walls that were "painfully bare and staring"!
   The braided rug was one that "Anne had never seen before."

(In the original story, "painfully bare and staring" has no exclamation point after it.)

STEP THREE: **Add direct quotes to your essay**

Student instructions for Step Three:

Now go back to the essay you assembled in the last writing session. Add at least one direct quote to each of the three literary analysis paragraphs. These direct quotes should not be more than 12–15 words each but should be at least 4–6 words.

When you are finished, check the punctuation of your quotes against the rules above.

Once you have proofread your essay, show it to your instructor.

HOW TO HELP THE STUDENT WITH STEP THREE

If the student has difficulty finding appropriate quotes, ask her to look at each sentence in her descriptive paragraphs, and then go to the paragraph of *Anne of Green Gables* which gave her the information in that sentence. Her quote should come from that paragraph.

Sample paragraphs using direct quotes might resemble the following:

Anne desperately wants to stay at Green Gables, but Marilla insists that they need to have a boy instead. She tells Anne that there is no place for a girl at Green Gables. "We want a boy to help Matthew on the farm," she says to Anne. "A girl would be of no use to us."

Anne wanted to have a home, and she thought that Green Gables would be her new home. She begged Marilla for the chance to stay. She said, "If I were very beautiful and had nut-brown hair would you keep me?" Marilla wanted a boy to help on the farm, though, so she refused to listen.

Marilla doesn't want to keep Anne because Anne talks too much and is hard to understand. Marilla likes her life to be peaceful and orderly; she doesn't like children who "have so much to say." Anne would make her life noisy and chaotic.

Marilla wanted a boy to help, but she also wanted her life to stay quiet and predictable. She knew that Anne would talk too much, and it bothered her that she didn't understand Anne. "There's something I don't understand about her," she said to Matthew. Because of this, she wanted to send Anne "straight-way back to where she came from."

Matthew is on Anne's side. He calls her a "real interesting little thing" and tells Marilla that it would be "kind of a pity to send her back". He wants her to stay, and he thinks that he and Marilla could be good for Anne.

Matthew told Marilla that they should keep Anne. Marilla said that Anne would be "no good" to them, but Matthew answered, "We might be some good to her". He offered to hire a boy to help on the farm instead. He wasn't willing to argue with Marilla, but Marilla began to doubt herself.

Week 25 Rubric
Brief Literary Essay

Organization

1 The essay should begin with a short summary of the story's plot.
2 Next should come a transitional sentence, explaining that the essay will now discuss the characters.
3 Next should come the explanation of what Anne wants, and why she cannot have it.
4 Next should come the explanation of what Marilla wants, and how Anne would keep her from having it.
5 The essay should end by explaining how Matthew helps and/or hinders Anne and/or Marilla.
6 Each of the three literary analysis paragraphs should contain a direct quote from the story, related to the observations in the paragraph.

Mechanics

1 Each sentence should make sense on its own when read aloud.
2 Possessive forms should be written properly.
3 Verb tense should be consistent throughout.
4 Subjects and verbs must be in agreement.
5 Antecedents of pronouns should be clear.
6 Unnecessary repetition of the same nouns, adjectives, and proper names should be avoided.
7 The title of the story should be in quotation marks if used; the book title should be italicized or underlined.
8 Direct quotes should be incorporated into full sentences and should be properly punctuated.

Week 26: Idea Stories

Day One: Read

Focus: Reading

Today's work should be done independently. The student's instructions are reproduced below for your convenience.

STEP ONE: Understand the background

Today's story, "The Bowmen," was written by the Welsh author Arthur Machen (1863–1947). Machen was best known as a writer of suspense and fantasy.

You're probably familiar with the word *fantasy,* but you might not know that "fantasy" is a formal *genre label.* "Genre" means "category." It is the name we use for a particular type or form of literature; works that use similar forms, or have similar purposes, belong in the same genre. *Mystery* is a genre, because mysteries have the same form (a puzzle is solved by the end of the book). *Comedy* is a genre, because although funny stories may have very different forms, they all have the same purpose—to make you laugh.

Fantasy takes place in a world that doesn't exist. The writer Orson Scott Card defined fantasy as "all stories that take place in a setting contrary to known reality."[55] A world where a ring can make you invisible is a fantastical world. So is a world where animals talk, people fly, magical spells work, and swords are drawn from stones.

"The Bowmen" is a fantasy story set in a very real time: World War I. World War I was particularly devastating for Britain (of which Wales is a part); almost a million British soldiers were killed in the war. Machen wrote the story in 1914, near the beginning of the war.

There is some British slang in the story that you may not completely understand, but that won't affect your understanding of the story. However, you might want to be familiar with the following terms:

Allied. World War I was fought between two groups of countries, the Allied Powers (Britain, France, Italy, and the Russian Empire) and the Central Powers (the German Empire, the Austro-Hungarian Empire, the Ottoman Empire, and the Kingdom of Bulgaria).

The Retreat of the Eighty Thousand. The British troops were forced to retreat from the French border at the Battle of Mons, on August 23, 1914 (just a month before this story was published).

55. Orson Scott Card, *How to Write Science Fiction and Fantasy* (Writers Digest Books, 2001), p. 17.

The Censorship. The British government read the letters sent home by soldiers and crossed out any sentences (or whole paragraphs) that seemed to give away information about the war.

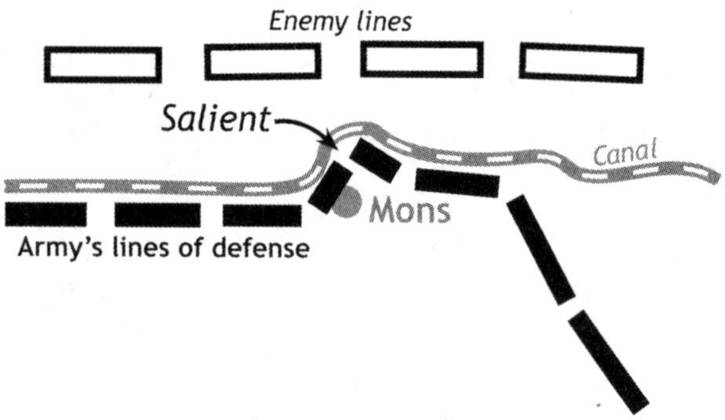

Sedan. Machen uses this term to mean "absolute defeat." In 1870, the French were forced to surrender to the Germans at Sedan, France. This led to the ultimate defeat of France in the Franco-Prussian War. All of Machen's readers in 1914 would have known about Sedan.

Sidney Street. In 1911, London police had a famous shootout on Sidney Street with a group of robbers.

Bisley. The British National Rifle Association used to meet at a field called Bisley Common to practice their shooting.

Agincourt. At the Battle of Agincourt in 1415, an outnumbered English army led by Henry V defeated a much larger French force.

Salient. A salient is a place in a battlefield where the territory held by one army juts into the territory of the other army, like a peninsula. The salient is surrounded by enemy forces on three sides.

STEP TWO: Read

Read and enjoy.

Day Two: Think

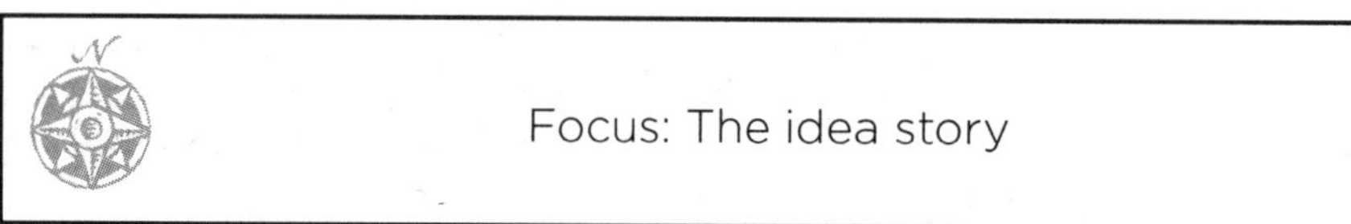

Today, the student will examine how this story works; tomorrow, he will write about the story. You will help the student with Steps One and Two by carrying on a dialogue. The student will finish Step Three independently.

Note that *St.* is the correct abbreviation for the word "saint." The student may write either *Saint George* or *St. George.*

STEP ONE: Identify the protagonist and antagonist

Carry on the following dialogue with the student. If the student answers as suggested, continue on with the main dialogue and skip the optional dialogue; if the student is confused, use the optional dialogue.

MAIN DIALOGUE **OPTIONAL DIALOGUE**

Instructor: What is the definition of "protagonist"? Try to answer without looking at your Literary Terms chart. If you can't, turn to the chart and read the definition out loud.

Student: The character who wants to get, become, or accomplish something

Instructor: In the last three stories you've studied, you've seen three different kinds of protagonists and antagonists. This story introduces you to a fourth kind. In this story, who is the protagonist? Hint: it isn't a single person.

Student: The English army

(If student is unsure)

Instructor: What two armies are fighting, at the beginning of this story?

Student: The English and German armies

Instructor: Which army is the author more in sympathy with (which army does he want to win)?

Student: The English

Instructor: The English army is the protagonist.

Instructor: What is the definition of "antagonist"? Try to answer without looking at your Literary Terms chart. If you can't, turn to the chart and read the definition out loud.

Student: The character, force, or circumstance that opposes the protagonist

Instructor: What is opposing the English army?

Student: The German army

Instructor: The German army is the antagonist. Now read me the definitions of "hero/heroine" and "villain" from your Literary Terms Chart.

Student: Hero/heroine: a central character with admirable qualities. Villain: an antagonist with evil motives.

Instructor: In this story, the protagonist is definitely heroic—and the antagonist is villainous. For one thing, the protagonist—the English army—is outnumbered. In many stories, the hero looks, at first glance, weaker and less powerful than the enemy. Can you think of at least two stories, movies, or books in which the hero has less power than the villain?

Suggested answers:

David and Goliath, The Lord of the Rings, The Brave Little Toaster, Snow White and the Seven Dwarves, Shiloh, A Little Princess, The Wonderful Wizard of Oz . . .

[the list is endless]

Instructor: Arthur Machen suggests to you that the English are heroic in several different ways. Look back at the story and find two places where the writer describes the English soldiers as admirable. (In other words, find two places where he uses complimentary adjectives or phrases to describe them.) Also look for two places where he writes of the Germans in less than complimentary ways.

If the student cannot find these places, you may give him specific paragraphs within which to search, using the key below:

The heroic protagonist:

Paragraph 3: The men showed bravery by joking about the shells and calling them names; they are described as "good Englishmen" and as brothers.

Paragraph 5: Stout hearts

Paragraph 15: The bowmen who come to the aid of the English are shining like angels (implication: angels only help the righteous).

The villainous antagonist:

Paragraph 5: German cannons are a "seven-times-heated hell."

Paragraph 18: German officers have a "guttural scream" and shoot the reluctant soldiers on their own side.

Paragraph 20: Germans are a "heathen horde"

Instructor: In Step One of your workbook, write down two or three sentences explaining how the English appear to be heroic, while the Germans appear to be villains.

SAMPLE ACCEPTABLE ANSWERS:

> *The outnumbered English army is courageous and cheerful, even when it is afraid. The English soldiers think of each other as brothers. The Germans are a heathen horde whose officers shoot their own soldiers.*
>
> OR
>
> *The English are described as good and as brotherly. Even their artillery is described as good. The German artillery, though, is described as a "seven-times-heated hell," and the Germans themselves as heathens.*

Note: If the student talks about the "army" as the protagonist, remind him that "army" is singular because it represents one unit; the pronoun "it" should be used. If the student talks about "soldiers," the pronouns "them" and "they" are correct.

STEP TWO: **Identify the idea in the story**

Instructor: Now that you've identified the protagonist and antagonist, you should ask yourself the next basic question: What do they want? In this story, they want the same thing. What is it?

Student: To win the battle [war]

Instructor: Can they both win?

Student: No

Instructor: That is a very simple want, and a very uncomplicated conflict. In the past few weeks, you've practiced writing essays about conflict—what characters want and what blocks them from getting it. But if you wrote an essay about what the armies want and what keeps them from getting it, you'd have a very short and boring (and obvious) essay. This story has a different purpose than the other stories you've read for this course. Instead of describing how a character grapples with a problem and overcomes it, this story explores an idea. Read me the definition of an "idea story" from your workbook.

Student: A story that solves a problem, explores a what-if, or answers a question

Instructor: An idea story can be centered around a thought, a theory, a speculation, or a question. But the main focus of the story is the idea—not the characters. The characters only exist to help make the idea clear. Now finish this sentence for me: "The Bowmen" describes **what** would happen **if** . . .

Student: Saint George came to help the English

Instructor: On the lines in Step Two of your workbook, describe in three or four sentences how Saint George was summoned, and what happened when he arrived.

SAMPLE ACCEPTABLE ANSWERS:

One of the English soldiers summoned St. George by accident when he said a Latin motto out loud. St. George brought shining bowmen to fight against the Germans. The German forces were wiped out, but there were no wounds on them.

OR

One of the English soldiers remembered reading St. George's motto on a restaurant plate. He said it out loud—and St. George came to help the English army. He brought with him a whole force of shining archers. The German army was defeated, and the English were saved.

OR

An English soldier remembered the motto Adsit Anglis Sanctus Georgius, *"May St. George be a present help to the English." He said the motto out loud as he fired at the Germans. Then he heard thousands of voices shouting "St. George!" St. George's bowmen had come to help the English, and the Germans were defeated.*

Note to Instructor: If the student uses the Latin motto, it should be underlined (italicized) to show that the words are in another language.

STEP THREE: **Learn about the story's effect**

Student instructions for Step Three:

An idea story can have a powerful effect on readers. Take a few minutes now and read the following excerpts about the reaction of British readers to "The Bowmen."

Now read Arthur Machen's own account of how his story was turned into legend.

Finish today's work by making a few notes on the lines below about the story's effect. Write two or three sentences describing how "The Bowmen" affected the English public, and then one or two sentences describing Arthur Machen's reaction. Try to use a few of Machen's own words (in quotes) in your answer.

When you are finished, show your work to your instructor.

HOW TO HELP THE STUDENT WITH STEP THREE

The student's sentences should resemble the following:

By 1915, readers had begun to believe that "The Bowmen" was a true story. People claimed that they had seen angels on the battlefield, and that the angels had helped drive back the Germans. Arthur Machen himself had never expected to hear much more about his story. He insisted that the story was "pure invention," but the rumor went on growing like a "snowball."

After "The Bowmen" was published, rumors began to spread that the story was true. Witnesses insisted that they had seen angels on the battlefield. A parish priest even wrote to Arthur Machen, asking where he had heard the story. Machen insisted that he had made the story up as "light fiction," but rumors continued.

Although it was fiction, "The Bowmen" was soon thought to be true. Other versions of the story followed, with St. George, a cloud, and shining shapes frightening the Germans. Machen explained that the story was "pure invention," but readers did not believe him.

Day Three: Write

Focus: Writing about an idea story

Today's essay will include a summary and a paragraph or two about the protagonists and antagonists. It will also include two new elements: a brief look at the story's main idea, and a description of the story's effect on its readers.

STEP ONE: **Write the summary**

Student instructions for Step One:

> Begin by writing a brief narrative summary of the story. This summary should be three to five sentences in length. You may find it useful to use some or all of the sentences you wrote in Day Two, Step Two.
>
> In the first sentence, mention both the name of the story and the author.
>
> When you are finished, check your work with your instructor.

HOW TO HELP THE STUDENT WITH STEP ONE

The student may use either present or past tense for the summary, but should keep the same tense all the way through. The title of the story should be placed in quotation marks.

If the student gets bogged down in detail, point him back to the sentences written in Day Two, Step Two. The summary should tell about the danger the English were in, the summoning of St. George, and the result.

The narration should resemble one of the following:

> *In "The Bowmen" by Arthur Machen, the English army is fighting against the Germans. They are outnumbered and about to be defeated. One of the English soldiers remembers a Latin motto and says it out loud. This summons St. George and the Agincourt bowmen to the aid of the English, and the Germans are defeated.*

> *Arthur Machen wrote "The Bowmen" in 1914, during World War I. In the story, English soldiers were fighting against the Germans, but they were badly outnumbered. One of the English soldiers summoned St. George by accident, and St. George brought shining bowmen to fight against the Germans. The German forces were wiped out, but there were no wounds on them.*

> *In Arthur Machen's story "The Bowmen," English soldiers were fighting the Germans in World War I. An English soldier remembered the motto* Adsit Anglis Sanctus Georgius, *"May St. George be a present help to the English." He said the motto out loud as he fired at the Germans. Then he heard thousands of voices shouting "St. George!" St. George's bowmen had come to help the English, and the Germans were defeated.*

STEP TWO: **Write about the idea**

Student instructions for Step Two:

> In Day Two, you learned that "The Bowmen" is an idea story. Instead of writing about the protagonist, antagonist, and conflict, you'll use the central paragraphs of your essay to discuss the main idea of the story.
>
> "The Bowmen" describes what would happen if St. George came to help the English. This central part of your essay should tell *why* St. George appeared when he was summoned.

The story hints at two reasons. The first has to do with the motto on the plate; the second, with the character qualities of the English and German armies (you've already written briefly about this in Step One of the last lesson, so you may want to make use of those sentences).

Try to write a paragraph of four to six sentences describing why St. George appeared, covering both of these reasons. If you have trouble, ask your instructor for help.

When you are finished, check your work with your instructor.

HOW TO HELP THE STUDENT WITH STEP TWO

The student has not been given much guidance about interpreting the motto on the plate; if possible, encourage him to think independently about this. If he can't come up with an answer, you may tell him that St. George was the patron saint of the English (according to legend, he had a special responsibility to protect the English from danger).

You may need to remind the student that, in this story, the English army is heroic and the German army villainous.

The paragraphs should resemble one of the following:

St. George was the patron saint of the English, so he appeared in order to protect the English army from destruction. In the story, the English army also deserved to be protected because of their heroism. They were brotherly, courageous, and cheerful, but the Germans were a heathen horde whose officers even shot their own soldiers.

The Latin motto on the plate refers to the legend that St. George is the special protector of the English people. He appears because the army is in great danger. He also appears to help the English soldiers because they are good and brotherly; even their artillery is described as good. The Germans, on the other hand, are cruel and heathen.

St. George came to help the English army because he was the patron saint of the English people. He had a special duty to keep the English safe. The English army also was admirable and heroic. The soldiers were brotherly and brave, making jokes and singing even though they were in great danger. The German army was villainous. Even their artillery is described as a "seven-times-heated hell," and the Germans themselves are described as heathens. In the story, St. George appeared to help the heroic English against the wicked Germans.

STEP THREE: **Write about the story's effect**

Student instructions for Step Three:

Now conclude your essay with the paragraph you wrote in Step Three of yesterday's lesson. You should now have a three-paragraph essay.

Read your entire essay out loud. Eliminate any unnecessary repetition. Check your punctuation and spelling. If any sentences sound awkward, correct them.

When you are finished, show your entire essay to your instructor.

HOW TO HELP THE STUDENT WITH STEP THREE

You may need to remind the student to use consistent tense throughout the first two paragraphs. Both paragraphs should use either the present *or* the past tense. The third paragraph should be in the past tense, no matter what tense is used in the first two paragraphs; it talks about what happened in the definite past (1915), instead of what happens in the world of the story.

A sample acceptable essay might be:

Arthur Machen wrote "The Bowmen" in 1914, during World War I. In the story, English soldiers were fighting against the Germans, but they were badly outnumbered. One of the English soldiers summoned St. George by accident, and St. George brought shining bowmen to fight against the Germans. The German forces were wiped out, but there were no wounds on them.

St. George came to help the English army because he was the patron saint of the English people. He had a special duty to keep the English safe. The English army also was admirable and heroic. The soldiers were brotherly and brave, making jokes and singing even though they were in great danger. The German army was villainous. Even their artillery is described as a "seven-times-heated hell," and the Germans themselves are described as heathens. In the story, St. George appeared to help the heroic English against the wicked Germans.

By 1915, readers had begun to believe that "The Bowmen" was a true story. People claimed that they had seen angels on the battlefield, and that the angels had helped drive back the Germans. Arthur Machen himself had never expected to hear much more about his story. He insisted that the story was "pure invention," but the rumor went on growing like a "snowball."

Check the completed essay using the following rubric.

Week 26 Rubric
Brief Literary Essay

Organization

1 The essay should begin with a short summary of the story's plot.
2 The first paragraph must contain the title of the story and the name of the author.
3 The next paragraph should begin with a statement about St. George as patron saint and protector of the English.
4 The paragraph should then point out that the heroic English deserved to be saved.
5 The essay should end with a paragraph describing the story's effect on its readers.
6 The final paragraph should contain a few of Machen's own words in quotation marks.

7 The first two paragraphs should be in the same tense, either present or past; the final paragraph should be in the past tense.

Mechanics

1 Each sentence should make sense on its own when read aloud.
2 Possessive forms should be written properly.
3 Verb tense should be consistent throughout.
4 Subjects and verbs must be in agreement.
5 Antecedents of pronouns should be clear; pronouns should agree with the antecedents in number (army=singular=it, soldiers=plural=them).
6 Unnecessary repetition of the same nouns, adjectives, and proper names should be avoided.
7 The title of the story should be in quotation marks.
8 Direct quotes should be incorporated into full sentences and should be properly punctuated.
9 Either "St. George" or "Saint George" should be used.
10 If the Latin motto is quoted, it should be underlined (italicized).

Day Four: Reviewing Terms and Forms

Focus: Summarizing a narrative by choosing the main events and listing them chronologically

In this last lesson of the unit, the student will review literary terms and construct a basic essay-writing chart. The student will complete today's work independently, but the instructions are reproduced below for your convenience.

STEP ONE: **Add to the Literary Terms chart**

Write the following definitions on your Literary Terms chart, using the same format as your other definitions.

genre: a particular type or form of literature; works that use similar forms or have similar purposes

fantasy: a genre in which stories are set in a world that doesn't exist

Now choose three colored pencils. Use one colored pencil to represent "character," the second to represent "structure," and the third to represent "language."

With the first colored pencil, underline the definitions of *hero/heroine, protagonist, antagonist, villain*, and *supporting character.* All of these definitions have to do with the characters in stories.

With the second colored pencil, underline the definitions of *conflict, inversion, surprise story, fantasy,* and *genre.* All of these definitions have to do with the ways stories are put together, or structured.

With the third pencil, underline the definitions of *simile, metaphor,* and *synecdoche.* All of these definitions have to do with how words are used within the story.

STEP TWO: Construct the Essay Chart

In the last four weeks, you've practiced four different ways to write a literary essay. There are many other ways to write an essay, but following the methods you've been practicing will help you start to write about literature on your own.

Copy the following chart onto your own paper and put it in the Reference section of the Composition Notebook. When you need to write about a novel or story, you can follow the steps on this chart to get you started.

1. Write a basic narrative summary.
2. Who is the protagonist? What does he or she want?
   Write several sentences answering these questions.
3. Who or what is keeping the protagonist from getting what he or she wants? What does the antagonist want? Write several sentences answering these questions.

IF ANSWERS ARE INTERESTING (CHARACTERS HAVE REAL STRUGGLES), then ask	IF ANSWERS ARE BORING (CHARACTERS HAVE SIMPLE WANTS), then ask
4. What scenes show the conflict between protagonist and antagonist? Write several sentences describing these scenes. 5. Is the protagonist a hero? If so, how do you know? Is the antagonist a villain? If so, how do you know? 6. Is there a supporting character? If so, does he or she help or hinder?	4. Does the story solve a problem, explore a what-if, or answer a question? If so, 4a. What is the problem? OR 4b. What is the "what if"? OR 4c. What is the question?

Part V

RESEARCH
WEEKS 27–31

Overview of Weeks 27–31

The student now knows how to construct a basic outline; how to put together chronological narrations, descriptions, biographical sketches, sequences, and basic literary essays (the topoi); and how to alter sentences with basic transformations of nouns, adjectives, and verbs. In this five-week unit, the student will review and add to those skills.

These weeks focus on two skills in particular. First, now that the student has learned how to do a one-level outline, she will be introduced to the basics of two-level outlines (a skill she'll continue to develop in the next level of this course). Second, the student will continue to practice the topoi, but will now add footnotes and citations to the compositions.

There is more than one accepted way to document information. The three most common methods are probably Turabian, MLA, and Chicago. Each method uses a slightly different form for both citations and bibliographical references. The student will be taught MLA format, but Chicago and Turabian formats will also be provided in this instructor guide for your reference.

Week 27: Two-Level Outlining

Day One: Introduction to Two-Level Outlining

Focus: Understanding the function of the second level of an outline

In Week 2, the student used a passage from *The Story of Canada* to study one-level outlines. Today, she'll use it to see how a two-level outline is constructed.

STEP ONE: Understand the two-level outline

Student instructions for Step One:

Five hundred years ago, 60 million bison—or buffalo, as they are more often called—roamed the grasslands of North America. They meant life itself to plains nations like the Blackfoot of what is now southern Alberta. The Blackfoot moved slowly across the land, following the herds and carrying with them everything they had. They hunted deer and antelope, they grew tobacco, and they gathered wild turnips and onion. But for centuries it was the buffalo that provided for the Blackfoot people. Buffalo hides made their tipis and their clothing. Buffalo sinews were their thread. Buffalo bones made clubs and spoons and needles. They even used dried buffalo dung as fuel for their campfires. To the Blackfoot, buffalo meat was "real" meat and nothing else tasted so good. They trusted the buffalo to keep them strong.

The Blackfoot had always gone on foot, using dogs to help carry their goods, for there were no horses in North America until Spanish colonists brought them in the 1500s. Soon after that, plains people captured animals that had gone wild, or stole them in raids. They traded the horses northward and early in the 1700s, horses came to the northern plains. Suddenly the Blackfoot were a nation on horseback. How exciting it was, learning to ride a half-wild mustang and galloping off to the horizon![56]

In Week Two, you used this passage to study one-level outlines. Today, you'll use it to see how a two-level outline is constructed.

In a two-level outline, the main Roman-numeral points still sum up the central idea of the paragraph. However, you'll now add *subpoints* under each main point. These subpoints are each given a capital letter:

---

56. Janet Lunn and Christopher Moore, *The Story of Canada* (Key Porter Books, 1992), p. 313.

I. Main point
  A. First subpoint
  B. Second subpoint
  C. Third subpoint
II. Main point
  A. First subpoint
  B. Second subpoint

Each of the subpoints should provide a specific piece of information from the paragraph that relates *directly* to the main idea.

The best way to find subpoints is to first find your main point, and then ask yourself: What additional information does the paragraph give me about each of the people, things, or ideas in the main point?

Let's see how this works for the passage above. For the first paragraph, the main point you chose back in Week 2 might have sounded something like this:

I. The Blackfoot people used buffalo for food, clothing, and many other purposes.

There are two major people, things, or ideas in that point: the Blackfoot people, and the buffalo. In order to find your subpoints, ask two questions: What other important thing does the paragraph tell me about buffalo? And what other important thing does the paragraph tell me about the Blackfoot's *use* of the buffalo?

The answers to those questions are: The paragraph tells you how many buffalo there were—60 million. And it also tells you that the Blackfoot used the buffalo to keep them strong.

The two-level outline of the paragraph might read like this:

I. The Blackfoot people used buffalo for food, clothing, and other purposes.
  A. There were 60 million buffalo in North America.
  B. The Blackfoot relied on the buffalo to keep them strong.

Often, beginners will try to to use the capital-letter subpoints to give specific details about the paragraph:

I. The Blackfoot people used buffalo for food, clothing, and other purposes.
  A. They hunted deer and antelope too.
  B. They made clothing from buffalo.
  C. They ate buffalo meat.
  D. They made clubs and spoons and needles from buffalo bones.

These are actually details about exactly *how* the Blackfoot used the buffalo to keep themselves strong. Details like this would only appear in a three-level outline, which you won't practice until a later level of this course.

I. The Blackfoot people used buffalo for food, clothing, and other purposes.
  A. There were 60 million buffalo in North America.
  B. The Blackfoot relied on the buffalo to keep them strong.
    1. They made clothing from buffalo.
    2. They ate buffalo meat.
    3. They made clubs and spoons and needles from buffalo bones.

Try to remember this (you'll get plenty of practice in the next few lessons): Each capital-letter subpoint should make an independent statement relating directly to something in the main Roman-numeral point. So you'll need to leave out unnecessary detail.

A two-level outline of the second paragraph might begin with the main point "The Blackfoot tribe learned to use horses in the 1700s." In that case, the subpoints should answer the questions "What is the most important additional information that this paragraph gives me about the Blackfoot? What is the most important additional information that it gives me about the horses?"

An acceptable outline might look like this:

II. The Blackfoot tribe learned to use horses in the 1700s.
  A. They had always gone on foot before.
  B. The horses were brought to North America by Spanish colonists.

HOW TO HELP THE STUDENT WITH STEP ONE

Step One should be completed independently by the student. However, here are two additional pieces of information for you:

1. Many guides to outlining will tell you that you should never have an A unless you have a B, and that you should never use 1 unless you use 2. While this might be a useful guide when you're constructing your own outlines to write from, it's not workable when you're outlining someone else's material; the writer might not have provided two subpoints per main point, and it's pointless to make one up in order to preserve some sort of ideal outline form.

2. There may be several different ways to outline any given paragraph. If the student can give good reasons why she's chosen her main points and subpoints, don't worry about whether she's constructed the best possible outline.

STEP TWO: **Practice the two-level outline**

Note to Instructor: You will see that the actual text to be outlined is included. Since you will be carrying on a dialogue with the student about the passage, be sure to read it in its entirety:

Student instructions for Step Two:

> Read the following paragraph, taken from a history of East Asia, describing life in China after the Mongols invaded and seized power.
>
> Life in China under the Mongols was much like life in China under earlier alien rulers. Once order was restored, people did their best to get on with their lives. Some suffered real hardship. Many farmers had their lands expropriated; others were forced into slavery or serfdom, perhaps transported to a distant city, never to see their family again. Yet people still spoke Chinese, followed Chinese customary practices in arranging their children's marriages or dividing their family property, made offerings at local temples, celebrated New Year and other customary festivals. . . . Teachers still taught students the classics; scholars continued to write books; and books continued to be printed.[57]
>
> You will now construct a two-level outline of this paragraph. Begin by finding the main point and writing it down, using the Roman numeral I. When you are finished, check your work with your instructor. If you have difficulty, ask your instructor for help.
>
> Once you have found the main point of the paragraph, your instructor will help you find your subpoints.

---

57. Patricia Buckley Ebrey, Anne Walthall, and James B. Palais, *Pre-Modern East Asia to 1800: A Cultural, Social, and Political History* (Houghton Mifflin, 2006), p. 198.

HOW TO HELP THE STUDENT WITH STEP TWO

The student should begin by finding the main point. This is a descriptive paragraph, giving details about the pattern of daily life under Mongol rule. The main point is simply:

I. Life in China under the Mongols

The point can be expressed in different ways; for example,

I. Life after the Mongol conquest of China

I. China under Mongol rule

I. How people in China lived under Mongol rule

etc.

If the student copies the first (topic) sentence, remind her to use her own words. You may also point out that the second half of the sentence ("much like life in China under earlier alien rulers") mentions a topic ("earlier rulers") that isn't addressed anywhere else in the paragraph, so it should be left out of the main point.

If the student has a difficult time finding the main point, ask "Which single sentence in the paragraph sums up the experiences of all the different people under Mongol rule?" If she chooses the second sentence, ask "If the first sentence were missing, would you understand the topic of the paragraph?" The answer should be no, because the information that China was now under the Mongols is central to the details that follow. Only the first sentence sums up the entire paragraph.

Once the student has found the main point, ask the following questions to help her construct her two-level outline.

First subpoint

Instructor: There are two proper names in your main point. What are they?

Student: China and the Mongols

Instructor: Remember, each one of your subpoints should make a statement about something in your main point. The third and fourth sentences of the paragraph tell you specifically about the effect that the Mongols had on daily life. Was it a good or bad effect?

Student: Bad

Instructor: There are three specific bad things mentioned that happened to people under the Mongol rule. What are they?

Student: People lost their land, were forced into slavery, and were sent to distant cities.

Instructor: Those are details. See if you can sum up by saying "Under the Mongols, life was . . ."

Student: Hard [difficult, filled with suffering, a hardship, etc]

Instructor: That is your first subpoint. Write it down now.

Second subpoint

Instructor: The first subpoint tells you that life was difficult under the Mongols. The second subpoint is a contrast. Even though life was difficult, some things continued on as always. Tell me what four of those things are.

> *Student: People spoke Chinese, followed Chinese customs, made offerings, celebrated festivals, taught students, wrote books, printed books.*

Instructor: Those are details. See if you can sum up by saying "Despite the Mongol conquest . . ."

> *Student: Despite the Mongol conquest, Chinese traditions continued [life continued as always in China, people still followed Chinese customs, the Chinese lifestyle remained the same, etc.].*

Instructor: That is your second subpoint. Write it down now.

For your reference, a full three-level outline of the paragraph might look like this:

I. Life in China under the Mongols
   A. Under the Mongols, life was difficult
      1. Lands expropriated
      2. Slavery and serfdom
      3. Transport to distant cities
   B. Despite the Mongol conquest, Chinese traditions continued
      1. Chinese language spoken
      2. Chinese customs observed
      3. Festivals celebrated
      4. Students taught
      5. Books written, printed

Day Two: Outlining Exercise

Focus: Finding the central topics and subtopics in each paragraph of a chronological narrative in history

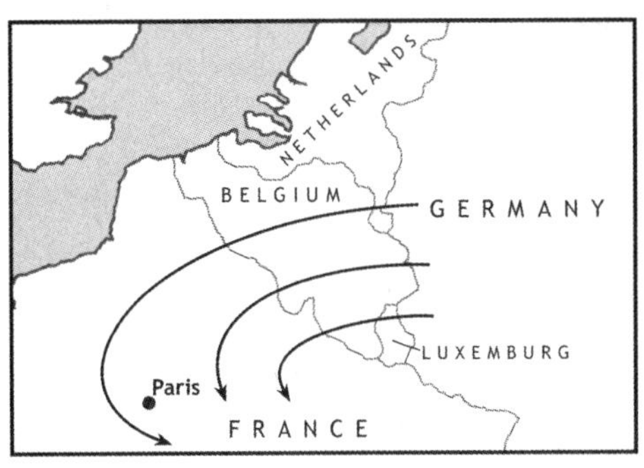

STEP ONE: **Read (Student Responsibility)**

Student instructions for Step One:

Read the following excerpt about the beginning months of World War I, from *The World War* by Albert E. McKinley et al.

STEP TWO: **Construct a one-level outline**

Student instructions for Step Two:

> Begin by finding the main idea in each of the three paragraphs.
>
> This excerpt is a chronological narrative about a past event. When you practiced making one-level outlines earlier in this course, you learned that you can ask the following questions about a chronological narrative:
>
> 1. What is the main thing or person that this section is about? *Or* Is the section about an idea?
> 2. Why is that thing or person important? *Or* What did that thing or person do/what was done to it? *Or* What is the idea?
>
> Sometimes, chronological narratives include descriptions. For a paragraph of description, you should ask:
>
> What part of the place does this paragraph focus on? *Or* What aspect or part of the whole does this section describe?
>
> As you look for the main idea in each paragraph, try to identify whether the paragraph is primarily a chronological narrative or a description. Then, ask the appropriate questions.
>
> If you have trouble, don't hesitate to ask your instructor for help. And when you are finished, check your main points with your instructor before going on.

HOW TO HELP THE STUDENT WITH STEP TWO

The student has already practiced one-level outlines extensively, so this assignment shouldn't be too difficult. However, the paragraphs do contain a lot of information, so you may need to help the student sort through the details to find the main points.

The student has been given the task of deciding whether it would be more productive to ask the simple question "What aspect or part of the whole does this section describe?" or whether it would be better to ask the two-part "What is the main thing that this section is about? Why is that thing important?"

If necessary, you may help the student by pointing out that the first and third paragraphs contain *actions.* Whenever an action is involved, the two-part question should be asked. The second paragraph contains no present actions, just speculation about how a German attack *might* work. The third paragraph refers to the German decision to attack from the northeast, but the rest of the paragraph is devoted to explaining what the northeast was like. The second and third paragraphs are both descriptive.

Suggested answers (the student's answers should resemble the following but don't need to be identical):

I. The German leaders getting ready to attack France OR Germany planned to invade France OR The German plan OR The plan of the German leaders

II. The French frontier OR The frontier of France nearest to Germany

III. The northeast of France OR The northeastern frontier of France

III. The neutrality of Belgium and Luxemburg OR The decision to ignore neutrality of Belgium and Luxemburg

If the student struggles with this assignment, use the following dialogue:

Paragraph 1
Instructor: Who is the most important actor in this paragraph? Hint: they're mentioned in the first sentence.

Student: The German leaders

Instructor: What are the German leaders getting ready to do?

Student: Attack France

Instructor: Everything else in the paragraph has to do with the German plan to attack France. That is your main point.

Paragraph 2
Instructor: Although this paragraph talks about invasion and attack, is there any actual invasion and attack going on?

Student: No

Instructor: There is no real action in this paragraph. Instead, it describes the landscape of a country. Which country?

Student: France

Instructor: What part or aspect of France does the paragraph describe?

Student: The frontier

Instructor: That is your second main point.

Paragraph 3
Instructor: This paragraph is a contrast to the previous paragraph. The previous paragraph described the frontier nearest France. What part or aspect of France does this paragraph describe?

Student: The northeast OR *The northeastern frontier*

Instructor: That is your third main point.

Paragraph 4
Instructor: What is the most important thing in this paragraph? Hint: it has to do with both Belgium and Luxemburg.

Student: Neutrality

Instructor: The entire paragraph is about the neutrality of those two countries. That is your final main point.

STEP THREE: **Construct a two-level outline**

Student instructions for Step Three:

Now go back and try to find two subpoints in each paragraph. Remember: the subpoints should make independent statements that relate *directly* to the main point.

Below, you will see questions and hints that will help you find the subpoints in each paragraph. Use these and construct your own two-level outline on your own paper.

When you are finished, check your work with your instructor.

I. Germany planned to invade France
  A. This point has to do with the timing of the invasion
  B. This point has to do with the pace of the invasion
II. The French frontier OR The frontier of France nearest Germany
  A. The first important characteristic of the French frontier
  B. The second important characteristic of the French frontier
III. The northeast of France OR The northeastern frontier of France
  A. The first important thing that the northeast frontier lacked
  B. The second important thing that the northeast frontier lacked
IV. The neutrality of Belgium and Luxemburg OR The decision to ignore neutrality of Belgium and Luxemburg
  A. This point has to do with France's relationship to the neutrality
  B. This point has to do with Germany's relationship to the neutrality

HOW TO HELP THE STUDENT WITH STEP THREE

The student will not be asked to do independent two-level outlining until the next level of this course. The hints given should point her towards the correct answers. If necessary, use the sample outline below to prompt her.

I. Germany planned to invade France
  A. Planned to attack France before the Russians
  B. Success dependent on speed
II. The French frontier OR The frontier of France nearest Germany
  A. The frontier had military obstacles
  B. The frontier had natural obstacles
III. The northeast of France OR The northeastern frontier of France
  A. No natural barriers
  B. No fortifications
IV. The neutrality of Belgium OR The decision to ignore Belgian neutrality
  A. France depended on Belgian neutrality
  B. The Germans decided to ignore it

Day Three: Outlining Exercise

Focus: Finding the central topics and subtopics in each paragraph of a chronological narrative in science

STEP ONE: **Read (Student Responsibility)**

Student instructions for Step One:

Read the following excerpt about changing views of the solar system, from *Earth's Changing Environment.*

STEP TWO: **Construct a one-level outline**

Student instructions for Step Two:

Begin by finding the main idea in each of the four paragraphs.

This passage is a chronological narrative, because it explains in chronological order the ideas that different scientists have had about the relationship between the Earth and the rest of the universe. You'll probably find it most useful to ask this version of the two questions you've been using:

1. What is the central idea in this passage?
2. Who held that idea?

Try those two questions now.

When you've finished your one-level outline, check your work with your instructor. If you have trouble finding the main idea, ask your instructor for help.

HOW TO HELP THE STUDENT WITH STEP TWO

Each of the paragraphs in today's passage contains information about (1) a theory and (2) the thinkers who held that theory. The main point for each paragraph should mention both.

By this point, the student should be outgrowing the need for dialogue to find the main point. However, if necessary you may use the explanations below to guide the student.

I. Ancient people believed the Earth was one of a kind OR People once believed the Earth was one of a kind

1. What is the central idea in this passage?

The central idea in this passage is that the Earth was one of a kind. That the other heavenly bodies were thought to be "of a different nature," that the earth was considered to be at the center, and that the planets were "wanderers" are all details about this idea—in all of these ways, the Earth was unlike everything else around it.

2. Who held that idea?

The belief was held by ancient people. This is implied, not stated, but is clear because the belief was held "for centuries" by "most believers" and "was generally thought." "Aristotle" is not a good answer because he was only one of many who believed this. To use the adverb "once" also places the belief in the past.

In this first paragraph, none of the three details about the central idea seem to be the "most" distinctive, so all should appear only in the second level of the outline.

II. Most thinkers thought the earth was motionless at the center of the universe OR The geocentric theory of most ancient thinkers

1. What is the central idea in this passage?

The theory of geocentrism is mentioned in every single sentence, so it is clearly the governing idea. The student may either simply use the word "geocentrism," or may include the explanation of what geocentrism is.

2. Who held that idea? OR What made that idea most distinctive?

"Most thinkers" held this idea; as in the paragraph before, this means "ancient thinkers."

III. The new ideas of Copernicus OR Copernicus believed the earth was a planet

1. What is the central idea in this passage?

There are two central ideas connected to Copernicus: that the Earth rotates on an axis, and that the Earth orbits around the sun. These are separate ideas, so it is simplest for the student to sum up with "The new ideas of Copernicus" rather than listing each idea—the details about the ideas should go in the subpoints.

However, if the student wishes to be more specific about the central idea: the Earth's rotation and its orbit are both related to the earth's identity as a planet *rather than as the motionless center of the universe.*

2. Who held that idea? OR What made that idea most distinctive?

The focus of the paragraph is clearly Copernicus.

IV. Kepler's planetary laws OR Kepler's law of elliptical orbits

1. What is the central idea in this passage?

The passage mentions that Kepler developed three planetary laws, but then only develops one—elliptical orbits—in detail. It is acceptable for the student to use either as the central idea.

2. Who held that idea? OR What made that idea most distinctive?

Kepler's name must appear in the main point; the most distinctive of the planetary laws is clearly the law governing elliptical orbits, but it is not necessary for the student to include this information.

STEP THREE: **Construct a two-level outline**

Student instructions for Step Three:

> Now go back and try to find two or three subpoints in each paragraph. Remember: the subpoints should make independent statements that relate *directly* to the main point.

Below, you will see hints that will help you find the subpoints in each paragraph. Use these and construct your own two-level outline on your own paper.

When you are finished, check your work with your instructor.

I.
  A. Where it was
  B. What others were like
  C. What others did

II.
  A. What it did at the center
  B. Who developed this
  C. Who accepted it

III.
  A. What it does
  B. What it and others do

IV.
  A. What shape it is
  B. How Earth's is a little different

HOW TO HELP THE STUDENT WITH STEP THREE

The hints given should point the student towards the correct answers. If necessary, use the sample outline below to prompt her.

I. Ancient people believed the Earth was one of a kind
  A. Earth at the center
  B. Other heavenly bodies of a different nature
  C. The planets, or wanderers

II. Most thinkers thought the Earth at the center of the universe OR The geocentric theory of most ancient thinkers
  A. Earth motionless at the center
  B. Developed by Ptolemy of Alexandria
  C. Accepted by all astronomers

III. The new ideas of Copernicus OR Copernicus believed the earth was a planet
  A. The Earth rotates on its axis
  B. Earth and other planets revolve around Sun

IV. Kepler's planetary laws OR Kepler's laws of elliptical orbits
  A. A planet's orbit is an ellipse
  B. Earth has a more circular orbit

Day Four: Outlining Exercise

Focus: Finding the central topics and subtopics in each paragraph of a description

STEP ONE: Read (Student Responsibility)

Student instructions for Step One:

The following passage is excerpted from a longer piece about three giant tree species that grow in California: the Monterey cypress, the common redwood, and the giant redwood.

STEP TWO: Understand how to construct a two-level outline (Student Responsibility)

Student instructions for Step Two:

You have been practicing two-level outlining by first constructing a one-level outline and then adding subpoints to each main point. That's a good way to practice two-level outlining for the first time, because it breaks the task down into smaller, manageable parts. Most often, though, you'll find it easier to find the main point and subpoints of each paragraph at the same time.

As you begin, remember that this passage is a *description*. When you outline a description, you can usually find the main topic of each paragraph by asking two questions:

1. What is the most important thing in this paragraph?
2. What aspect or part of the whole does this paragraph describe?

Look at the first paragraph of your reading now. The first sentence tells you what the paragraph is about; the most important thing in the paragraph is the species giant redwood, the *Sequoia gigantea*. So you would start to construct your outline by writing down:

I. Giant redwoods

Now you need to figure out what aspect or part of the species *Sequoia gigantea* is being described.

You can identify this aspect or part, and start to find your subpoints at the same time, by underlining each phrase that tells you something about giant redwoods, like this:

The paragraph tells you seven things about the giant redwoods:

They are the most famous of the giant trees.
They grow in the Mariposa valley.
They grow in groups and as single trees.
They are survivors of an almost extinct race.

They are very large.
They are 30–36 feet around.
They are 400–450 feet high.

(Notice that you wouldn't include the information about the fallen redwood tree that's large enough for a rider on horseback to ride through; that is a specific detail about *one* tree, not a piece of information about the whole species, "giant redwoods.")

The underlined phrases tell you where and how giant redwoods grow, what their reputation (fame) is like, what they're descended from, and what size they are. In other words, this is an *overall description of giant redwoods.* When you studied descriptions in Part II, you learned that a scientific description (like a description of a natural object) often begins with an introductory paragraph that gives a basic definition and overview of the object or phenomenon under study (page 153). This paragraph gives an overall survey of giant redwoods. So you would want to finish your main point by changing it to:

I. About giant redwoods OR Introduction to giant redwoods

Your list of underlined phrases helped you to identify the main point in the passage; now, you can turn those phrases into subpoints.

In the list below, the phrases have been grouped together by subject. The first three subjects have been listed for you; try to summarize the fourth subject in your own words. Write your answer in the blank before continuing on.

PHRASES	*SUBJECT*
They are the most famous of the giant trees.	*The fame of the trees*
They grow in the Mariposa valley.	*Where and how they grow*
They grow in groups and as single trees.	
They are survivors of an almost extinct race.	*Survivors of their race*
They are very large.	
They are 30–36 feet around.	____________________
They are 400–450 feet high.	

What did you write for the fourth subject?

Your answer should have been either *Their size* or *How big they are.*

Listing the phrases helps you to find the main point for each paragraph; it also helps you to figure out what subpoints are in the paragraph. A finished two-level outline for the first paragraph might look like this:

I. About the giant redwoods
  A. The fame of the trees
  B. Where and how they grow
  C. Survivors of their race
  D. Their size

You will not do three-level outlines until the end of the next level of this course, but (for your reference) here is what a three-level outline would look like.

I. About the giant redwoods
  A. The fame of the trees
  B. Where and how they grow
    1. In the Mariposa valley
    2. Some in groups
    3. Some as single trees
  C. Survivors of their race
  D. Their size
    1. One fallen tree
    2. 30–36 feet wide
    3. 400–450 feet high

STEP THREE: **Construct a two-level outline**

Student instructions for Step Three:

Now work on a two-level outline of each remaining paragraph by following the method described in Step Two. For each paragraph:

1. Find the most important thing in the paragraph.
2. Underline each phrase in the paragraph that tells you something important about it.
3. Finish your main point by answering the question "What aspect or part is being described?"
4. Group the important phrases together by subject. Each subject should give you a subpoint.

In the worksheet below, at least one of these steps has been completed for each paragraph. Using these hints, finish the remaining steps and construct your two-level outline.

When you are finished, check your work with your instructor. And if you have difficulty, ask your instructor for help.

HOW TO HELP THE STUDENT WITH STEP THREE:

The student's completed work should resemble the answers below. Remember that the student may have slightly different answers. However, it is important that the student not pick out minor details as important to the passage. The central piece of information in each sentence has been underlined below; additional phrases shouldn't be underlined.

It is possible that the student may choose another phrase as central to the sentence. For example, below we have suggested

Even then it <u>refused to fall</u>, so exactly erect had it grown, and some two days more were required to get it down.

It would not be unreasonable for the student to choose instead

Even then it refused to fall, so exactly <u>erect had it grown</u>, and some two days more were required to get it down.

The refusal to fall and the position of the tree are directly related to each other; either one could serve as the subpoint highlighting that particular quality of the tree. However, the student should not choose

Even then it <u>refused to fall</u>, so exactly <u>erect had it grown</u>, and some two days more were required to get it down.

When choosing subpoints, the student *must* attempt to avoid underlining phrases that simply repeat or reinforce other underlined phrases.

SUGGESTED ANSWERS

One of these old giants was cut, many years ago, by <u>boring holes through it</u> with a pump auger, the holes just touching each other, until the entire wood was cut away. Even then

it refused to fall, so exactly erect had it grown, and some two days more were required to get it down. This was accomplished by driving wedges into one side by means of heavy logs used as battering rams, until it toppled over. A house has been built on the stump. A section twenty feet in diameter has been sawed off and exhibited in many places.

PHRASES	*SUBJECT*
Boring holes	*Holes bored in tree*
Refused to fall	*Tree refused to fall*
Driving wedges into one side	*Wedges driven into tree*
House built on stump	*After the tree fell*
Section sawed off and exhibited	

II. Cutting down one giant redwood
- A. Holes bored through it
- B. Tree refused to fall
- C. Wedges driven into tree
- D. After the tree fell

These "big trees" are survivors from a past era. . . . All the older trees are hollow, the central wood having decayed out to a great height. They have branches only near the top, and the foliage is scanty, so making the tree appear much like a tall shaft. The wood of these "big trees" is coarse and rather weak. Even if it were not right and wise to preserve the few still growing as monuments of the past, little use could be made of the wood as timber. The bark is thick and hard, though somewhat fibrous, varying from twelve to fifteen inches in thickness, and probably one reason why these trees have survived is its protection.

PHRASES	*SUBJECT*
Older trees are hollow	*Trees are hollow*
Branches only near the top	*Branches only near top*
Coarse and rather weak	*Coarse and weak*
Little use could be made of the wood	
Bark is thick and hard	*Thick hard bark*

III. How the tree is made OR The wood of the giant redwood
- A. Trees are hollow [OR Decays out from the bottom]
- B. Branches only near the top
- B. Coarse and weak
- C. Thick hard bark

The common redwood alone possesses value for timber. This is so valuable as to threaten its early extinction as a forest tree. The lumber is cut and sawed into lengths for logs in the usual way, and the wood is adapted to all uses in the construction of frame buildings. The trees are so large that the logs are usually split with wedges into quarters, and then these are sawed into lumber for inside finishing in the manner known as "quarter sawing," which makes the edge of the grain show in every board. The color is a deep red, much like cherry, only not quite so dark, and the wood works easily and smoothly, so making fine finishings.

PHRASES	*SUBJECT*
Value for timber	*Value for timber*
Cut and sawed into lengths for logs	*The logs OR How the wood is used*
Wood is adapted.	
Logs are usually split with wedges.	
Color is a deep red.	*Deep red color*
Wood works easily and smoothly.	*Wood is easy to work*

IV. The wood of the common redwood
A. Value for timber
B. The logs OR How the wood is used
C. Deep red color
D. Wood is easy to work

WEEK 28: DOCUMENTATION

Day One: Outlining Exercise

Focus: Finding the central topics and selected subtopics in a chronological narrative that includes descriptions of character and place

STEP ONE: **Read (Student Responsibility)**

Student instructions for Step One:

The following passage comes from Jacob Abbott's classic biography *History of King Charles the First of England*. Charles I was born in 1600. His father, James VI of Scotland, was the closest living relative to Queen Elizabeth I of England; so, when Elizabeth died in 1603, James became James VI of Scotland and James I of England at the same time.

Charles's mother was Anne of Denmark, and he had an older brother (Henry, the heir to the Scottish and eventually English throne) and an older sister, also named Elizabeth.

Charles I would become King of England in 1625. During his reign, a great civil war was fought in England. In 1649, Charles I became the only king of England to be executed for treason.

STEP TWO: **Identify the form of each paragraph**

Student instructions for Step Two:

This passage combines three different forms that you've studied in previous weeks: a chronological narrative of past events, a place description, and a description of a person.

Go back now and write, in the margin next to each paragraph, a label that identifies each paragraph's form. Use the labels "narrative," "place," and "person." When you're finished, check your answers with your instructor.

HOW TO HELP THE STUDENT WITH STEP TWO

The student should have identified the paragraphs as follows:

narrative	Young Charles was very weak and feeble in his infancy. . . .
narrative	It was only about two years after Charles's birth that Queen Elizabeth died. . . .
place	One of the chief residences of the English monarchs is Windsor Castle . . .
narrative	Here King James held his court after his arrival in England . . .
narrative	Soon after this, when he was perhaps five or six years of age . . .
person	The same cause operated to make him not agreeable as a companion . . .
narrative	When he was about twelve years of age, too, his brother Henry died. . . .
narrative	In the mean time his health and strength rapidly improved . . .

If the student has misidentified a paragraph, simply tell him the correct answer and then point out the following:

The narrative paragraphs all begin at one point in time, and then move forward to a future point in time.

The paragraph labelled as "place" is a simple description of the location, purpose, and structure of Windsor Castle.

The paragraph labelled as "person" describes aspects of Charles's personality—his temper, jealousy, and unpopularity. This is not chronological narrative because it is a description of Charles at *one point in time.*

STEP THREE: **Construct a one-level outline**

Student instructions for Step Three:

> Construct a one-level outline on your own paper, using the questions suggested below to identify the main topic of each paragraph. When you're finished, check your answers with your instructor.
>
> I. What part of Charles I's life is discussed?
> II. What was the most important thing that happened?
> III. What is described?
> IV. What was the most important thing that happened?
> V. What part of Charles I's life is discussed?
> VI. What aspect of Charles I is described?
> VII. What was the most important thing that happened?
> VIII. What was the most important thing that happened?

HOW TO HELP THE STUDENT WITH STEP THREE

The student's finished outline should resemble the following. The hints given in the workbook should point the student in the right direction, but you may prompt him if necessary.

I. Charles's infancy OR Charles as a baby OR Charles was a weak and feeble baby
II. King James became king of England

("Queen Elizabeth died" is not the main point, because everything else in the passage has to do with James becoming king; Queen Elizabeth's death is merely the cause of James's kingship.)

III. Windsor Castle

IV. Charles arrived in England OR Charles travelled to Windsor Castle

V. Charles's boyhood OR Charles as a boy

VI. Charles's disposition OR What Charles was like OR Why Charles was unpopular

VII. Charles became heir to the throne

("Charles became Prince of Wales" isn't the main point because it is a result of Charles becoming heir to the throne. "Henry died" isn't the main point because the rest of the paragraph talks about Charles, not Henry; Henry's death is merely the cause of Charles's becoming heir.)

VIII. Charles's health and strength improved OR Charles got stronger OR Charles grew into a healthy young man

STEP FOUR: **Construct a two-level outline of selected paragraphs**

Student instructions for Step Four:

> Now expand the first four points on your outline by adding subpoints. Use the hints below. When you're finished, check your answers with your instructor.
>
> I.
> A. This happened first
> B. This happened second
> C. This is how people felt about it
>
> II.
> A. This happened first
> B. This happened second
> C. This happened third
>
> III.
> A. The first aspect discussed
> B. The second aspect discussed
> C. The third aspect discussed
>
> IV.
> A. This happened first
> B. This happened second
> C. This happened third

HOW TO HELP THE STUDENT WITH STEP FOUR

The student's answers should resemble the following. The hints given in the workbook should point the student in the right direction, but you may prompt him if necessary.

I. Charles's infancy OR Charles as a baby OR Charles was a weak and feeble baby
A. He was immediately baptized.
B. He lived but was weak.

C. No one was very concerned.

II. King James became king of England

A. Queen Elizabeth died.

B. A messenger arrived.

C. James went to England.

("Anne and the children went a little later" is not a main point; it is a detail about James's journey to England, since he and his queen and the two older children went as a unit.)

III. Windsor Castle

A. Location OR Where it was

B. Function OR Purpose

C. Layout OR What it looked like OR How it was built

IV. Charles arrived in England OR Charles travelled to Windsor Castle

A. James sent for Charles.

("Here James held his court" is a transition between the descriptive paragraph before and the current paragraph, not a subpoint.)

B. Charles made a slow journey.

C. Charles arrived OR Charles arrived at the age of four.

Day Two: Documentation

Focus: Citing source material properly

In the next few lessons, the student will work on developing a chronological narration that includes a place and character description—all forms that have been practiced already, and now need to be reviewed. But this time, the student will work on finding her own information: taking notes from sources and using it as she writes.

Before she can do this, she'll need to spend some time learning how to use those sources properly.

Today's lesson covers the correct form for footnotes, endnotes, in-text citations, and Works Cited pages.

There is more than one accepted style for citations and bibliographies. The style taught here is MLA (Modern Language Association), which is widely accepted and straightforward. For your reference, here is how a citation for the same book appears in each of the major citation styles:

MLA — Bauer, Susan Wise. *The Story of the World: Ancient Times, from the Earliest Nomads to the Last Roman Emperor.* Charles City, Va.: Well-Trained Mind Press, 2006.

APA — Bauer, Susan Wise. (2006). *The story of the world: Ancient times, from the earliest nomads to the last Roman emperor.* Charles City, Va.: Well-Trained Mind Press.

CHICAGO Bauer, Susan Wise. 2006. *The story of the world: ancient times, from the earliest nomads to the last Roman emperor.* Charles City, Va.: Well-Trained Mind Press.

HARVARD BAUER, SUSAN WISE. (2006). *The story of the world: ancient times, from the earliest nomads to the last Roman emperor.* Charles City, Va., Well-Trained Mind Press.

TURABIAN Bauer, Susan Wise. *The Story of the World: Ancient Times, from the Earliest Nomads to the Last Roman Emperor.* Charles City, Va.: Well-Trained Mind Press, 2006.

At this stage, it is best for the student to learn one documentation style thoroughly and get into the habit of using it. Variations can be covered in the high-school years.

Correct citation form for all of these styles can be found at WorldCat (http://worldcat.org). Use the search box to locate a text, and then click on the "Cite/Export" command. The screen that pops up will show how a text should be cited in each style.

The student will work independently until Step Four is completed; his directions are reproduced below for your convenience. A key to the final exercise is found at the end of this lesson.

STEP ONE: **Understand footnotes (Student Responsibility)**

Student instructions for Step One:

> This book makes use of footnotes. Every quote is followed by a superscript number that comes *after* the closing quotation marks.
>
> "When you use someone else's words or ideas in your research paper, you *must* give credit."[58]
>
> The superscript number leads to the footnote. Footnotes should be written like this:
>
> Author's name, *Title of Book* (Publisher, date of publication), p. #.
>
> If there are two authors, list them like this:
>
> Author name and author name, *Title of Book* (Publisher, date of publication), p. #.
>
> If your quote comes from more than one page of the book you're quoting, use "pp." to mean "pages" and put a hyphen between the page numbers.
>
> Author's name, *Title of Book* (Publisher, date of publication), pp. #-#.
>
> Sometimes a book has been revised and put out in a new edition. If the book is a second (or third, or fourth, etc.) edition, put that information right after the title.
>
> Author's name, *Title of Book,* number of edition (Publisher, date of publication), p. #.
>
> You can find all the information you need on the copyright page of the book (usually the second

58. Laurie Rozakis, *Schaum's Quick Guide to Writing Great Research Papers,* 2nd ed. (McGraw-Hill, 2007), p. 117.

or third page in the book). On the following copyright page, look down until you see "Library of Congress Cataloging-in-Publication Data." This will always give you the author, title, edition (all in the second line of the data), and the date (on the next to last line). Underline each piece of information now. Then look back up the page to the top and find the name of the publisher. Underline it now.

If you're using a regular word processing program, footnotes are easy to insert; there's a specific command on one of your menus that will automatically put the footnotes in and adjust the rest of the text on the page. The only thing you'll have to do is make sure that the text in the footnote is smaller than the text in your paper (usually about 2 points—in this book, the font is 12 point for the text and 10 point for the footnotes).

STEP TWO: **Understand endnotes and in-text citations (Student Responsibility)**

Student instructions for Step Two:

If you're using a plain text program or handwriting your papers, footnotes can be much harder to place. There are two other acceptable ways to document quotes.

The first is endnotes:

"Otherwise, you're stealing their work."[1]

An endnote is written exactly like a footnote, except that the note is placed at the end of the paper instead of down at the bottom of the page where the quote occurs. The endnotes are usually headed like this:

ENDNOTES

[1] Laurie Rozakis, *Schaum's Quick Guide to Writing Great Research Papers,* 2nd ed. (McGraw-Hill, 2007), p. 117.

For a short paper, the endnotes can be placed on the last page. For a longer paper, you would want to have an entirely separate page headed ENDNOTES.

The second alternative is an in-text citation. With an in-text citation, you write the last name of the author, the date of the book, and the page number in parentheses after the closing quotation mark, but before the period.

"Learn how to avoid literary theft by documenting your sources correctly" (Rozakis, 2007, p. 117).

All of the other publication information about the book goes on the Works Cited page (which you'll find out about in a minute).

While you can use any of these three methods, I like footnotes the best. Endnotes force the reader to flip to the end of the paper to see where your quote came from (and when you flip, you lose your place). In-text citations clog up your writing and distract the reader.

STEP THREE: **Understand the Works Cited page (Student Responsibility)**

Student instructions for Step Three:

The Works Cited page should be a separate page at the end of your paper. On it, you should list, in alphabetical order by last name of author, all of the books that you've quoted from (even if there's only one). The Works Cited page looks like this:

WORKS CITED

Rozakis, Laurie. *Schaum's Quick Guide to Writing Great Research Papers,* 2nd ed. New York: McGraw-Hill, 2007.

You'll see that there are three major differences between the way you list a book on the Works Cited page, and the way you list it in a footnote or endnote.

First, when you list a book on the Works Cited page, you list it alphabetically by the last name of the author. In the Works Cited section of this book, you'll see:

Riley, Franklin Lafayette. *General Robert E. Lee after Appomattox.* New York: The Macmillan Company, 1922.

Rogers, Julia Ellen. *Trees That Every Child Should Know: Easy Tree Studies for All Seasons of the Year.* New York: Doubleday, 1909.

Rozakis, Laurie. *Schaum's Quick Guide to Writing Great Research Papers,* 2nd ed. New York: McGraw-Hill, 2007.

Scalzi, John. *The Rough Guide to the Universe.* London: Rough Guides, 2003.

Schiff, Stacy. *Cleopatra: A Life.* New York: Little, Brown and Company, 2010.

Schom, Alan. *Napoleon Bonaparte.* New York: HarperCollins, 1997.

As you can see, "Rozakis" comes alphabetically between Rogers and Scalzi. This is in case the reader suddenly thinks "Wait, wasn't there a quote from a book by Laurie Rozakis? What was the book? How can I find it?" All the reader has to do is go to the Works Cited page and find "Rozakis" to get answers.

Second, you'll see that the publisher gets an additional identification: by city, not just by name. I'm not sure that I can think of a good reason why. Possibly, in the days before the internet, it was difficult to locate a publisher unless you knew what city's Yellow Pages to look in? Whatever the reason, the form has stuck.

If the publisher is in a huge and very well known city—New York, Los Angeles, London, Chicago—you just need to list the city. But for other cities, you should list both the city and the state, like this:

Bauer, Susan Wise. *Writing with Skill, Level 1.* Charles City, Va.: Well-Trained Mind Press, 2012.

When you write a citation, you shouldn't use the postal code abbreviation for the state (VA). Instead, you should use the following standard abbreviations (and yes, these are silly and pointless rules):

Ala.	Alaska	Ariz.	Ark.	Calif.	Colo.
Conn.	Del.	Fla.	Ga.	Hawaii	Idaho
Ill.	Ind.	Iowa	Kan.	Ky.	La.
Maine	Md.	Mass.	Mich.	Minn.	Miss.
Mo.	Mont.	Neb.	Nev.	N.H.	N.J.
N.M.	N.Y.	N.C.	N.D.	Ohio	Okla.
Ore.	Pa.	R.I.	S.C.	S.D.	Tenn.
Texas	Utah	Vt.	Va.	Wash.	W. Va
Wis.	Wyo.				

Sometimes the publisher provides an address in the first few pages of the book. But if you can't find it, the simplest way to find the city is to use WorldCat, the largest online library reference tool.

To use WorldCat, go to http://www.worldcat.org. Type the title of the book and the author's last name into the search box. If you were to type *Schaum's Quick Guide to Writing Great Research Papers Rozakis* into the box and hit "Search," here's what would come up:

All the information you need for your Works Cited page is right there: title, author, publisher, date, and city (New York).

To sum up, here's how Works Cited entries should be formatted:

WORKS CITED

Author last name, author first name. *Title.* Publisher city: publisher, publisher date.

STEP FOUR: **Practice documentation**

Student instructions for Step Four:

Using your word processing program, type the following paragraph and footnote each quote properly, using the page images and copyright pages provided. Attach a properly formatted Works Cited page, doing whatever additional research is necessary. Not all of the copyright pages below are in the exact same format—see if you can find the information you need.

If you are not using a word processing program, you may use endnote format instead.

When you are finished, check your work with your instructor.

HOW TO HELP THE STUDENT WITH STEP FOUR

KEY TO STEP FOUR

Most ideas are not completely original; we "use ideas from other people all the time" and "weave them into our working and academic lives."[1] But we should also give credit to the authors whose words we use. After all, they came up with the ideas first—and spent plenty of blood, sweat, and tears doing so. And don't forget that "failure to properly credit your sources could get you in big trouble, whether it's an intentional omission or not."[2] The correct format is important as well. As Dick Francis once wrote, in a novel on a completely different subject: "If you get the form of things right . . . every peril can be tamed."[3]

---

[1] Colin Neville, *The Complete Guide to Referencing and Avoiding Plagiarism* (Open University Press, 2007), p. 4.

[2] Kelly Garbato, *13 Lucky Steps to Writing a Research Paper* (Peedee Publishing, 2005), p. 141.

[3] Dick Francis, *Break In* (Berkley Publishing Group, 1986), p. 193.

WORKS CITED

Francis, Dick. *Break In.* New York: Berkley Publishing Group, 1986.

Garbato, Kelly. *13 Lucky Steps to Writing a Research Paper.* Overland Park, Kan.: Peedee Publishing, 2005.

Neville, Colin. *The Complete Guide to Referencing and Avoiding Plagiarism.* New York: Open University Press, 2007.

Day Three: Avoiding Plagiarism

Focus: Understanding common knowledge and proper documentation

In the last lesson, the student learned proper documentation for direct quotes. In this lesson, he will learn that whenever he uses someone else's words and ideas in paraphrase, he should also give credit to the original author.

However, if the words and ideas he's using are "common knowledge," he doesn't need to footnote. Today, he will learn more about this principle.

Steps One and Two will be completed independently. The student's directions are reproduced below for your convenience.

STEP ONE: **Understand the definition of plagiarism (Student Responsibility)**

Student instructions for Step One:

> If you use someone else's words or ideas without giving them credit, you are *plagiarizing.* (The word comes from the Latin noun *plagiarius*, or "kidnapper"—you're "kidnapping" someone else's work and pretending that it is your own.)
>
> The simplest form of plagiarism is copying someone else's exact words. Imagine that you were collecting information to write your own chronological narration about Charles I of England and came across this passage in Jacob Abbott's biography:
>
> ---
>
> (Look down at the footnote and notice something important: the *second* time you quote from a book, you don't need to write all the same information in the footnote. You can just write the last name of the author and the page number of the quote.)
>
> If you used this information in your own chronological narration, you would *not* want to write:
>
> > Charles I ascended the scaffold for his execution. He spent a few minutes in prayer, and then stretched out his hands. The executioner swung the axe and beheaded him.
>
> The second sentence of your paragraph would use the exact same words as the third sentence of Jacob Abbott's paragraph. Using Abbott's words without acknowledging him would be plagiarism. Instead, you would want to write

Charles I ascended the scaffold for his execution. He "spent a few minutes in prayer, and then stretched out his hands."[1] The executioner swung the axe and beheaded him.

---

[1] Jacob Abbott, *History of King Charles the First of England* (Henry Altemus Company, 1900), p. 282.

To avoid plagiarism, you have to put quotation marks around the words that are taken directly from Abbott's biography and also provide a footnote.

But plagiarism can also happen if you use someone's ideas without giving them credit—even if you change the words.

Here's an example. In 2006, a major publisher in New York, called Little, Brown & Co. published a novel called *How Opal Mehta Got Kissed, Got Wild, and Got a Life.* The novel was written by a college freshman named Kaavya Viswanathan. She got a lot of attention for writing a novel at such a young age—but before long, a number of readers started to point out that the ideas and scenes in Viswanathan's book were very, very close to ideas and scenes in novels by four other writers. Here are some examples of the similarities:

Viswanathan's book	Other books
"He had too-long shaggy brown hair that fell into his eyes, which were always half shut. His mouth was always curled into a half smile, like he knew about some big joke that was about to be played on you." (p. 48)	"He's got dusty reddish dreads that a girl could never run her hands through. His eyes are always half-shut. His lips are usually curled in a semi-smile, like he's in on a big joke that's being played on you but you don't know it yet." (Megan McCafferty, *Sloppy Firsts* [Random House, 2001], p. 23)
"Five department stores, and 170 specialty shops later, I was sick of listening to her hum along to Alicia Keys . . ." (p. 51)	"Finally, four major department stores and 170 specialty shops later, we were done." (McCafferty, p. 237)
"Poster reads, 'If from drink you get your thrill, take precaution—write your will.'" (p. 118)	"Warning reads, 'If from speed you get your thrill / take precaution—make your will.'" (Salman Rushdie, *Haroun and the Sea of Stories* [Granta Books, 1991], p. 35)
"And I'll tell everyone that in eighth grade you used to wear a 'My Little Pony' sweatshirt to school every day," I continued. Priscilla gasped. "I didn't!" she said, her face purpling again. "You did! I even have pictures," I said. "And I'll make it public that you named your dog Pythagoras . . ." Priscilla opened her mouth and gave a few soundless gulps . . . "Okay, fine!" she said in complete consternation. "Fine! I promise I'll do whatever you want. I'll talk to the club manager. Just please don't mention the sweatshirt. Please." (p. 282)	"And we'll tell everyone you got your Donna Karan coat from a discount warehouse shop." Jemima gasps. "I didn't!" she says, colour suffusing her cheeks. "You did! I saw the carrier bag," I chime in. "And we'll make it public that your pearls are cultured, not real . . ." Jemima claps a hand over her mouth . . . "OK!" says Jemima, practically in tears. "OK! I promise I'll forget all about it. I promise! Just please don't mention the discount warehouse shop. Please." (Sophie Kinsella, *Can You Keep a Secret?* [Random House, 2005], p. 350)

Viswanathan's book	Other books
"The whole time, Frederic (I wondered if anyone dared call him Freddie) kept picking up long strands of my hair and making sad faces. 'It must go,' he said. 'It must all go.' And it went. Not all of it, because after four inches vanished, I started making panicked, whimpering sounds that touched even Frederic's heart . . ." (p. 57)	"Meanwhile, Paulo was picking up chunks of my hair and making this face and going, all sadly, 'It must go. It must all go.' And it went. All of it. Well, almost all of it. I still have some like bangs and a little fringe in back." (Meg Cabot, *The Princess Diaries* [HarperCollins, 2001], p. 128)
"Every inch of me had been cut, filed, steamed, exfoliated, polished, painted, or moisturized. I didn't look a thing like Opal Mehta. Opal Mehta didn't own five pairs of shoes so expensive they could have been traded in for a small sailboat. She didn't wear makeup or Manolo Blahniks or Chanel sunglasses or Habitual jeans. . . . She never owned enough cashmere to make her concerned for the future of the Kazakhstani mountain goat population. I was turning into someone else." (p. 59)	"There isn't a single inch of me that hasn't been pinched, cut, filed, painted, sloughed, blown dry, or moisturized. . . . Because I don't look a thing like Mia Thermopolis. Mia Thermopolis never had fingernails. Mia Thermopolis never had blond highlights. Mia Thermopolis never wore makeup or Gucci shoes or Chanel skirts. . . . I don't even know who I am anymore. It certainly isn't Mia Thermopolis. *She's turning me into someone else.*" (Cabot, p. 12)

If just *one* of these similarities had been in Viswanathan's book, someone might have pointed it out—but most readers would have assumed that it was just coincidence. But because there were so many scenes borrowed from other writers (these are only a few), Viswanathan's publisher admitted that plagiarism had taken place and withdrew the book from publication.

As you can see, plagiarism can happen when entire ideas are taken from another writer—even if some, or even most, of the words have been changed.

So another way to write that paragraph about Charles I's execution might be like this:

> Charles I ascended the scaffold for his execution. He prayed for a few moments, and then he extended his hands in a sign.[1] The executioner swung the axe and beheaded him.
>
> ---
>
> [1] Jacob Abbott, *History of King Charles the First of England* (Henry Altemus Company, 1900), p. 282.

In this version, Jacob Abbott's words "spent a few minutes in prayer, and then stretched out his hands" have been rephrased as "He prayed for a few moments, and then extended his hands in a sign." But because the idea of Charles's praying and then stretching out his hands originally came from Abbott, the footnote is still necessary.

So do you have to use footnotes for every single idea in your next chronological narration?

No. You don't have to use a footnote for ideas, or facts, or details, or any other information that is considered "common knowledge."

STEP TWO: **Understand the concept of "common knowledge" (Student Responsibility)**

Student instructions for Step Two:

If a piece of information is widely known by a large group of people, it is called "common knowledge." You don't have to footnote common knowledge.

Here's an example: Jacob Abbott's biography of Charles I begins with this paragraph:

> King Charles the First was born in Scotland. It may perhaps surprise the reader than an English king should be born in Scotland.[59]

You could begin your own chronological narrative with:

> Charles I was born in Scotland.

without having to footnote. Hundreds of historians know that Charles I was born in Scotland. Every biography of Charles I points out that Charles was born in Scotland. You could have discovered this without ever picking up Jacob Abbott's book. That is common knowledge.

Figuring out what is common knowledge and what isn't can be tricky. Generally, the following are considered to be common knowledge:

Historical dates	"Charles I was born in 1600."
Historical facts	"Columbus claimed the New World for Spain."
Widely accepted scientific facts	"Lava erupts out of volcanoes."
Geographical facts	"Mount Everest is 29,029 feet above sea level."
Genealogical facts	"Charles I was the father of Charles II."
Definitions	"Honey is made out of nectar."
Proverbs and sayings	"A penny saved is a penny earned."
Well-known theories and ideas	"Snow happens when water in the atmosphere condenses and freezes."
Anything that can be learned through the senses	"Cyanide smells like almonds."
	"During a solar eclipse, the moon blocks the sun."

Here's one more example—a paragraph from my own book *The History of the Medieval World*, about the Frankish king Clovis.

> He settled on the old Roman town Lutetia Parisiorum, the Seine, and began to reinforce its walls. He issued a set of Latin laws for his domain, the Pactus Legis Salicae; the laws were very specific in forbidding the old Germanic traditions of blood revenge, instead substituting fines and penalties for clan-based revenge killings.[1]
>
> ---
>
> [1] Roger Collins, *Early Medieval Europe, 300–1000*, 2nd ed. (St. Martin's Press, 1999), p. 36.

I didn't footnote the first sentence because it's simply a historical fact. In the second sentence, the *existence* of the Latin laws is also a simple historical fact as well. But it was in Roger Collins's book that I first found the idea that Clovis's fines and penalties were intended to completely get rid of blood revenge. Just looking at the laws themselves, I would not have come up with that explanation. So I gave Roger Collins credit in a footnote.

---

59. Abbott, p. 13.

If you aren't sure whether or not to insert a footnote, use one! As you read and write more, you will develop a better sense of what is and isn't common knowledge.

STEP THREE: **Practice!**

Student instructions for Step Three:

Mark each sentence CK (for "common knowledge") or NF (for "needs footnote). When you're finished, check your answers with your instructor. Don't worry if you have trouble deciding; even scholars often disagree over whether or not a particular piece of information should be documented. Your instructor will explain the answers if necessary.

HOW TO HELP THE STUDENT WITH STEP THREE

Suggested correct answers are provided below. If necessary, explain the reasoning behind each answer to the student.

Don't worry too much if the student has difficulty grasping this concept. It will take time, experience, and maturity for the student to come to a full understanding of the difference between common knowledge and information that needs to be documented. This lesson is just a first introduction to the concept.

1. __CK__ To show his supremacy over the kings he had vanquished, Zheng took the title First Sovereign Qin Emperor, or Qin Shi Huangdi.[60]
This is a historical event, so it isn't necessary to footnote it; however, it's not incorrect to add a footnote, since the particular spelling of the name is probably drawn from one particular source.

2. __CK__ When a chameleon is cold, certain cells called iridocytes allow more light to enter the skin.[61]
Widely accepted scientific theories do not need to be footnoted.

3. __CK__ The Greek cities were bounded by natural barriers: mountain ridges, clefts in the rocky land, or ocean.[62]
Geographical facts are common knowledge.

4. __NF__ In August 1941, Roosevelt and Churchill met off the coast of Newfoundland and released to the world the Atlantic Charter, setting forth noble goals for the postwar world, saying their countries "seek no aggrandizement, territorial or other," and that they

---

60. Arthur Cotterell, *Ancient China* (Penguin, 2005), p. 16.
61. Sandra Alters and Brian Alters, *Biology: Understanding Life* (John Wiley & Sons, 2006), p. 707.
62. Susan Wise Bauer, *The History of the Ancient World* (W. W. Norton, 2007), p. 371.

respected "the right of all peoples to choose the form of government under which they will live."[63]

The specific information in the Atlantic Charter needs to be documented, as do the direct quotes.

5. __CK__ An earthquake is a trembling or shaking of the ground caused by a sudden release of energy stored in the rocks below the Earth's surface.[64]

   This is a definition; it doesn't need a footnote.

6. __CK__ The Declaration of Independence was adopted by Congress on July 2, and officially proclaimed July 4, 1776.[65]

   Historical event; doesn't need a footnote.

7. __NF__ Special water storage cells in peat moss allow the peat to absorb and retain up to 90% of its dry weight in water.[66]

   This is not a generally known fact; in addition, the exact percentage of 90% is something that had to be studied and documented in a particular experiment.

8. __NF__ Nebuchadnezzar built a seventy-foot-wide path from the central temple complex of Babylon to the ceremonial Ishtar Gate.[67]

   The detail that the path was seventy feet wide takes this quote out of the realm of common knowledge; it draws on a particular archaeological study.

9. __CK__ Many chameleons are shades of green and brown, which adds to the look of a live or dead leaf.[68]

   Common knowledge because it can be learned through the senses.

10. __CK__ Peat moss is used in gardening as mulch; it is layered around trees or plants to protect the roots from temperature fluctuation and to retain moisture, control weeds, and enrich the soil.[69]

    These are widely known uses of peat moss, but it isn't incorrect for the student to add a footnote.

11. __NF__ The ancient Chinese believed that dragons inhabited every river, lake, and sea and also lived high in the sky among the rainclouds.[70]

---

63. Howard Zinn, *A People's History of the United States* (HarperCollins, 2010), p. 412.
64. Kenneth R. Lang, *The Cambridge Guide to the Solar System* (Cambridge University Press, 2003), p. 122.
65. Zinn, p. 77.
66. Alters, p. 641.
67. Bauer, *History of the Ancient World*, p. 447.
68. Alters, p. 707.
69. Alters, p. 641.
70. Cotterell, p. 17.

This isn't a historical event or something that anyone can figure out; it's a summary of information found in particular Chinese writings which can only be read by experts.

12. ___NF___ The 1906 San Francisco earthquake would have measured 8.3 on the Richter scale, and the one that occurred there in 1989 measured 6.9.[71]
The exact measurements here were determined by an expert, so this is not general knowledge. When details *are given about historical events, a footnote is usually needed.*

13. ___CK___ Wood bursts into flames at 500 degrees Fahrenheit, iron melts at 2,000 degrees, and steel is contorted into weird shapes at 2,500 degrees.[72]
These are scientific facts which can be determined independently and are known by many people.

14. ___NF___ Thirty-foot waves battered the city and a nine-foot storm surge inundated it.[73]
These particular details could only be gathered from eyewitnesses and reports, so they need footnoting.

15. ___NF___ The First Emperor built an impressive tomb guarded by thousands of life-size terra-cotta warriors.[74]
This is a historical fact.

16. ___NF___ A magnitude 8 earthquake releases as much energy as detonating 6 million tons, or 6 billion kilograms, of trinitrotoluene, TNT.[75]
This is specialized knowledge that requires an expert to figure out exactly how much energy is released by two separate events; needs documentation.

Day Four: Taking Notes

Focus: Collecting information

There's one more skill the student needs to practice before writing another chronological narrative: taking notes on sources.

When the student first learned how to write narratives, descriptions, and sequences, all of the source information was provided in a list, and no documentation was required; this allowed

71. Lang, p. 122.
72. Philip L. Fradkin, *The Great Earthquake and Firestorms of 1906* (University of California Press, 2005), p. 16.
73. Fradkin, p. 19.
74. Cotterell, p. 16.
75. Lang, p. 122.

the student to concentrate on mastering one skill at a time. Now that the student has had some practicing in writing narratives, descriptions, and sequences, he can begin to collect his own source information.

Steps One and Two will be completed independently. The student's instructions are provided below for your reference.

STEP ONE: **Examine a sample of note-taking (Student Responsibility)**

Student instructions for Step One:

> Think all the way back to the first chronological narrative you wrote this year—about Alexander the Great. You were instructed to use a list of main events and details to write your narrative. That list included:
>
> **Taught by Aristotle from ages 13–16**
>
> Most famous philosopher in the world at this time
> Gave Alexander lifelong thirst for knowledge
> Interested in medicine, philosophy, history
>
> Those details were taken from several different histories. Here are excerpts from three of the sources that tell us about Alexander and Aristotle. The first two are biographies of Alexander; the third is a history of philosophy that talks about Aristotle.
>
> ---
>
> When I read these paragraphs, I took notes on the details about Aristotle's tutoring of Alexander the Great and used those notes to make the list in your lesson.
>
> You'll notice that I left out most of the information in the paragraphs. When you take notes, you must stay focused on *one particular topic or idea* and only write down the information that's directly related to that topic or idea. Otherwise, you'll end up simply copying most of your source. When I took notes on these paragraphs, I kept in mind that I only wanted details about *when and what Aristotle taught Alexander.* I ignored everything else.
>
> Here's what my notes looked like:

Foreman, Laura. *Alexander the Conqueror: The Epic Story of the Warrior King*. Cambridge, Mass.: Da Capo, 2004.

"authority on constitutional law, politics, poetry and rhetoric" and other scientific fields (43)
"father of the scientific method" (43)

O'Brien, John Maxwell. *Alexander the Great: The Invisible Enemy.* New York: Routledge, 1994.

"trained in medicine and evidently passed these skills on" to Alexander (19)
"Alexander maintained a lifelong interest in these subjects" (19)

Ueberweg, Friedrich, George S. Morris, Henry B. Smith, Philip Schaff, Noah Porter, and Vincenzo Botta. *A History of Philosophy: From Thales to the Present Time.* New York: C. Scribner & Company, 1872.

"most influential tutor of Alexander from the thirteenth to the sixteenth years" of Alexander's life (137)

I looked at these notes when making the list for your lesson.

Notice that I didn't footnote any of this information. That's because I only used historical facts and was careful not to use the exact words of any of my sources.

STEP TWO: **Learn proper form for taking notes (Student Responsibility)**

Student instructions for Step Two:

When you take notes, you should follow four simple rules.

1. Always write down the full bibliographical information of your source (author, full title, city of publisher, publisher, date) as if you were entering it on a Works Cited page.
2. Always quote directly and use quotation marks around the exact words of your source. You can combine this with brief paraphrases that sum up information you're not going to quote directly (as I did above for the Laura Foreman book).
3. Always write the page number of quotes right next to the words themselves.
4. If you are reading a book or resource online, *never* copy and paste words into your notes. Type them out yourself (this will force you to pick only the most important information).

This will help you write more efficiently—if you don't write down the full bibliographical information and page number *as you go*, you will end up having to go back and find it later—and you may have trouble locating the book or the page.

Most important, though, these rules will help you avoid plagiarism. If you write down the *exact words* that the source uses and then look at your notes as you write, you'll be able to avoid accidentally using another person's words without giving them credit.

There are two acceptable ways to take notes. Traditionally, students have been taught to take notes on 3x5 cards and then arrange the cards in order when they start to write. You can still use 3x5 cards for your notes. Use a different card for each quote, write the full bibliographical information about the source on the *first* card, and then just write the author's last name at the top of each remaining card.

However, now that most students use word processors, using 3x5 cards isn't necessary; typing your notes can be much more efficient than handwriting them. I took my notes above by creating a document in my word processor. I typed the full information for each book before I started to take notes on it. Then I made a list of important quotes (with page numbers!) under each book's title.

STEP THREE: **Practice taking notes**

Student instructions for Step Three:

Take notes on the following source, using proper form as illustrated above. You can choose to use either 3x5 cards or a word processing document.

All of your notes should be focused on one subject: the major events in Julius Caesar's life between January 49 BC and his death. You should list at least seven but no more than ten events.

Here are a couple of hints to help you keep your list of events to a manageable length. First, only list *Caesar's* actions or actions that *directly* affected him. Second, if a paragraph tells you that Caesar fought in three or four different places, or did three or four different things, don't write a sentence for each. For example, at the top of page xiv, you will see this paragraph:

> During the next twelve months, by a series of rapid military movements, Caesar secured Sicily, the great granary of the republic, conquered the senatorial forces in Spain, and finally, at Pharsalia, achieved a decisive victory over Pompey and his entire army.

The major event in this paragraph is that Caesar was victorious—in three different places. So you could write:

Caesar conquered Sicily, the "senatorial forces in Spain," and Pompey. (xiv)

You can use this as one of your events.

If you have trouble, ask your instructor for help. When you're finished, show your notes to your instructor. Then hold on to them; you'll use them again next week.

The date of this book isn't on the copyright page, but it was published in 1901. Use the first listed city as the city of publication. And notice that "With Notes, Dictionary, and a Map of Gaul" is a subtitle. Even though a semicolon is used on the copyright page, when you write a book title you should insert a colon between the title and subtitle.

HOW TO HELP THE STUDENT WITH STEP THREE

At the top of the page of notes, or on the first 3x5 card, the student should have written the bibliographical information in this exact format:

> Harkness, Albert. *Caesar's Commentaries on the Gallic War: With Notes, Dictionary, and a Map of Gaul.* New York: American Book Company, 1901.

Following this, the student should have listed a series of direct quotes and brief paraphrases, all covering the major events in Julius Caesar's life between January 49 BC and his death. (If the student has used 3x5 cards, each quote should be on a separate card, and each card should say "Harkness" at the top.) There should be at least seven but no more than ten events.

The senate told Caesar "to resign the governorship of both Gauls and disband his army." (xiii)

Caesar found out about the senate's decree "at Ravenna, on the 10th of January, 49 BC." (xiii)

Caesar "crossed the Rubicon . . . and advanced into Italy." (xiii)

As he marched through Italy, "town after town threw open its gates" to him. (xiii)

Caesar reached the capital "sixty days after the edict of the senate." (xiii)

Caesar conquered Sicily, the "senatorial forces in Spain," and Pompey. (xiv)

In the next four years, Caesar fought "successively in Egypt," Pontus, Numidia, and Spain. (xiv)

Back in Rome, Caesar "corrected abuses, enriched the public treasury, reformed the calendar" and tried to unify the empire. (xiv)

Caesar was "loaded with titles and honors" and "declared dictator for life." (xiv)

He was "assassinated in the senate house, on the 15th of March, 44 BC." (xiv)

Caesar's writings included "Commentaries on the Gallic and the Civil War." (xv)

If the student has difficulty locating the most important events, ask him to answer the following questions in 20 or fewer words, quoting directly from the text.

What did the senate tell Caesar to do?
What did Caesar do in response?
What five places did Caesar fight in?
What did Caesar do at home?
What position of power did he achieve?
What happened to him in 44 BC?

Week 29: Writing from Notes: Chronological Narrative of a Past Event, Description of a Person, Description of a Place

Day One: Practicing the Topos, Part One: Taking Notes

Focus: Collecting information

The student started off last week by outlining a a chronological narrative about Charles I of England that included a personal description and a description of a place. This week, she will write a chronological narrative about Julius Caesar that follows the same pattern.

Like the narrative about Charles I, the finished composition will have eight paragraphs. Six of those paragraphs will be chronological narrative, one will be a paragraph describing Caesar, and one will be a paragraph describing the city of Ravenna as it appeared during Caesar's stay there. The chronological narrative will begin with Caesar at Ravenna, the news he got there, and his decision to cross the Rubicon. It will end with his death.

The student must use footnotes (or endnotes) as she writes, and will need to include a Works Cited page at the end. For each part of the paper—chronological narrative, personal description, place description—she should take notes from at least two different sources. The notes from last week can serve as one source for the chronological narrative. Five more sources are provided in the student text.

Today, the student will take notes for the composition. She will begin writing in the next session.

STEP ONE: **Take notes for the chronological narrative**

Student instructions for Step One:

> Remember to focus on Caesar and his actions, rather than on others. Do not list more than ten statements.

HOW TO HELP THE STUDENT WITH STEP ONE

The student's notes should resemble the following. They do not have to be identical, but there should not be more than ten statements. If the student has more, encourage her to eliminate unnecessary details that do not apply to Caesar (for example, it isn't important to know that Pompey was killed in Egypt, or that Pompey refused to disband his army; one or two of the specifics of Caesar's reforms could be listed, but all of them do not need to be described).

Delphian Society. The Delphian Course. Chicago: The Society, 1913.

Caesar "completed his Gallic campaign" in 49 BC. (480)

The senate was afraid of Caesar and "asked him to disband his soldiers." (480)

Caesar refused and "crossed the Rubicon, the stream north of Rome." (480)

Caesar entered Rome and "brought order instead of turmoil to the city." (480)

Pompey and his army opposed Caesar but Pompey was defeated and "treacherously slain." (480)

Caesar "believed that Rome should be the capital of a great empire" and gave citizenship to "the Gauls, Spaniards, and other provincials." (480)

Caesar made the senate larger and "brought into it men from various parts of Italy and the provinces." (481)

Caesar employed "idle men" for "public works" and abolished "imprisonment for debt." (481)

Brutus and others wanted "to restore the old republic" by getting rid of Caesar. (481)

In 44 BC, Caesar was assassinated because of "the mistaken conceptions of eighty senators." (481)

STEP TWO: **Take notes for the personal description**

Student instructions for Step Two:

> Again, remember to focus on Caesar, not on others. You should have no more than 14 total statements between the two sources.

HOW TO HELP THE STUDENT WITH STEP TWO

The student's notes should resemble the following. They do not have to be identical, but there should not be more than 14 total statements. You may need to remind the student that a personal description can include character as well as appearance. The details about his friend "young Curio" should be eliminated, since they are more about Curio than about Caesar.

West, Willis Mason. Ancient History to the Death of Charlemagne. Boston, Mass.: Allyn and Bacon, 1902.

Caesar had "gracious courtesy and unrivaled charm" that attracted even his enemies. (381)

He had "forbearance and love" for his friends. (381)

He worked hard and had "genius, understanding, memory, taste, reflection, industry, exactness." (381)

Caesar could carry on "many activities" at the same time. (381)

He was ambitious, strong, and "broad-minded." (381)

Caesar was ambitious and also "preferred statesmanship" to "mere fighting." (381)

Goldsworthy, Adrian Keith. Caesar: Life of a Colossus. New Haven, Conn.: Yale University Press, 2006.

Caesar was "kind, generous, and inclined to forget grudges." (3)

Caesar was "willing to be utterly ruthless" and was vain, "especially of his appearance." (3)

Even when he was young, Caesar was "absolutely convinced of his own superiority." (3)

He was "brighter and more capable" than the other senators. (3)

Caesar's portraits show that he was "stern and strong" with a lined face, and that his hair was "thinning." (61)

Caesar's portraits show "power, experience and monumental self-confidence." (61)

The historian Suetonius said that Caesar was tall, pale, and slender, with "very dark, piercing eyes." (61)

STEP THREE: **Take notes for the place description**

Student instructions for Step Three:

> You shouldn't include more than ten statements between the two sources. You can include a sentence or two about the islands around Ravenna, since these islands affected Ravenna itself.

HOW TO HELP THE STUDENT WITH STEP THREE

The student's notes should resemble the following. They do not have to be identical, but there should not be more than 14 total statements.

Symonds, John Addington. Sketches and Studies in Southern Europe, Vol. 2. New York: Harper & Brothers, 1880.

Ravenna stood "in the centre of a huge lagoon" like Venice. (110)

The houses of Ravenna were "built on piles" and there were "canals instead of streets." (110)

Ravenna was surrounded by a "vast morass" with "low islands" rising out of it. (110)

The islands around Ravenna were covered with "vines and fig-trees and pomegranites" and were fruitful. (110)

Like in Venice, the "people went about in gondalas" and barges brought "fresh fruit or meat and vegetables." (110)

Cadell, W. A. A Journey in Carniola, Italy, and France in the Years 1817, 1818, Vol. 2. Edinburgh: Archibald Constable and Co., 1820.

There was "a great scarcity of fresh water" in Ravenna. (42)

Ravenna was "intersected with canals" where sea water flowed. (42)

Strabo called Ravenna the "largest city in the marshes." (42)

According to Strabo, the city of Ravenna was "entirely built of wood" and filled with canals and bridges. (42)

Gladiators were trained at Ravenna because the "place is so healthy." (43)

The canals of Ravenna are cleaned out by "sea-water at the flow of the tide," which carries the mud away. (43)

Vines grow quickly in Ravenna but "die at the end of four or five years." (43)

Day Two: Practicing the Topos, Part Two: The Chronological Narrative

Focus: Writing a chronological narrative of a past event

In previous lessons, whenever the student has been assigned a chronological narrative, she has also been given a list of events in chronological order. This week, the student will begin by putting together her own list of events.

STEP ONE: **Arrange notes in chronological order**

Student instructions for Step One:

> You took notes about Caesar's actions from two books, *The Delphian Course* and *Caesar's Commentaries on the Gallic War.* In this step, you'll put the notes from both books together into one chronological list, cutting out unnecessary repetition.
>
> Here's an example. From *Caesar's Commentaries,* you might have written down the following three events:
>
> Caesar found out about the senate's decree "at Ravenna, on the 10th of January, 49 BC." (xiii)
>
> Caesar "crossed the Rubicon . . . and advanced into Italy." (xiii)

As he marched through Italy, "town after town threw open its gates" to him. (xiii)

From *The Delphian Course,* you might have written down:

Caesar "completed his Gallic campaign" in 49 BC. (480)

The senate was afraid of Caesar and "asked him to disband his soldiers." (480)

Caesar refused and "crossed the Rubicon, the stream north of Rome." (480)

Putting those two lists together so that all of the events are in order would look like this:

Caesar "completed his Gallic campaign" in 49 BC. (480)

The senate was afraid of Caesar and "asked him to disband his soldiers." (480)

Caesar found out about the senate's decree "at Ravenna, on the 10th of January, 49 BC." (xiii)

Caesar refused and "crossed the Rubicon, the stream north of Rome." (480)

~~Caesar "crossed the Rubicon . . . and advanced into Italy." (xiii)~~

As he marched through Italy, "town after town threw open its gates" to him. (xiii)

After putting the events in order, you would delete any notes that repeat the same information (like the crossed-out note above). If a note repeats *some* information but also provides new facts, you may leave it. For example, in the following:

In 44 BC, Caesar was assassinated because of "the mistaken conceptions of eighty senators." (481)

He was "assassinated in the senate house, on the 15th of March, 44 BC." (xiv)

the two notes repeat that Caesar was assassinated in 44 BC, but the first note tells you *who* and the second tells you *where* and *when.*

If you're using a word processor, create a new document and cut and paste information from both lists of events into it. If you're using note cards, simply arrange the cards in order and set aside the ones that have repeated information.

Notice that in the list above it's very obvious which notes are from *Caesar's Commentaries* (the page numbers are all in Roman numerals) and which ones are from the *Delphian Course* (they all come from page 480 or 481). But if the two sources had similiar page numbers, you'd want to add a source or author name to each note to keep you from mixing them up by accident:

Caesar refused and "crossed the Rubicon, the stream north of Rome." (Delphian Society, 480)

As he marched through Italy, "town after town threw open its gates" to him. (Harkness, xiii)

Your last instruction: if it isn't completely clear what events happened first, just make an intelligent guess.

If you have trouble, ask your instructor for help.

HOW TO HELP THE STUDENT WITH STEP ONE

The student's completed list should resemble the following (these are given as possibilities; the student may choose other points or leave out some of these as long as she ends up with the required number of events):

Caesar "completed his Gallic campaign" in 49 BC. (480)

The senate was afraid of Caesar and "asked him to disband his soldiers." (480)

The senate told Caesar "to resign the governorship of both Gauls and disband his army." (xiii)

Caesar found out about the senate's decree "at Ravenna, on the 10th of January, 49 BC." (xiii)
~~*Caesar "crossed the Rubicon . . . and advanced into Italy." (xiii)*~~
Caesar refused and "crossed the Rubicon, the stream north of Rome." (480)
As he marched through Italy, "town after town threw open its gates" to him. (xiii)
Caesar reached the capital "sixty days after the edict of the senate." (xiii)
Caesar entered Rome and "brought order instead of turmoil to the city." (480)
Pompey and his army opposed Caesar but Pompey was defeated and "treacherously slain." (480) Caesar conquered Sicily, the "senatorial forces in Spain," and Pompey. (xiv)
In the next four years, Caesar fought "successively in Egypt," Pontus, Numidia, and Spain. (xiv)
Back in Rome, Caesar "corrected abuses, enriched the public treasury, reformed the calendar" and tried to unify the empire. (xiv)
Caesar "believed that Rome should be the capital of a great empire" and gave citizenship to "the Gauls, Spaniards, and other provincials." (480)
Caesar made the senate larger and "brought into it men from various parts of Italy and the provinces." (481)
Caesar employed "idle men" for "public works" and abolished "imprisonment for debt." (481)
Caesar was "loaded with titles and honors" and "declared dictator for life." (xiv)
Brutus and others wanted "to restore the old republic" by getting rid of Caesar. (481)
In 44 BC, Caesar was assassinated because of "the mistaken conceptions of eighty senators." (481)
He was "assassinated in the senate house, on the 15th of March, 44 BC." (xiv)
Caesar's writings included "Commentaries on the Gallic and the Civil War." (xv)

The student may have some trouble figuring out where to put notes that sum up Caesar's actions over a long period of time; for example,

> Back in Rome, Caesar "corrected abuses, enriched the public treasury, reformed the calendar" and tried to unify the empire. (xiv)

was happening at the same time as

> Caesar "believed that Rome should be the capital of a great empire" and gave citizenship to "the Gauls, Spaniards, and other provincials." (480)

The student can choose whatever order seems most logical for statements like this. She'll work more on the grouping of events in the next step.

STEP TWO: **Divide notes into main points**

Student instructions for Step Two:

Look one more time at that list of details about Alexander the Great back on pages 52–54.

Taught by Aristotle from ages 13–16
Most famous philosopher in the world at this time
Gave Alexander lifelong thirst for knowledge
Interested in medicine, philosophy, history
Father assassinated in 336
Assassin was bodyguard, Pausanias
Pausanias then killed by rest of bodyguard
Succeeded his father to the throne
Twenty years old
Had all of his rivals to the throne murdered
Greek cities rebelled, had to reconquer them

Now that you've had some experience in outlining, you should recognize this format. It's a two-level outline, without the numbers and letters.

I. **Taught by Aristotle from ages 13–16**
A. Most famous philosopher in the world at this time
B. Gave Alexander lifelong thirst for knowledge
C. Interested in medicine, philosophy, history

So right from the beginning of this course, you've been using an outline to write your compositions.

Before you can write your chronological narrative about Caesar, you need to make yourself an outline. You're going to do this by dividing your list of events up into five groups and giving each group a phrase or sentence that explains what it's about.

Here's an example. Imagine that these are the first eight notes that you have on your list.

Caesar "completed his Gallic campaign" in 49 BC. (480)
The senate was afraid of Caesar and "asked him to disband his soldiers." (480)
The senate told Caesar "to resign the governorship of both Gauls and disband his army." (xiii)
Caesar found out about the senate's decree "at Ravenna, on the 10th of January, 49 BC." (xiii)
Caesar refused and "crossed the Rubicon, the stream north of Rome." (480)
As he marched through Italy, "town after town threw open its gates" to him. (xiii)
Caesar reached the capital "sixty days after the edict of the senate." (xiii)

Caesar entered Rome and "brought order instead of turmoil to the city." (480)

The first four events are all leading up to the senate's decree, so you can group them all together and describe them like this:

I. The senate's decree to Caesar
Caesar "completed his Gallic campaign" in 49 BC. (480)
The senate was afraid of Caesar and "asked him to disband his soldiers." (480)
The senate told Caesar "to resign the governorship of both Gauls and disband his army." (xiii)
Caesar found out about the senate's decree "at Ravenna, on the 10th of January, 49 BC." (xiii)

These events will be the basis for the first paragraph of your chronological narrative.

(The events at the beginning of your list may not be identical, but you can still use "The senate's decree to Caesar" as your first point.)

Now look at the next four events. What title or description would you give them?

After you've settled on a title or description, divide the remaining events into three more groups. Give each group a title or description. If you're using a word processor, give the titles Roman numerals and type them into your document, using the same format as above:

II. Title for second group of notes
  event
  event
  event
III. Title for third group of notes
  event
  event
  event

and so on. If you're using note cards, write each title on a separate note card and place it in front of the group of cards that it describes.

If you have trouble dividing the events into groups or giving them titles and descriptions, your instructor will help you.

When you're finished, show your work to your instructor before going on.

HOW TO HELP THE STUDENT WITH STEP TWO

The student's five points should resemble the following.

I. The senate's decree to Caesar
  Caesar "completed his Gallic campaign" in 49 BC. (480)
  The senate was afraid of Caesar and "asked him to disband his soldiers." (480)
  The senate told Caesar "to resign the governorship of both Gauls and disband his army." (xiii)
  Caesar found out about the senate's decree "at Ravenna, on the 10th of January, 49 BC." (xiii) (This could also go at the beginning of the next section.)

II. Caesar marches to Rome OR Caesar crosses the Rubicon OR Caesar defies the senators
  Caesar refused and "crossed the Rubicon, the stream north of Rome." (480)
  As he marched through Italy, "town after town threw open its gates" to him. (xiii)
  Caesar reached the capital "sixty days after the edict of the senate." (xiii)
  Caesar entered Rome and "brought order instead of turmoil to the city." (480)

III. Caesar's victories in battle OR Caesar's fights OR Caesar's wars
  Pompey and his army opposed Caesar but Pompey was defeated and "treacherously slain." (480) (This could also go at the end of the previous section.)
  Caesar conquered Sicily, the "senatorial forces in Spain," and Pompey. (xiv)
  In the next four years, Caesar fought "successively in Egypt," Pontus, Numidia, and Spain. (xiv)

IV. Caesar's work of governing OR Caesar's work at home OR What Caesar did for Rome

Back in Rome, Caesar "corrected abuses, enriched the public treasury, reformed the calendar" and tried to unify the empire. (xiv)

Caesar "believed that Rome should be the capital of a great empire" and gave citizenship to "the Gauls, Spaniards, and other provincials." (480)

Caesar made the senate larger and "brought into it men from various parts of Italy and the provinces." (481)

Caesar employed "idle men" for "public works" and abolished "imprisonment for debt." (481)

V. Caesar's assassination OR The plot against Caesar

Caesar was "loaded with titles and honors" and "declared dictator for life." (xiv) (This could also go at the end of the previous section.)

Brutus and others wanted "to restore the old republic" by getting rid of Caesar. (481)

In 44 BC, Caesar was assassinated because of "the mistaken conceptions of eighty senators." (481)

He was "assassinated in the senate house, on the 15th of March, 44 BC." (xiv)

Caesar's writings included "Commentaries on the Gallic and the Civil War." (xv)

If the student has difficulty with this assignment, use the following dialogues. Since each student's list of events will be slightly different, you may need to adapt the dialogues.

If the student has included an event which does not seem easy to group with *any* other events in the list, suggest that the event be left out; it is clearly not central to the narrative.

II.

Instructor: This set of notes all has to do with an important action that Caesar took. What is that important action?

Student: He crossed the Rubicon OR *He marched to Rome* OR *He defied the senators.*

Note to Instructor: All of the above answers are correct because each one simply puts the focus on a different aspect of Caesar's actions.

III.

Instructor: In each of the events in this group, Caesar is doing the same thing. What is he doing?

Student: He is fighting.

Instructor: "Caesar's fights" or "Caesar's wars" is a good way to phrase your main point for this section.

Note to Instructor: The details about Caesar's actions fall into two clear categories: Caesar's wars, and Caesar's administration of the empire. If the student has mixed these two categories together in the chronological list of events, help her to divide the events into two separate groups.

IV.

Instructor: The previous group of events was all about Caesar's actions as a military leader. This group of events is all about another aspect of Caesar's work as a leader. What kind of work is Caesar doing as he builds up the treasury, gives citizenship, and enlarges the senate?

> *Student: Governing* OR *Taking care of things at home*

Instructor: "Caesar's work of governing" or "Caesar's work at home" would both be good main points.

Note to Instructor: If the student has trouble coming up with a name for Caesar's domestic work, give her one of the suggested answers; don't allow her to become frustrated.

V.

Instructor: What is the most important thing that happens to Caesar in this last group of events?

> *Student: He is assassinated.*

Instructor: "Caesar's assassination" is the topic of this last section.

STEP THREE: **Write the chronological narrative**

Student instructions for Step Three:

> Take a minute to review the Chronological Narrative of a Past Event chart in the Reference section of your notebook.
>
> Using the outline you have created, write a five-paragraph chronological narrative about Julius Caesar. Write one paragraph for each main point. Your narrative should be at least 200 words but not longer than 400.
>
> Do not use the exact words of your sources unless you use quotation marks and a footnote (or endnote). If you describe something that is common knowledge (like a historical event) in your own words, you do not need to provide a footnote. But if you use an idea that is not common knowledge, be sure to use a footnote even if you put the idea into your own words. If you're not sure, provide a footnote (better safe than plagiarizing!).
>
> Be sure to quote directly from each source at least once.
>
> Review these examples before you write.
>
> *Source material:*
>
> In 44 BC, Caesar was assassinated because of "the mistaken conceptions of eighty senators." (481)
>
> *Common knowledge, no footnote needed:*
>
> Caesar was assassinated by the senators of Rome in 44 BC.
>
> *Needs a footnote because it uses the exact words of the source:*
>
> "In 44 BC, the mighty Caesar fell."[1]
>
> ---
>
> Delphian Society, *The Delphian Course* (The Society, 1913), p. 481.
>
> *Needs a footnote because it is the writer's specific idea that the senators made a mistake:*

Caesar was assassinated in 44 BC because of "the mistaken conceptions of eight senators."[1]

Delphian Society, *The Delphian Course* (The Society, 1913), p. 481.

When you are finished, show your composition to your instructor.

HOW TO HELP THE STUDENT WITH STEP THREE

Beginning writers usually tend to overdocument. It's fine for the student to use more footnotes than necessary, but try to point out places where the student has documented common knowledge (historical facts, names, places, dates).

An acceptable narrative might resemble the following:

After Caesar finished fighting in Gaul in 49 BC, he was very powerful. The senate was afraid of him, and told him to "disband his soldiers."[1] He found out about this decree when he was at the city of Ravenna, on January 10.

Instead of disbanding his soldiers, Caesar crossed the Rubicon and headed towards Rome. It took him 60 days to get to Rome, and the towns along the way welcomed him. When he arrived at Rome, he "brought order instead of turmoil."[2]

The Roman senator Pompey was still against Caesar, but Caesar's army defeated Pompey's, and Pompey was killed. After this, Caesar had to fight in Sicily and in Spain to defend his power. He also carried on wars in Egypt, Pontus, and Numidia.

Back at home, Caesar tried to bring unity to the empire.[3] He made men who lived in Gaul, Spain, and other parts of the empire full citizens. He allowed them to be part of the senate as well. He made other reforms, too, such as adding to the treasury and putting "idle men" to work on public projects.[4]

Caesar was so successful that he was given many honors and was also made dictator for life. But many of the senators, including Brutus, wanted to get rid of him. On the 15th of March, 44 BC, Caesar was assassinated.

---

[1] *Delphian Society,* The Delphian Course *(The Society, 1913), p. 480.*

[2] *Delphian Society, p. 480.*

[3] *Albert Harkness,* Caesar's Commentaries on the Gallic War: With Notes, Dictionary, and a Map of Gaul *(American Book Company, 1901), p. xiv.*

[4] *Delphian Society, p. 481.*

Check the student's work using the following rubric.

Week 29 Rubric
Chronological Narrative of Past Events

Organization

1 Events should be in chronological order.
2 The composition should have five paragraphs, each dealing with one main point on the outline.
3 Two or more time words should be used.
4 The composition should use more than 200 but fewer than 400 words.

Mechanics

1 Each sentence should make sense on its own when read aloud.
2 Each proper name should be capitalized.
3 Dates should be written properly.
4 Direct quotes and unique ideas should be documented with footnotes.
5 Footnotes should be written correctly.
6 Direct quotes from the source material should be surrounded by quotation marks.

Day Three: Practicing the Topos, Part Three: The Personal Description

Focus: Writing a description of a person

The passage about Charles I that the student outlined at the beginning of last week was a chronological narrative that also included a description of a place (Windsor Castle) and a person (Charles I as a young man). Now that the student has put together a basic chronological narrative, she will add these elements to make a complete composition.

Today, the student will use her notes on Caesar's character and person to write a description of him.

The student is not required to show you her work for Steps One and Two, but suggestions for helping the student are included.

STEP ONE: **Review the elements of a personal description**

Student instructions for Step One:

Before you begin to write, go back and read through the Description of a Person chart in the Reference section of your notebook.

This should remind you that a description of a person can include much more than simple physical appearance. Glance back now at the notes you took on Willis Mason West's *Ancient History to the Death of Charlemagne* and Adrian Keith Goldsworthy's *Caesar: Life of a Colossus*. On a scratch piece of paper, jot down the aspects found in the Description of a Person chart that your notes also include.

For example, if you wrote

> Caesar had "gracious courtesy and unrivaled charm" that attracted even his enemies. (381)

in your notes on *Ancient History to the Death of Charlemagne*, you would jot down

Character qualities
What others think

on your scratch paper.

You could also use "behaviors" or even "expressions of face and body" to classify that particular quote. Don't worry too much about which exact aspect is the "right" one; the goal here is to make sure that you cover several different aspects in your description.

When you're finished, you should have at least three or four aspects written down. If you have fewer than three, go back to the souce material and look for quotes that illustrate at least one more aspect of Caesar.

If you have trouble, ask your instructor for help.

HOW TO HELP THE STUDENT WITH STEP ONE

Possible aspects are listed below. If necessary, suggest one or two to the student.

West, Willis Mason. *Ancient History to the Death of Charlemagne.* Boston, Mass.: Allyn and Bacon, 1902.

Caesar had "gracious courtesy and unrivaled charm" that attracted even his enemies. (381)	Character qualities, behaviors, expressions of face and body, what others think
He had "forbearance and love" for his friends. (381)	Character qualities
He worked hard and had "genius, understanding, memory, taste, reflection, industry, exactness." (381)	Talents and abilities, mind/ intellectual capabilities, self-disciplines
Caesar could carry on "many activities" at the same time. (381)	Talents and abilities

He was ambitious, strong, and "broad-minded." (381)	Mind/intellectual capabilities
Caesar was ambitious and also "preferred statesmanship" to "mere fighting." (381)	Character qualities, habits

Goldsworthy, Adrian Keith. *Caesar: Life of a Colossus*. New Haven, Conn.: Yale University Press, 2006.

Caesar was "kind, generous, and inclined to forget grudges." (3)	Character qualities, behaviors
Caesar was "willing to be utterly ruthless" and was vain, "especially of his appearance." (3)	Character qualities, behaviors
Even when he was young, Caesar was "absolutely convinced of his own superiority." (3)	Character qualities, mind/intellectual capabilities
He was "brighter and more capable" than the other senators. (3)	Mind/intellectual capabilities
Caesar's portraits show that he was "stern and strong" with a lined face, and that his hair was "thinning." (61)	Physical appearance, portrayals, expressions of face and body
Caesar's portraits show "power, experience and monumental self-confidence." (61)	Portrayals, expressions of face and body, character qualities
The historian Suetonius said that Caesar was tall, pale, and slender, with "very dark, piercing eyes." (61)	Physical appearance, what others think, expressions of face and body

STEP TWO: **Plan the personal description**

Student instructions for Step Two:

> Look again at your Description of a Person chart. Notice that there are two suggestions in the "Remember" column. Before you go on, turn back to Weeks 17 and 18 in your text. Read the instructions for Days Two and Three in each week.
>
> As you write your description of Caesar, you will slant it in either a positive or negative direction. (You'll review using a governing metaphor in a later lesson.)
>
> Choose three or four nouns, adjectives, or verbs used in your notes, and look them up in your thesaurus. Make a list of possible synonyms, both positive and negative. For example, if you took the following note:
>
>> Caesar had "gracious courtesy and unrivaled charm" that attracted even his enemies. (381)

you might decide to look up "gracious." You would find the synonyms:

gallant, chivalrous, mannerly, polished; suave, smug, glib, oily-tongued, ingratiating.

If you wanted to slant your description positively, you could then write

> Caesar had a gallant courtesy and "unrivaled charm."[1]

[1]Willis Mason West, *Ancient History to the Death of Charlemagne* (Allyn and Bacon, 1902), p. 381.

If you chose to slant the description in a negative direction, you could write instead

> Caesar had a smug, oily-tongued courtesy.

Since the original description was positive, you would probably want to leave off the direct quote from the source.

Aim to have at least three slanted words in your description, along with at least two direct quotes (you'll have to choose these carefully so that they go with the slant you've decided to use).

Once you've listed the synonyms you might make use of, you'll be ready to move on to the third step.

HOW TO HELP THE STUDENT WITH STEP TWO

If the student has difficulty finding the right adjectives, nouns, or verbs in the thesaurus, suggest looking up the following key words.

ORIGINAL WORD	POSITIVE KEY WORDS	NEGATIVE KEY WORDS
forbearance	patience, self-control	indulgence, weakness
exactness	precision, accuracy	rigidity, fussiness
ambitious	enthusiastic, eager	aggressive, pushy
ruthless	uncompromising, determined	harsh, merciless
convinced of superiority	certain, secure	arrogant, boastful
monumental	unshakeable, tremendous	excessive, unreasonable

STEP THREE: **Write the personal description**

Student instructions for Step Three:

Now use your notes and your list of synonyms to write a description of Caesar. Follow these guidelines:

1. Your description should be at least 50 and not more than 100 words long.
2. The description should be clearly slanted in a positive (admiring) or negative (critical) direction.
3. You should include at least one direct and one indirect quote.
4. The description should cover at least three different aspects of Caesar.

When you are finished, show your work to your instructor.

HOW TO HELP THE STUDENT WITH STEP THREE

Acceptable descriptions might resemble the following:

Caesar was powerful and serious, with a lined face and thinning hair.[1] *He had a reputation for patience and politeness; he was an ambitious man, but he was also kind, benevolent, and "inclined to forget grudges."*[2] *He was a diligent, energetic worker, able to do many things at once. He had a great deal of self-confidence, because he was more intelligent than most other senators.*[3]

---

[1] *Adrian Keith Goldsworthy,* Caesar: Life of a Colossus *(Yale University Press, 2006), p. 61.*
[2] *Goldsworthy, p. 3.*
[3] *Goldsworthy, p. 3.*

Note to Instructor: It is correct to use "Ibid." for a citation that is exactly the same as the one directly before it, but the student will learn this at a later date.

Caesar was tall, thin, and balding, but he was still obsessed with his own looks.[1] *He was arrogant about his own intelligence, and worked unceasingly to push his own self-serving agendas. He was willing to show "forbearance and love" to his friends, but to his enemies he was harsh and completely without pity.*[2]

---

[1] *Adrian Keith Goldsworthy,* Caesar: Life of a Colossus *(Yale University Press, 2006), p. 3.*
[2] *Willis Mason West,* Ancient History to the Death of Charlemagne *(Allyn and Bacon, 1902), p. 381.*

Check the student's work using the following rubric.

Week 29 Rubric
Description of a Person

Organization

1 The description should include at least three of the aspects listed on the Description of a Person chart.
2 The description should be at least 50 and not more than 100 words.
3 The description should use appropriate adjectives, nouns, and verbs to slant the description in a positive or negative direction.
4 At least one direct and one indirect quote should be used (it is not necessary to cite *both* sources, however).

Mechanics

1 Each sentence should make sense on its own when read aloud.
2 Each proper name should be capitalized.
3 Possessive forms should be written properly.
4 Personal pronouns should have clear antecedents and be of the proper gender.
5 Verb tense should be consistent throughout.
6 Subjects and verbs must be in agreement.
7 Footnotes should be properly formatted and should come at the ends of the sentences which contain the source material.

Day Four: Practicing the Topos, Part Four: The Place Description

Focus: Writing a description of a place

The final element of this week's composition is a description of the city of Ravenna, where Caesar heard about the senate's decree. After the student writes this description, she will assemble the full composition, give it a title, and attach a Works Cited page.

STEP ONE: Review the elements of a place description

Student instructions for Step One:

Turn to the Description of a Place chart in the Reference section of your Composition Notebook and read through it. If you don't remember some of the elements on the chart, go back in your text to the following lessons and read through the instructions:

Purpose: Week 8, Day Three
Space and distance words: Week 8, Day Four
Point of view: Week 9, Days Three and Four
Metaphors and similes: Week 10, Days Three and Four

When you are finished with your review, glance back over the notes you took on ancient Ravenna. On the lines below, jot down possible answers:

What purpose will this description serve? ____________________
What point of view will I use? ____________________
Which three space and distance words will be most useful? ____________________
What metaphor or simile could I use? ____________________

If you can answer these questions without help, go ahead. If you need help, though, your instructor can give you options to choose from.

HOW TO HELP THE STUDENT WITH STEP ONE

If the student needs help answering these questions, use the following prompts.

Purpose

If necessary, use the following dialogue:

Instructor: Your description of Ravenna could serve one of two different purposes. Imagine that you're Caesar. You've just finished a long, difficult campaign in Gaul. Finally, you've come to a place where you can rest and gather the energy to go home—to Rome, where you think the people will welcome you with celebration. In this scenario, Ravenna is a place of . . .

> *Student: Peace, rest, plenty . . . [etc]*

Note to Instructor: Prompt the student with the above answers if necessary.

Instructor: Which details should you include in the description to make Ravenna sound like a place of peace and rest?

> *Student: The vines and fig trees and pomegranates, the fruitful islands, the barges with fresh fruit and meat and vegetables, the healthy air, and the clean canals*

Instructor: Now imagine that you're Caesar, and that you're only staying in Ravenna because you're not sure that Rome will welcome you. You don't want to be in Ravenna. Compared with Rome, Ravenna is a dingy, muddy waystation that you're stuck in and can't wait to leave. What details would you include in a description that makes Ravenna sound like a dingy, muddy, waystation?

> *Student: It is surrounded by a vast swamp, there's not very much fresh water, vines die, and Ravenna is a marsh.*

Instructor: Make a note of the purpose your description will serve.

Point of view

Any point of view could be used, but the impersonal (from above) and moving (as though walking through) points of view will be the most useful because they allow the student to describe more parts of the city. Suggest that the student choose one of those two.

Space and distance words

Suggest that "in/at the middle of" might be useful, since Ravenna is in the middle of a swamp. If the student needs additional guidance, point her towards the list of "interlocking relationship" words in Appendix I.

Metaphor or simile

If necessary, use one of the following prompts. Metaphors are difficult for many beginning writers; you should feel free to simply give the student one or more answers if she begins to get frustrated.

Prompt #1

Ravenna is in the center of a marsh. It's a little surprising to find a city right in the center of a marsh. So you could use a metaphor to finish the following sentence: "Ravenna sat in the center of a swamp like a ____________ in the middle of a ____________________." Think of something that you'd be happy to find in the middle of something else.

Possible answers

Like caramel in the middle of a chocolate
Like a flower in the middle of a patch of thorns
Like an oasis in the middle of a desert

Prompt #2

Ravenna has canals running through it. The canals are like roads, but they're not made out of stone or dirt. They are like roads of . . .

Possible answers

Roads of water
Roads of liquid
Roads in the sea

Prompt #3

The islands around Ravenna are *fruitful.* You could use a metaphor to finish the following sentence: "The islands around Ravenna were as fruitful as a______________." Think of something that yields lots of things to eat.

Possible answers

As fruitful as a garden
As fruitful as an orchard
As fruitful as a supermarket

STEP TWO: **Write the place description**

Student instructions for Step Two:

> Using your notes, and making reference to the answers you wrote down above, write your description now. Follow these guidelines:
>
> 1. Your description should be at least 40 and not more than 90 words long.
> 2. The purpose of the description should be clear from the adjectives and nouns you use.
> 3. You should include at least one direct quote.
> 4. Your point of view should be consistent throughout.
> 5. The description should include one metaphor or simile.
> 6. The description should make use of at least two space and distance words.

HOW TO HELP THE STUDENT WITH STEP TWO

Acceptable descriptions might resemble the following:

(Impersonal point of view, purpose to show Ravenna as restful)

Ravenna stood at the center of a swamp, like a flower in the middle of a briar patch. It was the largest city around.[1] *Canals filled with clean seawater flowed through the city. Its houses sat up above the moving water, with sea breezes blowing through them. All around the city lay islands, covered with "vines and fig-trees and pomegranates," providing plenty of fresh food for every table.*[2]

---

[1] *W. A. Cadell,* A Journey in Carniola, Italy, and France in the Years 1817, 1818, *Vol. 2 (Archibald Constable and Co., 1820), p. 42.*

[2] *John Addington Symonds,* Sketches and Studies in Southern Europe, *Vol. 2 (Harper & Brothers, 1880), p. 110.*

(Moving point of view, purpose to show Ravenna as dingy and muddy)

Ravenna sat in the middle of a huge swamp. Low, muddy islands surrounded it. There was very little fresh water. The houses were "entirely built of wood" and sat up on rickety stilts above the sea.[1] *Canals cut through the city like roads of dirty water.*

---

[1] *W. A. Cadell,* A Journey in Carniola, Italy, and France in the Years 1817, 1818, Vol. 2 *(Archibald Constable and Co., 1820), p. 42.*

Check the student's work using the following rubric.

Week 29 Rubric
Description of a Place

Organization

1 The description should use appropriate adjectives and verbs to convey the purpose of the description.
2 At least two space and distance words and phrases should be used.
3 Point of view should remain consistent.
4 The description should be at least 40 and not more than 90 words long.
5 At least one direct quote should be included.
6 There should be at least one metaphor or simile in the description.

Mechanics

1 Each sentence should make sense on its own when read aloud.
2 Verbs should have consistent tense (all past or all present).
3 Subjects and verbs should be in agreement.
4 Each proper name should be capitalized.
5 Possessive forms should be written properly.
6 Personal pronouns should have clear antecedents and be of the proper gender.
7 Verb tense should be consistent throughout.
8 Footnotes should be properly formatted and should come at the ends of the sentences which contain the source material.

STEP THREE: **Assemble and title the composition**

Student instructions for Step Three:

First, insert your place description into your chronological narrative.

The place description should be its own paragraph, and should come right after the paragraph where you mention Ravenna. If you didn't mention Ravenna in your chronological narrative, you'll need to go back and insert the fact that Caesar was at Ravenna after his Gallic campaign/when he heard of the senate's decree. You may also need to write a transitional sentence at the beginning of your place description, relating Caesar's experiences to the description. For example, if you've decided to show that Ravenna was a boring, backwater place to be, you might want to start your paragraph with a sentence like:

> Caesar was anxious to get to Rome, but instead he was forced to wait in Ravenna.

Second, insert your personal description into your chronological narrative.

You can choose where to put the personal description, as long as it doesn't break the flow of the narrative. For example, if you have three paragraphs describing, in order, Caesar's crossing the Rubicon, going through Italy, and then arriving in Rome, you wouldn't want to put the description of Caesar in between any of those paragraphs. That would be like forcing Caesar to stop marching towards Rome in order to give an interview. The most natural place for the description is probably near the end of the composition, either right before or right after the paragraphs describing Caesar's achievements. You may need to provide a transitional sentence or phrase such as "At this time in his life, Caesar was . . ."

Third, title your composition with one of the following:

Julius Caesar's Rise to Power in Rome
Julius Caesar Becomes Dictator
Julius Caesar Takes Control of Rome

Your title should be centered at the top of your first page.

When you are completely finished, make sure that your paper is double-spaced and that the footnotes are in the proper place. (Student papers done on a word processor should always be double-spaced.) If your paper is more than one page long, insert a page number at the bottom left or bottom center of each page.

If you have trouble with this assignment, ask your instructor for help. When you are finished, show your work to your instructor.

HOW TO HELP THE STUDENT WITH STEP THREE

The student may need help with transitional sentences. You may suggest the following:

"Caesar was exhausted from his battles and needed to rest in Ravenna."
"Ravenna was a peaceful place for Caesar and his men to wait."
"Caesar waited impatiently in Ravenna."
"Caesar stayed in Ravenna, but he couldn't wait to leave."
"By this point in his life, Caesar's character was fully formed."
"Caesar was now in his fifties."

The student's final composition should resemble the following:

Julius Caesar Takes Control of Rome

After Caesar finished fighting in Gaul in 49 BC, he was very powerful. The senate was afraid of him, and told him to "disband his soldiers."[1] He found out about this decree when he was at the city of Ravenna, on January 10.

Ravenna stood at the center of a swamp, like a flower in the middle of a briar patch. It was the largest city around.[2] Canals filled with clean seawater flowed through the city. Its houses sat up above the moving water, with sea breezes blowing through them. All around the city lay islands, covered with "vines and fig-trees and pomegranates," providing plenty of fresh food for every table.[3]

Instead of disbanding his soldiers, Caesar left Ravenna, crossed the Rubicon, and headed towards Rome. It took him sixty days to get to Rome, and the towns along the way welcomed him. When he arrived at Rome, he "brought order instead of turmoil."[4]

The Roman senator Pompey was still against Caesar, but Caesar's army defeated Pompey's, and Pompey was killed. After this, Caesar had to fight in Sicily and in Spain to defend his power. He also carried on wars in Egypt, Pontus, and Numidia.

Back at home, Caesar tried to bring unity to the empire.[5] He made men who lived in Gaul, Spain, and other parts of the empire full citizens. He allowed them to be part of the senate as well. He made other reforms, too, such as adding to the treasury and putting "idle men" to work on public projects.[6]

By this time, Caesar was in his fifties. He was powerful and serious, with a lined face and thinning hair.[7] He had a reputation for patience and politeness; he was an ambitious man, but he was also kind, benevolent, and "inclined to forget grudges."[8] He was a diligent, energetic worker, able to do many things at once. He had a great deal of self-confidence, because he was more intelligent than most other senators.[9]

Caesar was so successful that he was given many honors and was also made dictator for life. But many of the senators, including Brutus, wanted to get rid of him. On the 15th of March, 44 BC, Caesar was assassinated.

---

[1] *Delphian Society,* The Delphian Course *(The Society, 1913), p. 480.*

[2] *W. A. Cadell,* A Journey in Carniola, Italy, and France in the Years 1817, 1818, *Vol. 2 (Archibald Constable and Co., 1820), p. 42.*

[3] *John Addington Symonds,* Sketches and Studies in Southern Europe, *Vol. 2 (Harper & Brothers, 1880), p. 110.*

[4] *Delphian Society, p. 480.*

[5] *Albert Harkness,* Caesar's Commentaries on the Gallic War: With Notes, Dictionary, and a Map of Gaul *(American Book Company, 1901), p. xiv.*

[6] *Delphian Society, p. 481.*

[7] *Adrian Keith Goldsworthy,* Caesar: Life of a Colossus *(Yale University Press, 2006), p. 61.*

[8] *Goldsworthy, p. 3.*

[9] *Goldsworthy, p. 3.*

Notes to Instructor:

1. The student has been told to double-space and use page numbers. Proper manuscript format will be taught more explicitly in the second level of this course; the focus of this first level remains on basic skill-building.
2. The student has been given titles to choose from. Titling will be taught more explicitly in the second level of this course.
3. Although it is not necessary for the student to continue to use this many footnotes, the focus of this unit has been proper documentation of sources; it is appropriate for the beginner to overuse citations. The student will continue to develop this skill in future levels of this course.

STEP FOUR: Attach the Works Cited page

Student instructions for Step Four:

> You only have one page left to add.
>
> Center the title "Works Cited" at the top of a new page. Beneath this title, aligned with the left-hand margin, list all of the sources you cited in your composition. Use the proper format:
>
> Author last name, Author first name. *Title.* City of publication: Publisher, date.
>
> Single-space each entry, but double-space *between* each entry. This Works Cited page will be the last page of your composition. (It does not need to have a page number.)
>
> Ask your instructor to check your Works Cited page when you are finished.

HOW TO HELP THE STUDENT WITH STEP FOUR

The student's completed Works Cited page should resemble the following. It should only include the sources cited in the student's paper.

WORKS CITED

Cadell, W. A. A Journey in Carniola, Italy, and France in the Years 1817, 1818, *Vol. 2. Edinburgh: Archibald Constable and Co., 1820.*

Delphian Society. The Delphian Course. *Chicago: The Society, 1913.*

Goldsworthy, Adrian Keith. Caesar: Life of a Colossus. *New Haven, Conn.: Yale University Press, 2006.*

Harkness, Albert. Caesar's Commentaries on the Gallic War: With Notes, Dictionary, and a Map of Gaul. *New York: American Book Company, 1901.*

Symonds, John Addington. Sketches and Studies in Southern Europe, *Vol. 2. New York: Harper & Brothers, 1880.*

West, Willis Mason. Ancient History to the Death of Charlemagne. *Boston, Mass.: Allyn and Bacon, 1902.*

The student has now written a fully documented paper with three separate elements. Be sure to acknowledge this accomplishment—put the paper on the refrigerator, show it to relatives, make a special folder for it, etc.

Week 30: Writing from Notes: Sequence: Natural Process, Scientific Description

Day One: Outlining Exercise

Focus: Finding the central topics and selected subtopics in each paragraph of a sequence of events

Today's assignment will combine outlining with a brief review of the form of a sequence; during the remaining lessons of this week, the student will work on taking notes for and writing a properly documented sequence.

STEP ONE: Read (Student Responsibility)

Student instructions for Step One:

Read the following passage about how the human body controls and uses the act of breathing.

STEP TWO: Identify the form of each paragraph

Student instructions for Step Two:

This passage is a sequence describing a natural process. When you studied the form of sequences, you learned that the following elements are often present:

Introduction/summary
Scientific background
Step-by-step process
Repetition of the process

In this particular passage, there is no scientific background or repetition. Instead, the passage describes two *different* (but related) step-by-step processes, and also provides a description.

Mark each paragraph as introduction, first process, or second process. When you are finished, check your work with your instructor before going on.

HOW TO HELP THE STUDENT WITH STEP TWO

The student has been asked to identify the element of the sequence that each paragraph belongs to. He should have written the following answers in the margins next to each paragraph:

Paragraph 1	*Introduction/summary*
Paragraph 2	*First process [oxygen entering the body]*
Paragraph 3	*First process [oxygen entering the body]*
Paragraph 4	*Second process [lungs filtering out impurities]*

STEP THREE: **Construct a one-level outline**

Student instructions for Step Three:

> The last time you outlined a sequence of natural events, you asked yourself the following questions:
>
> What is this paragraph introducing me to?
>
> Which stage of the process does this paragraph describe?
>
> In this stage of the process, what is the first, or most important, or biggest thing that happens?
>
> Ask yourself the appropriate question about each paragraph of your reading in order to find the main point. If you have trouble, ask your instructor for help. When you are finished, check your work with your instructor.

HOW TO HELP THE STUDENT WITH STEP THREE

The student's outline should resemble the following:

Suggested answers:

I. Delivering oxygen to the cells OR Oxygen and the cells OR Breathing
II. Oxygen enters the body OR Oxygen moves into the bronchial tree
III. Oxygen goes into the bloodstream OR Oxygen is distributed through the body
IV. Filtering out impurities OR Impurities filtered out of the air

If necessary, use the following dialogues to help the student:

Paragraph 1
Instructor: This paragraph introduces you to a process. What is the end result of this process?

Student: Oxygen goes to the cells.

Paragraph 2
Instructor: This paragraph describes the first part of the process. How far does oxygen get, in this first sequence of events?

Student: Into the bronchial tree OR *Into the body*

Paragraph 3
Instructor: In this part of the first process, where does the oxygen go?

Student: Into the bloodstream OR *Through the body*

Paragraph 4
Instructor: This last paragraph describes a second step-by-step process. What is filtered out during this process?

Student: Impurities

Note to Instructor: If the student answers "Dust, dirt, smoke, and germs," say "What is the general name that the paragraph uses for all of those things?"

STEP FOUR: **Construct a two-level outline**

Student instructions for Step Four:

> Now go back and try to find the subpoints in paragraphs 2 and 3.
> In a sequence, the subpoints in each paragraph should outline the major *steps* in the step-by-step process. The subpoints should not give descriptive details *about* those steps; instead, the subpoints should *name* those steps in order.
> You should find two subpoints in the second paragraph, and three in the third paragraph. When you are finished, check your work with your instructor.

HOW TO HELP THE STUDENT WITH STEP FOUR

Constructing full two-level outlines is a skill that will be further developed in the next level of this course. The purpose of today's assignment is to prepare the student to write his own sequence of natural events from notes over the next two days.

The student's answers should resemble the following:

Suggested answers:

I. Delivering oxygen to the cells OR Oxygen and the cells OR Breathing
II. Oxygen enters the body OR Oxygen moves into the bronchial tree
  A. Air is inhaled through nose or mouth
  B. Oxygen moves through bronchial tree
III. Oxygen goes into the bloodstream OR Oxygen is distributed through the body
  A. Oxygen enters the bloodstream
  B. Carbon dioxide leaves the bloodstream
  C. Oxygen goes through the body

The student has already been told that there are two subpoints in the second paragraph and three in the third; he should not require dialogue to find these. If he includes details, remind him that *only* steps in the processes should appear in the outline. The descriptions of the trachea, bronchi, alveoli, and capillaries do not belong in a two-level outline.

Day Two: Practicing the Topos, Part One: Taking Notes

Focus: Collecting information

Today, the student will take notes for a descriptive sequence of his own.

The information for each source, properly formatted, should be written at the top of the page where the student is taking notes (or, if he is using 3x5 cards, on the first card). If necessary, remind the student to use quotation marks to surround the exact words of the source, and to always put the page number in parentheses after each quote.

The student will complete the first two steps independently. His instructions are included for your convenience. If necessary, he should read the instructions for Week 28, Day Four to remind himself of the proper form for taking notes.

STEP ONE: **Review the elements of a sequence and a scientific description (Student Responsibility)**

Student instruction for Step One:

> Before you begin to take notes, turn to the Sequence: Natural Process chart in the Reference section of your notebook and read through it. Then turn back to Week 22, Day 2, and read the instructions about constructing a sequence of natural events.
>
> Next, turn to the Scientific Description chart in the Reference section of your notebook and review the elements of a scientific description. Finally, turn back to Week 12, Day 3, and read the instructions about writing a scientific description.

STEP TWO: **Make a preliminary plan (Student Responsibility)**

Student instruction for Step Two:

> In the next lesson, you'll write a descriptive sequence that includes a scientific description. Since you are combining two forms, you will not need to include every element of both.
>
> Your sequence should explain the process of digestion. This sequence should have an introduction, a step-by-step explanation of the process, and a conclusion that discusses the repetition of the process. You should also include a brief scientific description of one or more digestive organs. This scientific description should describe each part of the organ(s), should take a particular point of view, and should include figurative langage (a simple simile is fine).
>
> Before you begin to take notes, read through both of the sources provided to get an overview of digestion. Then, decide which organ(s) you will describe as part of your composition. (This will keep you from taking unnecessary notes; if you're not going to describe an organ, you don't need to write down all of the details about it.)

STEP THREE: **Take notes**

Student instructions for Step Three:

> Take notes on the following two sources, using proper form. You can choose to use either 3x5 cards or a word processing document.
>
> You will see two different kinds of information in these sources: the different steps of digestion, and descriptions of the organs and what they do. When you are simply listing the steps of digestion, you do not need to quote directly. These steps fall under the heading of "widely accepted scientific facts." Scientific facts are generally considered to be common knowledge.
>
> However, if you're using the same words that the source uses to describe an organ or a part of the process, you should use a direct quote.
>
> For example, your notes on page 318 of *Real Things in Nature* might look like this:
>
>> Food goes from the gullet to the stomach and is dissolved by gastric juice. (318)
>> Food turns into "a soft mass, like very thick soup." (318)
>
> It is a widely accepted scientific fact that food goes from gullet to stomach, and that gastric juices then dissolve it. But the particular description of the dissolved food as a "soft mass" and the simile "like very thick soup" belong to Edward Holden; you should use quotation marks to set this off.
>
> Do not take more than 15 notes on either source!
>
> When you are finished with your notes, show them to your instructor.

HOW TO HELP THE STUDENT WITH STEP THREE

The student's notes should resemble the following (although the student should have no more than 15 notes for each source). If the student has difficulty, allow him to look at a few of the answers; he may need an example in order to get started.

The student will find it simplest to choose the small intestine as the organ to describe in detail; he can also add another organ (the gullet, stomach, or teeth) if he chooses to.

Holden, Edward S. *Real Things in Nature.* New York: The Macmillan Company, 1910.

> Food goes from the gullet to the stomach and is dissolved by gastric juice. (318)
> Food turns into "a soft mass, like very thick soup." (318)
> This is called chyme (319)
> Chyme mixes with bile and goes to the small intestine. (319)
> In the small intestine, chyme becomes a "cream-like liquid" and is called chyle. (319)
> Undigested food goes to the bowels. (319)
> Food is moistened by saliva in the mouth. (320)
> The gullet pushes food down with rings of muscle. (320)
> Food doesn't fall down like a brick "down a chimney." (320)
> The gullet is "a small tube full of rings of muscle." (320)
> Chyme takes one to four hours to move to the small intestine. (320)
> The stomach is empy three or four hours after eating. (320)

The small intestine is "coiled up in folds." (321)
The small intestine would be 20 feet long if stretched out. (321)
The chyme is pushed along the intestine with rings of muscle. (321)
Chyle in the intestines is "sucked up, by thousands of small tubes." (321)
Some chyle goes into the blood, some is mixed with lymph. (321)

Frost, John. *The Class Book of Nature.* Hartford, Conn.: Belknap and Hamersley, 1839.

The stomach is a "hollow bag" that holds "about three pints of fluid." (219)
Food is crushed by the teeth and mixed with saliva. (219)
The gullet pushes the food down. (219)
Food goes from the stomach to the intestines. (219)
The intestines are folded up and are "five or six yards long." (219)
The intestines are covered on the inside by villi. (220)
The outside of the intestines is "smooth and shining" and kept moist. (220)
There are muscles between the inside and outside of the intestines. (220)
The muscles push the food foward. This is called *peristaltic* motion. (220)
The teeth and saliva make the food into a "soft pulp" (223)
In the stomach the food is mixed with gastric juices. (223)
Gastric juices make the food into a "half fluid state" which is gray and called chyme. (223)
Chyme goes into the small intestines and is mixed with fluid. (224)
Chyme turns white and is called chyle. (224)
Chyle is mixed with bile that separates "the *nutritious* from the useless parts." (224)
The villi are the mouth of the lacteals. (224)
Lacteals take the chyle to glands. (224)
The chyle goes into the veins. (224)

Day Three: Practicing the Topos, Part Two: Write

Focus: Writing a descriptive sequence combined with a scientific description

Today the student will use his notes to write a descriptive sequence of digestion, combined with a scientific description of at least one of the organs used for digestion.

The subject matter of this composition is simpler than the subject matter of last week's Julius Caesar composition. The student has also been given much less explicit guidance on how to structure and write the paper. The simpler content should allow the student to work a little more independently on organizing the paper.

STEP ONE: **Write the description**

Student instructions for Step One:

> Start by writing your description.
>
> Go through your notes and mark with a highlighter (or underline) the notes that describe particular organs. Then, use those notes and the illustrations in the source texts to write a description, following these guidelines:
>
> 1. The description must focus on one particular digestive organ.
> 2. The description must be at least two sentences and 40 words in length.
> 3. The description should have a consistent point of view.
> 4. The description should tell what at least two parts of the organ look like and what they do.
> 5. At least one metaphor or simile should be used.
>
> You may use a direct quote, but this is not a requirement. Remember to footnote the exact words or ideas of the source material, but not generally accepted scientific facts.
>
> If you have trouble with your description, ask your instructor for help. When you're finished, show your description to your instructor.

HOW TO HELP THE STUDENT WITH STEP ONE

The student's notes will differ from the sample answers provided, but the following notes are descriptive:

Holden, Edward S. Real Things in Nature. *New York: The Macmillan Company, 1910.*

> *The gullet pushes food down with rings of muscle. (320)*
> *Food doesn't fall down like a brick "down a chimney." (320)*
> *The gullet is "a small tube full of rings of muscle." (320)*
> *The small intestine is "coiled up in folds." (321)*
> *The small intestine would be 20 feet long if stretched out. (321)*
> *The chyme is pushed along the intestine with rings of muscle. (321)*

Frost, John. The Class Book of Nature. *Hartford, Conn.: Belknap and Hamersley, 1839.*

> *The stomach is a "hollow bag" that holds "about three pints of fluid." (219)*
> *The intestines are folded up and are "five or six yards long." (219)*
> *The intestines are covered on the inside by villi. (220)*
> *The outside of the intestines is "smooth and shining" and kept moist. (220)*
> *There are muscles between the inside and outside of the intestines. (220)*
> *The muscles push the food foward. This is called* peristaltic *motion. (220)*

Notice that there can be some overlap between description and sequence of events—describing what an organ *does* belongs in both categories. You may need to point this out.

The student should probably choose either the gullet or the intestine to describe.

If the student has difficulty thinking of a metaphor, remind him to go back and look at the illustrations; he can then try to think of something that has the same visual appearance. You may also use the following dialogue:

For the gullet:
Instructor: Your source says that food doesn't fall down the gullet "as a brick falls down a chimney." Let's think of another way to put this. What other object might fall? What other long tube-like shape might you drop something down?

Note to Instructor: If necessary, suggest that the student think about dropping something down a well.

For the intestines:
Instructor: Look at page 318 of *Real Things in Nature.* Do you see how the intestines are folded in on each other, back and forth? Something firefighters use is also folded in this way. What is it?

Student: A fire hose

Instructor: That could be your metaphor.

When the student is finished, check his work using the following rubric:

Week 30 Rubric
Scientific Description

Organization

1 The description should describe what at least two parts of the organ look like and what function they have.
For the gullet: the tube and the rings of muscle
For the intestines: the coiled folds, the length, the muscles, the villi, the outside
2 The description should have a clear point of view—either from above (impersonal, outside) or moving through or around (in other words, the student can describe the organ from the point of view of the food moving through it).
3 At least one metaphor or simile should be used.
4 The final description should be at least 40 words and two sentences in length.

Mechanics

1 Each sentence should make sense on its own when read aloud.
2 Verb tense should be consistent throughout.
3 Subjects and verbs must be in agreement.
4 Possessive forms should be written properly.
5 If used, footnotes should be properly formatted and should come at the ends of the sentences which contain the source material.
Author first and last name, *Title of book* (Publisher, date), p. #.

STEP TWO: **Write the sequence**

Student instructions for Step Two:

> Now you'll use the same strategy you used for your Julius Caesar paper to arrange your notes and write your sequence.
>
> Go back to your notes and rearrange them so that all of the events involved in digestion are listed in order. If you're using a word processor, create a new document and cut and paste information from both lists of events into it. If you're using note cards, simply arrange the cards in order and set aside the ones that have repeated information. You can cut the notes that simply give description, since your description is already written.
>
> Be sure not to lose track of which notes go with which source.
>
> Once you've arranged all of your events in order, go back and divide them into groups. Each group of events should cover a different stage of digestion.
>
> Give each group a Roman numeral and a title or description.
>
> Then write your composition. Write one paragraph for each main point. Do not use the exact words of your sources unless you use quotation marks and a footnote. If you describe a scientific fact in your own words, you do not need to provide a footnote. If you're not sure, use a footnote.
>
> Your completed sequence should be at least 150 words in length. Use at least one direct quote.
>
> If you have trouble with any of these steps, ask your instructor for help. If not, you can wait to show your composition to your instructor until it is assembled.

HOW TO HELP THE STUDENT WITH STEP TWO

The student's rearranged notes, divided into events and titled, should resemble the following:

I. Food in the mouth
   Food is crushed by the teeth and mixed with saliva. (219)
   The teeth and saliva make the food into a "soft pulp" (223)
   Food is moistened by saliva in the mouth. (320)

II. Food goes to the stomach OR Food becomes chyme
   The gullet pushes food down with rings of muscle. (320)
   Food goes from the gullet to the stomach and is dissolved by gastric juice. (318)
   In the stomach the food is mixed with gastric juices. (223)
   Food turns into "a soft mass, like very thick soup." (318)
   Gastric juices make the food into a "half fluid state" which is gray and called chyme. (223)
   This is called chyme (319)

III. Food goes to the small intestine OR Chyme becomes chyle
   Food goes from the stomach to the intestines. (219)
   The stomach is empy three or four hours after eating. (320)
   Chyme takes one to four hours to move to the small intestine. (320)

The chyme is pushed along the intestine with rings of muscle. (321)
The muscles push the food foward. This is called *peristaltic* motion. (220)
Chyme goes into the small intestines and is mixed with fluid. (224)
Chyme mixes with bile and goes to the small intestine. (319)
Chyle is mixed with bile that separates "the *nutritious* from the useless parts." (224)
In the small intestine, chyme becomes a "cream-like liquid" and is called chyle. (319)
Chyme turns white and is called chyle. (224)

IV. Chyle goes into the body
Chyle in the intestines is "sucked up, by thousands of small tubes." (321)
Some chyle goes into the blood, some is mixed with lymph (321)
Lacteals take the chyle to glands. (224)
The chyle goes into the veins. (224)

V. What happens to the rest
Undigested food goes to the bowels. (319)

The student's final composition should have either four or five paragraphs (it isn't necessary for the student to include the last detail about the undigested food). If the student has trouble organizing the events, suggest that he divide them into four groups and classify them according to which organ is being used: mouth and teeth, stomach, small intestine, rest of the body.

STEP THREE: **Assemble the composition**

Student instructions for Step Three:

> Now insert your description into your sequence at the most appropriate place—probably where the organ is first mentioned.
>
> Attach a Works Cited page where you list the bibliographical information for the book or books you cited in your paper.
>
> Give your paper a title, centered on the first page. (Nothing fancy—"Human Digestion" is fine.)
>
> Make sure that your paper is double-spaced. If it is more than one page in length, not including the Works Cited page, give the pages numbers. If there is only one page, you do not need to give it the number "1."
>
> When you are finished, show your work to your instructor.

HOW TO HELP THE STUDENT WITH STEP THREE

Check the student's composition using the following rubric.

Week 30 Rubric
Sequence of a Natural Event, Including a Scientific Description

Organization

1 The final composition should be at least 190 words long.
2 There should be either five or six paragraphs.
3 Each paragraph in the sequence should describe what happens to the food in one stage of the digestive process.
4 The scientific description should be placed after the first mention of the organ it describes.
5 Ideas or images from the source material should be footnoted. Scientific facts do not need footnotes. At least one direct quote should be included and footnoted.
6 A Works Cited page must be attached.

Mechanics

1 Each sentence should make sense on its own when read aloud.
2 Possessive forms should be written properly.
3 Each paragraph should have at least two sentences.
4 Verb tense should be consistent throughout.
5 Subjects and verbs must be in agreement.
6 Footnotes should be properly formatted.
7 The paper should be double-spaced.
8 If there is more than one page (not including the Works Cited page), the pages should be numbered.
9 The title should be centered at the top of the first page.
10 A separate Works Cited page should be attached (even if only one source is included on it) and properly formatted.

Author last name, Author first name. *Title of book.* City of publication: Publisher, date.

Day Four: Copia Exercise

Focus: Main verbs and infinitives

STEP ONE: **Review**

Student instructions for Step One:

> Take a few minutes now to read down your Sentence Variety chart. When you are finished, rewrite the following sentences (freely adapted from Edward Holden's *Real Things in Nature*). Each sentence contains a phrase or clause that can be easily transformed, using the principles you've already learned.
>
> If you have difficulty, ask your instructor for help. When you are finished, check your work with your instructor.

HOW TO HELP THE STUDENT WITH STEP ONE

The correct transformations are listed below. If the student has trouble, tell him which phrase needs to be transformed (these are underlined for your reference). If necessary, you may also tell him which transformation needs to be done.

Underneath the skin is a layer of fat, and under the fat are the muscles.
Transformation: Noun to descriptive adjective

> *Under the skin is a fat layer, and under the fat are the muscles.*

The outer layer of our skin is dead and is continually being worn away.
Transformation: Passive verb to active verb

> The outer layer of our skin is dead and is continually wearing away.

The science of physiology teaches us the uses of all the parts of the body.
Transformation: Indirect object to object of the preposition

The science of physiology teaches the uses of all the parts of the body to us.

The muscles of our body make it possible for us to move, to walk, and to stand erect.
Transformation: Infinitives to participles

The muscles of our body make moving, walking, and standing erect possible.

STEP TWO: **Understand how to transform main verbs into infinitives (Student Responsibility)**

Student instructions for Step Two:

In the last copia exercise that you did (back in Week 22), you learned that a main verb can be followed by an infinitive (a verb form that starts with "to"). You also learned that an infinitive can be changed to a participle, and vice versa.

infinitive
The star begins to grow hungry for a new energy source.
participle
The star begins growing hungry for a new energy source.

With your pencil, underline the word "begins" twice (in both sentences). This is the main verb of the sentence.

A main verb can be followed by an infinitive (or participle) that completes its meaning. But you can also transform a main verb *into* an infinitive or participle. Read the following two sentences out loud, listening the differences in sound.

We breathe whether we think about it or not.

We continue to breathe whether we think about it or not.

With your pencil, underline the word "breathe" in the first sentence twice. Write "main verb" above it. In the second sentence, underline "continue" twice. Write "main verb" above it. Then underline "to breathe" once and write "inf." above it.

In the second sentence, the main verb has been changed to an infinitive. But since that leaves the sentence without a main verb, a *new* main verb has to be provided.

This changes the meaning of the sentence a little bit. If I had decided to use other main verbs, the meaning of the sentence would change yet again.

We remember to breathe whether we think about it or not.
We don't forget to breathe whether we think about it or not.
We need to breathe whether we think about it or not.

You can also add adjectives and nouns, if necessary, to help connect the main verb to the infinitive.

adjective
We are able to breathe whether we think about it or not.

noun
We have the ability to breathe whether we think about it or not.

When you change the main verb to an infinitive, you have the opportunity to add another level or shade of meaning to your sentence.

STEP THREE: **Add to the Sentence Variety chart (Student Responsibility)**

Student instructions for Step Three:

Write the following principle and illustrations on the next line of your Sentence Variety chart.

main verb ⟷ *infinitive*	*I usually plan ahead.* *I usually need to plan ahead.* *I usually manage to plan ahead.*

STEP FOUR: **Practice sentence variety**

Student instructions for Step Four:

In the following sentences, transform each main verb into an infinitive. Rewrite each sentence twice, providing a new main verb each time.

HOW TO HELP THE STUDENT WITH STEP FOUR

Possible answers might be:

Chyme moves from the stomach into the small intestine.
Chyme begins to move from the stomach into the small intestine.
Chyme continues to move from the stomach into the small intestine.
Chyme needs to move from the stomach into the small intestine.

Babies learn to use their muscles as they grow.
Babies have to learn how to use their muscles as they grow.
Babies try to learn how to use their muscles as they grow.
Babies want to learn how to use their muscles as they grow.

You should understand how your body works.

You should try to understand how your body works.
You should plan to understand how your body works.
You should choose to understand how your body works.

If the student has difficulty coming up with new main verbs, you may prompt him with this list of verbs that take infinitives.

agree	appear	arrange	ask	
begin				
care	cease	choose	claim	continue
decide	deserve			
expect				
fail				
hesitate	hope			
intend				
learn	love			
manage				
need				
offer				
plan	prepare			
refuse				
seem	start			
tend	try			
wait	want	wish		

Week 31: Writing from Notes: Biographical Sketch, Description of a Person

Day One: Outlining Exercise

Focus: Finding the central topics and selected subtopics in each paragraph of a biographical sketch

STEP ONE: **Read (Student Responsibility)**

Student instructions for Step One:

Read the following biographical sketch of physicist Marie Curie, born in 1867. Marie Curie won two Nobel prizes, one in physics in 1903 and the second in chemistry in 1911; she was the first person to win two Nobel prizes.

Piezoelectricity is an electrical charge that is produced when pressure is put on certain kinds of crystals (such as quartz and tourmaline). "Ecole Superieure de Physique et de Chimie" is French for "College of Physics and Chemistry."

STEP TWO: **Construct a one-level outline**

Student instructions for Step Two:

When outlining a biographical sketch, the most useful question you can ask yourself is "What aspect of the person's life or character does this paragraph focus on?" In Week 18, you asked yourself this question while outlining a biographical sketch of the painter Jan Brueghel; in Week 19, you asked the same question for a biographical sketch of Edgar Allan Poe.

That question will work very well for the first two paragraphs of the sketch. For the last three paragraphs, however, you may need to take a slightly different approach.

Each one of these paragraphs progresses chronologically through events in Marie Curie's life. Each paragraph also covers a certain span of time. One way for you to sum up each paragraph would be: List the period of time that the paragraph covers. For example, the third paragraph could be given the title:

III. Curie's life between secondary school and 1894

That's not a very exciting main point, but it's a very accurate summing up of the main purpose of the paragraph.

But you could also sum up the paragraph by going back to a question you've used for many other outlines: What is the most important thing that happens to Marie Curie in this paragraph?

She begins her university education. The paragraph tells you everything that leads up to Curie's university entrance, but the whole point of those details is that Curie finally made it to the university and began to study physics and mathematics.

Now do a one-level outline of this passage. For paragraphs three through five, provide two main points—one that sums up the period of time, and one that tells the most important thing that happens in the paragraph. Write the outline like this:

III. Curie's life between secondary school and 1894 OR
Curie begins her university education

(You can use those main points for III.)

If you have difficulty, ask your instructor for help. When you're finished, show your work to your instructor.

HOW TO HELP THE STUDENT WITH STEP TWO

The student's outline should resemble the following:

I. Curie's family OR Curie's early life
II. Secondary school OR Curie's early schooling
III. Curie's life between secondary school and 1894 OR
Curie begins her university education
IV. Curie's life between 1894 and 1897 OR
Marie Curie marries Pierre Curie
V. Curie's life between 1904 and 1906 OR
Curie becomes a physics professor

If necessary, use the following dialogues to help the student

Paragraph 1

Instructor: This paragraph tells you about three people. Who are they?

Student: Marie Curie, her father, and her mother

Instructor: They are all members of the same . . .

Student: Family

Instructor: This paragraph is all about Marie Curie's family.

Paragraph 2

Instructor: Both sentences in this paragraph talk about the same subject. Hint: it's the word that is repeated three times.

Student: School

Instructor: This paragraph is about Marie Curie's secondary school experience.

Paragraph 4
Instructor: When do the first and last events of the paragraph happen?

> *Student: 1894 and 1897*

Instructor: So you could use "Curie's life between 1894 and 1897" as your main point. What is the most important single event that happens in the passage? It affects every single sentence—for example, Marie Curie could not have gotten a lab room for her experiments if this event hadn't happened.

> *Student: She marries Pierre Curie.*

Paragraph 5
Instructor: When do the first and last events of the paragraph happen?

> *Student: 1904 and 1906*

Instructor: So you could use "Curie's life between 1904 and 1906" as your main point. The most important event that happens in this passage isn't actually about Pierre Curie. Remember, the sketch is about *Marie*. The details about Pierre are only there to explain what happens to Marie. What is the most important event that happens *to Marie* in this passage?

> *Student: She becomes a professor.*

Instructor: She becomes not just a professor, but a physics professor—the first woman at her university to do so.

STEP THREE: **Construct a two-level outline**

Student instructions for Step Three:

> Now go back and add subpoints to your outline for points III, IV, and V only.
>
> In a biographical sketch that progresses chronologically, the subpoints are likely to be the most important events in each paragraph. Try to list ONLY the events that are *directly related* to the main points that tell the most important thing that happens in the paragraph. So, for the third paragraph, ONLY include those events that are directly related to Curie's beginning her university education. (That means that Bronya's education and marriage shouldn't be subpoints. Those events are indirectly related to Curie's own education, so those would appear in a more detailed outline.)
>
> Try to use only four subpoints for III, three subpoints for IV, and three subpoints for V.

HOW TO HELP THE STUDENT WITH STEP THREE

The student's answers should resemble the following:

III. Curie's life between secondary school and 1894 OR
Curie begins her university education

A. Marie and Bronya decided to go to Paris.
B. Curie became a governess.
C. Curie went to Paris in 1890.
D. Curie studied physics and mathematics.
IV. Curie's life between 1894 and 1897 OR
Marie Curie marries Pierre Curie
A. Met Pierre in 1894
B. Was given a room for her experiments in his building
C. Had her first daughter in 1897
V. Curie's life between 1904 and 1906 OR
Curie becomes a physics professor
A. Pierre was appointed as a professor.
B. Pierre was killed in an accident.
C. Marie was given Pierre's position.

There is some room for interpretation in this part of the outlining process, but the student should remember that subpoints must be *directly* related to the main point. In IV, where Pierre lived is irrelevant to the main point, but the date of the marriage and the honeymoon could be included. In V, Pierre's papers are irrelevant to the main point; Marie's part-time teaching could be considered relevant. If the student chooses to use one of these as subpoints in place of the suggested subpoints, accept the answer.

Day Two: Practicing the Topos, Part One: Taking Notes

Focus: Collecting information

Today, the student will take notes for a biographical sketch of the French queen Marie Antoinette. She should write the information for each source, properly formatted, at the top of the page where she's taking notes (or, if he's using 3x5 cards, on the first card). Quotation marks should surround the exact words of the source, and the page number should always be placed in parentheses after each quote.

STEP ONE: **Review the elements of a biographical sketch and description of a person (Student Responsibility)**

Student instructions for Step One:

> Before you begin to take notes, turn to the Biographical Sketch chart in the Reference section of your notebook and read through it. Then turn back to Week 19, Day Two, and Week

20, Day Two and read the instructions in both of those lessons.

Next, turn to the Description of a Person chart in the Reference section of your notebook and review the elements of a personal description. Finally, turn back to Week 16, Day Two; Week 17, Day Two; and Week 18, Day Two. Read the instructions about writing descriptions in all three of those lessons.

Remember—your biographical sketch will include selected aspects from the Description of a Person chart.

STEP TWO: **Make a preliminary plan**

Student instructions for Step Two:

In the next two lessons, you'll take notes and write a biographical sketch that includes selected aspects from the Description of a Person chart.

You will have three major choices to make as you take notes and write. Here's a summary of your choices:

1. What will the focus be?
   First option: A chronological listing of major life events
   Second option: A brief summary of life events, followed by a survey of the subject's accomplishments and achievements
2. What aspects from the Description of a Person chart will you include?
3. Which of the following strategies will you use? (You have to pick one.)
   First option: Slant your description (and sketch) in either a positive or negative direction by using appropriate adjectives, nouns, and verbs.
   Second option: Choose an overall metaphor to give clues about the character of your subject.

Before you begin to take notes, read through all of the sources provided on pp. 422–429 to get an overview of the subject of Marie Antoinette. Then, make a tentative decision about each of these choices. (You may change your mind later, but this will help focus your note-taking so that you don't write down too many unnecessary details.)

HOW TO HELP THE STUDENT WITH STEP TWO

If the student has difficulty, you may make the following suggestions.

1. The first focus will be easier than the second; the sources are focused more on Marie's life and her difficulties than on her achievements. Note too that the sources suggest a structure that talks first about Marie's triumphant entrance into Paris as a girl, and last about her ride to the guillotine as a woman; these two events frame the other facts about her life.
2. The sources lend themselves best to: physical appearance, what others think, character qualities, challenges and difficulties, clothing, dress, economic status, fame, notoriety, prestige, expressions of face and body.
3. Either strategy will work. For the first option, the student could portray Marie as callous, clueless, ignorant, noble, martyred. For the second, the student could use the metaphor of a trapped animal. (Further guidance is provided on Day Four.)

STEP THREE: **Take initial notes from an encyclopedia**

Student responsibility for Step Three:

In the next two steps, you will take notes on the following sources, using proper form. You can choose to use either 3x5 cards or a word processing document.

The first source is an article from the *Chambers's Encyclopedia*, a well-respected British encyclopedia. When you're writing about a new subject, an encyclopedia is often the best place to start. Encyclopedia entries give you a succinct summary of the most important facts about your subject, and this will give you some idea of the topics that your composition should cover.

In most cases, you won't want to cite the encyclopedia article itself in your final composition. Instead, use it to make an initial list of facts.

If you use *World Book*, *Encyclopedia Britannica*, or another recognized encyclopedia, you can trust the facts you find there. If you use Wikipedia to make your initial list of facts, you must check every one of them with a published source before using it in your composition. Wikipedia can be a useful first stop when you're first investigating something unfamiliar. But unlike a recognized encyclopedia, Wikipedia doesn't require any sort of expertise or training for its contributors, and there is no systematic fact-checking. So always confirm all information discovered on Wikipedia with at least one independent source.

Now read through the following article and write down, in list form, the most important events in Marie Antoinette's life. Since the entire article comes from page 326, you do not need to put the page number next to each event.

Try to list *only* historical facts that can be classified as common knowledge.

When you're finished, show your notes to your instructor before going on.

HOW TO HELP THE STUDENT WITH STEP THREE

The purpose of this step is to give the student a basic framework of historical knowledge. Encyclopedias should usually not be quoted directly, and if the student is writing about topics she knows well, this step may not be necessary. Both in this step and in future uses of the encyclopedia, encourage the student to list only those facts which are common knowledge.

For this encyclopedia entry, the list of facts should resemble the following:

Marie Antoinette de Lorraine, full name
Youngest daughter of the German emperor Francis I and the queen of Austria, Maria Theresa
Born at Vienna on Nov. 2, 1755
Betrothed to the Dauphin at 14
Married at Versailles at 15
Dauphin became Louis XVI in May 1774.
Her enemies circulated rumors and stories about her.
Her good name was damaged by the diamond necklace affair in 1785.
Her two favorite ministers were condemned for overspending.
She opposed the Assembly of Notables in 1788.
She opposed the assembling of the States-General in 1789.

The Assembly of Notables said she had caused France's financial trouble.
The Revolution began in May 1789.
There was an attempted assassination on October 6, 1789, in Versailles.
She tried to make herself popular.
She decided to flee.
Louis didn't want to go at first, but then agreed.
They fled at night on June 20, 1791.
They were recognized and captured at Varennes.
Marie was put in the Temple, a fortress in Paris.
She was moved to prison on August 1, 1793.
The Revolutionary Tribunal condemned her on Oct. 15, 1793.
She was guillotined on Oct. 16.

The following pieces of information are not historical facts—they are interpretations and would need to be footnoted (and shouldn't be included in this list). Simply tell the student, when necessary, which facts to include. It will take time for her to develop this sense.

> "Her lack of ceremony and hatred for rigid etiquette scandalised the court at Versailles."
>
> "Her faults, as a queen, were a certain levity of disposition, a girlish love of pleasure, banquets, fine dress, an aristocratic indifference to general opinion, and a lamentable incapacity to see the actual misery of France."
>
> ". . . she made some spasmodic efforts to gain the goodwill of the populace by visiting the great factories of the capital and by seeming to take an interest in the labours of the workmen, but the time was gone by for such weak efforts to succeed."
>
> "Louis XVI had a dim sense of kingly duty and honour."
>
> "From this time, Marie's attitude became heroic; but the French people could not rid themselves of the suspicion that she was secretly plotting with the allies for the invasion of the country."
>
> ". . . subjected to most sickening humiliations."

STEP FOUR: **Take additional notes from other sources**

Student instructions for Step Four:

> Now take additional notes on the aspects and events you intend to use in your sketch.
>
> Remember, historical events are generally considered to be common knowledge. However, if you use the writer's specific interpretation of those events, be sure to use a direct quote.
>
> In the encyclopedia article above, for example, you would not need to footnote the fact that Marie and Louis fled on June 20, 1791; that they were captured in Varennes; or that Marie was imprisoned in the Temple fortress. However, if you decided to write that Marie had a heroic attitude during all of this, you would be using the encyclopedia's own interpretation. Not everyone agrees that Marie was being heroic—but everyone agrees that she fled on June 20.
>
> So your notes might look like this:

> Marie and Louis XVI fled on June 20, 1791.
> They were captured in Varennes.
> "Marie's attitude became heroic" during her imprisonment. (326)

(As noted above, it's usually better not to quote directly from an encyclopedia—this is just an example.)

Do not take more than 15 notes on any single source. You can always go back to the source while you're writing if you need more information.

When you are finished with your notes, show them to your instructor.

HOW TO HELP THE STUDENT WITH STEP FOUR

The student's notes should resemble the following (although the student should have no more than 15 notes for each source). If the student has difficulty, allow her to look at a few of the answers; she may need an example in order to get started.

The sources in this exercise are lengthier than in previous exercises, so the student may have difficulty picking and choosing. If necessary, encourage her to focus only on the titles and aspects she decided to include when making her preliminary plan. Remind her that she can return to the sources at any time. You may also need to point out that the student should not be making detailed notes on Louis XVI—just on Marie. (This is a biographical sketch, not a narrative of chronological events.)

Abbot, Willis J. Notable Women in History. *Philadelphia: The John C. Winston Co., 1913.*

Marie married the Dauphin of France in 1770 when she was 15. (147)

She made a triumphant progression to Versailles for her wedding. (147)

The "roads were strewn with flowers" and "nobility and country folk turned out to do her honor." (147)

The ladies at Versailles hated Marie for being "too free in her manners." (148)

She had a "girlish sense of humor" and laughed at the court for being "the most artificial society in all Europe." (148)

She had maids to pull off her stockings at night and to tie her night cap. (148)

32 people were killed in fireworks celebrating the marriage, and this made her more unpopular. (148)

The people of France "resented the king's bringing a princess" of Austria to "be their future queen." (148)

"The queen's girdle" was a tax on bread and wine that went to the queen. (148–149)

Marie "remitted this tax" in 1774, but the people soon forgot. (149)

The "Countess de la Motte" convinced Cardinal Rohan to buy an expensive necklace for the queen and give the necklace to her. (149)

The swindler had a forged invoice and also brought a look-alike to meet with the cardinal. (149–150)

The cardinal thought the necklace had gone to the queen, but the "Countess" stole it. (150)

The queen knew nothing about this, but the people of France blamed her anyway. (150)

Marie broke down and wept and "became solitary" and was in a "broken and pathetic state." (150)

Tytler, Sarah. Marie Antoinette: The Woman and the Queen. *London: Marcus Ward & Co., 1883.*

Marie left home in 1770 on April 21 to go to France. (32)

She "covered her face with her hands" and cried when she left. (33)

The Empress wrote her many "earnest, affectionate letters" by special messenger, and the letters were burned "as soon as read." (33)

She had blue eyes and fair hair. (34)

She rode in a state carriage "flaming with crimson and gold, surmounted by wrought and tinted wreaths and nosegays of flowers." (34)

She was greeted with "salutes from regiments of cavalry," "cannon from the ramparts," bells, and fountains filled with wine. (34)

She was "quick, kind, and tender-hearted." (34)

When she went to the guillotine, "every house was closed and every window shut." (213)

Some people insulted her, but others greeted her. (213)

She had "one last look" at her home and "was visibly moved." (213)

The guillotine "was in the Place de la Revolution," and the people had put "a female figure of Liberty" there. (213–214)

She said, "Courage! I have served an apprenticeship to it for a long time; there is no fear of my losing it at this moment." (214)

She ascended the scaffold alone and said, "Lord, enlighten and soften my executioners." (214)

"Her head was shown to the people," and she was buried "in an open coffin among quick-lime." (214)

France paid 31 francs for her burial. (214)

Bishop, M. C. The Prison Life of Marie Antoinette. *London: Kegan Paul, Trench, Trübner & Co., 1893.*

When she first came to Paris the "enthusiastic people . . . could not sufficiently admire and love her." (172)

Now she was on a cart with a "plank for a seat." (172)

Madame le Brun said that she was "tall, admirably made, rather fat" with small hands and feet. (172)

She walked well and "carried her head gracefully." (172)

She had royal dignity and majesty, but she was also sweet in appearance. (172–173)

She had irregular features and a "long and narrow oval face." (173)

Her eyes were small and "almost blue." (173)

She had an "intelligent and soft" expression. (173)

She had a "well cut" nose and full lips. (173)

She had a brilliant complexion and transparent skin. (173)
She had "the imposing and majestic air of a goddess." (173)
She was 38 when she died. (173)
Her hair lost its color after she was taken prisoner. (173)

Day Three: Practicing the Topos, Part Two: Organizing the Biographical Sketch

Focus: Using notes to construct an outline

Today, the student will prepare to write a biographical sketch by turning her notes into an outline and dividing the outline into paragraphs. Tomorrow, she'll finish the assignment by writing the sketch, complete with footnotes and Works Cited page.

These first-year assignments are spread across several days because the student is taught the "long way" to take notes, assemble them, and write a composition. As the student grows more practiced, she'll be able to shorten the process and carry it out more efficiently.

STEP ONE: **Arrange notes in order**

Student instructions for Step One:

> Now go back to the notes you took from the encyclopedia article about Marie Antoinette. These basic facts will serve as the skeleton of your outline. Copy them and paste them into a new word processing document (or arrange the 3x5 cards into order, one fact on each card).
>
> You'll now put each one of the additional notes you took underneath the corresponding fact from the encyclopedia article. Copy and paste the additional notes into your document, or arrange the cards in order behind the correct note card from the encyclopedia article.
>
> For example, imagine that the first six facts in your encyclopedia list are these:
>
> Youngest daughter of the German emperor Francis I and the queen of Austria, Maria Theresa
> Born at Vienna on Nov. 2, 1755
> Betrothed to the dauphin at 14
> Married at Versailles at 15
> Dauphin became Louis XVI in May 1774.
> Her enemies circulated rumors and stories about her.
>
> Suppose that the first few notes you took from Sarah Tytler's *Marie Antoinette* and M. C. Bishop's *The Prison Life of Marie Antoinette* look like this:
>
> Tytler, Sarah. *Marie Antoinette: The Woman and the Queen.* London: Marcus Ward & Co., 1883.
> Marie left home in 1770 on April 21 to go to France. (32)
> She "covered her face with her hands" and cried when she left. (33)

The Empress wrote her many "earnest, affectionate letters" by special messenger, and the letters were burned "as soon as read." (33)
She had blue eyes and fair hair. (34)
She rode in a state carriage "flaming with crimson and gold, surmounted by wrought and tinted wreaths and nosegays of flowers." (34)

Bishop, M. C. *The Prison Life of Marie Antoinette.* London: Kegan Paul, Trench, Trübner & Co., 1893.

When she first came to Paris the "enthusiastic people . . . could not sufficiently admire and love her." (172)
Now she was on a cart with a "plank for a seat." (172)
Madame le Brun said that she was "tall, admirably made, rather fat" with small hands and feet. (172)

Five of the notes give details about Marie's arrival in France for her wedding. You would place all of them underneath "Married at Versailles at 15," like this:

Married at Versailles at 15
Marie left home in 1770 on April 21 to go to France. (32)
She "covered her face with her hands" and cried when she left. (33)
The Empress wrote her many "earnest, affectionate letters" by special messenger, and the letters were burned "as soon as read." (33)
She rode in a state carriage "flaming with crimson and gold, surmounted by wrought and tinted wreaths and nosegays of flowers." (34)
When she first came to Paris the "enthusiastic people . . . could not sufficiently admire and love her." (172)

Dauphin became Louis XVI in May 1774

Because the detail about the Empress's letters happens *after* Marie arrives in France, you would want to move it to the end of the list.

The detail about the plank for the seat would go later in your list of facts, in the section dealing with Marie's execution.

You may notice that the details about Marie's appearance don't seem to be connected to any particular fact from the encyclopedia article. A personal description can come at several different places in the biographical sketch. Create a separate list called "Personal description" and assemble all the details about her appearance underneath that heading:

Personal description
She had blue eyes and fair hair. (34)
Madame le Brun said that she was "tall, admirably made, rather fat" with small hands and feet. (172)

If you're using a word processing program, it isn't necessary to put the last name of the author in front of every single page number as long as you can glance back at your original list and confirm which note belongs to which source. (That's why you *copy and paste* instead of *cut and paste*—you want to leave your original notes to use as reference.)

When you're finished assembling your notes in order, show them to your instructor.

HOW TO HELP THE STUDENT WITH STEP ONE

Although the student's specific notes will differ, her completed list should resemble the following:

Marie Antoinette de Lorraine, full name

Youngest daughter of the German emperor Francis I and the queen of Austria, Maria Theresa

Born at Vienna on Nov. 2, 1755

Betrothed to the Dauphin at 14

Married at Versailles at 15

Marie left home in 1770 on April 21 to go to France. (32)

She "covered her face with her hands" and cried when she left. (33)

She made a triumphant progression to Versailles for her wedding. (147)

She rode in a state carriage "flaming with crimson and gold, surmounted by wrought and tinted wreaths and nosegays of flowers." (34)

She was greeted with "salutes from regiments of cavalry," "cannon from the ramparts," bells, and fountains filled with wine. (34)

The "roads were strewn with flowers" and "nobility and country folk turned out to do her honor." (147)

When she first came to Paris the "enthusiastic people . . . could not sufficiently admire and love her." (172)

The ladies at Versailles hated Marie for being "too free in her manners." (148)

She had a "girlish sense of humor" and laughed at the court for being "the most artificial society in all Europe." (148)

She had maids to pull off her stockings at night and to tie her night cap. (148)

The people of France "resented the king's bringing a princess" of Austria to "be their future queen." (148)

32 people were killed in fireworks celebrating the marriage, and this made her more unpopular. (148)

The Empress wrote her many "earnest, affectionate letters" by special messenger, and the letters were burned "as soon as read." (33)

Dauphin became Louis XVI in May 1774.

"The queen's girdle" was a tax on bread and wine that went to the queen. (148–149)

Marie "remitted this tax" in 1774, but the people soon forgot. (149)

Her enemies circulated rumors and stories about her.

Her good name was damaged by the diamond necklace affair in 1785.

The "Countess de la Motte" convinced Cardinal Rohan to buy an expensive necklace for the queen and give the necklace to her. (149)

The swindler had a forged invoice and also brought a look-alike to meet with the cardinal. (149–150)

The cardinal thought the necklace had gone to the queen, but the "Countess" stole it. (150)

The queen knew nothing about this, but the people of France blamed her anyway. (150)

Marie broke down and wept and "became solitary" and was in a "broken and pathetic state." (150)

Her two favorite ministers were condemned for overspending.

She opposed the Assembly of Notables in 1788.

She opposed the assembling of the States-General in 1789.

The Assembly of Notables said she had caused France's financial trouble.

The Revolution began in May 1789.

There was an attempted assassination on October 6, 1789, in Versailles.

She tried to make herself popular.

She decided to flee.

Louis didn't want to go at first, but then agreed.

They fled at night on June 20, 1791.

They were recognized and captured at Varennes.

Marie was put in the Temple, a fortress in Paris.

She was moved to prison on August 1, 1793.

Her hair lost its color after she was taken prisoner. (173)

The Revolutionary Tribunal condemned her on Oct. 15, 1793.

She was guillotined on Oct. 16.

Now she was on a cart with a "plank for a seat." (172)

When she went to the guillotine, "every house was closed and every window shut." (213)

Some people insulted her, but others greeted her. (213)

She had "one last look" at her home and "was visibly moved." (213)

The guillotine "was in the Place de la Revolution," and the people had put "a female figure of Liberty" there. (213–214)

She said, "Courage! I have served an apprenticeship to it for a long time; there is no fear of my losing it at this moment." (214)

She ascended the scaffold alone and said, "Lord, enlighten and soften my executioners." (214)

"Her head was shown to the people," and she was buried "in an open coffin among quick-lime." (214)

France paid 31 francs for her burial. (214)

She was 38 when she died (173)

Personal description

She had blue eyes and fair hair. (34) (Could also go under "Married at Versailles at 15")

She was "quick, kind, and tender-hearted." (34) (Could also go under "Married at Versailles at 15")

Madame le Brun said that she was "tall, admirably made, rather fat" with small hands and feet. (172)

She walked well and "carried her head gracefully." (172)

She had royal dignity and majesty, but she was also sweet in appearance. (172–173)

She had irregular features and a "long and narrow oval face." (173)
Her eyes were small and "almost blue." (173)
She had an "intelligent and soft" expression. (173)
She had a "well cut" nose and full lips. (173)
She had a brilliant complexion and transparent skin. (173)
She had "the imposing and majestic air of a goddess." (173)

STEP TWO: **Divide notes into main points (Student Responsibility)**

Student instructions for Step Two:

Now look over your assembled list of notes. Your next step is to divide them into main points, as you did with your notes on Julius Caesar and the process of digestion.

At least three of the facts from the encyclopedia should be followed by three or more details taken from your additional sources. Other facts will have no details at all, as in the following example (the encyclopedia facts are bolded):

Marie was put in the Temple, a fortress in Paris.
She was moved to prison on August 1, 1793.
Her hair lost its color after she was taken prisoner. (173)
The Revolutionary Tribunal condemned her on Oct. 15, 1793.
She was guillotined on Oct. 16.
Now she was on a cart with a "plank for a seat." (172)
When she went to the guillotine, "every house was closed and every window shut." (213)
Some people insulted her, but others greeted her. (213)
She had "one last look" at her home and "was visibly moved." (213)

Your next task: Divide your list into main points.

Each encyclopedia fact that has three or more details after it should be a separate paragraph. But where there are lists of encyclopedia facts with no details, you will need to decide how many facts to put in the same paragraph. Sometimes the only uniting theme in a paragraph of a biographical sketch is that the events all happened within a certain span of time. Remember, from the first lesson this week, that "Between Year X and Year Y" can be a perfectly good way to organize a paragraph!

So as you work on organizing the list into main points, you can use your best judgment. How many facts should you put into a list? Should you organize them by timespan, or look for another way to tie them together?

Try to use between six and eight divisions (not more than eight), not including the personal description. For right now, leave the personal description alone at the bottom of your list. In Step Four, you'll decide where to place it.

If you have trouble, just use your best judgment.

STEP THREE: **Title the main points**

Student instructions for Step Three:

When you have finished dividing your list into main points, give each main point a name.

Everywhere that a fact from the encyclopedia and details from your other sources form a separate, single paragraph, give that main point the name of the encyclopedia fact: for example,

II. Married at Versailles at 15

for

Married at Versailles at 15

Marie left home in 1770 on April 21 to go to France. (32)

She "covered her face with her hands" and cried when she left. (33) . . .

But for main points that contain one or more encyclopedia facts, you will need to choose a name.

Choosing a name will often show you that you need to go back and rethink your divisions. For example, imagine that you had chosen the following division of main points:

V.

Her two favorite ministers were condemned for overspending.

She opposed the Assembly of Notables in 1788.

She opposed the assembling of the States-General in 1789.

The Assembly of Notables said she had caused France's financial trouble.

The Revolution began in May 1789.

VI.

There was an attempted assassination on October 6, 1789, in Versailles.

She tried to make herself popular.

She decided to flee.

You could give Section V the title "Trouble in the government" or "Marie and the French government"—except that the French Revolution doesn't really fit in. But change your division slightly:

V. Marie and the French government

Her two favorite ministers were condemned for overspending.

She opposed the Assembly of Notables in 1788.

She opposed the assembling of the States-General in 1789.

The Assembly of Notables said she had caused France's financial trouble.

VI.

The Revolution began in May 1789.

There was an attempted assassination on October 6, 1789, in Versailles.

She tried to make herself popular.

She decided to flee.

and it fits perfectly. (You can borrow this title and use it in your own assignment.)

You can use "Marie's life from Year X to Year Y" as one title—but *only one.* Your other titles should sum up the events or give the central event.

If you have difficulty, ask your instructor for help. When you're finished, show your work to your instructor before going on.

HOW TO HELP THE STUDENT WITH STEP THREE

The student's finished work should resemble the following:

I. Early life

Marie Antoinette de Lorraine, full name

Youngest daughter of the German emperor Francis I and the queen of Austria, Maria Theresa

Born at Vienna on Nov. 2, 1755

Betrothed to the Dauphin at 14

II. Married at Versailles at 15

Marie left home in 1770 on April 21 to go to France. (32) . . .

III. Becomes queen of France

Dauphin became Louis XVI in May 1774.

"The queen's girdle" was a tax on bread and wine that went to the queen. (148–149)

Marie "remitted this tax" in 1774, but the people soon forgot. (149)

Her enemies circulated rumors and stories about her.

IV. Her good name was damaged by the diamond necklace affair in 1785.

The "Countess de la Motte" convinced Cardinal Rohan to buy an expensive necklace for the queen and give the necklace to her. (149) . . .

V. Marie and the French government

Her two favorite ministers were condemned for overspending.

She opposed the Assembly of Notables in 1788.

She opposed the assembling of the States-General in 1789.

The Assembly of Notables said she had caused France's financial trouble.

VI. Marie and the French Revolution

The Revolution began in May 1789.

There was an attempted assassination on October 6, 1789, in Versailles.

She tried to make herself popular.

She decided to flee.

Louis didn't want to go at first, but then agreed.

They fled at night on June 20, 1791.

They were recognized and captured at Varennes.

VII. Imprisonment and trial

Marie was put in the Temple, a fortress in Paris.

She was moved to prison on August 1, 1793.

Her hair lost its color after she was taken prisoner. (173)

The Revolutionary Tribunal condemned her on Oct. 15, 1793.

VIII. She was guillotined on Oct. 16.

Now she was on a cart with a "plank for a seat." (172) . . .

Personal description

She had blue eyes and fair hair. (34) . . .

Other divisions are possible; for example, "They were recognized and captured at Varennes" could just as well go at the beginning of section VII as at the end of Section VI. If the student's titles and divisions seem to work well together, accept them.

The student may choose to combine encyclopedia facts and details from her notes into one section. For example, I and II could be structured like this:

I. Early life

Marie Antoinette de Lorraine, full name

Youngest daughter of the German emperor Francis I and the queen of Austria, Maria Theresa

Born at Vienna on Nov. 2, 1755

II. Married at Versailles at 15

Betrothed to the Dauphin at 14

Marie left home in 1770 on April 21 to go to France. (32) . . .

In this version, "Betrothed to the Dauphin at 14" becomes one of the details about Marie's marriage at 15. This makes as much logical sense as the first version.

If the student has difficulty, use the suggested titles above to prompt her; for example, say "Which events happened to Marie as queen of France, before the affair of the diamond necklace?"

Where encyclopedia facts and notes come in the same section (as in VII above), it is acceptable for the student to list them all at the same level of importance:

VII. Imprisonment and trial

Marie was put in the Temple, a fortress in Paris.

She was moved to prison on August 1, 1793.

Her hair lost its color after she was taken prisoner. (173)

The Revolutionary Tribunal condemned her on Oct. 15, 1793.

Technically, "Her hair lost its color" is a third-level outline detail that would be assigned an Arabic numeral (B.1) in a finished outline, but the student has not yet studied three-level outlines. The focus of this exercise is on overall organization.

STEP FOUR: **Place the personal description**

Student instructions for Step Four:

> As your final step in constructing this outline, decide where to place the description of Marie Antoinette. Cut and paste it into the outline. Give it the appropriate Roman numeral, and renumber the sections that follow. (If this isn't clear, ask your instructor.)
>
> Now your outline is complete. Tomorrow, you'll use it to write the final biographical sketch.

HOW TO HELP THE STUDENT WITH STEP FOUR

The personal description can go anywhere in the outline EXCEPT:

between I & II (because most of the description is clearly about Marie as a grown woman, not as a 15-year-old girl);

or between IV and V (because the necklace episode and Marie's troubles with the French government *both* made her unpopular, so to insert the description here would break up two very closely related paragraphs in an awkward way).

Wherever the personal description goes, it should be numbered and the following points renumbered, as in the example below:

V. Marie and the French government
VI. Personal description
VII. Marie and the French Revolution
VIII. Imprisonment and trial
IX. She was guillotined on Oct. 16.

The finished outline should have no more than nine points.

Day Four: Practicing the Topos, Part Three: Writing the Biographical Sketch

Focus: Writing from notes organized into an outline

Encourage the student to work independently today. She should show you her composition when it is completely finished, including Works Cited page.

STEP ONE: **Write (Student Responsibility)**

Student instructions for Step One:

Using your notes, write your biographical sketch. Give it the simple title "Marie Antoinette" and follow these guidelines:

1. Write one paragraph for each main point on your outline.
2. Each paragraph should have at least two sentences.
3. The finished composition should be at least 450 words.
4. Use footnotes if you are quoting directly or using ideas from another writer. Historical facts do not need to be documented.
5. Use at least four direct quotes.
6. Quote at least once from each of your three sources.
7. In your descriptive paragraph, use verbs, adjectives, and adverbs to either slant

the description in a positive or negative way, or to support a metaphor that you have chosen.

Remember that you do not have to include everything in your notes. Pick and choose among the details.

Make sure that your paper is double-spaced and that the pages are numbered.

STEP TWO: **Assemble Works Cited page (Student Responsibility)**

Student instructions for Step Two:

On a separate sheet of paper, center the title "Works Cited" at the top of the page. List your sources below in alphabetical order, in proper format.

STEP THREE: **Proofread**

Student instructions for Step Three:

Read your composition out loud. If any sentences sound awkward or unclear, work on rewriting them. Check for correct spelling and punctuation. (If you use the name of a month, spell it out rather than abbreviating.) Check the format of your footnotes.

When you are finished, show your work to your instructor.

HOW TO HELP THE STUDENT WITH STEP THREE

Listen to the student; if she is proofreading silently, remind her to read out loud.

The student's final composition might resemble the one below. You will notice that the prose style is not particularly elegant, and that paragraphs begin and end abruptly. This example is intended to reproduce realistically the level of prose that many students are capable of at this point. The focus in this year's study has been on structure; the goal of this assignment is to walk the student through the steps of researching, organizing, writing, and documenting a composition independently. In the more advanced levels of this course, when the student has had enough practice to do these steps comfortably, more attention will be paid to transitions, phrasing, and other style issues.

In the example below, the descriptive paragraph is slanted in a positive direction (this will be the natural choice for most students).

Marie Antoinette

Marie Antoinette was born in 1755 in Vienna. She was the youngest daughter of the Emperor Francis I and the Queen of Austria, Maria Theresa. At the age of 14, she was betrothed to the French prince.

When she was 15 years old, Marie left home to be married. The people of France greeted her with enthusiasm. She rode to Versailles in a "crimson and gold" carriage and was greeted with "salutes from regiments of cavalry," bells, and fountains filled with wine.[1] But once she was at the palace she became unpopular. She laughed at the court, and the ladies of the court thought that she was "too free in her manners."[2] The French people also resented her because she was Austrian but she would become a French queen.

Marie's husband, the Dauphin, became king in May 1774. Marie was now queen, but her enemies went on telling stories and spreading rumors about her.

In 1785, Marie became even more unpopular because of a scam involving a diamond necklace. A swindler calling herself the "Countess de la Motte" convinced Cardinal Rohan to buy a diamond necklace for Marie.[3] The "Countess" then brought a girl who looked like Marie to meet the Cardinal. Then the "Countess" took the necklace herself. Marie Antoinette knew nothing about this, but the French people blamed her anyway.

Marie also had difficulty with the French government. She was opposed to the Assembly of Notables meeting in 1788, and as soon as the Assembly of Notables met, they blamed her for France's financial troubles.

At this time, Marie was dignified and majestic in appearance. She had brilliant, transparent skin and an intelligent expression. She was a little bit heavy, but she had delicate, graceful hands and feet. Her face was oval, with a well-shaped nose and "full lips."[4]

In 1789, the French Revolution began. Just five months later, an assassin tried to kill Marie at Versailles. She decided to flee from France and convinced Louis to go with her. They tried to escape from the country but they were captured on June 20, 1791, and taken back to Paris.

At first, Marie was imprisoned in the Temple, a Paris fortress. On August 1, two years after her capture, she was moved to prison. On October 15, 1793, the Revolutionary Tribunal condemned her to death.

The day after, Marie was taken to the guillotine on a cart with a "plank for a seat."[5] When she arrived at the guillotine, which was at the Place de la Revolution, she climbed the scaffold alone and said, "Lord, enlighten and soften my executioners."[6] She was beheaded and buried in quick-lime. Marie was only 38 when she died.

---

[1] *Sarah Tytler,* Marie Antoinette: The Woman and the Queen *(Marcus Ward & Co., 1883), p. 34.*

[2] *Willis J. Abbot,* Notable Women in History *(The John C. Winston Co., 1913), p. 148.*

[3] *Abbot, p. 149.*

[4] *M. C. Bishop,* The Prison Life of Marie Antoinette *(Kegan Paul, Trench, Trübner & Co., 1893), p. 173.*

[5] *Bishop, p. 172.*

[6] *Sarah Tytler, p. 214.*

WORKS CITED

Abbot, Willis J. *Notable Women in History.* Philadelphia: The John C. Winston Co., 1913.

Bishop, M. C. *The Prison Life of Marie Antoinette.* London: Kegan Paul, Trench, Trübner & Co., 1893.

Tytler, Sarah. *Marie Antoinette: The Woman and the Queen.* London: Marcus Ward & Co., 1883.

When the student's composition is finished, check it using the following rubric.

Week 31 Rubric
Biographical Sketch with Personal Description

Organization

1 The sketch should have nine paragraphs. Each paragraph should have at least two sentences.
2 The paragraph of description should not be placed between the original paragraphs I and II or IV and V.
3 The paragraph of description should have a clear positive or negative slant OR should use a governing metaphor.
4 The sketch should be at least 450 words in length.
5 The sketch should progress forward chronologically through the events of Marie Antoinette's life.
6 The sketch should include at least four direct quotes, making use of all three sources.

Mechanics

1 Each sentence should make sense on its own when read aloud.
2 Each proper name should be capitalized.
3 Possessive forms should be written properly.
4 Personal pronouns should have clear antecedents and be of the proper gender.
5 Verb tense should be consistent throughout.
6 Subjects and verbs must be in agreement.
7 Direct quotes should be properly footnoted.
8 The Works Cited page should be organized alphabetically and entries formatted properly.
9 The paper must be double-spaced and the pages must be numbered.

Part VI

BEGINNING LITERARY CRITICISM: POETRY WRITING ABOUT POEMS WEEKS 32–34

Overview of Weeks 32–34

In Part IV of this course, the student practiced basic literary criticism by writing about stories. In the next three weeks, she will practice the same skills on poetry.

Poetry is very different than fiction. In poetry, the writer pays just as much attention to the *form* of the words as to the *content*; the sound and rhythm of every single syllable are important. And the words the writer chooses are absolutely central to the poem's meaning. In poetry, the words can't be separated from the ideas.

Because poems are so much shorter than stories, each word becomes much more important. To pack as much meaning as possible into fewer words, poets use many different strategies: meter, rhyme, alliteration, metaphors, similes, and much more.

When the student begins to write about poems, she will write about their meaning. But since meaning and words are so closely tied together, she'll also have to write about the words and techniques that the poet uses. In the next three weeks, the student will practice putting these elements together into short essays about poems.

This brief unit is not intended as a literature study; explanations of the forms used are included, but the unit doesn't offer a survey of poetic forms or techniques. (This is usually covered in a literature study.) The unit has two purposes: to give the student beginning direction in how to approach a poem and what questions to ask; and to make the student more alert to the rhythms and sounds of the English language overall.

WEEK 32: SOUND

Day One: Read

Focus: Reading

The student's first step is to read.

Although today's work will be done independently, check to make sure that the student has looked up unfamiliar words in the dictionary and has also followed the reading directions closely.

Student instructions for Step One:

> Turn to Appendix IV. The first poem you'll see is "The Bells," by Edgar Allan Poe. You should know something about Poe; you wrote a biographical sketch about him back in Week Nineteen. However, you don't really need to know anything about Poe to understand this poem.
>
> Start by reading "The Bells" four times from beginning to end, closely following these instructions.
>
> STEP ONE: Read silently
>
> Read the poem silently and slowly. Stop and look up the meanings and pronunciations of all words you don't know.
>
> STEP TWO: Read out loud
>
> Go to a private place and read the poem out loud, at a normal pace, listening to the sounds. (You can do this in front of a sibling or someone else if you'd rather, but most people prefer to be alone.)
>
> STEP THREE: Read for punctuation
>
> Read the poem out loud again. This time, pay attention to the punctuation marks. Pause briefly at each comma and dash. Pause for a longer time at each period. When there's an exclamation point, raise your voice.
>
> STEP FOUR: Read for effect
>
> Read the poem out loud one more time, as quickly as possible. If you can, record yourself and listen to the recording.

Day Two: Analyze

Focus: Understanding how sound is used in the poem

The purpose of this lesson is not to cover every single device used in the poem, but to make the student more alert to sounds within poetry.

The student will need four different colored pencils.

STEP ONE: **Examine the overall form**

Student instructions for Step One:

> In poetry, words and meaning are tied together—so before you can write anything about the poem's meaning, you have to become familiar with the words and techniques the poet uses.
>
> Let's start with the overall form of the poem. It's divided into four *stanzas,* or groups of lines. On your Literary Terms chart in the Reference section of your notebook, add the following definition.
>
> stanza: a group of lines within a poem
>
> "The Bells" is *free verse,* meaning that Edgar Allan Poe did not force the poem to follow a strict pattern of rhythm and rhyme. Look at the first three lines of the poem. In the margin next to the poem, write how many syllables each line has. (If you have trouble, ask your instructor for help.)
>
> Do you see how unequal the lines are?
>
> In the same way, Poe doesn't follow a particular pattern of rhyme. Look at the sounds that end the first five lines of the first stanza, and the sounds that end the first five lines of the second stanza:

I.		II.	
	bells		bells
	bells		bells
	foretells		foretells
	tinkle		night
	night		delight

> There's plenty of rhyming here, but in the first stanza, lines 4 and 5 don't rhyme; in the second, they do. The pattern isn't the same.
>
> Before moving on, show the number of syllables you came up with to your instructor.

HOW TO HELP THE STUDENT WITH STEP ONE

You may need to remind the student that a syllable is the smallest part of a word—the part that takes one beat or clap to say. You can illustrate by saying the word *tin-tin-na-bu-la-tion,* pausing at each dash. Clap your hands as you say each syllable (six claps for the six syllables).

The student should have written the following number of syllables next to the first three lines of the poem:

7 Hear the sledges with the bells—
3 Silver bells!
13 What a world of merriment their melody foretells!

STEP TWO: **Understand onomatopoeia**

Student instructions for Step Two:

> Instead of regular rhythm and rhyme, this poem is all about sound—at least four different kinds of sound.
>
> The first kind of sound this poem uses is *onomatopoeia*—when a word sounds like its meaning. Say the word "groan" out loud and notice how the word itself sounds like the sound a groaning person would make. Read the following onomatopoeic words out loud, listening carefully to yourself: *pop, crunch, meow, boom, slurp, buzz.*
>
> On your Literary Terms chart in the Reference section of your notebook, add the following definition.
>
> onomatopoeia: when a word sounds like its meaning
>
> It may help you remember the term to know that *onoma* is Greek for "name" and *poiein* is Greek for "to make," so an onomatopoeic word is a name that's been made to go along with its meaning. In the first stanza, Poe made up the word *tintinnabulation* to represent bells ringing. You can find it in the dictionary now—but Poe was the first to use it.
>
> Go through "The Bells" now with your first colored pencil and underline each onomatopoeic word. If the word repeats within the same stanza, you only need to underline it the first time.
>
> When you are finished, show your work to your instructor before going on.

HOW TO HELP THE STUDENT WITH STEP TWO

The student should have underlined the following onomatopoeic words in the poem (only the lines with underlined words are reproduced). If he missed one, point it out and have him underline it.

There is room for disagreement here; if the student identifies an additional word as onomatopoeia, accept it as long as he is able to explain his reasoning.

I
How they <u>tinkle</u>, tinkle, tinkle,
To the <u>tintinnabulation</u> that so musically wells
From the <u>jingling</u> and the <u>tinkling</u> of the bells.

II
What a <u>gush</u> of euphony voluminously wells!
To the rhyming and the <u>chiming</u> of the bells!

III
How they scream out their affright!
They can only shriek, shriek,
How they clang, and clash, and roar!
By the twanging,
And the clanging,
In the jangling,
In the clamor and the clangor of the bells!

IV
Hear the tolling of the bells—
Is a groan.
In that muffled monotone,
And their king it is who tolls;
To the throbbing of the bells— (optional; there is disagreement over this word)
To the moaning and the groaning of the bells.

STEP THREE: **Look for repetition**

Student instructions for Step Three:

> The poem also uses *exact repetition.* When you repeat the same word several times in a row, you create a new sound effect.
>
> The most obvious repetition in this poem is found in the final lines of each stanza, when Poe writes the word *bells* over and over again—seven times in the first stanza, ten in the second, eight in the third, and in the fourth stanza three times, three times again, and then seven times. And that's not even counting all the *other* times he writes the word *bells.*
>
> Go through the poem with a second colored pencil and underline every place where words are repeated more than one time in a row—*not* including the word "bells." Some words may be underlined twice if you've already underlined them in the first step.
>
> On the lines below, write the answer to these two questions:
>
> What series of words occurs more than once?
>
> Where does it occur, and how many times?
>
> When you are finished, show your work to your instructor before going on.

HOW TO HELP THE STUDENT WITH STEP THREE

The student should have underlined the following repeated words.

I
How they tinkle, tinkle, tinkle,
Keeping time, time, time,

III
They can only shriek, shriek,
Leaping higher, higher, higher

IV
And who, tolling, tolling, tolling,
And he rolls, rolls, rolls,
Rolls
Keeping time, time, time,
Keeping time, time, time,
Keeping time, time, time,
As he knells, knells, knells

The repetition *time, time, time* occurs in the first stanza once, and in the fourth stanza three times.

STEP FOUR: **Look for repeated rhymes**

Student instructions for Step Four:

> The poem uses *repeated rhymes*. These don't always come at the end of the lines; sometimes they occur in the middle, or in the next to last word. But the sameness of the sounds creates a third kind of sound effect.
>
> Look at the first stanza. The first line ends with the word *bells*. With your third colored pencil, underline all occurences of the word *bells* as well as the words *foretells* and *wells*. The repetition of those rhyming sounds affects the meaning of the poem.
>
> Go through the entire poem and with your third colored pencil underline all the words that have repeated rhyming sounds. Some words may end up being underlined twice. In the first stanza, for example, you would underline *tinkle, tinkle, tinkle* for a second time, as well as *oversprinkle* and *twinkle*—and the first occurence of *tinkle* should be underlined three times, since that word is also an example of onomatopoeia.
>
> When you're finished, show your work to your instructor.

HOW TO HELP THE STUDENT WITH STEP FOUR

When the student is finished with underlining, his poem should resemble the version below. Note that internal rhymes, such as the long *o* sound in "molten-golden notes," have not been underlined. This is an introductory exercise, so the student isn't required to identify internal rhymes, but if he underlines these words, accept them as well.

"The Bells"
Edgar Allan Poe

I
Hear the sledges with the bells—
Silver bells!
What a world of merriment their melody foretells!
How they tinkle, tinkle, tinkle,
In the icy air of night!
While the stars that oversprinkle

All the heavens, seem to twinkle
With a crystalline delight;
Keeping time, time, time,
In a sort of Runic rhyme,
To the tintinnabulation that so musically wells
From the bells, bells, bells, bells,
Bells, bells, bells—
From the jingling and the tinkling of the bells.

II
Hear the mellow wedding bells,
Golden bells!
What a world of happiness their harmony foretells!
Through the balmy air of night
How they ring out their delight!
From the molten-golden notes,
And all in tune,
What a liquid ditty floats
To the turtle-dove that listens, while she gloats
On the moon!
Oh, from out the sounding cells,
What a gush of euphony voluminously wells!
How it swells!
How it dwells
On the Future! how it tells
Of the rapture that impels
To the swinging and the ringing
Of the bells, bells, bells,
Of the bells, bells, bells, bells,
Bells, bells, bells—
To the rhyming and the chiming of the bells!

III
Hear the loud alarum bells—
Brazen bells!
What a tale of terror, now, their turbulency tells!
In the startled ear of night
How they scream out their affright!
Too much horrified to speak,
They can only shriek, shriek,
Out of tune,
In a clamorous appealing to the mercy of the fire,

In a mad expostulation with the deaf and frantic fire,
Leaping higher, higher, higher,
With a desperate desire,
And a resolute endeavor,
Now-now to sit or never,
By the side of the pale-faced moon.
Oh, the bells, bells, bells!
What a tale their terror tells
Of Despair!
How they clang, and clash, and roar!
What a horror they outpour
On the bosom of the palpitating air!
Yet the ear it fully knows,
By the twanging,
And the clanging,
How the danger ebbs and flows:
Yet the ear distinctly tells,
In the jangling,
And the wrangling,
How the danger sinks and swells,
By the sinking or the swelling in the anger of the bells—
Of the bells—
Of the bells, bells, bells, bells,
Bells, bells, bells—
In the clamor and the clangor of the bells!

IV
Hear the tolling of the bells—
Iron Bells!
What a world of solemn thought their monody compels!
In the silence of the night,
How we shiver with affright
At the melancholy menace of their tone!
For every sound that floats
From the rust within their throats
Is a groan.
And the people—ah, the people—
They that dwell up in the steeple,
All Alone
And who, tolling, tolling, tolling,
In that muffled monotone,
Feel a glory in so rolling

On the human heart a stone—
They are neither man nor woman—
They are neither brute nor human—
They are Ghouls:
And their king it is who tolls;
And he rolls, rolls, rolls,
Rolls
A paean from the bells!
And his merry bosom swells
With the paean of the bells!
And he dances, and he yells;
Keeping time, time, time,
In a sort of Runic rhyme,
To the paean of the bells—
Of the bells:
Keeping time, time, time,
In a sort of Runic rhyme,
To the throbbing of the bells—
Of the bells, bells, bells—
To the sobbing of the bells;
Keeping time, time, time,
As he knells, knells, knells,
In a happy Runic rhyme,
To the rolling of the bells—
Of the bells, bells, bells:
To the tolling of the bells,
Of the bells, bells, bells, bells—
Bells, bells, bells—
To the moaning and the groaning of the bells.

STEP FIVE: **Find examples of alliteration**

Student instructions for Step Five:

> The poem uses *alliteration.* Alliteration happens when two or more words within a group of words begin with the same sound or sounds.
>
> On your Literary Terms chart in the Reference section of your notebook, add the following definition.
>
> alliteration: when words begin with the same sound or sounds
>
> In the first stanza, "merriment" and "melody" show alliteration. So does the phrase "Runic rhyme." With your fourth colored pencil, circle the opening *m*'s and *r*'s of these words.
>
> Now go through the next three stanzas and circle the opening letters of any words that

show alliteration. Look for words that occur in the same line. Don't circle the opening letters of repeated words.

Now glance back over your underlinings and circles and notice how many words in this poem have been carefully chosen for their *sound*.

When you are finished, show your work to your instructor.

HOW TO HELP THE STUDENT WITH STEP FIVE

The student should have circled the opening sounds of the bolded words in the lines below:

II
What a world of **happiness** their **harmony** foretells!
Oh, from out the **sounding cells,**

III
Brazen bells!
What a **tale** of **terror,** now, their **turbulency tells**!
In a mad expostulation with the deaf and **frantic fire,**
With a **desperate desire,**
Now—**now** to sit or **never,**
What a **tale** their **terror tells**
How they **clang,** and **clash,** and roar!
How the danger **sinks** and **swells,**
By the **sinking** or the **swelling** in the anger of the bells—
In the **clamor** and the **clangor** of the bells!

IV
What a world of solemn **thought their** monody compels!
At the **melancholy menace** of their tone!
From the rust within **their throats**
All Alone
In that **muffled monotone,**
On the **human heart** a stone-
In a sort of **Runic rhyme,**
In a happy **Runic rhyme,**

Day Three: Think

Focus: Connecting form and meaning

Today you will talk to the student about the poem; talking will prepare the student for tomorrow's writing assignment.

In the first step, the student is told "Most poems don't begin and end in the same place. Something happens, or *changes*, during the poem." This is an excellent starting place for the beginning writer—but, like all general statements, this one has plenty of exceptions. Of course there are poems that don't have forward movement, but many of those poems are *about* the lack of movement.

Instead of confusing the student with a too-complex introduction to poetry, I've chosen to start with this very basic and sweeping statement. When the student is more comfortable writing about poetry, a more nuanced and complex method can be introduced.

STEP ONE: **Understand the difference between stories and poems (Student Responsibility)**

Student instructions for Step One:

> When you learned how to write about stories, you started out by writing a summary of events—a plot summary. But although some poems tell stories, many others do not. Instead, they describe experiences, places, sensations, objects, moods, emotions, feelings, ideas, and many other things.
>
> Think about "Rikki-Tikki-Tavi," the first story you read when you were learning how to write about literature. That story had a very clear beginning (Rikki-tikki-tavi went to live with the family), middle (the cobras wanted the family out of the bungalow), and end (Rikki killed the cobras). Compare that with the first six lines of "The Daffodils," by the nineteenth-century poet William Wordsworth:
>
> I wander'd lonely as a cloud
> That floats on high o'er vales and hills,
> When all at once I saw a crowd,
> A host, of golden daffodils;
> Beside the lake, beneath the trees,
> Fluttering and dancing in the breeze.
>
> How would you write a "plot summary" of that poem? You couldn't, because you can't really find a protagonist, antagonist, or conflict in "The Daffodils." The poet is, instead, just looking at the daffodils.
>
> So how do you begin to write about a poem? Instead of asking "What happens?" ask yourself "How does this poem move forward?"
>
> Most poems don't begin and end in the same place. Something happens, or *changes,* during the poem. For a very simple (and ridiculous) example, consider this:
>
> There was an old man from Peru,
> Who dreamed he was eating his shoe.
> He woke in the night
> With a terrible fright,
> And found it was perfectly true.
>
> At the beginning of the poem, the old man from Peru doesn't know that he's eating his shoe. At the end, he does. Things have changed.
>
> In the next two steps, your instructor will carry on a dialogue with you. During these dialogues, you'll fill out the charts below. These charts will help you construct your short essay tomorrow.

STEP TWO: **Examine the movement of the poem**

Carry on the following dialogue with the student.

Instructor: First, we're going to try to identify the movement of a poem. You can usually find clues to this movement by looking for repetition. This poem is *full* of repetition. What word is repeated more than any other?

Student: Bells

Instructor: So we'll start by looking at the bells. Movement happens when something in the poem is repeated—but changes slightly each time. In this poem there are four different kinds of bells. Look at the first three stanzas only. What kind of bell is each stanza about?

Student: Sledge bells, wedding bells, alarm bells

Note to Instructor: If the student says "Silver bells" or "Golden bells," say "That's the material the bell is *made out of.* Look at the first line to tell me what kind of bell it *is.*"

Instructor: Write those answers on the lines in your workbook. Now, for the first three stanzas only, what is the bell made out of?

Student: Silver, gold, brass.

Instructor: Write those answers on the lines in your workbook. You've seen the same repetition in the first and second lines of each stanza—a kind of bell in the first line, and the material it's made of in the second. There's also repetition in the third line of each stanza. Read the third line of each stanza out loud.

Student: What a world of merriment their melody foretells! What a world of happiness their harmony foretells! What a tale of terror, now, their turbulency tells!

Instructor: On the lines in your workbook, write the emotion named in each stanza. Now let's look at the fourth stanza. One of those three answers is missing. Which one is it?

Student: The kind of bell

Note to Instructor: If the student can't answer, continue on to the next question anyway.

Instructor: What are the bells made of?

Student: Iron

Instructor: What emotion is named?

Student: Solemnity ["Solemn thought" is acceptable]

Instructor: It looks as though Poe wants you to decide for yourself what kind of bells these are. Any guesses?

Student: [Answers will vary. If the student guesses "Funeral," say "Probably so!" and continue on with the dialogue as written.]

Instructor: Out of the four bells, which one is made of the most valuable metal?

Student: The golden/wedding bells

Instructor: So in the poem, the second stanza—the wedding—is the high point. Write "wedding day" on the last blank under II. in your workbook. Now look back to the first stanza. Silver is valuable—just not quite as valuable as gold. And merriment is a wonderful emotion—but it's not quite as deep as happiness. What time of life, or period of life, comes before the wedding day, is precious (although not quite as precious as getting married), and is filled with merriment?

Student: Childhood or *youth*

Note to Instructor: If the student cannot answer, say "This would be the time when you are too *young* to get married."

Instructor: Write that on the last blank under I. Now look back at your answers so far. We have childhood, wedding day . . . and then do things get better or worse?

Student: Worse

Instructor: Absolutely! Bronze is worth less than gold *or* silver.? Happiness turns into terror. An alarm starts to ring. What part of life do you think *this* is?

Student: [Answers will vary, but should be some variation on "old age," "aging," "getting sick," "getting older." If necessary, prompt the student by saying "If you were young in the first stanza, and then older in the second stanza, what might still be happening? You are still getting . . ."]

Note to Instructor: If the student says "Getting married was a bad idea" (or some variation), say, "But that's not a part of life."

Instructor: Write "getting older" on the last blank under III. Now it's time to come to a conclusion about the fourth stanza. It should be pretty clear now why those iron bells are so mournful. What comes after getting older . . . and older . . . and older?

Student: Death

Instructor: Write "death" [or "dying"] on the last blank under IV. What kind of bells are these?

Student: Funeral bells

Instructor: Now you've seen the movement of the poem. It moves through *time*. Do you remember which three words were repeated once in Stanza I—and then *three times* in Stanza IV? Look back at the last lesson if you don't remember.

Student: Time, time, time

Instructor: In both the first and last stanzas, the poem tells you that it is moving through *time*.

Note to Instructor: The student's completed chart should resemble the following:

	I.	II.	III.	IV.
KIND	*Sledge*	*Wedding*	*Alarm*	*Funeral*
MATERIAL	*Silver*	*Gold*	*Bronze*	*Iron*
EMOTION	*Merriment*	*Happiness*	*Terror*	*Solemn thought*
TIME	*Childhood/youth*	*Wedding day*	*Old age*	*Death*

STEP THREE: **Understand the connection between form and meaning**

Carry on the following dialogue with the student.

Instructor: Let's look now at how the form of the poem—the words and the patterns—affect its meaning. In the first stanza, read out loud every underlined word except for *bells* and the word that rhymes with it—*wells*.

Student: Tinkle, tinkle, tinkle, night, oversprinkle, twinkle, delight, time, time, time, rhyme, tintinnabulation, jingling, tinkling

Instructor: Every single one of those words has a variation of the same vowel sound. What is it?

Student: I

Instructor: Every word has either a short or long *i* sound in it. The poem uses this sound to represent "merry childhood." The i-sound words are all very light and cheerful: sprinkle, delight, jingling, tinkling. "Twinkle" is a childish word as well. What nursery rhyme does it remind you of?

Student: "Twinkle, Twinkle, Little Star."

Instructor: On your chart, write "Childhood" next to "Time" and "-i" next to "vowel sound." Write "tinkle, oversprinkle, twinkle, delight, jingling, tinkling" on the line that follows "Words used." Write "light, cheerful, reminds me of a nursery rhyme" on the lines that follow "Effect." We will do this for the next three stanzas as well.

Note to Instructor: For the next three stanzas, remind the student to fill out the chart as you progress through the dialogues. If you are unsure what to include, look at the key below and prompt the student as necessary.

Instructor: Now look at the second stanza. Read me all the underlined words that do *not* rhyme with *bells*.

Student: Night, delight, notes, tune, floats, gloats, moon, swinging, ringing, rhyming, chiming

Instructor: There are still some words with i-vowels in that list, but the poem tells you that it's moving on to the next time period by introducing new vowel sounds. What vowel is it?

Student: O

Note to Instructor: The long *o* and *oo* sounds both fall into the category of o-sounds.

Instructor: The o sounds are slower [draw the word out] and more grown-up. Some critics have called them "richer" and "more resonant" than the i sounds—meaning that they last longer and have more power.

Note to Instructor: You can encourage the student to find his own adjectives for these longer -o sounds, but it is acceptable for him to simply write "slower, richer, more resonant" on his chart.

Instructor: Look at the third stanza. This stanza has both i-vowel sounds and o-vowel sounds. Read me the words with i-vowel sounds.

Student: Night, affright, fire, higher, desire

Note to Instructor: If the student includes *scream* and *shriek,* explain that these are e-sounds, not i-sounds. *Fire* is an i-sound that includes an r-sound.

Instructor: What words have long *o* and *oo* sounds?

Student: Tune, moon, roar, outpour, knows, flows

Instructor: Notice how each stanza repeats the sounds from the stanza before—and then adds new sounds as well. What words in this stanza have the same vowel sound as *scream*?

Student: Speak, shriek

Instructor. What does someone say when they scream in fright?

Student: Eek!

Instructor: The stanza uses these vowels to show alarm and terror. It also introduces a second new vowel sound—the one in the syllable *ang.* What words have the *ang* sound in them?

Student: Clang, twanging, clanging, jangling, wrangling, clangor

Instructor: These sounds represent a bell clanging. So the two new vowel sounds both remind you that bells are clanging in terror and fright. Now look at the underlined words in the final stanza. Which ones have the same vowel sound as *groan*?

Student: Tolling, tone, floats, throats, alone, monotone, rolling, stone, rolls, moaning, groaning

Instructor: The second stanza had some of those long *o* sounds in it—but they were mixed with *oo*-sounds and plenty of *i*-sounds. This last stanza is filled with groaning [draw the word out] and moaning sounds—because that's what you do at a funeral.

Note to Instructor: The student's completed chart should resemble the following. Prompt him where necessary.

I	**TIME:** *Childhood*	**VOWEL SOUND** *i*
WORDS USED	*Tinkle, night, oversprinkle, twinkle, delight, time, time, time, rhyme, tintinnabulation, jingling, tinkling*	
EFFECT	Light, cheerful, reminds me of a nursery rhyme, childish	
II	**TIME:** *Wedding day*	**VOWEL SOUND** *o*
WORDS USED	*Notes, tune, floats, gloats, moon*	
EFFECT	Slower, richer, more resonant	
III	**TIME:** *Growing older*	**VOWEL SOUND** *ee and ang*
WORDS USED	*Scream, speak, shriek, clang, twanging, clanging, jangling, wrangling, clangor*	
EFFECT	Alarm, terror, fright, clanging bell	
IV	**TIME:** *Death*	**VOWEL SOUND** *o*
WORDS USED	*Tolling, tone, floats, throats, alone, monotone, rolling, stone, rolls, moaning, groaning*	
EFFECT	Groaning and moaning	

Day Four: Write

Focus: Writing about the poem

Although Step One should be completed independently, you may need to review the proper form for quoting a poem.

STEP ONE: Understand proper form for quoting a poem (Student Responsibility)

Student instructions for Step One:

> Before you begin to write, read carefully through the following instructions on how to quote poetry directly.
>
> When you cite a classic poem—one that has been reprinted in many different places over many different years—you don't need to give an actual book title along with publication

information and page numbers. Instead, you need to identify the poem clearly in the introduction to your essay (we'll cover that in Step Three) and then include, in parentheses after the quote, the number of the line within the poem that your quote is drawn from:

> The poem describes the "moaning and the groaning of the bells" (113).

To the right of "The Bells" in your poetry appendix, you'll see line numbers that occur every five lines. In very long poems, you will often find line numbers printed in the text to make citatation easier. (For shorter poems, you'll have to count the lines yourself.)

Notice that the parenthesis goes outside the closing quotation mark, but inside the closing punctuation mark.

If you quote two or three consecutive lines from a poem, use a forward slash mark followed by a space to show the division between the lines. Use exactly the same punctuation as the original except in the last line; you should just drop the punctuation on that line.

For example:

> "The Bells" describes the "people" who live in the steeple as "neither man nor woman—/ They are neither brute nor human—/ They are Ghouls" (86–88).

Notice that the quote keeps the dashes after *woman* and *human* but drops the semicolon after *Ghouls*.

If you quote four or more lines from a poem, double-space down, indent twice, and reproduce the lines exactly as they appear in the poem. This is called a "block quote" and looks like this:

> The king of the Ghouls tolls the bell and does much more:
> And his merry bosom swells
> With the paean of the bells!
> And he dances and he yells;
> Keeping time, time, time (93-96).

Notice that there are no quotation marks. Indenting twice shows that you are quoting, so the punctuation isn't needed.

In a block quote, you can drop the last punctuation mark, just as in a shorter quote. In the original, there is a comma after the last "time." That comma has been dropped. Since the quote ends after the line citation, a period goes after the closing parenthesis.

STEP TWO: **Write one paragraph for each stanza**

Student instructions for Step Two:

Put your two charts side by side with your marked-up copy of the poem. Use these to write four paragraphs about the poem, one for each stanza. Each paragraph should tell the reader (not necessarily in this order):

1. The type of bell/what the bell is made of/why this is important
2. The time of life the bell represents
3. The emotion/state of mind in the stanza
4. What words, sounds, and rhymes in the passage help to make this clear

Here is an example for you: the first paragraph, written about the first stanza. You can use this first paragraph in your own composition, and model your other three paragraphs after it.

> The bells in the first stanza are silver sleigh bells, which represent childhood. Silver isn't as expensive as gold, but it is still valuable—just as

> youth is valuable, but not as important as the next phase of life. The silver bells are merry and delighted, like children at play. The poem uses *i*-sounds, cheerful verbs such as "twinkle," and phrases like "jingling and tinkling" (14) to make us think about childhood.

Make a run at three paragraphs of your own. (You can also write your own first paragraph, if you'd rather.) Your paragraphs can be as simple as the example, or use much more detail.

In each paragraph, quote at least once from the stanza you are writing about. Your quote should have at least three words in it; you can quote single words (as in the example above) but this doesn't count towards your total.

At least one of your quotes should be four or more lines and set as a block quote.

When you are finished, show your work to your instructor.

HOW TO HELP THE STUDENT WITH STEP TWO

The example given is simple, but represents the prose you can realistically expect from a student at this level. A more detailed and subtle paragraph might sound like this:

> *In the first paragraph of "The Bells," the poet uses both short and long sounds of the vowel* i *to represent the merriment and delight of childhood. The silver sledge bells "tinkle, tinkle, tinkle" (4) in a lighthearted fashion, and the stars above "twinkle/ With a crystalline delight," (7–8) reminding us of the nursery rhyme "Twinkle, Twinkle, Little Star." The silver that makes up the bells is a valuable metal, but not as precious as gold—also reminding us that childhood is precious, but not as valuable as adulthood.*

It is important not to demand that beginning writers, making their first attempt to analyze poems, produce paragraphs like the one above. If the paragraphs are grammatical and cover the requirements in the assignment, don't worry about awkward constructions, repetitions, and missing transitions; these skills will be covered in further levels of this course. Requiring a beginner to perform at a high level the first time out will simply paralyze him.

It is completely reasonable at this stage for the student to produce sentence-by-sentence imitations of the sample paragraph. For example, an acceptable second paragraph on the second stanza might be:

> *The bells in the second stanza are golden wedding bells, which represent the wedding day. Gold is even more valuable than silver. This shows us that the wedding day is more valuable than childhood. The wedding bells are slower, richer, and more resonant than the silver bells. The poem uses o-sounds in words such as "floats" and "gloats," and phrases like "molten-golden notes" (20) to make us think about the happiness of the wedding day.*

In fact, if the student has difficulty, you should encourage him to imitate the model, sentence by sentence. Writing about poems is excruciatingly difficult for many young students; they may need to copy a model many times before feeling comfortable enough to strike out on their own.

Copying the model won't stifle their creativity. Eventually, it will give them the confidence to exercise it.

When the student shows you his paragraphs, do not criticize them in detail. Instead, check to see that the following criteria have been met:

1. There are four paragraphs.
2. Each paragraph mentions:
   a. The time of life (childhood/marriage/old age/death)
   b. The emotion (merriment/happiness/terror/solemnity)
   c. The words or sounds specific to that paragraph (i/o/e *and* ang/long o)
   d. At least one word in the stanza that helps with the effect
3. Each paragraph quotes the stanza it discusses at least once, in the correct format described above. At least one of the quotes should be more than three lines and set in block format.

STEP THREE: **Write an introduction and assemble your essay**

Student instructions for Step Three:

> You should now have four paragraphs discussing the four stanzas of "The Bells"—but you don't yet have an essay.
>
> In order to have an essay, you need an introduction and conclusion.
>
> Your introduction only needs to be one sentence long (although you can make it longer if you want to). It should include the following information:
>
> 1. The name and the author of the poem. Remember that the titles of poems are put in quotation marks, while the titles of books are italicized (or underlined, if you're writing by hand).
> 2. The main topic, idea, or theme of the poem.
>
> If you have difficulty, ask your instructor for help.
>
> When you are finished, put your introduction at the beginning of your essay. It can either stand as its own paragraph or else be the first line of your existing first paragraph. Read your composition out loud, listening for awkward phrases and sentences that might not make sense. Then read it one more time silently, looking for misspelled words and incorrect punctuation.
>
> When you are finished, show your composition to your instructor.

HOW TO HELP THE STUDENT WITH STEP THREE

The introduction should be simple and straightforward; if the student begins to include too much information (for example, discussion about the vowel sounds and how they affect the poem), remind her that the introduction shouldn't repeat information found later in the essay.

Acceptable introductions might be:

> *In "The Bells," Edgar Allan Poe describes four stages of life, from childhood through death.*
>
> *The poem "The Bells," by Edgar Allan Poe, uses four different kind of bells to stand*

for the four stages of life.

Edgar Allan Poe's poem "The Bells" has four stanzas. Each stanza is about the sounds made by a different kind of bell, and each bell represents a different part of life.

If the student needs additional help, give him this template:

In (poem), (the author) describes (four whats?).

Remind him that the four bells are not the main theme of the poem—they *represent* the main theme.

When the student is finished, check his essay using the following rubric.

Week 32 Rubric
Brief Poem Essay

Organization

1 The essay should begin with an introduction that gives the poem's title, the author, and the information that the poem is about the four stages of life.
2 There should be four paragraphs, one for each stanza.
3 Each paragraph should mention the time of life, the type of bell, the emotion/mood of the stanza, the vowel sounds used, and at least one specific word that contains that vowel sound.
4 Each paragraph should contain a direct quote from the poem.
5 At least one quote should be four lines or longer.

Mechanics

1 Each sentence should make sense on its own when read aloud.
2 Possessive forms should be written properly.
3 Verb tense should be consistent throughout.
4 Subjects and verbs must be in agreement.
5 Antecedents of pronouns should be clear.
6 Unnecessary repetition of the same nouns, adjectives, and proper names should be avoided.
7 The title of the poem should be in quotation marks.
8 Direct quotes should be incorporated into full sentences and should be properly punctuated.
9 Quotes longer than three lines should be set as blocks.

SUMMARY OF CORRECT FORMAT FOR QUOTING A POEM:

For one to three lines of poetry:

Use quotation marks.

In the third stanza, the alarm bells "shriek, shriek" (42).

For more than one line, place a slash followed by a space at the end of each line.

Keep ending punctuation in all lines but the last.

End the quote with " (line number).

Use ellipses to show where words have been left out

In the third stanza, the alarm bells "shriek, shriek,/ Out of tune . . . / In a mad expostulation with the deaf and frantic fire" (42–45).

For four or more lines of poetry:

Block indent ten spaces from the left margin and reproduce the poem as written.

In the third stanza, the alarm bells
shriek, shriek,
Out of tune,
In a clamorous appealing to the mercy of the fire,
In a mad expostulation with the deaf and frantic fire (42–45).

Place (line number) after the final period.

If the last line does not end with a period, cut original punctuation and use (line number).

If the quote starts halfway through a line, indent the first line but do not use ellipses.

If an entire line is eliminated, use a line of ellipses.

In the third stanza, the alarm bells
shriek, shriek,
Out of tune,
In a clamorous appealing to the mercy of the fire,
....
Leaping higher, higher, higher (42–46).

Week 33: Meter

Day One: Read

Focus: Reading

Today's work on "Ozymandias," by Percy Bysshe Shelley, will be done independently. However, check to make sure that the student has looked up unfamiliar words in the dictionary and has also followed the reading directions closely.

Student instructions for Day One:

STEP ONE: Read silently

Read the poem silently and slowly. Stop and look up the meanings and pronunciations of all words you don't know.

STEP TWO: Read out loud

Go to a private place and read the poem out loud, at a normal pace, listening to the sounds. (You can do this in front of a sibling or someone else if you'd prefer.) Pause briefly at the end of each line so that you can hear the rhythm of the poem's individual lines.

STEP THREE: Read for punctuation

Read the poem out loud again. This time, pay attention to the punctuation marks. Pause briefly at each comma and dash. Pause for a longer time at each period. When there's an exclamation point, raise your voice.

Do not stop at the end of a line if there is no punctuation. So you would read "Near them on the sand, [PAUSE] half sunk, [PAUSE] a shattered visage lies." But you would read, "Two vast and trunkless legs of stone Stand in the desert [NO PAUSE].

STEP FOUR: Read for dialogue

Read the poem out loud one more time. This time, use three different voices: one for the narrator (the "I" in the first line), a second for the traveller, and a third for the words on the pedestal (Ozymandias).

Day Two: Analyze

Focus: Understanding meter and sonnet form

Last week's poem was free verse; the lines did not follow a regular pattern of rhythm or rhyme. This week, the student will study the opposite: a sonnet, which has an extremely *strict* pattern of both rhythm *and* rhyme.

STEP ONE: **Understand meter (Student Responsibility)**

Student instructions for Step One:

The rhythm that a poem follows is called its *meter*. The word "meter" means "measure," and to find the meter of a poem you measure each line by counting the syllables.

That's not all you do, though. To find meter, you also have to learn the difference between *stressed* and *unstressed* syllables.

Say the following words out loud. Emphasize the bolded syllables by making your voice just a little more forceful, but use a normal tone of voice on the syllables in regular type.

an a lyze
hum ming bird
to **ma** to
fan **tas** tic
mem **or** i al
vo lun **teer**
po li **ti** cian

The bolded syllables above are stressed syllables—places where your voice naturally wants to put more emphasis. Most English words have one syllable that should be stressed. If you stress the wrong syllable, the word sounds odd. Read these words again, once more emphasizing the bolded syllable.

an **a** lyze
hum **ming** bird
to ma to
fan tas **tic**
mem or **i** al
vo **lun** teer
po **li** ti cian

When you put the stress on a different syllable, the word sounds awkward and wrong.

The meter of a line of poetry is created by a particular pattern of stressed and unstressed syllables. Read the lines of the following poems out loud, stressing each bolded syllable.

Come **live** with **me** and **be** my **love**	(Christopher Marlowe)
Now **came** still **eve**ning **on,** and **twi**light **gray**	(John Milton)
What a **world** of **merriment** their **melody** fore**tells**	(Edgar Allan Poe)
Like the **leaves** of the **for**est when **Sum**mer is **green**	(Lord Byron)

In the first two lines, the syllables fall into this pattern:

unstressed **stressed** unstressed **stressed** unstressed **stressed**

Each one of these pairs of syllables is called a **foot.** The first line has four feet, and the second line has five.

foot foot foot foot
(Come **live**) (with **me**) (and **be**) (my **love**)
foot foot foot foot foot
(Now **came**) (still **eve**) (ning **on**), (and **twi**) (light **gray**)

If all of the feet in a line of poetry have the pattern of unstressed **stressed**, the meter of the poem is **iambic**.

Iambic is one of the most common meters, but there are many others. In the third line of poetry above, each foot has the pattern

stressed unstressed **stressed** unstressed **stressed** unstressed

If all of the feet have this pattern of **stressed** unstressed, the meter of the poem is **trochaic.**

The last line above is in **anapestic** meter, which has this pattern:

unstressed unstressed **stressed** unstressed unstressed **stressed**

As you can see, a foot can have either two or three syllables in it.

So far, you've learned the following two definitions:

meter: the rhythmical pattern of a poem
foot: a set of syllables that follows a certain pattern of stress and unstress

Write both definitions on your Literary Terms chart.

STEP TWO: **Understand iambic pentameter**

Student instructions for Step Two:

On the copy of the poem printed below, mark the stressed and unstressed syllables in each line. Use an accent mark (′) to show a stressed syllable and a circumflex (˘) to show an unstressed syllable, like this:

˘ ′ ˘ ′ ˘ ′ ˘ ′
Come **live** with **me** and **be** my **love**

These are the most common marks used to show meter.

The first line is done for you. If you have difficulty, ask your instructor for help.

Each line in this poem has five feet (pairs of stressed and unstressed syllables):

˘ ′ ˘ ′ ˘ ′ ˘ ′ ˘ ′
(I met) (a trav) (eller from) (an an) (tique land)
1 2 3 4 5

This meter is called *iambic pentameter.* "Iambic" tells you that each foot has two syllables that follow the pattern of unstressed **stressed**. "Pentameter" tells you that there are five feet in each line, for a total of ten syllables. (*Penta* comes from the Greek word for "five.")

Iambic pentameter often just sounds like natural speech, which is why Shakespeare uses iambic pentameter for so much of the dialogue in his plays. Read these four lines from *Henry V,* Act IV, Scene iii out loud, stressing the syllables with accent marks.

˘ ′ ˘ ′ ˘ ′ ˘ ′ ˘ ′ ˘
We few, we happy few, we band of brothers:

˘ ′ ˘ ′ ˘ ′ ˘ ′ ˘ ′
For he today that sheds his blood with me,

Shall be my brother: be he ne're so vile,

This day shall gentle his condition.

(You might notice that there's an extra syllable at the end of the first line and a missing syllable at the end of the fourth. Because iambic pentameter sounds so natural, poets often expand or shorten the lines where necessary.)

When a poet writes in iambic pentameter, you can usually assume that he wants you to pay more attention to the meaning than to the rhythm. The rhythm of the poem is very regular, but it fades into the background so that you can concentrate on the words and images themselves.

When you are finished with this lesson, show your poem marked with stresses and unstressses to your instructor.

HOW TO HELP THE STUDENT WITH STEP TWO

The student's marked poem should resemble the following:

"Ozymandias"
Percy Bysshe Shelley

I met a traveller from an antique land

Who said: "Two vast and trunkless legs of stone

Stand in the desert. Near them on the sand,

Half sunk, a shattered visage lies, whose frown

And wrinkled lip and sneer of cold command

Tell that its sculptor well those passions read

Which yet survive, stamped on these lifeless things,

The hand that mocked them and the heart that fed.

And on the pedestal these words appear:

'My name is Ozymandias, King of Kings:

Look on my works, ye mighty, and despair!'

Nothing beside remains. Round the decay

Of that colossal wreck, boundless and bare,

The lone and level sands stretch far away".

This poem has very regular meter, but you will see that in lines 12 and 13 it is possible to read the fourth foot as a reversal of the meter, from iambic (unstressed **stressed**) to trochaic (**stressed** unstressed). Either choice is correct.

STEP THREE: **Understand rhyme scheme**

Student instructions for Step Three:

> Last week's poem had irregular rhythm; this week's poem has extremely regular rhythm. Last week's poem also had irregular rhyme; plenty of words in it rhymed, but there was no way to predict where those rhymes would be.
>
> This week's poem has a very particular *rhyme scheme.* A rhyme scheme is a pattern of repeating rhymes. You find a rhyme scheme by giving the ending sound in each line of the poem a different letter of the alphabet.
>
> Look at this example, from Edward Lear's *Book of Nonsense:*
>
> There was an Old Man with a beard, A
> Who said, "It is just as I feared! A
> Two Owls and a Hen, B
> Four Larks and a Wren, B
> Have all built their nests in my beard!" A
>
> The first line of the poem ends with the sound *-eard,* so we give that sound the letter A. Every time a line ends with *-eard,* no matter what the word itself is, we give that line the same letter.
>
> The first two lines have the same rhyme, but the third line ends with a different sound: *-en.* This is the second ending sound in the poem, so we give it the second letter of the alphabet: B.
>
> Turn back to your marked copy of the poem and assign each ending sound a letter of the alphabet. Write those letters at the end of each line on the blank provided.
>
> When you are finished, write the following definition of rhyme scheme on your Literary Terms chart.
>
> rhyme scheme: a pattern of repeating rhyme marked with letters of the alphabet
>
> Then check your work with your instructor.

HOW TO HELP THE STUDENT WITH STEP THREE

The rhyme scheme of "Ozymandias" is ABAB ACDC EDE FEF.

STEP FOUR: **Understand sonnet form**

Student instructions for Step Four:

"Ozymandias" is a *sonnet.* On your Literary Terms chart, write the following definition:

sonnet: a 14-line poem written in iambic pentameter

All sonnets are 14-line poems written in iambic pentameter, but there are several different variations on this pattern. The two most common variations are known as the Italian and English sonnet forms.

You don't have to memorize the following definitions and information; just read it carefully.

An "Italian sonnet" has two parts. The first eight lines ("octet") present a problem, an idea, an argument, or a situation. The last six lines ("sestet") give a solution, offer an answer, or complete the idea. Usually, the ninth line contains an obvious change, or shift, between the two parts of the poem; this is called a "turn."

The rhyme scheme for the Italian sonnet is almost always ABBAABBA for the first eight lines. The last six lines can be rhymed in a number of different ways (for example, CDCDCD or CDCEDC), but they never have more than three total rhymes.

An "English sonnet" has three parts. Like an Italian sonnet, an English sonnet has an octet (first eight lines) which goes in one direction. The "turn" that introduces a new direction for the poem comes in the next four lines ("quatrain"). Then the poem ends with two lines (a "couplet") that sums up the poem with a rhyming conclusion.

The rhyme scheme for an English sonnet is most often ABABCDCD EFEF GG.

These are just general rules, and poets often do not follow them exactly. However, when a poet decides to break the rules, you should always pay attention. The change often is a signal to you that you should look more closely at the lines that depart from the regular pattern.

With this in mind, look at "Ozymandias" again. Write brief answers to the following questions on the lines provided. If you have difficulty, ask your instructor for help.

When you are finished, show your answers to your instructor.

HOW TO HELP THE STUDENT WITH STEP FOUR

Suggested answers and explanations are below. If the student has difficulty, use the questions provided to prompt her.

For your information, an Italian sonnet is sometimes known as "Petrarchan," and an English sonnet is often called "Shakespearean," after the most influential poets using these forms. You will often see these terms used interchangeably.

In what line does the change of meaning happen?

ANSWER: *Line 9*

EXPLANATION: In both forms described, the turn or change begins in line 9, so the student should not have another option.

QUESTION FOR STUDENT: "In both the Italian and English sonnets, what line starts the quatrain or sestet that has the change of meaning in it?"

Does the poem follow the English or Italian rhyme scheme more closely?

ANSWER: *English*

EXPLANATION: Although the end of the sonnet doesn't follow either scheme, the

ABAB ACDC pattern of the octet is closest to the ABAB CDCD pattern of the English sonnet.

QUESTION FOR STUDENT: "Just look at the first four lines. Which rhyme scheme do they match?"

Which lines break the pattern?

ANSWER: *Lines 5–8 and the entire sestet*

EXPLANATION: The end of the octet rearranges the English sonnet rhyme scheme slightly, but the last six lines depart completely from any of the patterns provided.

Looking only at the meaning of the sonnet, not the rhyme scheme, how would you classify this sonnet? Is it closer to an Italian or English sonnet?

ANSWER: *Italian*

EXPLANATION: In an English sonnet, the last two lines would provide a summary or conclusion. In this poem, the last three lines all talk about the wreck of the statue; the last two lines are not separate.

QUESTION FOR STUDENT: "Do the last two lines provide a clear summary of the poem?"

What makes the sonnet *different* from the form you did *not* choose?

ANSWER: *The last two lines do not provide a clear conclusion.*

Day Three: Think

Focus: Connecting form and meaning

In the two steps of today's lesson, carry on the following dialogues with the student. During these dialogues, the student will write brief answers to be used in tomorrow's essay.

STEP ONE: Identify the voices within the poem

Instructor: At the beginning of the poem, someone is speaking. What pronoun refers to that person?

Student: I

Instructor: That is the first voice in the poem. We can call that voice either "the narrator" or "the poet." Write those down on the first line, after the number 1. Who is the second speaker in the poem—the second character to say something?

Student: The traveller

Note to Instructor: If necessary, you can say "The speaker's words are in quotation marks."

Instructor: Where's he from?

Student: An antique land

Instructor: Write "traveller" after the number 2. Whose is the third voice you hear in the poem?

Student: Ozymandias

Note to Instructor: If necessary, you can say "Whose voice does the traveller hear when he reads the words on the pedestal?"

Instructor: Write that after the number 3. Now you've identified the three voices in the poem, but there's one more question you should think about. Whose voice is the most important to the poem?

Student: Ozymandias's

Note to Instructor: If the student is unsure, say "Which one of the three voices is the poem actually *about*?"

Instructor: Where is Ozymandias's voice heard—or, in this case, written?

Student: On a pedestal

Instructor: Who reads the pedestal?

Student: The traveller

Instructor: Who listens to the traveller's story?

Student: The narrator [poet]

Instructor: Who reads—or hears—the *narrator's* voice?

Student: I do or *The reader*

Instructor: Ozymandias can only speak to the traveller, and the traveller can only speak to the narrator, and the narrator can only speak to you. So you can't hear what Ozymandias says except through how many other voices?

Student: Two

Instructor: Does this make Ozymandias seem more powerful or less powerful?

Student: Less powerful

Note to Instructor: If necessary, say "Is a king powerful if he can never talk to his people directly?"

Instructor: What title does Ozymandias give himself?

Student: King of kings

Instructor: Does this title go along with or contradict the power that Ozymandias actually *has* in the poem?

Student: Contradicts

Instructor: On the next two lines after the number 3, try to write that observation down in your own words.

Note to Instructor: The student should write down a sentence or two that resembles one of the following:

Ozymandias says he is the king of kings, but *he can only talk to us through two other voices.*

Although Ozymandias says he is powerful, *he can't talk to us directly.*

Ozymandias says that he is powerful, *but he doesn't even have enough power to tell us about himself without two other voices in the way.*

If the student has difficulty, give her the bolded part of one of these sentences and let her finish the sentence herself.

STEP TWO: **Examine the movement of the poem**

Instructor: Last week, you learned that most poems do not begin and end in the same place. Most poems have *movement*. This poem has two different kinds of movement. The first one is physical. Imagine that you're the traveller, walking through the desert. What is the first thing you see? Quote from the poem as you answer.

Student: Two vast and trunkless legs of stone

Instructor: You walk a little farther. What do you see lying on the sand?

Student: A shattered visage

Instructor: Then walk a little farther. What do you see now?

Student: The pedestal

Instructor: Walk past the pedestal. What is the last thing you see?

Student: The lone and level sands stretch far away.

Instructor: The poem has movement because the traveller seems to be walking along and describing each thing he sees as he comes to it. On the first set of lines in your paper, write down the order of the things the traveller sees and describes, in this format: "First, the traveller sees. . . . Then, he sees. . . ." and so on. Use complete sentences and quote from the poem, using quotation marks.

Note to Instructor: The student's notes should resemble the following: *"First the traveller sees 'two vast and trunkless legs of stone.' Then he sees a 'shattered visage' lying on the sand. Next he sees a pedestal. Then, when he walks past the pedestal he sees 'lone and level sands' stretching far away."*

Instructor: There's a second kind of movement in the poem as well. First, the poem concentrates on describing one particular scene. Then, the poem moves in another direction by giving you a different point of view on that scene. Let's start with the first eight lines. What object do these eight lines—the "octet" of the sonnet—describe?

Student: The statue OR The wrecked statue

Instructor: Write that on the second set of lines, beginning with "The octet . . ."

Note to Instructor: The student's answer should be "The octet of the sonnet describes the wrecked statue."

Instructor: In the next six lines, the poem gives you another point of view about the statue—Ozymandias. What do those six lines tell you about how Ozymandias saw himself?

Student: He saw himself as King of Kings.

Instructor: Write that on the second set of lines, beginning with "The sestet . . ."

Note to Instructor: The student's answer should be "The sestet of the sonnet tells us that Ozymandias saw himself as King of Kings."

Instructor: The first eight lines tell about the wreck of the statue; the last six contrast the wreck with the ancient king's hopes that his works would last forever. Did they last forever?

Student: No.

Day Four: Write

Focus: Writing about the poem

Today the student will assemble his essay.

Sonnets are difficult poems to write about. The suggestions and examples given below are realistic for most students writing at this level. More advanced students are welcome to produce a more sophisticated (and longer) essay, but students should not yet be *required* to write more detail than is found below.

STEP ONE: **Write one paragraph for each aspect of the poem (Student Responsibility)**

Student instructions for Step One:

> Put all your answers in front of you, along with your copy of the poem. Use these to write three paragraphs about the poem.
>
> In the first paragraph, explain in what way the poem is like an English sonnet, and in what way the poem is like an Italian sonnet. (You do not need to explain what English and Italian sonnets are—you can assume that your reader will know this.)
>
> In the second paragraph, describe the two kinds of movement that are in the poem. Use at least two direct quotes.
>
> In the third paragraph, explain the three different voices in the poem and who they belong to. Explain what this tells us about Ozymandias.

STEP TWO: **Write an introduction and conclusion**

Student instructions for Step Two:

> The introduction to the poem should sum the story of the poem up briefly; it should tell you what the basic storyline, or plot, or subject matter of the poem is. A conclusion is a little different. Conclusions tell you what you've *learned* about the poem.
>
> Think of it this way: An introduction just gives you a surface acquaintance with the poem (like an introduction to a person doesn't tell you much more than what the person looks and sounds like). But a conclusion looks beneath the surface of the poem and tells you what *message* the poet is giving you.
>
> Now write one sentence that introduces the poem by giving its name, author, and overall meaning. Your sentence can begin like this:
>
> "Ozymandias," by Percy Bysshe Shelley, tells about . . .
>
> This sentence will stand on its own as the introductory paragraph to your brief essay. (In a short assignment like this, it is acceptable to have a one-sentence paragraph.)
>
> Then write a concluding sentence that begins like this:
>
> The form of the poem, the movement of the poem, and the voices of the poem all point out . . .
>
> If you have difficulty, ask your instructor for help.

HOW TO HELP THE STUDENT WITH STEP TWO

If the student has difficulty with the introduction, say "If someone asked you to say in one sentence what the poem is about, what would you say?" If the student still struggles, say, "*Who* is the poem about?"

If the student has difficulty with the conclusion, say "What is the contrast in the poem?" If the student still struggles, say "Where do you see a difference between something real and something imagined?"

Examples of an acceptable introduction and conclusion are found below.

STEP THREE: **Assemble and proofread your essay**

Student instructions for Step Three:

> Put your introduction at the beginning of your essay and your conclusion at the end. Read the composition out loud, listening for awkward phrases and sentences that might not make sense. Then read it one more time silently, looking for misspelled words and incorrect punctuation. Be sure that you have quoted from the poem directly at least twice in the essay.
>
> When you are finished, show your composition to your instructor.

HOW TO HELP THE STUDENT WITH STEP THREE

An acceptable composition may resemble the following.

"Ozymandias"

"Ozymandias," by Percy Bysshe Shelley, is a sonnet about a king who thought he was mighty—but whose kingdom completely disappeared.

The sonnet that does not exactly follow the form of either an English or Italian sonnet. The rhyme scheme of the poem is closer to an English sonnet, but the last four lines of the octet are a little bit different. The last six lines are completely different. The meaning of the poem follows an Italian sonnet more closely. The first eight lines tell the reader about the wrecked statue in the desert. In the ninth line, the turn or change begins. The next five lines tell about the king's hopes that his works would last forever.

There are two kinds of movement in the poem. The first is the physical movement of the traveller. He walks through the desert and sees first "two vast and trunkless legs of stone" (2) and then a "shattered visage" (4). Third, he sees the pedestal with Ozymandias's words written on it. Finally, he walks past the pedestal and sees nothing but "lone and level sands" stretching far away (14). The second kind of movement gives us two different points of view. The first point of view describes the wrecked statue lying in the desert. Then the point of view shifts, and we find out exactly what Ozymandias thought about himself. He saw himself as King of Kings, and he thought that his works would last forever.

The poem has three different voices. The first voice is the poet himself. The second voice belongs to the traveller who tells the poet about the statue. The third voice belongs to Ozymandias himself. Even though Ozymandias calls himself the King of Kings, he doesn't even have enough power to talk to us through two other voices.

The form of the poem, the movement of the poem, and the voices of the poem all point out the difference between what Ozymandias thought would happen and what really happened.

Check the student's work using the following rubric.

Week 33 Rubric
Brief Poem Essay

Organization

1 The essay should begin with an introduction that gives the poem's title, the author, and the information that the poem is about an ancient king whose kingdom disappeared.
2 There should be five paragraphs total.
3 The conclusion should make a statement about the conflict between Ozymandias's expectations and what really happened.
4 The essay should include at least two direct quotes from the poem.

Mechanics

1 Each sentence should make sense on its own when read aloud.
2 Possessive forms should be written properly.
3 Verb tense should be consistent throughout.
4 Subjects and verbs must be in agreement.
5 Antecedents of pronouns should be clear.
6 Unnecessary repetition of the same nouns, adjectives, and proper names should be avoided.
7 The title of the poem should be in quotation marks.
8 Direct quotes should be incorporated into full sentences and should be properly punctuated.

WEEK 34: NARRATIVE

Day One: Read

Focus: Reading

Note to Instructor: This is the last week of regular lessons. During the final two weeks of the course, the student will work independently on a final writing project. You will need to schedule a library trip for next week, when the student will begin to do research for this final project.

This week, the student will write about the final poem in Appendix IV: "The Charge of the Light Brigade" by Alfred, Lord Tennyson.

This poem is based on a historical event. On Day Three the student will learn about the historical background. Today he will concentrate on the sound and rhythm of the poem.

Today's work will be done independently. However, if the student has trouble understanding 3/4 time (Step Three), you may need to help him by finding and playing one of the following pieces of music:

"The Blue Danube" by Johann Strauss
"Morning Mood" by Edvard Grieg
"Greensleeves" or "What Child Is This?"
"Take Me Out to the Ballgame"
"Waltzing with Bears"
"The Tennessee Waltz"
"How Much Is That Doggie in the Window?"
"Edelweiss" and "My Favorite Things" (from the movie *The Sound of Music*)
"The Times They Are a-Changin'" (Bob Dylan or Peter, Paul, and Mary)
"Time in a Bottle" (Jim Croce)
"You Light Up My Life"

Listen to make sure that the student is reading out loud in Steps Two–Four. Check to make sure that the student is up and walking around for Step Four.

The student's directions are reproduced below for your convenience.

Student instructions for Day One

STEP ONE: Read silently

Read the poem silently and slowly. Stop and look up the meanings and pronunciations of all words you don't know.

STEP TWO: Read out loud

Go to a private place and read the poem out loud, at a normal pace, listening to the sounds. (You can do this in front of someone else if you'd prefer.) Pause briefly at the end of each line so that you can hear the rhythm of the poem's individual lines.

STEP THREE: Read for rhythm

Read the poem out loud again. This time, pay attention to the rhythm of the poem.

You'll learn more about the poem's meter in the next lesson, but for the purposes of reading the poem out loud, all you need to remember is that much of the poem is in 3/4 time.

If you play an instrument, you already know what this means—the rhythm of the poem is 1-2-3, 1-2-3, 1-2-3, 1-2-3. Even if you don't take music lessons, though, 3/4 time is easy to understand. All you need to do is sway back and forth. Sway to the right and say "One, two, three!" Then sway to the left and say "One, two, three!" Do this a few more times and you'll be chanting in 3/4 time.

If you still can't quite hear 3/4 time, try listening to a piece of music. There are plenty of classical music pieces written in 3/4 time: "The Blue Danube" by Johann Strauss and "Morning Mood" by Edvard Grieg are just two. The folk songs "Greensleeves" (same tune as the hymn "What Child Is This?"), "Take Me Out to the Ballgame," "Waltzing with Bears," "The Tennessee Waltz," and "How Much Is That Doggie in the Window?" are all 3/4 time. So are "Edelweiss" and "My Favorite Things," from the movie *The Sound of Music*. The 1960s classic "The Times They Are a-Changin'" is in 3/4 time; so are the 1970s songs "Time in a Bottle" and "You Light Up My Life." (If you don't know these, your parents probably do.)

When you read the poem this time, try to chant it in regular 3/4 time. (Sway back and forth if necessary.) You'll notice that every once in a while, a line will be missing the last beat or two. Just count the last one or two beats silently in your head. (In music, this would be like a rest.)

For example, here's how the first four lines should sound:

(Sway left for a count of 1-2-3) (Sway right for a count of 1-2-3)
Half a league, half a league
(Sway left, 1-2-3) (Sway right, 1-2-3; the third beat will be silent)
Half a league onward,
(Sway left, 1-2-3) (Sway right, 1-2-3) (Sway left, 1-2-3; the second and third beats will be silent)
All in the valley of Death
(Sway right, 1-2-3) (Sway left, 1-2-3; the third beat will be silent)
Rode the six hundred

STEP FOUR: Read for motion

The rhythm of the poem mimics the galloping rhythm of a horse (a gallop also has three beats). For your final reading of the poem, you don't have to gallop, but you do have to get up and move.

Once again, read the poem in regular 3/4 time. But this time, walk around the room (or your house, or your yard), taking one step for each beat. Whenever you get to the end of a line that's missing a beat or two, stop dead in your tracks and count the remaining beats in your head. Then begin again.

Here's how the first four lines would work:

(Take three steps) (Take three steps)
Half a league, half a league
(Take three steps) (Take two steps and then pause for one beat)
Half a league onward,
(Take three steps) (Take three steps) (Take one step and then pause for two beats)
All in the valley of Death
(Take three steps) (Take two steps and then pause for one beat)
Rode the six hundred

Day Two: Analyze

Focus: Understanding ballad form

STEP ONE: **Identify complete and incomplete dactyls**

Student instructions for Step One:

If you did yesterday's reading carefully, you already know what the metrical pattern of this poem is from the following feet:

(**Half** a league), (**half** a league) . . .
(**All** in the) (**val**ley of) . . .

Each complete foot in the poem has three syllables and follows this pattern:

(**stressed** unstressed unstressed)

Remember, last week you learned about the following meters:

iambic (unstressed **stressed**)
trochaic (**stressed** unstressed)
anapestic (unstressed unstressed **stressed**)

The meter of this poem is a new one:

dactylic (**stressed** unstressed unstressed)

Dactylic meter is one of the most rhymic poetic patterns. (In fact, the word **po-**e-try itself is dactylic!) Say the following phrases out loud and listen to the dactylic pattern in each:

higgledy-piggledy
patty cake, patty cake
honor and glory and power and
I was out walking one morning

In "The Charge of the Light Brigade," Tennyson uses the dactylic meter very regularly—and when he leaves a dactyl incomplete (like at the end of the line "**Rode** the six **hund**red [missing beat]), he does so on purpose.

Your first step today will be to mark the stressed and unstressed syllables in each line of the poem. (This may seem tedious, but it forces you to read slowly and analytically, paying attention to each syllable.) As you mark the syllables, look for incomplete feet (feet with fewer than three syllables). Circle each incomplete foot.

The first four lines are done for you.

HOW TO HELP THE STUDENT WITH STEP ONE

1
Half a league, half a league,
Half a league **onward**,
All in the valley of **Death**
Rode the six **hundred**.
"Forward, the Light Brigade!
"Charge for the guns!" he said:
Into the valley of **Death**
Rode the six **hundred**.

2
"Forward, the Light Brigade!"
Was there a man dismay'd?
Not tho' the soldier knew
Someone had **blunder'd:**
Theirs not to make reply,
Theirs not to reason why,
Theirs but to do and die:
Into the valley of **Death**
Rode the six **hundred**.

3
Cannon to right of them,
Cannon to left of them,
Cannon in front of them
Volley'd and **thunder'd;**
Storm'd at with shot and shell,
Boldly they rode and well,
Into the jaws of Death,
Into the mouth of Hell
Rode the six **hundred**,

4
Flash'd all their sabres bare,
Flash'd as they turn'd in air,
Sabring the gunners there,

Charging an army, while
All the world **wonder'd:**
Plunged in the battery-smoke
Right thro' the line they broke;
Cossack and **Russian**
Reel'd from the sabre stroke
Shatter'd and **sunder'd**.
Then they rode back, but not
Not the six **hundred**.

5
Cannon to right of them,
Cannon to left of them,
Cannon be**hind them**
    Volley'd and **thunder'd;**
Storm'd at with shot and shell,
While horse and hero fell,
They that had fought so well
Came thro' the jaws of Death
Back from the mouth of Hell,
All that was left of them,
    Left of six **hundred.**

6
When can their glory fade?
O the wild charge they made!
    All the world **wondered.**
Honor the charge they made,
Honor the Light Brigade,
    Noble six **hundred.**

STEP TWO: Identify rhyme scheme

Student instructions for Step Two:

"The Charge of the Light Brigade" has an irregular rhyme scheme. There is a pattern to the rhymes—but the pattern changes from stanza to stanza.

Go back to the copy of the poem you marked up in the previous step. Look at the ending words of each line. Some of those ending words rhyme with other words in the same stanza. Some of the ending words don't have *any* matching rhyme within the stanza.

Underline the ending words that rhyme with at least one other ending word within the stanza. (Don't do anything to the ending words that have no match.) Then, give each rhyming sound a letter. Write that letter after each line that ends with the sound.

For example, Stanza 2 would look like this:

"Forward, the Light Brigade!"	A
Was there a man dismay'd?	A
Not tho' the soldier knew	
Someone had blunder'd:	B
Theirs not to make reply,	C
Theirs not to reason why,	C
Theirs but to do and die:	C
Into the valley of Death	
Rode the six hundred.	B

"Brigade" and "dismay'd" rhyme with each other and have the same ending sound. "Brigade" is the first rhyming word in the stanza, so the "-aid" sound at the end is given the letter A.

"Knew" doesn't rhyme with any other word, so it is neither underlined nor given a letter.

"Blunder'd" and "hundred" rhyme. (Well, close enough. Sometimes the ending sounds of words are *so* close that you *think* the poet intended a rhyme—but there's a tiny bit of difference. You can decide whether or not these "near rhymes" are *actual* rhymes. There isn't necessarily a right answer; this is a judgment call.) "Blunder'd" is the second rhyming word in the stanza, so the sound at the end is given the letter "B."

"Reply," "why," and "die" all rhyme and are given the letter C.

"Death" doesn't rhyme with anything, so it isn't underlined or given a letter.

Now do this with the other stanzas in the poem (you can copy our answers for Stanza 2). Note: when a word rhymes only with itself, such as the repetition of *Death* in Stanza 1, this is generally not considered part of a rhyme scheme. If three lines ended with *Death, breath, Death,* that would be considered part of a rhyme scheme.

When you are finished, fill out the following chart by listing the rhyme scheme for each stanza beneath the stanza number. (Leave out the unrhymed lines.) The second stanza is done for you.

Show your work to your instructor.

HOW TO HELP THE STUDENT WITH STEP TWO

The ends of the lines should resemble the following:

league,
onward,
Death
hundred. A
Brigade!
said: A
Death
hundred. A

Brigade!" A
dismay'd? A
knew
blunder'd: B
reply, C
why, C
die: C
Death
hundred. B

them,
them,
them
thunder'd; A
shell, B
well, B
Death,
Hell B
hundred. A

bare, A
air, A
there, A
while
wonder'd: B
smoke C
broke; C
Russian
stroke C
sunder'd. B
not
hundred. B

them,
them,
them
thunder'd; A
shell, B
fell, B
well B
Death
Hell, B

them,
hundred. A

fade? A
made! A
wondered. B
made, A
Brigade, A
hundred. B

The finished chart should be:

1	2	3	4	5	6
A	A	A	A	A	A
A	A	B	A	B	A
A	B	B	A	B	B
	C	B	B	B	A
	C	A	C	B	A
	C		C	A	B
	B		C		
			B		
			B		

STEP THREE: Understand ballad form

Student instructions for Step Three:

> You've already studied one poem written in free verse and one sonnet—two forms you'll see very often as you continue to write about poetry. This week's poem is another very common form: a *ballad.*
>
> A ballad is a poem that tells a story, usually a heroic or tragic one. Ballads don't have one particular form, which makes them different from sonnets. A sonnet always has the same form (14 lines, iambic pentameter), but the *content* of the sonnet can be anything the poet chooses. A ballad always has the same *content* (a heroic or tragic story), but the poet can use different *forms* to tell that story.
>
> Many ballads are written in sets of four lines called *quatrains,* from the Latin word for "four." These stanzas are from "The Rime of the Ancient Mariner," a ballad written by Samuel Taylor Coleridge:
>
> The fair breeze blew, the white foam flew,
> The furrow followed free;
> We were the first that ever burst
> Into that silent sea.

Down dropped the breeze, the sails dropped down,
'Twas sad as sad could be;
And we did speak only to break
The silence of the sea!

All in a hot and copper sky,
The bloody sun, at noon,
Right up above the mast did stand,
No bigger than the moon.

Day after day, day after day,
We stuck, nor breath nor motion;
As idle as a painted ship
Upon a painted ocean.

Water, water, every where,
And all the boards did shrink;
Water, water, every where,
Nor any drop to drink.

This ballad also has one of the most common rhyme schemes for ballads; the second and fourth lines of each quatrain rhyme with each other, while the first and third lines don't rhyme at all. We describe this rhyme scheme as ABCB.

Here's a stanza from another famous ballad, "Paul Revere's Ride" by Henry Wadsworth Longfellow:

You know the rest. In the books you have read
How the British regulars fired and fled;
How the farmers gave them ball for ball,
From behind each fence and farmyard wall,
Chasing the redcoats down the lane,
Then crossing the fields to emerge again
Under the trees at the turn of the road,
And only pausing to fire and load.

In this ballad, the stanzas are made up of *two* quatrains, and the rhyme scheme is AABBCCDDEE—each pair of lines rhymes.

Many ballads also have a refrain—a line that is repeated exactly, or with slight variation, throughout the poem. Sometimes this refrain is part of the quatrain, and sometimes it is an extra, fifth line. These stanzas are from "The Lady of Shalott" by Tennyson; the refrain lines are underlined.

She left the web, she left the loom,
She made three paces through the room,
She saw the water-lily bloom,
She saw the helmet and the plume,
    <u>She looked down to Camelot</u>.
Out flew the web and floated wide;
The mirror cracked from side to side;
"The curse is come upon me," cried
    <u>The Lady of Shalott</u>.

In the stormy east-wind straining,
The pale yellow woods were waning,
The broad stream in his banks complaining,
Heavily the low sky raining
    Over towered Camelot;
Down she came and found a boat
Beneath a willow left afloat,
And round about the prow she wrote
    The Lady of Shalott.

In each stanza, the first refrain is an additional, fifth line. The second refrain is just the fourth line of the quatrain.

Notice that this ballad uses yet another rhyme scheme: AAAABCCCB.

Now that you've seen three examples of ballads, look back at the poem you marked up in Steps One and Two. First, go through the copy of the poem below and draw a square bracket around each quatrain that you can find. Not every line in the poem belongs to a four-line quatrain, but many do. The first quatrain is done for you.

Second, circle every repeated line or phrase that you can find in the poem. The repetition may be exact (as in "The Lady of Shalott") or have a variation ("down to Camelot" "towered Camelot"). The first set of repetitions is circled for you.

Finally, write the following definition in your Literary Terms chart:

ballad: a poem that tells a story, usually a heroic or tragic one

When you are finished, check your work with your instructor.

HOW TO HELP THE STUDENT WITH STEP THREE

The student's finished work should resemble the following. If the student misses a circled or bracketed line, simply tell him which stanza the missing repetition or quatrain is found in.

You may need to remind the student to read the lesson carefully before doing the exercise.

1

Half a league, half a league,
Half a league onward,
All in the valley of Death
Rode the six hundred.
"Forward, the Light Brigade!
"Charge for the guns!" he said:
Into the valley of Death
Rode the six hundred.

2

"Forward, the Light Brigade!"
Was there a man dismay'd?
Not tho' the soldier knew
Someone had blunder'd:
Theirs not to make reply,
Theirs not to reason why,
Theirs but to do and die:
Into the valley of Death
Rode the six hundred.

3

Cannon to right of them,
Cannon to left of them,
Cannon in front of them
Volley'd and thunder'd;
Storm'd at with shot and shell,
Boldly they rode and well,
Into the jaws of Death,
Into the mouth of Hell
Rode the six hundred.

4

Flash'd all their sabres bare,
Flash'd as they turn'd in air,
Sabring the gunners there,
Charging an army, while
All the world wonder'd:
Plunged in the battery-smoke
Right thro' the line they broke;
Cossack and Russian
Reel'd from the sabre stroke
Shatter'd and sunder'd.
Then they rode back, but not
Not the six hundred.

5

Cannon to right of them,
Cannon to left of them,
Cannon behind them
Volley'd and thunder'd;
Storm'd at with shot and shell,
While horse and hero fell,
They that had fought so well
Came thro' the jaws of Death
Back from the mouth of Hell,
All that was left of them,
Left of six hundred.

6

When can their glory fade?
O the wild charge they made!
All the world wondered.
Honor the charge they made,
Honor the Light Brigade,
Noble six hundred.

Day Three: Think

Focus: Connecting form and meaning

In the first two steps, you will talk to the student about the poem; talking will prepare the student for tomorrow's writing assignment. In the third step, the student will also take notes on the poem's historical background.

The student should not be expected to do this sort of analysis on his own. The exercise has two purposes: to make him more aware of the relationship between meaning and rhyme, rhythm, and repetition; and to give him practice in writing about poems.

STEP ONE: **Examine the movement of the poem**

Carry on the following dialogue with the student. If the student answers as suggested, continue on with the main dialogue and skip the optional dialogue; if the student is confused, use the optional dialogue.

Examples of what the student's completed exercises should look like are in bold type after each instruction.

MAIN DIALOGUE **OPTIONAL DIALOGUE**

Instructor: Let's start by thinking about the movement of the poem. When you read the poem on Day One, you learned that the rhythm of the poem mimics a horse's gallop. Right away, this tells you that the horses are galloping *somewhere.* The repetition in the poem gives you clues about where this might be. What is the first repeated phrase?

Student: Half a league

Instructor: "League" is an old word for how far a man could walk in an hour—usually about three miles. Tennyson could have written "A league and a half" or even "Four and a half miles." Why do you think he repeats "half a league, half a league, Half a league" like this?

Student: It shows more forward movement.

(Doesn't have any idea)

Instructor: Watch me as I read. [Stand up and take one large step forward as you say] "One and a half leagues." Now watch this. [Take three steps forward, one for each repetition of the phrase.] "Half a league, half a league, Half a leage onward." Which one has more energy and movement forward?

Student: The second

Instructor: So he uses this to show progressive forward movement.

Instructor: Write "forward movement" on the first blank in your workbook.

"Half a league, half a league, half a league onward" shows forward movement.

Instructor: Now tell me the second repeated phrase you come to.

Student: "In the valley of Death"

Instructor: This tells you where the forward movement was happening. Write that on the second blank in your workbook.

Where? In the valley of Death.

Instructor: The third repeated phrase in the stanza is "Rode the six hundred." In what other stanzas does this phrase—or a variation—occur?

Student: All of them

Instructor: This is the refrain of the ballad. Now, the final repeated phrase in the stanza doesn't occur again until Stanza 2. What is it?

Student: "Forward, the Light Brigade!"

Instructor: This completes the movement of the first two stanzas. Write that phrase in the third blank.

In what direction? Forward the Light Brigade!

Instructor: Now look at the third stanza. The third stanza is mising the word "forward." Instead, the repeated phrases are mostly about what?

Student: Cannon

Instructor: Where are the cannon?

Student: To the right, left, and in front of them

Instructor: In the square under Stanza 2, draw three X's to represent the Light Brigade. Then draw circles to represent the cannon. When you are done, show me your drawing.

Note to Instructor: The drawing should resemble the following:

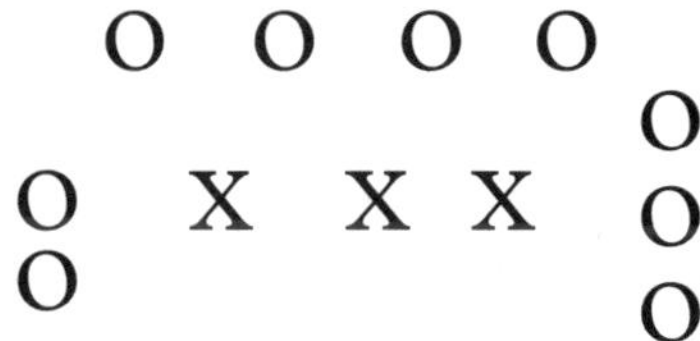

Instructor: In this stanza, the phrase "Into the valley of Death" has been changed a little bit. What is it now?

Student: "Into the jaws of Death"

Instructor: What do the cannon look like in your drawing?

Student: Jaws

Instructor: Is the Light Brigade still moving forward?

Student: No

Instructor: So the forward movement has . . .

Student: Stopped.

Instructor: The repetition of "Cannon to right of them, Cannon to left of them, Cannon in front of them" tells you that the Light Brigade has arrived at its destination. Write that on the first line beneath the heading "Stanza 3."

The Light Brigade has now reached its destination.

Instructor: Then answer the second question as well.

They are trapped in the jaws of Death.

Note to Instructor: If the student is confused, say "Remember, the 'valley of Death' was changed. What was it changed to?"

Instructor: The poet then uses another phrase to describe the jaws of Death. What is it?

Student: "The mouth of Hell"

Instructor: Write that on the third line.

The jaws of Death are also the mouth of Hell.

Instructor: Then answer this one last question. Do people normally get out of the jaws of Death or escape the mouth of Hell?

Student: No.

Instructor: Write that on the final line.

Most people do not escape the mouth of Hell.

Instructor: Now look at Stanza 4. What repetition do you see in Stanza 4?

Student: "Not the six hundred" OR *Just the refrain*

Instructor: There is no other repetition in this stanza. Does repetition start again in Stanza 5?

Student: Yes

Instructor: The lack of repetition tells you that the Light Brigade is now at the center of the poem—and the center of the charge. Write that answer into your workbook.

The lack of repetition shows that the Light Brigade has arrived at the center of the poem.

Instructor: What are they doing there at the center?

Student: Fighting

Instructor: What happens to them?

Student: Some of them are killed.

(Doesn't know)

Instructor: Do they all come back out of the valley of death?

Student: No

Instructor: What happens to the ones who don't come back?

Student: They are killed.

Instructor: Write that down in your workbook.

Two things happen there: they are fighting; some of them are killed.

Instructor: Now look at Stanza 5. If the Light Brigade moved forward in Stanzas 1 and 2, and arrived at the jaws of Death and the center of the poem in Stanzas 3 and 4, what are they doing in Stanza 5?

Student: Coming back out

(Doesn't know)

Instructor: Read line 47 out loud. Where are they coming from?

Student: "Back from the mouth of Hell"

Instructor: Write that on the first line after the heading "Stanza 5."

Finally, they come back from the mouth of Hell.

Instructor: There are six repeated lines in this poem. What other stanza do they occur in?

Student: Stanza 3

Instructor: Write "Stanza 4" on the top blank in your workbook. On the left blank, write "Stanza 3." What should you write on the right blank?

Student: Stanza 5.

Instructor: The structure of the poem mimics the movement of the Light Brigade—they move forward and then back again through the same place. So does the poem. There is one change in the repetition of the first three lines that tells you the Light Brigade has moved in the opposite direction. What is the change?

Student: "Cannon behind them"

Instructor: This shows that the Light Brigade has turned around. Now look at the final stanza. There's only one repeated line. What is it?

Student: "Noble six hundred"

Instructor: What did that line sound like when it occurred in the first stanza?

Student: "Rode the six hundred"

Instructor: What has the six hundred become?

Student: Noble.

Instructor: Fill in the blanks under Stanza 6 as best you can.

Physically, the Light Brigade moved forward into the valley of Death and then back out again. In the eyes of others, they moved from being just the six hundred to the noble six hundred.

Note to Instructor: Prompt the student as necessary.

STEP TWO: **Understand the relationship between form and meaning**

Carry on the following dialogue with the student.

Instructor: Look at the rhyme scheme chart you made yesterday. Which stanza has the most rhyming lines in it?

Student: Stanza 4

Instructor: In the last step you also saw that Stanza 4 has the least . . .

Student: Repetition

Instructor: The increased number of rhymes is another clue that you've come to the center of the poem. Which two stanzas are the most *alike* in rhyme scheme?

Student: Stanzas 3 and 5

Instructor: The only difference is that there's one more B rhyme in Stanza 5. On the top blank in your workbook, write "Stanza 4 has most rhyming lines." On the blank on the right side, write "Stanza 5 reflects Stanza 3." What do you think you should write on the left side?

Student: Stanza 3 reflects Stanza 5.

Instructor: The rhyme scheme and the repetition both do the same thing—they tell you that you've arrived at the Light Brigade's destination, and that next the Light Brigade will turn around and go back the way it came. Now look at one last thing—the incomplete feet in the poem. Look at Stanza 1 and read me, in order, the incomplete feet that you circled yesterday.

Student: Onward, Death, hundred, Death, hundred

Instructor: The first stanza gives you a hint about what the rest of the poem is going to be about—the six hundred riding onward into death. Write those five words on the blank in your workbook. Now do the same for the second stanza. What did you write down?

Student: Blunder'd, Death, hundred

Instructor: Tennyson is using the incomplete feet to draw your attention to key words in the poem. The Light Brigade was sent into the valley by accident. That blunder led to the deaths of hundreds. Now, a poet will often use a strategy in one part of a poem and not in other parts. If you look at Stanzas 3, 4, and 5, you can see that Tennyson isn't using incomplete feet in the same way. Read me the incomplete feet, in order, from all three stanzas.

Student: Thundered, hundred, wondered, Russian, sundered, hundred, hind them, thundered, hundred

Instructor: That doesn't have any particular pattern—but remember, Tennyson is already using repetition and rhyme scheme to tell you how Stanzas 3, 4, and 5 fit together. He doesn't need to use rhythm as well. But look at Stanza 6. Write down the incomplete feet. What do you have?

Student: Wondered, hundred

Instructor: "Wonder" has two meanings. One is to be in awe of something. What is the other?

Student: To ask a question OR *To be confused* OR *To not know something*

Note to Instructor: If the student is confused, say "What do you mean when you say, 'I wonder if . . . ?' "

Instructor: The death of the Light Brigade was caused because of a wrong order. Tennyson is telling you that there's still a question about how something like this could have happened. Now you'll find out more about this by reading about the historical background of the poem.

STEP THREE: **Investigate the historical background**

Student instructions for Step Three:

> The charge of the Light Brigade took place during the Battle of Balaklava, during the Crimean War (1853–1856). The Crimean War was fought between Russia and the allied armies of Turkey, England, and France.
>
> Read through the following account of the Battle of Balaklava, from Dorothy Donnell Calhoun's *The Book of Brave Adventures.* You will see from the tone of the book that it's intended for slightly younger readers, but Calhoun gives the clearest and most readable account of the battle that I could find.
>
> After you read the account, go back and take notes on the events of the Battle of Balaklava. Tomorrow, when you write your composition, you will write one paragraph on the historical background of the poem. Prepare for this by first listing 14–15 events leading to and during the battle. Be sure to focus on the Battle of Balaklava itself, rather than on details of the Crimean War.
>
> These events should not use the exact wording of the text. Historical events are common knowledge, so if you do not use the exact wording of the text, you do not need to use quotation marks or document the information. For example, you might write:
>
> > The Light Brigade was a British cavalry regiment. (125)
>
> Then go back and list three or four details that you can use to make your paragraph more vivid. These details may use the exact words of the source. Your paragraph will need to include at least one direct quote, so be sure to use quotation marks to surround the exact words of the text.
>
> The publication information for the book is:
>
> > Calhoun, Dorothy Donnell. *The Book of Brave Adventures.* New York: The Macmillan Company, 1915.
>
> If you need help, ask your instructor. When you're finished, show your work to your instructor.

HOW TO HELP THE STUDENT WITH STEP THREE

The student's list of events and details should resemble the following. There should not be more than 15 events and 4 details listed, and all should relate to the Battle of Balaklava, not to the larger Crimean War.

Events:

The Light Brigade was a British cavalry regiment. (125)
The Allied forces fighting against the Russians landed at the Crimea. (125)
The British and French troops met the Russians at Balaklava. (126)
The Allies had a camp on top of the hills at Balaklava. (126)
The French and English drove the Russians away from the camp. (126)
The Russians took twelve cannon with them. (126)
Lord Raglan told Lord Lucern to keep the Russians from taking the rest of the cannon from the hill. (126–127)
Lord Lucern thought he was supposed to attack the Russians who were in the valley. (127)
Russian troops surrounded the valley and were at the end with guns. (127)
Lord Lucern passed the order on to Lord Cardigan, captain of the Light Brigade. (129)
All of the soldiers knew there was a mistake, but they went into the valley anyway. (129)
They were shot at from the front and from both sides. (130)
Hundreds were killed. Only 195 survived. (132) [Note: Modern accounts say 450]

Sample details:

At Balaklava, "Low hills surrounded a green plain." (126)
Lord Raglan "wrote a hasty note to Lord Lucern who was directing the battle in the valley." (126)
Lord Lucern was "amazed at such an order." (127)
The "gray uniforms of the Russian troops" dotted the hills of the valley. (127)
The Light Brigade had "been taught to obey orders without questioning them." (129)
The Brigade faced "the shriek of bullets and the roar of shells." (130)
As they rode back out of the valley, their "red uniforms were black with dust and powder smoke." (132)

If necessary, show the student part of your list in order to give him a clearer sense of what the assignment requires.

Day Four: Write

Focus: Writing about the poem

Today, the student will arrange a copy of the poem, answers to the Day Three exercises, and the list of historical events and details in front of him. He will then write a composition using all three of these resources.

He does not need to show his composition to you until he is finished, but he may ask for help at any time. At the end of the student instructions, you will see a sample composition. If the student struggles with any of the paragraphs, show him one or two sentences from the sample composition. This will demonstrate how he should use his Day Three exercises to construct the paragraphs.

The student instructions are reproduced below for your reference.

Student instructions for Day Four:

> STEP ONE: Write a chronological narrative describing the Battle of Balaklava
>
> Your first paragraph will give the historical background of "The Charge of the Light Brigade." (Notice that although you experienced the poem *first,* the reader of your essay will not have the poem in front of him; he is relying solely on your interpretation. He can't understand your interpretation unless he knows the background, so you will present this information first.)
>
> This paragraph will simply be a brief chronological narrative of a past event—something you've had plenty of practice in writing. Glance back at your Chronological Narrative of a Past Event chart and your list of time words. Then write a paragraph of at least 120 but not more than 200 words, explaining the events of "The Charge of the Light Brigade." Try to use at least two time words. You must include at least one direct quote, properly footnoted.
>
> You will need an introductory sentence that tells the reader the connection between the poem and the historical background. You may use this introductory sentence:
>
> > "The Charge of the Light Brigade" tells the story
> > of a battle that took place during the Crimean War.
>
> or else write your own.
>
> STEP TWO: Explain the movement of the poem
>
> Now write either two or three more short paragraphs, explaining the movement of the poem. These paragraphs should total at least 175 but not more than 300 words. Use the poem itself and your answers from Step One of yesterday's lesson. You may also glance back over your Day Two work if you need additional ideas.
>
> You will need a sentence that connects this paragraph with the historical background. You may use this introductory sentence:
>
> > When writing his poem about the Light Brigade,
> > Tennyson chose to use the rhythm of a horse galloping.
>
> or else write your own.
>
> Your paragraphs should describe what happens in each stanza, and should tell how the repetitions of the poem help show the movement of the Light Brigade.
>
> Your paragraphs should quote directly from the poem at least three times, using properly formatted line numbers.
>
> If you have trouble getting started, ask your instructor to prompt you.
>
> STEP THREE: Explain how the meter and rhyme scheme of the poem support its meaning
>
> Your composition will conclude with a paragraph describing how Tennyson uses meter and rhyme scheme. Begin with rhyme scheme, and then explain how the incomplete feet in the poem add to the poem's meaning. This paragraph should be at least 120 and not more than 200 words.
>
> You will need a transitional sentence at the beginning of this paragraph. You may use this sentence:
>
> > Tennyson uses both rhyme and meter to add extra levels of meaning to the poem.
>
> or else write your own.
>
> In your paragraph, explain how the rhyme schemes in Stanzas 3, 4, and 5 reinforce the central position of Stanza 4. Also tell the reader that the poem is written in dactylic meter and that some feet are incomplete. Then, explain what these incomplete feet do.

STEP FOUR: Assemble and proofread the composition

Give the composition a title ("'The Charge of the Light Brigade,' by Alfred, Lord Tennyson" is fine). Proofread it for spelling and grammar mistakes. Check to see that your footnotes and poem line numbers are properly formatted.

Since this composition has only one citation, it is not necessary to do a separate Works Cited page.

When you are ready, give your composition to your instructor to read.

HOW TO HELP THE STUDENT WITH DAY FOUR

An acceptable final composition might resemble the following.

"The Charge of the Light Brigade," by Alfred, Lord Tennyson

The charge of the Light Brigade took place during the Crimean War. British and French troops were fighting in the Crimea. A British camp at Balaklava was captured by the Russians. Then the British and French drove the Russians away from the camp, but the Russians took twelve cannon with them. One of the British officers, Lord Raglan, told another officer, Lord Lucern, to keep the Russians from taking any more cannon. Lord Lucern thought that he was supposed to attack the larger force of Russians in the valley nearby. He was "amazed at such an order"[1] but passed it on to the captain of the Light Brigade, a British cavalry regiment. The soldiers knew that the order was wrong, but they went into the valley anyway. Over four hundred of them were killed.

When writing his poem about the Light Brigade, Tennyson chose to use the rhythm of a horse galloping. The poem begins with the phrases "Half a league, half a league, Half a league" (1–2) which show the forward movement of the horses. In Stanzas 1 and 2, they move forward into the "valley of Death" (3). In Stanza 3, the Light Brigade reaches its destination—the valley, surrounded by the cannon. Tennyson calls this the "jaws of Death" (24) and the "mouth of Hell" (25). It is a place that most people do not escape.

In Stanza 4, the lack of repetition shows that the Light Brigade has arrived at the center of the poem. Two things happen here: the Light Brigade fights, and many are killed. Finally, in Stanza 5, the Light Brigade retreats from the valley the same way it came. Stanzas 3 and 5 have similar repetition. This shows that the Light Brigade moved forward into the valley and then back out again. Finally, Stanza 6 shows that the Brigade has also moved from being just six hundred soldiers, to being six hundred noble soldiers.

Tennyson uses both rhyme and meter to add extra levels of meaning to the poem. The most rhymes in the poem are found in Stanza 4, which is also the center of the poem. Stanzas 3 and 5, on either side, have reflecting rhyme schemes, showing that the Light Brigade went into the valley in Stanza 3 and back out the same way in Stanza 5. The meter of the poem is dactylic, but

Tennyson leaves some of the feet incomplete. In Stanzas 1, 2, and 5, the incomplete dactyls hint at meaning. In Stanza 1, they tell us that the 600 will go onward to death; in Stanza 2, they tell us that a blunder brought death to hundreds; and in Stanza 3, they suggest that there are still questions about how the Light Brigade got the orders.

[1] Dorothy Donnell Calhoun, *The Book of Brave Adventures* (The Macmillan Company, 1915), p. 127.

Check the student's finished composition, using the following rubric.

Week 34 Rubric
Brief Poem Essay

Organization

1 The essay should be at least 415 but no more than 700 words.
2 There should be either four or five paragraphs.
3 The first paragraph should give a brief chronological narrative about the poem's events and should include two time words and one direct quote.
4 The second and third (and fourth, if used) paragraphs should explain the movement of the poem by describing what happens in each stanza. These paragraphs should also tell how the repetition of the poem helps show the movement of the Light Brigade. They should include at least three direct quotes from the poem.
5 The final paragraph should describe how the rhyme scheme and the incomplete feet add meaning to the poem.

Mechanics

1 Each sentence should make sense on its own when read aloud.
2 Possessive forms should be written properly.
3 Verb tense should be consistent throughout.
4 Subjects and verbs must be in agreement.
5 Antecedents of pronouns should be clear.
6 Unnecessary repetition of the same nouns, adjectives, and proper names should be avoided.
7 The title of the poem should be in quotation marks.
8 Direct quotes should be incorporated into full sentences and should be properly punctuated.
9 Poem quotes should be properly attributed.
10 Secondary sources should be properly footnoted.

Part VII

FINAL PROJECT WEEKS 35–36

Overview of Weeks 35–36

Over the past 34 weeks, the student has practiced many separate skills: outlining; putting together narrations, descriptions, and sequences; writing basic literary essays on both stories and poems; and changing sentences around by transforming nouns, adjectives, and verbs.

In these last two weeks, the student will put those skills to use by writing an actual composition—on any topic. The student will decide on the form of the composition, pick the subject, find resources, read up on the topic, take notes, write the composition, and add the footnotes.

You will need to schedule a library trip for Week 35. If the student is not familiar with the library catalog and shelves, introduce the student to the reference librarian and ask the librarian to give the student a brief orientation. (By the way, reference librarians do *not* feel put upon when asked to do this. Don't hesitate to use their expertise.)

Instead of giving four days' worth of assigments, each week is divided up into a number of steps, with a suggestion of how many hours the student should spend on each step. You can decide whether to spread these hours over several days, or concentrate them into one or two days of single-minded work. The student can always spend more hours (but not fewer!) and go more deeply into the subject.

The final composition must:

1. Put together at least two of the topoi the student has learned to write.
2. Be at least 1000 words in length.
3. Make use of at least three sources.
4. Include footnotes and a Works Cited page.

General rubrics are provided for your use in Appendix V.

Week 35: Finding and Researching Your Topic

The Final Project, Part One: Finding and Researching Your Topic

This week, the student may work independently and show you her chosen resources once she has completed all of these steps. However, you should be prepared to offer help for each step if the student asks. Suggestions for helping the student are found below.

The times listed may be increased or decreased, according to your own judgment.

STEP ONE: **Decide which topoi to include** 1/2 hour

Student instructions for Step One:

> Turn to the Reference section of your Composition Notebook and review the forms of the seven topoi you have learned this year. They are:
>
> Chronological Narrative of a Past Event
> Chronological Narrative of a Scientific Discovery
> Description of a Place
> Scientific Description
> Description of a Person
> Biographical Sketch
> Sequence: Natural Processes
>
> Before going on, read the columns under "Procedure" and "Remember" for each topos.
>
> 
>
> Now, make a tentative decision about which topoi you will use for your paper. You *must* use a minimum of two (but don't try to include more than four, even if you're feeling ambitious).
>
> You've already practiced combining a chronological narrative of past events with a description of a place (Week 11, Ivan the Terrible and St. Basil's Cathedral), combining a chronological narrative of a scientific discovery with a scientific description (Week 15, the discovery and description of deep-ocean hydrothermal vents), a chronological narrative of past events that includes a personal description and a description of a place (Week 29, Julius Caesar), and a sequence of natural events that includes a scientific description (Week 30, digestion). You've also learned that a biographical sketch can include a personal description as one

of the aspects covered (Week 31, Marie Antoinette). You can use one of these combinations, or choose your own.

As you choose the topoi, also make a decision about the subject you'll write about. If possible, choose a subject that's related to your other studies.

Example: I might like to write about X-rays, which were discovered in 1895 by Wilhelm Roentgen. I could combine a chronological narrative of a scientific discovery with a description of Roentgen, or with a biographical sketch of Roentgen. Or I could combine the chronological narrative with a sequence, describing exactly how X-rays work. Or I could write a biographical sketch of Roentgen that includes a sequence describing how X-rays work. I pick the combination of chronological narrative and sequence—but I might change my mind once I start researching, if I find out that writing a sequence will require me to know a lot more about physics than I do. In that case I might decide to do a biographical sketch of Roentgen instead.

Your instructor can help you if you're having trouble deciding on your topoi or coming up with a subject. And remember: you can always change your mind when you start researching.

HOW TO HELP THE STUDENT WITH STEP ONE

If necessary, suggest one of the following additional combinations:

Chronological narrative of a past event plus description of a place (optional: also include description of a person)

Biographical sketch including description of a place

Scientific description plus biographical sketch

Chronological narrative of a scientific discovery plus description of a person

If the student has trouble coming up with a topic, try using the following websites for ideas:

http://www.pbs.org/wgbh/aso/databank/
http://science.discovery.com
http://science.discovery.com/convergence/100discoveries/big100/big100.html
http://www.famoushistoricalevents.net/
http://www.fordham.edu/halsall/

As a final resort, you may assign one of the following topics:

The Battle of Hastings plus a description of the battlefield and/or a description of William the Conqueror

Biographical sketch of George Washington plus a description of Mount Vernon

Chronological narrative of the discovery of the cell nucleus by Robert Brown in 1831, along with a scientific description of the nucleus

A scientific description of the Earth's core combined with a biographical sketch of Richard Oldham, who first theorized that the Earth has a liquid core

STEP TWO: **Collect resources** 2 hours

Student instructions for Step Two:

Your next task is to collect at least five books that deal generally with your subject. You won't need to use all five when you write, but you'll probably find that at least one or two of the books turns out to be unsuitable, so choosing five makes it more likely that you'll end up with three good resources.

For this assignment, you may not use websites. A published book may have errors in it, but it has been inspected and edited by professionals who are *not* the author. A website, on the other hand, doesn't have to be inspected or edited by anyone. A writer can put anything up on a website, and unless you're an expert yourself, you won't be able to tell what's true and what's false. (You'll learn more about this in future levels of this course.)

The only exception: you *may* use e-book versions of standard published works. These have been edited and proofread in the same way as the print versions.

Here are a few suggestions to help you find your five resources.

1. Start by reading encyclopedia articles on your subject. These will give you a useful overview and alert you to the topics you should cover as you write. Note down two or three important names, places, or details.

Remember that you may use online versions of standard encyclopedias such as Britannica or World Book. You may *not* use Wikipedia. Wikipedia is not professionally edited or fact-checked. Anyone can post anything on Wikipedia. Usually, other users will identify and remove mistakes—but if you happen to use Wikipedia five minutes after someone has posted bad information (which people sometimes do just for fun), you won't realize that you're writing down false facts.

Example: I look up Wilhelm Roentgen in the Encyclopedia Britannica and find out that he won the first Nobel prize for physics in 1901; that a unit of radiation called a roentgen *is named after him; and that he called his discovery "X-rays." I jot down "Nobel prize," "roentgen," and "X-rays."*

2. Visit your library. Look up the names, places, or details in the library catalog. (Ask the reference librarian for help if you don't know how to use the catalog. Reference librarians *want* to help you. That's why they became reference librarians.) Then go and pull at least ten books off the shelves.

Example: I search for "Wilhelm Roentgen" in the catalog of the York County Library. I see one title that might be useful—it's described as "juvenile literature," which means it won't be a complicated college-level text:

Gherman, Beverly. *The Mysterious Rays of Dr. Röntgen*

When I look over to the left of the catalog page, I see that I can find out more about three different subjects:

Roentgen, Wilhelm Conrad, 1845-1923—Juvenile literature
X-rays—Juvenile literature
Physicists—Germany—Biography—Juvenile literature

I click on each link to find more books, but the same book keeps coming up again and again. So I type "X-ray" into the search box and find:

McClafferty, Carla Killough. *The Head Bone's Connected to the Neck Bone: The Weird, Wacky, and Wonderful X-Ray*

When I type "roentgen" in the search box, I find:

Adler, Robert E. *Medical Firsts: From Hippocrates to the Human Genome*

And when I type "Nobel prize" into the search box I find:

Worek, Michael, editor. *Nobel: A Century of Prize Winners*

> *That's only four books, but it's a start. I go find each book and look on either side of them on their shelves to find books on related topics. I look in the index of these surrounding books for* "Roentgen" *and* "X-ray." *If I find a reference in the index, I take the surrounding books as well.*
>
> 3. Flip through the books. Eliminate those that are too complicated (remember, you're just writing a short essay, not a research paper—you don't want to end up with an overwhelming amount of information) or only have a sentence or two on your topic. Try to end up with five that you can check out and take home.

HOW TO HELP THE STUDENT WITH STEP TWO

You may need to help the student navigate the library catalog and shelves. Also take responsibility for introducing the student to the reference librarian and asking for help, since the student may be too shy to do this herself.

The student has been given instructions for library use only, since one of the goals of this course is to accustom young writers to using published, edited works for reference. However, if your library is poor (or nonexistent), you may use books.google.com as a last resort; (See Week 3, Day Two, p. 31, for previous suggestions about how to use Google Books.)

Typing any of the search terms into the books.google.com search engine will produce a long list of books. You will need to help the student scan down the books to find juvenile or young adult titles suitable for this project. Most books which are available for preview will allow you to read at least a chapter online for free; this will often be sufficient for the student's purposes. You may also buy a complete e-book of many titles. Older books which are out of copyright are often available for free. These resources are fine, but the student should use at least one contemporary title as well.

STEP THREE: **Do initial reading** — 4–5 hours

Student instructions for Step Three:

> Sit down with your five books and read them. If the entire book is on your topic, try to read the whole thing. If there is only a chapter or page on your topic, only read that chapter or page. Don't take notes yet. If you take notes too early, you end up writing down a lot of information you won't need. This week's task is to get an overview of your topic.

HOW TO HELP THE STUDENT WITH STEP THREE

Keep an eye on the student to make sure she is reading instead of staring into space.

STEP FOUR: **Choose final resources** — 1/2 hour

Student instructions for Step Four:

> Pick the two or three books that you will find useful. If necessary, change your topoi so that they match the information available to you. For example, if your library has lots of biographical information about Roentgen but nothing on your level about X-rays, you'll probably

want to do a biographical sketch and a description—even if you had originally planned to do a sequence and a scientific description.

You'll finish your work next week. It is always easier to write about a topic if you've read about it first—and then let the information sit in your mind for a few days. Researching at the last minute often makes your paper sound rushed and superficial. (Remember this when you get to college!)

Show your collected books to your instructor.

HOW TO HELP THE STUDENT WITH STEP FOUR

Check the student's resources to make sure that they are not too long and complicated. At least one of the books should have brief *summaries* of information. If all of the books are detailed, book-length studies, the student will have difficulty choosing only the important details needed for a brief composition.

WEEK 36: WRITING YOUR FINAL COMPOSITION

The Final Project, Part Two: Taking Notes and Writing the Composition

This week, plan on checking the student's work after each step. Your inspection doesn't need to be detailed, but you should make sure that the student is not cutting corners. You may also need to encourage the student to review the lessons listed if he seems uncertain about the assignment.

STEP ONE: **Make a preliminary plan** — 1/2 hour

Student instructions for Step One:

Now that you've settled on a subject and two or three topoi, you're almost ready to start taking notes. But unless you know exactly what information you're looking for, you'll be tempted to take too many notes on too many different details. So before you go on to the note-taking step, stop for a minute and make a preliminary plan.

Making a preliminary plan means that you decide what *sorts* of details you'll need to fill out your composition. You've practiced making a preliminary plan in several previous lessons. For this project, glance down the list below. Choose the topoi you'll be using and make decisions about the information you'll need to complete them successfully. Answer each question by jotting down phrases or short sentences on a piece of paper. (Do *not* simply answer the questions in your head!)

If necessary, go back to the lessons listed to review the meaning of each question.

Chronological narrative of a past event
Week 4, Days Three–Four; Week 6, Days Three–Four

- What is the theme of the narrative—its focus?
- What are its beginning and ending points?
- Will you use dialogue? Who will speak?

Chronological narrative of a scientific discovery
Week 5, Days Three–Four; Week 7, Days Three–Four;

- Will you need a background paragraph explaining the circumstances before the discovery?
- Can you quote from the scientist's own words?

Description of a place

Week 8, Days Three–Four; Week 9, Days Three–Four; Week 10, Days Three–Four

What purpose will this description fulfill?
What is your point of view?
What metaphors or similes will make the description more vivid?

Scientific description

Week 12, Days Three–Four; Week 13, Days Three–Four; Week 14, Days Three–Four

What are the parts of the object or phenomenon?
What is your point of view? Will you use more than one?
What figurative language can make the description more visual?

Description of a person

Week 16, Days Two–Three; Week 17, Days Two–Three; Week 18, Days Two–Three

What aspects will be included?
Will you slant the description in a positive or negative direction?
Will you use an overall metaphor to give clues about the person's character?

Biographical sketch

Week 19, Days Two–Three; Week 20, Days Two–Three

What will the focus be—life events, or the subject's accomplishments/work?
If life events, which ones will be included?
If accomplishments/work, will they be listed chronologically or by topic?
What aspects from the Description of a Person chart should be included?

Sequence: natural process

Week 21, Days Two–Three; Week 22, Days Two–Three

What other elements will you include?
Introduction/summary?
Scientific background?
Repetition of the process?

HOW TO HELP THE STUDENT WITH STEP ONE

Check to make sure that the student has actually written down the answers to all questions.

STEP TWO: **Take notes** — **3–4 hours**

Student instructions for Step Two:

Keeping your answers to Step One nearby, take notes from at least three of your resources. If you need to review the correct form, reread Week 28, Days Two–Four.

The number of notes you will take will vary. However, for a short composition you should try never to take more than 20 notes from any individual source.

HOW TO HELP THE STUDENT WITH STEP TWO

Check to make sure that the student's notes are properly formatted, that he has taken notes from at least three resources, and that there are no more than 20 notes for each source.

STEP THREE: **Write the topoi** 3 hours

Student instructions for Step Three:

> Place your notes in order. If you need to review this process, reread Week 29, Days Two–Three. You may also want to reread Week 30, Days Two–Three, and Week 31, Days Two–Four.
>
> Use your notes to write each topos. Write the topoi one at a time; you will assemble them in the final step.
>
> You should quote directly from each of your three sources at least one time. If you need to review proper documentation, reread Week 28, Day Two.

HOW TO HELP THE STUDENT WITH STEP THREE

Check each topoi using Appendix V, General Rubrics.

Make sure that the student has quoted directly from each source at least one time.

STEP FOUR: **Assemble the composition** 1/2 hour

Student instructions for Step Four:

> Put your topoi together into a complete composition.
>
> Read your composition out loud. Listen for awkward phrases and abrupt transitions. You may need to insert sentences linking the topoi together.
>
> Read your composition one more time silently, looking for mistakes in spelling, grammar, and punctuation.
>
> Make sure that all direct quotes and anything which is not common knowledge is footnoted.
>
> Assemble your Works Cited page. If you need to review the form, reread Week 28, Day Two.
>
> Give your composition a simple title (the name of the event, person, place, or process is fine).
>
> Make sure your composition has page numbers.
>
> Show your completed work to your instructor.

HOW TO HELP THE STUDENT WITH STEP FOUR

Do one final check for grammar, spelling, and punctuation.
Listen for awkward transitions. If necessary, point them out to the student.
Check the format of the Works Cited page.
Use the appropriate General Rubric to evaluate the structure and mechanics.

When the student has completed this lesson, the course is finished. If you would like a certificate of completion, fill out and mail the certificate on the last page of the student workbook to us at:

Well-Trained Mind Press
18021 The Glebe Lane
Charles City, VA 23030
Attn: WWS Completion Certificate

Include a self-addressed, stamped envelope. I will sign the certificate personally and return it.

Appendix I

TOPOI

Chronological Narrative of a Past Event

Definition: A narrative telling what happened in the past and in what sequence

Procedure

1. Ask, Who did what to whom? (Or, What was done to what?)
2. Create main points by placing the answers in chronological order.

Remember

1. Select your main events to go with your theme.
2. Make use of time words.
3. Consider using dialogue to hold the reader's interest.

Chronological Narrative of a Scientific Discovery

Definition: A narrative telling what steps or events led to a discovery, and in what sequence

Procedure

1. Ask, What steps or events led to the discovery?
2. Ask, In what sequence did these steps or events happen?
3. Create main points by placing the answers in chronological order.

Remember

1. May need a background paragraph explaining the circumstances that existed before the discovery.
2. Make use of time words.
3. If possible, quote directly from the scientist's own words.

Description of a Place

Definition: A visual description of a physical place

Procedure

1. Ask, What specific purpose should this description fulfill?

Remember

1. Make use of space and distance words and phrases.

Procedure	Remember
2. Choose a point of view.	2. Consider using vivid metaphors and similes.

Scientific Description

Definition: A visual and structural description of an object or phenomenon

Procedure	Remember
1. Describe each part of the object or phenomenon and tell what it is made from.	1. Consider using figurative language to make the description more visual.
2. Choose a point of view.	2. Consider combining points of view.

Description of a Person

Definition: A description of selected physical and non-physical aspects of a person

Procedure	Remember
1. Decide on which aspects will be included. They may include: Physical appearance Sound of voice What others think Portrayals Character qualities Challenges and difficulties Accomplishments Habits Behaviors Expressions of face and body Mind/intellectual capabilities Talents and abilities Self-disciplines Religious beliefs Clothing, dress Economic status (wealth) Fame, notoriety, prestige Family traditions, tendencies	1. Descriptions can be "slanted" using appropriate adjectives. 2. An overall metaphor can be used to organize the description and give clues about character.

Biographical Sketch

Definition: A chronological summary of the important events in a person's life combined with description of aspects of the person

Procedure

1. Decide on the life events to list in the chronological summary.
2. Choose aspects from the Description of a Person chart to include.

Remember

1. The main focus can be on the subject's work/accomplishments.
   a. Listed chronologically
   b. Listed by subject/topic

Sequence: Natural Process

Definition: A step-by-step description of a cycle that occurs in nature

Procedure

1. Describe the natural process chronologically, step by step.
2. Decide which other elements to include.
   a. Introduction/summary
   b. Scientific background
   c. Repetition of the process

Remember

Appendix II

WEEKLY RUBRICS

Week 1 Narration Rubric

Organization

1 Events should be in chronological order.

2 If two or more events are listed in a single sentence, they should have a cause and effect relationship.

For example:

The Pepins didn't know what to do, so they went next door to ask Mr. Bradshaw is acceptable; they went next door *because* they didn't know what to do.

The Pepins had toads in their shoes, and they went next door is not acceptable. There is no clear causal relationship between the two sentences.

Mechanics

1 Each sentence should make sense on its own when read aloud.

2 Each proper name should be capitalized.

Week 1 Challenge Narration Rubric

Organization

1 Events should be in chronological order.
2 If two or more events are listed in a single sentence, they should have a cause and effect relationship.
3 The summary must not be more than eight sentences in length.
4 It should mention the little man, the goose, Dullhead, the king, and the princess; the other characters do not need to be named as long as the series of events is clear.
5 It should end with Dullhead's marriage to the princess.

Mechanics

1 Each sentence should make sense on its own when read aloud.
2 Each proper name should be capitalized.
3 The student may choose to capitalize *King* and *Princess* (since the story does) or to leave them lowercase, but should be consistent throughout the story.

Week 3 Narration Rubric

Organization

1 Events should be in chronological order.
2 If two or more events are listed in a single sentence, they should have a cause and effect relationship.
3 The summary should end with a statement about Helen's new understanding of words/names.

Mechanics

1 Each sentence should make sense on its own when read aloud.
2 Each proper name should be capitalized.
3 Either first or third person should be used consistently throughout.

OPTIONAL

4 Quotation marks should be used to set off words that are spelled out to Helen.

Note: The student is probably not familiar with the grammar rule governing #4. The rule is: When words are referred to as words, they are set off with either quotation marks or italics. "Word as word" means that the focus is on the word *itself,* not on the meaning, so:

I felt water on my hand.

She spelled "water" on my hand.

You may explain this rule to the student if you choose, but if you think the student will be confused, feel free to ignore it.

Week 4 Narration Rubric

Organization

1 Events should be in chronological order.
2 If two or more events are listed in a single sentence, they should have a cause and effect relationship.
   For example:
   The dragons were everywhere, and everyone killed them
   is acceptable; because the dragons were everywhere, everyone killed them.
   The newspapers called the dragons lizards at first, and everyone killed them
   is not acceptable. There is no causal relationship between the two sentences.
3 Each event of major importance should be in the summary (if it were missing from the original passage, the narrative would no longer make sense).

Mechanics

1 Each sentence should make sense on its own when read aloud.
2 Each proper name should be capitalized.

Week 4/5 Rubric
Chronological Narrative of Past Events

Organization

1 Events should be in chronological order.
2 Three or more time words should be used.
3 The composition should use more than 150 but fewer than 300 words.

Mechanics

1 Each sentence should make sense on its own when read aloud.
2 Each proper name should be capitalized.
3 The exact words of the source material should not be used in every sentence.

Week 5 Rubric
Chronological Narrative of Scientific Discovery

Organization

1. Events should be in chronological order.
2. The paragraph giving "background information" should be the first or second paragraph in the composition.
3. Three or more time words should be used.
4. The composition should use more than 150 but fewer than 300 words.

Mechanics

1. Each sentence should make sense on its own when read aloud.
2. Each proper name should be capitalized.
3. Possessive forms should be written properly. (Note that the possessive of "Phipps" is "Phipps's.")
4. The exact words of the source material should not be used in every sentence.

Week 6 Narration Rubric

Organization

1. Events should be in chronological order.
2. If two or more events are listed in a single sentence, they should have a cause and effect relationship.

   For example:

   Wart ate a magic mouse and turned into an owl

   is acceptable, because the mouse turned Wart into the owl.

   Archimedes taught the Wart to fly and the Wart could see like an owl

   is not acceptable. There is no causal relationship between the two sentences.
3. Each event of major importance should be in the summary (if it were missing from the original passage, the narrative would no longer make sense).

Mechanics

1. Each sentence should make sense on its own when read aloud.
2. Each proper name should be capitalized. (Note that "Wart" is a proper name in this context. It may be written either as "Wart" or "the Wart," since White uses both.)
3. Personal pronouns should have clear antecedents and be of the proper gender (Archimedes and the Wart are "he," while the mouse is "it").

Week 6 Rubric
Chronological Narrative of Past Events

Organization

1 Events should be in chronological order.
2 Two or more time words should be used.
3 The composition should use more than 150 but fewer than 300 words.

Mechanics

1 Each sentence should make sense on its own when read aloud.
2 Each proper name should be capitalized.
3 At least one line of dialogue should be included; dialogue and dialogue tags should be properly punctuated.

Week 7 Narration Rubric

Organization

1 Events should be in chronological order.
2 If two or more events are listed in a single sentence, they should have a cause and effect relationship.

For example:

After he was wound up, Tik-Tok could think, talk, and walk

is acceptable.

The Shaggy Man recognized Tik-Tok, and Betsy wound him up

is not acceptable. There is no causal relationship between the two sentences.

3 Each event of major importance should be in the summary (if it were missing from the original passage, the narrative would no longer make sense).

Mechanics

1 Each sentence should make sense on its own when read aloud.
2 Each proper name should be capitalized.
3 Personal pronouns should have clear antecedents and be of the proper gender (Tik-Tok is "he," while Polychrome and the Rose Princess are both "she").

Week 7 Rubric
Chronological Narrative of Scientific Discovery

Organization

1 Events should be in chronological order.
2 The paragraph giving "background information" (heliocentric vs. geocentric world view) should be the first or second paragraph in the composition.
3 Two or more time words should be used.
4 The composition should use more than 150 but fewer than 300 words.

Mechanics

1 Each sentence should make sense on its own when read aloud.
2 Each proper name should be capitalized.
3 Possessive forms should be written properly.
4 The exact words of the source material should not be used in every sentence.
5 At least one direct quote should be included; quote and accompanying dialogue tags should be properly punctuated.

Week 8 Narration Rubric

Organization

1 Sentences should describe the world at the time the story takes place.
2 If two or more details are listed in a single sentence, they should be related.
For example:
The kingdom was filled with mountains, and caverns were below the mountains
is acceptable;
Caverns were under the mountains, and the goblins caused mischief
is not acceptable. There is no stated relationship between the caverns and the goblins.

Mechanics

1 Each sentence should make sense on its own when read aloud.
2 Each proper name should be capitalized.
3 Possessive forms should be written properly.
4 Personal pronouns should have clear antecedents and be of the proper gender.
5 Consistent verb tense should be used throughout.
For example, the student should not write
The kingdom was full of mountains, and caverns are in the mountains
because the first verb is in the simple past and the second is in the simple present.
The kingdom is full of mountains, and caverns are in the mountains and
The kingdom was in the mountains, and caverns were in the mountains
are both acceptable.

Week 8 Description Rubric

Organization

1 The description should use appropriate adjectives and verbs to convey a sense of vastness.

EXAMPLE: *The castle sits on top of a* ***gigantic*** *rock whose sides* ***plunge steeply*** *down.*

2 The description should mention both the castle itself and the landscape.

3 At least four space and distance words and phrases should be used.

EXAMPLE: Far **below** the castle, **to the right**, a white road stretches **into** the distance.

4 The composition should use at least three and not more than seven sentences.

Mechanics

1 Each sentence should make sense on its own when read aloud.

2 Verbs should have consistent tense (all past or all present).

Rows of windows line the white walls, and spires reach sharply upwards is acceptable.

Rows of windows lined the white walls, and spires reach sharply upwards is not.

Week 9 Narration Rubric

Organization

1 The summary should describe the park, with a single sentence at the end describing the final event.
2 A time word should link the final sentence to the rest of the summary.
3 Details of conversations should not be listed.
4 If two or more details are listed in a single sentence, they should be related.
For example,
Flowers were trees, and flowerbeds were made of petals
is acceptable;
Flowers were trees, and a little round man sat on a bench
is not.

Mechanics

1 Each sentence should make sense on its own when read aloud.
2 Each proper name should be capitalized.
3 Possessive forms should be written properly.
4 Personal pronouns should have clear antecedents and be of the proper gender.
5 Consistent verb tense should be used throughout.

Week 9 Description Rubric

Organization

1 The descriptions should use appropriate adjectives and verbs to convey peacefulness (or at least the absence of violence!).
2 At least two space and distance words and phrases should be used in each description.
3 Point of view should remain consistent throughout each description.
4 The details described should differ in each description, depending on the point of view.

Mechanics

1 Each sentence should make sense on its own when read aloud.
2 Verbs should have consistent tense (all past or all present).
3 Subjects and verbs should be in agreement.

Week 10 Narration Rubric

Organization

1 Events should be in chronological order.
2 If two or more events are listed in a single sentence, they should have a cause and effect relationship.
3 Each event of major importance should be in the summary (if it were missing from the original passage, the narrative would no longer make sense).
4 Vital details should be listed immediately after (or in the same sentence as) the connected event.
5 The summary should not be more than four sentences long.

Mechanics

1 Each sentence should make sense on its own when read aloud.
2 Each proper name should be capitalized.
3 Personal pronouns should have clear antecedents and be of the proper gender.
4 Consistent verb tense should be used throughout.

Week 11 Narration Rubric

Organization

1 Events should be in chronological order.

2 If two or more events are listed in a single sentence, they should have a cause and effect relationship.

For example:

Tom woke up Sid, and Sid ran downstairs for Aunt Polly

is acceptable; Sid ran downstairs because Tom woke him up.

Tom woke up Sid and Aunt Polly came upstairs

is not acceptable. There is no obvious causal relationship between the two events.

3 Each event of major importance should be in the summary (if it were missing from the original passage, the narrative would no longer make sense).

It is acceptable for the student to describe the exact method by which the tooth was pulled; although it would make sense to just say "Aunt Polly pulled the tooth," this is one of the most memorable parts of the passage.

Mechanics

1 Each sentence should make sense on its own when read aloud.

2 Each proper name should be capitalized.

3 Personal pronouns should have clear antecedents and be of the proper gender.

4 Verb tense should be consistent throughout.

Week 11 Rubric
Chronological Narrative of a Past Event Incorporating Description of a Place

Organization

1 Events should be in chronological order.
2 Two or more time words should be used.
3 There should be a clear connection between an event that shows Ivan IV's power and the construction of the cathedral.
4 The description of the cathedral should immediately follow the main event "Ordered the building of a new church to celebrate his military victories."
5 At least one metaphor or simile should be used in the description of the cathedral.
6 At least two space and distance words should be used.
7 The description should be written from the point of view of an outside, impersonal observer.
8 The composition should be at least 150 and not more than 350 words.

Mechanics

1 Each sentence should make sense on its own when read aloud.
2 Each proper name should be capitalized.
3 Possessive forms should be written properly.
4 Verbs should be in consistent tense.
5 Subjects and verbs should be in agreement.
6 The exact words of the source material should not be used in every sentence.
7 At least one direct quote should be included; the quote and accompanying dialogue tags should be properly punctuated.

Week 12 Summary of Narrative Fiction Rubric

Organization

1 Events should be in chronological order.
2 If two or more events are listed in a single sentence, they should have a cause and effect relationship.
3 Dr. Mortimer's story should be distinct from the events actually taking place at Baker Street.
4 The second part of the summary should describe Mortimer and Holmes having a conversation, not the details of the scene recounted by Mortimer.

Mechanics

1 Each sentence should make sense on its own when read aloud.
2 Each proper name should be capitalized.
3 Personal pronouns should have clear antecedents and be of the proper gender: for example, in the sentences "Mortimer wanted Baskerville to go to London. Before he could leave . . . ," the antecedent of "he" is unclear.
4 Verb tense should be consistent throughout.
5 The perfect past (pluperfect) should be correctly used: "When Dr. Mortimer had finished" or "After Dr. Mortimer had told his story" indicates that Dr. Mortimer's story happened *before* the scene at Baker Street.

Week 12 Rubric Scientific Description

Organization

1 The description should include at least three or four major parts of the volcano.
2 The description should explain what each part of the volcano is made from.
3 At least one metaphor or simile should be used.
4 The description should be at least 200 words long but no longer than 400 words.

Mechanics

1 Each sentence should make sense on its own when read aloud.
2 Verbs should have consistent tense (all past or all present).
3 Possessive forms should be written properly.
4 Subjects and verbs should be in agreement.

Week 13 Rubric
Summary of Narrative Fiction

Organization

1 Events should be in chronological order; the two events in the first story should occur before and after the events in the second story.
2 The summary must mention the poor brother, the rich brother, the dwarves, and the merchant; other characters may or may not be present.
3 If two or more events are listed in a single sentence, they should have a cause and effect relationship.
4 The summary should not be longer than six sentences.

Mechanics

1 Each sentence should make sense on its own when read aloud.
2 Each proper name should be capitalized.
3 Personal pronouns should have clear antecedents and be of the proper gender.
4 Verb tense should be consistent throughout.
5 Subjects and verbs must be in agreement.

Week 13 Rubric
Scientific Description

Organization

1 The description should explain what the eruption looks like from the perspective of at least three of the five senses: sight, sound, smell, taste, touch.
2 The description should be at least 150 words and no longer than 300 words.

Mechanics

1 Each sentence should make sense on its own when read aloud.
2 Each proper name should be capitalized.
3 Personal pronouns should have clear antecedents and be of the proper gender.
4 Verb tense should be consistent throughout.
5 Subjects and verbs must be in agreement.
6 Adjectives and adverbs should refer to heat, sound, light, and dark.

Week 14 Rubric
Summary of Narrative Fiction

Organization

1 Events should be in chronological order.
2 The summary must mention the two extraordinary events in the passage.
3 The summary should not also cover the first and last paragraphs.
4 If two or more events are listed in a single sentence, they should have a cause and effect relationship.
5 The summary should not be longer than six sentences.

Mechanics

1 Each sentence should make sense on its own when read aloud.
2 Each proper name should be capitalized.
3 Personal pronouns should have clear antecedents and be of the proper gender.
4 Verb tense should be consistent throughout.
5 Subjects and verbs must be in agreement.
6 Any predicate nominatives or adjectives must agree with their subjects in person, number, and gender.

Week 14 Rubric
Scientific Description

Organization

1 The description should describe what at least three separate parts of Mars are made from, what they look like, and what function they have.
2 The description should include at least one present point-of-view description of at least one part of Mars from the perspective of at least three of the five senses: sight, sound, smell, taste, touch.
3 At least one metaphor or simile should be used.
4 The final description should be at least 200 words and no longer than 500 words.

Mechanics

1 Each sentence should make sense on its own when read aloud.
2 Each proper name should be capitalized.
3 Personal pronouns should have clear antecedents and be of the proper gender.
4 Verb tense should be consistent throughout.
5 Subjects and verbs must be in agreement.

Week 15 Rubric
Summary of Narrative Fiction

Organization

1 Events should be in chronological order.
2 If two or more events are listed in a single sentence, they should have a cause and effect relationship.
3 The summary should not go into detail about Danny's actions in tracking Big Red and the bear.
4 The summary should not be longer than four sentences.

Mechanics

1 Each sentence should make sense on its own when read aloud.
2 Each proper name should be capitalized.
3 Personal pronouns should have clear antecedents and be of the proper gender.
4 Verb tense should be consistent throughout.
5 Subjects and verbs must be in agreement.
6 Any predicate nominatives or adjectives must agree with their subjects in person, number, and gender.

Week 15 Rubric
Chronological Narrative of a Scientific Discovery Incorporating Description of a Place

Organization

1 Events in the narrative should be in chronological order.
2 Two or more time words should be used.
3 The events of the 1977 expedition should be included, as well as at least one other main event on the list.
4 The description should make use of one or both points of view: removed, present.
5 Present point-of-view descriptions should incorporate at least three of the five senses: sight, sound, smell, taste, touch.
6 Removed point-of-view descriptions should describe each part of the object or phenomenon and tell what it is made of.
7 At least one metaphor or simile may be used.
8 The entire composition should be at least 250 and no longer than 550 words.

Mechanics

1 Each sentence should make sense on its own when read aloud.
2 Each proper name should be capitalized.
3 Possessive forms should be written properly.
4 Personal pronouns should have clear antecedents and be of the proper gender.
5 Verb tense should be consistent throughout.
6 Subjects and verbs must be in agreement.
7 The exact words of the source material should not be used in every sentence.
8 At least one direct quote should be included; quote and accompanying dialogue tags should be properly punctuated.

Week 16 Rubric
Description of a Person

Organization

1 At least five but no more than eight of the aspects listed on the Description of a Person chart should be used.
2 Physical appearance of the character should be included.
3 The entire composition should be at least 200 and no longer than 600 words.

Mechanics

1 Each sentence should make sense on its own when read aloud.
2 Each proper name should be capitalized.
3 Possessive forms should be written properly.
4 Personal pronouns should have clear antecedents and be of the proper gender.
5 Verb tense should be consistent throughout.
6 Subjects and verbs must be in agreement.
7 The following words may not be used: *nice, good, bad, beautiful, lovely, attractive, handsome, pretty, ugly, sparkling, twinkling, soft, loud, famous, poor, rich, smart,* and *dumb.*

Week 17 Rubric
Description of a Person

Organization

1 The description should include the eight qualities/aspects listed on the chart from Step Two.

2 Qualities listed in the same sentence should be related. For example,

He spent money on elaborate parties and gave away money

is acceptable, because both of those actions show wastefulness.

He spent money and worried about his looks

is not, because wastefulness and vanity are different qualities.

3 The description should be negative.

4 The entire composition should be at least 100 and no longer than 250 words.

Mechanics

1 Each sentence should make sense on its own when read aloud.

2 Each proper name should be capitalized.

3 Possessive forms should be written properly.

4 Personal pronouns should have clear antecedents and be of the proper gender.

5 Verb tense should be consistent throughout.

6 Subjects and verbs must be in agreement.

Week 18 Rubric
Description of a Person

Organization

1 The description should include at least three of the qualities/aspects listed on the Description of a Person chart.

2 Qualities listed in the same sentence should be related. For example,

He was often sick, and the ulcer on his leg made him short-tempered

is acceptable, because the ulcer is a kind of sickness.

He was short-tempered, and his gold mane began to turn gray

is not, because his temper and his hair are unrelated.

3 The description should use at least four of the words from the student's list of verbs, adjectives, and nouns.

4 The entire composition should be at least 50 and no longer than 150 words.

5 The composition may include imaginary scenes and actions not described in the source excerpts.

Mechanics

1 Each sentence should make sense on its own when read aloud.

2 Each proper name should be capitalized.

3 Possessive forms should be written properly.

4 Personal pronouns should have clear antecedents and be of the proper gender.

5 Verb tense should be consistent throughout.

6 Subjects and verbs must be in agreement.

7 At least one adverb should be used (in the above samples, "**dangerously** short-tempered" and "he devoured his meals **greedily**").

Week 19 Rubric
Biographical Sketch

Organization

1 The sketch should begin with an introductory statement about Daniel Boone.
2 The chronological narrative should have at least four but not more than eight events from the chronological list, including Boone's birth and death. These events should be listed in chronological order.
3 One aspect of Boone should be described.
4 The paragraph(s) of description should be placed near a related event. Appearance can be described either at the beginning or end of the composition.
5 The sketch should be at least 125 but not more than 400 words in length.
6 The composition should not use the exact words of the source material.

Mechanics

1 Each sentence should make sense on its own when read aloud.
2 Each proper name should be capitalized.
3 Possessive forms should be written properly.
4 Personal pronouns should have clear antecedents and be of the proper gender.
5 Verb tense should be consistent throughout.
6 Subjects and verbs must be in agreement.

Week 20 Rubric
Biographical Sketch

Organization

1 The sketch should begin with a brief chronological narrative. This should be at least 50 and not more than 150 words. The chronological narrative can either cover all of Shakespeare's life in one paragraph, or can cover birth to 1599 in the first paragraph and 1613–1616 in a paragraph at the end of the composition.
2 The events in the narrative should be listed in chronological order.
3 The sketch should contain three paragraphs describing Shakespeare's works. The three paragraphs should either describe the works in the order they were composed, or should describe them by type (history, comedy, tragedy).
4 At least six but not more than ten plays should be named.
5 The sketch should give specific details about each play listed.
6 The sketch should not use the exact words of the source material.

Mechanics

1 Each sentence should make sense on its own when read aloud.
2 Each proper name should be capitalized.
3 Possessive forms should be written properly.
4 Personal pronouns should have clear antecedents and be of the proper gender.
5 Verb tense should be consistent throughout.

When the student is talking about Shakespeare's life, past tense should be used. When she is describing the action of a play, she may use either past or present tense—but she should always use the *same* tense when describing a play.

Shakespeare wrote many comedies that end with a wedding. In The Taming of the Shrew *(1596), a young woman with a bad temper marries a man with an even worse temper.* As You Like It *has both serious and funny elements.* Twelfth Night *weaves together high comedy and low comedy.*

is correct. The first verb is past because it describes something Shakespeare did in the past. The other verbs, describing the actions in the plays, are all present tense.

Shakespeare wrote many comedies that end with a wedding. In The Taming of the Shrew *(1596), a young woman with a bad temper married a man with an even worse temper.* As You Like It *had both serious and funny elements.* Twelfth Night *weaves together high comedy and low comedy.*

is not correct because the first two play descriptions use past tense while the third uses present.

6 Subjects and verbs must be in agreement.

Week 21 Rubric
Sequence: Natural Process

Organization

1 There is no specific word count for this exercise, but it should be either five or six paragraphs in length.
2 The paragraphs should be, in order: hydrogen stars (optional), the beginning of the death process, red giant, planetary nebula, white dwarf, black dwarf.
3 Within each paragraph, the events should be listed in chronological order.
4 Each paragraph should contain some descriptive detail about the star at that stage (color, temperature, size, mass, etc.).
5 The sequence should not use the exact words of the source material.

Mechanics

1 Each sentence should make sense on its own when read aloud.
2 Possessive forms should be written properly.
3 Each paragraph should have at least two sentences.
4 Verb tense should be consistent throughout.
5 Subjects and verbs must be in agreement.

Week 22 Rubric
Sequence: Natural Process

Organization

1 There is no specific word count for this exercise, but it should be six paragraphs in length.
2 The paragraphs should be, in order: Embryo/egg, hatchling/young, mature, reproduction, old age.
3 Within each paragraph, the events should be listed in chronological order.
4 Each paragraph should contain some descriptive detail about the octopus at that stage (behavior, habits, appearance).
5 The sequence should not use the exact words of the source material.

Mechanics

1 Each sentence should make sense on its own when read aloud.
2 Possessive forms should be written properly.
3 Each paragraph should have at least two sentences.
4 Verb tense should be consistent throughout.
5 Subjects and verbs must be in agreement.

Week 22 Rubric
Sequence of a Natural Event with Brief Description

Organization

1 There is no specific word count for this exercise, but it should contain the following elements, in order: introduction, scientific knowledge, description (this may also go after the step-by-step process), step-by-step process, repetition.
2 Within each paragraph of the step-by-step process, the events should be listed in chronological order.
3 The description should contain at least three details about the octopus's appearance.
4 The exact words of the source material should not be used.

Mechanics

1 Each sentence should make sense on its own when read aloud.
2 Possessive forms should be written properly.
3 Possessive forms should be written properly.
4 Each paragraph should have at least two sentences.
5 Verb tense should be consistent throughout.
6 Subjects and verbs must be in agreement.

Week 23 Rubric
Brief Literary Essay

Organization

1 The essay should begin with an introduction to the world of the story.
2 Next should come the explanation of what Rikki wants and why.
3 Next should come the explanation of what the cobras want and why.
4 Next should come a chronological description of the scene where Rikki kills Nag, including the reason why Nag went into the bathroom.
5 The essay should end with a chronological description of the scene where Rikki kills Nagaina, including the reason why Nagaina went into the house.

Mechanics

1 Each sentence should make sense on its own when read aloud.
2 Possessive forms should be written properly.
3 Verb tense should be consistent throughout
4 Subjects and verbs must be in agreement.
5 Rikki-tikki-tavi may be abbreviated as Rikki.
6 Antecedents of pronouns should be clear.
7 The titles of short stories should be in quotation marks; the titles of books, italicized (in handwriting, underlined).

Week 24 Rubric
Brief Literary Essay

Organization

1 The essay should begin with a short summary of the story's plot.
2 Next should come the explanation of Madame Loisel's wish to be rich and admired.
3 Next should come the explanation of Madame Loisel's pride and embarrassment.
4 The essay should end by explaining that her life changed forever because the second set of wants was stronger than the first.

Mechanics

1 Each sentence should make sense on its own when read aloud.
2 Possessive forms should be written properly.
3 Verb tense should be consistent throughout.
4 Subjects and verbs must be in agreement.
5 Antecedents of pronouns should be clear.
6 Unnecessary repetition of the same nouns, adjectives, and proper names should be avoided.
7 The title of the story should be in quotation marks if used.
8 The title "Madame" may be written out or abbreviated as "Mme."

Week 25 Rubric
Brief Literary Essay

Organization

1 The essay should begin with a short summary of the story's plot.
2 Next should come a transitional sentence, explaining that the essay will now discuss the characters.
3 Next should come the explanation of what Anne wants, and why she cannot have it.
4 Next should come the explanation of what Marilla wants, and how Anne would keep her from having it.
5 The essay should end by explaining how Matthew helps and/or hinders Anne and/or Marilla.
6 Each of the three literary analysis paragraphs should contain a direct quote from the story, related to the observations in the paragraph.

Mechanics

1 Each sentence should make sense on its own when read aloud.
2 Possessive forms should be written properly.
3 Verb tense should be consistent throughout.
4 Subjects and verbs must be in agreement.
5 Antecedents of pronouns should be clear.
6 Unnecessary repetition of the same nouns, adjectives, and proper names should be avoided.
7 The title of the story should be in quotation marks if used; the book title should be italicized or underlined.
8 Direct quotes should be incorporated into full sentences and should be properly punctuated.

Week 26 Rubric
Brief Literary Essay

Organization

1 The essay should begin with a short summary of the story's plot.
2 The first paragraph must contain the title of the story and the name of the author.
3 The next paragraph should begin with a statement about St. George as patron saint and protector of the English.
4 The paragraph should then point out that the heroic English deserved to be saved.
5 The essay should end with a paragraph describing the story's effect on its readers.
6 The final paragraph should contain a few of Machen's own words in quotation marks.
7 The first two paragraphs should be in the same tense, either present or past; the final paragraph should be in the past tense.

Mechanics

1 Each sentence should make sense on its own when read aloud.
2 Possessive forms should be written properly.
3 Verb tense should be consistent throughout.
4 Subjects and verbs must be in agreement.
5 Antecedents of pronouns should be clear; pronouns should agree with the antecedents in number (army=singular=it, soldiers=plural=them).
6 Unnecessary repetition of the same nouns, adjectives, and proper names should be avoided.
7 The title of the story should be in quotation marks.
8 Direct quotes should be incorporated into full sentences and should be properly punctuated.
9 Either "St. George" or "Saint George" should be used.
10 If the Latin motto is quoted, it should be underlined (italicized).

Week 29 Rubric
Chronological Narrative of Past Events

Organization

1 Events should be in chronological order.
2 The composition should have five paragraphs, each dealing with one main point on the outline.
3 Two or more time words should be used.
4 The composition should use more than 200 but fewer than 400 words.

Mechanics

1 Each sentence should make sense on its own when read aloud.
2 Each proper name should be capitalized.
3 Dates should be written properly.
4 Direct quotes and unique ideas should be documented with footnotes.
5 Footnotes should be written correctly.
6 Direct quotes from the source material should be surrounded by quotation marks.

Week 29 Rubric
Description of a Person

Organization

1 The description should include at least three of the aspects listed on the Description of a Person chart.
2 The description should be at least 50 and not more than 100 words.
3 The description should use appropriate adjectives, nouns, and verbs to slant the description in a positive or negative direction.
4 At least one direct and one indirect quote should be used (it is not necessary to cite *both* sources, however).

Mechanics

1 Each sentence should make sense on its own when read aloud.
2 Each proper name should be capitalized.
3 Possessive forms should be written properly.
4 Personal pronouns should have clear antecedents and be of the proper gender.
5 Verb tense should be consistent throughout.
6 Subjects and verbs must be in agreement.
7 Footnotes should be properly formatted and should come at the ends of the sentences which contain the source material.

Week 29 Rubric
Description of a Place

Organization

1 The description should use appropriate adjectives and verbs to convey the purpose of the description.
2 At least two space and distance words and phrases should be used.
3 Point of view should remain consistent.
4 The description should be at least 40 and not more than 90 words long.
5 At least one direct quote should be included.
6 There should be at least one metaphor or simile in the description.

Mechanics

1 Each sentence should make sense on its own when read aloud.
2 Verbs should have consistent tense (all past or all present).
3 Subjects and verbs should be in agreement.
4 Each proper name should be capitalized.
5 Possessive forms should be written properly.
6 Personal pronouns should have clear antecedents and be of the proper gender.
7 Verb tense should be consistent throughout.
8 Footnotes should be properly formatted and should come at the ends of the sentences which contain the source material.

Week 30 Rubric
Scientific Description

Organization

1 The description should describe what at least two parts of the organ look like and what function they have.
   For the gullet: the tube and the rings of muscle
   For the intestines: the coiled folds, the length, the muscles, the villi, the outside
2 The description should have a clear point of view—either from above (impersonal, outside) or moving through or around (in other words, the student can describe the organ from the point of view of the food moving through it).
3 At least one metaphor or simile should be used.
4 The final description should be at least 40 words and two sentences in length.

Mechanics

1 Each sentence should make sense on its own when read aloud.
2 Verb tense should be consistent throughout.
3 Subjects and verbs must be in agreement.
4 Possessive forms should be written properly.
5 If used, footnotes should be properly formatted and should come at the ends of the sentences which contain the source material.
   Author first and last name, *Title of book* (Publisher, date), p. #.

Week 30 Rubric
Sequence of a Natural Event, Including a Scientific Description

Organization

1 The final composition should be at least 190 words long.
2 There should be either five or six paragraphs.
3 Each paragraph in the sequence should describe what happens to the food in one stage of the digestive process.
4 The scientific description should be placed after the first mention of the organ it describes.
5 Ideas or images from the source material should be footnoted. Scientific facts do not need footnotes. At least one direct quote should be included and footnoted.
6 A Works Cited page must be attached.

Mechanics

1 Each sentence should make sense on its own when read aloud.
2 Possessive forms should be written properly.
3 Each paragraph should have at least two sentences.
4 Verb tense should be consistent throughout.
5 Subjects and verbs must be in agreement.
6 Footnotes should be properly formatted.
7 The paper should be double-spaced.
8 If there is more than one page (not including the Works Cited page), the pages should be numbered.
9 The title should be centered at the top of the first page.
10 A separate Works Cited page should be attached (even if only one source is included on it) and properly formatted.

Author last name, author first name. *Title of book.* City of publication: Publisher, date.

Week 31 Rubric
Biographical Sketch
with Personal Description

Organization

1 The sketch should have nine paragraphs. Each paragraph should have at least two sentences.
2 The paragraph of description should not be placed between the original paragraphs I and II or IV and V.
3 The paragraph of description should have a clear positive or negative slant OR should use a governing metaphor.
4 The sketch should be at least 450 words in length.
5 The sketch should progress forward chronologically through the events of Marie Antoinette's life.
6 The sketch should include at least four direct quotes, making use of all three sources.

Mechanics

1 Each sentence should make sense on its own when read aloud.
2 Each proper name should be capitalized.
3 Possessive forms should be written properly.
4 Personal pronouns should have clear antecedents and be of the proper gender.
5 Verb tense should be consistent throughout.
6 Subjects and verbs must be in agreement.
7 Direct quotes should be properly footnoted.
8 The Works Cited page should be organized alphabetically and entries formatted properly.
9 The paper must be double-spaced and the pages must be numbered.

Week 32 Rubric
Brief Poem Essay

Organization

1 The essay should begin with an introduction that gives the poem's title, the author, and the information that the poem is about the four stages of life.
2 There should be four paragraphs, one for each stanza.
3 Each paragraph should mention the time of life, the type of bell, the emotion/mood of the stanza, the vowel sounds used, and at least one specific word that contains that vowel sound.
4 Each paragraph should contain a direct quote from the poem.
5 At least one quote should be four lines or longer.

Mechanics

1 Each sentence should make sense on its own when read aloud.
2 Possessive forms should be written properly.
3 Verb tense should be consistent throughout.
4 Subjects and verbs must be in agreement.
5 Antecedents of pronouns should be clear.
6 Unnecessary repetition of the same nouns, adjectives, and proper names should be avoided.
7 The title of the poem should be in quotation marks.
8 Direct quotes should be incorporated into full sentences and should be properly punctuated.
9 Quotes longer than three lines should be set as blocks.

Week 33 Rubric
Brief Poem Essay

Organization

1 The essay should begin with an introduction that gives the poem's title, the author, and the information that the poem is about an ancient king whose kingdom disappeared.
2 There should be five paragraphs total.
3 The conclusion should make a statement about the conflict between Ozymandias's expectations and what really happened.
4 The essay should include at least two direct quotes from the poem.

Mechanics

1 Each sentence should make sense on its own when read aloud.
2 Possessive forms should be written properly.
3 Verb tense should be consistent throughout.
4 Subjects and verbs must be in agreement.
5 Antecedents of pronouns should be clear.
6 Unnecessary repetition of the same nouns, adjectives, and proper names should be avoided.
7 The title of the poem should be in quotation marks.
8 Direct quotes should be incorporated into full sentences and should be properly punctuated.

Week 34 Rubric
Brief Poem Essay

Organization

1 The essay should be at least 415 but no more than 700 words.
2 There should be either four or five paragraphs.
3 The first paragraph should give a brief chronological narrative about the poem's events and should include two time words and one direct quote.
4 The second and third (and fourth, if used) paragraphs should explain the movement of the poem by describing what happens in each stanza. These paragraphs should also tell how the repetition of the poem helps show the movement of the Light Brigade. They should include at least three direct quotes from the poem.
5 The final paragraph should describe how the rhyme scheme and the incomplete feet add meaning to the poem.

Mechanics

1 Each sentence should make sense on its own when read aloud.
2 Possessive forms should be written properly.
3 Verb tense should be consistent throughout.
4 Subjects and verbs must be in agreement.
5 Antecedents of pronouns should be clear.
6 Unnecessary repetition of the same nouns, adjectives, and proper names should be avoided.
7 The title of the poem should be in quotation marks.
8 Direct quotes should be incorporated into full sentences and should be properly punctuated.
9 Poem quotes should be properly attributed.
10 Secondary sources should be properly footnoted.

Appendix III

Literary Terms

hero/heroine: a central character with admirable qualities.
protagonist: the character who wants to get, become, or accomplish something.
antagonist: the character, force, or circumstance that opposes the protagonist.
villain: an antagonist with evil motives.
conflict: the clash between protagonist and antagonist.
simile: a comparison that uses "like," "as," or similar words.
metaphor: a comparison that speaks of one thing in terms of another.
synecdoche: a kind of metaphor that uses a part to represent the whole.
inversion (plot): an unexpected revelation that reverses the meaning or action of the story.
surprise story: a story that uses inversion to change the reader's point of view.
supporting character: a character who helps, supports, or hinders the protagonist or antagonist.
genre: a particular type or form of literature; works that use similar forms or have similar purposes.
fantasy: a genre in which stories are set in a world that doesn't exist.
stanza: a group of lines within a poem.
onomatopoeia: when a word sounds like its meaning.
alliteration: when words begin with the same sound or sounds.
meter: the rhythmical pattern of a poem.
foot: a set of syllables that follows a certain pattern of stress and unstress.
rhyme scheme: a pattern of repeating rhyme marked with letters of the alphabet.
sonnet: a 14-line poem written in iambic pentameter.
ballad: a poem that tells a story, usually a heroic or tragic one.

Appendix IV

Sentence Variety Chart

descriptive adjectives	←→	nouns	an eloquent man a man of eloquence
passive verb	←→	active verb	The kingdom was ruled by its king. The king ruled his kingdom.
indirect object	→	object of the preposition	The mother gave the baby a bottle. The mother gave a bottle to the baby.
infinitives	←→	participles	The truth needs saying. The truth needs to be said.
main verb	←→	infinitive	I usually plan ahead. I usually need to plan ahead. I usually manage to plan ahead.

Appendix V

General Rubrics

Mechanics Rubric: All

1. Each sentence should make sense on its own when read aloud.
2. Possessive forms should be written properly.
3. Verb tense should be consistent throughout.
4. Subjects and verbs must be in agreement.
5. Antecedents of pronouns should be clear.
6. Unnecessary repetition of the same nouns, adjectives, and proper names should be avoided.
7. The titles of poems or short stories should be in quotation marks.
8. Direct quotes should be incorporated into full sentences and should be properly punctuated.
9. Poem quotes should be properly formatted and attributed.
10. Secondary sources should be properly footnoted:
    First name, last name, *Title of book* (Publisher, year of publication), p. xx.
11. The Works Cited page should be separate and should be properly formatted. Entries should be alphabetized and single-spaced, with double spaces separating entries. "Works Cited" should be centered at the top.
    Last name, first name. *Title of book.* City of publication: Publisher, year.
12. Compositions of more than one page should have page numbers.
13. Typed compositions should be double-spaced.
14. If used, the title should be centered at the top of the first page.

Summary of Narrative Fiction Organization

1. Events should be in chronological order.
2. If two or more events are listed in a single sentence, they should have a cause and effect relationship.

3. Each event of major importance should be in the summary (if it were missing from the original passage, the narrative would no longer make sense).

Summary of Descriptive Fiction
Organization

1. If two or more details are listed in a single sentence, they should be related.
2. Details of conversations should not be listed.
3. Any events should be connected to the description by a time word.

Chronological Narrative of Past Events
Organization

1. Events should be in chronological order.
2. Time words should be used to create transitions.
3. A clear theme should be used to sort through and choose events.
4. Dialogue may be used.

Chronological Narrative of Scientific Discovery
Organization

1. Events should be in chronological order.
2. The paragraph giving "background information" should be the first or second paragraph in the composition.
3. Time words should be used.
4. If possible, the scientist's own words should be quoted.

Description of a Place
Organization

1. The description should use appropriate adjectives and verbs to convey the purpose of the description.
2. Space and distance words and phrases should be used.
3. Point of view should remain consistent: from above, from inside, from one side or angle, or moving through/around.
4. A vivid metaphor or simile should be used when possible.

Scientific Description
Organization

1. The description should make use of one or both points of view: removed, present.
2. Present point-of-view descriptions should incorporate at least three of the five senses: sight, sound, smell, taste, touch.

3. Removed point-of-view descriptions should describe each part of the object or phenomenon and tell what it is made of.
4. At least one metaphor or simile may be used.
5. The description should cover each part of the object or phenomenon.

Description of a Person
Organization

1. The description should include at least five but no more than eight of the aspects listed on the Description of a Person chart.
2. The description may be slanted in a positive or negative direction.
3. A governing metaphor may be used to organize the description.

Biographical Sketch
Organization

1. The sketch should include selected aspects from the Description of a Person chart.
2. The focus may be on:
   a. Life events, listed chronologically.
   b. The subject's work/accomplishments, listed chronologically.
   c. The subject's work/accomplishments, listed by subject/topic.

Sequence: Natural Process
Organization

1. Each step in the process should be described in order.
2. Ideas or images from the source material should be footnoted. Scientific facts do not need footnotes.
3. One or more of the following must be included:
   a. Introduction/summary.
   b. Scientific background.
   c. Repetition of the process.